AF471240

Film Review
2006-2007

Uma's Ulla: Ms Thurman barnstorms her way onto
a new career arc in Susan Stroman's dynamic if
stage-bound *The Producers* (from Sony Pictures)

Film Review 2006-2007

JAMES CAMERON-WILSON

Founding father: F. Maurice Speed 1911-1998

Reynolds & Hearn Ltd
London

To Alex Grundon, for encouraging me to vent
my passion for the cinema on his radio shows

Acknowledgements

The author would like to convey his considerable
appreciation to the following, without whom this
book would not have been achievable: Charles Bacon,
Reuben Barnes, Ewen Brownrigg, Juliet Cameron-
Wilson, Joel Finer, Marcus Hearn, Tony Hillman,
Keira, Scot Woodward Myers, Daniel O'Brien,
Carolynn Reynolds, Richard Reynolds, George
Savvides, Ailsa Scott, Mansel Stimpson (in particular),
David Nicholas Wilkinson and Derek Winnert.

Thank you all.

Film World Diary pictures: Rex Features
In Memoriam pictures: The Tony Hillman Collection
All other pictures © their respective distributors

First published in 2006 by
Reynolds & Hearn Ltd
61a Priory Road
Kew Gardens
Richmond
Surrey TW9 3DH

© James Cameron-Wilson 2006

A CIP catalogue record for this book
is available from the British Library.

ISBN 1 905287 28 3

Designed by James King.

Printed and bound in Great Britain by Biddles Ltd,
King's Lynn, Norfolk.

Contents

Introduction

The bottom line is that cinema is here to entertain. And as the small screen relies more and more on game shows and far-fetched reality TV, so the cinema's remit is all the more crucial: to bring large-scale, narrative-driven spectacle to the masses. But the bigger the budget, the more dependent the studios become on providing something with a guaranteed return. The cost of prints, marketing, special effects and stars like Will Ferrell, Vince Vaughn and Reese Witherspoon is more than merely daunting. It's bordering on economic suicide. Nonetheless, the marketplace has never been more crowded with titles, to which the packed contents of this book offer testament (last year, for the first time, the publishers were forced to add on twelve pages).

It's no longer unusual for ten, eleven or even twelve films to open in London in one week, forcing the more comprehensive newspapers to hire one, two or even three critics to cover the releases. And therein lies a quandary. As Hollywood bows to commercial pressure to produce more sequels than ever before – and then tops these up with remakes – so critics become more and more disillusioned. Some of my colleagues – not me – routinely sit through four films a day, sometimes four days a week. Quite how they find the time to write their reviews is beyond me. As a freelance critic, I am obliged by economic forces to see one film and then review it as many times as possible (my record is crafting seven separate pieces for one title). Over time I have spread my views across the media of books, television, radio, newspapers, magazines, public appearances and the Internet. Once, I even served a two-year term as a 'dial-a-film-critic'.

Critics *en masse* must be dreading the summer of 2007. This is the period when Hollywood will be unleashing *Spider-Man 3*, *Shrek 3*, *Pirates of the Caribbean: At World's End*, *Ocean's Thirteen*, *Fantastic Four 2*, *Evan Almighty* (the sequel to *Bruce Almighty*), *Harry Potter and the*

Order of the Phoenix, *The Bourne Ultimatum* (with Matt Damon reprising his role as Jason Bourne), *Rush Hour 3* and *Alien Vs. Predator 2*, the sequel to the sequel combo. Hollywood has become one big soap opera in which stars are paid enormous sums of money to duplicate previous performances, while all the other screens are jammed with cartoons assembled from computers. At the time of writing, three of the six highest-grossing films of the year are animated, while four out of the top ten are sequels. And at eleventh place is *Scary Movie 4*, a strong contender for worst film of the new millennium. But not only are movies beginning to look more and more alike, their structure is becoming increasingly formulaic. If it's a comedy, there has to be flatulence; if it's a horror film, there has to be a prologue; if it's any damned film it has to come with its own deranged orchestra.

Understandably, then, critics are being driven to new extremes of vilification. I've witnessed normally sane individuals to denounce publicly *The Da Vinci Code*, *The Omen* and *Poseidon* as the worst films ever made. Of course, they are no such thing, but they are heartless, mechanical and misjudged. Even so, there are moments in *The Da*

Vinci Code that are quite engaging. But the expectations that came with the Holy Trinity of Tom Hanks, Ron Howard and Dan Brown were too much to live up to. At least it wasn't a sequel (its own follow-up is in pre-production, though).

In 2005 Hollywood produced 17 sequels; this year that number rose to 21. Next year, the figure promises to be higher still, with ten sequels being belched out between the Memorial Day weekend and mid-August, the prime time for box-office domination. The wonder is that audiences still buy this stuff. But, hey, *Film Review* is not aimed at the mindless, popcorn-guzzling masses, which is why a movie like *Brokeback Mountain* is on the cover. So, to end on a positive note, it was heartening to see *Brokeback*, *Capote*, *Crash*, *Good Night, And Good Luck* and *Munich* – films dealing with homosexuality, creative ethics, racism, social intolerance and terrorism – all nominated for best picture Oscars. Likewise, it's encouraging that actors like George Clooney and Brad Pitt are willing to set aside their huge salaries to make meaningful, provocative and grown-up movies. It comes with a price, but it's worth it.

James Cameron-Wilson
July 2006

Steven Spielberg (in baseball cap) on the set of *Munich*, with Daniel Craig, Hanns Zischler and Eric Bana

Estimable infamy: Catherine Keener and Philip Seymour Hoffman in Bennett Miller's Oscar-winning *Capote*

Top 20 UK Box-Office Hits
July 2005 – June 2006

1. Harry Potter and the Goblet of Fire
2. The Chronicles of Narnia: The Lion,
   The Witch and the Wardrobe
3. Pirates of the Caribbean:
   Dead Man's Chest*
4. Charlie and the Chocolate Factory
5. The Da Vinci Code*
6. Ice Age: The Meltdown
7. Wallace & Gromit:
   The Curse of the Were-Rabbit
8. War of the Worlds
9. King Kong
10. Madagascar
11. X-Men: The Last Stand*
12. Nanny McPhee
13. Mission: Impossible III
14. Pride and Prejudice
15. Chicken Little
16. Superman Returns*
17. Wedding Crashers
18. The Fantastic Four
19. The Polar Express
20. Walk the Line

Still on release

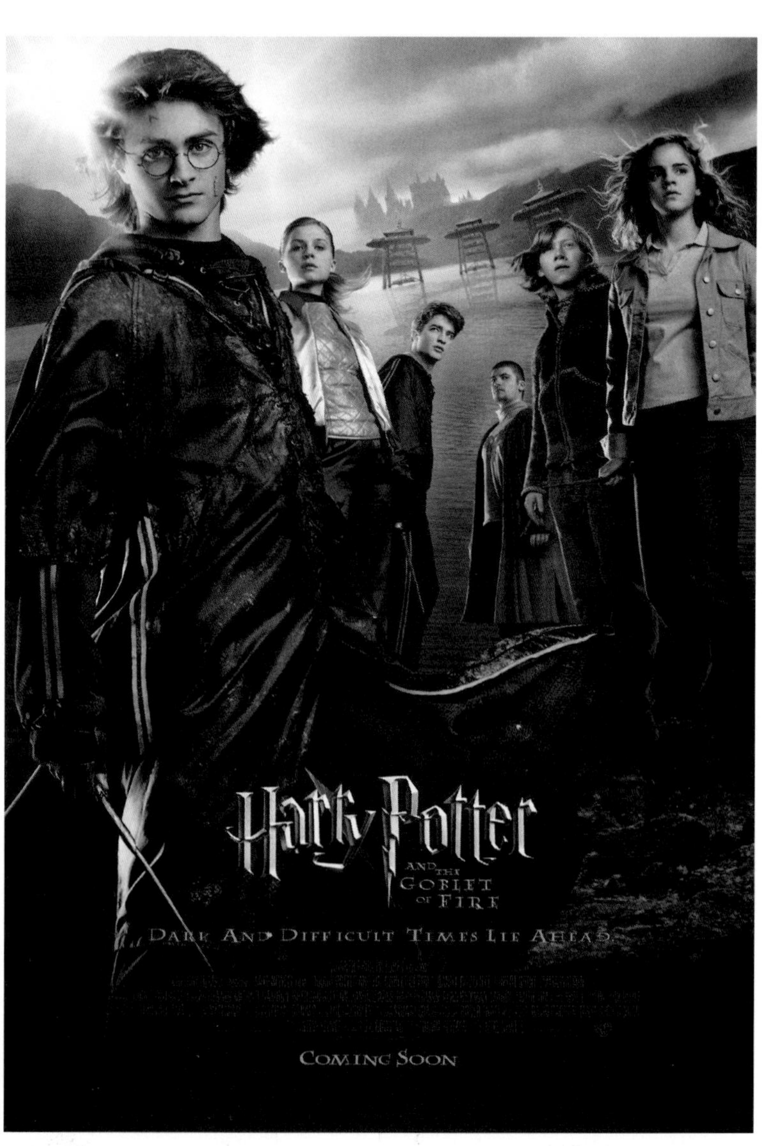

Top 10 Box-Office Stars
Star of the Year: Johnny Depp

With the plethora of franchises and cartoons crowding the box-office, it's almost impossible to value the worth of a star these days. In real terms, J.K. Rowling, C.S. Lewis and Roald Dahl would seem to be the biggest draws, or, on another plane, Harry Potter, Aslan and Willy Wonka. Still, one can't deny the timeless, sexless and sexual appeal of Johnny Depp, with *Pirates of the Caribbean: Dead Man's Chest* breaking almost every record invented. That puts Keira Knightley pretty high, too, taking into consideration the breakout success of *Pride & Prejudice*. But otherwise it's business as usual with Tom One and Tom Two and, still giggling, Jim Carrey.

JC-W

2. Tom Cruise
3. Tom Hanks
4. Keira Knightley
5. Steve Martin
6. Jim Carrey
7. Jodie Foster
8. Martin Lawrence
9. Orlando Bloom
10. Clive Owen

Releases of the Year

This section contains details of all the films released in Great Britain from 1 July 2005 to the end of June 2006 – the period covered by all the reference features in this book.

Leading actors are normally credited with the roles they played, followed by a summary of supporting players. Where an actor further down a cast list is of special interest then his/her role is generally credited as well.

For technical credits the normal abbreviations operate, and are as follows: Dir – for Director; Pro – for Producer; Ex Pro – for Executive Producer; Co Pro – for Co-Producer; Ass Pro – for Associate Producer; Line Pro – for Line Producer; Scr – for Screenwriter; Ph – for Cinematographer; Ed – for Editor; Pro Des – for Production Designer; and M – for composer.

Abbreviations for the names of film companies are also obvious when used, such as Fox for Twentieth Century Fox, and UIP for Universal International Pictures. The production company (or companies) is given first, the distribution company last.

Information at the foot of each entry is presented in the following order: running time/ country of origin/year of copyright/ date of British release/British certification.

Reviewers: **Charles Bacon, Ewen Brownrigg, James Cameron-Wilson, Juliet Cameron-Wilson, Scot Woodward Myers, Ian Paton, George Savvides, Mansel Stimpson and Derek Winnert**

Star ratings

★★★★★ **Wonderful**
★★★★ **Very good**
★★★ **Good**
★★ **Mediocre**
★ **Insulting**

The Adventures of Greyfriars Bobby ★★★★

Modest, old-fashioned but heart-felt, John Henderson's treatment of the story of the 19th century Edinburgh dog devoted to his master beyond the grave has virtues similar to those found in Paul Marcus's *Heidi*. The historical facts are followed but embroidered by giving a central role to a poor boy who loses his mother and wins the dog's heart. Social issues come in too with a factory owner and a hard-hearted Charity Commissioner presented as villains whose comeuppance we await eagerly. There are some good performances but what gives real distinction to the piece is the cameo towards the close by Christopher Lee as the Lord Provost, Sir William Chambers of dictionary fame. The film's climax in which he features is highly predictable but Lee has such presence and plays with such sincerity that the scene is extremely touching. MS

• *James Brown* James Cosmo, *Ewan Adams* Oliver Golding, *Maureen Gray* Gina McKee, *Duncan Smithie* Sean Pertwee, *Minister Lee* Greg Wise, *Coconut Tam* Ardal O'Hanlon, *The Lord Provost* Christopher Lee, *Laurie* Ron Donachie, *with* Ian Richardson, Thomas Lockyer, William MacBain, Kirsty Mitchell, Ronald Pickup, Suzanne Dance.

• *Dir* John Henderson, *Pro* Christopher Figg, *Ex Pro* Mark Bentley, Charles Armitage, Robert Whitehouse, Walter Nimmo, Maggie Monteith and Nigel Goldsack, *Screenplay* Henderson, Richard Matthews and Neville Watchurst, *Ph* John Ignatius, *Pro Des* Simon Holland, *Ed* David Yardley, *M* Mark Thomas, *Costumes* Ali Mitchell.

Piccadilly Pictures/Ursus Films/Edina Film Prods/Noel Gay Motion Pictures-The Works UK.
105 mins. UK. 2005. Rel: 10 February 2006. Cert. PG.

The Adventures of Sharkboy and Lavagirl in 3-D ★★★

In this *Wizard of Oz* meets *The NeverEnding Story* fable, young imagineer and artist Max (Cayden Boyd ably adopting the mantle of a post-millennial Barret Oliver) has created the planet Drool and its resident superheroes Sharkboy and Lavagirl. Together they keep at bay the evil menace of Mr Electricidad. When fiction bursts forth into reality, and the all-too-real Sharkboy and Lavagirl take Max to Drool, he must face both the delights and the dangers of his creations… The story was actually conceived by director Robert Rodriguez's then seven-year-old son Racer and jumps between the fantastic and mundane in the way only a child's imagination can. Rich with visual panache, it is a film for children but will equally delight adults who haven't completely smothered their own sense of innocent wonder. SWM

• *Sharkboy* Taylor Lautner, *Lavagirl* Taylor Dooley, *Max* Cayden Boyd, *Mr Electric/Tobor/Ice Guardian/Mr Electricidad* George Lopez, *Max's dad* David Arquette, *Max's mom* Kristen Davis, *Linus/Minus* Jacob Davich, *Marissa/Ice Princess* Sasha Pieterse, *Sharkboy's Dad* Rico Torres, *Sharkboy (aged 5)* Rebel Rodriguez, *Sharkboy (aged 7)* Racer Rodriguez, *Lug* Rocket Rodriguez.

• *Dir, Ph, Ed* and *Special Effects* Robert Rodriguez, *Pro* Rodriguez and Elizabeth Avellan, *Ex Pro* Bob Weinstein and Harvey Weinstein, *Screenplay* Robert Rodriguez and Marcel Rodriguez, from a story by Robert and Racer Rodriguez, *M* Robert Rodriguez, John Debney and Graeme Revell, *Art Dir* Jeanette Scott and Steve Joyner, *Costumes* Nina Proctor.

Columbia Pictures/Dimension Films/Troublemaker Studios-Columbia TriStar.
93 mins. USA. 2005. Rel: 26 August 2005. Cert. U.

Aeon Flux ★★★

In 2011 a virus wipes out 99 per cent of the world's population and five million survivors wall themselves into the sheltered city of Bregna. Four centuries later nature has reclaimed the planet and a high-tech administration keeps the remaining populace in place. Yet not everybody is happy with having traded freedom for a gilded cage, and ace rebel Aeon Flux is only too thrilled to be selected to assassinate Bregna's inviolate chairman, Trevor Goodchild… There is much to enjoy in this po-faced take on the animated MTV series, not least the nifty costume design and awesome reconstruction of Bregna itself. There's also some really cool stuff to satisfy sci-fi *aficionados*, such as the ability to produce eavesdropping drinking water, the modification of feet into hands (ideal for rock-climbing) and grass that can literally transform itself into a bed of blades. Eventually, though, the film implodes under a weight of cartoon silliness, which is only exacerbated by bizarre cameos from Frances McDormand and Pete Postlethwaite. However, on a scale of *Elektra* to *Catwoman*, *Aeon Flux* is in a class of its own. JC-W

• *Aeon Flux* Charlize Theron, *Trevor Goodchild* Marton Csokas, *Oren Goodchild* Jonny Lee Miller, *Sithandra* Sophie Okonedo, *Handler* Frances McDormand, *Keeper* Pete Postlethwaite, *Una Flux* Amelia Warner, *with* Caroline Chikezie, Nikolai Kinski, Phil Hay, Robin Gooch and (uncredited) Stuart Townsend.

• *Dir* Karyn Kusama, *Pro* Gale Anne Hurd, David Gale, Gary Lucchesi, Greg Goodman and Martha Griffin, *Ex Pro* Tom Rosenberg and Van Toffler, *Screenplay* Phil Hay and Matt

Fantastic voyage: Taylor Dooley and Taylor Lautner in Robert Rodriguez' *The Adventures of Sharkboy and Lavagirl in 3-D* (from Sony Pictures)

Manfredi, based on characters created by Peter Chung, *Ph* Stuart Dryburgh, *Pro Des* Andrew McAlpine, *Ed* Peter Honess, Plummy Tucker and Jeff Gullo, *M* Graeme Revell, *Costumes* Beatrix Aruna Pasztor.

Lakeshore Entertainment/Valhalla Motion Pictures/MTV Films-UIP.
92 mins. USA. 2005. Rel: 17 February 2006. Cert. 15.

After Midnight ★★

Optimistically billed as a cross between *Cinema Paradiso* and *Jules et Jim*, this Italian offering by Davide Ferrario, part comedy, part drama, comes from a man who clearly loves movies. However, only silent cinema aficionados will be thrilled by seeing old footage of Turin and unmemorable moments from Keaton shorts (Turin's Museum of Cinema is no substitute for an old-style movie-house). Furthermore, the actors cannot inject much life into the romantic triangle, which finds a waitress oddly unable to choose between the museum's timid but sincere night watchman and an unfaithful thief. A voice-over commenting on life, story telling and cinema itself tries to be clever but is merely banal and the resolution of the story is singularly unpersuasive. Sincere it undoubtedly is, but it's also sadly ineffective. Original title: *Dopo mezzanotte*. MS

• *Martino* Giorgio Pasotti, *Amanda* Francesca Inaudi, *Angelo, the Angel of Falchera* Fabio Troiano, *Barbara* Francesca Picozza, *Narrator* Silvio Orlando, *Martino's grandfather* Pietro Eandi, *fast food owner* Andrea Romero, *Bruno the night watchman* Giampiero Perone.

• *Dir, Pro* and *Screenplay* Davide Ferrario, *Line Pro* Ladis Zanini, *Ph* Dante Cecchin, *Pro Des* Francesca Bocca, *Ed* Claudio Cormio, *M* Fabio Barovero, Banda Ionica and Daniele Sepe, *Costumes* Paola Ronco.

Medusa Motion Picture-Yume Pictures.
92 mins. Italy. 2003. Rel: 9 December 2005. Cert. 15.

Alien Autopsy ★★

On a trip to Cleveland in Ohio, Ray Santilli accidentally comes across some highly confidential footage about aliens, which he brings back to England. But when he screens the film to his friends, he finds that it has disintegrated. The only thing left for him to do is to re-create the footage… Ant and Dec, the likeable TV duo, make an impressive feature film debut in this comedy based on true events. However, Will Davies' baffling script can't make up its mind whether it is a send-up or a faithful account of the story and, finally, the film falls between two stools. GS

• *Gary Shoefield* Ant McPartlin, *Ray Santilli* Declan Donnelly, *Morgan Banner* Bill Pullman, *Laszlo Voros* Götz Otto, *Harvey* Harry Dean Stanton, *Melik* Omid Djalili, *Jasmine* Morwenna Banks, *Gary's manager* Jimmy Carr, *with* John Shrapnel, Madaleine Moffatt, John Cater, David Threlfall, Jonathan Coy, Shane Rimmer, Orson Bean.

• *Dir* Jonny Campbell, *Pro* Will Davies, Barnaby Thompson

and Fiona Dwyer, *Ex Pro* Michael Kuhn, Ray Santilli, Gary Shoefield and James Spring, *Screenplay* Davies, *Ph* Simon Chaudoir, *Pro Des* Grenville Horner, *Ed* Oral Norrie Ottey, *M* Murray Gold, *Costumes* Rhona Russell.

Warner/Qwerty Films/Ealing Studios/N1 European Film Produktions-Warner.
95 mins. UK/USA/Germany. 2006. Rel: 7 April 2006. Cert. 12A.

American Dreamz ★★★½

Having secured a second term as President of the United States, Joe Staton decides to take it easy for a bit and discovers a passion for newspapers, taken aback by their content (there's more than one kind of Iraqi?). However, Staton's momentary disappearance from the world stage causes his approval ratings to plummet, so to boost his popularity he's put forward as a guest judge on the world's most watched TV show, *American Dreamz*, a talent contest hosted by a belligerent Englishman. And one of the finalists happens to be a show tune-loving suicide bomber… Dumb presidents, reality TV, Middle Eastern terrorists… All this is familiar stuff in celluloid satire, but the conceit of *Paradise Now* meets *Pop Idol* is too good to ignore. And there's some great dialogue here, delivered with skill by an accomplished cast (Hugh Grant as Simon Cowell, Dennis Quaid as George W., Mandy Moore as Britney…). It's very broad, quite silly and not exactly original, but there are enough genuine belly laughs to counter allegations of superficiality. JC-W

• *Martin Tweed* Hugh Grant, *President Joe Staton* Dennis Quaid, *Sally Kendoo* Mandy Moore, *Chief of Staff* Willem Dafoe, *William Williams* Chris Klein, *First Lady* Marcia Gay Harden, *Martha Kendoo* Jennifer Coolidge, *Accordo* Judy Greer, *Ittles* John Cho, *Chet Krogl* Seth Meyers, *Nazneen Riza* Shohreh Aghdashloo, *Omer* Sam Golzari, *Iqbal Riza* Tony Yalda, *with* Bernard White, Noureen Dewulf, Marley Shelton, Lawrence Pressman, Christianne Klein, Andrew Divoff, James Gleason, Trey Parker, Carmen Electra.

• *Dir* and *Screenplay* Paul Weitz, *Pro* Paul Weitz, Rodney Liber and Andrew Miano, *Ex Pro* Chris Weitz and Kerry Kohansky, *Ph* Robert Elswit, *Pro Des* William Arnold, *Ed* Myron Kerstein, *M* Stephen Trask, *Costumes* Molly Maginnis.

Universal/Depth of Field-UIP.
107 mins. USA. 2006. Rel: 21 April 2006. Cert. 12A.

An American Haunting ★½

Red River, Tennessee; 1817-1822. Shortly after wealthy landowner John Bell is accused of loan-sharking, his family comes under the spell of an unearthly curse. It's Bell's teenage daughter Betsy who gets the worst of it, though, being repeatedly tormented at midnight by an angry and unseen entity… Allegedly based on a true incident, *An American Haunting* blows its credibility in its first act. Opening with a girl being chased by an apoplectic orchestra, the film seems bent on trotting out every cliché in the canon. Yes, the first scene is actually a dream and yes, we have flashbacks, slow

Idol hands: Dennis Quaid and Hugh Grant in Paul Weitz' topical, funny *American Dreamz* (from UIP)

motion, cheesy false alarms and endless creaking doors. Consequently, the film quickly tries the patience, ending up as a series of repetitive and monotonous spectral visitations. Still, by casting the 71-year-old Donald Sutherland and the 56-year-old Sissy Spacek as the parents of young children immediately dispels any plausibility. In 1817, a man of Sutherland's age would more than likely be dead or at the very least a doddering grandfather. JC-W

• *John Bell* Donald Sutherland, *Lucy Bell* Sissy Spacek, *Richard Powell* James D'Arcy, *Betsy Bell* Rachel Hurd-Wood, *James Johnston* Matthew Marsh, *John Bell Jr* Thom Fell, *with* Zoë Thorne, Gaye Brown, Miquel Brown, Vernon Dobtcheff, Philip Hurd-Wood.

• *Dir* and *Screenplay* Coutney Solomon, from the novel *The Bell Witch – An American Haunting* by Brent Monahan, *Pro* Solomon, Christopher Milburn and André Rouleau, *Ex Pro* Allan Zeman, Julien Rémillard, Maxime Rémillard, Simon Franks and Zygí Kamasa, *Co-Pro* Andreí Boncea, *Ph* Adrian Biddle, *Pro Des* Humphrey Jaeger, *Ed* Richard Comeau, *M* Caine Davidson, *Costumes* Jane Petrie.

Allan Zeman/Midsummer Films/Remstar Prods/ AfterDark Films-Redbus.
90 mins. UK/Canada/USA/Romania. 2005. Rel: 14 April 2006. Cert. 15.

Another Public Enemy ★★

Transformed into a crusading public prosecutor, former slob and detective Kang Chul-joong sets his sights on an old schoolmate, now the head of a giant corporation. While the latter got off scot-free from his misdemeanours in childhood, he is now dealing in much bigger and more dangerous waters… Sequels don't come much weirder than this. Sharing the same director, actors and character names as the 2002 *Public Enemy*, this heavy-handed drama changes direction with a portentous whiff of self-adjustment. Substituting thrills with high-handed moralizing, the sequel could not be more dull or pompous. While there are a few sequences that deliver – particularly a couple of car chases directed by *Tell Me Something*'s Chang Yoon-hyun – the rest is a cold commentary on global capitalism. Original title: *Gonggongeui Jeok 2*. EB

• *Kang Chul-joong* Sol Kyung-gu, *Han Sang-woo* Jung Jun-ho, *Captain Uhm* Kang Shin-il, *investigator* Park Geun-hyeong, *with* Byeon Heui-bong, Im Seung-dae, Park Sang-wook, Eom Tae-ung, Jeong Gyu-su, Yun Heui-jeong, Lee Mun-shik, Yu Hae-jin.

• *Dir* Kang Woo-suk, *Guest Directors* Kim Sang-Jin and Chang Yoon-hyun, *Pro* Jung Sun-young, *Screenplay* Kim Huei-jae, *Ph* Kim Seong-bok, *Pro Des* Jo Seong-weon, *Ed* Go Im-pyo, *M* Han Jae-gweon, *Costumes* Oh Gyeong-ah, *Action Choreography* Jeong Du-hong and Yu Sang-seob.

Cinema Service/Chungmuro Fund-Tartan Films. 148 mins. South Korea. 2005. Rel: 30 September 2005. Cert. 15.

Appleseed ★½

Earth; 2131. Following the devastation of World War III, a utopia emerges in the form of the city of Olympia. There, the population is divided into human beings and 'bioroids', clones produced from genetic engineering. But when terrorists threaten the future of the bioroids, elite warrior Deunan Knute is entrusted with the task of retrieving the clones' essential data – dubbed Appleseed… Another dystopia, another Magna opus. But, while the characters' movements have been superimposed onto the motion of real 'actors', the faces remain crude and twee, resulting in bland imagery. Quite frankly, in the wake of the atmospheric grace of Hayao Miyazaki and the technical sophistication of Pixar, only the most undemanding adherents of anime will take much pleasure in this. EB

• *Voices*: *Deunan Knute* Ai Kobayashi, *Briareos* Jurota Kosugi, *Hitomi* Yuki Matsuoka. *English version*: *Deunan* Jennifer Proud, *Briareos* James Lyon, *Hitomi* Mia Bradly

• *Dir* Shinji Aramaki, *Pro* Sori, Hidenori Ueki and Naoko Watanabe, *Ex Pro* Sumiji Miyake, *Screenplay* Haruka Handa and Tsutomu Kamishiro, based on the manga by Masamune Shirow, *Pro Des* Shinji Aramaki, *M* Tetsuya Takahashi and Boom Boom Satellites; tracks performed by Paul Oakenfold, Basement Jaxx, Carl Craig Vs. Adult, Akufen, Atom TM, T. Raumschmiere, and Ryuichi Sakamoto, *Sound* Koji Kasamatsu, *Character Design* Masaki Yamada.

Micott & Basara, TBS, Geneon Entertainment, Yamato, Toho, TYO, Digital Frontier Inc., MBS-Optimum Releasing. 105 mins. Japan/South Korea. 2004. Rel: 19 August 2005. Cert. 12A.

Aquamarine ★★

Florida; the present. As Hailey prepares to move to Australia with her mom, she has to make the most of her precious last weekend with her best friend, Claire. However, it turns out to be the weekend of a lifetime when the girls stumble across a mermaid, Aquamarine, and try to help her find true love… There's a great story in here somewhere, but it's already been told – twice, in *Splash* and *A Little Mermaid*. This edition, aimed squarely at young girls of very little brain, is charmless, silly and gauche. Hamstrung by way too much giggling and screaming, weak puns (Aquamarine curses, 'that's bullshark!') and a dull visual palette, the film is artless in the extreme. Still, Emma Roberts (niece of Julia) and the pop singer JoJo have some appeal and could go on to better things. JC-W

• *Claire* Emma Roberts, *Hailey* Joanna 'JoJo' Levesque, *Aquamarine* Sarah Paxton, *Raymond Calder* Jake McDorman, *Cecilia* Arielle Kebbel, *Ginny* Claudia Karvan, *Leonard* Bruce Spence, *Marjorie* Tammin Sursok, *with* Roy Billing, Julia Blake, Shaun Micallef.

• *Dir* Elizabeth Allen, *Pro* Susan Cartsonis, *Co-Pro* Steven R. McGlothen, *Screenplay* John Quaintance and Jessica Bendinger, from the novel by Alice Hoffman, *Ph* Brian J. Breheny, *Pro Des* Nelson Coates, *Ed* Jane Moran, *M* David Hirschfelder, *Costumes* Sally Sharpe.

Fox 2000 Pictures/Storefront Pictures-Fox. 103 mins. USA. 2006. Rel: 23 June 2006. Cert. PG.

Arakimentari ★★★★

This documentary feature by Travis Klose from New York offers an insightful portrait of the Japanese photographer Nobuyoshi Araki, now in his sixties. This energetic widower sees sex as central to life and is famed for his pornographic images that have challenged Japan's sexual prudery. He's equally well known as a major artist. Klose allows for a range of reactions ('He's a monster' says one man; 'he's a gentleman' says one of his models) and lets his film reflect the artist's personality. Araki's love for his late wife is vividly conveyed and there are interesting comments from Björk and from Takeshi Kitano, the latter envying Araki his confidence in his talent. Stronger structuring would have made it even better, but this is a good movie stylishly filmed. MS

• *With*: Nobuyoshi Araki, Takeshi Kitano, Björk, Daido Moriyama, Richard Kern, Komari, Shino, Yoshiko Kamikura.

• *Dir* Travis Klose, *Pro* Jason Fried, *Ex Pro* Regis Trigano, *Ph* Brian Burgoyne, *Ed* Masako Tsumura, *M* DJ Krush, *Sound* Aaron Mendez.

Cicada Project/Troopers Films-Tartan Films. 74 mins. USA. 2004. Rel: 5 August 2005. No Cert.

The Aristocrats ★★★½

Did you hear the one about the family that traipsed into the office of a talent agent? Well, it's one way of beginning a joke that, until now, has been a professional confidentiality among stand-up comedians. It's not a particularly funny joke but it does allow the teller an enormous degree of improvisational liberty, and the smuttier the action the better. The reason that the story – let's call it 'The Aristocrats' – has been an inside joke for so long is because it's too filthy and outrageous to unload onto a conventional audience. Consequently, this slickly edited, most unusual documentary is as much about the changing face of obscenity as it is about stand-up comedy. Yet, even as an 88-minute documentary about a single joke – retold in a variety of different versions, in mime, in magic and even as part of an acrobatic act – it is a most enlightening, entertaining and offensive experience. JC-W

• *With*: Jason Alexander, Hank Azaria, Billy the Mime, Drew Carey, George Carlin, Carrot Top, Billy Connolly, Tim Conway, Andy Dick, Phyllis Diller, Carrie Fisher, Whoopi Goldberg, Gilbert Gottfried, Eric Idle, Eddie Izzard, Amazing Jonathan, Paul Krassner, Lisa Lampanelli, Richard Lewis, Bill Maher, Howie Mandel, Chuck McCann, Michael McKean, Eric Mead, Larry Miller, Martin Mull, Taylor Negron, Otto & George, Rick Overton, The Passing Zone, Penn & Teller, Emo Philips, Kevin Pollak, Paul Reiser, Andy Richter, Don Rickles, Chris Rock, Rita Rudner, Bob Saget, Harry Shearer, Sarah Silverman, The Smothers Brothers, David Steinberg, Jon Stewart, Larry Storch, Dave Thomas, Fred Willard, Robin Williams, Steve Wright, Paul Provenza.

• *Dir* and *Ex Pro* Paul Provenza and Penn Jillette, *Pro* Peter Adam Golden, *Co-Pro* Ken Krasher Lewis, *Ed* Provenza and Emery Emery, *M* Gary Stockdale, *South Park Animation* Trey Parker and Matt Stone.

ThinkFilm/Mighty Cheese-Pathé.
88 mins. USA/Canada. 2004. Rel: 9 September 2005. Cert. 18.

Arsène Lupin ★★★

The hero of many past films, mainly French but including Hollywood productions of the thirties, the principled thief Arsène Lupin follows Zorro in returning to our screens. The period adventures depicted here carry a touch of Dumas although set much later (the coda is in 1913) and the plot encompasses a quest for a hidden necklace, vengeance sought for a father's murder, political plotting and a romantic triangle. Director Jean-Paul Salomé displays energy and enthusiasm and Kristin Scott Thomas is stylish as ever, but the tone is all over the place and the fast pace only serves to make the movie seem desperately overlong at 130 minutes. Less would have been more here and Romain Duris so striking in *The Beat That My Heart Skipped* is entirely forgettable in the title role. MS

• *Arsène Lupin* Romain Duris, *Joséphine Balsamo, Comtesse de Cagliostro* Kristin Scott Thomas, *Beaumagnan* Pascal Greggory, *Clarisse de Dreux Soubise* Eva Green, *with* Robin Renucci, Patrick Toomey, Mathieu Carrière, Philippe Magnan, Marie Bunel, Philippe Lemaire, Francoise Lepine, Jessica Boyde, Gaelle Vincent, Guillaume Huet, Adele Csech, Aurelien Wilk.

• *Dir* Jean-Paul Salomé, *Pro* Stephane Marsil, *Ex Pro* Alain Peyrollaz, *Screenplay* Salome and Laurent Vachaud, freely inspired by Maurice Leblanc's *La Comtesse De Cagliostro, Ph*

Pascal Ridao, *Pro Des* Francoise Dupertuis, *Ed* Marie-Pierre Renaud, *M* Debbie Wiseman, *Costumes* Pierre-Jean Larroque.

Hugo Films/TF1 Films/M6 Films, etc-Cinefile World.
130 mins. France/UK/Spain/Italy. 2004. Rel: 9 September 2005. Cert. 15.

Ask the Dust ★★½

Moving to Los Angeles from Colorado, aspiring writer Arturo Bandini is afraid that his inexperience of life will hamper his creative potential. However, an association with the editor and writer H.L. Mencken, and the publication of a short story in the latter's *American Mercury* magazine, boosts his confidence. Then Bandini meets the Mexican firebrand Camilla Lopez, a woman with more than her share of life's experience… Returning to the Chandler-speak of *Chinatown*, Oscar-winning scenarist Robert Towne heats up the 1939 novel of John Fante. But even though this is Fante's semi-autobiographical *magnum opus*, it's hard to take a film seriously with lines like, `whadya say we bust outta this joint tomorrow?' And with Dublin's Colin Farrell as Fante's alter ego and South Africa standing in for Depression-era Los Angeles, the film doesn't exactly exude authenticity. Nonetheless, there is considerable sexual tension between Farrell and Salma Hayek, which helps elevate this steamy tale of doomed love out of the trenches of dime novel literature. JC-W

• *Arturo Bandini* Colin Farrell, *Camilla Lopez* Salma Hayek, *Hellfrick* Donald Sutherland, *Mrs Hargreaves* Eileen Atkins, *Vera Rifkin* Idina Menzel, *Sammy* Justin Kirk, *with* Jeremy Crutchley, Ronald France, Dion Basco.

• *Dir* and *Screenplay* Robert Towne, *Pro* Tom Cruise, Paula Wagner, Don Granger and Jonas McCord, *Ex Pro* Redmond Morris, Mark Roemmich, David Selvan, Andreas Schmid, Andy Grosch and Chris Roberts, *Ph* Caleb Deschanel, *Pro Des* Dennis Gassner, *Ed* Robert K. Lambert, *M* Ramin Djawadi and Heitor Pereira; tracks performed by Django Reinhardt, Artie Shaw, and Jess Harnell, *Costumes* Albert Wolsky.

Paramount Classics/Capitol Films/Cruise/Wagner/VIP Medienfonds 3/Ascendant-Pathé.
117 mins. USA/Germany/South Africa. 2005. Rel: 2 June 2006. Cert. 15.

Asylum ★★

England/Wales; the 1950s. Imprisoned in a marriage dead from the neck down, Stella Raphael accompanies her husband to his new post as deputy superintendent of a psychiatric hospital in the north of England. There, bored to distraction, she becomes acquainted with Edgar, a handsome, charismatic inmate who has been assigned to repair their greenhouse. Then, before she can stop herself, she enters into a sexual liaison with the mental patient… Intellectually, *Asylum* is one of the cinema's more interesting explorations of insanity. It is also rather novelistic in its telling, with neatly packaged chapters, impeccably crafted visual prose and characters that stick rigidly to the page. In fact, 'rigid' defines the entire movie, a melodramatic tale slowed down to the pace of a

tea dance. As Edgar, the New Zealand actor Martin Csokas
needed to be more a force of nature, while Natasha Richardson
conceals her sexual dementia beneath a veneer of fastidious
petulance. JC-W

• *Stella Raphael* Natasha Richardson, *Peter Cleave* Ian McKellen,
Edgar Stark Martin Csokas, *Max Raphael* Hugh Boneville,
Brenda Raphael Judy Parfitt, *Nick* Sean Harris, *Dr Jack
Straffen* Joss Ackland, *Charlie Raphael* Guy Lewis, *with* Wanda
Ventham, Anna Keaveney, Sarah Thurstan, Maria Aitken,
Hazel Douglas, Andy de la Tour.

• *Dir* David Mackenzie, *Pro* Mace Neufeld, David E. Allen
and Laurie Borg, *Ex Pro* Michael Barlow, Natasha Richardson,
Robert Rehme, Chris Curling, Steven Markoff, Bruce McNail,
Harmon Kaslow and John Buchanan, *Co-Pro* David Collins,
Screenplay Patrick Marber, from the 1996 novel by Patrick
McGrath, *Ph* Giles Nuttgens, *Pro Des* Laurence Dorman, *Ed*
Colin Monie, *M* Craig Armstrong, *Costumes* Consolata Boyle.

Paramount Classics/Seven Arts/Samson Films-
Momentum Pictures.
99 mins. USA/Ireland. 2004. Rel: 9 September 2005.
Cert. 15.

Atash ★★★

There's some significance in this being an Israeli/Palestinian
co-production but this debut feature by the talented Tawfik
Abu Wael is essentially about patriarchy. It's shown as the
dominant factor in the lives of a Palestinian family who rely
for survival on the making of charcoal because they live in

an isolated valley following the disgrace caused by one of the
daughters being raped. This prize-winning film is clearly a
work of art, but the characters are largely inarticulate and that
seriously limits the film's ability to delve fully into the father's
conflicts. It also means that at 110 minutes the piece is hard-
going, easier to admire than to enjoy. Those eager to endorse
the questioning of patriarchal societies will approve, and rightly
so, but they will hardly receive fresh insights. English title:
Thirst. MS

• *father* Hussein Yassin Mahajne, *mother* Amal Bweerat, *Shukri*
Ahamad Abed Ed Gani, *Gamila* Roba Blal, *Halima* Jamila Abu
Hussein.

• *Dir and Screenplay* Tawfik Abu Wael, *Pro* Avi Kleinberger, *Ph*
Asaf Sudry, *Pro Des* Boaz Katzenelson, *Ed* Galit Shaked-Shaul,
M Wissam M. Gibran.

Atash Partnership/Hot Vision-Axion Films.
110 mins. Israel. 2003. Rel: 25 November 2005. Cert. 12A.

Bad News Bears ★★★

A long, long time ago, Morris Buttermaker pitched two
thirds of an inning in the majors. Now he works as a pest
exterminator to pay for the rent on his trailer and to finance
a lifestyle of booze and loose women. So, he's none too happy
when he's bribed to coach twelve hopeless, mismatched kids in
the fine art of baseball… *The Mighty Ducks*, *Hardball*, *Kicking
and Screaming*… this sub-genre is getting out of hand. Still,
this is directed by Richard Linklater and arrives from the
keyboard of Glenn Ficarra and John Requa, they who brought

us *Bad Santa*. Any promise of schmaltzy underdog heroics is banished when Billy Bob, as Buttermaker, peers at his young charges and observes, 'you guys look like the last shit I took.' Racist, size-ist and even moderately sadistic, Thornton's Buttermaker is a deliciously un-PC creation, if not quite as unredeemable as Willie Soke in *Bad Santa*. It's a shame, then, that the climax is so slackly paced and drawn-out, robbing a subversive black comedy of a befittingly anarchic coda. JC-W

• *Morris Buttermaker* Billy Bob Thornton, *Roy Bullock* Greg Kinnear, *Liz Whitewood* Marcia Gay Harden, *Amanda Whurlitzer* Sammi Kane Kraft, *Kelly Leak* Jeffrey Davies, *Tanner Boyle* Timmy Deters, *Mike Engelberg* Brandon Craggs, *Toby Whitewood* Ridge Canipe, *Timmy Lupus* Tyler Patrick Jones, *Prem Lahiri* Aman Johal, *with* Troy Gentile, Jeffrey Tedmori, Kenneth 'K.C.' Harris, Carlos Estrada, Emmanuel Estrada.

• *Dir* Richard Linklater, *Pro* Linklater and J. Geyer Kosinski, *Ex Pro* Marcus Viscidi, *Co-Pro* Bruce Heller, *Screenplay* Bill Lancaster, Glenn Ficarra and John Requa, *Ph* Rogier Stoffers, *Pro Des* Bruce Curtis, *Ed* Sandra Adair, *M* Edward Shearmur; Bizet; tracks performed by John Fogerty, Los Straitjackets, Young-Holt Trio, Ted Nugent, Grand Funk Railroad, Motion City Soundtrack, Alice Cooper, Eric Clapton, Phantom Planet, Simple Plan, Ben Kweller, and Senses Fail, *Costumes* Karen Patch.

Paramount/Media Talent Group/Detour Filmproduction-UIP.
113 mins. USA. 2005. Rel: 12 August 2005. Cert. 12A.

The Ballad of Jack & Rose ★★★

An island off the east coast of the USA; 1986. There is an intriguing ambiguity at the heart of Rebecca Miller's lyrical, sad and unusual film. And with the director's own husband, Daniel Day-Lewis, playing the enigmatic Jack, the mystery is all the more marked. Pictured at the outset lying in a meadow with his 16-year-old daughter, Day-Lewis's Jack looks like a young man in love. But soon his misplacement becomes evident. With his Scottish accent, tattoos, prominent earring and stooped lope, he is an anachronism, a washed-up hippy on the beach of commercial advancement. Sharing an idyllic retreat with Rose, theirs would seem to be an ambrosian existence. But Jack is floundering on shattered dreams and neither he nor Rose is physically or mentally in good shape. An elegiac drama of lost hope, the film is a parable of how the materialism of the 1990s was already cutting a swathe through the aspirations of the eco-combatant. At times a little precious, the film is nonetheless a poetic and bewitching fable, extremely well played. JC-W

• *Jack Slavin* Daniel Day-Lewis, *Kathleen* Catherine Keener, *Rose Slavin* Camilla Belle, *Marty Rance* Beau Bridges, *Gray* Jason Lee, *Red Berry* Jenna Malone, *Thaddius* Paul Dano, *Rodney* Ryan McDonald, *Miriam Rance* Susanna Thompson.

• *Dir* and *Screenplay* Rebecca Miller, *Pro* Lemore Syvan, *Ex Pro* Jonathan Sehring, Caroline Kaplan and Graham

King, *Co-Pro* Melissa Marr, *Line Pro* Brian Bell and Jenny Schweitzer, *Ph* Ellen Kuras, *Pro Des* Mark Ricker, *Ed* Sabine Hoffman, *M* Michael Rohatyn, *Costumes* Jennifer von Mayrhauser.

IFC/Initial Entertainment/Elevation Filmworks-Entertainment.
111 mins. USA. 2004. Rel: 31 March 2006. Cert. 15.

Ballet Russes ★★★★

Visually this feature-length documentary is akin to a television programme but the material is fascinating. Although old footage of ballet extracts is included, it's less a dance work than a history of two companies, one billed as 'the original Ballet Russe' and the other as the 'Ballet Russe de Monte Carlo', and of their fortunes from the 1930s to the 1960s. From triumph (despite rivalry) to eventual decline, the story told revolves around striking personalities and what is recalled is informative, gossipy and engaging. The speakers are mainly former dancers of advanced years but they are so lively and enthusiastic – some still teach today – that *Ballets Russes* becomes a touching document about strong interests making for a lively old age. As such the film's appeal does not depend on special enthusiasm for dance. MS

• *With*: Barbara Arms, Irina Baronova, Yvonne Chouteau, Yvonne Craig, Frederic Franklin, Alan Howard, Nathalie Krassovska, Alicia Markova, Nina Novak, Marc Platt, Wakefield Poole; *narrator* Marian Seldes.

• *Dir* Daniel Geller and Dayna Goldfine, *Pro* Geller, Goldfine, Jonathan Dana, Robert Hawk and Douglas Blair Turnbaugh, *Assoc Pro* Celeste Schaefer Snyder, *Screenplay* Geller, Goldfine, Schaefer Snyder and Gary Weimberg, *Ph* Geller, *Ed* Geller, Goldfine and Weimberg, *M* Todd Boekelheide and David Conte.

Geller/Goldfine/National Endowment for the Arts-Revolver Entertainment.
118 mins. USA. 2005. Rel: 21 April 2006. Cert. PG.

Basic Instinct 2 ★

Having relocated to London, best-selling novelist Catherine Tramell sets her sights on top psychiatrist Dr Michael Glass. Accomplished, handsome and committed to his brief of confidentiality, he is the perfect subject for her next book. But will he succumb to her treacherous charms? Director Michael Caton-Jones has admitted that he did this for the money and it looks like everybody was in it for the dough. The tragedy is that this high-class trash is more boring than shocking, whereas the original was at least entertaining. While much attention has been lavished on the London locales, the capital has seldom looked so anodyne. Indeed, the whole thing seems trapped – embalmed – between the covers of an indifferent Jackie Collins potboiler. JC-W

• *Catherine Tramell* Sharon Stone, *Dr Michael Glass* David Morrissey, *Roy Washburn* David Thewlis, *Dr Milena Gardosh* Charlotte Rampling, *Adam Tower* Hugh Dancy, *Michelle*

Broadwin Flora Montgomery, *Denise Glass* Indira Varma, *Dr Jakob Gerst* Heathcote Williams, *Henry Rose* Terence Harvey, *with* Stan Collymore, Neil Maskell, Jan Chappell, Iain Robertson.

• *Dir* Michael Caton-Jones, *Pro* Mario F. Kassar, Andrew G. Vajna and Joel B. Michaels, *Ex Pro* Moritz Borman, Matthias Deyle, Denise O'Dell and Mark Albela, *Co-Pro* Laura Viederman, *Assoc Pro* James Middleton, *Screenplay* Leora Barish and Henry Bean, *Ph* Gyula Pados, *Pro Des* Norman Garwood, *Ed* John Scott and Isván Király, *M* John Murphy, Costumes Beatrix Aruna Pasztor.

Mario F. Kassar & Andrew G. Vajna/MGM/C2/ Intermedia- Entertainment.
113 mins. USA/UK/Germany. 2006. Rel: 31 March 2006. Cert. 18.

Battle in Heaven ★★★★

Perhaps the most surprising and astonishing Mexican film since *El Topo* in 1971, Carlos Reygadas's *Battle in Heaven* defies conventional cinematic narrative and captures a disturbing, off-centre picture of Mexico City today. At its centre is the unsmiling, disconcertingly absent-minded figure of Marcos, a security guard-cum-chauffeur who is all belly and unflinching gaze. After being fellated in the film's opening sequence, Marcos retires to the subway to sell clocks and jelly when we discover that he has recently been complicit in the death of a baby that he kidnapped with his wife. In between standing around Mexico City not doing much of anything, Marcos indulges in various acts of lacklustre sex, with a prostitute, with his alarmingly overweight wife and with himself in front of the TV while watching football. Much of the action is off-camera, but what Reygadas allows us to see are some remarkable still lifes: the tears of the fellating prostitute, the faithful gathering in the forecourt of the city's imposing basilica, a couple of drunks urinating into the open boot of a car, an overhead shot of a massive traffic intersection, an old man ambling through the subway clutching a bag of his own urine… A bold, powerful, pungent work of cinema. JC-W

• *Marcos* Marcos Hernández, *Ana* Anapola Mushkadiz, *Berta, Marcos' wife* Berta Ruiz, *David* David Bornstein, *Viky* Rosalinda Ramírez, *police inspector* Juan Soria `El Abuelo.'

• *Dir* and *Screenplay* Carlos Reygadas, *Pro* Reygadas, Philippe Bober, Jaime Romandia and Susanne Marian, *Ph* Diego Mártinez Vignatti, *Art Dir* Elsa Ruiz Pirinoli and Daniela Schneider, *Ed* Benjamin Mirguet, Adoración G. Elipe and Nicolas Schmerkin, *M* John Tavener, J.S. Bach and Marcha Cordobesa.

The Coproduction Office/NoDream Cinema/Arte France Cinéma-Tartan Films.
97 mins. Mexico/France/Germany/Belgium/The Netherlands. 2005. Rel: 28 October 2005. Cert. 18.

The Beat That My Heart Skipped ★★★★

Paris; today. A real estate hustler, Thomas Seyr is not beyond using rats or even a frying pan to extract rent owed him. He is like his father, a ruthless, smooth-talking character living a life of immorality. Hell, he even sleeps with his best friend's wife. Then, a chance encounter introduces him to Mr Fox, a music impresario who once championed Thomas's late mother, a concert pianist. Suddenly, Thomas becomes obsessed with polishing his long-forgotten skills on the Steinway… Adapted from James Toback's little-seen 1978 film *Fingers*, *The Beat…* is a kinetic character study streaked with conflicting agendas. Ultimately, a clash between Tom's male and female temperaments – funnelled from his father and his mother – the film is a rollercoaster of contemporary ambiguity. As Tom, Romain Duris recalls a young De Niro – rather than Harvey Keitel, who starred in *Fingers* – and provides an unpredictable, seductive dynamism. And how refreshing to see the French borrowing from 'Hollywood' and making it their own. JC-W

• *Thomas Seyr* Romain Duris, *Robert Seyr* Niels Arestrup, *Miao-Lin* Linh-Dan Pham, *Chris* Emmanuelle Devos, *Aline* Aure Atika, *Fabrice* Jonathan Zaccaï, *Sami* Gilles Cohen, *Minskov* Anton Yakovlev, *Minskov's girlfriend* Mélanie Laurent, *Mr Fox* Sandy Whitelaw.

• *Dir* Jacques Audiard, *Pro* Pascal Caucheteux, *Screenplay* Audiard and Tonino Benacquista, *Ph* Stéphane Fontaine, *Pro Des* François Emmanuelli, *Ed* Juliette Welfling, *M* Alexandre Desplat; J.S. Bach, Liszt, Mozart, Chopin, Brahms; tracks performed by Sporto Kantes, telepopmusik, Bloc Party, 2square, The Kills, A.S. Dragon, and Electrocute, *Costumes* Virginie Montel.

Why Not Prods/SEDIF/France 3 Cinéma/Canal Plus-Artificial Eye.
107 mins. France. 2005. Rel: 4 November 2005. Cert. 15.

Beautiful Boxer ★★★½

Asanee Suwan is excellent in this film's leading role, that of a kick-boxer whose career was undertaken to build up funds to pay for a long desired sex-change operation. This may sound highly fanciful but is in fact a story taken from real life. 2000's *The Iron Ladies* also had roots in reality but in contrast to the tone of outrageous comedy favoured there, the approach here is sensitive and even sensual with the emphasis on the drama. Less happily the film outstays its welcome and serves up a cliché-ridden sub-plot about a devoted coach dying of cancer. Nevertheless, this film works well as a piece sympathetically supportive of individuals accepting their sexuality in order to become what they want to be rather than what others expect. MS

• *Nong Toom/Parinaya Charoemphol* Asanee Suwan, *Pi Chart* Sorapong Chatree, *Nong Toom's mother* Orn-Anong Panyawong, *Nong Toom's father* Nukkid Boonthong, *Nat* Sitiporn Niyom, *herself* Kyoko Inoue, *Jack, the reporter* Keagan Kang.

• *Dir* and *Pro* Ekachai Uekrongtham, *Ex Pro* Phaiboon Damrongchaiyatham, *Screenplay* Ekachai Uekrongtham and Desmond Sim Kim Jin, based on the life of Parinya Charoenphol, *Ph* Choochart Nantitanyatada, *Pro Des* Nopphadol

Arkart, *Ed* Dusanee Puinongpho, *Costumes* Tasakorn Tragulpadektrai.

GMM Pictures-Tartan Films.
118 mins. Thailand. 2003. Rel: 21 October 2005. Cert. 15.

Bee Season ★★★

The Naumanns are a smart, affluent Jewish family of high-achievers living in a salubrious suburb of Oakland, California. Saul Naumann is a theology professor, Miriam a scientist, their son Aaron a talented musician and their nine-year-old daughter, Eliza, something of a whiz with words. When Eliza wins the championship at her school spelling bee, her father transfers his attentions from Aaron to Eliza, in order to prepare her for the competitive road to the national spelling finals... A stylish film with a big head, *Bee Season* is the sort of intellectual challenge that you want to take home with you and puzzle over. A complex narrative laced with compelling ideas, it constantly piques the interest although it does take some underdeveloped shortcuts (such as Aaron's sudden conversion to Krishnaism). For all its faults, though, *Bee Season* should be applauded for exploring such an arcane pocket of American dogma. It's interesting, too, that Richard Gere – a dedicated Vajrayana Buddhist – should tackle a role that explores the Kabbalah so thoroughly. JC-W

• *Saul Naumann* Richard Gere, *Miriam Naumann* Juliette Binoche, *Eliza Naumann* Flora Cross, *Aaron Naumann* Max Minghella, *Chali* Kate Bosworth, *Kabbalah guide* Mitch Sisskind, *with* Joan Mankin, Piers Mackenzie, Lorri Holt.

• *Dir* Scott McGehee and David Siegel, *Pro* Albert Berger and Ron Yerxa, *Ex Pro* Arnon Milchan and Peggy Rajski, *Screenplay* Naomi Foner Gyllenhaal, from the novel by Myla Goldberg, *Ph* Giles Nuttgens, *Pro Des* Kelly McGehee, *Ed* Lauren Zuckerman, *M* Peter Nashel, *Costumes* Mary Malin.

Fox Searchlight/Regency Enterprises/Bona Fide-Fox.
104 mins. USA?Germany. 2005. Rel: 27 January 2006.
Cert. 12A.

The Benchwarmers ★★

Perennial losers Gus, Richie and Clark never got to play baseball as kids, so were dubbed 'benchwarmers' for sitting out every game they attended. Then fellow nerd Mel, now a billionaire, hires baseball legend Reggie Jackson to train the trio to play against the local Little Leaguers, the sons of the bullies who once tormented our heroes... Like many an Alan Sandler production, *The Benchwarmers* is crass, vulgar, infantile, offensive, sentimental and mean-spirited. Which is precisely why America's great unwashed loves Adam Sandler. But is it funny? Well, some of it, if only because director Dugan and writers Covert and Swarsdon throw so much at the screen, some of it has to stick. But for the most part it's stupid on a big budget. JC-W

• *Gus* Rob Schneider, *Richie* David Spade, *Clark* Jon Heder, *Mel* Jon Lovitz, *Jerry* Craig Kilborn, *Liz* Molly Sims, *Wayne* Tim Meadows, *Howie* Nick Swardson, *with* Erinn Bartlett, Amaury Nolasco, Reggie Jackson, Jackie Sandler, Jared Sandler, Rachel Hunter, Terry Crews, Patrick Schwarzenegger,

Dennis Dugan, Charles Dugan, Lochlyn Munro.

• *Dir* Dennis Dugan, *Pro* Adam Sandler and Jack Giarraputo, *Ex Pro* Barry Bernardi and Allegra Clegg, *Co-Pro* Nick Swardson and Derek Dauchy, *Screenplay* Allen Covert and Nick Swardson, *Ph* Thomas Ackerman, *Pro Des* Perry Andelin Blake, *Ed* Peck Prior and Sandy Solowitz, *M* Waddy Wachtel, *Costumes* Mary Jane Fort.

Revolution Studios/Happy Madison-Columbia TriStar.
85 mins. USA. 2005. Rel: 2 June 2006. Cert. 12A.

Bewitched ★

With his career in freefall, egotistical movie star Jack Wyatt is persuaded to star in a TV remake of the popular 1960s' sitcom *Bewitched*. However, to ensure that he is not upstaged, he hires an unknown – Isabel Bigelow – to play his necromantic wife. But little does Jack realise that his nose-wiggling co-star happens to possess some very real supernatural powers of her own... The premise – and cast – did sound promising. Yet there's little magic to be found in a production that feels so forced and depressingly devoid of wit. Nicole Kidman has seldom come off so one-dimensional, Will Ferrell is a ranting bore and dear old Shirley MacLaine is just embarrassing. FYI: Kidman previously played a witch in *Practical Magic*, while Kristin Chenoweth, who plays Isabel's new friend and neighbour, Maria, portrayed a witch on TV's *Wicked*. JC-W

• *Isabel Bigelow* Nicole Kidman, *Jack Wyatt* Will Ferrell, *Iris Smythson* Shirley MacLaine, *Nigel Bigelow* Michael Caine, *Richie* Jason Schwartzman, *Maria Kelly* Kristin Chenoweth, *Uncle Arthur* Steve Carell, *with* Heather Burns, Jim Turner, Stephen Colbert, David Alan Grier.

• *Dir* Nora Ephron, *Pro* Douglas Wick, Lucy Fisher, Penny Marshall and Nora Ephron, *Ex Pro* James W. Skotchdopole, Steven H. Berman and Bobby Cohen, *Screenplay* Nora Ephron and Delia Ephron, *Ph* John Lindley, *Pro Des* Neil Spisak, *Ed* Tia Nolan, *M* George Fenton, *Costumes* Mary Zophres.

Columbia-Columbia TriStar.
102 mins. USA. 2005. Rel: 19 August 2005. Cert. PG.

Big Momma's House 2 ★

FBI Agent Malcolm Turner goes undercover again as Big Momma, this time posing as a nanny in order to expose the suspected designer of a deadly computer 'worm'... This sequel is Martin Lawrence's desperate attempt for another hit five years after the original. The first film had a few funny scenes whereas here the lazy and totally unbelievable script lacks any credibility and is utterly devoid of laughs. It is very similar to that equally unfunny Vin Diesel vehicle *The Pacifier* and is a total waste of Lawrence's talents and of our time. GS

• *Malcolm Turner/Big Momma* Martin Lawrence, *Sherrie* Nia Long, *Leah Fuller* Emily Procter, *Kevin* Zachary Levi, *Tom Fuller* Mark Moses, *Molly* Kat Dennings, *Carrie* Chloë Grace Moretz, *with* Dan Lauria, Jascha Washington, Mark Joy, William Ragsdale.

• *Dir* John Whitesell, *Pro* David T. Friendly and Michael Green, *Ex Pro* Martin Lawrence, Jeffrey Kwatinetz and Arnon Milchan, *Screenplay* Don Rhymer, *Ph* Mark Irwin, *Pro Des* Craig Stearns, *Ed* Priscilla Nedd Friendly, *M* George S. Clinton, *Costumes* Debrae Little.

Fox/Regency Enterprises/Deep River/Firm Films-Fox. 98 mins. USA. 2006. Rel: 10 February 2006. Cert. PG.

The Big White ★★★

The 'Big White' is Alaska but the hue is definitely black in this sweet comedy about facial disfigurement, mental illness and misplaced cadavers. On the brink of Chapter 11 bankruptcy, mild-mannered travel agent Paul Barnell is cold, desperate and concerned about the deteriorating mental health of the wife he adores. Then he stumbles across a corpse in a dumpster and sees a chance to collect on the $1m insurance on his missing brother. So he deposits the stiff in the wilderness, covers it in bacon and waits for the local wildlife to removes all traces of identity… Initially, *The Big White* seems to be following in the noble tradition of such 'immovable body' classics as *The Trouble With Harry* and *Weekend at Bernie's*. Quickly, however, the film shifts into *Raising Arizona* and *Fargo* gear, what with the bleak terrain, fumbled kidnapping attempts and Coen brothers' regular Holly Hunter stealing the film wholesale. Indeed, it is the actors who save the day, drawing major laughs out of some skilfully engineered physical comedy. JC-W

• *Paul Barnell* Robin Williams, *Margaret Barnell* Holly Hunter, *Raymond Barnell* Woody Harrelson, *Ted Watters* Giovanni Ribisi, *Tiffany* Alison Lohman, *Gary* Tim Blake Nelson, *Jimbo* W. Earl Brown, *Cam* William Merasty, *with* Marina Stephenson Kerr, Ralph Alderman, Frank Adamson.

• *Dir* Mark Mylod, Pro Chris Roberts, Christopher Eberts and David Faigenblum, *Ex Pro* Jane Barclay, Hannah Leader, Michael Birnbaum, Andreas Schmid, Andy Grosch, John Schimmel and Kia Jam, *Screenplay* Colin Friesen, *Ph* James Glennon, *Pro Des* Jon Billington, *Ed* Julie Monroe, *M* Mark Mothersbaugh.

Ascendant Pictures/Capitol Films/Rising Star-Momentum. 105 mins. USA/UK/Canada/Germany. 2004. Rel: 24 March 2006. Cert. 15.

A Bittersweet Life ★★★★½

Seoul; the present. Kim Sun-woo is very much in charge of the swanky hotel he runs for underworld kingpin Kang. But when Sun-woo is entrusted with tailing the boss's young girlfriend (Hee-soo), he takes matters into his own hands – to disastrous ends… A masterful balancing act between the understated and the extreme, Kim Jee-woon's fourth feature is a modern *noir* classic. Its power lies in the face of young Lee Byung-hun, a beautiful man whose unflappable serenity is punctuated by spectacular acts of athletic combat. And he is well matched by a colourful ensemble of villains (Kim Young-chul's stately godfather is a major plus), although Shin Mina in the pivotal role of Hee-soo lacks the ethereal quality her character demands (in spite of a climactic luminescent smile). Original title: *Dal Kom Han In-saeng*. JC-W

Life's a drag: Martin Lawrence goes under several covers in John Whitesell's desperate and lazy *Big Momma's House 2* (from Fox)

• *Kim Sun-woo* Lee Byung-hun, *Boss Kang* Kim Young-chul, *Hee-soo* Shin Mina, *Chairman Baek* Whang Jung-min, *Moon-suk* Kim Roi-ha, *with* Moon Chong-hyuk, Lee Ki-young, Oh Dalsoo.

• *Dir* and *Screenplay* Kim Jee-woon, *Pro* Oh Jung-wan and Lee Eugene, *Ex Pro* Park Dong-ho, *Ph* Kim Ji-yong, *Pro Des* Ryu Sung-hee, *Ed* Choi Jae-geun, *M* Dal Palan and Chang Young-gyu, *Costumes* Cho Sang-kyung, *Sound* Choi Tae-young, *Action Choreography* Chung Du-hong.

CJ Entertainment/CTIC-Tartan Films.
118 mins. South Korea. 2005. Rel: 20 January 2006.
Cert. 18.

Black Sun ★★★★★

Told magnificently on the soundtrack in his own words, this is the true story of how French painter and filmmaker Hugues de Montalembert was blinded by muggers in New York in 1978 at the age of 36. It's an absorbing, humbling and uplifting account of a man coming to terms and philosophising about life in the process and it soon becomes clear that de Montalembert is someone truly remarkable and quite without self pity. Daringly, Gary Tarn, whose first feature this is, opts not for conventional reconstruction but for stylised images. They reflect the Frenchman's state of mind, the emphasis being mainly on abstract designs or on visuals which correspond to what he came to 'see' when his brain created its own impressions of locations and even of people. This approach ensures that *Black Sun* is not a work that could have functioned fully on radio and, since Tarn's own musical score is another key factor, he has produced a brilliantly original work. It's at once narrative and meditation and a combination of film and music that yields a work of art of a new kind. The nearest thing to it is Derek Jarman's *Blue* (1993) but, whereas that remained an avant-garde exercise highly specialised in its appeal, this unique work has the power to reach and to touch a far wider audience. MS

• *Dir, Ph, Ed, M* and *Sound* Gary Tarn, *Pro* John Battsek, *Ex Pro* Alfonso Cuarón, Andrew Ruhemann and Frida Torresblanco, *Story* Hugues de Montalembert.

• *With*: Hugues De Montalembert.

Alfonso Cuarón/Land Media/Passion Pictures-ICA Projects.
75 mins. UK/USA. 2005. Rel: 5 May 2006. No Cert.

Blinded ★★

Looking for part-time work, Danish backpacker Mikael 'Mike' Hammershoi arrives at the bleak outpost of Black's farm in the Scottish borders. There, he's employed by the grim, blind Francis Black to tip old farm machinery into a `mud hole.' While treated with disdain by the farmer, Mikael finds a more sympathetic reception from Francis's young wife… A number of adjectives spring to mind while watching *Blinded*, not least 'stilted', 'static' and 'soporific'. A muted melodrama inspired by Emile Zola's *Thérèse Raquin*, this

first-time effort from director Eleanor Yule is like an Agatha Christie potboiler slipped a dose of Horlicks. Visually, it's quite arresting (particularly considering the film's minuscule budget), but a meddlesome, misjudged score and a series of awkward dramatic moments (in which every indiscretion is stumbled upon by the wrong person at the wrong time), kill it stone dead.
JC-W

• *Francis Black* Peter Mullan, *Rachel Black* Jodhi May, *Mike Hammershoi* Anders W. Berthelsen, *Bella Black* Phyllida Law, *Caroline Lamar* Samantha Bond, *Lachie McNeill* Kenny Ireland, *with* Kate Donnolly, Ralph Riach, Jan Wilson.

• *Dir* and *Screenplay* Eleanor Yule, *Pro* Oscar van Heek, *Ph* Jerry Kelly, *Pro Des* Mark Leese, *Ed* James Hamilton, *M* Malcolm Lindsay, *Costumes* Ali Mitchell, *Sound* Giles Lamb, Douglas McDougall and Michael MacKinnon.

Oscar Films/New Found Film/Scottish Television/National Lottery-Guerilla Films.
92 mins. UK. 2004. Rel: 30 September 2005. Cert. 15.

Born Into Brothels: Calcutta's Red Light Kids ★★★★

This documentary feature came about because of Zana Briski's concern for the inhabitants of Calcutta's Red Light District. This made her known to those living there and enabled her to film them. She wanted in particular to explore the plight of children born to prostitutes who find it difficult to obtain education because of their background and who, if female, may be under pressure to follow in their mother's footsteps. Made with Ross Kauffman, this move is unexceptional as film-making (it could be more effectively structured) but as a human document it is enormously powerful and compelling, the children wonderfully natural before the cameras coming across as human beings whose potential may be stifled by the situation in which they find themselves. MS

• *Dir, Pro* and *Ph* Ross Kauffman and Zana Briski, *Ex Pro* Geralyn White Dreyfous, *Co-Ex Pro* Pamela Tanner Boll, *Ed* Kauffman and Nancy Baker, *Assoc Pro* Ellen Peck, *M* John McDowell.

HBO/Cinemax Documentary Films-ICA Projects.
85 mins. USA/Canada. 2004. Rel: 2 September 2005.
No Cert.

Born to Fight ★★★

Deaw is a Special Forces police officer who, having witnessed the murder of his partner, takes a break from work. While he is attending a charity event in a small village at the Thai/Burmese border, guerrillas take over the village and hold everybody hostage. Deaw has no option but to organise an escape… This amazing martial arts film comes from Thailand and is very much in the style of the recent *Ong Bak*. Rittikrai's film is predictable but quite thrilling and the astounding stunts are quite exceptional. Stay until the final credits to see how some of these brilliant and extremely dangerous stunts were choreographed. Original title: *Ked Ma Lui*. GS

• *Moo* Amornthep Waesaeng, *Deaw* Dan Chupong, *General Yang* Noppol Gomarachun, *Daew's sister* Kesarin Ekatawatkul, *Yang's lieutenant* Suntisuk Phromsiri, *Tub* Piyapong Piw-on.

• *Dir* Panna Rittikrai, *Pro* Prachya Pinkaew and Sukanya Vongsthapat, *Ex Pro* Somsak Techaratanaprasert, *Screenplay* Rittikrai, Thanapat Taweesuk and Morakot Kaewthanee, *Ph* Surachet Tongmee, *Pro Des* Dusit Yapakawong, *Ed* Triple-X CG and Thanapat Taweesuk, *M* Atomix Clubbing, *Stunt Coordinator* Bunlu Srisaeng, *Action Coordinator* Panna Rittikrai

Sahamongkolfilm-Momentum Pictures.
95 mins. Thailand. 2004. Rel: 2 September 2005. Cert. 18.

Bread and Tulips ★

Taking *Shirley Valentine* as its prototype, this Italian feature made in 2000 won awards in Italy but is so incredibly naff that not even the engaging leading lady, Licia Maglietta, can save it. Totally improbable in its contrivances, it has as heroine a housewife, Rosalba, who, left behind during a family holiday when the coach departs, ends up in Venice making a new life for herself and finding a lover in the elderly Fernando, a role that wastes Bruno Ganz. Inept comedy dominates the first half as Rosalba's husband sends a plumber instead of a private investigator to trace her, but the second part of this farrago is a would-be touching love story. Some I know have enjoyed it as a tongue-in-cheek fairy tale, but others share my view that the film is the epitome of banality. MS

• *Rosalba Barletta* Licia Maglietta, *Fernando Girasoli* Bruno Ganz, *Costantino* Giuseppe Battiston, *Grazia* Marina Massironi, *Mimmo* Antonio Catania, *Fermo* Felice Andreasi, *Adele* Tatiana Lepore.

• *Dir* Silvio Soldini, *Pro* Daniele Maggioni, *Screenplay* Soldini and Doriana Leondeff, *Ph* Luca Bigazzi, *Art Dir* Paola Bizzarri, *Ed* Carlotta Cristiani, *M* Giovanni Venosta, *Costumes* Silvia Nebiolo.

Monogatari/Istituto Luce Spa-MatCine.
116 mins. Italy/Switzerland. 2000. Rel: 23 September 2005. Cert. 12A.

Breakfast on Pluto ★★★★½

Breakfast on Pluto is the simple story of a boy who wants to be a girl in search of his biological mother and, ultimately, himself. Abandoned as a baby, Patrick 'Kitten' Braden grows up as the foster son of a conventional, world-weary housewife in

Life's a drag II: Cillian Murphy scrubs up surprisingly well in Neil Jordan's bold and original *Breakfast on Pluto* (from Pathé)

the village of Tyreelin, near the border of Northern Ireland. As Ireland struggles to find its identity amid the nocturnal assassinations and car bombs, Patrick is only too aware of who he is but is not entirely sure where he is going. If only he could find the 'Phantom Lady', his real mammy… Like Neil Jordan's criminally overlooked *The Butcher Boy* (1997), *Breakfast on Pluto* is a vivid adaptation of a best-selling novel by Patrick McCabe. Unfolding during the volatile late 1960s and early 1970s, the film is rich in cultural and historical allusion, embroidered with the kitsch songs of the period and pitted with the brutal outbursts of violence of the time. Yet through all this, Patrick Braden remains true to himself and is brilliantly realised by Cillian Murphy in a revelatory performance. A cinematic *tour-de-force*, *Pluto* is a bold, moving, blackly comic and dramatically original work. JC-W

• *Patrick 'Kitten' Braden* Cillian Murphy, *Bertie* Stephen Rea, *John Joe Kenny* Brendan Gleeson, *Father Liam* Liam Neeson, *Eily Bergin* Eva Birthistle, *PC Wallis* Ian Hart, *Mr Silky String* Bryan Ferry, *Billy Hatchet* Gavin Friday, *Ma Braden* Ruth McCabe, *Patrick aged ten* Conor McEvoy, *Peepers Egan* Patrick McCabe, *Jackie Timlin* Eamonn Owens, *Charlie* Ruth Negga, *with* Liam Cunningham, Laurence Kinlan, Steven Waddington, Mary Coughlan, Tony Devlin, Mary Ryan, Kathryn Pogson, Britta Smith, Doreen Keogh, Tom Hickey.

• *Dir* Neil Jordan, *Pro* Jordan, Alan Moloney and Stephen Woolley, *Ex Pro* François Ivernel, Cameron McCracken, Brendan McCarthy and Mark Woods, *Line Pro* Jo Homewood, *Assoc Pro* Susan Mullen, *Screenplay* Jordan and Patrick McCabe, *Ph* Declan Quinn, *Pro Des* Tom Conroy, *Ed* Tony Lawson, *M* Anna Jordan, *Costumes* Eimer Ni Mhaoldomhnaigh.

Pathé/Bord Scannán na hÉireann/Irish Film Board-Pathé. 128 mins. Ireland/UK. 2005. Rel: 13 January 2006. Cert. 15.

Brick ★★

Although he and Emily have broken up, school outsider Brendan Frye still burns a candle for her. Then, when she rings him out of the blue, he is concerned that she is in trouble. As it happens, Emily has disappeared and Brendan braces himself for an investigation that is bound to reap a whole lotta trouble… Film buff Rian Johnson penned this tribute to *film noir* and the American detective movie fresh out of college. Seven years later the completed film won the Special Jury Prize at Sundance for 'Originality of Vision.' Setting his story in high school was a smart move and there's certainly a *frisson* when the Kingpin's mom serves apple juice to his collaborators. The film is also cold, self-satisfied and wilfully abstruse and though Johnson reveals a confident style and an artist's eye, *Brick* never succeeds at being anything more than a novel idea well done. JC-W

• *Brendan Frye* Joseph Gordon-Levitt, *Laura* Nora Zehetner, *The Pin* Lukas Haas, *Tugger* Noah Fleiss, *The Brain* Matt O'Leary, *Emily* Emilie de Ravin, *Dode* Noah Segan, *V.P. Trueman* Richard Roundtree, *Kara* Meagan Good, *with* Brian White, Jonathan Cauff, Reedy Gibbs.

• *Dir* and *Screenplay* Rian Johnson, *Pro* Ram Bergman and Mark G. Mathis, *Ex Pro* Lisa Johnson, Craig Johnson, Norman Dreyfuss and Marcie Campbell, *Co-Pro* Dana Lustig, Susan Dynner and Angela Roessel, *Assoc Pro* Raymond Izaac, *Ph* Steve Yedlin, *Pro Des* Jodie Tillen, *Ed* not credited, *M* Nathan Johnson, *Costumes* Michele Posch, *Sound* Jonathan Miller.

Bergman Lustig/Focus Features-Optimum Releasing. 109 mins. USA. 2005. Rel: 12 May 2006. Cert. 15.

Brokeback Mountain ★★★

In the summer of 1963, Jack Twist and Ennis Del Mar are hired as sheepherders on the forbidding slopes of Brokeback Mountain, Wyoming. Cut off from the rest of the world, they form a profound solidarity, a largely unspoken bond that leads to a rare intimacy. But, by its very nature, their affinity must remain a lifelong secret… Adapted from Annie Proulx's short story published in *The New Yorker*, *Brokeback Mountain* is a brave, beautiful film. It's also refreshingly understated, achingly sensitive and enriched with arresting detail. Even so, it's a film that cannot escape some fundamental problems with its structure. Spanning twenty years, it is inevitably episodic and the focus of the two men's relationship is diluted in a squall of melodramatic incident. There's a domestic here, a fisticuffs there and Heath Ledger – in a courageous piece of casting, to be sure – always seems to be acting. Gustavo Santaolalla's music is also preeningly saccharine, ultimately reducing a tough tale of male camaraderie to a picturesque but unconvincing tract. JC-W

• *Ennis Del Mar* Heath Ledger, *Jack Twist* Jake Gyllenhaal, *Lureen Newsome* Anne Hathaway, *Alma* Michelle Williams, *Joe Aguirre* Randy Quaid, *Cassie* Linda Cardellini, *L.B. Newsome* Graham Beckel, *Lashawn Malone* Anna Faris, *Alma Jr, aged 19* Kate Mara, *Jack's mother* Roberta Maxwell, *John Twist* Peter McRobbie, *with* David Trimble, Tom Carey, Mary Liboiron, Brooklyn Proulx, Sarah Hyslop, Jacey Kenny, Cayla Wolever, David Harbour.

• *Dir* Ang Lee, *Pro* Diana Ossana and James Schamus, *Ex Pro* William Pohlad, Larry McMurtry, Michael Costigan and Michael Hausman, *Co-Pro* Scott Ferguson, *Screenplay* Larry McMurtry and Diana Ossana, *Ph* Rodrigo Prieto, *Pro Des* Judy Becker, *Ed* Geraldine Peroni and Dylan Tichenor, *M* Gustavo Santaolalla, *Costumes* Marit Allen.

Focus Features/River Road Entertainment/Alberta Film Development Program-Entertainment. 134 mins. USA/Canada. 2005. Rel: 30 December 2005. Cert. 15.

Broken Flowers ★★★★★

Don Johnston has made his fortune in computers and now leads a life of ease. However, Don's peace is periodically punctuated by visits from his neighbour, Winston, a hard-working father of five. Then, when Don receives an unsigned letter from an old girlfriend claiming that he's a father, Winston prepares a meticulous road trip for him. Reluctantly,

Don sets off to try and find the mother of his theoretical son… After an absence of six years (discounting *Coffee and Cigarettes*, his anthology of shorts), Jim Jarmusch returns with his most mature film to date. Virtually designed as a series of still lifes, respectful of its silences and rich with telling touches, *Broken Flowers* is a fascinating anthropological study of contemporary America. Bill Murray, even more minimalist than in *Lost in Translation*, proves himself to be a past master as a listener, weighing every eccentric facet he encounters with an imperceptible astonishment. It's a film where every detail counts, and the details – subtle clues to the essence of a character or scene – are consummately orchestrated. This is Jarmusch's masterpiece. JC-W

• *Don Johnston* Bill Murray, *Winston* Jeffrey Wright, *Laura* Sharon Stone, *Dora* Frances Conroy, *Carmen* Jessica Lange, *Penny* Tilda Swinton, *Sherry* Julie Delpy, *Carmen's assistant* Chloë Sevigny, *Mona* Heather Alicia Simms, *Ron* Christopher McDonald, *Lolita* Alexis Dziena, *Sun Green* Pell James, *the kid* Mark Webber, *with* Brea Frazier, Dared Wright, Suzanne Hevner.

• *Dir and Screenplay* Jim Jarmusch, from an idea by Bill Raden and Sara Driver, *Pro* Jon Kilik and Stacey Smith, *Co-Pro* Ann Ruark, *Ph* Frederick Elmes, *Pro Des* Mark Friedberg, *Ed* Jay Rabinowitz, *M* Mulatu Astatke; Fauré; tracks performed by The Greenhornes, Holly Golightly, Jackie Mittoo, The Tennors, The Allman Brothers Band, Sleep, Marvin Gaye, and The Brian Jonestown Massacre, *Costumes* John Dunn.

Focus Features/Five Roses/BAC Films-Momentum Pictures. 105 mins. USA/France. 2005. Rel: 21 October 2005. Cert. 15.

The Brothers Grimm ★★½

Amazingly, this is Terry Gilliam's first completed film since *Fear and Loathing in Las Vegas* in 1998. And it is so very Gilliam, being a visionary, phantasmagorical, frequently brilliant original marred by unfettered buffoonery and lack of narrative discipline. Transporting the folklorists Jacob and Wilhem Grimm into a world of cinematic fiction, historical fact and European mythology, Gilliam has created an illusory domain of cackling witches, diabolical curses and malevolent forests. Here, Wilhelm and Jacob Grimm spread stories of terrifying demons and exploit the gullible for their own material gain, becoming apocryphal heroes who vanquish their own devilish creations. Then they are removed to the woebegone village of Marbaden, a community suffering from a very real curse… Putting on screen a thrilling evocation of the Grimms' own realm of remote hamlets and possessed woods, Gilliam reveals the full extent of his cinematic mastery. Yet, again, he over eggs his own pudding, expanding his unique vision into a Pythonesque spectacle of hammy acting and bloated theatrics. And it was all so promising… JC-W

• *Wilhem Grimm* Matt Damon, *Jacob Grimm* Heath Ledger, *Cavaldi* Peter Stormare, *Angelika* Lena Headey, *Delatombe* Jonathan Pryce, *Mirror Queen* Monica Bellucci, *with* Harry Gilliam, Roger Ashton-Griffiths, Mackenzie Crook, Richard Ridings, Julian Bleach, Bruce McEwan, Petr Vrsek.

• *Dir* Terry Gilliam, *Pro* Charles Roven and Daniel Bobker, *Ex Pro* Bob Weinstein, Harvey Weinstein, Jonathan Gordon and Andrew Rona, *Co-Pro* Jake Myers and Michael Solinger, *Assoc Pro* Mishka Cheyko, *Screenplay* Ehren Kruger, *Ph* Newton Thomas Sigel and Nicola Pecorini, *Pro Des* Guy Hendrix Dyas, *Ed* Lesley Walker, *M* Dario Marianelli, *Costumes* Gabriella Pescucci and Carlo Poggioli, *Visual Effects* Kent Houston.

Mosaic Media Group/Dimension Films/MGM-Buena Vista International. 118 mins. USA/Czech Republic. 2005. Rel: 4 November 2005. Cert. 12A.

The Business ★★½

Malaga, Spain; the 1980s. Raised in the high-rise squalor of London's East End, Frankie is advised by his ne'er-do-well father to stay away from 'crime, women and drugs'. But by Frankie's reckoning that doesn't leave him much, so when he's adopted by an English crime lord on Spain's Costa-del-Crime, he feels immediately at home… Loud, flashy and predictable, *The Business* is an unashamed hybrid of *Lock Stock…*, *Sexy Beast* and *GoodFellas*. With its voice-over, freeze frames and bountiful soundtrack of familiar pop standards, it plunders a tried-and-tested formula with a couldn't-give-a-shit bravura. And it looks great (fire engine-red sports cars set against cobalt-blue skies), while the salty, blackly humorous dialogue comes thick and fast. There's also a charismatic performance from Tamar Hassan (reminiscent of a wide-boy Antonio Banderas) and a snivelling turn from Geoff Bell (in the Joe Pesci part), although a villain of the calibre of Ben Kingsley (in *Sexy Beast*, say) is sadly missing. JC-W

• *Frankie* Danny Dyer, *Charlie* Tamer Hassan, *Sammy* Geoff Bell, *Carly* Georgina Chapman, *Ronnie* Eddie Weber, *Danny* Adam Bolton, *Shirley* Linda Henry, *Sonny* Roland Manookian, *with* Arturo Venegas, Camille Coduri, Martin Marquez.

• *Dir* and *Screenplay* Nick Love, *Pro* Allan Niblo and James Richardson, *Ex Pro* Rob Morgan and Rupert Preston, *Co-Pro* Andy Eliot, *Line Pro* Charlie Woodhouse, *Ph* Damian Bromley, *Pro Des* Paul Burns, *Ed* Stuart Gazzard, *M* Ivor Guest; tracks performed by Duran Duran, Frankie Goes To Hollywood, Mary Jane Girls, The Cult, Loose Ends, Rick James, Simple Minds, Martha and the Muffins, The Buggles, A Flock of Seagulls, Belouis Some, Shannon, David Bowie, Talk Talk, The Knack, Roxy Music, Orchestral Manoeuvres in the Dark, Adam & the Ants, and Blondie, *Costumes* Andrew Cox.

Vertigo Films/Monkey Prods-Pathé. 95 mins. UK/Spain. 2005. Rel: 2 September 2005. Cert. 18.

Cache

See *Hidden*.

Calvaire ★★★

Having extricated himself from the suffocating embrace of a nursing home (where all the female residents seemingly lust after him), travelling crooner Marc Stevens heads south for Christmas. But then his van breaks down in the remote region of Fagne, Belgium, and he is forced to spend the night at the Bartel Inn. Bartel, a genial, one-joke comedian, welcomes his guest with promises of hearty meals and mechanical expertise. But he also warns Marc to go nowhere near the local village, although he can't bring himself to say why… While its antecedents include such seminal touchstones as *Deliverance* and *The Texas Chain Saw Massacre*, *Calvaire* is the antithesis of the American horror film. Stripped of the standard prologue, false alarms, scary music (in fact, there's no 'incidental' music at all) and the traditional screaming damsel-in-distress, this is very primal cinema. Almost matter-of-fact in its 'key' moments, it is all the more disquieting for playing its hand outside the margins of what is accepted. This is really elemental horror, although not quite in the European league of *Funny Games* and *Switchblade Romance*. English title: *The Ordeal*. JC-W

• *Marc Stevens* Laurent Lucas, *Paul Bartel* Jackie Berroyer, *Robert Orton* Philippe Nahon, *Boris* Jean-Luc Couchard, *Mademoiselle Vicky* Brigitte Lahaie, *Madame Langhoff* Gigi Coursigni, *Thomas Orton* Philippe Grand'Henry.

• *Dir* Fabrice du Welz, *Pro* Vincent Tavier and Eddy Géradon-Luyckx, *Ex Pro* Tavier, Michaël Gentile and Eddy Géradon-Luyckx, *Screenplay* du Welz and Romain Protat, *Ph* Benoit Debie, *Art Dir* Emmanuel Demeulemeester, *Ed* Sabine Hubeaux, *M* Vincent Cahay, *Costumes* Géraldine Picron.

The Film/La Parti/Tarantula/Studio Canal-Tartan Films. 91 mins. France/Belgium/Luxemburg. 2004. Rel: 9 December 2005. Cert. 18.

Capote ★★★½

On 15 November, 1959, two men walked into a farmhouse in Kansas and shot dead a family of four. Fascinated by such an act of meaningless violence, the novelist Truman Capote set about exploring the case in an article that, over the course of four years, turned into the non-fiction novel *In Cold Blood*. American literature and, indeed, Capote, were never to be the same again… Anybody with a passing knowledge of Capote, *In Cold Blood* or the killers Perry Smith and Dick Hickock cannot but be intrigued by this creditable exploration of the dynamics of journalism and its effect on the people it portrays. At once exploiting Smith as a subject yet drawn to him as a human being, Capote is traumatised by a case that at first merely piqued his intellectual curiosity. As the eccentric writer, with all his effete tics and mannerisms in place, Philip Seymour Hoffman is mesmerising, while Catherine Keener and Chris Cooper lend a gravitas to the more conventional characters that inhabit his world. If, at times, the film is a little dry, it is redeemed by its pictorial poise and enormous humanity. JC-W

• *Truman Capote* Philip Seymour Hoffman, *Nelle Harper Lee* Catherine Keener, *Perry Smith* Clifton Collins Jr., *Alvin Dewey* Chris Cooper, *Jack Dunphy* Bruce Greenwood, *William Shawn* Bob Balaban, *Marie Dewey* Amy Ryan, *Dick Hickock* Mark

Pellegrino, *with* Allie Mickelson, Marshall Bell, Araby Lockhart, John MacLaren.

• *Dir* Bennett Miller, *Pro* Caroline Baron, William Vince and Michael Ohoven, *Ex Pro* Dan Futterman, Philip Seymour Hoffman, Kerry Rock and Danny Rosett, *Assoc Pro* Kyle Mann, Dave Valleau, Emily Ziff and Kyle Irving, *Line Pro* Jacques Méthé, *Screenplay* Futterman, from the book by Gerald Clarke, *Ph* Adam Kimmel, *Pro Des* Jess Gonchor, *Ed* Christopher Tellefsen, *M* Mychael Danna, *Costumes* Kasia Walicka Maimone, *Sound* Ron Bochar.

United Artists/Sony Pictures Classics/A-Line Pictures/ Cooper's Town-Columbia TriStar. 114 mins. USA/Canada. 2005. Rel: 24 February 2006. Cert. 15.

The Car Keys ★★

Aspiring filmmaker Laurent Baffie misplaces his car keys and decides this is the perfect jumping off point for his first movie. But who will he get to star and how will he raise the money? In search of a suitable formula, Baffie solicits for advice on camera. He pesters the famous for their collaboration; he seeks ideas from the clientele of his local. What *The Car Keys* lacks in cohesion and discipline, it fails to make up for in energy and originality. Some surreal gags – such as the door in Laurent's Paris apartment opening straight onto the beach – only work for their novelty; but are then repeated again and again like the desperate waving of a drowning man. Original title: *Les clefs de bagnole*. JC-W

• *Laurent* Laurent Baffie, *Daniel* Daniel Russo, *Pascal* Pascal Sellem, *with* Karine Lyachenko, Dani, Alain Chabat, Gérard Depardieu, Michel Galabru, Ticky Holgado, Claude Berri, Alain Sarde, Pierre Arditi, Yvan Attal, Daniel Auteuil, Jean-Marc Barr, Richard Berry, Jean-Claude Brialy, Guillaume Canet, Eric Cantona, Antoine de Caunes, Gérard Darmon, Jean-Pierre Darroussin, Gérard Jugnot, Gérard Lanvin, Samuel Le Bihan, Vincent Lindon, Thierry Lhermitte, Eddy Mitchell, Vincent Perez, Pierre Richard, Jean Rochefort, Patrick Timsit, Roschdy Zem, Sophie Marceau, Guillaume Depardieu, Jean-Pierre Marielle, Venus Williams, etc.

• *Dir, Pro* and *Screenplay* Laurent Baffie, *Ph* Philippe Vène, *Art Dir* Baptiste Glaymann, *Ed* Anne Lafarge and Bridget O'Driscoll, *M* Ramon Pipin.

Laurent Baffie Prods/Canal Plus-Tartan Films. 94 mins. France. 2003. Rel: 8 July 2005. No Cert.

Casanova ★★★½

Venice; 1753. With his reputation for womanising threatening the moral fabric of Venice, Giacomo Casanova is forced to find a bride. But no sooner has he committed himself to the honour of a previously unattainable virgin, than he falls heavily for the charms of one Francesca Bruni. However, Francesca is not only already engaged to a wealthy Genoese merchant, but she despises everything Casanova stands for… With its witty dialogue, breezy pace, mouth-watering locations and effervescent score (Corelli, Rameau, Albinoni), *Casanova* is an unexpected delight. Recalling the knockabout period comedies of Richard Lester in the 1970s, the film makes up in canny plotting what it lacks in sexual disclosure. Indeed, anybody expecting sheer raunch will be disappointed, although we do witness a fair proportion of Oliver Platt. Good, too, to see Jeremy Irons on comic form, while Sienna Miller makes a spunky heroine. While an easy film to knock (the critics had a heyday), it's an even easier film to enjoy. JC-W

• *Giacomo Casanova* Heath Ledger, *Francesca Bruni* Sienna Miller, *Bishop Pucci* Jeremy Irons, *Papprizzio* Oliver Platt, *Andrea Bruni* Lena Olin, *Lupo* Omid Djalili, *Donato* Stephen Greif, *Dalfonso* Ken Stott, *Victoria* Natalie Dormer, *with* Helen McCrory, Leigh Lawson, Tim McInnerny, Charlie Cox, Phil Davis, Paddy Ward, Lauren Cohan, Niall Buggy.

• *Dir* Lasse Hallström, *Pro* Mark Gordon, Betsy Beers and Leslie Holleran, *Ex Pro* Su Armstrong, Adam Merims and Gary Levinsohn, *Co-Pro* Guido Cerasuolo, *Screenplay* Jeffrey Hatcher and Kimberly Simi, from a story by Simi and Michael Cristofer, *Ph* Oliver Stapleton, *Pro Des* David Gropman, *Ed* Andrew Mondshein, *M* Alexandre Desplat; Albinoni, Corelli, Durante, Handel, Rameau, Vivaldi, etc, *Costumes* Jenny Beavan.

Touchstone Pictures-Buena Vista International. 111 mins. USA. 2005. Rel: 17 February 2006. Cert. 12A.

The Cave ★★

A group of American cave explorers are hired to investigate a cave, which is found near the ruins of a 13th century abbey in the middle of a Romanian forest... Bruce Hunt's film is well crafted and the script has some fun lines like 'respect the cave' and 'there is no rescue team – we are the rescue team', but ultimately it's all quite predictable. However, *The Cave* is not totally unwatchable thanks to its attractive cast – even if there is a little too much wooden acting. Comparisons are inevitable to the similar but vastly superior *The Descent*. GS

• *Jack* Cole Hauser, *Top Buchanan* Morris Chestnut, *Tyler* Eddie Cibrian, *Briggs* Rick Ravanello, *Dr Nicolai* Marcel Iures, *Strode* Kieran Darcy-Smith, *Kim* Daniel Dae Kim, *Kathryn* Lena Headey, *Charlie* Piper Perabo.

• *Dir* Bruce Hunt, *Pro* Richard Wright, Michael Ohoven, Tom Rosenberg, Gary Lucchesi and Andrew Mason, *Ex Pro* Marco Mehlitz, Neil Bluhm and Judd Malkin, *Co-Pro* Robert Bernacchi and James McQuaide, *Screenplay* Michael Steinberg and Tegan West, *Ph* Ross Emery, *Pro Des* Pier Luigi Basile, *Ed* Brian Berdan, *M* Johnny Klimek and Reinhold Heil, *Costumes* Wendy Partridge, *Sound* Dane A. Davis, *Visual Effects* James McQuaide, Gary Beach and Payam Shohadai, *Creature Design* Patrick Tatopoulos.

Screen Gems/Lakeshore Entertainment/Cinerenta/ City Prods-Entertainment.97 mins. Germany/USA/ Australia. 2005. Rel: 26 August 2005. Cert. 12A.

Lust in Venice: Lena Olin and Heath Ledger share a mint in Lasse Hallström's witty, breezy *Casanova* (from Buena Vista International)

The Cave of the Yellow Dog ★★★★★

Part-documentary and part-narrative drama, this is the story of a nomadic Mongolian family of five who find themselves adopted by a wild dog. The eldest daughter, Nansaa, befriends the canine stranger with glee, but her father tells her that she must return it to the wild… In a season when most of what passes for cinema comes out of a computer, it's revitalizing to encounter something brimming with the minutia of humanity. Little more than a series of snapshots of nomadic Mongolian life, the film accumulates an enormous resonance punctuated with moments of extraordinary beauty and spontaneous humour. Seldom has the camera seemed so invisible, as the children, half asleep, play in their bed or as their parents go about their business of chopping wood, making cheese and skinning sheep. And out of all this a very real story emerges, set in a world still barely touched by the twentieth century. A small masterpiece. Original title: *Die Höhle des gelben Hundes*.
JC-W

• *With*: Urindorj Batchuluun, Batbayar Batchuluun, Nansaa Batchuluun, Buyandulam Daramdadi Batchuluun.

• *Dir* and *Screenplay* Byambasuren Davaa, inspired by a story by Gantuya Lhagva, *Pro* Stephen Schesch, *Ex Pro* Natalie Lambsdorff, *Ph* Daniel Schönauer, *Ed* Sarah Clara Weber, *M* Ganpurev Dagvan.

X-Verleih/Schesch Filmproduktion-Tartan Films. 93 mins. Germany. 2005. Rel: 30 June 2006. Cert. U.

Charlie and the Chocolate Factory ★★★★

Long isolated from his own family, the extravagant confectioner Willy Wonka launches a worldwide contest to find an heir to his candy empire. Five lucky children win the 'Golden Tickets' and embark on a bizarre tour of Willy's world… Erasing all memories of the 1971 adaptation of Roald Dahl's classic children's novel (starring Gene Wilder), Tim Burton has channelled into the core of Dahl's sensibility and added his own distinctive spin. Inventing a backstory for Wonka that explains the chocolatier's eccentric *modus operandi*, Burton has presented a rounded, gob-smacking fantasy that appeals on a number of simultaneous levels. The production design may be the star, but there are some sublime extras here, down to the smallest non-sequiter. Johnny Depp, in his fourth collaboration with the director, is somewhat swamped by the grandiose machinery of Burton's invention, although the actor's bizarre serving of Michael Jackson mixed with Marilyn Manson is not without its pleasures. The film could have been darker – the children are monstrous and deserve a harsher comeuppance – but it will certainly appeal to a humungous cross-section of the young-at-heart. JC-W

• *Willy Wonka* Johnny Depp, *Charlie Bucket* Freddie Highmore, *Grandpa Joe* David Kelly, *Mother Bucket* Helena Bonham Carter, *Father Bucket* Noah Taylor, *Mrs Beauregarde* Missi Pyle, *Mr Salt* James Fox, *Oompa-Loompas* Deep Roy, *Dr Wonka* Christopher Lee, *Violet Beauregarde* AnnaSophia Robb, *Mr Teavee* Adam Godley, *Mrs Gloop* Franziska Troegner, *Veruca Salt* Julia Winter, *Mike Teavee* Jordan Fry, *Augustus Gloop* Philip Wiegratz, *Grandma Georgina* Liz Smith, *Grandma Josephine* Eileen Essell, *Grandpa George* David Morris, *Narrator* Geoffrey Holder, *with* Nitin Ganatra, Shelley Conn, Chris

Heir of the dog: Nansaa Batchuluun inherits a canine friend in Byambasuren Davaa's picturesque and exhilarating *The Cave of the Yellow Dog* (from Tartan Films)

Cresswell, Mark Heap, Roger Frost, Oscar James, Debora Weston, Annette Badland.

• *Dir* Tim Burton, *Pro* Brad Grey and Richard D. Zanuck, *Ex Pro* Patrick McCormick, Felicity Dahl, Michael Siegel, Graham Burke and Bruce Berman, *Screenplay* Jon August, *Ph* Philippe Rousselot, *Pro Des* Alex McDowell, *Ed* Chris Lebenzon, *M* Danny Elfman, *Costumes* Gabriella Pescucci, *Sound* Steve Boeddeker.

Warner/Village Roadshow/Plan B/Theobald Film-Warner. 114 mins. USA/UK/Australia. Rel: 29 July 2005. Cert. PG.

Cheaper by the Dozen 2 ★½

Afraid that his extensive brood is drifting away from the family nest, Tom Baker arranges a nostalgic trip to Lake Winnetka, Michigan. However, the family vacation turns into a nightmare when the competitive paterfamilias discovers that his childhood rival, Jimmy Murtaugh, has bought up most of the waterfront property… At one point Steve Martin's Tom Baker announces that, 'every dad is entitled to one hideous shirt – and one horrible sweater.' And every star is entitled to one lousy sequel to an iffy remake. But what with this and *Mixed Nuts*, *The Out-of-Towners*, *The Pink Panther* and the *Father of the Bride* couplet, Steve Martin has blotted his copybook big time. Bonnie Hunt supplies some long-suffering sparkle, but Martin's wild-and-crazy-guy act is rheumatic. Besides, there's something rather queasy about watching a 60-year-old man goof off with all his pre-pubescent kids. The rest is just mechanical mediocrity. JC-W

• *Tom Baker* Steve Martin, *Jimmy Murtaugh* Eugene Levy, *Kate Baker* Bonnie Hunt, *Charlie Baker* Tom Welling, *Nora Baker-McNulty* Piper Perabo, *Sarina Murtaugh* Carmen Electra, *Anne Murtaugh* Jaime King, *Lorraine Baker* Hilary Duff, *Eliot Murtaugh* Taylor Lautner, *Sarah Baker* Alyson Stoner, *Bud McNulty* Jonathan Bennett, *Jake Baker* Jacob Smith, *with* Liliana Mumy, Morgan York, Kevin G. Schmidt, Forrest Landis, Brent Kinsman, Alexander Conti, Melanie Tonello, Damon Runyan, Adam Shankman, Shawn Levy.

• *Dir* Adam Shankman, *Pro* Shawn Levy and Ben Myron, *Ex Pro* Shankman, Jennifer Gigbot and Garrett Grant, *Screenplay* Sam Harper, *Ph* Peter James, *Pro Des* Cary White, *Ed* Christopher Greenbury and Matthew Cassel, *M* John Debney, *Costumes* Joseph G. Aulisi.

Fox/21 Laps-Fox. 93 mins. USA. 2005. Rel: 26 December 2005. Cert. PG.

Chicken Little ★½

A shortsighted chicken with self-confidence issues kicks up a brouhaha when he announces to the citizens of Oakey Oaks that the sky is falling. But when no evidence to the fact is forthcoming, the false alarm is put down to the intervention of an acorn. Then the tentacled aliens arrive… Disney's first in-house computer-animated feature (after the company's break-up with Pixar), *Chicken Little* is little short of a travesty. Taking the old fable of the brave, misunderstood chick, Disney have shaved it of any charm it might've had and turned it into a

crass, all-American and all too-familiar farce. Thus Little is transformed into a pint-sized, bespectacled, accident-prone weakling who tries to win friends and influence people on the baseball field. Worse still, real aliens are introduced into the mix in a crude attempt to cash-in on the *War of the Worlds*. With its tired referencing of other movies, obvious musical cues and unbearable characters (Runt of the Litter is a particular irritant), this really is a dishonour to the memory of Walt. JC-W

• *Voices*: *Chicken Little* Zach Braff, *Buck Cluck* Garry Marshall, *Abby Mallard* Joan Cusack, *Runt of the Litter* Steve Zahn, *Foxy Loxy* Amy Sedaris, *Mayor Turkey Lurkey* Don Knotts, *dog announcer* Harry Shearer, *Mr Woolensworth* Patrick Stewart, *Principal Fetchit* Wallace Shawn, *Melvin, alien dad* Fred Willard, *Tina, alien mom* Catherine O'Hara, *with* Adam West, Patrick Warburton, Mark Walton, Mark Dindal, Dan Molina.

• *Dir* Mark Dindal, *Pro* Randy Fullmer, *Assoc Pro* Peter Del Vecho, *Screenplay* Steve Bencich, Ron J. Friedman and Ron Anderson, from a story by Dindal and Mark Kennedy, *Pro Des* David Womersley, *Ed* Dan Molina, *M* John Debney; tracks performed by Barenaked Ladies, Five for Fighting, Patti LaBelle and Joss Stone, The Cheetah Girls, C & C Music Factory, REM, and Diana Ross, *Sound* Robert L. Sephton.

Walt Disney Pictures-Buena Vista International. 80 mins. USA. 2005. Rel: 10 February 2006. Cert. U.

The Child ★★★

Sonia, 18, has just given birth to a baby boy, Jimmy. But when she hooks up with the child's father, Bruno, he couldn't appear less interested. Living each day as it comes, Bruno seems more concerned about how he'll flog his next assignment of stolen goods… Some seem surprised that the Dardenne brothers' drab, virtually unwatchable *Rosetta* won the Palme d'Or at the 1999 Cannes festival. This, their sixth feature, also snagged the Palme d'Or and while plagued with problems of credibility, is a more understandable winner. A powerful evocation of European realism, it conveys a world of quiet desperation and certainly pulls no punches. Yet some of the details rankle: can a girl who's just given birth really crave sex? Can a nine-day-old baby be so resistant to crying? Be that as it may, *The Child* is a telling, uncompromising and pertinent commentary on the underbelly of Belgian society. Original title: *L'Enfant*. JC-W

• *Bruno* Jérémie Renier, *Sonia* Déborah François, *Steve* Jérémie Segard, *young thug* Fabrizio Rongione, *plainclothes officer* Olivier Gourmet, *Bruno's mother* Mireille Bailly.

• *Dir* and *Screenplay* Jean-Pierre and Luc Dardenne, *Pro* Jean-Pierre and Luc Dardenne and Denis Freyd, *Line Pro* Olivier Bronckart, *Ph* Alain Marcoen, *Art Dir* Igor Gabriel, *Ed* Marie-Hélène Dozo, *Costumes* Monic Parelle.

Les Films du Fleuve/Archipel 35/Arte France Cinéma/ Canal Plus-Artificial Eye. 95 mins. Belgium/France. 2005. Rel: 10 March 2006. Cert. 12A.

The Chronicles of Narnia: The Lion, The Witch and the Wardrobe ★★

While playing hide-and-seek with her three siblings in a rambling country mansion, ten-year-old Lucy Pevensie retreats into a large, ornate wardrobe. Within, she finds a magical forest blanketed with snow and there meets a friendly faun, a half-man, half-goat. It is the latter, Mr Tumnus, who warns Lucy of the invincible White Witch, who has turned the parallel universe of Narnia into an eternal winter… One of the most hyped films in recent memory, Disney's mammoth transmogrification of the C.S. Lewis classic is neither beast nor fowl. Boasting some of the most gobsmacking CGI effects to date, the film cannot escape from being just a computer-generated phenomenon. Indeed, it is an unwieldy attempt to bridge the commercial gap between *Shrek* and *The Lord of the Rings*, piling on the battles, mythical creatures and staggering New Zealand landscapes with the calculating onslaught of a franchise machine. The fact remains that director Adamson is no Peter Jackson – and he can't direct children. You'll believe a graphic can roar, but you probably won't care.
JC-W

• *White Witch* Tilda Swinton, *Mr Tumnus* James McAvoy, *Professor Kirke* Jim Broadbent, *Lucy Pevensie* Georgie Henley, *Edmund Pevensie* Skandar Keynes, *Peter Pevensie* William Moseley, *Susan Pevensie* Anna Popplewell, *Ginarrbrik* Kiran Shah, *Father Christmas* James Cosmo, *Mrs Pevensie* Judy McIntosh, *Mrs MacReady* Elizabeth Hawthorne.

• *Voices*: *Aslan* Liam Neeson, *Mr Beaver* Ray Winstone, *Mrs Beaver* Dawn French, *Mr Fox* Rupert Everett, *Gryphon* Cameron Rhodes, *Philip the Horse* Philip Steuer, *Vardan* Jim May, *Wolf* Sim Evan-Jones.

• *Dir* Andrew Adamson, *Pro* Mark Johnson and Philip Steuer, *Ex Pro* Adamson and Perry Moore, *Co-Pro* Douglas Gresham (stepson of C.S. Lewis), *Screenplay* Adamson, Ann Peacock, Christopher Markus and Stephen McFeely, *Ph* Donald M. McAlpine, *Pro Des* Roger Ford, *Ed* Sim Evan-Jones and Jim May, *M* Harry Gregson-Williams, *Costumes* Isis Mussenden, *Visual Effects* Dean Wright.

Walt Disney Pictures/Walden Media-Buena Vista International. 140 mins. USA. 2005. Rel: 8 December 2005. Cert. PG.

Cinderella Man ★★★★★

In his youth, James J. Braddock was a hero, a boxing phenomenon. But his take of $8,000 a fight has slipped to $50, his hand is broken and his family relocated to a run-down, one-room flat in New Jersey. Then, as the Depression is crippling the spirit of America, Braddock has his boxing licence revoked… Few American filmmakers working today can tell a story as well as Ron Howard. Paying as much attention to the little details (Mae Braddock watering down the milk, a coin pressed mid-fight behind Braddock's ear) as to the broad sweep of his narrative, Howard has created a classic fable that it as much about its period – the Great Depression – as the larger-than-life characters who inhabit it. Russell Crowe – who refused a stunt double after dislocating

The ugly stepbrother: Craig Bierko gives Russell Crowe grief in Ron Howard's exhilarating classic fable, *Cinderella Man* (from Buena Vista International)

his shoulder – is surprisingly low-key out of the ring, but still holds the screen with a palpable focus. And the production design, photography, costumes, etc, are second to none, contributing to a work of cinematic excellence. JC-W

• *James J. Braddock* Russell Crowe, *Mae Braddock* Renée Zellweger, *Joe Gould* Paul Giamatti, *Max Baer* Craig Bierko, *Jimmy Johnston* Bruce McGill, *Mike Wilson* Paddy Considine, *Joe Jeanette* Ron Canada, *Ford Bond* David Huband, *Corn Griffin* Art Binkowski, *John Henry Lewis* Troy Amos-Ross, *Art Lasky* Mark Simmons, *with* Connor Price, Ariel Waller, Rosemarie DeWitt, Nicholas Campbell, Chuck Shamata, Rance Howard, Clint Howard, Ken James, Gavin Grazer, Craig Warnock, Peter MacNeil, Darrin Brown, Beau Starr.

• *Dir* Ron Howard, *Pro* Howard, Brian Grazer and Penny Marshall, *Ex Pro* Todd Hallowell, *Assoc Pro* Louisa Velis and Kathleen McGill, *Screenplay* Cliff Hollingsworth and Akiva Goldsman, *Ph* Salvatore Totino, *Pro Des* Wynn Thomas, *Ed* Mike Hill and Dan Hanley, *M* Thomas Newman, *Costumes* Daniel Orlandi, *Boxing Choreography* Nick Powell, *Boxing Stunts* Steve Lucescu.

Universal/Miramax/Imagine Entertainment/Parkway Prods-Buena Vista International. 144 mins. USA. 2005. Rel: 9 Septermber 2005. Cert. 12A.

Clean ★★★½

Like our own Michael Winterbottom, France's Olivier Assayas makes a point of not repeating himself. Here he has a story set in Canada, Paris and (briefly) London about a once popular

Chinese rock singer, Emily (Maggie Cheung), determined to get off drugs. Her aim is to claim back her young son from the late father's parents (Nick Nolte and Martha Henry) who have him in their care. Beautifully shot by Eric Gautier, the film is anxious not to be sentimental. It succeeds, but it also keeps us at a distance since Emily, first seen when already an addict, doesn't fully claim our sympathy. A somewhat open ending and rather too much music are additional minor drawbacks, but Assayas does show his admiration for a woman no longer young who has the courage to change her life. MS

• *Emily Wang* Maggie Cheung, *Albrecht Hauser* Nick Nolte, *Elena* Béatrice Dalle, *Irene Paolini* Jeanne Balibar, *Vernon* Don McKellar, *Rosemary Hauser* Martha Henry, *Lee* James Johnston, *Jay* James Dennis, *Jean-Pierre* Remi Martin, *Sandrine* Laetitia Spigarelli, *with* Tricky, Liz Densmore, David Roback, Emily Haines.

• *Dir* and *Screenplay* Olivier Assayas, *Pro* Edouard Weil, Xavier Giannoli, Xavier Marchand and Niv Fichman, *Ex Pro* Aline Perry and Rupert Preston, *Ph* Eric Gautier, *Pro Des* François-Renaud Labarthe and Bill Fleming, *Ed* Luc Barnier, *M* David Roback, Tricky, and Brian Eno; *Costumes* Anaïs Romand.

Rectangle Prods-Vertigo Films.
110 mins. France/UK/Canada. 2004. Rel: 1 July 2005. Cert. 15.

A Cock and Bull Story ★★★★

Steve Coogan and Rob Brydon are in make-up getting on each other's nerves. Brydon reckons his part in the new film adaptation of *Tristram Shandy* is a co-starring lead. Coogan begs to differ. However, with the daily vicissitudes of the film business, anything could pan out… While capturing the random, comic and episodic spirit of Laurence Sterne's iconoclastic literary classic *Tristram Shandy*, *A Cock and Bull Story* is also a critic's wet dream. A highly original and incisive satire of the filmmaking process and the world of Steve Coogan, it is simultaneously a stylish and hilarious mosaic of 18th century farce and of contemporary comic improvisation. As in Jim Jarmusch's *Coffee and Cigarettes*, Coogan plays himself as a smug, conceited celebrity, in this case endowed with a girlfriend, a new baby and a running rivalry with co-star Rob Brydon, who also plays himself. Fact, fictionalised fact and compromised fiction blur into a bizarre, entertaining homage to a novel that, in the 18th century, turned literature on its head. Indeed, of the all the cinematic adaptations of impossible books (including *Naked Lunch* and *Fear and Loathing in Las Vegas*), this is probably the most successful. JC-W

• *Walter Shandy/Tristram Shandy/Steve Coogan* Steve Coogan, *Uncle Toby/Rob Brydon* Rob Brydon, *Elizabeth Shandy* Keeley Hawes, *Susannah/Shirley Henderson* Shirley Henderson, *Dr Slop* Dylan Moran, *Mark, the director* Jeremy Northam, *Jenny Coogan* Kelly Macdonald, *Widow Wadman/Gillian Anderson* Gillian Anderson, *Corporal Trim* Raymond Waring, *Jennie* Naomie Harris, *Simon, the producer* James Fleet, *Ingoldsby* Mark Williams, *Joe, the screenwriter* Ian Hart, *Adrian* Roger Allam, *Ed* Benedict

Wong, *Greg* Greg Wise, *Anita* Ronni Ancona, *Gary, the journalist* Kieran O'Brien, *with* Stephen Fry, Mark Tandy, Jack Shepherd, Mary Healey, Stephen Rodrick, Stuart Wilson.

• *Dir* Michael Winterbottom, *Pro* Winterbottom and Andrew Eaton, *Ex Pro* Kate Ogborn, Julia Blackman, Jeff Abberley, David M. Thompson, Tracey Scoffield and Henry Normal, *Co-Pro* Anita Overland and Wendy Brazington, *Screenplay* Martin Hardy, *Ph* Marcel Zyskind, *Pro Des* John Paul Kelly, *Ed* Peter Christelis, *M* Michael Nyman, Erik Nordgren, Schumann, Handel, J.S. Bach, Purcell, asnd Christopher Barnett, *Costumes* Charlotte Walter.

BBC Films/EM Media & Revolution Films/Baby Cow Prods/Scion Films-Redbus Film Distribution.
94 mins. UK. 2005. Rel: 20 January 2006. Cert. 15.

Cockles & Muscles ★★★

Cote d'Azur, France; the present. What is hoped to be a resuscitating family holiday for Béatrix and Marc and their son Charly doesn't exactly turn out to plan. There is some confusion as to Charly's burgeoning sexuality, while the molluscs that Marc and Béatrix consume seem to have a disconcerting effect on their behaviour… The wonderful thing about the French is that when they make a farce, they people it with plausible characters. Here, we totally believe in the domestic dynamics of this family, as Béatrix strives to be `modern' in her outlook, Marc combats the perils of inactivity and Charly spends way too much time in the shower. Still, while *Cockles & Muscles* is always a pleasure to watch, it doesn't attain the laugh quotient it may have been hoping for. In oenological terms, it's more a cheeky Sauvignon Blanc than a rich, rewarding port. Original title: *Crustacés et Coquillages*. US title: *Mariscos Beach*. JC-W

• *Béatrix* Valeria Bruni Tedeschi, *Marc* Gilbert Melki, *Didier* Jean-Marc Barr, *Mathieu* Jacques Bonnaffé, *Martin* Édouard Collin, *Charly* Romain Torres, *Laura* Sabrina Seyvecou, *with* Yannick Baudin, Julien Weber, Sebastien Cormier, Marion Roux.

• *Dir and Screenplay* Olivier Ducastel & Jacques Martineau, *Pro* Nicolas Blanc, *Assoc Pro* Robert Guediguian, *Ph* Matthieu Porot-Delpech, *Pro Des* Lise Petermann, *Ed* Dominique Gallieni, *M* Philippe Miller, *Costumes* Anne-Marie Giacalone, *Choreography* Sylvie Giron.

Agat Films & Cie/Bac Films/Cofimage 16/Canal Plus-Peccadillo Pictures.
94 mins. France. 2004. Rel: 14 April 2006. Cert. 15.

Confetti ★½

In a ploy to boost their readership, the publisher and editor of the bridal magazine *Confetti* cook up an event they call 'Most Original Wedding of the Year.' And so three couples compete for the prize of a ghastly suburban house, namely Sam and Matt (who intend to turn their big day into a Busby Berkeley show-stopper), Michael and Joanna (a pare of naturists who aim to wed in the altogether) and Josef and Isabelle (who envisage a sort of wedding-cum-Wimbledon)… Dragging the mockumentary out for yet another airing, writer-director Debbie Isitt (*Nasty Neighbours*) emphasises all the problems of the genre. Drowning the action in cheesy musical numbers and encouraging her cast to ham it up mercilessly, Isitt seems keener to resurrect the spirit of the *Carry On* films than pay homage to *This is Spinal Tap*. Jimmy Carr is very funny as the publisher and Vincent Franklin and Jason Watkins make the most of their camp wedding planners (modelled on the pop artists Gilbert and George), but the rest is soundly depressing. JC-W

• *Matt* Martin Freeman, *Sam* Jessica Stevenson, *Josef* Stephen Mangan, *Isabelle* Meredith MacNeill, *Michael* Robert Webb, *Joanna* Olivia Colman, *Archie Heron* Vincent Franklin, *Gregory Hough* Jason Watkins, *Vivien* Felcity Montagu, *Antoni* Jimmy Carr, *Sam's mum* Alison Steadman, *Snoopy* Mark Wootton, *Jen* Sarah Hadland, *Sam's dad* Ron Cook, *with* Selina Cadell, Julia Davis, Nickolas Grace, Mark Heap, Helen Ryan, Peter Isitt, Barbara Isitt.

• *Dir* and *Screenplay* Debbie Isitt, *Pro* Ian Flooks and Ian Benson, *Ex Pro* David M. Thompson, Lee Thomas, Andrew Taylor, Oliver Edwards and Joe Oppenheimer, *Ph* Dewald Aukema, *Pro Des* Chris Roope, *Ed* Nicky Ager, *M* Paul Englishby, *Costumes* Deirdre Clancy.

BBC Films/Fox Searchlight/Wasted Talent/Screen West Midlands-Fox.
99 mins. UK/USA. 2006. Rel: 5 May 2006. Cert. 15.

The Constant Gardener ★★★★

A self-effacing and rather ineffectual figure working for the British High Commission in Kenya, Justin Quayle finds his life transformed when he becomes romantically involved with Tessa, a conscientious live wire bent on saving Africa. Once in Kenya, Tessa starts ruffling some old-school feathers and would appear to be a voracious flirt. Her meddling results in her death and Justin is determined to find out who killed her – and why… At the grand old age of 74, John le Carré has become the Graham Greene of the new millennium. Yet even as this is the tale of a low-level diplomat in a forgotten corner of the British empire, it is a topical, kinetic and truly international movie. An Anglo-German-Canadian co-production directed by a Brazilian, scored by a Spaniard and set in Africa, it is still an extremely British tale of intrigue, subterfuge and New Labour incompetence. Fernando Meirelles, who directed the multi-Oscar-nominated *City of God*, takes the staple ingredients of the Cold War milieu and gives them a decidedly cinematic, immediate spin. With a hand-held camera and panoramic views of cold, grey London and a burnished, luminous Kenya, Meirelles charges Le Carré's pertinent novel with a jolt of compelling, contemporary vitality. JC-W

• *Justin Quayle* Ralph Fiennes, *Tessa Quayle* Rachel Weisz, *Sandy Woodrow* Danny Huston, *Sir Bernard Pellegrin* Bill Nighy, *Lorbeer* Pete Postlethwaite, *Arnold Bluhm* Hubert Koundé, *Ghita Pearson* Archie Panjabi, *Sir Kenneth Curtiss* Gerard McSorley, *Gloria Woodrow* Juliet Aubrey, *Arthur Hammond* Richard McCabe, *with* Daniele Harford, Keith Pearson, John Sibi-Okumu, Donald Sumpter, Nick Reding, Jacqueline Maribe, Donald Apiyo, Anneke Kim Sarnau, Mumbi Kaigwa, Chris Payne, Jeffrey Caine, Rupert Simonian, Claire Simpson.

• *Dir* Fernando Meirelles, *Pro* Simon Channing Williams, *Ex*

Dead funny: The eponymous *Corpse Bride* – voiced by Helena Bonham Carter – from Warner

Pro Gail Egan, Robert Jones, Donald Ranvaud, Jeff Abberley and Julia Blackman, *Co-Pro* Tracey Seaward, Henning Molfenter and Thierry Potok, *Screenplay* Jeffrey Caine, *Ph* César Charlone, *Pro Des* Mark Tildesley, *Ed* Claire Simpson, *M* Alberto Iglesias; tracks performed by Ayub Ogada, Bomas of Kenya, Cibelle, Rachel Weisz, and Necessary Noise, *Costumes* Odile Dicks-Mireaux.

Focus Features/UK Film Council/National Lottery-UIP. 128 mins. UK/Germany/Canada. 2005. Rel: 11 November 2005. Cert. 15.

Corpse Bride ★★★★★

Adapted from a Russian folk tale, *Corpse Bride* is a miraculous combination of the original, the witty and the innovative. Taking stop-motion animation to a whole new level, the film tells the story of an arranged marriage in a depressed Victorian town that, fortuitously, turns out to be a godsend for its timid protagonists. Victor, the sole scion of the grossly upwardly mobile Nell and William Van Dort, is to be married off to Victoria, the only child of the aristocratic but destitute Finis and Maudeline Everglot. Unable to master his vows at the wedding rehearsal, Victor goes off into the woods to practise. Perfecting the ritual, Victor triumphantly places his bride's wedding ring onto what he thinks is a twig, only to find that he has fixed the token onto the skeletal finger of a young female cadaver. And so Victor has become inadvertently betrothed to a corpse… Punctuated with musical numbers penned by Tim Burton regular Danny Elfman (*The Nightmare Before Christmas*), and voiced by a wonderful cast of British talent and Johnny Depp, the film is a delirious delight. Loaded with verbal and visual puns and pictorially awe-inspiring, this is a genuine triumph of human imagination. JC-W

• **Voices**: *Victor Van Dort* Johnny Depp, *Corpse Bride* Helena Bonham Carter, *Victoria Everglot* Emily Watson, *Finis Everglot* Albert Finney, *Barkis Bittern* Richard E. Grant, *Maudeline Everglot* Joanna Lumley, *Pastor Galswells* Christopher Lee, *Mrs Plum/black widow spider* Jane Horrocks, *Nell Van Dort* Tracey Ullman, *William Van Dort/Mayhew/Paul, the head watier* Paul Whitehouse, *with* Michael Gough, Enn Reitel, Deep Roy, and *Bonejangles* Danny Elfman.

• *Dir* Mike Johnson and Tim Burton, *Pro* Burton and Allison Abbate, *Ex Pro* Jeffrey Auerbach and Joe Ranft, *Screenplay* John August, Caroline Thompson and Pamela Pettler, *Ph* Pete Kozachik, *Pro Des* Alex McDowell, *Ed* Jonathan Lucas and Chris Lebenzon, *M* Danny Elfman, *Sound* Martin Cantwell and Steve Boeddeker, *Animation* Anthony Scott.

Warner/Tim Burton/Laika Entertainment-Warner. 77 mins. UK/USA. 2005. Rel: 21 October 2005. Cert. PG.

Crash ★★★★★

LA Detective Graham Waters observes that the inhabitants of his city have lost the simple, human ability of touch, noting that, 'we crash into something just so that we feel OK.' It's a metaphor that fits nicely into the first scene, in which a routine traffic accident turns into a racial altercation between a Mexican and an Asian (or, as it happens, a Puerto Rican and a Korean). The ripple effect waxes and wanes over the next few hours until leading, inevitably, to an act of unalterable tragedy… Paul Haggis, scripter of *Million Dollar Baby*, was in Los Angeles when he was carjacked at gunpoint. After he'd recovered his nerves and changed all the locks in his house, he started to think about the men who had taken his car. Rather than condemn them out of hand, he tried to understand them. The result is this passionate, multi-levelled drama in which all the villains are the other guy. Sagely, Haggis has said that we all hate to be judged but see no contradiction in judging others. Thus, he has fashioned a *Short Cuts* on racism, in which even the most liberal characters find they are victim of an indoctrinated prejudice. How can a DA bestow a medal on a heroic fireman who happens to be an Iraqi called Saddam? How can a racist cop abuse his privileges one day and risk his life for a complete stranger the next? Consummately plotted, flush with irony and superbly acted, *Crash* is a film to take home and ponder over in the small hours. If it has any faults, its preachiness shows through on occasion, but it's a human, intelligent sermon that should be compulsory viewing at schools throughout the planet. JC-W

• *Jean Cabot* Sandra Bullock, *Officer Graham Waters* Don Cheadle, Officer Ryan Matt Dillon, *Ria* Jennifer Esposito, *Flanagan* William Fichtner, *District Attorney Rick Cabot* Brendan Fraser, *Thayer Cameron* Terrence Howard, *Anthony* Chris `Ludacris' Bridges, *Christine Thayer* Thandie Newton, *Tom Hansen* Ryan Phillippe, *Daniel Ruiz* Michael Peña, *Peter* Larenz Tate, *Shaniqua* Loretta Devine, *Karen* Nona Gaye, *Lara Ruiz* Ashlyn Sanchez, *Dorri* Bahar Soomekh, *Graham's mother*

Collision course: Matt Dillon in his Oscar-nominated performance as a racist cop in Paul Haggis's moving and provocative *Crash* (from Pathé)

Beverly Todd, *Farhad* Shaun Toub, *with* Karina Arroyave, Art Chudabala, Tony Danza, Keith David, James Haggis, Bruce Kirby, Jack McGee, Greg Joung Paik, Marina Sirtis, Kathleen York.

• *Dir* Paul Haggis, *Pro* Haggis, Cathy Schulman, Don Cheadle, Bob Yari, Mark R. Harris and Bobby Moresco, *Ex Pro* Andrew Reimer, Tom Nunan, Jan Körbelin and Marina Grasic, *Co-Pro* Betsy Danbury, *Screenplay* Haggis and Bobby Moresco, *Ph* J. Michael Muro, *Pro Des* Laurence Bennett, *Ed* Hughes Winborne, *M* Mark Isham, *Costumes* Linda Bass.

Bob Yari Prods/DEJ Prods/BlackFriar's Bridge/Harris Company/Bull's Eye Entertainment-Pathé.
112 mins. USA/Germany/Australia. 2004.
Rel: 12 August 2005. Cert. 15.

C.R.A.Z.Y. ★★★½

C.R.A.Z.Y. is about an album, or at least about how music defines and informs our lives. For Gervais Beaulieu, a traditional father prone to siring sons, Patsy Cline means as much to him as Bowie does to Zac, Gervais' fourth boy. Born on Christmas Day in 1960, Zachary Beaulieu is literally dropped on his head and from then on exhibits a sensitivity lacking in his siblings. Zac's mother believes he is endowed with a gift to heal, Gervais thinks he is soft. Over the ensuing twenty years, Zac grows up at right angles to his family, seeking to find out who he truly is beyond the conventions of a changing world… The cinematic equivalent of crazy paving, this fourth feature from the Montreal-born Jean-Marc Vallée reveals a world-class talent. Knowing the latent power of a child's face and skilfully blending music and imagery, Vallée orchestrates a magnificent tale of domestic catharsis. However, by the halfway mark, *C.R.A.Z.Y.* begins to follow an all-too-familiar path of pop-driven nostalgia, and by the end the effect is more dazzling than emotionally enriching. Still, Marc-André Grondin is quite remarkable as the 15-to-21-year-old Zac. JC-W

• *Gervais Beaulieu* Michel Côté, *Zachary Beaulieu, aged 15-21* Marc-André Grondin, *Laurianne Beaulieu* Danielle Proulx, *Zachary Beaulieu, aged 6-8* Émile Vallée, *Raymond Beaulieu, aged 22-28* Pierre-Luc Brillant, *Christian Beaulieu, aged 24-30* Maxime Tremblay, *Antoine Beaulieu, aged 21-27* Alex Gravel, *Michelle, aged 15-22* Natacha Thompson, *Yvan Beaulieu, aged 15-16* Félix Antoine Despatie, *with* Johanne Elbrun, Mariloup Wolfe, Francis Ducharme.

• *Dir* and *Co-Pro* Jean-Marc Vallée, *Pro* Pierre Even, *Ex Pro* Jacques Blain and Richard Speer, *Assoc Pro* Nicole Hilaréguy, *Screenplay* Vallée and François Boulay, *Ph* Pierre Mignot, *Visual Design* Patrice Bricault-Vermette, *Ed* Paul Jutras, *M* tracks performed by David Bowie, Elvis Presley, Jean-Marc Vallée, Patsy Cline, The Stories, The Cure, Charles Aznavour, Jefferson Airplane, Pink Floyd, Giorgio Moroder, etc, *Costumes* Ginette Magny, *Sound* Martin Pinsonnault.

Circus Communications/Crazy Films/Télèfilm Canada-Soda Pictures.
126 mins. Canada. 2005. Rel: 21 April 2006. Cert. 15.

Crossing the Bridge – The Sound of Istanbul ★★★★

In total contrast to his German drama *Head-On* with its forceful in-your-face style, the Turkish director Fatih Akin now offers this engagingly atmospheric documentary set in Istanbul. In theory it's a film about the musical mix in a city where East meets West and pop music reflects both (the range extends from psychedelic underground to the Saz tradition with songs in Kurdish, a language that had been banned in Turkey for political reasons not long ago). The artists are mainly much younger than those in *Buena Vista Social Club*, but their music comes across as less commercialised and more political than in the West. Furthermore, although lacking any strong shape, the film beguiles through its views of Istanbul quite marvellously photographed in colour by Hervé Dieu. A word too for Andrew Bird's editing. Inevitably the music is central, but this is filmmaking of real quality that captures the flavour of the city.
MS

• *With*: Alexander Hacke, Baba Zula, Orient Expressions, Duman, Replikas, Erkin Koray, Ceza, Istanbul Style Breakers, etc.

• *Dir* and *Screenplay* Faith Akin, *Pro* Akin, Klaus Maeck, Andreas Thiel, Sandra Harzer-Kux and Christian Kux, *Line Pro* Tina Mersmann, *Ph* Hervé Dieu, *Ed* Andrew Bird.

Pictorion Pictures/NFP-Soda Pictures.
90 mins. Germany/Turkey. 2005. Rel: 24 February 2006. Cert. 12A.

Crying Fist ★★

South Korea; the present. Kang Tae-sik was a silver-winning boxer in the 1990 Beijing Asian Games but has now fallen on hard times. Separated from his wife and chased by creditors, he finds himself on the street, offering passers-by a chance to punch him for money. Meanwhile, Yoo Sang-hwan lands in juvenile detention after mugging and almost killing a wealthy pensioner. Filled with rage, he takes up boxing to let off steam, but – initially, at least – his temper is no substitute for his poor technique. Inevitably, these two misfits are destined for a face-off in the ring… A nice idea, this, but one that works against itself dramatically. For a boxing film to succeed, one has to root for one of the combatants, but neither of these low-lifes is very sympathetic. In addition, the fight choreography is so frenetic that it's hard to tell one pugilist from another, while the muddy, jaundiced photography is another minus. Original title: *Jumeogi unda*.
JC-W

• *Kang Tae-sik* Choi Min-shik, *Yoo Sang-hwan* Ryoo Seung-beom, *Won-tae* Lim Won-hee, *Sang-chul* Chun Ho-jin, *Yong-dae* Oh Dal-su, *Sun-joo* Seo Hye-rin, *Kang Se-jin* Lee Jun-gu.

• *Dir* Ryoo Seung-wan, *Pro* Syd Lim, *Ex Pro* Kim Dong-joo, *Co-Pro* JD Han, *Screenplay* Ryoo and Jeon Cheol-hong, *Ph* Cho Yong-kyu, *Pro Des* Park Il-hyun, *Ed* Nam Na-young, *M* Bang Jun-suk.

ShowEast/Sio Film/Bravo Entertainment-
Contender Entertainment.
121 mins. South Korea. 2005. Rel: 9 December 2005.
Cert. 15.

Cry Wolf ★★½

At an American high school, following a murder in nearby woods, eight students start spreading lies on the Internet about a serial killer called The Wolf. But when a mysterious figure wearing a ski mask appears on campus and the students' friends start disappearing one by one, it seems that the rumour they have spread was not too far from the truth... The acting is inconsistent but newcomer Jeff Wadlow's stylish CinemaScope film keeps the suspense going until the end with clever plotting and an unexpected twist. GS

• *Owen* Julian Morris, *Dodger* Lindy Booth, *Tom* Jared Padalecki, *Randall* Jesse Janzen, *Rich Walker* Jon Bon Jovi, *Mercedes* Sandra McCoy, *Regina* Kristy Wu, *Mr Matthews* Gary Cole, *with* Jane Beard, Paul James, Ethan Cohn, Anna Deavere Smith.

• *Dir* Jeff Wadlow, *Pro* Beau Bauman, *Ex Pro* David Bartis and Doug Liman, *Screenplay* Wadlow and Bauman, *Ph* Romeo Tirone, *Pro Des* Martina Buckley, *Ed* Seth Gordon, *M* Michael Wandmacher, *Costumes* Alysia Raycraft.

Rogue Pictures/Hypnotic Pictures-Optimum Releasing.
90 mins. USA. 2005. Rel: 13 January 2006. Cert. 12A.

Curious George ★★★

On a jungle expedition to find a gigantic idol, Ted the museum curator befriends a little monkey. When the monkey follows him back to New York, Ted's life is turned upside down as the little primate's innate curiosity causes constant havoc... At one point Arnold Schwarzenegger was lined up to play the Man with the Yellow Hat in this perennial children's favourite. Well, thank God that didn't happen. Under the auspices of producer Ron Howard, the simplicity and charm of the original books (co-written and drawn by the husband and-wife team of Margret and H.A. Rey) have been preserved here in simple line drawings. While today's more savvy youth will hardly be blown away by the shenanigans of George, the ingenuity of the mischievous monkey is not without its appeal. Young children in particular should be enthralled by George's adventures, while Will Ferrell brings just the right amount of ironic shading to Ted without overwhelming the character. JC-W

• *Voices*: *Ted/The Man in the Yellow Hat* Will Ferrell, *Maggie* Drew Barrymore, *Bloomsberry Jr* David Cross, *Clovis* Eugene Levy, *Miss Plushbottom* Joan Plowright, *Mr Bloomsberry* Dick Van Dyke, *cab driver* Michael Sorich, *Ivan* Ed O'Ross, *with* Frank Welker, Billy West, Kath Soucie, Clint Howard.

• *Dir* Matthew O'Callaghan, *Pro* Ron Howard, Jon Shaprio and David Kirschner, *Ex Pro* Bonne Radford, Ken Tsumura, James Whitaker and David Bernardi, *Screenplay* Ken Kaufman, from a story by Kaufman and Mike Werb, *Pro Des* Yarrow Cheney, *Ed* Julie Rogers, *M* Heitor Pereira; songs written and performed by Jack Johnson.

Universal/Imagine Entertainment-UIP.
87 mins. USA/Germany. 2006. Rel: 26 May 2006. Cert. U.

Danny the Dog

See *Unleashed*.

The Dark ★½

Shortly after Adelle and her daughter Sarah arrive in Wales from New York, Adelle is haunted by a prescient nightmare. The next day, she and Sarah are reunited with James, Sarah's father. He's an artist who's secluded himself in a cliff-top farmhouse the better to focus on his work. Then, shortly afterwards, Sarah disappears... Even by the parameters of the dog-eared horror B-movie, *The Dark* is wearisomely wrong-headed. In spite of the presence of the steely Maria Bello and direction from Alberta's John Fawcett (whose *Ginger Snaps* was funny and fiercely original), *The Dark* cannot escape the shortcomings of its script. Even before we get to know the three main protagonists, `the horror' kicks in, providing a scenario that is ludicrously improbable. Yet the film strives for a kitchen sink realism at constant odds with the panoply of its cheap shock effects. JC-W

• *Adelle* Maria Bello, *James* Sean Bean, *Sarah* Sophie Stuckey, *Dafydd* Maurice Roëves, *Ebrill* Abigail Stone, *with* Richard Elfyn, Caspar Harvey, Eluned Jones.

• *Dir* John Fawcett, *Pro* Jeremy Bolt and Paul W.S. Anderson, *Ex Pro* Robert Kulzer and Steve Christian, *Co-Pro* Robert How, *Screenplay* Paul Tamasy and Stephen Massicotte, from the novel *Sheep* by Simon Maginn, *Ph* Christian Sebaldt, *Pro Des* Eve Stewart, *Ed* Chris Gill, *M* Ed Butt, *Costumes* Ffion Elinor.

Constantin Film/Impact Pictures/Isle of Man Film-Momentum.
93 mins. UK/Germany. 2005. Rel: 7 April 2006. Cert. 15.

Dark Water ★★★

The dark water first appears on the ceiling of Dahlia Williams' new bedroom. She's just moved to an apartment block on New York's Roosevelt Island and it's been raining non-stop for days. She's in the throes of an ugly divorce and is fighting for custody of her five-year-old daughter, Ceci. Initially resenting the move, Ceci immediately changes her mind when she befriends a little girl who lives in the deserted flat above... Considering the plethora of remakes of Asian horror films about creepy children with big black hair, writer Yglesias and director Salles have been wise to pare down the clichés of the original (Hideo Nakata's 2002 film of the same name). But by exchanging the horror of the first film for a more psychological dynamic, they have lost the former's scariness. Even so, the remake is a better film, exceptionally well acted by Ms Connelly and elegantly photographed by Brazil's Affonso Beato. If it sags in the middle and the production values gloss over the human immediacy, the pay-off is unusually chilling. JC-W

• *Dahlia Williams* Jennifer Connelly, *Mr Murray* John C. Reilly, *Jeff Platzer* Tim Roth, *Mr Veeck* Pete Postlethwaite, *Kyle* Dougray Scott, *Mrs Finkle* Camryn Manheim, *Ceci* Ariel Gade,

Within these walls: Maria Bello takes a peek in John Fawcett's fatally misjudged *The Dark* (from Momentum Pictures)

Natasha/young Dahlia Perla Haney-Jardine, *with* Debra Monk, Elina Löwensohn, Matt Lemche.

• *Dir* Walter Salles, *Pro* Bill Mechanic, Roy Lee and Doug Davison, *Ex Pro* Ashley Kramer, *Co-Pro* Diana Pokorny, *Screenplay* Rafael Yglesias, *Ph* Affonso Beato, *Pro Des* Therese DePrez, *Ed* Daniel Rezende, *M* Angelo Badalamenti, *Costumes* Michael Wilkinson, *Sound* Frank Gaeta.

Touchstone Pictures/Pandemonium/Vertigo Entertainment-Buena Vista International. 104 mins. USA/Japan. 2005. Rel: 22 July 2005. Cert. 15.

Date Movie ★

Unable to find a husband due to her big thighs, amateur diarist Julia Jones goes to see a date doctor called Hitch. He organises to have her back shaved and the fat sucked out of her butt and then, sure enough, a handsome Englishman falls for her previously buried charms. However, Julia's father objects to the liaison because the boyfriend is not an African-American-Japanese-Indian Jew… This actually sounds better on paper. On screen, it's an embarrassing mishmash of old gags and fatist, homophobic gibes. Considering how many well-intentioned films never find a distributor, it's soul-destroying to see something so amateurish and deadly unfunny get a wide release. When a character is said `to get a lot of tail' and we cut to a shot of him being swished by the tail of a lion, you know you're on a losing wicket. JC-W

• *Julia Jones* Alyson Hannigan, *Grant Funkyerdoder* Adam Campbell, *Roz Funkyerdoder* Jennifer Coolidge, *Hitch* Tony

Cox, *Andy* Sophie Monk, *Bernie Funkyerdoder* Fred Willard, *Frank Jones* Eddie Griffin, *with* Lil Jon, Carmen Electra, Marie Matiko, Judah Friedlander, Josh Meyers.

• *Dir* Aaron Seltzer, *Pro* Paul Schiff and Jason Friedberg, *Ex Pro* Arnon Milchan, *Screenplay* Seltzer and Friedberg, *Ph* Shawn Maurer, *Pro Des* William Elliott, *Ed* Paul Hirsch, *M* David Kitay, *Costumes* Alix Friedberg.

Regency Enterprises/New Regency-Fox. 82 mins. USA. 2006. Rel: 24 February 2006. Cert. 12A.

Dave Chappelle's Block Party ★★★½

A block party is a street concert and this particular festival of high spirits unfolded in Brooklyn, September 2004. Apparently inspired by the block party chronicled in Mel Stuart's seminal music documentary *Wattstax* (1973) – covering the shindig held in LA to `celebrate' the riots – stand-up comic Dave Chappelle orchestrated a similar event as a valentine to New York and hip-hop. Chappelle himself is on terrific form and director Michel Gondry (*Eternal Sunshine of the Spotless Mind*) is prudent enough to sublimate his more typical stylistic flourishes. And so we have Chappelle doing a flawless impersonation of Mr T, giving out `golden tickets' (à la Willy Wonka) to residents of his hometown in Ohio, the process of rehearsal and the magnificent acts themselves, from a terrific rendition of `Killing Me Softly' from the specially reunited Fugees to Kanye West performing `Get 'Em High.' A truly uplifting experience. CB

• *With*: Dave Chappelle, Kanye West, Mos Def, The Fugees,

Erykah Badu, Jill Scott, Big Daddy Kane, John Legend, Martin Luther, Pharoahe Monch, Andre 4000, etc.

• *Dir* Michel Gondry, *Pro* Dave Chappelle, Bob Yari, Mustafa Abuelhija and Julie Fong, *Ex Pro* Greg Manocherian, Doug Levine and Skot Bright, *Ph* Ellen Kuras, *Pro Des* Lauri Faggioni, *Ed* Sarah Flack and Jeff Buchanan, *M* Corey Smith.

Rogue Pictures/Bob Yari Prods/Pilot Boy/Kabuki Brothers Films-Optimum Releasing.
102 mins. USA. 2006. Rel: 30 June 2006. Cert. 15.

The Da Vinci Code ★★★½

While in Paris for a lecture on the language of symbols, American professor Robert Langdon finds himself a chief suspect in the murder of a curator in the Louvre. However, he manages to escape the clutches of the police thanks to the intervention of a mysterious — and very pretty — cryptologist, Sophie Neveu. Together, they start to unravel a conspiracy that appears to lead to the very founding of Christianity… Leonardo Da Vinci has little to do with the film version of Dan Brown's literary blockbuster and more's the pity. It's the brushes with the great man that provides this phenomenon with its credentials, rather than the banal subterfuge, mediocre chase scenes and corrupt bishops. Once boiled down to its essentials, *The Da Vinci Code* is a decent enough thriller overblown with a sense of its own importance. With smaller stars, a quieter orchestra and fewer preposterous red herrings, it could have been rather special. As it is, the effect is like drinking real orange juice with the juice removed. While the pith is very exciting, you do need the fluid to swallow it. P.S. The scene in which Langdon and Neveu walk towards Westminster Abbey and Parliament Square morphs into a Medieval version of itself is worth the price of admission alone. JC-W

• *Robert Langdon* Tom Hanks, *Sophie Neveu* Audrey Tautou, *Sir Leigh Teabing* Ian McKellen, *Bishop Aringarosa* Alfred Molina, *Silas* Paul Bettany, *Captain Bézu Fache* Jean Reno, *Vernet* Jürgen Prochnow, *Remy Jean* Jean-Yves Berteloot, *Lieutenant Collet* Etienne Chicot, *Jacques Sauniere* Jean-Pierre Marielle, *with* Marie-Françoise Audollent, Seth Gabel, Denis Podalydès, Clive Carter, Serretta Wilson.

• *Dir* Ron Howard, *Pro* Brian Grazer and John Calley, *Ex Pro* Todd Hallowell and Dan Brown, *Screenplay* Akiva Goldsman, *Ph* Salvatore Totino, *Pro Des* Allan Cameron, *Ed* Dan Hanley and Mike Hill, *M* Hans Zimmer, *Costumes* Daniel Orlandi, *Sound* Daniel Pagan.

Columbia Pictures/Imagine Entertainment-
Columbia TriStar.
148 mins. USA. 2006. Rel: 19 May 2006. Cert. 12A.

Daybreak ★★½

As an admirer of Ingmar Bergman I thought that no Swedish film could be too gloomy for my taste, but this bleak piece of Scandinavian angst, dealing with the troubled lives of its leading characters over a period of some twenty four hours, is relentless enough to feel contrived. A married surgeon has an affair with the wife of a colleague who becomes pregnant, a jealous divorcee threatens her former husband and his new wife and a bricklayer jeopardises his marriage through his obsession with work including that undertaken for a tragic couple who want to be cut off from the world. The performances are good but as everything piles up in the second half one looks in vain for some sign that director Bjorn Runge might recognise his material as better suited to black comedy than to solemn tragedy. Original title: *Om Jag Vander Mig Om*. MS

• *Agnes* Pernilla August, *Rickard* Jakob Eklund, *Sofie* Marie Richardsson, *Mats* Leif Andrée, *Jonas* Johan Kvarnström, *Olof* Peter Andersson, *Anita* Ann Petrén, *with* Sanna Krepper, Ingvar Hirdwall, Marika Lindstrom, Magnus Krepper.

• *Dir* and *Screenplay* Björn Runge, *Pro* Clas Gunnarsson, *Ex Pro* Mattias Nohrborg, *Ph* Ulf Brantås, *Art Dir* Catarina Schiller, *Ed* Lena Dahlberg, *M* Ulf Dageby, *Costumes* Anna Agren.

Auto Images-Metrodome.
108 mins. Sweden. 2004. Rel: 16 September 2005. Cert. 15.

Dear Wendy ★★★

The mining town of Estherslope, somewhere in America's South-East; today. Wendy is a gun, a double-action pearl-handled revolver to be precise. When Dick buys Wendy as a birthday present for Huey, he presumes she is a toy. He then thinks she is too good for Huey, so he keeps her and is surprised by the self-confidence she brings him. A staunch pacifist, Dick decides to round up the town's losers and provide them with the same self-assurance, on the strict proviso that they never show their weapons in public. Dick calls his new gang The Dandies… Filmed in Denmark (at an abandoned military base), *Dear Wendy* is like a timeless Western, a dreamy period piece set in the present. The Dandies don old-fashioned costumes and sport antique firearms, at odds with the modern weaponry favoured by the police. A quirky condemnation of the freedom to bear arms, the film's outcome is inevitable, although it does allow for considerable suspense. The climax itself is off-the-wall — a deranged sting in an otherworldly allegory — but then the film's originality is not in question. JC-W

• *Dick* Jamie Bell, *Krugsby* Bill Pullman, *Freddie* Michael Angarano, *Sebastian* Danso Gordon, *Clarabelle* Novella Nelson, *Susan* Alison Pill, *Stevie* Mark Webber, *Marshall Walker* William Hootkins, *with* Trevor Cooper, Matthew Géczy, Teddy Kempner.

• *Dir* Thomas Vinterberg, *Pro* Sisse Graum Jørgensen, *Ex Pro* Peter Garde, Peter Aalbæk Jensen, Bo Ehrhardt and Birgitte Hald, *Co-Pro* Marie Cecilie Gade, *Screenplay* Lars Von Trier, *Ph* Anthony Dod Mantle, *Pro Des* Karl Juliusson, *Ed* Mikkel E.G. Nielsen, *M* Benjamin Wallfisch, *Costumes* Annie Perier, *Sound* Kristian Eidnes Andersen.

Lucky Punch/Nimbus Zentropa/Pain Unlimited/Danish Film Institute-Metrodome.
105 mins. Denmark/Germany/France/UK/Norway/ Sweden. 2004. Rel: 5 August 2005. Cert. 15.

Los Debutantes ★★

Following the death of their mother, small-town siblings Silvio and Victor Guzman move north to Santiago. Treating Victor to a prostitute's attentions as a 17th birthday present, Silvio finds a job at the brothel, fetching and carrying for the crooked tycoon Don Pascual. But little does he know that young Victor has fallen hard for one of Pascual's strippers, who also happens to be Pascual's mistress... Cinematically, Chile is a distant cousin to Brazil, Argentina and Mexico but is ripe for global occupation. Debutant director Andres Waissbluth certainly unveils the capacity that his country has for undiluted sex and production values and reveals his own potential as a confident filmmaker. However, his movie's slavering allegiance to Western cinema and repetitive structure makes a potentially interesting exercise in *film noir* a wearisome endurance test. Just as the story kicks in, we cut back to an earlier incident, which is then unfolded via the perspective of another character. Waissbluth has coaxed powerful, naked performances from his actors but his screenplay is derivative, implausible, undeveloped and tedious. JC-W

• *Gracia Perez* Antonella Ríos, *Silvio Guzman* Néstor Cantillana, *Victor Guzman* Juan Pablo Miranda, *Don Pascual* Alejandro Trejo, *Don Marco* Eduardo Barril, *Danilo* Roberto Farías.

• *Dir* Andres Waissbluth, *Pro* Sebastian Freund, *Ph* Arnaldo Rodriguez, *Art Dir* Sebastían Muñoz, *Ed* Galut Alarcón, *M* Cristián Heyne, *Costumes* Carolina Espina, *Sound* Cristián Freund.

Retaguardia Films/ZooFilm & Audio-Revolver Entertainment.
114 mins. Chile. 2003. Rel: 15 July 2005. Cert. 18.

Derailed ★★★½

Chicago; the present. Stuck in a stagnating marriage, advertising executive Charles Schine takes a small risk with a woman he has just met. Like him, Lucinda Harris lives in a world of corporate pressure and only sees her other half on holidays and special occasions. Making a brief yet solid connection, Charles and Lucinda take a hotel room, but before they've even undressed they are mugged by an unseen assailant. She is raped and he is beaten to a pulp... This is one corker of a story and with Clive Owen providing a credible and charismatic central presence, at times the suspense is almost unbearable. With a daughter on a dialysis machine, and his work on the line, Schine's life is thrown into a spin just as he's trying to pull his act together. As the woman who shares his nightmare, Jennifer Aniston breaks away from the mannered fluff of her recent performances, while Vincent Cassel makes a charming, shocking villain. If only the film had stopped sooner – and spent more time on the details of Schine's domestic crisis – it could've been a classic high-concept thriller. JC-W

• *Charles Schine* Clive Owen, *Lucinda Harris* Jennifer Aniston, *LaRoche* Vincent Cassel, *Deanna Schine* Melissa George,

Det. Church Giancarlo Esposito, *Winston Boyko* RZA, *Dexter* Xzibit, *Elliot Firth* Tom Conti, *Sam Griffin* David Morrissey, *with* Addison Timlin, Rachel Blake, Richard Leaf, Georgina Chapman, Sam Douglas.

• *Dir* Mikael Håfström, *Pro* Lorenzo di Bonaventura, *Ex Pro* Harvey Weinstein, Bob Weinstein and Jonathan Gordon, *Co-Pro* Mark Cooper, *Assoc Pro* Jeremy Steckler, *Screenplay* Stuart Beattie, from the novel by James Siegel, *Ph* Peter Biziou, *Pro Des* Andrew Laws, *Ed* Peter Boyle, *M* Edward Shearmur; tracks performed by Strong Army Steady, Xzibit, Jellyroll, JD & the Straight Shot, Planet Funk, Free Murder, Aslyn, Pink, and Rular Rah, *Costumes* Natalie Ward.

Weinstein Co./Miramax/Bonaventura Pictures-Buena Vista International.
107 mins. USA/UK. 2005. Rel: 3 February 2006. Cert. 15.

The Descent ★★½

In the Appalachian mountains, six women meet up to embark on a life-affirming cave expedition. Led by the gung-ho Juno, they find themselves in a network of caves that, supposedly, have never been explored before. But shortly after their exit route becomes blocked, they discover signs of previous life and something else entirely... Previously, writer-director Neil Marshall delivered the illogical and hackneyed *Dog Soldiers* (2001), a Scottish werewolf movie crossed with *Assault On Precinct 13*. Here, he switches gender and pumps in testosterone where oestrogen dare not flow. Unfortunately, he gives us little time to get to know these ballsy women, other than Sarah, who's recuperating from a horrific car crash that took her husband and daughter. While Marshall creates an atmosphere of some credibility (with Scotland standing in for a wet and overcast North Carolina), and presents a gutsy heroine in the form of the Oriental Natalie Mendoza, he blows it in the final act. Resorting to frenetic cutting and pantomimic gore, he reduces an intriguing concept into an incomprehensible shambles. JC-W

• *Sarah* Shauna Macdonald, *Juno* Natalie Mendoza, *Beth* Alex Reid, *Rebecca* Saskia Mulder, *Holly* Nora-Jane Noone, *Sam* MyAnna Buring, *Paul* Oliver Milburn.

• *Dir* and *Screenplay* Neil Marshall, *Pro* Christian Colson, *Ex Pro* Paul Smith, *Co-Pro* Paul Ritchie, *Assoc Pro* Ivana MacKinnon, *Ph* Sam McCurdy, *Pro Des* Simon Bowles, *Ed* Jon Harris, *M* David Julyan, *Costumes* Nancy Thompson.

Celador Films-Pathé.
99 mins UK. 2005 Rel: 8 July 2005. Cert. 18.

Deuce Bigalow: European Gigolo ★★

T.J. Hicks, Deuce's former pimp, is implicated in the murders of Europe's most successful gigolos. So, to help his friend clear his name and find the real murderer, Bigalow returns to his old profession... I must admit that I found myself laughing at some truly awful jokes in the beginning (such as when Deuce remembers how his wife was killed by sharks in Mexico, with only her leg uneaten). But the film soon runs out of steam

– and jokes – when Rob Schneider, who also wrote the script, attempts to offend almost everyone – be they blind, black, homosexual or a dwarf. GS

• *Deuce Bigalow* Rob Schneider, *T.J. Hicks* Eddie Griffin, *Gaspar Voorsboch* Jeroen Krabbé, *Heinz Hummer* Til Schweiger, *Chadsworth Buckingham III* Douglas Sills, *Rodrigo* Carlos Ponce, *Gian-Carlo* Charles Keating, *Eva* Hanna Verboom, *with* Alex Dimitriades, Oded Fehr, Topper, SuChin Pak, Jimmy Gardner, Zoë Telford, Rachel Stevens, Johnny Vaughan.

• *Dir* Mike Bigelow, *Pro* Jack Giarraputo, Adam Sandler and John Schneider, *Ex Pro* Glenn S. S. Gainor, *Co-Pro* Nathan T. Reimann and Tom McNulty, *Screenplay* Rob Schneider, David Garnett and Jason Ward, based on characters created by Schneider and Harris Goldberg, *Ph* Marc Felperlaan, *Pro Des* Benedict Schillemans, *Ed* Peck Prior and Sandy Solowitz, *M* James L. Venable, *Costumes* Linda Bogers.

Columbia/Happy Madison-Columbia TriStar. 83 mins. USA. 2005. Rel: 30 September 2005. Cert. 15.

The Devil and Daniel Johnston ★★★★

What makes this so distinctive amongst documentary features about singers is the fact that director Jeff Feuerzeig puts before us not merely a singer/songwriter whose work confronts the sadness in his own life but someone who comes across as a manic depressive with a religious mission. Because of this you don't have to appreciate Daniel Johnston's music to find this a thoroughly intriguing portrait. A rebel reacting against extremely religious parents is not unusual, but this one is an extraordinary figure being religious himself now and believing that his role is to promote Jesus in his performances. In tracing his career the film, made with flair and assurance, confronts Johnston's mental problems and breakdowns but celebrates his survival. The interviews are good, too. MS

• *With*: Daniel Johnston, Mabel and Bill Johnston, Kathy McCarty, Jeff Tartakov, Gibby Haynes, Jad and David Fair, Matt Groening.

• *Dir* Jeff Feuerzeig, *Pro* Henry S. Rosenthal, *Ex Pro* Ted Hope, *Ph* Fortunato Procopio, *Ed* Tyler Hubby, *M* Daniel Johnston, *Sound* James LeBrecht.

This Is That/Complex Corp./Henry S. Rosenthal- 109 mins. USA. 2005. Rel: 5 May 2006. Cert. 12A.

The Devil's Rejects ★★★

Seventy-five corpses are unearthed at the unholy homestead of the deranged, inbred Firefly family. As heavily armed police surrounds the property, Otis and Baby escape by a secret tunnel. Later, they hole up at a run-down motel and, joined by their father, part-time clown Colonel Spaulding, they continue their vocation of teasing, humiliating, torturing and butchering whosoever they should meet… An unrelenting homage to the splatter genre of the 1970s, *The Devil's Rejects* is a sequel to Rob Zombie's berserk, nightmarish *House of 1000 Corpses* (2003). Here, he ups the horror a few more notches, proudly producing

the nastiest movie of the year. Blending in elements of *The Wild Bunch* and *Bonnie and Clyde* for good measure, Zombie follows his creed of 'more is more' and produces a classic, of sorts. His actors seem deliriously uninhibited, the mayhem is pretty imaginative (in one scene a woman is forced to wear the face of her recently skinned husband) and the soundtrack a rich compendium of golden oldies (Three Dog Night, Lynyrd Skynyrd, even David Essex). Misogynistic and unevenly acted, this will run at late-night cinema clubs for years to come. JC-W

• *Captain Spaulding* Sid Haig, *Otis B. Driftwood* Bill Moseley, *Baby Firefly* Sheri Moon Zombie, *Tiny* Matthew McGrory, *Charlie Altamont* Ken Foree, *Sheriff John Wydell* William Forsythe, *Mother Firefly* Leslie Easterbrook, *Roy Sullivan* Geoffrey Lewis, *Rondo* Danny Trejo, *Clevon* Michael Berryman, *with* Dave Sheridan, Lew Temple, Kate Norby, Priscilla Barnes, Jossara Jinaro, P.J. Soles, Dave Sheridan, E.G. Daily, Tom Towles, Deborah Van Valkenburgh, Ginger Lynn Allen, Chris Ellis, Mary Woronov, Daniel Roebuck, Duane Whitaker, Sean Murphy, and (uncredited) *Sheriff Ken Dwyer* Steve Railsback.

• *Dir* and *Screenplay* Rob Zombie, *Pro* Michael Ohoven and Marco Mehiltz, Andy Gould and Mike Elliott, *Ex Pro* Peter Block, Michael Paseornek, Michael Burns and Guy Oseary, *Assoc Pro* Ali Forman, *Ph* Phil Parmet, *Pro Des* Anthony Tremblay, *Ed* Glenn Garland, *M* Tyler Bates; tracks performed by Blind Willie Johnson, The Allman brothers Band, Three Dog Night, Terry reid, Kitty Wells, Buck Owens, Elvin Bishop, Otis Rush, Steely Dan, The James Gang, David Essex, Joe Walsh, Muddy Waters, Lynyrd Skynyrd, etc, *Costumes* Yasmine Abraham, *Sound* Scott Sanders, *Visual Effects* Robert Kurtzman.

Lions Gate Films/Cinerenta/Firm Films- Momentum Pictures. 109 mins. USA/Canada/Germany. 2005. Rel: 5 August 2005. Cert. 18.

Diameter of the Bomb ★★★½

This is a justifiably grim view of an incident in Jerusalem in 2002 when a bomb blew up a bus. Featuring interviews with friends and family of the victims together with home movies of those who died, the film also extends to comparable material about the suicide bomber himself. Despite this latter element the film is too harrowing to be read as supportive of violence: indeed the very title comes from a poem about the circle of pain emanating from such a bombing extending far beyond those directly involved to encompass questions concerning our world today and whether or not the idea of God is refuted. However, the filmmakers inappropriately opt for elements of dramatisation: a music score that seeks to build up tension and reconstructions that we are invited to see as the real thing. Despite its ambitions, this is ultimately less effective than that other documentary about violence on a bus, *Bus 174* (2002). MS

• *Dir* Steven Silver and Andrew Quigley, *Pro* Claude Bonin, Paul Goldin and Georgina Townsley, *Ex Pro* Paul Trijbits, Nick Fraser, Tom Perlmutter, Eric Michel, Simon Franks and Zygi

Kamasa, *Ph* Noel Smart, *Ed* Andrew Quigley, *M* Christian Henson.

Rainmaker Films/National Film Board of Canada/UK Film Council/BBC-Lionsgate UK.
86 mins. UK/Canada. 2005. Rel: 31 March 2006. Cert. 12A.

DIG! ★★

As rock documentaries go, *DIG!* strikes an incongruous melody. The concert footage itself is frustratingly abridged, the personalities repugnant and the filmmaking style freewheeling and raw. The thrust of the piece concerns the rivalry of the bands The Brian Jonestown Massacre and The Dandy Warhols. But as the arc of the Dandys' success in Europe gains some interest, the film cuts back to the tantrums of Anton Newcombe, the arrogant and self-destructive force behind Jonestown. Filmed over a period of seven years, *DIG!* could have been something special under a more disciplined editor. At 110 minutes, it's another ramshackle exploration of the mindless mayhem produced by that familiar and vicious cocktail of drugs and ego. JC-W

• *With*: The Brian Jonestown Massacre, The Dandy Warhols. *Narrator*: Courtney Taylor.

• *Dir, Pro* and *Ed* Ondi Timoner, *Co-Pro* Vasco Lucas Nunes and David Timoner, *Assoc Pro* Tim Rush and Jeff Frey, *Ph* Ondi Timoner, Vasco Lucas Nunes and David Timoner.

Interloper Films-Tartan Films.
110 mins. USA. 2004. Rel: 1 July 2005. Cert. 15.

Domino ★

The daughter of the Oscar-nominated actor Laurence Harvey, Domino was born into privilege, became a model and then decided to get her kicks as a bounty hunter in Los Angeles. Trailed by a television crew, Domino and her seedy colleagues become the victims of a scam engineered by bail bondsman Claremont Williams III. Soon, the FBI, the Mob, rival bounty hunters and god knows who else are involved in the mess… Tony Scott doesn't so much direct *Domino* as cut it to shreds and then hurl the pieces back at the audience. With dialogue repeated and then typed across the screen, with close-ups, zooms, desaturated colour, revolving cameras, flashbacks and every conceivable cliché of modern filmmaking, the film is exhausting to watch. It's also highly unpleasant and jammed with silly, instantly disposable characters, while Keira as Domino just doesn't convince as a tough cookie: she simply looks petulant. As a fictionalised account of the real-life Domino Harvey (who died from an overdose in her bath in June of 2005), the film serves as a mean-spirited epitaph. JC-W

• *Domino Harvey* Keira Knightley, *Ed Moseby* Mickey Rourke, *Choco* Edgar Ramirez, *Claremont Williams* Delroy Lindo, *Lateesha Rodriguez* Mo'Nique, *Kimmie* Mena Suvari, *Lashandra Davis* Macy Gray, *Sophie Wynn* Jacqueline Bisset, *Drake Bishop* Dabney Coleman, *Taryn Mills* Lucy Liu, *Mark Heiss*

Christopher Walken, *Alf* Rizwan Abbasi, *himself* Ian Ziering, *himself* Brian Austin Green, *Burke Beckett* Peter Jacobson, *Frances* Kel O'Neill, *himself* Jerry Springer, *Wanderer* Tom Waits, *Domino aged eight* Tabitha Brownstone, *with* Joseph Nunez, Shondrella Avery, Dale Dickey, Lew Temple, T.K. Carter, Charles Paraventi, Jack McGee.

• *Dir* Tony Scott, *Pro* Scott and Samuel Hadida, *Ex Pro* Toby Emmerich, Victor Hadida, Skip Chaisson, Barry Waldman, Zach Schiff-Abrams and Lisa Ellzey, *Co-Pro* Peter Toumasis and David Hadida, *Screenplay* Richard Kelly, from a story by Kelly and Steve Barancik, *Ph* Dan Mindel, *Pro Des* Chris Seagers, *Ed* William Goldenberg and Christian Wagner, *M* Harry Gregson-Williams, Junkie XL, Hybrid, and Toby Chu, *Costumes* B.

Samuel Hadida/Scott Free/Davis Films-Entertainment.
127 mins. USA/France. 2005. Rel: 14 October 2005. Cert. 15.

Don't Come Knocking ★★½

Although now shorter than when screened at Cannes, this new film from Wim Wenders was poorly received and ultimately that's justified since it becomes pretentious, tiresome and improbably reliant on coincidences. Like Jarmusch's *Broken Flowers*, it's about a discontented middle-aged man reconnecting with his past, including here a former love and two children of whose existence he had been unaware. Sam Shepard – who wrote the screenplay – is less than ideally cast in the lead role but there are good players here (it's a particular pleasure to see again Eva Marie Saint as assured as ever). Add a good music score, lovely images and a real feel for the American setting (Butte, Montana, is the main location) and it's a real shame that script and story collapse in the second half. MS

• *Howard Spence* Sam Shepard, *Doreen* Jessica Lange, *Sutter* Tim Roth, *Earl* Gabriel Mann, *Sky* Sarah Polley, *Amber* Fairuza Balk, *Howard's mother* Eva Marie Saint, *with* James Gammon, George Kennedy, Marley Shelton, Rodney A. Grant, Tim Matheson, Julia Sweeney, Kurt Fuller.

• *Dir* Wim Wenders, *Pro* Peter Schwartzkopff, Karsten Brünig and In-ah Lee, *Ex Pro* Wenders and Jeremy Thomas, *Co-Pro* Carsten Lorenz, *Screenplay* Sam Shepard, from a story by Shepard and Wenders, *Ph* Franz Lustig, *Pro Des* Nathan Amondson, *Ed* Peter Przygodda and Oli Weiss, *M* T-Bone Burnett, *Costumes* Caroline Eselin-Schaeffer, *Sound* Claude Letessier.

HanWay/Reverge Angle International/Arte France Cinéma-Columbia TriStar.
110 mins. Germany/France/UK/USA. 2005.
Rel: 28 April 2006. Cert. 15.

Doom ★★★

On a remote research facility on Mars, communication has been lost with the scientists who work there. Suspecting the worst, the powers-that-be mobilize a unit of the Rapid

Response Tactical Squad headed by the gung-ho `Sarge.' Once there, the Marines discover a scenario beyond their worst nightmares… Let's get one thing straight. This is an adaptation of a computer game starring The Rock. And there are characters with comic-book personalities who say things like, 'We got us a game,' and, 'Let's see if we can find the body that goes with that arm.' So, obviously *Doom* is not taking itself too seriously. Of its genre – the video-game-to-movie milieu – it's a marked improvement on the likes of *Street Fighter*, *Wing Commander* and *Resident Evil*. Indeed, the kick-ass moment is not when The Rock picks up a state-of-the-art cannon and blows a hole in the ceiling, it's when Rosamund Pike, in a flash of devastating exposition, explains, `but ten per cent of the human gene is still unmapped!' Derivative but fun. JC-W

• *John Grimm* aka *Reaper* Karl Urban, *Samantha Grimm* Rosamund Pike, *Destroyer* DeObia Oparei, *Goat* Ben Daniels, *Sarge* The Rock, *Duke* Raz Adoti, *Portman* Richard Brake, *Mac* Yao Chin, *the Kid* Al Weaver, *Pinky* Dexter Fletcher, *with* Brian Steele, Robert Russell, Sara Houghton.

• *Dir* Andrzej Bartkowiak, *Pro* Lorenzo di Bonaventura and John Wells, *Ex Pro* John D. Schofield, *Co-Ex Pro* Laura Holstein and Jeremy Steckler, *Screenplay* David Callaham and Wesley Strick, *Ph* Tony Pierce-Roberts, *Pro Des* Stephen Scott, *Ed* Drek G. Brechin, *M* Clint Mansell, *Costumes* Carlo Poggioli, *Special Effects* Kit West and Jon Farhat, *Creatures* John Rosengrant.

Universal/Distant Planet-UIP.
104 mins. UK/Czech Republic/Germany/USA. 2005.
Rel: 2 December 2005. Cert. 15.

Down in the Valley ★★★★

The San Fernando Valley is as much a character as its star-crossed lovers in this melancholy tale of a forbidden liaison. With its pastures, freeways, rolling hills and urban wasteland, the Valley embodies the clash of the old and new as a multitude of sensibilities attempt to function side by side. Harlan Caruthers represents a simpler, more romantic, bygone era, and as such is something of an innocent, a characteristic reinforced by his boyish good looks. In many ways, October is more emotionally mature than the man twenty years her senior, but she is drawn to his easy charm and the lost world he represents. At times, *Down in the Valley* is like an asphalt *Badlands*, with its sprawling vistas, romantic soundtrack and winsome, camera-friendly protagonists. And beneath the lyrical idyll beats a note of impending tragedy. It's hard to imagine another actor who could fill Harlan's boots so effectively. Edward Norton not only convinces as a man-child, but seems as comfortable on a horse as he does cocking a Colt Peacemaker. JC-W

• *Harlan Fairfax Caruthers* Edward Norton, *October `Tobe'* *Sommers* Evan Rachel Wood, *Wade Sommers* David Morse, *Lonnie Sommers* Rory Culkin, *Charlie* Bruce Dern, *Steve* John Diehl, *April* Kat Dennings, *with* Hunter Parrish, Aviva, Aaron Fors, Geoffrey Lewis, Elizabeth Peña, Ty Burrell.

• *Dir* and *Screenplay* David Jacobson, *Pro* Holly Wiersma, Edward Norton, Adam Rosenfelt and Stavros Merjos, *Ex Pro*

Sam Nazarian, *Co-Pro* Bill Migliore, Marc Schaberg and Mike Upton, *Ph* Enrique Chediak, *Pro Des* Franco-Giacomo Carbone, *Ed* Lynzee Klingman and Edward Harrison, *M* Peter Salett, *Costumes* Jacqueline West.

Element Films/Class 5/Sundance Institute-Icon.
112 mins. USA. 2004. Rel: 26 May 2006. Cert. 15.

Dreamer ★★★★

Originally dubbed *Dreamer: Inspired by a True Story* (a rather pointless and unwieldy title), this is the enchanting but entirely fictitious story of a family pulled together by the resolve of a ten-year-old girl. The only child of the disillusioned horse trainer Ben Crane, Cale has grown up listening to tales of equestrian heroism at the knee of her grandfather, Pop. One day, she insists on accompanying her father to work, an event that leads to his dismissal when, unnerved by the presence of his daughter, he is unable to put down an injured filly. Instead, he adopts it, a move that – initially, at least – turns out to be a mixed blessing… Extremely well acted by the four principals, *Dreamer* is a sentimental tale rooted in reality. While the horse gallops off with the story, it is Ben's reconnection to his dreams that fuels the emotions. Beautifully shot in Kentucky (where else?), and underpinned by some deft plotting, *Dreamer* is a little gem. Incidentally, the film was inspired by the true story of the racehorse Mariah's Storm, a filly whose career came to a premature end in 1993. JC-W

• *Ben Crane* Kurt Russell, *Cale Crane* Dakota Fanning, *Pop Crane* Kris Kristofferson, *Lilly Crane* Elisabeth Shue, *Balon* Luis Guzmán, *Manolin Vallarta* Freddy Rodriguez, *Everett Palmer* David Morse, *Prince Sadir* Oded Fehr, *with* Ken Howard, Holmes Osborne, Adam Tomei.

• *Dir* and *Screenplay* John Gatins, *Pro* Mike Tollin and Brian Robbins, *Ex Pro* Ashok Amritraj, Jon Jashni, Bill Johnson, Stacy Cohen and Caitlin Scanlon, *Ph* Fred Murphy, *Pro Des* Brent Thomas, *Ed* David Rosenbloom, *M* John Debney, *Costumes* Judy Ruskin Howell, *Horse wrangler* Rusty Hendrickson.

DreamWorks/Hyde Park Entertainment/Brass Hat Films-Entertainment.
105 mins. USA/UK. 2005. Rel: 21 October 2005. Cert. U.

The Dukes of Hazzard ★½

Georgia; the present. Luke and Bo Duke are cousins and best friends. Luke chases the ladies; Bo drives his faithful Dodge Charger with a passion. Theirs is an aimless existence until, when their farm is confiscated by the unscrupulous Boss Hogg, they find themselves fighting for the future of Hazzard County… This being an update of the popular 1979-1985 TV series, it's weird to consider that such a show existed within living memory. It's even odder to think that anybody would see fit to reinvent it. With its package of rednecks, imbecilic cops, God-fearing hillbillies and leggy bimbettes, not to mention its criminal element of moonshine (illicitly distilled liquor), the film feels very much of another era. Indeed, there is a strong whiff of *Smokey and the Bandit* about it, a case accentuated by the presence of Burt Reynolds. There's also much wit in the naming of characters – a racer named Pricket, a sheriff called Anus (or is it Enos?) – a lot of very loud music and the time-honoured complement of barroom brawls, half-baked puns and all that endless racing through the back roads of Georgia. To say that *The Dukes of Hazzard* is repetitive is to understate the matter. *The Dukes of Hazzard* is redundant and numbingly repetitive. JC-W

• *Luke Duke* Johnny Knoxville, *Bo Duke* Seann William Scott, *Daisy Duke* Jessica Simpson, *Jefferson Davis 'Boss' Hogg* Burt Reynolds, *Governor Jim Applewhite* Joe Don Baker, *Pauline* Lynda Carter, *Uncle Jesse L. Duke* Willie Nelson, *Deputy Enos Strate* Michael Weston, *Billy Prickett* James Roday, *with* Junior Brown, Alice Greczyn, Steve Lemme, M.C. Gainey, Jay Chandrasekhar, Andrew Prine, Rip Taylor.

• *Dir* Jay Chandrasekhar, *Pro* Bill Gerber, *Ex Pro* Eric McLeod, Dana Goldberg and Bruce Berman, *Screenplay* John O'Brien, based on characters created by Gy Waldron, *Ph* Lawrence Sher, *Pro Des* Jon Gary Steele, *Ed* Lee Haxall and Myron Kerstein, *M* Nathan Barr; tracks performed by Jerry Reed, The Allman Brothers Band, Waylon Jennings, Willie Nelson, Jimmy Vaughan, Bo Diddley, Lynyrd Skynyrd, Air Supply, Junior Brown, Blues Explosion, BT Express, ZZ Top, AC/DC, The James Gang, Jessica Simpson, Nancy Sinatra, Southern Culture On the Skids, etc, *Costumes* Genevieve Tyrrell.

Warner/Village Roadshow-Warner.
103 mins. USA/Australia. 2005. Rel: 24 August 2005. Cert. 12A.

Dumplings ★★★★

If there's an appetite, there's a market. And in this age of the instant fix and the super-rich, the beautiful, self-confident and independent 'Aunt Mei' has cornered a very lucrative business. She cooks the most expensive dumplings in Hong Kong, using the best flour, extra ginger and a very special ingredient. In fact, Mei is her own best advertisement, her dumplings being an elixir of rejuvenation… Director Fruit Chan exhibits both an aesthetic and psychological grip on his subject that is rare in contemporary cinema. With its mischievous score, idiosyncratic camera angles and blackly comic sight gags, *Dumplings* only slowly reveals its hand before Grand Guignol comedy kicks in. While fainter-hearted viewers may find themselves reaching for the sick bag, others cannot deny that this is a most bewitching – and even enlightening – *divertissement*. Original title: *Gaauji*. JC-W

• *Qing Li* Miriam Yeung, *Aunt Mei* Bai Ling, *Sije Li* Tony Ka-Fai Leung, *Connie* Meme, *Kate* Miki Yeung, *Kate's mother* Wong So-Fun.

• *Dir* Fruit Chan, *Pro* Peter Ho-Sun Chan, *Ex Pro* Eric Tsang, *Assoc Pro* Patricia Cheung, *Screenplay* Lilian Lee, *Ph* Christopher Doyle, *Pro Des* Yee Chung-Man, *Ed* Tin Sam Fat and Chan Ki-Hop, *M* Chan Kwong Wing, *Costumes* Dora Ng, *Sound* Kinson Tsang.

Applause Pictures-Tartan Films.
90 mins. Hong Kong. 2004. Rel: 16 June 2006. Cert. 18.

Eight Below ★★★½

As the biggest storm in 25 years descends on Antarctica, survival guide Jerry Shepard is forced to leave his eight sledge dogs (six huskies and two malamutes) behind at the US National Science Research Base. Considering that the dogs had just saved the life of visiting geologist Davis McClaren, Jerry finds this unacceptable. However, he finds his hands are tied… As Disney wildlife adventures go, this is a return to form for the critically beleaguered company. With its uncompromising depiction of the harsh conditions of Antarctica, the film pulls few punches even if the real facts of the case (which occurred in 1958) are somewhat sweetened for the family tooth. Still, with the magnificent snowscapes, the handsome huskies and Paul Walker's bottomless blue eyes, this is a visual treat. The human dynamic is also well played, with Bruce Greenwood bringing a thoughtful gravitas to the geologist and Moon Bloodgood providing an attractive turn as the bush pilot who might just provide a romantic distraction. The action scenes are also exceptionally well done, completing the recipe for a rousing, moving and exciting package. Filmed in Canada, Greenland and Norway. Previously known as *Antarctica*. JC-W

• *Jerry Shepard* Paul Walker, *Davis McClaren* Bruce Greenwood, *Katie* Moon Bloodgood, *Charlie Cooper* Jason Biggs, *Dr Andy Harrison* Gerard Plunkett, *Mindo* August Schellenberg, *Eve McClaren* Wendy Crewson, *with* Belinda Metz, Connor Christopher Levins, Duncan Fraser.

• *Dir* Frank Marshall, *Pro* David Digilio and Patrick Crowley, *Ex Pro* Todd Lieberman, Masaru Kakutani, Frank Marshall, Christine Iso, Roy Lee, Gary Barber and Roger Birnbaum, *Screenplay* David DiGilio, 'suggested' by the 1983 Japanese film *Nankyoku Monogatari*, *Ph* Don Burgess, *Pro Des* John Willett, *Ed* Christopher Rouse, *M* Mark Isham, *Costumes* Jori Woodman.

Walt Disney Pictures/Spyglass Entertainment/Mandeville Films-Buena Vista International.
120 mins. USA. 2005. Rel: 20 April 2006. Cert. PG.

Election ★★

As the chairman of Hong Kong's largest Triad prepares to retire, a vicious power play erupts between his strongest successors, Lok and Big D. While the latter uses bribes and intimidation to win votes, Lok is subtler in corralling support. But when Lok is democratically elected chairman, Big D threatens to set up a rival gang… Anybody intrigued by the workings of the Hong Kong Triad may be diverted by this complex, occasionally violent genre piece. However, the shadowy characterisations and convoluted plotting will put off more general filmgoers. There's an effective, distinctive guitar-driven score and a powerful pay-off, but the underdeveloped portrayal of Lok seriously undermines the emotional equilibrium of the piece, resulting in substantial monotony. Original title: *Hak Sewui*. JC-W

• *Lok* Simon Lam, *Big D* Tony Leung Ka-Fai, *Jimmy* Louis Koo, *Jet* Nick Cheung, *Mr So* Cheung Siu Fai, *Big Head* Lam Suet, *with* Lam Ka Tung, Wong Tin Lam, Tam Ping Man, Maggie Shiu.

• *Dir* Johnnie To, *Pro* To and Dennis Law, *Screenplay* Yau Nai Hoi and Yip Tin Shing, *Ph* Cheng Siu Keung, *Art Dir* Tony Yu, *Ed* Patrick Tam, *M* Lo Tayu, *Costumes* Stanley Cheung.

Milkway Image/One Hundred Years of Film-Optimum Releasing.
99 mins. Hong Kong. 2005. Rel: 9 June 2006. Cert. 18.

Elizabethtown ★★★★★

Drew Baylor is the designer of a new shoe that has lost Mercury Worldwide $927 million. But, just before he takes his own life, Drew finds out that his father has died. Then, on the way to Elizabethtown, Kentucky, to supervise his father's cremation, he meets Claire Colburn, a warrior of optimism… Cameron Crowe's sixth feature in 16 years, *Elizabethtown* bears all the hallmarks of this exceptional filmmaker: that is, it's smart, sassy, sad, charming, heartfelt, unexpected and a cinematic *tour-de-force*. Crowe knows how to write a good line, how to knock a scene on its head and how to peel back the fabric and find another, more interesting layer beneath. He's also a consummate craftsman, cutting his narrative into a mosaic of magical, sometimes even iconic moments. As Drew, Orlando Bloom gives the best performance of his career, as an American Everyman stunned into being a passive observer with just enough charm left to spill over the edges: it's a confident, relaxed and affable turn, complementing the dazzling peak of Kirsten Dunst's own remarkable body of work. In addition, the supporting cast (Sarandon, Baldwin, Greer), songs, photography and editing are all in a class of their own. In short,

Elizabethtown is a life-affirming, all-enveloping celluloid odyssey that repeatedly spits humour in the face of death. JC-W

• *Drew Baylor* Orlando Bloom, *Claire Colburn* Kirsten Dunst, *Holly Baylor* Susan Sarandon, *Phil* Alec Baldwin, *Bill Banyon* Bruce McGill, *Heather Baylor* Judy Greer, *Ellen* Jessica Biel, *Jessie* Paul Schneider, *Aunt Dora* Paula Deen, *with* Loudon Wainwright, Gailard Sartain, Jed Rees, Alice Marie Crowe, Patty Griffin.

• *Dir* and *Screenplay* Cameron Crowe, *Pro* Crowe, Tom Cruise and Paula Wagner, *Ex Pro* Donald J. Lee Jr, *Ph* John Toll, *Pro Des* Clay A. Griffith, *Ed* David Moritz, *M* Nancy Wilson; Henry Purcell; tracks performed by The Hollies, The Concretes, Tom Petty and The Heartbreakers, Elton John, Helen Stellar, Ryan Adams, My Morning Jacket with Paul Schneider and Charlie Crowe, Jeff Finlin, Patty Griffin, Wheat, Lindsey Buckingham, The Hombres, I Nine, The Temptations, James Brown, U2, Simple Minds, etc, *Costumes* Nancy Steiner.

Paramount/Cruise/Wagner/Vinyl Films-UIP.
123 mins. USA. 2005. Rel: 4 November 2005. Cert. 12A.

L'Enfant

See *The Child*.

Enron: The Smartest Guys in the Room ★★★★

The story of Enron is not yet over. While the name has become synonymous with greed and fraud in the US, not many people are entirely aware of the facts. This slick, fascinating documentary puts that to rights and in the tradition of *All the President's Men* is a mystery-thriller that beggars belief. Based on the book by Bethany McLean and Peter Elkind, the

Peaking on the phone: Orlando Bloom and Kirsten Dunst in Cameron Crowe's charming, sassy and unexpected *Elizabethtown* (from UIP)

documentary is a superb piece of story-telling – and with a superb story to tell – with incredible access to commentators, insiders, experts and private video footage of the villains of the piece, Jeff Skilling and Ken Lay. Before its demise in December 2001, Enron was the seventh largest company in the United States. And yet Enron, a company that fooled banks, stock analysts and reporters, seemed to be making money out of thin air. As its schemes consistently went belly-up – a $2.8 billion power plant in India, a broadband merger with Blockbuster – its stock kept on rising. Bluff was Enron's main strategy and its ambition to make more and more money – at the cost of the ordinary working man – is likely to shape the face of the American economy for years to come. JC-W

• *With:* Ken Lay, Jeff Skilling, Senator Fritz Hollings, Linda Lay, Peter Elkind, Bethany McLean, Max Eberts, Jim Chanos, Harvey Rosenfield, Loretta Lynch, etc. *Narrator:* Peter Coyote.

• *Dir* and *Screenplay* Alex Gibney, *Pro* Gibney, Jason Kliot and Susan Motamed, *Ex Pro* Mark Cuban, Todd Wagner and Joana Vicente, *Co-Pro* and *Ed* Alison Ellwood, *Ph* Maryse Alberti, *M* Matt Hauser; tracks performed by Tom Waits, Dusty Springfield, Billie Holiday, Judy Garland, Marilyn Manson, Philip Glass, Black Eyed Peas, Traffic, The Cardigans, Julie London, Phantom Planet, Los Straitjackets, Oingo Boingo, and Red Hot Chili Peppers, *Research* Crystal Whelan.

2929 Entertainment/HDNet Films-Redbus.
109 mins. USA. 2005. Rel: 28 April 2006. Cert. 15.

Errance ★½

As Lou undergoes a traumatic childbirth, her husband Jacques is getting drunk in the mountains. Contrite and buoyed by an optimism for the future, Jacques promises Lou a future of sunshine on the Mediterranean coast. There, he becomes involved in a dodgy real estate business and falls back on his old drinking and womanising ways… Why do people make films like this? With its drab visual palette (think the 1960s, squalor, rain and ghastly fashions), irredeemable protagonist and dead-end milieu, *Errance* is no fun. While the performances are fine, the film is hardly relieved by its monotonous story, if one can even call it that. Divided into three parts – set in the countryside, by the beach and in 'the big city' – the film is not only contrived but also repetitive. Above all, though, it's hard to fathom why a woman of Lou's capability, connections and beauty would stick by such a violent, alcoholic and unfaithful loser. JC-W

• *Lou* Laetitia Casta, *Jacques* Benoit Magimel, *Johnny* Yann Goven, *Cesar* Mattéo Tardito, *Vicky* Valerie Dashwood, *Roman* Sagamore Stevenin.

• *Dir* Damien Odoul, *Pro* Gérard Lacroix, *Screenplay* Odoul and Antoine Lacomblez, *Ph* Pascale Granel, *Pro Des* Michel Vandestien, *Ed* Gwenola Heaulme, *Costumes* Annie Thiellement.

Morgane Prods/Gérard Lacroix/Arte France Cinéma/

Canal Plus-Tartan Films.
100 mins. France. 2002. Rel: 22 July 2005. No Cert.

Everything ★★

Excellent performances from Ray Winstone and Jan Graveson cannot save this totally unlikely tale of a man frequenting a London prostitute. He visits not for the usual services but to talk and his strange behaviour would certainly ensure that he would be shown the door permanently. Here he is allowed back and a bond develops. The man's actual purpose (not too difficult to guess) is only revealed in the final minutes of the film which, irritatingly shot with a hand-held camera, is almost a two-hander that would have been more suited to a stage play or even to a work for radio. The players undoubtedly deserved better but the director, Richard Hawkins, did not, since he is also the writer. MS

• *Richard* Ray Winstone, *Naomi* Jan Graveson, *Ed, Naomi's pimp* Ed Deedigan, *Tanya* Katherine Clisby, *with* Andy Buckley, Lindy Sellars, Lois Winstone.

• *Dir* and *Screenplay* Richard Hawkins, *Pro* Oliver Potterton and Ed Deedigan, *Ex Pro* Geoffrey M. Freeman, *Co-Pro* Michelle Redfern and Ed Deedigan, *Ph* Ole Bratt Birkeland, *Pro Des* Christophe Spurling, *Ed* Oliver Potterton, *M* Tom Ingleby and Damon Albarn, *Costumes* Suzy Peters.

High st.films/Kandu Arts/Sustainable Development-Soda Pictures.
91 mins. UK. 2004. Rel: 7 October 2005. Cert. 18.

Everything is Illuminated ★★

Jonathan Safran Foer is an odd little chap, a young Jewish American who doesn't say much and collects miscellaneous items which he seals in a zip lock bag and hangs on his bedroom wall. Then, one day, he decides to track down the woman who may have saved his grandfather from the Nazis during the Second World War. And so, aided by a pair of curious Ukrainians (one of whom, the driver, claims to be blind), he sets off into the grasslands of the former Soviet Union… Liev Schreiber is a terrific actor and this, his directorial debut, is obviously a deeply personal project and a huge labour of love. Adapted from Jonathan Safran Foer's *A Very Rigid Secret* first published in *The New Yorker* (and later expanded into the eponymous novel), Schreiber's film starts promisingly with its jokey, surreal prologue and Magritte-inspired imagery. Then it seems to shift into a single eccentric gear from which it refuses to disengage. The result, driven by an invasive Balkan orchestra, reveals a desperation to be `offbeat' and results in an exercise of insufferable whimsy. JC-W

• *Jonathan Safran Foer* Elijah Wood, *Alex* Eugene Hutz, *grandfather* Boris Leskin, *leaf blower* Jonathan Safran Foer, *Sammy Davis Jr Jr* Mikki and Mouse, *Augustine* Tereza Veselková, *Lista* Laryssa Lauret, *Baruch, young grandfather* Lukáš Král, *young Lista* V ra Šindelá ová.

• *Dir* and *Screenplay* Liev Schreiber, *Pro* Marc Turtletaub and Peter Saraf, *Ex Pro* Matthew Stillman, *Ph* Matthew Libatique,

Pro Des Mark Geraghty, *Ed* Craig McKay and Andrew Marcus, *M* Phil Cantelon, *Costumes* Michael Clancy.

Warner Independent Piuctures/Big Beach-Warner.
105 mins. USA. 2005. Rel: 25 November 2005. Cert. 12A.

Evil Aliens ★

There's news of an alien abduction on the Welsh island of Scalleum. So the questionable cable programme *Weird Worlde* send their most unscrupulous team to cover the story. And to make sure it's sexy, the crew fabricate crop circles and don silly space suits. But there is something really nasty and unnatural going down… They don't come much more amateur than this, a mishmash of the pantomimic, the vulgar and the very, very cheap. Bad taste is one thing, crude inanity something else entirely. CB

• *Michelle Fox* Emily Booth, *Ricky Anderson* Samuel Butler, *Cat Williams* Jennifer Evans, *Gavin Gorman* Jamie Honeybourne, *Jack Campbell* Peter McNeil O'Connor, *Bruce Barton* Nick Smithers, *Candy Vixen* Jodie Shaw, *Llyr Williams* Chris Adamson, *Howard Marsden* Norman Lovett, *with* Chris Thomas, Mark Richard Williams.

• *Dir, Screenplay* and *Ed* Jake West, *Pro* Tim Dennison, *Ex Pro* Quentin Reynolds, *Ph* Jim Solan, *Pro Des* Neil Jenkins, *M* Richard Wells, *Costumes* Cal Westbrook, *Makeup Effects* Life Creations, *Digital Effects* Llyr Williams.

Falcon Media-ContentFilm.
93 mins. UK. 2004. Rel: 10 March 2006. Cert. 18.

The Exorcism of Emily Rose ★★★½

Having recently won a scholarship to the University of Minnesota, 19-year-old Emily Rose undergoes a traumatic night when she is assaulted by an unseen force and starts seeing demons everywhere. Diagnosed as suffering from 'psychotic-epileptic disorder', Emily is prescribed a sedative, but merely deteriorates and is sent home to be overseen by a local Catholic priest. When she dies in his care, hard-nosed agnostic lawyer Erin Bruner is persuaded to defend him… Basically a courtroom drama punctuated by horrifying flashbacks, *The Exorcism of Emily Rose* is both scary and thought provoking. Powered by consummate acting rather than cheesy special effects, the film avoids many of the clichés of the horror genre, although there's still a few too many. Nonetheless, this is probably the most intelligent film about exorcism since a certain release in 1973 kept all of us up at night. Incidentally, there never was an Emily Rose. The real subject was Anneliese Michel, a 16-year-old German girl who died during an exorcism in the early 1970s (around the time of the release of *The Exorcist*). JC-W

• *Erin Bruner* Laura Linney, *Father Richard Moore* Tom Wilkinson, *Ethan Thomas* Campbell Scott, *Emily Rose* Jennifer Carpenter, *Karl Gunderson* Colm Feore, *Judge Brewster* Mary Beth Hurt, *Dr Briggs* Henry Czerny, *Dr Adani* Shohreh Aghdashloo, *Jason* Joshua Close, *with* Kenneth Welsh, Duncan Frazer,

Shriek 2: Jennifer Carpenter suffers *The Exorcism of Emily Rose*, the second film based on the curious case of Anneliese Michel (from Columbia TriStar)

J.R. Bourne.

• *Dir* Scott Derrickson, *Pro* Paul Harris Boardman, Tripp Vinson, Beau Flynn, Tom Rosenberg and Gary Lucchesi, *Ex Pro* Andre Lamal, Terry McKay, David McIlvain and Julie Yorn, *Screenplay* Derrickson and Harris Boardman, *Ph* Tom Stern, *Pro Des* David Brisbin, *Ed* Jeff Betancourt, *M* Christopher Young, *Costumes* Tish Monaghan, *Make-up/Visual Effects* Keith Vanderlaan.

Screen Gems/Lakeshore Entertainment/Firm Films-Columbia TriStar.
119 mins. USA. 2005. Rel: 25 November 2005. Cert. 15.

Extraño ★★★★½

This is a slow-moving and demanding work like Fred Kelemen's *Abendland* of 1999 and would be a masterpiece if only its purpose were a shade clearer. Even without that, Santiago Loza's first feature, a meditation on life and its fragility, is remarkable. He concentrates not on a plot but on two characters, a middle-aged surgeon (Julio Chávez), a loner who has in effect withdrawn from life, and a younger woman (Valeria Bertuccelli) awaiting the birth of her child but living alone until these two become lovers. Loza's genius is to cast these roles perfectly and then to present the players as though they were real people living their lives. This extends to capturing their interior being and admirers of Bresson and/or Ozu could well find *Extraño* wholly engrossing. It's a genuine work of art. MS

• *Erika* Valeria Bertuccelli, *Axel* Julio Chávez, *Laura* Raquel Albéniz, *with* Chunchuna Villafañe, Jorge Prado, Eva Bianco, Lautaro Bengoechea.

• *Dir* and *Screenplay* Santiago Loza, *Pro* Ana Laura Bonet,
Francesca Feder and María Galarza, *Ph* Willi Behnisch,
Pro Des Alejandra Taubin, *Ed* Ana Poliak, *Sound*
Martin Grignaschi.

Viada Producciones/Æternan Films, etc-ICA Projects.
81 mins. Argentina/France/Netherlands/Switzerland.
2003. Rel: 24 March 2006. No Cert.

Factotum ★★★

Henry Chinaski harbours no delusions about his lifestyle of
drinking, womanising and betting on the horses. But, if he
puts in a few hours of work, he reckons he's owed the loose
change to subsidise his living. Taking odd jobs in factories
and warehouses, and picking up women in bars, he still
finds time to record his thoughts in short stories and a long
gestating, half-finished novel. But nobody seems interested in
publishing his writing, which, to Chinaski, proves he's doing
something right... Largely drawn from Charles Bukowski's
second, semi-autobiographical novel of the same name,
Factotum is predictably episodic and aimless, albeit infused
with a strong wry humour and urban poetry. Matt Dillon,
adopting a gruff, rasping voice, is something of a revelation
here, providing an engaging combination of thug, artist and
lost soul. And there's strong support from Lili Taylor and
Marisa Tomei, in selfless, almost masochistic turns. FYI:
Tomei's first line on screen was, 'you're drunk', which she
addressed to Matt Dillon in *The Flamingo Kid* (1984). Here,
Dillon meets her in a bar where she's already been drinking
heavily. JC-W

• *Henry Chinaski* Matt Dillon, *Jan* Lili Taylor, *Laura* Marisa
Tomei, *Manny* Fisher Stevens, *Pierre* Didier Flamand, *Jerry*
Adrienne Shelly, *Grace* Karen Young, *Tom Lyons* Tony
Endicott.

• *Dir* Bent Hamer, *Pro* and *Screenplay* Hamer and Jim Stark,
Ex Pro Christine Kunewa Walker, *Assoc Pro* Rainer Mockert
and Karl Baumgartner, *Ph* John Christian Rosenlund, *Pro
Des* Eve Cauley Turner, *Ed* Pål Gengenbach, *M* Kristin
Asbjørnsen, *Sound* Petter Fladeby.

Jim Stark/Norwegian Film Fund/Norwegian Film
Institute/Canal Plus, etc-Icon.
93 mins. Norway/USA/Germany/Italy/France. 2005.
Rel: 18 November 2005. Cert. 15.

Failure to Launch ★★

With his dashing good looks, effortless charm and fun-loving
nature, Tripp is the modern woman's model dreamboat. But
Tripp, for all his romantic flair and seeming generosity, has
one major setback: he still lives with Mom and Dad. So, in
desperation, Tripp's parents hire a woman to lure their son
away from the domestic fold... Had Matthew McConaughey
or Sarah Jessica Parker had a fraction of the comic acumen
of, say, Cary Grant and Carole Lombard, then they may have
overcome the schematic mechanism of this leaden, formulaic
farce. As it is, McConaughey has never come off as more
smug, arrogant or insufferable, while Parker seems madly

miscast as the hard-nosed siren pulling his strings. Only an
amusing subplot featuring Zooey Deschanel – as a sexually
repressed killjoy – saves the film from being a total bomb.
JC-W

• *Tripp* Matthew McConaughey, *Paula* Sarah Jessica Parker,
Kit Zooey Deschanel, *Ace* Justin Bartha, *Demo* Bradley Cooper,
Al Terry Bradshaw, *Sue* Kathy Bates, *Jeffrey* Tyrel Jackson
Williams, *Bud* Stephen Tobolowsky, *with* Katheryn Winnick,
Robert Corddry, Kate McGregor-Stewart.

• *Dir* Tom Dey, *Pro* Scott Rudin and Scott Aversano, *Ex
Pro* Ron Bozman, *Screenplay* Tom J. Astle and Matt Ember,
Ph Claudio Miranda, *Pro Des* Jeremy Conway, *Ed* Steven
Rosenblum, *M* Rolfe Kent, *Costumes* Ellen Mirojnick.

Paramount/Scott Rudin/Aversano-UIP.
96 mins. USA. 2006. Rel: 31 March 2006. Cert. 12A.

Familia Rodante ★★★★

A total contrast to his contemporary drama *El Bonaerense*, this
appealing new work finds the Argentinean filmmaker Pablo
Trapero creating an agreeable fiction out of his childhood
memories. Casting his own octogenarian grandmother in the
leading role, he invites us to share the travails of a journey
in a camper. It's undertaken by four generations of one
family setting out to attend a wedding taking place near the
border with Brazil. The film has been described as a comedy
but the mishaps on the road and the family tensions that
develop while travelling afford quiet pleasures of recognition
rather than hearty laughter. The film's affectionate approach
compensates for it being a lightweight piece and also for
its uncertainty as to how to bow out at the close. Indeed,
the movie generates a warmth so rare in cinema today that
watching it is an extremely welcome experience. Aka *Rolling
Family*. MS

• *Emilia* Graciana Chironi, *Marta* Liliana Capurro, *Claudia*
Ruth Dobel, *Oscar* Bernardo Forteza, *Paola* Laura Glave,
Nadia Leila Gómez.

• *Dir* and *Screenplay* Pablo Trapero, *Pro* Pablo Trapero,
Donald Ranvaud and Robert Bevan, *Ex Pro* Martina Gusman
and Hugo Castro Fau, *Ph* Guillermo Nieto, *Pro Des* Sergio
Hernández, *Ed* Nicolás Goldbart, *M* León Gieco, Hugo Díaz
and Juanjo Soza, *Costumes* Marisa Urruti, *Sound*
Martín Grignatchi.

Matanza Cine/Lumina Films/Paradis Film/Pandora Film
Produktion/ Videofilmes Producoes Artisticas-Artificial Eye.
103 mins. Argentina/France/Germany/UK/Spain. 2004.
Rel: 18 November 2005. Cert. 15.

The Family Stone ★★★★

Christmas is approaching and handsome Manhattan executive
Everett Stone is impatient to introduce his girlfriend,
Meredith, to his parents and four siblings. However, Meredith
and the family Stone clash in spite of their united best
efforts. Uptight, overly manicured and insecure, Meredith

immediately falls prey to the Stones' bohemian informality, while they mistake her fear for standoffish disapproval… On the written page, *The Family Stone* looks too silly for words. Yet it's so deftly written and played that the events unfold with toe-curling plausibility – and with an equal measure of laughs. It would be impossible to single out any one performance – everybody is so good – although Sarah Jessica Parker deserves merit for creating such an insufferable stuffed shirt. Memorable highlights include the Christmas Eve dinner sequence (in which Meredith digs herself into an appallingly homophobic grave) and the hilarious morning after the night before. In another's hands, *The Family Stone* could so easily have degenerated into farce; here, it's a human comedy of enormous emotional engagement. JC-W

• *Julie Morton* Claire Danes, *Sybil Stone* Diane Keaton, *Amy Stone* Rachel McAdams, *Everett Stone* Dermot Mulroney, *Kelly Stone* Craig T. Nelson, *Meredith Morton* Sarah Jessica Parker, *Ben Stone* Luke Wilson, *Thad Stone* Ty Giordano, *Patrick Thomas* Brian White, *Brad Stevenson* Paul Schneider, *with* Savannah Stehlin, Jamie Kaler, Robert Dioguardi.

• *Dir* and *Screenplay* Thomas Bezucha, *Pro* Michael London, *Ex Pro* Jennifer Ogden, *Ph* Jonathan Brown, *Pro Des* Jane Ann Stewart, *Ed* Jeffrey Ford, *M* Michael Giacchino, *Costumes* Shay Cunliffe.

Fox 2000-Fox.
103 mins. USA. 2005. Rel: 2 December 2005. Cert. PG.

Fantastic Four ★★½

Returning from an intergalactic expedition, five scientists find their DNA irreparably altered. Inventor Dr Reed Richards discovers that he has acquired a remarkable ability to stretch his limbs, Sue Storm can turn herself invisible, her brother Johnny can transform himself into a human fireball and Ben Grimm is, well, a walking wall. Dubbed the `Fantastic Four' by the media, the quartet employ their new powers for the greater good – and to forestall the evil machinations of their boss, Victor Von Doom, who has acquired a few unearthly faculties himself… *Fantastic Four* is cheesy, over-the-top and a little too close to *X-Men* for comfort, but at least it doesn't take itself seriously. With a babe like Jessica Alba playing a director of genetic research, how could it? And dig those surnames: Storm, Grimm and Von Doom. Being the longest-running series in Marvel Comics' history, one might have hoped for something more special, but as popcorn-lite it's got fun high on its agenda and is refreshingly unpretentious. JC-W

• *Dr Reed Richards/Mr Fantastic* Ioan Gruffudd, *Sue Storm/The Invisible Woman* Jessica Alba, *Johnny Storm/The Human Torch* Chris Evans, *Ben Grimm/The Thing* Michael Chiklis, *Victor Von Doom/Dr Doom* Julian McMahon, *Alica Masters* Kerry Washington, *Leonard* Hamish Linklater, *with* Kevin McNulty, Stan Lee, Peggy Gormley, C.B. Hackworth.

• *Dir* Tim Story, *Pro* Bernd Eichinger, Avi Arad and Ralph Winter, *Ex Pro* Stan Lee, Kevin Feige, Chris Columbus, Mark Radcliffe and Michael Barnathan, *Co-Pro* Ross Fanger, *Screenplay*

Mark Frost and Michael France, *Ph* Oliver Wood, *Pro Des* Bill Boes, *Ed* William Hoy, *M* John Ottman, *Costumes* José I. Fernandez, *Sound* Charles Maynes.

Fox/Constantin Film/Marvel Enterprises/1492-Fox.
105 mins. USA. 2005. Rel: 22 July 2005. Cert. PG.

The Fast and the Furious: Tokyo Drift ★★★

With original stars Vin Diesel jumping ship after part one (though he has a cameo here) and Paul Walker after part two, you wouldn't expect much from the second sequel – but this isn't at all bad as far as slick, brain-in-neutral action is concerned. Lucas Black is the American who goes to Japan and gets mixed up with drift racing and the Yakuza, Brian Tee the local Drift King he comes up against. The actors give bright, lively turns, Justin Lin's direction is dynamic and imaginative, the Tokyo setting makes it come up fresh as a new pin and it's all surppringly effective, thrilling and exciting. And yes, it does what it says on the tin – it's fast and furious. DW

• *Sean Boswell* Lucas Black, *Twinkie* Bow Wow, *Neela* Nathalie Kelley, *D.K.* Brian Tee, *Han* Sung Kang, *Morimoto* Leonardo Nam, *Major Boswell* Brian Goodman, *Uncle Kamata* JJ Sonny Chiba, *Clay* Zachery Bryan, *with* Nikki Griffin, Jason Tobin, Keiko Kitagawa, Lynda Boyd, Vincent Laresca, and (uncredited) *Dominic Toretto* Vin Diesel.

• *Dir* Justin Lin, *Pro* Neal H. Moritz, *Ex Pro* Clayton Townsend, Ryan Kavanaugh, Lynwood Spinks, *Co-Pro* Amanda Cohen, *Screenplay* Chris Morgan, *Ph* Stephen F. Windon, *Pro Des* Ida Random, *Ed* Fred Raskin and Kelly Matsumoto, *M* Brian Tyler, *Costumes* Sanja Milkovic Hays.

Universal/Relativity Media-UIP.
104 mins. USA. 2006. Rel: 16 June 2006.
Cert. 12A.

Fate ★★★½

Even more directly than Hungary's *Pleasant Days*, this Turkish movie, superbly photographed in colour and made with flair by Demirkubuz, draws on the Camus novel *The Outsider*. The setting is now Istanbul in the 1990s but the central figure, Musa, well played by Serdar Orçin, displays the same absence of feeling as Camus's Meursault, be it over his mother's death, marrying Sinem his fellow clerk or facing death himself when found guilty of murders he did not commit. His indifference can be seen as challenging the hypocrisy of those who feign feelings or as representing an emptiness of soul present in all human beings. The story illustrating this has its improbabilities (would Sinem want to marry a man so unresponsive?), but if not always persuasive the piece is certainly thought provoking. Original title: *Yazgi*. MS

• *Musa Demircan* Serdar Orçin, *Sinem* Zeynep Tokus, *Naim* Demir Karahan, *Necati* Engin Günaydin, *with* Feridun Koç, Necmi Aykar, Sehsuvar Aktas, Nazan Kirilmis, Turkan Ince, Apo Demirkubuz.

• *Dir, Pro, Screenplay* and *Ed* Zeki Demirkubuz, inspired by

L'Etranger by Albert Camus, *Ph* Ali Utku, *Art Dir* Bahar Evgin, *M* Gustav Mahler.

Mavi Filmcilik/Esef Pilsen-BFI.
118 mins. Turkey. 2001. Rel: 3 February 2006. Cert. 15.

Fateless ★★½

The future Nobel Prize winner Imre Kertész was just 14-years-old when he was deported from Budapest to the concentration camps of Auschwitz, Buchenwald and Zeitz. This is his story... It's easy to spot that this is the directorial debut of a cinematographer. The film is a little measured in its pacing, overly earnest and maybe too pretty for its own good. Watching it is like leafing through a series of arty, black-and-white photographs, handpicked for a glossy coffee table book on the Holocaust. Like his protagonist and scenarist, Lajos Koltai was born in Budapest and so, understandably, connects with his subject. But the (true) story of Jews being torn from their homes, herded into cattle trucks and then starved in the hell holes of Auschwitz and Buchenwald has been told so many times, that to revisit such horrors seems an effort of obligation. Young Marcell Nagy provides a suitably picturesque visage on which to superimpose such atrocities, but the raw ugliness of it all seems to be missing. FYI: Lajos Koltai was nominated for an Oscar nominee for *Malèna* and went on to photograph the English-speaking *The Emperor's Club*, *Max* and *Being Julia*. Original title: *Sorstalanság*. JC-W

• *Gyuri Köves* Marcell Nagy, *Bandi Citrom* Áron Dimény, *Finn* Andras M. Kecskes, *Balszerencses* Jozsef Gyabronka, *Kollmann* Endre Harkanyi, *smoker* Béla Dóra, *American soldier* Daniel Craig, *pretty boy* Bálint Péntek.

• *Dir* Lajos Koltai, *Pro* Andras Hamori, Peter Barbalics, Ildiko Kemeny and Jonathan Olsberg, *Ex Pro* Laszlo Vincze, Bernd Hellthaler and Robert Buckler, *Screenplay* Imre Kertész, *Ph* Gyula Pados, *Pro Des* Tibor Lazar, *Ed* Hajnal Sello, *M* Ennio Morricone, *Costumes* Gyorgyi Szakacs.

Magyar Mozgókép Közalapítvány/Eurimages, etc-Dogwoof Pictures.
140 mins. Hungary/Germany/UK/Israel. 2005. Rel: 5 May 2006. Cert. 12A.

Favela Rising ★★★

This prize-winning documentary set in the favelas or ghettos of Rio de Janeiro is acceptable but nevertheless something of a disappointment. That's because of the sense of déjà vu. Like *Rize* it features music, here including hip hop and Afro-Brazilian rhythms, as a means of luring youngsters away from violent street life and drug gangs. But whereas *Rize* tellingly built up its social comment this film moves away from that aspect which was in any case better done in *Bus 174*. It then concentrates instead on Anderson Sa who inspired the musical programme, but he's far less fascinating than those two contrasted men central to *The Wild Parrots of Telegraph Hill* and *Grizzly Man* respectively. It also fails to encompass the full range of work of Afro Reggae, the cultural group named

after the music, so the picture we get is incomplete. MS

• *Dir* and *Pro* Jeff Zimbalist and Matt Mochary, *Ex Pro* Ravi Anne and Rich Lim, *Assoc Pro* José Junior and Tatiana Dorow, *Ph* and *Ed* Zimbalist, *M* Force Theory, written and performed by Sanford Livingston and Michael Furjanic, *Sound* Mike Furjanic.

Sidetrack Films/VOY Pictures-ICA Projects.
80 mins. USA. 2005. Rel: 10 March 2006. No Cert.

Fearless ★★★★

Tianjin, China; 1880. When his father is killed in a humiliating public duel, a young Huo Yuanjia swears to become the best fighter that he can. And so he grows up to be the unbeatable combatant of his dreams, but with tragic consequences... Jet Li is a wonderfully charismatic performer and his expert martial arts skills are put to great effect in this true story of the legendary martial arts master Yuanjia. In addition, Ronny Yu's striking film looks nothing short of spectacular with superb production values. The story itself is thrilling and exciting, leading to an unforgettable *Hamlet*-like finale. Original title: *Huo Yuan Jia*. GS

• *Huo Yuanjia* Jet Li, *Anno Tanaka* Nakamura Shidou, *Moon `Betty' Sun Li* Jinsun Dong Yong, *Yuanjia's father* Collin Chou, *Hercules O'Brien* Nathan Jones, *Mr Mita* Masato Harada, *with* Paw Hee Ching, Chen Zhihui, Tina Leung.

• *Dir* Ronny Yu, *Pro* Yu, Bill Kong, Jet Li and Yang Buting, *Co-Pro* Chui Po Chu and Han Sanping, *Screenplay* Christine To and Chris Chow, *Ph* Poon Hang Sang, *Pro Des* Kenneth Mak, *Ed* Virginia Katz and Richard Learoyd, *M* Shigeru Umebayashi, *Costumes* Thomas Chong, *Choreography* Yuen Wo Ping.

Hero China International/China Film Group/Beijing Film Studio-UIP.
103 mins. China/Hong Kong/USA. 2005. Rel: 23 June 2006. Cert. 15.

Feed ★★★

Sydney/Ohio; the present. Philip Jackson is a cyber crime investigator for the Australian police. Having tracked down a German cannibal who preyed on willing victims, he now turns his attention to something equally bizarre. On the website *Feeders & Gainers*, he encounters a man who gets his kicks force-feeding women to the point of morbid obesity. It appears to be a symbiotic arrangement – the 'gainer' gets an equal erotic charge from her weight increase – but is it legal? Even in the spirit of the progressive mainstreaming of perversion, *Feed* takes the biscuit, the cake and the entire banquet. A genuine curiosity item perched on the outer fringes of human indignity, the film is uneasy to forget and, depending on one's appetite, questionably digestible. Even so, it poses some intriguing counter-arguments to the media-drenched forum on anorexia and although it's not a very good film, it wields a powerful stick.
JC-W

• *Philip Jackson* Patrick Thompson, *Michael Turner/Feeder X* Alex O'Loughlin, *Deirdre* Gabby Millgate, *Richard* Jack Thompson, *Nigel* Matthew Le Nevez, *with* Rose Ashton, Sherly Sulaiman, Marika Aubrey, David Field, Connor Thompson.

• *Dir* Brett Leonard, *Pro* Melissa Beauford, *Ex Pro* Jack Thompson, Chris Foster, John Gregory and Greg Quail, *Screenplay* Kieran Galivin, from an idea by Alex O'Loughlin and Patrick Thompson, *Ph* Steve Arnold, *Pro Des* Jessamy Llewelyn, *Ed* Mark Bennett, *M* Gregg Leonard and Geoff Michael, *Costumes* Helen Mather, *Special Effects* David Trethewey.

Becker Films International/Honour Bright/All at Once-Showbox Media Group.
100 mins. Australia. 2005. Rel: 17 February 2006. Cert. 18.

Festival ★★

The Edinburgh Festival is gearing up for another season of madness, culture shock and disillusionment. Faith Myers accosts pedestrians with news of her one-woman show about Dorothy Wordsworth, TV star Sean Sullivan is in town to judge the best comedy act and a trio of existential Canadians have moved into a grand old house that has opened itself up as a hostelry. There's also a gentle giant with his show about a paedophile priest, a drunken Irish comic here for his ninth summer and a reporter for BBC Scotland who cannot play by the rules… A sort of *Happiness* for the largest arts jamboree in the world, *Festival* is a strangely poignant black comedy with a lot of strengths and some glaring weaknesses. Its stretches of comedy are embarrassing in their awfulness, the raw sex scenes uncomfortably human and the acting much better than the film deserves. Raquel Cassidy is a stand-out as the comedy star's long-suffering PA, Lucy Punch a scream as the artless but innately funny comedienne Nicky Romanowski and Lyndsey Marshal wide-eyed and touching as the actress who's in Edinburgh for the art. JC-W

• *Micheline Menzies* Amelia Bullmore, *Conor Kelly* Billy Carter, *Petra Loewenberg* Raquel Cassidy, *Dina* Megan Dodds, *Gordon Menzies* Duncan Duff, *Rick* Jonah Lotan, *Mary* Meredith MacNeill, *Sean Sullivan* Stephen Mangan, *Faith Myers* Lyndsey Marshal, *Joan Gerard* Daniela Nardini, *Tommy O'Dwyer* Chris O'Dowd, *Frida Finucane* Deirdre O'Kane, *Nicky Romanowski* Lucy Punch, *Brother Mike* Clive Russell, *with* Selina Cadell, Jimmy Chisholm, Gabriel Quigley, Frank Gilhooley, Steven Dick, Stuart Milligan, Dorothy Paul, Eileen Buresh, Monty Cantsin, Neil Fitzmaurice, Richard Ayoade, Sanjeev Singh Kohli, Tom Goodman-Hill, Peter McDonald, Neil McCormack, Stephen Davidson, Mark McDonnell.

• *Dir* and *Screenplay* Annie Griffin, *Pro* Christopher Young, *Ex Pro* Robert Jones, Caroline Leddy and Roger Shannon, *Ph* Daniel Cohen, *Pro Des* Tom Sayer, *Ed* William Webb, *M* Jim Sutherland, *Costumes* Gill Horn.

UK Film Council/FilmFour/Scottish Screen/
Young Pirate Films-Pathé.
107 mins. UK. 2005. Rel: 15 July 2005.
Cert. 18.

Fever Pitch

See *The Perfect Catch*.

Final Destination 3 ★★★½

As Wendy Christensen had foreseen, a terrible accident on a rollercoaster ride kills her boyfriend and several of her classmates. It is now a race against time for Wendy and the survivors of the crash to cheat death again – and again… Returning to the series after taking a break on number two, director James Wong raises the bar in horror sequels. The level of invention is on top form, with the invisible force of Death scouting around the mundane to forge instruments of indescribable destruction. So, be it a bench press, a melting frappuccino or a tube of suntan lotion, death will out. Wong also brings a surprising visual wit to his macabre scenarios, ensuring that there's plenty of life yet in this ingenious franchise. CB

• *Wendy Christensen* Mary Elizabeth Winstead, *Kevin Fischer* Ryan Merriman, *Ian McKinley* Kris Lemche, *Lewis Romero* Texas Battle, *Erin* Alexz Johnson, *Jason Wise* Jesse Moss, *Carrie Dreyer* Gina Holden, *with* Sam Easton, Crystal Lowe, Chelan Simmons.

• *Dir* James Wong, *Pro* Wong, Craig Perry, Warren Zide and Glen Morgan, *Ex Pro* Toby Emmerich, Richard Brener and Matt Moore, *Co-Pro* Art Schaefer, Screenplay Wong and Morgan, *Ph* Robert McLachlan, *Pro Des* Mark Freeborn, *Ed* Chris Willingham, *M* Shirley Walker, *Costumes* Gregory B. Mah.

New Line Cinema/Hard Eight Pictures/Practical Pictures/
Matinee Pictures-Entertainment.
92 mins. USA. 2006. Rel: 10 February 2006. Cert. 15.

Firewall ★★★

Security specialist Jack Stanfield is at the top of his field. Employed by the Seattle-based Landrock Pacific Bank, he has rendered the on-line finances of his employer inviolable. But even with his world-class knowledge of tracers, access codes and firewalls, he has overlooked one weak spot – himself. Taking Stanfield's family hostage, master criminal Bill Cox offers the lives of Stanfield's wife and children in exchange for a way into Landrock's computer network… Like top-of-the-range fast food, *Firewall* slips down a treat. The premise is a gem, all the right buttons are pushed and Paul Bettany is all the more chilling for reining in any villainous histrionics (indeed, he must be the politest killer in aeons). But not for one minute do we suspect that any real harm will come to our protagonists, and it's odd that no allusion is made to the fact that, at 63, Harrison Ford is rather old to be the father of an eight-year-old. FYI: Even at the tender age of ten, Jimmy Bennett is typecast: he was also held captive in last year's *Hostage*. JC-W

• *Jack Stanfield* Harrison Ford, *Bill Cox* Paul Bettany, *Beth Stanfield* Virginia Madsen, *Gary Mitchell* Robert Patrick, *Harry Romano* Robert Forster, *Arlin Forester* Alan Arkin, *Janet Stone* Mary Lynn Rajskub, *Sarah Stanfield* Carl Schroeder, *Andy Stanfield* Jimmy Bennett, *with* Matthew Currie Holmes, David Lewis, Nikolaj Coster Waldau, Ty Olsson.

Computer graphic: Harrison Ford fine-tunes his software in Richard Loncraine's formulaic but highly efficient *Firewall* (from Warner)

• *Dir* Richard Loncraine, *Pro* Armyan Bernstein, Jonathan Shestack and Basil Iwanyk, *Ex Pro* Brent O'Connor, Charlie Lyons, Dana Goldberg and Bruce Berman, *Screenplay* Joe Forte, *Ph* Marco Pontecorvo, *Pro Des* Brian Morris, *Ed* Jim Page, *M* Alexandre Desplat, *Costumes* Shuna Harwood, *Sound* Richard King.

Warner/Village Roadshow/Beacon Pictures/
Thunder Road-Warner.
104 mins. USA/Australia. 2006. Rel: 31 March 2006.
Cert. 12A.

Flightplan ★★★½

Kylie Pratt, a propulsion engineer based in Berlin, is accompanying the coffin of her husband on a plane headed for New York. With her is her six-year-old daughter, Julia, who has never flown before. Three hours into the journey, Kylie wakes from a brief slumber to find that her child is missing. Stranger still, Julia's name is not on the passenger list and nobody can even remember seeing her… Great concept for a movie, this, even though it's uncomfortably close to an amalgam of *The Forgotten* and *Red Eye*. Nonetheless, the cavernous shafts and alleyways of the fictitious Aalto Air E-474 make for a fresh and claustrophobic setting for a psychological thriller. It's a shame, then, that Robert Schwentke insists on drawing attention to his direction, although Jodie Foster repeatedly pulls us back into the human drama. There are also too many improbabilities. Why would a top aircraft engineer fly in economy? How come Julia, the American daughter of an aircraft engineer, had never flown

to America before? And on which flight have you ever come across nine simultaneously empty toilets? Forget this, though, and *Flightplan* is an original and suspenseful ride into every mother's worst nightmare. JC-W

• *Kylie Pratt* Jodie Foster, *Air Marshal Gene Carson* Peter Sarsgaard, *Captain Rich* Sean Bean, *Stephanie* Kate Beahan, *Obaid* Michael Irby, *Ahmed* Assaf Cohen, *Fiona* Erika Christensen, *Julia Pratt* Marlene Lawston, *therapist* Greta Scacchi, *with* Shane Edelman, Mary Gallagher, Haley Ramm, Brent Sexton, Judith Scott, John Benjamin Hickey, Gavin Grazer, Stephanie Faracy.

• *Dir* Robert Schwentke, *Pro* Brian Grazer, *Ex Pro* James Whitaker, Charles J.D. Schlissel, Robert DiNozzi and Erica Huggins, *Screenplay* Peter A. Dowling and Billy Ray, *Ph* Florian Ballhaus, *Pro Des* Alexander Hammond, *Ed* Thom Noble, *M* James Horner, *Costumes* Susan Lyall.

Touchstone Pictures/Imagine Entertainment-
Buena Vista International.
98 mins. USA. 2005. Rel: 25 November 2005. Cert. 12A.

The Fog ★½

Shortly after Elizabeth Williams returns to her birthplace of Antonio Island in Oregon, a series of strange deaths are reported. The island is also visited by a thick, unpredictable fog, which seems to arrive out of nowhere… With the likes of *Psycho*, *The Texas Chain Saw Massacre* and *Dawn of the Dead* having been given a modern makeover, the vault of great horror has pretty much run dry. So the new trend is to revamp more mediocre titles which either support a mild cult following or had some box-office success. John Carpenter's *The Fog* (1980) was a vaguely ludicrous and heavy-handed affair and the remake is only marginally more unsettling. It's also very dumb and formulaic. It's the sort of movie where, after a night of unbridled lovemaking, Maggie Grace sits bolt upright from a traumatic nightmare but manages first to cover her breasts with a sheet. However, she's a bright girl, because she tells us what a hallmark is. The rest is a lot of smoke, mirrors and fog. JC-W

• *Nick Castle* Tom Welling, *Elizabeth Williams* Maggie Grace, *Captain Blake* Rade Sherbedgia, *Spooner* DeRay Davis, *Tom Malone* Kenneth Welsh, *Father Malone* Adrian Hough, *Stevie Wayne* Selma Blair, *Dan the weatherman* Jonathon Young, *with* Sara Botsford, Cole Heppell, Mary Black.

• *Dir* Rupert Wainwright, *Pro* Debra Hill, David Foster and John Carpenter, *Ex Pro* Todd Garner, Dan Kolsrud and Derek Dauchy, *Screenplay* Cooper Layne, *Ph* Nathan Hope, *Pro Des* Michael Diner and Graeme Murray, *M* Graeme Revell, *Costumes* Monique Prudhomme.

Revolution Studios-Columbia TriStar.
99 mins. USA/Canada. 2005. Rel: 24 February 2006.
Cert. 15.

Football Days ★★½

Madrid; the present. Fresh out of prison, Antonio decides to form a seven-side football team to help the self-esteem of his six closest male friends. But things are not going well: Antonio's dreams of being a psychologist are proving to be pie-in-the-sky; Jorge's girlfriend has turned down his proposal of marriage; Miguel has been thrown out by his wife (after he lost their baby); Charlie's movie career is not all that it's cracked up to be; Gonzalo catches the clap after his first sexual experience in aeons; and Ramón is appalled when his wife becomes pregnant. Besides, none of them • can play football worth a damn… After a promising start, this frenetic farce – from the writer of the witty and innovative *The Other Side of the Bed* – just fails to find its feet. There are some very funny moments, a number of good lines and a steady brisk pace. However, the men are such moronic and insensitive egotists that's it hard to stay involved in their deteriorating lives. Original title: *Días de fútbol*; US title: *Soccer Days*. JC-W

• *Antonio* Ernesto Alterio, *Jorge* Alberto San Juan, *Violeta* Natalia Verbeke, *Carla* María Esteve, *Serafín* Fernando Tejero, *Ramón* Roberto Álamo, *Gonzalo* Secun de La Rosa, *Carlos* aka `Charlie' Pere Ponce.

• *Dir* and *Screenplay*, David Serrano, *Pro* Tomás Cimadevilla, *Ex Pro* Cimadevilla, José Herrero de Egaña and Ghislain Barrois, *Ph* Kiko de La Rica, *Art Dir* Beatriz San Juan, *Ed* Rori Sáinz de Rozas, *M* Miguel Malla.

Telespan/Picasso Estudios/Via Digital-Dogwoof Pictures.
113 mins. Spain. 2003. Rel: 12 August 2005.
Cert. 15.

Forty Shades of Blue ★½

Memphis, Tennessee; the present. Like a gazelle stunned by the lights of a headlight, Laura seems trapped in a perpetual trance. The young-ish Russian girlfriend of a legendary soul musician – and the mother of the latter's three-year-old son – she cannot seem to fit into the strange world orbiting her man. Then, out of the blue, she forms a tenuous connection with her stepbrother… At once inscrutable and arbitrary, Ira Sachs' second feature seems to be in as much of a daze as its leading protagonist, and any real drama seems purely accidental. Rip Torn is his gruff, charismatic self, but he's given too little to do, while the alarmingly thin Dina Korzun is maybe not as physically captivating as Sachs' camera thinks she is. The director's technique is also highly soporific – slow pans to right and left – while it seems odd that a film about a musician is so swollen with silence. JC-W

• *Alan James* Rip Torn, *Laura* Dina Korzun, *Michael James* Darren Burrows, *Lonni* Paprika Steen, *Duigan* Red West, *Celia* Jenny O'Hara, *with* Jerry Chipman, Andrew Henderson, Joanne Pankow.

• *Dir* Ira Sachs, *Pro* Sachs, Margot Bridger, Mary Bing, Jawal Nga and Donald Rosenfeld, *Ex Pro* Geoff Stier and Dioane Von Furstenberg, *Screenplay* Sachs and Michael Rohatyn, *Ph* Julian Whatley, *Pro Des* Teresa Mastropierro, *Ed* Affonso Gonçalves, *M* Dickon Hinchliffe, *Costumes* Eric Daman.

Charlie Guidance Prods/Flux Films/Tiny Dancer Films/ High Line/Sundance Institute-Artificial Eye.
109 mins. USA. 2004. Rel: 30 June 2004. Cert. 15.

The 40 Year Old Virgin ★★★★

As a nerdy fortysomething into action dolls – and who thinks it's finally time to dump his virginity – Steve Carell gives a thoroughly likeable performance in an often hilarious laddish comedy. The gleeful movie steers a confidently steady course round its gross-out situations, swearing and non-PC gags, and on to a touching, surprising romantic finale. And Carell has a great support team: there's a keen turn by Catherine Keener as the divorced single mother he fancies, while Paul Rudd, Romany Malco and Seth Rogen are hysterical as Carell's lewd workmates who uncover his secret and decide to help him out. Unusually, the film sustains its long running time, and is still funny on a second viewing, though the extra footage in the DVD version is too much. DW

• *Andy Stitzer* Steve Carell, *Trish* Catherine Keener, *David* Paul Rudd, *Jay* Romany Malco, *Cal* Seth Rogen, *Beth* Elizabeth Banks, *Nicky* Leslie Mann, *Paula* Jane Lynch, *with* Gerry Bednob, Shelley Malil, Kat Dennings, Loudon Wainwright.

• *Dir* Judd Apatow, *Pro* Judd Apatow, Clayton Townsend and Shauna Robertson, *Ex Pro* Steve Carell and Jon Poll, *Co-Pro* Seth Rogen, *Screenplay* Apatow and Carell, *Ph* Jack Green, *Pro Des* Jackson DeGovia, *Ed* Brent White, *M* Lyle Workman, *Costumes* Debra McGuire.

Universal/Apatow-UIP.
115 mins. USA. 2005. Rel: 2 September 2005. Cert. 15.

'4' ★★★

This debut feature from Moscow-born Ilya Khrzhanovsky heralds the arrival of a filmmaker who might follow in the footsteps of Tarkovsky. The first half intrigues as a prostitute, a piano tuner and a man in the meat business meet in a bar and spin fantasies about their lives. However, the second part, mainly featuring the girl now seen attending the village funeral of a sister, becomes ever slower and increasingly enigmatic. Ultimately the film becomes an endurance test, but the earlier scenes – finely photographed with an emphasis on long shot that echoes *The Magnificent Ambersons* – are original and sure-footed, cryptic yet engaging. Nevertheless, despite references to cloning, the director's assertion that his film is a protest about a society in which everybody is becoming like everyone else is more clear-cut than anything in his movie. Original title: *Chetyre*. MS

• *Marina* Marina Vovchenko, *Sonia* Irina Vovchenko, *Vera* Svetlana Vovchenko, *Marat* Konstantin Murzenko, *Misha* Anatoly Adoskin.

• *Dir* Ilya Khrzhanovsky, *Pro* Yelena Yatsura, *Screenplay* Vladimir Sorokin, *Ph* Alisher Khamidkhodzhaev and Alexander Ilkhovsky, *Art Dir* Shavkat Abdusalamov, *Ed* Igor Malakhov, *Costumes* Alexandra Timofeeva.

Yelena Yatsura/Filmcom/Russian Federal Agency for Culture and Film-ICA Projects. 126 mins. Russia/The Netherlands. 2004. Rel: 23 September 2005.

Four Brothers ★★

Talk about manipulative. And amoral. And confusing. And gratuitous. Working from some bizarre agenda about the unification of brothers of every race and lesser evils, John Singleton weaves his latest shoot-'em-up urban Western around the death of a little old lady (Dublin's Fionnula Flanagan). Murdered in a random grocery store hold-up, Evelyn Mercer happened to have just performed an act of sly humanitarianism. Dedicated to improving the hard streets of Detroit, she adopted four boys destined for hell – two black, two white – and taught them their ethics and table manners. Unfortunately, she appeared to have left out that two wrongs don't make a right and so the Sons of Evelyn set out to rough up Detroit in their quest for justice. Slick and preposterous, *Four Brothers* ploughs along with as much disdain for logic as the human lives it squanders. Clichés and bullets ricochet around the plot like exclamation marks, although the action sequences are pretty awesome. JC-W

• *Bobby Mercer* Mark Wahlberg, *Angel Mercer* Tyrese Gibson, *Jeremiah Mercer* André Benjamin (aka Andre 2000), *Jack Mercer* Garrett Hedlund, *Lt. Green* Terrence Howard, *Det. Fowler* Josh Charles, *Sofi* Sofia Vergara, *Evelyn Mercer* Fionnula Flanagan, *Victor Sweet* Chiwetel Ejiofor, *with* Taraji P. Henson, Barry Shabaka Henley, Kenneth Welsh, Shawn Singleton.

• *Dir* John Singleton, *Pro* Lorenzo di Bonaventura, *Ex Pro* Eic Kidney and Erik Howsam, *Screenplay* David Elliot and Paul Lovett, *Ph* Peter Menzies Jr, *Pro Des* Keith Brian Burns, *Ed* Bruce Cannon, *M* David Arnold, *Costumes* Ruth Carter.

Paramount/di Bonaventura Pictures-UIP. 108 mins. USA. 2005. Rel: 30 September 2005. Cert. 15.

Freedomland ★★★½

Arriving dazed at a hospital in New Jersey, nursery school teacher Brenda Martin appears to be the victim of a carjacking. With her hands cut to ribbons, and her reasoning bruised, she makes little sense until confronted by black police detective Lorenzo Council. He senses something is amiss and Brenda finally admits, falteringly, that her four-year-old son was in the back of the car... There's a lot to chew on in Richard Price's meaty adaptation of his own novel. And there's some high-calibre acting, although the emotional intensity is pitched at such a high level, watching the film can get quite wearisome. Juggling themes of racism, parenthood, loss, forgiveness, responsibility and even our place in God's master plan, *Freedomland* is the cinematic equivalent of a full battery charge. Even so, the film's power stays with you and Julianne Moore's climactic, naked *tour-de-force* is something of a remarkable career high. JC-W

• *Lorenzo Council* Samuel L. Jackson, *Brenda Martin* Julianne Moore, *Karen Collucci* Edie Falco, *Danny Martin* Ron Eldard, *Boyle* William Forsythe, *Felicia* Aunjanue Ellis, *Billy Williams* Anthony Mackie, *Marie* LaTanya Richardson Jackson, *Reverend Longway* Clarke Peters, *with* Peter Friedman, Domenick Lombardozzi, Philip Bosco, Brenda's attorney Richard Price, Sharon Washington, Leonard Thomas, Jasmin Walker.

• *Dir* Joe Roth, *Pro* Scott Rudin, *Ex Pro* Charles Newirth, *Screenplay* Richard Price, from his novel, *Ph* Anastas Michos, *Pro Des* David Wasco, *Ed* Nick Moore, *M* James Newton Howard, *Costumes* Ann Roth.

Revolution Studios/Scott Rudin-Columbia TriStar. 113 mins. USA. 2005. Rel: 28 April 2006. Cert. 15.

Friends With Money ★★★★

Close friends for all of their adult lives, Franny, Christine, Jane and Olivia are finding their loyalties battered as they approach middle age. While the first three have procured some success in their professional lives, Olivia has given up teaching and has resorting to cleaning other's people's houses to make ends meet. Olivia is also finding it hard to find a man, although Christine's own marriage is showing considerable signs of wear-and-tear... A superbly observed comic-drama of growing-up, old and apart in Los Angeles, *Friends With Money* reaffirms the standing of writer-director Nicole Holofcener. With dialogue that cuts to the bone and aches of autobiography, Holofcener's third film (she previously directed *Walking and Talking* and *Lovely & Amazing*) has the ring of truth one might find in a good novel or play. Yet this is a completely cinematic diversion, deftly directed and consummately played by four actresses at the top of their form. JC-W

• *Olivia* Jennifer Aniston, *Franny* Joan Cusack, *Christine* Catherine Keener, *Jane* Frances McDormand, *Aaron* Simon McBurney, *David* Jason Isaacs, *Mike* Scott Caan, *Matt* Greg Germann, *Marty* Bob Stephenson, *with* Ty Burrell, Romy Rosemont, Timm Sharp, Hailey Noelle Johnson, Elizabeth Keener, Hallie Foote.

• *Dir* and *Screenplay* Nicole Holofcener, *Pro* Anthony Bregman, *Ex Pro* Ted Hope, Anne Carey and Ray Angelic, *Ph* Terry Stacey, *Pro Des* Amy Ancona, *Ed* Robert Frazen, *M* Craig Richey; tracks performed by Rickie Lee Jones, Steve Glotzer, Neil Halstead, Cory Culinan, The Weepies, William Joseph Martin, Jean-Paul Renus, Big Red Button, and Doug Hall, *Costumes* Michael Wilkinson.

Sony Picture Classics/This is That-Columbia TriStar. 87 mins. USA. 2006. Rel: 26 May 2006. Cert. 15.

Frozen ★★

Two years after her sister, Annie, vanished without trace, Kath has become frozen in an internal void. Obsessed with unravelling the mystery surrounding her sister's disappearance, Kath steals a security camera videotape that reveals Annie's last recorded steps. And on the tape is an abstract image which Kath believes holds a clue… There are a lot of fine qualities evident in *Frozen*, Juliet McKoen's first full-length feature: the luminous, brittle photography of a wintry Morecambe Bay, the naked, understated performance of Shirley Henderson and an understanding of police procedure surrounding a missing person. Even so, there are gaps in the narrative that are bewildering (there is no sense of Kath's life outside her search for her sister) and a perverse obfuscation in the ultimate outcome. The film is also inexorably languorous and wilfully inscrutable. JC-W

• *Kath Swarbrick* Shirley Henderson, *Noyen Roy* Roshan Seth, *Elsie* Ger Ryan, *Steven* Richard Armitage, *Eddie* Ralf Little, *Jim* Jamie Sives, *Vellama* Shireen Shah, *Hurricane Frank* Sean Harris, *with* Lyndsey Marshal, Rebecca Palmer, Karl Johnson, George Costigan, Richard Ridings, Natalie Henderson, Neil Morrison.

• *Dir* and *Screenplay* Juliet McKoen, *Pro* Mark Lavender, *Co-Pro* Jim Hickey, *Line Pro* Rebecca Knapp, *Ph* Philip Robertson, *Pro Des* Loren Slater, *Ed* Paul Endacott, *M* Guy Michelmore, *Costumes* Bobby McCulla, *Sound* Tim Barker.

Liminal Films/Freedonia Films/National Lottery/Scottish Screen-Guerilla Films. 90 mins. UK. 2004. Rel: 27 January 2006. Cert. 15.

Fun With Dick and Jane ★

A happy-go-lucky guy with a million watt charm and can-do attitude finds himself unemployed. So, in order to maintain his lifestyle of widescreen TV and designer lawn, he turns to crime… There is a great post-Enron satire to be made from the 1977 comedy starring George Segal and Jane Fonda. But this remake isn't it. Black comedy is one thing, farce another. Basically a series of slapstick routines stitched around Jim

Carrey's ability to pull faces, this really is profoundly banal. And depressing. JC-W

• *Dick Harper* Jim Carrey, *Jane Harper* Téa Leoni, *Jack McCallister* Alec Baldwin, *Frank Bascombe* Richard Jenkins, *Veronica Cleeman* Angie Harmon, *Jack's receptionist* Stacey Travis, *Phyllis* Laurie Metcalf (uncredited), *with* John Michael Higgins, Richard Burgi, Carlos Jacott, Ralph Nader, Gavin Grazer, Clint Howard, Rick Overton, Chris Ellis.

• *Dir* Dean Parisot, *Pro* Brian Grazer and Jim Carrey, *Ex Pro* Peter Bart, Max Palevsky and Jane Bartelme, *Screenplay* Judd Apatow and Nicholas Stoller, *Ph* Jerzy Zielinski, *Pro Des* Barry Robinson, *Ed* Don Zimmerman, *M* Theodore Shapiro, *Costumes* Julie Weiss.

Columbia/Imagine Entertainment/JC 23 Entertainment-Columbia TriStar. 90 mins. USA. 2005. Rel: 20 January 2006. Cert. 12A.

Get Rich or Die Tryin' ★★

Inspired by the real-life story of the rapper 50 Cent, this is another familiar tale of growing up on the rough streets of the Bronx with guns, drugs and rap. Here, 50 Cent himself plays Marcus, a kid indoctrinated into violence from an early age. Indeed, he doesn't know who his father is and his mother is burnt to death by a rival drug dealer. So, at the tender age of 14, Marcus buys a gun and starts dealing drugs himself… It used to be Mickey Rooney and Judy Garland. Now it's Eminem and 50 Cent putting on a show – with coarser lyrics. The trouble is that new urban cinema is peopled by personalities with more attitude than acting smarts and here the drama just doesn't take off. Furthermore, this is an MTV production and it's hard to believe that this is from the same director who brought us *My Left Foot* and *In America*. Interestingly, a far more credible story of the influence of guns on urban culture was the English *Bullet Boy* starring Ashley Walters. Walters, himself a rapper with the band So Solid Crew, here co-stars as 50 Cent's friend Antwan and again displays a real screen presence. JC-W

Criminal remake: Jim Carrey and Téa Leoni in Dean Parisot's profoundly banal *Fun With Dick and Jane* (from Columbia TriStar)

• *Marcus* Curtis '50 Cent' Jackson, *Bama* Terrence Howard, *Charlene* Joy Bryant, *Levar* Bill Duke, *Majestic* Adewale Akinnuoye-Agbaje, *Antwan* Ashley Walters, *Katrina* Serena Reeder, *with* Omar Benson Miller, Viola Davis, Tory Kittles, Leon, Frank Pellegrino, Bubba.

• *Dir* Jim Sheridan, *Pro* Sheridan, Jimmy Iovine, Paul Rosenberg and Chris Lighty, *Ex Pro* Gene Kirkwood, Stuart Parr, Van Toffler, David Gale, Arthur Lappin and Daniel Lupi, *Screenplay* Terence Winter, *Ph* Declan Quinn, *Pro Des* Mark Geraghty, *Ed* Conrad Buff and Roger Barton, *M* Quincy Jones, Gavin Friday and Maurice Seezer, *Costumes* Francine Jamison-Tanchuck.

Paramount/Interscope/Shady/Aftermath and MTV Films-UIP.
116 mins. USA. 2005. Rel: 20 January 2006. Cert. 15.

Glastonbury ★★★

This documentary includes footage from every single Glanstobury festival of the last 30 years. In 1970 Michael Eavis, a young farmer, opened his 150-acre land to 1,500 people who came to watch rock and folk stars perform all weekend long. It started a tradition in which thousands of music and fun lovers now go every year to watch their favourite bands, get drunk, get wet and get stoned. Julien Temple has assembled masses of fascinating material for this very entertaining, acutely observed film. There is a plethora of interviews from the hostile locals to the stoned participants and it is occasionally very funny. Many stars are featured here, too – from Velvet Underground to Björk – the film suitably reaching its climax with David Bowie's "Heroes". It's perhaps too long but is still very enjoyable. GS

• *With*: Velvet Underground, Nick Cave and the Bad Seeds, Morrissey, Faithless, Melanie, Prodigy, Primal Scream, Richie Havens, Alabama 3, Billy Bragg, Cypress Hill, The Scissor Sisters, Radiohead, Babyshambles, David Gray, Björk, Stereo MCs, Coldplay, The Chemical Brothers, Dr John, Blur, Joe Strummer and the Mescaleros, ENO Orchestra, Ray Davies, Pulp, David Bowie, etc.

• *Dir* Julien Temple, *Pro* Robert Richards, *Ex Pro* Jeremy Thomas, Tracey Scoffield, Jane Hawley and Dave Henderson, *Ph* Ben Smithard, *Ed* Niven Howie and Tobias Zaldua, *M* see above, *Research* John Shearlaw.

BBC Films/HanWay Films/Emap Performance/ Newhouse Nitrate-Pathé.
138 mins. UK. 2006. Rel: 14 April 2006. Cert. 15.

Goal! ★★★½

Obsessed with football since growing up in a poor Mexican village, Santiago Muñez now tends gardens for the rich in Los Angeles. Spotted plying his athletic expertise by a Scottish scout, Santiago is invited to try out for Newcastle FC. The only problem is that Santiago has to get to England, he doesn't have enough money for the airfare and is an illegal immigrant in the US… Alan Shearer, Sven-Göran Eriksson

and David Beckham contribute cameos, Noel Gallagher provides new songs and the locations take in Mexico, Los Angeles, Newcastle and London. The *Rocky* of English football, *Goal!* is probably the first British film about the game to capture its high-stakes excitement. Taking over from the original director Michael Winterbottom, Danny Cannon (*Judge Dredd*, TV's *CSI: Crime Scene Investigation*) provides a slick, sweeping canvas on which to trot out the time-honoured clichés of the sports movie. And he has secured some first-rate performances: Marcel Iures is particularly good as the Eastern-European manager, a man of charismatic, distracted authority; while the Massachusetts-born Alessandro Nivola captures perfectly the cocky Englishness of the bad-boy star player. JC-W

• *Santiago Muñez* Kuno Becker, *Glen Foy* Stephen Dillane, *Gavin Harris* Alessandro Nivola, *Roz Harminson* Anna Friel, *Erik Dornhelm* Marcel Iures, *Barry Rankin* Sean Pertwee, *Bobby Redfern* Robert Dixon, *Mal Braithwaite* Gary Lewis, *Mercedes* Miriam Colón, *Hernan Muñez* Tony Plana, *with* Stephen Graham, Lee Ross, Kieran O'Brien, Ashley Walters, Frances Barber, Cassandra Bell, Christopher Fairbank, Alan Shearer, Sven-Göran Eriksson, David Beckham, Raúl Gonzalez Bravo, Zinedine Zidane.

• *Dir* Danny Cannon, *Pro* Mike Jefferies, Matt Barrelle and Mark Huffam, *Ex Pro* Peter Hargitay and Lawrence Bender, *Co-Pro* Danny Stepper, *Assoc Pro* Allen Hopkins, *Screenplay* Dick Clement and Ian La Frenais, from a story by Jefferies and Adrian Butchart, *Ph* Michael Barrett, *Pro Des* Laurence Dorman, *Ed* Chris Dickens, *M* Graeme Revell; Vivaldi; tracks performed by Gipsy Kings, Ballistic Brothers, Zero 7, Oasis, UNKLE, Kasabian, South, Supercharger, Grand National, Backyard Dog, The Bees, Paul Oakenfold, The Happy Mondays, And You Will Know Us By the Trail of Dead, Princess Superstar, Dirty Vegas, and The Perceptionists, *Costumes* Lindsay Pugh, *Sound* Tom Sayers, *Football Co-ordinator* Ian Carrington, *Football Choreography/Consultant* Andy Ansah.

milkshakefilms/Toshiba Entertainment/Little Magic Films-Buena Vista International.
118 mins. UK/USA/Japan. 2005. Rel: 30 September 2005. Cert. 12A.

Good Night, And Good Luck ★★½

The pioneering broadcaster Edward R. Murrow spoke his mind on air long before TV became the mind-numbing opium of the masses. But even in the 1950s, the editorial content of news shows was under threat from outside forces. The medium's liberty found its greatest jeopardy in the form of Senator Joseph McCarthy, whose crusade to weed out Communism threatened the livelihoods of many free-thinking Americans. But McCarthy had met his match in the fearless, principled Murrow… Exquisitely photographed in high-contrast black-and-white and stamped with a cut-glass performance from David Strathairn, *Good Night* flaunts its pedigree on its sleeve. It's also incredibly dry, wilfully rarefied and, considering the subject matter, all rather unexciting. As a filmmaker, George Clooney shows obvious intuition and intelligence, but next time he should hide his conceit and let the audience in on the action. JC-W

• *Edward R. Murrow* David Strathairn, *Shirley Wershba* Patricia Clarkson, *Fred Friendly* George Clooney, *Sig Mickelson* Jeff Daniels, *Joe Wershba* Robert Downey Jr, *William Paley* Frank Langella, *Don Hollenbeck* Ray Wise, *Jessie Zousmer* Tate Donovan, *Palmer Williams* Tom McCarthy, *Eddie Scott* Matt Ross, *John Aaron* Reed Diamond, *Charlie Mack* Robert John Burke, *Don Hewitt* Grant Heslov, *with* Rose Abdoo, Alex Borstein, Robert Knepper, Dianne Reeves, Glenn Morshower.

• *Dir* George Clooney, *Pro* Grant Heslov, *Ex Pro* Todd Wagner, Mark Cuban, Marc Butan, Jeff Skoll, Chris Salvaterra, Steven Soderbergh, Jennifer Fox and Ben Cosgrove, *Co-Pro* Simon Franks, Zygi Kamasa, Kiyotaka Ninomiya and Barbara Hall, *Co-Ex Pro* Samuel Hadida and Victor Hadida, *Screenplay* Clooney and Heslov, *Ph* Robert Elswit, *Pro Des* Jim Bissell, *Ed* Stephen Mirrione, *Costumes* Louise Frogley.

Warner Independent Pictures/2929 Entertainment/ Participant Prods/Section Eight-Redbus. 92 mins. USA/France/UK/Japan. 2005. Rel: 17 February 2006. Cert. PG.

Le Grand Voyage ★★★★

Modest yet well deserving of the awards it has received, this film by Ismaël Ferroukhi is an unusually brave first feature. That's because it is for much of the time a two-hander and a piece centred on a relationship rather than on dramatic events. Essentially a road movie, it sees a father (Mohamed Majd) and son (Nicolas Cazalé) travelling some three thousand miles from their home in the south of France to Saudi Arabia. Their goal is Mecca, for the father, a devout Muslim, is making a pilgrimage as required by the Koran, while his secular minded son is doing his duty by driving him. Ultimately there are memorable shots of Mecca itself but this is essentially a subtle study quite without sentimentality that shows two people of different outlook coming to a better understanding of each other. The importance of such a work in today's world climate is obvious, and the two leading players seem not to act but to be. A small film, perhaps, but very welcome. MS

• *Reda* Nicolas Cazalé, *the father* Mohamed Majd, *Mustapha* Jacky Nercessian, *old woman* Ghina Ognianova, *Khalid* Kamel Belghazi, *Ahmad* Atik Mohamed, *mother* Malika Mesrar El Hadaoui, *Italian customs official* François Baroni, *with* Krassi Kpacu, Kirill Kavadarkov, Blajo Wymenski.

• *Dir and Screenplay* Ismaël Ferroukhi, *Pro* Humbert Balsan, *Ph* Katell Djian, *Art Dir* Yves Bernard, Saïd Raïss, Abdelwahab Laâroussi, Youssef Raïs, Driss Aouglou and Ivan Andreev, *Ed* Tina Baz, *M* Fowzi Guerdjou, *Costumes* Christine Brottes.

Humbert Balsan/Ognon Pictures/ARTE France Cinéma/Casablanca Films-Peccadillo Pictures. 107 mins. France/Morocco. 2004. Rel: 14 October 2005. Cert. PG.

Frodo's Firm: Elijah Wood shows his tough side in Lexi Alexander's phoney, gratuitously violent *Green Street* (from UIP)

Green Street ★★

When a stash of cocaine is found in his personal effects, Harvard student Matt Buckner takes the fall for his well-connected roommate. Just two months away from his diploma, Matt packs his bags and heads to London to visit his sister, Shannon. There, he meets Shannon's brother-in-law, Pete, who is the ringleader of a 'firm' of football hooligans supporting West Ham United. Before Matt knows it, he tastes the blood of violence and decides he rather likes it… Interesting. A gratuitously violent film about English football hooligans directed by a German woman. And with an American intro and coda, *Green Street* could not be less convincing. Potted with improbabilities and saddled with phoney dialogue, the film – its dubious code of morality apart – is a mess. Not only does Charlie Hunnam brandish a hopeless Cockney accent, but you'd think that every Londoner east of the city spoke in Cockney rhyming slang. For more authentic films about organised football hooliganism, check out Alan Clarke's *The Firm* (1988) and Philip Davis's *I.D.* (1995). US title: *Green Street Hooligans*. JC-W

• *Matt Buckner* Elijah Wood, *Pete Dunham* Charlie Hunnam, *Shannon Dunham* Claire Forlani, *Bovver* Leo Gregory, *Steve Dunham* Marc Warren, *Nigel* David Alexander, *Jeremy Van Holden* Terence Jay, *Tommy Hatcher* Geoff Bell, *Carl Buckner* Henry Goodman, *with* Joel Beckett, Kieran Bew, Rafe Spall.

• *Dir* Lexi Alexander, *Pro* Gigi Pritzker and Deborah Del Prete, *Ex Pro* Alexander, Bill Allan, Patrick Aluise, Tom Hulme and Paul Schiff, *Co-Pro and Ph* Alex Buono, *Screenplay* Alexander, Dougie Brimson and Joshua Shelov, *Pro Des* Tom Brown, *Ed* Paul Trejo, *M* Christopher Franke, *Costumes* John Krausa, *Technical Adviser* Jon S. Baird.

Odd Lot Entertainment/Take Partnerships/ Baker Street Media-UIP. 109 mins. UK/USA. 2004. Rel: 9 September 2005. Cert. 18.

Greyfriars Bobby
See *The Adventures of Greyfriars Bobby*.

Grizzly Man ★★★★
Werner Herzog's documentary feature with an idiosyncratic voice over by the film-maker is a study of an obsessive, Timothy Treadwell, whose devotion to grizzly bears in Alaska led to his death and also to the death of a girlfriend, both being killed and eaten by a bear. Treadwell had himself taken hours of film footage and what we see here is partly his as selected by Herzog and partly Herzog's own as he talked to those who had known Treadwell. The film parallels *The Wild Parrots of Telegraph Hill*, being half a nature study and half a personal portrait but, where *Telegraph Hill*'s Mark Bittner is wholly engaging, Treadwell emerges as bizarre and narcissistic. Some questions about him are not asked, but Treadwell's mad dedication to his beliefs prompts from Herzog both valid criticism and recognition of a man who was in certain respects a kindred spirit. MS

• *With*: Timothy Treadwell, Amie Huguenard, Warren Queeney, Willy Fulton, Sam Egli, Marnie Gaede, Marc Gaede, Larry Van Daele, Franc Falico, Jewel Palovak, Val Dexter, Carol Dexter, Kathleen Parker.

• *Dir* Werner Herzog, *Pro* Erik Nelson, *Ex Pro* Billy Campbell, Tom Ortenberg, Kevin Beggs, Phil Fairclough and Andrea Meditch, *Co-Ex Pro* Jewel Palovak, *Assoc Pro* Alana Berry, *Ph* Peter Zeitlinger, *Ed* Joe Bini, *M* Richard Thompson.

Discovery Docs/Lions Gate-Revolver.
104 mins. USA. 2005. Rel: 3 February 2006. Cert. 15.

Guy X ★½
Qangattarsa, Greenland; June-December 1979. Having never left New Jersey, fresh army recruit Rudy Spruance is surprised to find himself in Greenland. He was bound for Hawaii, but a clerical error has left him abandoned in the middle of nowhere. As Colonel Woolwrap – commander of Greenland's US Army Air Force base – has been expecting his long-awaited Public Information Officer, he is in no mood to believe that Spruance is not his man... Presumably somebody thought John Griesemer's original novel would make a great movie. It's certainly got a unique setting – when was the last time somebody set a film on a US Army base in Greenland? But there's a troublesome air of the Europudding about the enterprise (albeit with an American-Canadian flavour). A wannabe *M*A*S*H*-cum-*Buffalo Soldiers*, the film is curiously absent of wit, while both the English-born Jeremy Northam and Natascha McElhone are fatally miscast as US military personnel. Without a rooting in reality – and devoid of suspense – the movie is like one those uncomfortable dreams that refuses to make any sense. JC-W

• *Rudy Spruance* Jason Biggs, *Sgt. Irene Teale* Natascha McElhone, *Colonel Woolwrap* Jeremy Northam, *Guy X* Michael Ironside, *Lavone* Sean Tucker, *Petri* Hilmir Snaer Gudnason, *Philly* Benz Antoine, *with* Buck Dreachman, Rob de Leeuw, Donny Falsetti, Harry Standjofski.

• *Dir* Saul Metzstein, *Pro* Sam Taylor, Mike Downey, Michael L. Cowan and Jason Piette, *Ex Pro* Stephen Daldry, Chris Auty, Neil Peplow, Peter James, James Simpson and Laura De Castro, *Line Pro* Mark Hubbard, *Screenplay* John Paul Chapple and Steve Attridge, from the novel *No One Thinks of Greenland* by John Griesemer, *Ph* François Dagenais, *Pro Des* Mike Gunn, *Ed* Ann Sopel, *M* Hilmar Örn Hilmarsson and Charlie Mole, *Costumes* Stewart Meachem.

Movision/The Film Consortium/UK Film Council/Tartan Films-Tartan Films.
101 mins. UK/Iceland/Canada. 2004. Rel: 14 October 2005. Cert. 15.

Half Light ★★½
Feeling responsible for the drowning of her only son, best-selling novelist Rachel Carlson takes up the lease on a windswept cottage in Scotland. There, she reckons, she can focus on her next book. But disturbing dreams, hallucinations and the appearance of a dashing lighthouse keeper rather get in the way... For a 43-year-old woman, Demi Moore is looking amazing. And so is Scotland, with its rugged beaches, wild horses and picturesque villages (although filmed in Wales). In fact, *Half Light* looks so good that it detracts from the business of scaremongering, providing characters that wouldn't seem out of place in a Joanne Trollope novel. The plot is a good one, though, even if it is a little too neat. And the opening rip-off of *Don't Look Now* (complete with piano-driven score, talking action figure, drowning and slow motion) is staggering in its impudence. JC-W

• *Rachel Carlson* Demi Moore, *Angus McCulloch* Hans Matheson, *Finlay Murray* James Cosmo, *Sharon Winton* Kate Isitt, *Morag* Therese Bradley, *Thomas* Beans Balawi, *Brian* Henry Ian Cusick, *Mary Murray* Joanne Hole, *with* Nicholas Gleaves, Michael Wilson, Nichola B.

• *Dir* and *Screenplay* Craig Rosenberg, *Pro* Joel B. Michaels, Steve Samuels, Garth H. Drabinsky and Clive Parsons, *Ex Pro* Andreas Schmidt, *Ph* Ashley Rowe, *Pro Des* Don Taylor, *Ed* Bill Murphy, *M* Brett Rosenberg, *Costumes* Ruth Myers.

Joel B. Michaels/Samuels Media/VIP Medienfonds 3/Rising Star-UIP.
110 mins. UK/Germany. 2004. Rel: 23 June 2006. Cert. 15.

Hard Candy ★★★★
Jeff, 32, picks up Hayley, 14, in an Internet chat room. Drawn by her taunting repartee and taste in literature and music, he suggests they meet for a coffee. While emphasising the legal ground rules, he nevertheless finds himself under Hayley's spell and invites her back to his place. Big mistake... If the sole purpose of *Hard Candy* is to provoke debate, then it more than accomplishes its brief. As the vicissitudes of plot tug the viewer this way and that, so Patrick Wilson and Ellen Page rise to the challenge. As Wilson (so bland in *Phantom of the Opera*) switches from urbane and charming to vulnerable and helpless, so Ms Page stakes out her own ground with

chilling conviction. Indeed, it is Ms Page (who in real life was 18 when she made this) who holds the screen, shifting from seductive, self-assured tomboy to cold-blooded predator. Male viewers are bound to initially side with Jeff but are then forced to reassess their own guilt-by-proxy. Brazenly thought-provoking drama, and extremely well played. JC-W

• *Jeff Kohlver* Patrick Wilson, *Hayley Stark* Ellen Page, *Juday Tokuda* Sandra Oh, *Janelle Rogers* Jennifer Holmes, *Nighthawks clerk* Gilbert John.

• *Dir* David Slade, *Pro* David W. Higgins, Richard Hutton and Michael Caldwell, *Ex Pro* Rosanne Korenberg, Paul G. Allen and Jody Patton, *Co-Pro* Brian Nelson and Hans Ritter, *Screenplay* Nelson, *Ph* Jo Willems, *Pro Des* Jeremy Reed, *Ed* Art Jones, *M* Molly Nyman and Harry Escott; songs performed by LFO, and Blonde Redhead, *Costumes* Jennifer Johnson.

Lions Gate/Vulcan/Launchpad-Lionsgate. 103 mins. USA. 2005. Rel: 16 June 2006. Cert. 18.

Harry Potter and the Goblet of Fire ★★½

Harry Potter is beginning to have seriously bad dreams and the scar on his forehead is hurting like hell. Then his name is entered into the Goblet of Fire, a magic tombola that selects a representative from each school to participate in a particularly gruelling and dangerous competition. In fact, to enter, you have to be at least 17, but Harry is 14… Daniel Radcliffe takes his shirt off, Ron Weasley tells Harry to 'piss off' and a friend of Harry's is killed. The *Harry Potter* franchise is growing up and in the process has lost its sense of fun and wonder. Instead, trapped entirely within the phantasmagorical realm of Hogwarts, it has become a nightmarish extended episode of an unstoppable licence to print money. There are some exciting sequences (notably Potter's encounter with a fire-breathing dragon), but the humour sounds some rather obvious notes and, by the very nature of the series, we know our hero will always be all right. Nevertheless, *The Goblet of Fire* still looks amazing – but we've come to expect that. JC-W

• *Harry Potter* Daniel Radcliffe, *Ron Weasley* Rupert Grint, *Hermione Granger* Emma Watson, *Rubeus Hagrid* Robbie Coltrane, *Lord Voldemort* Ralph Fiennes, *Albus Dumbledore* Michael Gambon, *Alastor 'Mad-Eye' Moody* Brendan Gleeson, *Lucius Malfoy* Jason Isaacs, *Sirius Black* Gary Oldman, *Professor Snape* Alan Rickman, *Professor McGonagall* Maggie Smith, *Peter Pettigrew* aka *Wormtail* Timothy Spall, *Draco Malfoy* Tom Felton, *Barty Crouch* Roger Lloyd Pack, *Victor Krum* Stanislav Ianevski, *Fleur Delacour* Clémence Poésy, *Cedric Diggory* Robert Pattinson, *Rita Skeeter* Miranda Richardson, *Cho Chang* Katie Leung, *Madame Olympe Maxime* Frances De La Tour, *Barty Crouch* Jr David Tennant, *Neville Longbottom* Matthew Lewis, *Igor Karkaroff* Pedja Bjelac, *Moaning Myrtle* Shirley Henderson, *with* Eric Sykes, Jarvis Cocker, Robert Hardy, David Bradley, Jeff Rawle, Margery Mason, Mark Williams, Geraldine Somerville, James Phelps, Oliver Phelps, Sheila Allen, Warwick Davis, Adrian Rawlins.
• *Dir* Mike Newell, *Pro* David Heyman, *Ex Pro* David Barron

and Tanya Seghatchian, *Co-Pro* Peter MacDonald, *Screenplay* Steve Kloves, from the novel by J.K. Rowling, *Ph* Roger Pratt, *Pro Des* Stuart Craig, *Ed* Mick Audsley, *M* Patrick Doyle, *Costumes* Jany Temime, *Creature Design* Nick Dudman, *Visual Effects* Jimmy Mitchell, *Special Effects* John Richardson.

Warner/Heyday Films/Patalex IV Prods-Warner. 156 mins. USA/UK. 2005. Rel: 18 November 2005. Cert: 12A

The Heart is Deceitful Above All Things ★★★

The title is a quote from the book of Jeremiah (17:9) and the central character is Jeremiah Leroy. Aged four, Jeremiah is dragged from the comfortable bosom of his foster parents and into the care of his mother, an unmarried 23-year-old prostitute. Jeremiah is all she has and so she enthusiastically shares her world of alcohol, drugs, sex and physical brutality with him. It is her life and Jeremiah is hers… A catalogue of emotionally numbing humiliation, this raw adaptation of J.T. Leroy's 'autobiography' is, in the apparent words of its subject, 'an amazing film – it feels like somebody hooked up the tube into my heart and into my brain and hit playback.' It's unsettling to see the director herself as Jeremiah's mother (in a performance of naked self-abandon), but she certainly understands the underbelly of the American dream gone awry. Here is a world of bruising contrast, where stretches of barren desert, heaving strip joints, fundamental Christianity and systematic child abuse make up the good ol' US of A. FYI: In January of 2006 Jeremiah Leroy was unmasked as the entirely fictitious creation of the musicians Laura Albert and Geoffrey Knoop. JC-W

• *Sarah* Asia Argento, *young Jeremiah, aged 7* Jimmy Bennett, *grandfather* Peter Fonda, *grandmother* Ornella Muti, *Luther* Kip Pardue, *older Jeremiah, aged 11* Dylan and Cole Spouse, *Aaron* John Robinson, *Chester* Jeremy Sisto, *with* Ben Foster, Michael Pitt, Jeremy Renner, Marilyn Manson, Matt Schulze, Hasil Adkins, Lydia Lunch.

• *Dir* Asia Argento, *Pro* Chris Hanley, Alain de la Mata, Roberta Hanley and Brian Young, *Ex Pro* Lilly Bright, Hamish McAlpine, Trish van Klaveren and Kevin Ragsdale, *Co-Pro* Jennifer L. Booth, *Screenplay* Argento and Alessandro Magania, *Ph* Eric Edwards, *Pro Des* Max Biscoe, *Ed* Jim Mol, *M* Billy Corgan, Sonic Youth and Marco Castoldi; tracks performed by Knoxville Girls, Danny Doll Rod, Terror at the Opera, André Williams, Sonic Youth, Hasil Adkins, The Subhumans, Vikkie Rae Jordan, Asia Argento, Ghost, Starlite Desperation, Pagoda, etc, *Costumes* Mel Ottenberg, *Sound* Sandy Gendlar, *Animation* Christine Cegavske.

Muse Prods/Bluelight/Wildbunch-Tartan Films. 98 mins. USA/UK/Japan/Italy/France. 2004. Rel: 15 July 2005. Cert. 15.

Hearts and Minds ★★★★★

When *Hearts and Minds* won the Oscar for best documentary in 1975 it caused an outrage. Bob Hope even demanded that the ceremony's producer Howard W. Koch issue a disclaimer. But then *Hearts and Minds* is not a funny film. The only laugh is when Hope himself, at a conference of POWs, quips, 'I like a captive audience.' The *Fahrenheit 9/11* of its day (but far less successful, due to the nervousness of its distributors – Columbia baled out completely), the film includes iconic footage of the Vietnam war (Colonel Loan's execution of a Vietcong suspect, the agony of the napalmed nine-year-old girl Kim Phuc) and extraordinary statements from the influential and the ignorant. Just as shocking as the sight of tortured Vietnamese soldiers and burning children is the revelations to camera. One soldier compares the thrill of bombing Vietnamese villages with that of a child playing with firecrackers, while senior military commander General Westmoreland explains that Oriental lives are not as important as American ones. Sagely, director Davis notes that America did learn from Vietnam, but that 9/11 inflicted an amnesic blow to the nation's head. Then came Iraq. A cinematic milestone. N.B. When *Hearts and Minds* was first shown in the UK in 1975, its release was so small that it wasn't even included in this annual. For the record, it is reviewed now. JC-W

• *With*: Georges Bidault, Clark Clifford, George Coker, Kay Dvorshock, Daniel Ellsberg, Randy Floyd, J.W. Fulbright, Brian Holden, Robert Muller, Khanh Nguyen, Walt Rostow, William C. Westmoreland.

• *Dir* Peter Davis, *Pro* Davis and Bert Schneider, *Assoc Pro* Tom Cohen and Richard Pearce, *Ph* Pearce, *Ed* Lynzee Klingman and Susan Martin, *Research* Brennon Jones, *Vietnam Consultant* Thomas C. Fox.

Rainbow Pictures-Metrodome.
111 mins. USA. 1974. Rel: 11 November 2005. Cert. 15.

Heidi ★★★½

This traditional take on Johanna Spyri's children's classic of the 1880s is done with such affection that one is prepared to overlook the weaknesses which include some inappropriate accents and some players below par. It's more important that Emma Bolger from *In America* eschews cuteness and makes the warm-hearted orphan Heidi a heroine blessed with good sense and determination. Slovenia and West Wales stand in well enough for the Swiss Alps and for Frankfurt, Max von Sydow determinedly underplays Heidi's reclusive grandfather and there are splendid contributions from Diana Rigg (sympathetic) and Geraldine Chaplin (enjoyably beastly). Those drawn to this material will not feel let down. MS

• *Uncle Alp* Max Von Sydow, *Heidi* Emma Bolger, *Mrs Rottenmeier, the housekeeper* Geraldine Chaplin, *Grandmamma* Diana Rigg, *Aunt Detie* Pauline McLynn, *Peter* Samuel Friend, *with* Jessica Claridge, Del Synott, Kellie Shjirley, Oliver Ford Davies, Caroline Pegg, Jessica James, Karl Johnson, Peter Wight.

• *Dir* Paul Marcus, *Pro* Martyn Auty, David Ball and Christopher Figg, *Ex Pro* H. Michael Heuser, James Atherton

and Michael Henry, *Screenplay* Brian Finch, from the novel by Johanna Spyri, *Ph* Peter Sinclair, *Pro Des* Tom McCullagh, *Ed* David Rees, *M* Jocelyn Pook, *Costumes* Mike O'Neill.

Piccadilly Pictures/Sure Fire Films/Suitable Viewing/ Storm Entertainment-The Works UK.
103 mins. UK/Italy/USA. 2005. Rel: 19 August 2005. Cert. U.

Hell ★★½

True tragedy, Anne tells us, cannot exist in the modern world because we now live in a godless society. So, Anne reasons, her life is a drama. However, three sisters, none of whom can maintain a healthy romantic relationship, live out a rough approximation of tragedy due to a traumatic event in their childhood, recalling, perhaps, the story of *Medea*... A stranger in a café reads a passage from a book to Céline and then runs off. In another café, Anne professes her love for her professor, who gets up and leaves with nary a word. Then, having accused her husband of being a liar, Sophie storms out of the room. Yep, *Hell* is that sort of movie: an enigmatic jigsaw of improbable and apparently disconnected events that can but leave the viewer in a state of utter frustration. Peppered with black humour and elegantly photographed, *Hell* recalls the distinction of Danis Tanovic's first film, *No Man's Land*, then drifts into abstruse pretension. A companion piece to Tom Tykwer's *Heaven* (2001), *Hell* is the second in a planned trilogy penned by Kieslowski protégé Krzysztof Piesiewicz. Original title: *L'Enfer*. JC-W

• *Sophie* Emmanuelle Béart, *Céline* Karin Viard, *Anne* Marie Gillain, *Sébastien* Guillaume Canet, *mother* Carole Bouquet, *Frédéric* Jacques Perrin, *Pierre* Jacques Gamblin, *father* Miki Manojlovic, *Louis* Jean Rochefort, *Julie* Maryam d'Abo, with Gaëlle Bona, Georges Siatidis, Françoise Bertin.

• *Dir* Danis Tanovic, *Pro* Drazen Bosnjak, Cedomir Kolar and Marc Baschet, *Screenplay* Krzysztof Piesiewicz, *Ph* Laurent Dailland, *Pro Des* Aline Bonetto, *Ed* Francesca Calvelli, *M* Tanovic and Dusko Segvic; Dvorak, *Costumes* Cariline De Vivaise.

A.S.A.P. Films/Sintra srl/Man's Film Prods/Bitters End/ France 2 Cinéma/Canal Plus-Momentum.
102 mins. France/Italy/Belgium/Japan. 2005. Rel: 21 April 2006. Cert. 15.

Herbie: Fully Loaded ★½

A former racing champion, Herbie is a white VW beetle with a mind and feelings of its own. But after many years of success, it would appear that this little car's time is up. Then, as it awaits demolition in a small, crowded junkyard, Maggie Peyton chooses it as her graduation present. However, Herbie proves to be more than a handful... This is a must-see movie – if clichés, repetition and boredom are your thing. Lindsay Lohan may have broken out of her teen-movie, chick-flick shell – but not for the better. There is no chemistry between her and Justin Long and the anticipated plot could be unravelled by a mentally challenged five-year-old. The film also lacks creativity and charm and leaves the viewer with an overwhelming desire to crush the 'love bug' themselves. On the other hand, it makes one appreciate the witty, intelligent and subtle filmmaking of *Grange Hill*. Juliet C-W

• *Maggie Peyton* Lindsay Lohan, *Kevin* Justin Long, *Ray Peyton Jr* Breckin Meyer, *Trip Murphy* Matt Dillon, *Ray Peyton Sr* Michael Keaton, *Sally* Cheryl Hines, *with* Jimmi Simpson, Jill Ritchie, Thomas Lennon, Robert Ben Garant.

• *Dir* Angela Robinson, *Pro* Robert Simonds, *Ex Pro* Charles Hirschhorn, Tracey Trench and Michael Fottrell, *Co-Pro* Lisa Stewart, *Screenplay* Thomas Lennon, Robert Ben Garant, Alfred Gough and Miles Millar, from a story by Lennon, Garant and Mark Perez, *Ph* Greg Gardiner, *Pro Des* Daniel Bradford, *Ed* Wendy Greene Bricmont, *M* Mark Mothersbaugh, *Costumes* Frank Helmer.

Walt Disney Pictures-Buena Vista International.
100 mins. USA. 2005. Rel: 5 August 2005.
Cert. U.

Hidden ★★★

Georges Laurent, the host of a literary TV show, and his wife, Anne, a publisher, lead a life of intellectual harmony in Paris. Then, out of the blue, the couple start receiving VHS tape recordings of their house. Gradually, Georges begins to suspect that this 'reign of terror' may have something to do with his long-forgotten adopted Algerian brother Majid… The Austrian director Michael Haneke has a talent for placing the viewer into the immediate reality of his drama. Here, he indulges himself with a number of extended still lifes of the protagonists' Parisian home (opposite the Rue Des Iris) and has harnessed two edgy performances from the accomplished Daniel Auteuil and Juliette Binoche. And this is typically diverting French drama, although the initial state of unease that Haneke builds up eventually dissipates as *Hidden* unravels into the emptiness of an intellectual exercise. Original title: *Caché*. JC-W

• *Georges Laurent* Daniel Auteuil, *Anne Laurent* Juliette Binoche, *Majid* Maurice Benichou, *George's mother* Annie Girardot, *chief editor* Bernard Le Coq, *Pierre* Daniel Duval, *Majid's son* Walid Afkir, *Mathilde* Nathalie Richard, *Yvon* Denis Podalydes.

• *Dir* and *Screenplay* Michael Haneke, *Line Pro* Michael Katz and Margaret Menegoz, *Co-Pro* Michael Weber and Valerio De Paolis, *Ph* Christian Berger, *Art Dir* Emmanuel de Chauvigny and Christoph Kanter, *Ed* Michael Hudecek and Nadine Muse, *Costumes* Lisy Christl.

Les Films du Losange/Wega Film/Bavaria Film/Art France Cinéma/StudioCanal-Artificial Eye.
118 mins. France/Austria/Germany/Italy. 2004. Rel: 27 January 2006. Cert. 15.

The Hidden Blade ★★★★

Save for the final scene (not just a cliché, but one that's wallowed in), this is a highly competent traditional samurai tale from the veteran director Yoji Yamada. It combines into a single narrative two stories of mid-19th century Japan by Shuhei Fujisawa whose work was also the basis of this film's predecessor, *The Twilight Samurai*. This one is part love story across a class barrier and part action tale involving a samurai ordered to seek out and kill an old friend regarded as a renegade. The combination may reduce the number of sword fights but here the characterisations and relationships matter as much as the action. It may not be a truly memorable film but, that last misjudged sequence apart, it's never less than efficient. Both leads, Takako Matsu as the low caste heroine and Masatoshi Nagase of *Mystery Train*, are pleasing. Original title: *Kakushi Ken: Oni No Tsume*. MS

• *Munezo Karagiri* Masatoshi Nagase, *Kie* Takako Matsu, *Samon Shimada* Hidetaka Yoshioka, *Yaichiro Hazama* Yukiyoshi Ozawa, *Shino* Tomoko Tabata, *Hazama's wife* Reiko Takashima, *Kansai Toda* Min Tanaka.

• *Dir* Yoji Yamada, *Pro* Takeo Hisamatsu, Hiroshi Fukazawa and Ichiro Yamamoto, *Ex Pro* Junichi Sakamoto, *Screenplay* Yamada and Yoshitaka Asama, *Ph* Mutsuo Naganuma, *Art Dir* Mitsuo Degawa, *Ed* Iwao Ishii, *M* Isao Tomita, *Costumes* Kazuko Kurosawa.

Shochiku/Nippon Television Network-Tartan Films.
132 mins. Japan. 2004. Rel: 2 December 2005. Cert. 15.

The Hills Have Eyes ★★

On a cross-country bonding vacation, the Carter family are stranded in the desert after the tyres on Big Bob's Suburban explode. Many miles from nowhere – and with no signal on their cell phones – the Carters find themselves at the mercy of something exceedingly nasty in them thar hills… Alexandre Aja's *Switchblade Romance* was arguably one of the most disturbing films of 2003. But few thought much of its ending. Here, Aja takes off from the gore-splattered climax of *Romance* and runs with it into the realms of a sub-Rob Zombie horror-western. With dumb, one-dimensional characters and an eye to Sergio Leone, Aja has taken something shocking (Wes Craven's original) and tamed it with hammy actors in over-the-top make-up. Consequently, the raw dementia of the 1977 classic is nowhere to be seen. FYI: The opening credit sequence of mutant babies supposedly misshapen form the effects of atomic testing in Nevada were actually lifted from photographs of infantile victims of Agent Orange in Vietnam. JC-W

• *Doug* Aaron Stanford, *Ethel* Kathleen Quinlan, *Lynn* Vinessa Shaw, *Brenda* Emilie De Ravin, *Bobby* Dan Byrd, *gas station attendant* Tom Bower, *Papa Jupiter* Billy Drago, *Lizard* Robert Joy, *Big Bob* Ted Levine, *Big Brain* Desmond Askew, *Ruby* Laura Ortiz.

• *Dir* Alexandre Aja, *Pro* Wes Craven and Marianne Maddalena, *Ex Pro* Frank Hildebrand, *Assoc Pro* Cody Zwieg, *Screenplay* Aja and Gregory Levasseur, *Ph* Maxime Alexandre, *Pro Des* Joseph Nemec III, *Ed* Baxter, *M* tomandandy, *Costumes* Danny Glicker, *Visual Effects* Jamison Goei, *Make-Up Effects* Gregory Nicotero and Howard Berger.

Family fun: Vinessa Shaw makes a point in Alexandre Aja's dumb, hysterical *The Hills Have Eyes* (from Fox)

Fox Searchlight Pictures/Dune Entertainment LLC-Fox. 107 mins. USA. 2006. Rel: 10 March 2006. Cert. 18.

A History of Violence ★★★★

To look at him, you wouldn't think Tom Stall had a history of violence. Living a Norman Rockwell existence in the small town of Millbrook, Indiana, Tom is blissfully married with a teenage son and six-year-old daughter. Then, out of the blue, two men turn up at Tom's friendly diner and pull a gun on him, a potentially ugly situation that Tom manages to thwart, resulting in the death of both strangers. Tom is declared a local hero, is much exposed on local TV and draws the attention of more bad men in dark suits. They think they know who Tom is and it isn't the man Tom says he is… Although an adaptation of the graphic novel by John Wagner and Vince Locke, *A History of Violence* is almost naturalistic in tone. And yet, should you look closely, everything is marginally off-kilter. The home-grown environment of Millbrook is almost corn-fed, the courteous face of evil a little unnatural, the colour palette slightly heightened. Within this frame is the hardcore marital union of Tom and Edie Small, a relationship fuelled by mutual respect, passion and human decency. Deliberately paced, even old-fashioned in its cadence, the film slips from moments of exaggerated grace to brutal outbursts of very contemporary violence. Its moral – that violence is the only way to combat violence – is contentious, but there's no doubting that David Cronenberg is back on form. JC-W

• *Tom Stall* Viggo Mortensen, *Edie Stall* Maria Bello, *Richie Cusack* William Hurt, *Carl Fogarty* Ed Harris, *Jack Stall* Ashton Holmes, *Leland Jones* Stephen McHattie, *Sheriff Sam Carney* Peter MacNeill, *William 'Billy' Orser* Greg Bryk, *Sarah Stall* Heidi Hayes, *with* Kyle Schmid, Sumela Kay, Gerry Quigley.

• *Dir* David Cronenberg, *Pro* Chris Bender and JC Spink, *Ex Pro* Roger E. Kass, Josh Braun, Toby Emmerich, Justis Greene, Kent Alterman and Cale Boyter, *Co-Pro* Jake Weiner, *Screenplay* Josh Olson, *Ph* Peter Suschitzky, *Pro Des* Carol Spier, *Ed* Ronald Sanders, *M* Howard Shore, *Costumes* Denise Cronenberg.

New Line Cinema/Benderspink-Entertainment. 95 mins. USA/Canada/Germany. 2005. Rel: 30 September 2005. Cert. 18.

The Honeymooners ★

In this misbegotten comedy based on America's much-loved sitcom of the fifties, Cedric the Entertainer and Mike Epps take over from Jackie Gleason and Art Carney as a New York bus driver with money-making schemes and his loyal neighbour and sidekick. They could be amusing if they had the right script, but the one they have is a non-starter with no conviction in either the fun-free gags or its creaky main story about racing a greyhound they find in a skip. Also fallen on hard times are very good actors like Gabrielle Union and Regina Hall, as the duo's long-suffering wives; Eric Stoltz as a scheming estate agent; John Leguizamo as their dog trainer; and Jon Polito as the dodgy racetrack owner. Fifty years on, supposedly one of the greatest TV shows of all time hits rock bottom as one of the Internet's 100 worst films of all time.

Maybe that's overstating it, but it's certainly a sad and sorry mess. And what's the title supposed to mean? FYI: Weirdly, a lot of it was filmed in Ireland. DW

• *Ralph Kramden* Cedric the Entertainer, *Ed Norton* Mike Epps, *Alice Kramden* Gabrielle Union, *Trixie Norton* Regina Hall, *William Davis* Eric Stoltz, *Kirby* Jon Polito, *Dodge* John Leguizamo, *Alice's mom* Carol Woods, *Vivek* Ajay Naidu, *Quinn* Kim Chan, *with* Arnell Powell, Doreen Keogh, Alice Drummond, Charlie Schultz.

• *Dir* John Schultz, *Pro* David T. Friendly, Marc Turtletaub, Eric C. Rhone and Julie Durk, *Ex Pro* Hal Ross, Cedric the Entertainer and Mike Epps, *Screenplay* Danny Jacobson, David Sheffield, Barry W. Blaustein and Don Rhymer, based on characters from the CBS Network series, *Ph* Shawn Maurer, *Pro Des* Charles Wood, *Ed* John Pace, *M* Richard Gibbs, *Costumes* Joan Bergin.

Paramount/Deep River/MMDP Munich Movie Development & Productionb GmbH & Co-UIP. 89 mins. USA/Germany. 2005. Rel: 2 September 2005. Cert. PG.

Hostel ★★½

After some drugs and a bit of hanky-panky in Amsterdam, American backpackers Paxton and Josh are tipped off that the women of Slovakia are even more beautiful and willing. So the randy Yanks and an Icelandic cohort check into a Slovakian hostel and find themselves sharing a room with a babelicious Russian and Czech. Of course, it's all too good to be true… Writer-director Eli Roth was surprised, nay *irritated*, when the British censor gave his first film, *Cabin Fever*, a 15 certificate. It had drugs, bad language, sex and a girl shaving the flesh off her legs. In revenge, Roth brings us *Hostel*, an 18-rated spin on *EuroTrip* and arguably the most gruesome, sadistic and nauseating film ever to be distributed by a major studio. The make-up effects are rather cheesy, the structure off-centre and the logic wanting, but the film certainly delivers the goods. There's a high T&A factor, the scenes of torture are unremitting and, to be fare, it's effective multiplex fodder (and debuted in the US at No. 1). But it ain't *Wolf Creek*. JC-W

• *Paxton* Jay Hernandez, *Josh* Derek Richardson, *Oli* Eythor Gudjonsson, *Natalya* Barbara Nedeljáková, *Svetlana* Jana Kaderabková, *Dutch businessman* Jan Vlasák, *American businessman* Rick Hoffman, *Kana* Jennifer Lim, *with* Keiko Seiko, Lubomir Bukovy, Jana Havlickova, Takashi Miike, Gabriel Roth.

• *Dir* and *Screenplay* Eli Roth, *Pro* Roth, Mike Fleiss and Chris Briggs, *Ex Pro* Boaz Yakin, Scott Spiegel and Quentin Tarantino, *Co-Pro* Daniel Frisch and Philip Waley, *Ph* Milan Chadima, *Pro Des* and *Costumes* Franco-Giacomo Carbone, *Ed* George Folsey Jr., *M* Nate Barr, *Make-Up Effects* Greg Nicotero and Howard Berger.

Next Entertainment/Raw Nerve-Columbia TriStar. 93 mins. USA/Czech Republic. 2005. Rel: 24 March 2006. Cert. 18.

Howl's Moving Castle ★★★★

Convinced that she is no beauty, Sophie, now 18, works long hours at the hat shop owned by her mother. One day, alone at the shop, she is visited by the Witch of the Waste who turns her into a 90-year-old woman – along with the curse of being unable to tell anybody about it. As her country turns to war, Sophie heads for the hills and boards the fearsome Moving Castle belonging to the wizard Howl… It may be a fallacy, but it seems the more sophisticated animation becomes, the more it loses its charm and magic. Hayao Miyazaki, who brought us *Princess Mononoke* (1997) and the Oscar-winning *Spirited Away* (2001), continues to charm with this phantasmagorical adventure based on the 1986 novel by the London-born Diana Wynne Jones. Welding a Japanese sensibility onto an imagined English Utopia, Miyazaki pays homage to anime, Disney and Terry Gilliam while whipping up a wildly imaginative scenario all his own. Steeped in an otherworldly atmosphere, and marbled with an understated humour, the film repeatedly takes one by surprise, while constantly amazing with its resourceful vision. Respecting its silences and well voiced by an Anglo-American cast (although it's a shame Christian Bale has Americanised his native Welsh brogue), the film may be a tad ambitious in its elephantine narrative but is nonetheless a captivating spectacle. Original title: *Hauru no ugoku shiro*. JC-W

• *Voices*: *Grandma Sophie Hatter* Jean Simmons, *Howl* Christian Bale, *Witch of the Waste* Lauren Bacall, *Madame Suliman* Blythe Danner, *young Sophie Hatter* Emily Mortimer, *Markl* Josh Hutcherson, *Calcifer* Billy Crystal, *Honey* Mari Devon, *Lettie* Jena Malone.

• *Dir* Hayao Miyazaki, *Pro* Toshio Suzuki, *Screenplay* Miyazaki and Noboru Yoshida, *Art Dir* Yoji Takeshige, *M* Joe Hisaishi, *Digital Animation* Mitsunori Kataama.

Tokuma Shoten/Studio Ghibli/Nippon Television Network-Optimum Releasing. 119 mins. Japan. 2004. Rel: 23 September 2005. Cert. U.

Hustle & Flow ★★½

Memphis, Tennessee; today. DJay is a pimp and drug dealer who shares his house with three 'bitches', one of whom is heavily pregnant, another saddled with a baby. His main income is supplied by Nola, a white girl who's willing to perform 'tricks' but is far from happy with her lot. Then DJay bumps into an old school friend, Key, who might just be able to harness DJay's poetic 'flow' to some marketable hip-hop beats… Writer-director Craig Brewer creates a credible atmosphere of urban malaise with his second feature and is blessed by a laudable turn from Terrence Howard, who, in spite of his character's peddling of dope and exploitation of female flesh, is not a cardboard villain. Indeed, we actually feel for this low-life, although it's hard to believe in his talent as a hip-hop luminary-in-waiting. It's also specious to swallow that DJay's only options are crime and celebrity. JC-W

• *DJay* Terrence Howard, *Key* Anthony Anderson, *Nola* Taryn Manning, *Shug* Taraji P. Henson, *Lexus* Paula Jai Parker, *Yevette* Elise Neal, *Arnel* Isaac Hayes, *Shelby* D.J. Qualls, *Skinny*

Black Chris `Ludacris' Bridges, *with* Juicy J, William `Poon' Engram, DJ Paul, Lindsey Roberts.

• *Dir* and *Screenplay* Craig Brewer, *Pro* John Singleton and Stephanie Allain, *Ex Pro* Dwight Williams, *Assoc Pro* Preson Holmes, *Ph* Amelia Vincent, *Pro Des* Keith Brian Burns, *Ed* Billy Fox, *M* Scott Bomar, *Costumes* Paul Simmons.

Paramount Classics/MTV Films/New Deal Entertainment/Crunk Pictures/Homegrown Pictures-UIP.
116 mins. USA. 2005. Rel: 11 November 2005. Cert. 15.

Ice Age: The Meltdown ★★★★

When the earth starts to warm up, the new climate proves to be a mixed blessing for its prehistoric inhabitants. But when the ice starts to crack beneath their feet, Manny the mammoth, Sid the sloth and Diego the sabre-tooth tiger urge their fellow critters to flee to higher ground. And it's a journey dogged with treacherous incident... Officially a sequel to Twentieth Century Fox's most successful cartoon (computer-animated or otherwise), *The Meltdown* recalls Disney's *Dinosaur* as much as anything. In the former, a dinosaur was raised by lemurs and had to join a perilous trek to safer ground. Here we have Elsie, a woolly mammoth raised by possums who has to join a perilous trek to safer ground... This aside, the sequel is a marked improvement on its predecessor, with wittier dialogue ('don't that put a stink in extinction?'), even more amazing visuals and more fully-fledged characters. JC-W

• **Voices:** *Manny* Ray Romano, *Sid* John Leguizamo, *Diego* Denis Leary, *Crash* Seann William Scott, *Eddie* Josh Peck, *Ellie* Queen Latifah, *Lone Gunslinger Vulture* Will Arnett, *Fast Tony* Jay Leno.

• *Dir* Carlos Saldanha, *Pro* Lori Forte, *Ex Pro* Christopher Meledandri and Chris Wedge, *Line Pro* Bob Gordon, *Screenplay* Peter Gaulke, Gerry Swallow and Jim Hecht, *Art Dir* Thomas Cardone, *Ed* Harry Hitner, *M* John Powell, *Sound* Randy Thom, *Character Design* Peter De Sève.

Cold lunch: Scrat finds his acorn in Carlos Saldanha's witty and entertaining *Ice Age: The Meltdown* (from Fox)

Twentieth Century Fox Animation/Blue Sky Studios-Fox. 90 mins. USA. 2006. Rel: 7 April 2006. Cert. U.

The Ice Harvest ★★

By aligning his brains with his partner's nerve, mob lawyer Charlie Arglist has pulled off the perfect crime: he's just walked away with $2,147,000 of his boss's cash. And while everybody in Wichita Falls, Kansas, is preparing for Christmas, all Charlie has to do is bide his time, act normal and prepare for his escape. Simple, no? John Cusack and Billy Bob Thornton made a wonderful double-act in Mike Newell's quirky and intelligent *Pushing Tin* (1999). Here, though, they're handed a couple of miserable ne'er-do-wells who speak in one-liners and breathe an unappealing self-loathing. Indeed, the film wears its *noir* label on its sleeve, while every character– save for Oliver Platt's obnoxious buffoon – attempts to operate as a pre-packaged stereotype. There is the occasional scene that works a treat but for the most part *The Ice Harvest* is frozen in a smart-ass stasis. JC-W

• *Charlie Arglist* John Cusack, *Vic Cavanaugh* Billy Bob Thornton, *Renata* Connie Nielsen, *Bill Guerrard* Randy Quaid, *Pete Van Heuten* Oliver Platt, *Sidney* Ned Bellamy, *Roy* Mike Starr, *with* Lara Phillips, Bill Noble, T.J. Jagodowski, Meghan Maureen McDonough, Caroline Gehrke.

• *Dir* Harold Ramis, *Pro* Albert Berger and Ron Yerxa, *Ex Pro* Robert Benton, Richard Russo and Glenn Williamson, *Co-Pro* Thomas Busch, *Screenplay* Russo and Benton, from the novel by Scott Phillips, *Ph* Alar Kivilo, *Pro Des* Patrizia von Brandenstein, *Ed* Lee Percy, *M* David Kitay, *Costumes* Susan Kaufmann, *Sound* Ron Bochar.

Focus Features/Bona Fide-UIP.
88 mins. USA. 2005. Rel: 3 February 2006. Cert. 15.

Imaginary Heroes ★★★

Matt Travis, outstanding swimmer and unrepentant bully, shoots his brains out. This incident cracks the fragile status quo of the Travis enclave and each member of Matt's family plunges into an emotional tailspin... A lugubrious contemplation of mortality, *Imaginary Heroes* is *Ordinary People* updated to the 21st century with a finely developed sense of irony. As scene follows scene (and they feel like scenes), a sense of unintentional suspense builds as we speculate which member of the fragmenting Travis brood will expire next. Sharply written, flabbily directed and superbly played, *Imaginary Heroes* fails to build any emotional momentum (or credibility), but keeps hitting home runs. Sigourney Weaver gives her best performance in aeons, Emile Hirsch supplies his standard young DiCaprio impression and a prize supporting cast shines when it can. But the film constantly fails to convince: no allusion is made to Tim's diminutive stature (he is a head shorter than his mother and father), the snow looks like foam and Vivaldi's *Spring Violin Concerto* is an unforgivable cliché (Sigourney's Sandy wouldn't have it in the house). Still, writer-writer Dan Harris is only 24 and is destined to go far. JC-W

• *Sandy Travis* Sigourney Weaver, *Tim Travis* Emile Hirsch, *Ben Travis* Jeff Daniels, *Penny Travis* Michelle Williams, *Matt Travis* Kip Pardue, *Marge Dwyer* Deirdre O'Connell, *Kyle Dwyer* Rayn Donowho, *Steph Connors* Suzanne Santo, *Vern* Jay Paulson, *Jack Johnson* Luke Robertson, *with* Lee Wilkof, Terry Beaver, Sara Tanaka, Rayn Patrick Bachand, Lori Yeghiayan, Stephen Rowe, Adam Lefevre.

• *Dir* and *Screenplay* Dan Harris, *Pro* Ilana Diamant, Art Linson and Frank Hübner, Gina Resnick and Denise Shaw, *Ex Pro* Moshe Diamant, Rudy Cohen and Jan Fantl, *Co-Pro* Deborah Lee, *Ph* Tim Orr, *Pro Des* Rick Butler, *Ed* James Lyons, *M* John Ottman and Deborah Lurie, *Costumes* Michael Wilkinson.

Signature Pictures International-Columbia TriStar.
111 mins. USA. 2004. Rel: 1 July 2005. Cert. 18.

Imagine Me & You ★★★★

London; today. Rachel has just married the ideal man, Hector, a handsome, sensitive charmer with a good job in the city. Meanwhile, Rachel's bridal florist, Luce, takes an unexpected interest in the couple and is invited round to dinner. There, Hector's best friend, Cooper, hits on Luce, only to discover she's gay... Having played a French exchange student in the sadly under-valued *Slap Her... She's French* (2000), the New Jersey-born Piper Perabo now perfects a near-flawless English accent. She may not be the most credible of B-list stars, but she's an attractive foil to a sublime ensemble of English players who buff Ol Parker's witty script to a fine polish (Celia Imrie: 'Coop – that trollop. He'd shag an open wound'). A skilful invasion of the Richard Curtis school of fantasy England, *Imagine Me & You* presents a welter of stereotypes but turns them neatly on their head. Parker is dealing in a well-trodden genre here, yet most of the time is one step ahead of the template. Essentially a feel-good romantic comedy in the vein of *Four Weddings*, *Imagine Me* aims primarily to entertain – which it does very well – but with a wry understanding of contemporary mores.
JC-W

• *Rachel* Piper Perabo, *Hector* Matthew Goode, *Luce* Lena Headey, *Heck* Matthew Goode, *Tessa* Celia Imrie, *Ned* Anthony Head, *Cooper* Darren Boyd, *Ella* Sue Johnston, *H* Boo Jackson, *Beth* Sharon Horgan, *Edie* Eva Birthistle, *Zina* Vinette Robinson, *Rob* Ben Miles, *priest* John Thompson, *Mrs Edwards* Mona Hammond, *with* Ruth Sheen, Philip Bird, Justine Mitchell, Gerard Horan, Kellie Bright.

• *Dir* and *Screenplay* Ol Parker, *Pro* Sophie Balhetchet, Barnaby Thompson and Andro Steinborn, *Ex Pro* Stefan Arndt, David Thompson, Jim Stern and Lynda La Plante, *Assoc Pro* Bill Shapter, *Ph* Ben Davis, *Pro Des* Eve Mavrakis, *Ed* Alex Mackie, *M* Alex Heffes, *Costumes* Consolata Boyle.

Ealing Studios/BBC Films/Cougar Films/Fragile Films/X Filme Creative/Focus Features-UIP.
94 mins. UK/Germany. 2005. Rel: 16 June 2006. Cert. 12A.

In Her Shoes ★★★★

For Maggie Feller, life has been easy. In spite of a predilection for ice cream, pancakes and unwholesome amounts of alcohol, she has retained a taut, leggy physique with a smile that could blind a horse. But her chronic untidiness, lying and kleptomania have finally become too much for sister Rose, and she is forced to find her own solution to her biggest problem: herself. Meanwhile, Rose, a high-flying lawyer, is obliged to trust her own romantic instincts in the chaotic wake of her younger sister... *In Her Shoes* is, in the cold light of day, all rather pat, manipulative and overly slick. Nonetheless, it could have been considerably sudsier and, where it matters, is movingly restrained. Indeed, its quieter moments wield the greatest emotional impact, while Cameron Diaz gives the performance of her career. Playing a highly unsympathetic character, and allowing the camera an unflattering proximity to her face, she reveals a commitment hitherto unseen. In support, Toni Collette is sharp, vulnerable and selfless, while Shirley MacLaine more than makes up for her embarrassing turn in *Bewitched*. JC-W

• *Maggie Feller* Cameron Diaz, *Rose Feller* Toni Collette, *Ella Hirsch* Shirley MacLaine, *Simon Stein* Mark Feuerstein, *Michael Feller* Ken Howard, *Sydelle Feller* Candice Azzara, *Mrs Lefkowitz* Francine Beers, *the 'Professor'* Norman Lloyd, *Lewis Feldman* Jerry Adler, *Amy* Brooke Smith, *Jim Danvers* Richard Burgi, *with* Anson Mount, Nicole Randall Johnson, Eric Balfour, Andy Powers, Marcia Jean Kurtz, Alan Blumenfeld, Jackie Geary, Dorothy Kelly, Joan Turner.

• *Dir* Curtis Hanson, *Pro* Hanson, Ridley Scott, Carol Fenelon and Lisa Ellzey, *Ex Pro* Tony Scott, *Co-Pro* Mari Jo Winkler-Ioffreda, *Screenplay* Susannah Grant, *Ph* Terry Stacey, *Pro Des* Dan Davis, *Ed* Craig Kitson and Lisa Zeno Churgin, *M* Mark Isham, *Costumes* Sophie de Rakoff.

Fox/Scott Free-Fox.
130 mins. USA/UK/Germany. 2005.
Rel: 11 November 2005. Cert. 12A.

Innocence ★★★½

Following a primal, watery initiation accompanied by the sound of a deep, subterranean pounding, Iris arrives at her new school in a coffin. Here, the children live in five houses in a wooded commune where the grown-ups are all but invisible. The children themselves hand down the rules and the only classes are natural history and ballet. It's an idyllic commune, albeit one with no seeming escape... *Innocence* will mean different things to different viewers. Indeed, the film's refusal to supply answers or even temporal or geographical markers is likely to infuriate many. And, much like the vernal state of presexuality itself, *Innocence* exists in a parallel universe of fantasy, memory and literary reference. Lewis Carroll, Enid Blyton, the photographs of Sally Mann and Peter Weir's *Picnic at Hanging Rock* collide in a mosaic of allusion and imagery. Whatever first-time director Lucile Hadzihalilovic is trying to say – this is actually an adaptation of Frank Wedekind's short story *Mine-Haha, The Corporal Education of Young Girls* – she does so with a bold, original voice. Stripping away the template of traditional narrative cinema – there is virtually no music and the film, utilising natural light, is shot on Super-16

– Hadzihalilovic is unquestionably a filmmaker of enormous promise. JC-W

• *Iris* Zoé Auclair, *Bianca* Bérangère Haubruge, *Alice* Léa Bridarolli, *Mademoiselle Eva* Marion Cotillard, *Mademoiselle Edith* Hélène de Fougerolles, *Laura* Olga Peytavi-Muller, *Selma* Alisson Lalieux, *Nadja* Ana Paloma-Diaz, *headmistress* Corine Marchand.

• *Dir* and *Screenplay* Lucile Hadzihalilovic, adapted from the novella *Mine-Haha, or the Corporal Punishment of Young Girls* by Frank Wedekind, *Pro* Patrick Sobelman, *Ph* Benoît Debie, *Pro Des* Arnaud de Moleron, *Ed* Adam Finch, *M* Richard Cooke, *Costumes* Laurence Benoît.

Ex Nihilo-Artificial Eye.
120 mins. France/Belgium/UK. 2004.
Rel: 30 September 2005. Cert. 15.

Inside Man ★★★★

Four men walk into a Wall Street bank, lock the door behind them and take 50 people hostage. Outside, recently promoted hostage negotiator Keith Frazier attempts to outwit the master criminal calling the shots. But the latter, Dalton Russell, has a plan and knows every loophole that Frazier can slip him… *Inside Man* boasts one of the finest screenplays about a bank heist ever written. With its brilliant premise, colourful dialogue, vivid characters, built-in suspense and wry humour, it is a director's dream. Shame, then, that in this instance the director is Spike Lee, who can't resist drawing attention to his *modus operandi*, be it rotating his camera around his protagonists, overdoing the Spielberg zoom (in which the camera tracks back as the lens zooms in) and cloaking vital dialogue in 'background' music. Still, Denzel Washington and Clive Owen dominate the screen with enormous power (Denzel laying on the charisma, Owen sharpening his acuity), providing a dramatic canvas that is cinematic nirvana. JC-W

• *Keith Frazier* Denzel Washington, *Dalton Russell* Clive Owen, *Madeline White* Jodie Foster, *Arthur Case* Christopher Plummer, *Captain John Darius* Willem Dafoe, *Bill Mitchell* Chiwetel Ejiofor, *Steve* Carlos Andrés Gómez, *with* Kim Director, James Ransome, Peter Frechette, Ken Leung.

• *Dir* Spike Lee, *Pro* Brian Grazer, *Ex Pro* Daniel M. Rosenberg, Jon Kilik, Karen Kehela Sherwood and Kim Roth, *Screenplay* Russell Gewirtz, *Ph* Matthew Libatique, *Pro Des* Wynn Thomas, *Ed* Barry Alexander Brown, *M* Terence Blanchard, *Costumes* Donna Berwick.

Universal/Imagine Entertainment/
40 Acres and a Mule-UIP.
129 mins. USA. 2006. Rel: 24 March 2006. Cert. 15.

Into the Blue ★★★

Jared Cole and his girlfriend Sam haven't had much luck finding treasure in the turquoise waters off the coast of New Providence in the Bahamas. Then, shortly after Jared's friend Bryce turns up with his new squeeze, the quartet stumble across a sunken galleon that could be the legendary, gold-laden *Zephyr*. But close by they also discover a plane containing a mammoth cargo of cocaine… In the good old days, *Into the Blue* would've passed muster as a B-movie every bit as good as the main feature. The underwater photography is sensational, the taut and bronzed bodies of the leads to die for and the plot more complex than one might have dared hope for. So, once you've checked your brain in at the door, sit back and enjoy the eye candy. JC-W

• *Jared Cole* Paul Walker, *Sam Nicholson* Jessica Alba, *Bryce Dunn* Scott Caan, *Amanda Collins* Ashley Scott, *Derek Bates* Josh Brolin, *Primo* Tyson Beckford, *Reyes* James Frain , *with* Dwayne Adway, Javon Frazer, Chris Taloa.

• *Dir* John Stockwell, *Pro* David A. Zelon, *Ex Pro* Peter Guber, Louis G. Friedman, Ori Marmur and Matt Luber, *Assoc Pro* Erin Mast, *Screenplay* Matt Johnson, *Ph* Shane Hurlbut, *Pro Des* Maia Javan, *Ed* Nicolas De Toth and Dennis Virkler, *M* Paul Haslinger, *Costumes* Leesa Evans.

MGM/Columbia Pictures/Mandalay Pictures-Fox.
109 mins. USA. 2005. Rel: 21 October 2005.
Cert. 15.

The Intruder ★

With locations ranging from France to Tahiti by way of Korea and with Agnès Godard as photographer, this film may look good but Claire Denis's idea of art is exactly what can give art a bad name. She expects us to be interested in characters presented without much background and with minimal dialogue and, while her tale of an aging man facing death but undergoing a heart transplant seems to be about fathers and sons, the story-telling (if you can call it that) is confusing and obscure. It's the kind of film described as 'dream-like', a phrase that sometimes hides a multitude of sins yet here fails to conceal them. This film is boring on every level except the visual and lasts for some two hours into the bargain. There's one shot – a tender close-up of a father with his young son – that lingers, but nothing else you would want to remembe. MS

• *Louis Trebor* Michel Subor, *Sidney* Grégoire Colin, *young Russian woman* Katia Golubeva, *pharmacist* Bambou, *Antoinette, customs officer* Florence Loiret-Caille, *with* Lolita Chammah, Beatrice Dalle, Alex Descas, Kim Dong-ho, Chang Se-tak, Park Hong-suk, Edwin Alin, Henri tetu Tetainanuarii, Jean-Marc Teriipaia, Anna Tetuaveroa.

• *Dir* Claire Denis, *Pro* Humbert Balsan, *Screenplay* Denis and Jean Pol Fargeau, *Ph* Agnes Godard, *Pro Des* Arnaud de Moleron, *Ed* Nelly Quettier, *M S.A.* Staples, *Costumes* Judy Shrewsbury, *Sound* Christophe Winding.

Humbert Balsan/Ognon Pictures/ARTE France-Tartan Films.
129 mins. France/South Korea. 2004.
Rel: 26 August 2005. No Cert.

Hostage to fortune: Jodie Foster cuts a deal in
Spike Lee's vivid, dramatic *Inside Man* (from UIP)

The Island ★★★½

In the year 2019, the entire globe has become contaminated, save for one last outpost, The Island. It is here that a few lucky winners of a daily lottery find themselves, while the rest remain in a strict, sterile facility in which every heartbeat is monitored. Lincoln Six-Echo dreams of the Island but is also plagued by harrowing nightmares, night terrors that suggest there might be more to his existence than he's permitted to know… Inspired by the story of Adam and Eve and a BBC documentary on cloning, *The Island* lunges into territory previously explored by *The Truman Show* and *The 6th Day* with a gung-ho bravura. Piling on his customary car chases and arsenal of high-tech destruction, Michael Bay (*Bad Boys*, *Armageddon*) refuses to let the tension flag, plugging any gaps with humour, moral meditations and in-jokes (Scarlett Johansson's clone Jordan Two-Delta is aghast to see a sky-high commercial of Scarlett Johansson plugging the Calvin Klein fragrance Eternity Moment). On the level of Hollywood's usual slam-bang action agenda, it's exhilarating stuff. Interestingly, *Blade Runner* was also set in the year 2019 and also featured 'replicants' of human beings. JC-W

• *Lincoln Six-Echo* Ewan McGregor, *Jordan Two-Delta* Scarlett Johansson, *Albert Laurent* Djimon Hounsou, *Merrick* Sean Bean, *Starkweather* Michael Clarke Duncan, *McCord* Steve Buscemi, *Jones Three Echo* Ethan Phillips, *chief of incubation* Max Baker, *Gandu Three Echo* Brian Stepanek, *Suzie* Shawnee Smith, *with* Siobhan Flynn, Glenn Morshower, Chris Ellis, Don Michael Paul, and (uncredited) *Charles Whitman* Kim Coates.

• *Dir* Michael Bay, *Pro* Bay, Walter F. Parkes and Ian Bryce, *Ex Pro* Laurie MacDonald, *Screenplay* Caspian Tredwell-Owen, Alex Kurtzman and Roberto Orci, *Ph* Mauro Fiore, *Pro Des* Nigel Phelps, *Ed* Paul Rubell and Christian Wagner, *M* Steve Jablonsky, *Costumes* Deborah L. Scott, *Visual Effects* Eric Brevig.

Warner/DreamWorks-Warner.
136 mins. USA. 2005. Rel: 12 August 2005. Cert. 12A.

Jarhead ★★★★

In August of 1990 Iraq invades Kuwait and so members of a hardened Marine corps are stationed in Saudi Arabia. And as more and more reinforcements arrive in the sun-baked no-man's-land, the soldiers become increasingly impatient to 'kick some Iraqi ass.' But as they wait, their testosterone is forced to find some less conventional outlets… War is hell but it's not always the hell you expect. Arguably the quintessential movie about the first Gulf War, *Jarhead* is a bold, hard-hitting and impeccably crafted (and acted) jolt of cinema. Playfully referencing the shadow of Vietnam (*Apocalypse Now*, The Doors, the bitterness), the film writes its own cultural agenda with help from more recent touchstones. Yet so successful is the film's portrayal of the build-up to the actual conflict in Kuwait, that when the engagement with the enemy finally arrives it is almost an anticlimax. P.S. 'Jarhead' is American military slang for a Marine. JC-W

• *Anthony Swofford* Jake Gyllenhaal, *Allen Troy* Peter Sarsgaard, *Chris Kruger* Lucas Black, *Lt. Col. Kazinski* Chris Cooper, *Staff Sergeant Skykes* Jamie Foxx, *Fergus O'Donnell* Brian Geraghty, *Cortez* Jacob Vargaz, *Escobar* Laz Alonso, *Fowler* Evan Jones, *Major Lincoln* Dennis Haysbert, *with* Scott

So here it is, Merry Xmas: Jake Gyllenhaal in Sam Mendes' bold, hard-hitting *Jarhead* (from UIP)

MacDonald, Damion Poitier, Donna Kimball.

• *Dir* Sam Mendes, *Pro* Douglas Wick and Lucy Fisher, *Ex Pro* Sam Mercer and Bobby Cohen, *Co-Pro* Pippa Harris, *Screenplay* William Broyles, Jr, from the autobiography by Anthony Swofford, *Ph* Roger Deakins, *Pro Des* Dennis Gassner, *Ed* Walter Murch, *M* Thomas Newman, *Costumes* Albert Wolsky, *Sound* Kyrsten Mate.

Universal/MP Kappa Prods/Neal Street Prods-UIP. 122 mins. USA/UK/Germany. 2005. Rel: 13 January 2006. Cert. 15.

The Jealous God ★★½

John Braine's novel of 1964 is much less well known than his *Room at the Top* but it's embraced here by filmmakers intent on finding tales that reflect life in the Pennine region of our north country. Good intentions, then, but this drama, self-conscious in its 1960s setting, plays like a piece for television. The story of a Catholic mother dominating her only son remaining unmarried and then taking against a prospective bride who is a Protestant could be worth telling – but not when it proves to be inept, unpersuasive and liable to lapse into melodrama. A fresh look at the Sixties could indeed be rewarding but this attempt at it merely proves that sincerity alone is not enough. MS

• *Vincent Dungarven* Jason Merrells, *Maureen* Denise Welch, *Laura* Mairead Carty, *Mrs Rosslea* Pamela Cundell, *Matthew* Andrew Dunn, *Mrs Dungarven* Marcia Warren, *Paul* William Ilkley, *with* Pia Gabriele, Robert Duncan, Tony Barton, Judy Flynn.

• *Dir, Pro* and *Screenplay* Steven Woodcock, *Ex Pro* Julie Woodcock, *Ph* Gordon MacGregor, *Pro Des* Christopher Sutton, *Ed* Heidi Stiene, *M* Michael Hammer.

North Country Pictures/Diva Theatre Prods-Miracle Communications. 95 mins. UK. 2005. Rel: 9 September 2005. Cert. 12A.

Junebug ★★★★½

When the British-born art dealer Madeleine travels to North Carolina to close a deal with a local artist, she stops by to visit the family of her new husband, George. As George himself reverts to his old predisposition for solitude, Madeleine is left at the mercy of her judgemental in-laws. Only George's heavily pregnant sister-in-law, Ashley, seems to appreciate Madeleine's grace and sophistication… Just when the comic conceit of meeting the parents seemed to be fizzling out with *Guess Who* and *Monster-in-Law*, along comes this delicate masterpiece. With a light touch it uncovers all the impending melodrama of culture collision, yet far from treating its protagonists with condescension, it illuminates the divide between the Deep South and urban enlightenment with compassion, heart and enormous humour. With its intelligent use of silences and mood-setting still lifes, the film builds up a tinderbox of anticipation as it traces the discomfort of these very real and recognisable characters. And with a pitch-perfect cast, it's impossible to single out any one performance, although it was Amy Adams – in the extrovert part of the garrulous, wide-eyed Ashley – who snared an Oscar nomination. JC-W

• *Ashley* Amy Adams, *Madeleine* Embeth Davidtz, *Johnny* Ben McKenzie, *George* Alessandro Nivola, *David Wark* Frank Hoyt Taylor, *Peg* Celia Weston, *Eugene* Scott Wilson, *Bernadette* Alicia van Couvering, *Bill Mooney* Will Oldham, *Sissy* Joanne Pankow.

• *Dir* Phil Morrison, *Pro* Mindy Goldberg and Mike S. Ryan, *Ex Pro* Mark P. Clein, Ethan D. Leder, Daniel Rappaport and Dany Wolf, *Screenplay* Angus MacLachlan, *Ph* Peter Donahue, *Pro Des* David Doernberg, *Ed* Joe Klotz, *M* Yo La Tengo; Haydn, Shostakovich, Schubert, Vivaldi, Alois Strohmayer; `Harmour Love' sung by Syreeta, *Costumes* Danielle Kays.

Epoch Films-Eureka Entertainment. 106 mins. USA. 2004. Rel: 14 April 2006. Cert. 15.

Just Friends ★★½

At school, Chris Brander was a dork, grossly overweight and besotted with his sexy best friend, Jamie. Ten years later and Chris has transformed himself, lost all the excess weight, become a major player in the music business and is a *bona fide* babe magnet. And yet he still lusts after Jamie – but is no longer the man that she once loved… Beneath the slapstick and sex gags, a very potent idea rests at the heart of this fitfully amusing farce. Why do we become who we are and are we really better now than our adolescent selves? Sadly, *Just Friends* is funnier in its first half, empowered by a nicely understated performance from Ryan Reynolds as a sarcastic but level-headed smart ass. There's a terrific routine, too, from Anna Faris as a cerebrally challenged Courtney Love clone, but then the film shifts into crass silliness from which it cannot recover. JC-W

• *Chris Brander* Ryan Reynolds, *Jamie Palamino* Amy Smart, *Samantha James* Anna Faris, *Dusty Dinkleman* Chris Klein, *Carol Brander* Julie Hagerty, *K.C.* Stephen Root, *Michael Brander* Christopher Marquette, *Clark* Fred Ewanuick, *Darla* Amy Matysio, *Mr Palamino* Barry Flatman, *with* Giacomo Beltrami, Wendy Anderson, Ty Olsson, Ashley Scott, Grace Kumble.

• *Dir* Roger Kumble, *Pro* Chris Bender and JC Spink, Michael Ohoven, William Vince, and Bill Johnson, *Ex Pro* Toby Emmerich, Richard Brener, Cale Boyter and Marco Mehlitz, *Co-Pro* Jake Weiner, *Screenplay* Adam `Tex' Davis, *Ph* Anthony B. Richmond, *Pro Des* Robb Wilson King, *Ed* Jeff Freeman, *M* Jeff Cardoni, *Costumes* Alexandra Welker.

New Line Cinema/Cinerenta a Benderspink and Cinezeta-Momentum Pictures. 94 mins. USA/Canada/Germany. 2005. Rel: 6 January 2005. Cert. 12A.

Just Like Heaven ★★★½

Elizabeth Masterson, a senior resident in a major San Francisco hospital, is so busy saving people's lives that she's saving her own life for later. David Abbott, who's in an emotional tailspin

Platonic sets: Ryan Reynolds and Amy Smart pair up in Roger Kumble's fitfully amusing *Just Friends* (from Momentum Pictures)

after his wife's death, has put his own life on hold. Then, when he moves into a new apartment on a short lease, he encounters Elizabeth's spirit, which is furious that he has moved into her space... Director Mark Waters has a nicely developed sense of comedy timing. After *Freaky Friday* and *Mean Girls*, he augments his comic canon with this slick, delightful and, yes, very funny romantic fantasy. Reese Witherspoon, grabbing the Meg Ryan baton with both hands, and Mark Ruffalo, grounding the ridiculous with a dishevelled sweetness, combine forces to create multiplex nirvana. In addition, the central conceit is a romantic dream, the dialogue sparkling and the production values shimmering. JC-W

• *Dr Elizabeth Masterson* Reese Witherspoon, *David Abbott* Mark Ruffalo, *Jack Houriskey* Donal Logue, *Abby Brody* Dina Waters, *Dr Brett Rushton* Ben Shenkman, *Darryl* Jon Heder, *Katrina* Ivana Milicevic, *with* Caroline Aaron, Rosalind Chao, Ron Canada, Willie Garson, Gabrielle Madé.

• *Dir* Mark Waters, *Pro* Laurie MacDonald and Walter F. Parkes, *Ex Pro* David Householter, *Co-Pro* Marc Levy, *Screenplay* Peter Tolan and Leslie Dixon, from the novel *If Only It Were True* by Marc Levy, *Ph* Daryn Okada, *Pro Des* Cary White,
Ed Bruce Green, *M* Rolfe Kent, *Costumes* Sophie de Rakoff.

DreamWorks/Parkes/MacDonald-UIP.
94 mins. USA. 2005. Rel: 30 December 2005. Cert. PG.

Just My Luck ★

Lindsay Lohan is the luckiest girl in the world whose two best friends are probably the prettiest girls in New York (poor casting, that). Then Lindsay meets Chris Pine (a Rob Lowe type), the unluckiest guy on the planet – until he meets Lindsay. So they kiss and Lindsay inherits all his miserable misfortune... If your idea of unbridled mirth is to see some poor sod have all the afflictions of the world rained down on them, then you'll find this a side-splitter. But slapstick, which reduces somebody as sometimes as talented as Lindsay Lohan to attack a foaming washing machine with a pair of trousers, is depressingly lame. JC-W

• *Ashley Albright* Lindsay Lohan, *Jake Hardin* Chris Pine, *Damon Phillips* Faizon Love, *Dana* Bree Turner, *Maggie* Samaire Armstrong, *Peggy Braden* Missi Pyle, *Katy* Mackenzie Vega, *themselves* McFly, *with* Carlos Ponce, Tovah Feldshuh, Jaqueline Fleming, Kevin Scanlon.

• *Dir* Donald Petrie, *Pro* Petrie, Arnon Milchan and Arnold Rifkin, *Ex Pro* Joe Caracciolo Jr., *Co-Pro* Ellen H. Schwartz and Marjorie Shik, *Screenplay* I. Marlene King and Amy B. Harris, from a story by King, Jonathan Bernstein, Mark Blackwell and James Greer, *Ph* Dean Semler, *Pro Des* Ray Kluga, *Ed* Debra Neil-Fisher, *M* Teddy Castellucci, *Costumes* Gary Jones.

Regency Enterprises/New Regency/Cheyenne Enterprises-Fox.
103 mins. USA. 2006. Rel: 30 June 2006. Cert. PG

Keeping Mum ★★★½

In the sleepy hamlet of Little Wallop, what should be a model life for the family of the Reverend Walter Goodfellow is turning a little sour. Walter himself is distracted by cooking up the perfect sermon, his wife is contemplating an affair with her American golfing coach, their 17-year-old daughter Holly is turning into a nymphomaniac and their son Petey is being bullied at school. Then, with the arrival of the new housekeeper, Grace Hawkins, everything starts to go mysteriously right… On one level, *Keeping Mum* is the perfect English black comedy. From its multi-purpose title, to its impeccable execution and ingenious narrative, it is an object lesson in the genre. Visually, it is safe and gorgeous, the music melodic but not intrusive and the performances skilfully understated. Indeed, Kristin Scott Thomas is a gem, at once credible and fortysomething yet still funny and beautiful in a class act. With Scott Thomas and Rowan Atkinson (again, playing the vicar) reunited from *Four Weddings*, this could be the bastard love child of the former. If *Keeping Mum* had been darker and funnier, it would've been a classic. JC-W

• *Reverend Walter Goodfellow* Rowan Atkinson, *Gloria Goodfellow* Kristin Scott Thomas, *Grace Hawkins* Maggie Smith, *Lance* Patrick Swayze, *Holly Goodfellow* Tamsin Egerton, *Petey Goodfellow* Toby Parkes, *Mrs Parker* Liz Smith, *Rosie Jones* Emilia Fox, *Mr Brown* James Booth, *with* Roger Hammond, Andrew Thomas Jones, Jack Ryan, Nazim Kourgli, Jack Zimmermann.

• *Dir* Niall Johnson, *Pro* Julia Palau and Matthew Payne, *Ex Pro* Steve Wilkinson, Anne Sheehan, Steve Christian, Marc Samuelson, Bertil Ohlssonand David Garrett, *Co-Pro* Nigel Wooll, *Screenplay* Johnson and Richard Russo, *Ph* Gavin Finney, *Pro Des* Crispian Sallis, *Ed* Robin Sales, *M* Dickon Hinchliffe, *Costumes* Vicki Russell.

Summit Entertainment/Isle of Man Film/Azure/ Tusk-Entertainment. 103 mins. UK/USA. 2005. Rel: 2 December 2005. Cert. 15.

The Ketchup Effect ★★★

In attempting to emulate another Swedish film, Lukas Moodysson's *Show Me Love* (1998), Teresa Fabik lowers the age of her troubled adolescents to 13 or so. Central is Sofie, a student at the high school where her father teaches. Anxious to be admired but upset if met by a sexual response, Sofie falls victim to fellow students who blacken her reputation while at home the absence of a mother makes her a difficult child… The cast is acceptable but the piece lacks weight because the tone is all over the place. Initially it's predominantly comic but later darkens as is necessary given that Sofie is driven to attempt suicide. But then, as though this were overly depressing, the film opts for an upbeat ending but one too easily achieved for credibility. It's a compromise which renders this film instantly forgettable although in its muddled way it's watchable enough. Original title: *Hip Hip Hora!* MS

• *Sofie* Amanda Renberg, *Krister* Björn Kjellman, *Amanda* Ellen Fjaestad, *Emma* Linn Persson, *with* Filip Berg, Marcus Hasselborg, Björn Davidson.

• *Dir* and *Screenplay* Teresa Fabik, *Pro* Lars Blomgren and Genya Kihlberg, *Ex Pro* Börje Hansson, Michael Obel,

Claes Olsson, Bertil Sandgren and Staffan Wallhem, *Ph* Par M. Ekberg, *Ed* Sofia Lindgren, *M* Jacob Groth, *Costumes* Lena Aspemar, *Sound* Bo Persson and Martin Dahl.

Filmlance/Swedish Film Institute, etc-Peccadillo Pictures. 90 mins. Sweden/Denmark/Finland. 2004. Rel: 10 March 2006. Cert. 18.

Kicking & Screaming ★

As Phil Weston relates, he was born a baby. Then as he grew up he found that his greatest rival was his father, who had to be better at everything. On the day that Phil proposes to his future wife, Barbara, his father introduces him to *his* new bride. And so it goes. Then, on a foolhardy whim, Phil agrees to coach a hopeless little league soccer team, The Tigers. Stupid really, when his father is coach of the triumphant Warriors. But then Phil Weston is a man of very little brain… Take a scenario already mined in *The Bad News Bears*, *The Mighty Ducks* and *Hardball*, throw in a running gag about coffee too hot to drink (that's a clever one) and to really guarantee a failsafe laugh base, insert musical cues referencing *Chariots of Fire* and *Rocky IV*. Few films this year, surely, can reach the creative lows of this moronic, derivative abuse of celluloid. JC-W

• *Phil Weston* Will Ferrell, *Buck Weston* Robert Duvall, *Mike Ditka* Mike Ditka, *Barbara Weston* Kate Walsh, *Sam Weston* Dylan McLaughlin, *Bucky Weston* Josh Hutcherson, *Janice Weston* Musetta Vander, *with* Steven Anthony Lawrence, Jeremy Bergman, Laura Kightlinger, David Bowe, Susan Barnes, Frank Cassavetes.

• *Dir* Jesse Dylan, *Pro* Jimmy Miller, *Ex Pro* Charles Roven, Judd Apatow and Daniel Lupi, *Screenplay* Leo Benvenuti and Steve Rudnick, *Ph* Lloyd Ahern, *Pro Des* Clayton R. Hartley, *Ed* Stuart Pappé and Peter Teschner, *M* Mark Isham, *Costumes* Pamela Withers-Chilton.

Universal/Mosaic Media-UIP. 94 mins. USA. 2005. Rel: 22 July 2005. Cert. PG.

Kidulthood ★★★½

When a classmate commits suicide after being bullied, the pupils of a West London school are given the day off. Far from using the time to deliberate over the girl's death, the kids take to the streets to shop and look for drugs, sex and other means of asserting their 'cool'… *Kidulthood* both benefits and suffers from the first-director syndrome, particularly being on such a low budget. But the film is to be commended for its freshness, the largely naturalistic performances and some nice cinematic touches. However, it's the subject matter that singles *Kidulthood* out, being an honest, terrifying portrait of 15-year-olds in contemporary London. While there's nothing new in the drugs, bullying, sex and robbery that inform these kids' lives, it's the accessibility to it in an age driven by technology and the Internet that is so disturbing. The film's villain is an unredeemable stereotype (played by scriptwriter Noel Clarke, no less), and the story is a tad schematic, but the language, cutting-edge music and guerrilla filmmaking on tourist-packed streets make this a vital piece of sociocultural cinema. JC-W

Arms and the man: Femi Oyeniran in Menhaj Huda's fresh, terrifying *Kidulthood* (from Revolver Entertainment)

• *Trife* Aml Ameen, *Alisa* Red Madrell, *Becky* Jaime Winstone, *Sam* Noel Clarke, *Claire* Madeleine Fairley, *Jay* Adam Deacon, *Lenny* Rafe Spall, *Moony* Femi Oyeniran, *Stella* Kate Magowan, *Trife* Aml Ameen, *Katie* Rebecca Martin, *Blake* Nicholas Hoult, *Vinnie* Adem Bayram, *Shaneek* Stefanie Di Rubbo, *Lenny* Rafe Spall, *Stella* Kate Magowan, *Mr Fineal* Christopher Villiers.

• *Dir* Menhaj Huda, *Pro* Huda, Damian Jones and George Isaac, *Ex Pro* Pierre Mascolo, Marco Costa, Tania Costa and Marcello Moscarello, *Co-Pro* Alexandra Stone, Ray Panthaki, Douglas Lochhead and Richard Lever, *Line Pro* Tim Cole, *Screenplay* Noel Clarke, *Ph* Brian Tufano, *Pro Des* Murray McKeown and Nick Tuft, *Ed* Victoria Boydell, *M* The Angel; tracks performed by CeeWhy, Akala, Shystie, The Streets, Dizzee Rascal, Roots Manuva, SkinnyMan, Audio Bullys, Lethal Bizzle, etc, *Costumes* Andy Blake.

Stealth Films/Cipher Films/TMC Films/
UK Film Council-Revolver Entertainment.
91 mins. UK. 2006. Rel: 3 March 2006. Cert. 15.

The King ★★★★

Fresh out of the US Navy, Elvis Valderez takes a motel room in Corpus Christi, Texas. Shortly afterwards he visits the Glad Tidings Baptist Church, hits on the virginal, 16-year-old Malerie Sandow and then approaches her father, Pastor David Sandow. The latter, recognising something in Elvis he does not like, tells the stranger to stay away from his family and his property... There is too much irony in *The King* for it to have sprung from the bosom of Hollywood. In fact, it's a collaboration between the New York writer Milo Addica (*Monster's Ball*, *Birth*) and the English documentary filmmaker James Marsh. Here, we have a Baptist minister (a solid William Hurt) who makes us uneasy, and a killer that we sympathise with. The Mexican Bernal, while playing an outsider, is still an odd choice for the role of the prodigal son, although his angelic features are a nice contrast to his actions. The sunny, ethereal music is another bonus as it plays with our emotions, telling us to feel one thing when we are perceiving something else entirely. The result is a film of inordinate power, like an unspeakable abomination with a serene, beatific smile.
JC-W

• *Elvis Valderez* Gael Garcia Bernal, *Pastor David Sandow* William Hurt, *Twyla Sandow* Laura Harring, *Malerie Sandow* Pell James, *Paul Sandow* Paul Dano, *with* Derek Alvarado, Veronica Bernal, Milo Addica.

• *Dir* James Marsh, *Pro* and *Screenplay* Marsh and Milo Addica, *Ex Pro* Edward R. Pressman, John Schmidt and Sofia Sondervan, *Line Pro* Susan Kirr, *Ph* Eigil Bryld, *Pro Des* Sharon Lomofsky, *Ed* Jinx Godfrey, *M* Max Avery Lichtenstein, *Costumes* Lee Hunsaker, *Sound* Tom Paul.

ContentFilm/FilmFour-Tartan Films.
105 mins. USA/UK. 2005. Rel: 19 May 2006. Cert. 15.

King Kong ★★★★

Having recently lost her job in vaudeville, Ann Darrow reluctantly agrees to drop everything and head to Singapore to star in a movie by the maverick director Carl Denham. But Denham has a secret agenda: to film on Skull Island, the last uncharted corner of the earth. And it's a monstrous place, dominated by an outsize, angry gorilla... Technically, this third version of Edgar Wallace and Merian C. Cooper's reworking of the *Beauty and the Beast* is awesome. The opening

Creature feature: Naomi Watts (at the feet of Kong) faces up to a tyrannosaurus in Peter Jackson's awesome, enthralling *King Kong* (from UIP)

alone, in which the skyline of 1930s' New York is viewed from a shantytown in Central Park, is sensational. Set to Al Jolson crooning 'I'm Sitting on Top of the World' the milieu of the Depression and the Big Apple is perfectly set up. The journey to Skull Island is less successful and could easily have been trimmed to ten minutes or less. But once there, the film takes off with one astounding set piece after another. Cinematic nirvana for the masses, the film is aided by a terrific turn by Naomi Watts who has to do much with little dialogue and nothing but a special effect to bounce off. At times unwieldy, the overall impact is enthralling and, ultimately, exhausting. JC-W

• *Ann Darrow* Naomi Watts, *Carl Denham* Jack Black, *Jack Driscoll* Adrien Brody, *Captain Englehorn* Thomas Kretschmann, *Preston* Colin Hanks, *Jimmy* Jamie Bell, *King Kong/Lumpy the Cook* Andy Serkis, *Hayes* Evan Parke, *Bruce Baxter* Kyle Chandler, *with* Lobo Chan, John Sumner, Craig Hall, Mark Hadlow, Peter Jackson, Lorraine Ashbourne.

• *Dir* Peter Jackson, *Pro* Jackson, Fran Walsh, Jan Blenkin and Carolynne Cunningma, *Co-Pro* Philippa Boyens and Eileen Moran, *Screenplay* Jackson, Walsh and Boyens, *Ph* Andrew Lesnie, *Pro Des* Grant Major, *Ed* Jamie Selkirk and Jabez Olssen, *M* James Newton Howard, *Costumes* Terry Ryan, *Visual Effects* Joe Letteri and Richard Taylor.

Universal/WingNut Films-UIP.
187 mins. USA/New Zealand. 2005.
Rel: 15 December 2005. Cert. 12A.

King's Game ★★★★

This political thriller from Denmark may not be individual enough to be memorable, but it's admirably efficient and certainly enjoyable. When just days before an election a party leader likely to win is seriously hurt in a car accident, the woman who looks set to be nominated in his place becomes subject to slanders in the media. Soon two journalists discover conspiracies that don't end there. Contemporary real-life parallels have been remarked on due to the film's talk of spin doctors and the like but it's actually reminiscent of *The Contender*(2000) and even of *Defence Of the Realm* (1985). This is a thoroughly reliable entertainment from one of the few Danish directors not into Dogme, Nikolaj Arcel. Original title: *Kongekabale*. MS

• *Ulrik Torp* Anders W. Berthelsen, *Erik Dreier* Jensen Søren Pilmark, *Lone Kjeldsen* Nastja Arcel, *Henrik Moll* Nicolas Bro, *Peter Schou* Lars Mikkelsen, *with* Ulf Pilgaard, Charlotte Munck, Lars Brygmann, Helle Fagralid, Kurt Ravn, Jens Jorgen Spottag, Jesper Langberg, Robert Hansen, Marianne Hogsbro.

• *Dir* Nikolaj Arcel, *Pro* Meta Louise Foldager, *Ex Pro* Bo Ehrhardt and Birgitte Hald, *Screenplay* Arcel and Rasmus Heisterberg, based on a novel by Niels Krause-Kjoer, *Ph* Rasmus Videbæk, *Pro Des* Niels Sejer, *Ed* Mikkel E. G. Nielsen, *M* Flemming Nordkrog and Henrik Munck, *Costumes* Helle Nielsen.

Nimbus Film/Zentropa Entertainments5 ApS/Film GEAR-Dogwoof Pictures.
107 mins. Denmark/Sweden/Norway. 2004. Rel: 23 September 2005. Cert. 12A.

Kinky Boots ★★★★

The title is a tad tawdry but *Kinky Boots* has charm and originality to spare. A grass roots, feel-good fable in the tradition of *The Full Monty* and *Calendar Girls*, this is a true story set in parallel worlds that could not be more different. When the meek, awkward Charlie Price inherits his father's antiquated shoe factory in Northampton, he knows a good brogue but is unversed in the ways of big business. As the future of his legacy looks set to implode, help arrives in the unlikely form of a large black drag queen from London's Soho… A paean to good old-fashioned craftsmanship, *Kinky Boots* trades on the nostalgia of England's north while injecting a liberal dose of rakish showbusiness. Although many British films have exploited this infallible formula, Julian Jarrold's directorial debut is rooted in enough reality to pull off its contrasting scenarios to rousing effect. Everything is just right. The numbers that Lola sings in his/her seedy club are sassy but fresh, the atmosphere of the factory claustrophobic and real and the supporting characters archetypal without being predictable. And Chiwetel Ejiofor (who we last saw as a Chicago gangster in *Four Brothers*) is a revelation as both a singer and a very fine lady. JC-W

• *Charlie Price* Joel Edgerton, *Lola* Chiwetel Ejiofor, *Lauren* Sarah-Jane Potts, *Nicola* Jemima Rooper, *Mel* Linda Bassett, *Don* Nick Frost, *Harold Price* Robert Pugh, *George* Ewan Hooper, *Mrs Cobb* Gwenllian Davies, *Jeannie* Kellie Bright, *with* Mona Hammond, Stephen Marcus, Geoffrey Streatfield, Leo Bill, Ilario Bisi-Pedro.

• *Dir* Julian Jarrold, *Pro* Nicholas Barton, Suzanne Mackie and Peter Ettedgui, *Co-Pro* Mairi Bett, *Screenplay* Geoff Deane and Tim Firth, *Ph* Eigil Byrd, *Pro Des* Alan Macdonald, *Ed* Emma Hickox, *M* Adrian Johnston; Rossini; tracks performed by Chiwetel Ejiofor, Kirsty MacColl, Lyn Collins, James Brown, Nina Simone, The Dub Pistols, Jemima Rooper, and David Bowie, *Costumes* Sammy Sheldon, *Choreography* Les Childs, *Singing Coach* Phil Bateman, *Drag Queen Consultant* Delbert 'Sandra' Bell.

Miramax/Harbour Pictures/Price Prods-Buena Vista International.
106 mins. UK/USA. 2005. Rel: 7 October 2005. Cert. 12A.

Kiss Kiss, Bang Bang ★★★½

On the run from police, small-time crook Harry Lockhart breaks into the audition for a new film and, sweating real angst, wins a screen test. Once in LA, he bumps into childhood flame Harmony Lane and, in the role of make-believe detective, finds himself in the middle of a real murder case… Shane Black – who, at 23, wrote the screenplay to *Lethal Weapon* – was obsessed with pulp detective fiction as a kid. Now, with his directorial debut, he brings the genre to the big screen and turns it on its head. Employing irreverent and witty dialogue, canny casting-against-type and a beguiling visual palette, he has created a tough, violent and hilarious diversion with a good number of genuine belly laughs. Unfortunately, Black also takes a few too many liberties with Downey Jr's tongue-in-cheek, gimmicky

Scissors, stone, scissors, *Kiss Kiss Bang Bang*: Val Kilmer and Robert Downey Jr play games in Shane Black's irreverent and witty homage (from Warner)

narration, which is more jarring than liberating (such as the resurrection of dead characters). Still, with Downey Jr on consummate form, Kilmer taking the piss out of his own persona and Monaghan proving to be an instant star (recalling the very young Kathleen Turner), this is a *bona fide* pleasure for fans of original, bracing cinema. JC-W

• *Harry Lockhart* Robert Downey Jr., *Perry van Shrike* aka `Gay Perry'* Val Kilmer, *Harmony Faith Lane* Michelle Monaghan, *Harlan Dexter* Corbin Bernsen, *Mr Frying Pan* Dash Mihouk, *Dabney Shaw* Larry Miller, *Flicka* Angela Lindvall, *Harry, aged nine* Indio Falconer Downey, *with* Rockmond Dunbar, Shannyn Sossamon, Josh Richman, Nancy Fish, Judie Aronson, Vincent Laresca.

• *Dir* and *Screenplay* Shane Black, *Pro* Joel Silver, *Ex Pro* Susan Levin and Steve Richards, *Co-Pro* Carrie Morrow, *Ph* Michael Barrett, *Pro Des* Aaron Osborne, *Ed* Jim Page, *M* John Ottman, *Costumes* Christopher J. Kristoff.

Warner/Silver Pictures-Warner.
102 mins. USA. 2005. Rel: 11 November 2005. Cert. 15.

Lady Vengeance ★★½

Sent to prison at the age of 19 for the murder of a six-year-old boy, Lee Geum-ja earns the reputation of an angel behind bars. Once outside – 13 years later – Geum-ja reveals a new side to her personality as she calls on the services of her fellow inmates to implement her revenge... There's no denying the opulent artistry of director Park Chan-Wook. However, here he's saddled himself with such an unengaging anti-heroine that it's hard to throw oneself into the plot's myriad confections. Everybody comments on Geum-ja's beauty, but Lee Young-ae hardly fits the bill (except, very occasionally, when she smiles). The rest of the film – like a Korean antithesis of *Amélie* – is perversely convoluted and very hard to follow. There are scenes, though, that you are unlikely to forget in a hurry, not least the video of a little girl being hanged and when Geum-ja shoots her daughter's new puppy. Original title: *Chin-jeol-han Geum-ja-ssi.* JC-W

• *Lee Geum-ja* Lee Young-ae, *Teacher Baek* Choi Min-sik, *Geun-shik* Kim Si-hu, *Chief Choi* Nam Il-woo, *preacher* Kim Byeong-ok, *Mr Chang* Oh Dai-su, *Park Yi-jeong* Lee Seung-shin.

• *Dir* Park Chan-Wook, *Pro* Lee Tae-hun, Cho Young-wuk and Lee Chun-young, *Ex Pro* Miky Lee, Park Dong-ho, Kim Joo-sung and Shin Shang-han, *Screenplay* Park and Chung Seo-kyung, *Ph* Chung-hoon, *Pro Des* Haw-sung, *Ed* Kim Sang-bum and Kim Jae-bum, *M* Cho Young-wuk, Costumes Cho Sang-*Martial Arts* Kwon Seung-ku.

CJ Entertainment/Moho Film-Tartan Films.
115 mins. South Korea. 2005. Rel: 10 February 2006. Cert. 18.

The Lake House ★★½

When Kate Forster reluctantly moves from the glass lake house in which she has lived for two years, she leaves a letter for the next tenant. However, he – successful architect Alex Burnham – is actually moving into an abandoned house never occupied by anybody outside his family. Even so, a correspondence ensues in which Kate and Alex find themselves inexorably drawn to each other – across a portal that defies rational physics... Whether or not one embraces the syrupy principles of this Mills & Boon crowd-pleaser depends entirely on personality. If you can accept Sandra Bullock as a lovelorn doctor and Keanu as a top Chicago planner, then you are halfway there. But it will take somebody with the brain of Stephen Hawking to work out the temporal logistics. Gorgeously photographed and intriguingly plotted, the film is adapted from the South Korean romance *Il Mare* (aka *Siworae*; 2000) and will have diehard romantics swooning in the aisles. JC-W

• *Alex Burnham* Keanu Reeves, *Dr Kate Forster* Sandra Bullock, *Morgan* Dylan Walsh, *Dr Anna Klyczynski* Shohreh Aghdashloo, *Simon Wyler* Christopher Plummer, *Henry Wyler* Ebon Moss-Bachrach, *Mona* Lynn Collins, *with* Willeke van Ammelrooy, Mike Bacarella,, Kevin Brennan.

• *Dir* Alejandro Agresti, *Pro* Doug Davison and Roy Lee, *Ex Pro* Mary McLaglen, Erwin Stoff, Dana Goldberg and Bruce Berman, *Co-Pro* Sonny Mallhi, *Screenplay* David Auburn, *Ph* Alar Kivilo, *Pro Des* Nathan Crowley, *Ed* Lynzee Klingman and Alejandro Brodersohn, *M* Rachel Portman, *Costumes* Deena Appel, *Sound* Frank Gaeta.

Warner/Village Roadshow/
Vertigo Entertainment-Warner.
98 mins. USA. 2006. Rel: 23 June 2006.
Cert. PG.

Land of the Dead ★★★

With the world taken over by the walking dead – or 'walkers', as they have become known – what's left of the living have barricaded themselves into a fortified city. As the elite attempt to maintain a facade of genteel comfort, the less fortunate struggle to survive on the streets... It's been twenty years since George A. Romero completed his terrifying trilogy with *Dawn of the Dead* (1985). Since then, the parameters of the horror movie have been moved all over the place, thanks in large part to *Scream*. Clearly taking this on board, Romero introduces a new note of self-conscious jokiness and in the process looses the raw power of his franchise. With its glossy production values and recognisable faces (the casting of Dennis Hopper as the villain is unimaginative and misjudged), the film just isn't scary. The zombies, though, are a hoot, and every time the film cuts away from its trite storyline, Romero's morbid creativity reaps dividends. FYI: As a deference to horror's new climate, Romero has cast Simon Pegg and Edgar Wright – the creators of *Shaun of the Dead* – as a pair of zombies who have their picture taken with partygoers. JC-W

• *Riley* Simon Baker, *Slack* Asia Argento, *Kaufman* Dennis Hopper, *Charlie* Robert Joy, *Cholo* John Leguizamo, *Big Daddy* Eugene Clark, *Pretty Boy* Joanne Boland, *with* Tony Nappo, Jennifer Baxter, Boyd Banks, Krista Bridges, Jonathan Whittaker, Peter Outerbridge, Tina Romero, Brian Renfro, Simon Pegg, Edgar Wright, Tom Savini.

• *Dir* and *Screenplay* George A. Romero, *Pro* Mark Canton, Peter Grunwald and Bernie Goldmann, *Ex Pro* Steve Barnett, Dennis E. Jones, Ryan Kavanaugh and Lynwood Spinks, *Ph* Miroslaw Baszak, *Pro Des* Arv Greywal, *Ed* Michael Doherty, *M* Reinhold Heil and Johnny Klimek, *Costumes* Alex Kavanagh.

Universal/Atmosphere Entertainment/Wild Bunch-UIP. 93 mins. USA/Canada/France. 2005. Rel: 23 September 2005. Cert. 15.

Lassie ★★½

When Sam Carraclough loses his job down the pits, he is forced to sell the family's prize asset, a beautiful collie. But Lassie cannot bear to be apart from the only family she knows and, against extraordinary odds, struggles to return to them... For 62 years now Lassie has endured as a canine American institution. However, the collie began as a Yorkshire creation in a 1938 short story by Eric Knight that first appeared in *The Saturday Evening Post*. Writer-director Charles Sturridge (TV's *Brideshead Revisited* and *Longitude*) attempts to bring Lassie home and draws his material from Knight's original novel (presciently titled *Lassie Come Home*; 1940). The result is a production strong on English scenery (albeit filmed in Ireland, Scotland and the Isle of Man) but weak on emotional heft. There is also an unevenness in the acting (Samantha Morton aims for kitchen sink realism, Peter O'Toole for the gods), and much dramatic stasis. Well intentioned to a fault, the film is never truly convincing (the snow looks like foam, the music is mechanical and intrusive), although it does display a simple charm. JC-W

• *The Duke of Rudling* Peter O'Toole, *Sarah Carraclough* Samantha Morton, *Sam Carraclough* John Lynch, *Joe Carraclough* Jonathan Mason, *Cilla* Hester Odgers, *Rowlie* Peter Dinklage, *Hynes* Steve Pemberton, *Daisy* Jemma Redgrave, *Hulton* Edward Fox, *French* John Standing, *Mapes* Gregor Fisher, *O'Donnell* Brian Pettifer, *Jeanie* Kelly Macdonald, *with* Gerry O'Brien, Jamie Lee, Robert Hardy, Nicholas Lyndhurst, Gabrielle Lloyd, Susie Lamb, Ken Drury, Angela Thorne, Peter Wight, Ian Mercer.

• *Dir* and *Screenplay* Charles Sturridge, *Pro* Sturridge, Ed Guiney and Francesca Barra, *Ex Pro* Steve Christian, Eric Ellenbogen, Louise Goodsill, Ralph Kamp, Andrew Lowe and Doug Schwalbe, *Co-Pro* Samuel Hadida and Victor Hadida, *Line Pro* Noëlette Buckley, *Ph* Howard Atherton, *Pro Des* John Paul Kelly, *Ed* Peter Coulson and Adam Green, *M* Adrian Johnston, *Costumes* Charlotte Walter.

Odyssey Entertainment/Isle of Man Film/Classic Media/ First Sight Films-Entertainment. 99 mins. Ireland/UK/France/USA. 2005. Rel: 16 December 2005. Cert. PG.

Last Days ★

Intentionally exploitative of Kurt Cobain's own demise, writer-director Gus Van Sant follows his fictional musician Blake as he wanders through the last days of his uninspired and supposedly out-of-control life... Presumably, the meandering camera work, disjointed scenes and non-existent plot are a metaphor for Blake's life. Unfortunately, just as Blake fails to connect to the people and events around him,

Vacational hazard: Queen Latifah and Gérard Depardieu ham it up in Wayne Wang's homespun *Last Holiday* (from UIP)

there's no connection formed between Blake and the viewer. I simply don't care about him – even though I *want* to care. This is filmmaking at its worst: pretentious, self-indulgent and lacking artistry or insight. Ultimately, one can only conclude that Blake's life was as meaningless as this movie. SWM

• *Blake* Michael Pitt, *Luke* Lukas Haas, *Asia* Asia Argento, *Scott* Scott Green, *Nicole* Nicole Vicius, *detective* Ricky Jay, *Donovan* Ryan Orion, *guy in club* Harmony Korine, *band in club* The Hermitt, *record executive* Kim Gordon, *elder Friberg #1* Adam Friberg, *elder Friberg # 2* Andy Friberg, *Yellow Book salesman* Thadeus A. Thomas, *tree trimmer* Chip Marks.

• *Dir, Screenplay* and *Ed* Gus Van Sant, *Pro* Dany Wolf, *Ph* Harris Savides, *Art Dir* Tim Grimes, *Costumes* Michelle Matland, *Sound* Leslie Shatz.

HBO Films/Meno Film Co-Optimum Releasing. 96 mins. USA. 2004. Rel: 2 September 2005. Cert. 15.

Last Holiday ★★

Told that she has just three weeks to live, New Orleans sales assistant Georgia Byrd decides to spend her last days in luxury. So she hightails it to the five-star Grand Hotel Pupp in Karlovy Vary to let her hair down and eat everything on the menu… Considering that Wayne Wang started out directing such nuanced pieces as *Chan is Missing*, *Eat a Bowl of Tea* and *Smoke*, it's increasingly baffling that he now lends his name to such flotsam as *Anywhere But Here*, *Maid in Manhattan* and *Because of Winn-Dixie*. He continues the downward trend with this folksy, predictable comedy-drama inspired by an old screenplay by none other than J.B. Priestley. Originally a very English vehicle for Alec Guinness (made in 1950), the remake has been given a Capraesque spin with a homespun sermon of living every day as if it's your last that sticks in the craw. Thankfully, Queen Latifah has learned to underplay her talents, but here to little avail. EB

• *Georgia Byrd* Queen Latifah, *Sean Matthews* LL Cool J, *Matthew Kragen* Timothy Hutton, *Chef Didier* Gérard Depardieu, *Ms Burns* Alicia Witt, *Senator Dillings* Giancarlo Esposito, *Rochelle* Jane Adams, *with* Mike Estime, Susan Kellerman, Ranjit Chowdhry, Michael Nouri, Smokey Robinson.

• *Dir* Wayne Wang, *Pro* Laurence Mark and Jack Rapke, *Ex Pro* Robert Zemeckis, Steve Starkey, Richard Vane, Peter S. Seaman and Jeffrey Price, *Screenplay* Price and Seaman, *Ph* Geoffrey Simpson, *Pro Des* William Arnold, *Ed* Deirdre Slevin, *M* George Fenton, *Costumes* Daniel Orlandi.

Paramount/Imagemovers/Laurence Mark-UIP. 111 mins. USA. 2005. Rel: 3 March 2006. Cert. 12A.

The Last Mitterrand ★★★½

That fine director from Marseilles, Robert Guédiguian, switches styles most successfully to give us this classically composed study of a French president, the late François Mitterand. It doesn't claim to be wholly factual but the portrait is intended as a true one. Looking back when already close to death, the president gives an interview to a journalist that offers a perspective on his life. The film sometimes questions his assertions but is generally admiring. On this level, however, there's a problem for those like myself who are not well versed in French political history because for us many references will be obscure (if you are knowledgable in this area you can safely increase the rating above). But the film is also a study of a great actor magnificent in old age and Michel Bouquet's performance makes this essential viewing. Original title: *Le Promeneur Du Champ De Mars*. MS

• *President François Mitterand* Michel Bouquet, *Antoine Moreau* Jalil Lespert, *Dr Jeantot* Philippe Fretun, *Jeanne* Anne Cantineau, *Judith* Sarah Grappin, *Mado* Catherine Salviat, *with* Jean-Claude Frissung, Philippe Lemercier, Genevieve Casile, Gisele Casadesus.

• *Dir* Robert Guédiguian, *Pro* Frank Le Wita, *Co-Ex Pro* Guédiguian and Marc de Bayser, *Screenplay* Gilles Taurand and Georges-Marc Benamou, based on Benamou's book *Le dernier Mitterrand*, *Ph* Renato Berta, *Art Dir* Michel Vandstien, *Ed* Bernard Sasia, *Costumes* Juliette Chanaud.

Film Oblige/Agat Films/Art France Cinéma/ Canal Plus-Pathé. 116 mins. France/Switzerland. 2004. Rel: 29 July 2005. Cert. PG.

The Legend of Zorro ★½

As the territory of California is about to join the United States (the year is 1850), Armand, an unscrupulous French aristocrat, plots to take over the terrain. However, Don Alejandro de la Vega – who fights for his fellow countrymen in the guise of the masked Zorro – smells a rat. But Alejandro's wife, Elena, has forbidden him to continue his life as an undercover law-enforcer and, in spite, turns to the affections of Armand himself… Not only is *The Legend of Zorro* – a sequel to 1998's *The Mask of Zorro* – an unwieldy, terminally silly farce, it is guilty of blatant plagiarism. Ripping off other movies with gay abandon (complete with a derivative, overblown score), it reaches a nadir when it steals a scene straight out of the 1965 western *Cat Ballou*. Slumped drunkenly against a wall on his horse, Zorro shares a bottle with his trusty steed, just as Lee Marvin did 40 years earlier. But this *Zorro* is not a spoof in the tradition of *Airplane!* and *The Naked Gun*, but a cumbersome, wearisome pantomime which plays like a cartoon without a hint of animation (except, perhaps, for the preposterous computer-generated stunts). JC-W

• *Don Alejandro de la Vega* aka *Zorro* Antonio Banderas, *Elena de la Vega* Catherine Zeta-Jones, *Count Armand* Rufus Sewell, *Jacob McGivens* Nick Chinlund, *Joaquin de la Vega* Adrian Alonso, *with* Julio Oscar Mechoso, Shuler Hensley, Michael Emerson, Alberto Reyes, Pedro Armendáriz, Mary Crosby, Leo Burmester.

Masked balls-up: Antonio Banderas cuts a swath
in Martin Campbell's cumbersome and wearisome
The Legend of Zorro (from Sony Pictures)

• *Dir* Martin Campbell, *Pro* Walter F. Parkes, Laurie MacDonald and Lloyd Phillips, *Ex Pro* Steven Spielberg, Gary Barber and Roger Birnbaum, *Co-Pro* John Gertz, *Screenplay* Roberto Orci and Alex Kurtzman, from a story by Orci, Kurtzman, Ted Elliott and Terry Rossio, *Ph* Phil Meheux, *Pro Des* Cecilia Montiel, *Ed* Stuart Baird, *M* James Horner, *Costumes* Graciela Mazon.

Columbia/Spyglass/Amblin-Columbia TriStar. 130 mins. USA. 2005. Rel: 28 October 2005. Cert. PG.

Lemming ★★½

Dominik Moll's third directorial venture has a fine cast, looks handsome and utilises a wide range of music but it split opinion at Cannes and, unlike many, I find myself siding with those who feel it doesn't work. That's because of the material which is all over the place as it tells of two married couples linked by the younger husband, an engineer, working for the older one whose relationship with his wife is embittered. Characteristically Moll provides Hitchcockian echoes but essentially this sets out as a psychological thriller, adopts symbolism (the lemming of the title which blocks a kitchen sink) and then becomes a supernatural tale halfway between a ghost story and a tale of possession. Moll wanted to leave the viewer unable to pinpoint a genre but in succeeding he ended up with a work in which for me the various elements cancel each other out leaving nothing that satisfies. MS

• *Alain Getty* Laurent Lucas, *Bénédicte Getty* Charlotte Gainsbourg, *Alice Pollock* Charlotte Rampling, *Richard Pollock* André Dussollier, *Nicolas Chevalier* Jacques Bonnaffé, *Francine* Veronique Affholder, *with* Michel Cassagne, Fabrice Robert, Natacha Boussaa.

• *Dir* Dominik Moll, *Pro* Michel Saint-Jean, *Screenplay* Moll and Gilles Marchand, *Ph* Jean-Marc Fabre, *Ed* Mike Fromentin, *M* David Sinclair Whitaker, *Costumes* Virginie Montel and Isabelle Pannetier.

Diaphana Films/ France 3 Cinéma/Canal Plus-Artificial Eye. 130 mins. France. 2005. Rel: 28 April 2006. Cert. 15.

The Libertine ★★½

Quoted by Tennyson and an inspiration to Voltaire, John Wilmot was the bad boy of the literary set in late 17th century England. Satirical to a point of insurrection, he taunted King Charles II and leched his way through the whorehouses of London, even though he was married (to a bride he had abducted). However, his real love was the theatre – and an actress with too much spirit even for him to defile... Peering directly at the camera, his face looming out of the gloom, John Wilmot declares, 'you will not like me... It's a bone-hard medical fact – and I put it about.' Stephen Jeffreys' play and this, his own adaptation, is full of such ribald innuendo and it gets dirtier by the minute. Johnny Depp, in one of his most extravagant parts yet, is a seductive, silver-tongued, gutter-mouthed monster who wields his provocative honesty like a spear. *The Libertine* looks wonderful – Rembrandt on a budget

– but loses its momentum when Wilmot turns to love and self-destruction. Indeed, after an invigorating start, the film shuffles to a crawl by the halfway mark. JC-W

• *John Wilmot, 2nd Earl of Rochester* Johnny Depp, *Elizabeth Barry* Samantha Morton, *Charles II* John Malkovich, *Elizabeth Malet* Rosamund Pike, *George Etherege* Tom Hollander, *Charles Sackville* Johnny Vegas, *Jane* Kelly Reilly, *Harris* Jack Davenport, *Alcock* Richard Coyle, *Countess* Francesca Annis, *Downs* Rupert Friend, *Molly Luscombe* Claire Higgins, *with* Paul Ritter, Stanley Townsend, Freddie Jones, Robert Wilfort, Niall Buggy, Peter Howell, T.P. McKenna.

• *Dir* Laurence Dunmore, *Pro* Lianne Halfon, John Malkovich and Russell Smith, *Ex Pro* Chase Bailey, Steve Christian, Marc Samuelson, Peter Samuelson, Ralph Kamp, Louise Goodsill, Donald Starr, Colin Leventhal and Daniel B. Taylor, *Line Pro* Mairi Bett, *Screenplay* Stephen Jeffreys, *Ph* Alexander Melman, *Pro Des* Ben Van Os, *Ed* Jill Bilcock, *M* Michael Nyman, *Costumes* Dien Van Straalen.

Weinstein Films/Isle of Man Film/Mr Mudd-Entertainment. 114 mins. USA/UK. 2005. Rel: 18 November 2005. Cert. 18.

Live and Become ★★★

Much applauded by some, this overlong film has great potential since its story covers unfamiliar territory. It's about Ethiopian Jews who as part of the airlift of 1985 known as 'Operation Moses' were repatriated and offered a new life in Israel, although being black there could create problems. This particular story concerns a boy of nine, Schlomo, whose widowed mother takes a desperate chance to give him a worthwhile life when she arranges for Schlomo to be substituted for a Jewish child who dies before he can take his arranged departure. Mainly set in Israel, the epic tale continues by taking Schlomo through his teenage years and on into adulthood throughout which time his attempts to pass as Jewish remain central. There are serious issues here but also romantic dramas akin to soap opera and a feel-good climax too contrived to be touching. Sincere though it is, this populist approach seems unworthy of the theme. Original title: *Va, vis et deviens.* MS

• *Yaël, Schlomo's Israeli mother* Yaël Abecassis, *Yoram, Schlomo's Israeli father* Roschdy Zem, *Schlomo as a man* Sirak M. Sabahat, *Schlomo as a boy* Mosche Agazai, *Schlomo as a teenager* Mosche Abebe, *Sarah* Roni Hadar, *Schlomo's real mother* Meskie Shibru Sivan, *Hana, Schlomo's Ethiopian Jewish mother* Mimi Abonesh Kebede.

• *Dir* Radu Mihaileanu, *Pro* Mihaileanu, Denis Carot, Marie Manmonteil, Riccardo Tozzi, Giovanni Stabilini, Marco Chimenz and Dominique Janne, *Ex Pro* Marek Rosenbaum and Itai Tamir, *Screenplay* Mihaileanu and Alain-Michel Blanc, *Ph* Remy Chevrin, *Art Dir* Eytan Levy, *Ed* Ludo Troch, *M* Armand Amar, *Costumes* Rona Doran.

Elzévir Films/Oï Oï Oï Prods/France 3 Cinéma/Eurimages/

Canal Plus-The Works.
149 mins. France/Italy/Belgium/Israel. 2005.
Rel: 30 December 2005. Cert. 12A.

Lobo ★½

Spain/France; the 1970s. Established in 1959 to combat
Franco's dictatorship and to fight for a state independent of
France and Spain, the Basque organisation ETA increasingly
resorted to violence. Disapproving of such tactics, Txema, a
Basque construction worker, took it upon himself to worm
his way into the heart of the group and expose them to the
secret police… As an exploration of the Basque Troubles
– drawn from 'real events' – *Lobo* could hardly be more dull.
With its procession of captions, nocturnal meetings and men
in leather jackets, it wilfully avoids any identifiable human
detail. It's also hard to know where the film's sympathies
lie, with the blank-faced 'hero', the gun-toting terrorists or
the unscrupulous police who look and behave like gangsters.
With its naff music and artless direction, *Lobo* recalls those
incredibly tedious Italian cop thrillers of the Seventies. Aka
Wolf. JC-W

• *Txema* aka `The Wolf' Eduardo Noriega, *Ricardo* José
Coronado, *Nelson* Patrick Bruel, *Amaya* Mélanie Doutey,
Begoña Silvia Abascal, *Pantxo* Santiago Ramos, *Asier* Jorge
Sanz, *Matías* Manuel Zarzo, *Comandante Palacios* Juan
Fernández.

• *Dir* Miguel Courtois, *Pro* Julio Fernández and Melchor
Miralles, *Line Pro* Miguel Torrente and Antonio Onetti,
Screenplay Onetti, *Ph* Néstor Calvo, *Art Dir* Luis Vallés, *Ed*
Guillermo Maldonado, *M* Francesc Gener, *Costumes* Pedro
Moreno and Victoria Velázquez.

Melchor Miralles & Julio Fernández/Mundo Ficción/
Castelao Prods-Dogwoof Pictures.
124 mins. Spain. 2004. Rel: 16 June 2006. Cert. 15.

The Longest Yard ★½

Six years after being banned from the NFL for throwing a
game, Paul 'Wrecking' Crewe has become a beer-swilling
slouch. When he crashes his girlfriend's expensive sports car
under the influence, he's sent down for three years at the
Allenville Federal Penitentiary in Texas. It transpires that
the prison's formidable warden, Hazen, has pulled a number
of strings to get Crewe there, so that the latter can coach a
team of inmates. Apparently, Hazen is looking for another
excuse to let his sadistic guards kick some penitentiary butt…
This is the second remake of Robert Aldrich's violent 1974
comedy-drama *The Longest Yard*, the first being the 2001
Mean Machine, with Vinnie Jones. And with the standard
requirements of an Adam Sandler vehicle – smug, smart-ass
protagonist, Rob Schneider cameo and rampant homophobia
– *The Longest Yard* is a headache-inducing scrum of prison
stereotypes and bone-crunching stunts. Sandler himself has
seldom been less endearing, while the grinding predictability
of the plot is pretty much laugh-free. JC-W

• *Paul 'Wrecking' Crew* Adam Sandler, *Caretaker* Chris

Rock, *Warden Hazen* James Cromwell, *Megget* Nelly, *Captain
Knauer* William Fichtner, *Nate Scarborough* Burt Reynolds,
Deacon Moss Michael Irvin, *Battle* Bill Goldberg, *with* Cloris
Leachman, Allen Covert, Bob Sapp, Nicholas Turturro, Dalip
Singh, David Patrick Kelly, Rob Schneider, Bill Romanowski,
Brian Bosworth, Terry Crews, Steve Austin, Kevin Nash,
Patrick Bristow, Ed Lauter, and (unbilled) *Lena* Courteney
Cox-Arquette.

• *Dir* Peter Segal, *Pro* Jack Giarraputo, *Ex Pro* Adam Sandler,
Van Toffler, David Gale, Barry Bernardi, Allen Covert, Tim
Herlihy, Michael Ewing and Albert S. Ruddy, *Co-Pro* Heather
Parry, *Screenplay* Sheldon Turner, based on the screenplay by
Tracy Keenan Wynn from a story by Albert S. Ruddy, *Ph*
Dean Semler, *Pro Des* Perry Andelin Blake, *Ed* Jeff Gourson,
M Teddy Castellucci; tracks performed by No Doubt, Lynyrd
Skynyrd, Jet, The Hollies, Public Enemy, D12 & Eminem,
Nelly, The Crystal Method, Creedence Clearwater Revival,
Big Head Todd & The Monsters with John Lee Hooker,
Wayne Hancock, Norman Greenbaum, Run DMC, Ludacris
& Lazy Eye, AC/DC, Red Hot Chili Peppers, etc, *Costumes*
Ellen Lutter, *Sound*
Derek Vanderhorst.

Columbia/Paramount/Happy Madison/MTV Films/
Callahan Filmworks-Columbia TriStar.
113 mins. USA. 2005. Rel: 9 September 2005. Cert. 12A.

Lord of War ★★½

Standing at the brink of a sea of spent bullet cartridges,
arms dealer Yuri Orlov tells us that there is now one firearm
for every twelve people on the planet. 'The question is,' he
continues, 'how do we arm the other eleven?' Ambitious,
greedy and amoral, Yuri wrestles with his conscience as his
knack for selling guns lifts him out of the ghetto of New
York's Little Odessa and into the jet stream of the very, very
rich… Andrew Niccol is a fine writer-director of ideas but
the ideas get in the way of the narrative in this, his third
directorial effort. With the opening credits following the
course of a bullet instead of a feather, this is Niccol's own
Forrest Gump, sweeping across decades and countries as our
hero nears his destiny. Like Gump, Orlov gets the girl of
his dreams, swaps jokes with world leaders and becomes
something of a media sensation. But Orlov deals in death and
while we have shared his most intimate thoughts, we cannot
share his moral justifications. Acerbic, stylish, disturbing and
often predictable, *Lord of War* is an unwieldy, dour satire that
leaves a really nasty taste in the mouth. JC-W

• *Yuri Orlov* Nicolas Cage, *Jack Valentine* Ethan Hawke, *Vitaly
Orlov* Jared Leto, *Ava Fontaine* Bridget Moynahan, *Simeon Weisz*
Ian Holm, *André Baptiste Snr* Eamonn Walker, *André Baptiste
Jr* Sammi Rotibi, *Uncle Dmitri* Eugene Lazarev, *with* Jean-
Pierre Nshanian, Tanya Finch, Donald Sutherland, Weston
Cage.

• *Dir and Screenplay* Andrew Niccol, *Pro* Niccol, Philippe
Rousselet and Norm Golightly, *Ex Pro* Fabrice Gianfermi,
Bradley Cramp, Michael Mendelsohn, James D. Stern,

The Weapon Man: Nicolas Cage stars in Andrew Niccol's stylish if predictable *Lord of War* (from Momentum Pictures)

Christopher Eberts, Gary Hamilton and Andreas Schmid, *Ph* Amir Mokri, *Pro Des* Jean Vincent Puzos, *Ed* Zach Staenberg, *M* Antônio Pinto, *Costumes* Elisaabetta Beraldo

Entertainment Manufacturing Co./Saturn Films/Rising Star/Endgame Entertainment, etc-Momentum Pictures. 121 mins. USA/Germany. 2005. Rel: 14 October 2005. Cert. 15.

Lords of Dogtown ★★

Dogtown, Venice, California; the 1970s. As a heatwave empties the swimming pools of Southern California, a rebel group of surfers take advantage of their new polyurethane wheels to start a skateboarding craze… If you like to watch skateboarding, you may get a kick out of this. A loose dramatisation of Stacy Peralta's documentary *Dogtown and Z-Boys*, *Lords of Dogtown* is scripted by Peralta himself and is directed by Catherine Hardwicke, the latter who made her debut with the perceptive and harrowing *thirteen* (2003). There is a lot of skateboarding action in *Lords of Dogtown* and there's a lot of fast-cut partying, some surfing, high jinks and low IQs. Rebecca DeMornay is still looking shapely at 43 – in the Holly Hunter part – and Heath Ledger does a wry impression of a young Val Kilmer, complete with omnipresent shades and wild hair. But considering that this is from the director of *thirteen*, it is surprisingly undramatic and ultimately rather tedious. A story would've been nice. JC-W

• *Jay Adams* Emile Hirsch, *Tony Alva* Victor Rasuk, *Stacy Peralta* John Robinson, *Sid* Michael Angarano, *Kathy Alva* Nikki Reed, *Skip Engblom* Heath Ledger, *Philaine* Rebecca DeMornay, *Topper Burks* Johnny Knoxville, *Mr Alva* Julio Oscar Mechoso, *Chino* Vincent Laresca, *Craig Stecyk* Pablo Schreiber, *Amelia* Sofia Vergara, *TV director* Stacy Peralta, *with* William Mapother, Elden Henson, Melonie Diaz, Matt Malloy, Bill Cusack, America Ferrera, Jay Adams, Tony Alva, Charles Napier, Bai Ling, Alexis Arquette, Rebecca Silva.

• *Dir* Catherine Hardwicke, *Pro* John Linson, *Ex Pro* Art Linson, David Fincher and Joe Drake, *Co-Pro* Ginger Sledge, *Screenplay* Stacy Peralta, *Ph* Elliot Davis, *Pro Des* Chris Gorak, *Ed* Nancy Richardson, *M* Mark Mothersbaugh, *Costumes* Cindy Evans.

Columbia/Linson Films/Senator International-Columbia TriStar. 106 mins. USA. 2005. Rel: 16 September 2005. Cert. 12A.

Los Debutantes

See *Debutantes, Los*.

Lost Embrace ★★★

Set in a Jewish quarter of Buenos Aires, Daniel Burman's feature is strong on atmosphere and not without autobiographical elements. Despite some bothersome hand-held camera work, it's engaging, but there's a conflict that weakens the over-all impact. Much of the piece is comedic centred on the inhabitants of a small shopping mall yet simultaneously it's the story of a son brought up by his mother and of his need for the father who returns after 16 years but whom he blames for letting down his mother. The lightness of the inconsequential comedy that takes up two thirds of the movie limits the impact of the drama, which calls for greater insight and more detailed dramatisation. It's all quite viewable nevertheless and pleasantly acted. MS

• *Ariel* Daniel Hendler, *Sonia* Adriana Aizenberg, *Elias* Jorge D'Elia, *Joseph* Sergio Boris, *Mitelman* Diego Korol, *Senior Saligani* Atilio Pozzobón, *Rita* Silvina Bosco, *Osvaldo* Isaac Fajn, *Marcos 'El Colorado'* Salo Pasik, *Estela* Melina Petriella, *Rabbi Benderson* Norman Erlich, *Grandmother* Rosita Londner.

• *Dir* Daniel Burman, *Pro* Diego Dubcovsky and Daniel Burman, *Ex Pro* Dubcovsky, *Screenplay* Marcelo Birmajer and Daniel Burman, *Ph* Ramiro Civita, *Art Dir* María Eugenia Sueiro, *Ed* Alejandro Brodersohn, *M* Cesar Lerner, *Costumes* Roberta Pesci, *Sound* Martin Grignaschi.

BD Cine/Paradis Films/Classic/Wanda Vision/
Canal Plus-Axiom Films.
99 mins. Argentina/France/Italy/Spain/Netherlands.
2003. Rel: 28 April 2006.
Cert. 15.

Love + Hate ★★

Northern England; today. Coming from a traditional Pakistani family, it is a big deal for the 17-year-old Naseema to start work in the big outside world. But her presence at the decorating shop where she's hired as a dogsbody upsets co-worker Adam, who's a died-in-the-wool racist. Gradually, though, Adam finds himself drawn to the pretty, unassuming outsider… Utilising improvisation and non-professional actors, TV director Dominic Savage aims for a hard-edged naturalism that merely emphasises his inexperience as a filmmaker. While his leading lady, Samina Awan, is a genuine find, the other actors fail to bring their roles to life, resulting in a major shortfall in emotional engagement. It's impossible to fathom what the bright and sensitive Naseema sees in Adam, a surly, awkward and inarticulate black hole of humanity. If we'd been given one glimpse of his soul, a shared interest – *anything* – then maybe we could've suspended our disbelief. The film is also visually uneven and implausibly rife with coincidence, while Rupert Gregson-Williams' lush, orchestral score is entirely out-of-place.
JC-W

• *Naseema* Samina Awan, *Adam* Tom Hudson, *Michelle* Nichola Burley, *Yousif* Wasim Zakir, *Pete* Peter O'Connor, *Derek* Dean Andrews, *Sean* Ryan Leslie, *Shane* Michael McNulty, *with* Aliya Bhatti, Mohammed Rafique, Kathy Sharples, Tracy Brabin.

• *Dir* and *Screenplay* Dominic Savage, *Pro* Neris Thomas, *Ex Pro* Robert Jones, David M. Thompson and Ruth Caleb, *Line Pro* Michas Kotz, *Ph* Barry Ackroyd, *Pro Des* Phil Rawsthorne, *Ed* David G. Hill and Nicolas Gaster, *M* Rupert Gregson-Williams; tracks perrformed by Shystie, Gary Lightbody, Stephen Fretwell, Snow Patrol, Ian Brown, and Keane, *Costumes* Justine Luxton.

UK Film Council/BBC Films/Momentum Pictures-
Verve Pictures.
86 mins. UK/Ireland. 2005. Rel: 5 May 2006.
Cert. 15.

Lower City ★★

Deco and Naldinho have been friends since childhood. Determined to put their past of petty crime behind them, they now operate a small cargo ship, but their earnings are meagre. Then they meet up with a pretty young prostitute, Karinna, and accept her services in lieu of her fare. Soon, neither can face life without her… It's hard to know why anyone would want to sit through this, unless, of course, they're potty about the underbelly of Brazil or are, perhaps, a South American casting director. As it happens, the performances are not at all bad (Lázaro Ramos in particular reveals a strong cinematic presence), while first-time director Sérgio Machado avoids many of the clichés of first-time directors. Nonetheless, his and Karim Ainouz' script is seriously underdeveloped, leaving a film without a plot peopled by characters we have no reason to care about. JC-W

• *Karinna* Alice Braga, *Deco* Lázaro Ramos, *Naldinho* Wagner Moura, *Luzinete* Maria Menezes, *Sirlene* Débora Santiago, *Zilu* Divina Valéria.

• *Dir* Sérgio Machado, *Pro* Mauricio Andrade Ramos and Walter Salles, *Assoc Pro* Donald Ranvaud and Robert Bevan, *Line Pro* Marcelo Torres, *Screenplay* Machado and Karim Ainouz, *Ph* Toca Seabra, *Pro Des* Marcos Pedroso, *Ed* Isabela Monteiro de Castro, *M* Carlinhos Brown and Beto Villares, *Costumes* Cristina Camargo and André Simonetti, *Actors' Coach* Fátima Toledo.

VideoFilms/Buena Onda-Verve Pictures.
97 mins. Brazil/UK. 2005. Rel: 2 December 2005. Cert. 18.

Lucky Number Slevin ★★★½

Slevin Kelevra is having an exceptionally bad day. He's lost his job, he's discovered that his apartment is condemned and he's caught his girlfriend *in flagrante delicto*. He then has his wallet stolen in the street. Stopping to take a shower at the flat of his friend Nick Fisher – the latter who has gone missing – Slevin is accosted by two goons who think that he is his friend. And his friend owes somebody $96,000… The irony of the film's title is that Slevin is anything but a lucky guy. But because he suffers from a rare condition that suppresses anxiety, he can't get too het up about it. Cast against type, Josh Hartnett makes a delightfully goofy leading man and is nicely complemented by Lucy Liu in another about-turn (here she's unusually fresh and perky). Good, too, to see Morgan Freeman as a baddy for once (although, wisely, he doesn't play the evil), while all and sundry are fed some delicious dialogue (Liu, defensively: 'So, I'm *short* for my height…'). Just as the 6'3" Hartnett makes a surprising foil for the 5' 3" Asian Liu, everything is refreshingly off-kilter here. But this is really director McGuigan and scripter Smilovic's show, whose combined forces of visual and literary wit provide a constantly satisfying skew-whiff thriller. JC-W

• *Slevin Kelevra* Josh Hartnett, *the Boss* Morgan Freeman, *the Rabbi* Ben Kingsley, *Lindsey* Lucy Liu, *Brikowski* Stanley Tucci, *Mr Goodkat* Bruce Willis, *Sloe* Mykelti Williamson, *Roth*

Danny Aiello, *Murphy* Robert Forster, *with* Kevin Chamberlin, Sam Jaeger, Peter Outerbridge, Bernard Kay.

• *Dir* Paul McGuigan, *Pro* Christopher Eberts, Chris Roberts, Ryler Mitchell, Robert Kravis, Anthony Rhulen and Kia Jam, *Ex Pro* Sharon Harel, Jane Barclay, Eli Klein, Andreas Schmid, Don Carmody, A.J. Dix and Bill Shively, *Screenplay* Jason Smilovic, *Ph* Peter Sova, *Pro Des* François Séguin, *Ed* Andrew Hulme, *M* J. Ralph, *Costumes* Odette Gadoury.

Weinstein Co./Ascendant Pictures/FilmEngine/ VIP 4/Capitol Films-Entertainment. 110 mins. USA/Canada/UK/Germany. 2005. Rel: 24 February 2006. Cert. 18.

Madagascar ★★★½

Life would seem to be just peachy for Alex, Marty, Melman and Gloria. A lion, zebra, giraffe and hippo leading the life of Riley at New York's Central Park Zoo, the critters have all the latest commodities and all the food they can eat. But, on Marty's tenth birthday, the zebra suffers a mid-life crisis and heads for Grand Central Station. So Alex, Melman and Gloria head off to rescue him and find that life can be a zoo out there… With four scriptwriters on hand and a stellar voice cast, *Madagascar* has plenty of good jokes and a generous comic brio. There are also some priceless minor creations (the chimps escape to catch a reading by Tom Wolfe, the penguins display a surprisingly sadistic streak), a fabulous soundtrack and state-of-the-art animation. The story's a little weak, there's not a lot of charm, but this is effortless escapism of the highest pedigree. JC-W

• *Voices*: *Alex* Ben Stiller, *Marty* Chris Rock, *Melman* David Schwimmer, *Gloria* Jada Pinkett Smith, *Julien* Sacha Baron

Cohen, *Maurice* Cedric the Entertainer, *Mort* Andy Richter *Skipper/Fossa* Tom McGrath, *Private* Christopher Knights, *Kowalski* Chris Miller, *Mason* Conrad Vernon.

• *Dir* Eric Darnell and Tom McGrath, *Pro* Mireille Soria, *Co-Pro* Teresa Cheng, *Screenplay* Darnell, McGrath, Mark Burton and Billy Frolick, *Pro Des* Kendal Cronkhite-Shaindlin, *Ed* H. Lee Peterson, *M* Hans Zimmer, *Visual Effects* Philippe Gluckman.

DreamWorks Animation-UIP. 86 mins. USA. 2005. Rel: 15 July 2005. Cert. U.

Mad Hot Ballroom ★★★½

Dig lightly and you'll find American youth obsessing about something. In Jeff Blitz's extraordinary *Spellbound* it was orthography, here it's ballroom dancing. Following the selection process of three New York elementary schools to compete in a citywide ballroom dancing competition, Marilyn Agrelo's debut feature is warm, immediate and entertaining. Here, we have a variety of eleven-year-olds, captured close-up as they try to master the moves of the foxtrot, the merengue and the tango. Of course, it's comical and cute at first but as the kids near their deadline, the dancing gets slicker. And so the idealistic offspring of poor immigrant families transform themselves from street fodder into little 'ladies and gentlemen'. Serving as a microcosm of the diversity of all human life – the students are largely Asian, Hispanic, black and from the Dominican Republic – the film is at its funniest and most enlightening as the kids air their opinions. 'Girls are alright,' states one boy. 'I buy their inner beauty and their outer beauty – but mainly their inner beauty.' It's a shame we don't get to know the students better – there are so many of them – but as a

Foxtrot cubs: A scene from Marilyn Agrelo's enlightening and utterly charming *Mad Hot Ballroom* (from Metrodome)

kaleidoscopic view of American youth it's utterly charming. JC-W

• *Dir* Marilyn Agrelo, based on an feature article by Amy Sewell, *Pro* Sewell and Agrelo, *Assoc Pro* W. Wilder Knight II, *Line Pro* Brian David Cange, *Ph* Claudia Raschke-Robinson, *Ed* Sabine Krayenbuhl, *M* Steven Lutvak and Joseph Baker.

• *With*: Pierre Dulaine, Yvonne Marceau, Otto Caooel, Danielle Quisenberry, Yomaira Reynoso, Allison Sheniak, Alyssa Polack, Leslie Freij, Louise Verdemare, Terri Mintzer, Lois Olshan, Susan Bahaloul, Ann Reinking.

Nickleodeon Movies/JustOne Prods-Metrodome. 105 mins. USA. 2005. Rel: 25 November 2005. Cert. U.

The Magician ★½

Melbourne; the recent past. With a masochistic eye for immortality, hitman Ray Shoesmith agrees to have a fly-on-the-wall documentary made about him. So, it's business as usual for a man who conducts his trade with a loaded pistol and isn't afraid to use it… Taking a concept already ploughed more fruitfully in *Man Bites Dog* and *The Last Horror Movie*, this is little more than a series of inane conversations with writer-director Scott Ryan as host. Like an emaciated hybrid of Willem Dafoe and Steve Buscemi, Ryan makes for ghoulish company but sheds paltry light on the complexity of the criminal condition. There's little actual violence and absolutely no suspense, but lots of gutter dialogue filmed in murky DV. JC-W

• *Raymond John Shoesmith* Scott Ryan, *Tony Rickards* Ben Walker, *Massimo 'Max' Totti* Massimiliano Andrighetto, *Benny* Kane Mason, *Edna* Nathaniel Lindsay, *garage victim* Adam Ryan.

• *Dir* and *Screenplay* Scott Ryan, *Pro* Ryan, Michele Bennett and Nash Edgerton, *Ex Pro* Gary Phillips and Mark Vennis, *Ph* Massimiliano Andrighetto, *Ed* Ryan, Nash Edgerton and Kristine Rowe, *Sound* Sam Petty.

Hopscotch/Moviehouse Entertainment/Film Finance Corporation Australia/Film Victoria/Blue-Tongue Films/Cherub Pictures/I Will Films-Trinity Filmed Entertainment. 85 mins. Australia. 2005. Rel: 5 May 2006. Cert. 15.

The Man ★★

Eugene Levy plays a talkative dental supply salesman who, after a case of mistaken identity, ends up as bag carrier for cynical maverick cop Samuel L. Jackson in his scheme to trap Luke Goss's gang of arms dealers. This frantic, familiar and formulaic buddy-action-comedy often betrays its desperation to please, while having little idea of how to go about it. But chucklesome moments of mild amusement do crop up now and again, and Levy and Jackson's pairing is inspired: so it's a pity it doesn't have a better showcase. However, Goss makes a surprisingly good British baddie. DW

• *Derrick Vann* Samuel L. Jackson, *Andy Fiddler* Eugene Levy, *Joey/Kane* Luke Goss, *Agent Peters* Miguel Ferrer, *Lt Rita Carbone* Susie Essman, *Booty* Anthony Mackie, *Diaz* Horatio Sanz, *Dara Vann* Rachael Crawford, *Kate Vann* Tomorrow Baldwin Montgomery, *with* Gigi Rice, Philip Akin, Christopher Murray, Leonard Thomas.

• *Dir* Les Mayfield, *Pro* Rob Fried, *Ex Pro* Toby Emmerich, Kent Alterman and Matthew Hart, *Co-Pro* Bill Straus, *Screenplay* Jim Piddock, Margaret Oberman and Steve Carpenter, *Ph* Adam Kane, *Pro Des* Carol Spier, *Ed* Jeffrey Wolf, *M* John Murphy, *Costumes* Delphine White.

New Line Cinema/Fried Films-Entertainment. 83 mins. USA. 2005. Rel: 9 September 2005. Cert. 12A.

Manderlay ★★★½

Alabama; 1933. As Grace travels through the American South with her father, she is stopped by a young black woman in obvious distress. The woman explains that at the plantation, Manderlay, a black man is about to be flogged. Taking the matter into her own hands, Grace resolves to set the workforce free – after all, it's seventy years since the abolition of slavery – and takes over the running of Manderlay… Lars von Trier has always courted controversy, both with his subject matter and *modus operandi*. And by confronting the unspeakable, and exploring new methods of storytelling, he opens up new avenues for thought and art. Love him or hate him, he's hard to ignore. This, the second episode of his *USA: Land of Opportunities* trilogy, is again shot on a large stage in Sweden (à la *Dogville*) with imaginary doors and stencilled lettering in place of exteriors. Yet once one has become accustomed to this perverse artifice, the power of the story and the performances take hold. Bryce Dallas Howard is extraordinary as Grace (replacing Nicole Kidman) and John Hurt's wry, mellifluous voice-over is once again sublime. JC-W

• *Grace Margaret Mulligan* Bryce Dallas Howard, *Timothy* Isaach De Bankolé, *Wilhelm* Danny Glover, *Grace's father* Willem Dafoe, *Thomas* Michaël Abiteboul, *Mam* Lauren Bacall, *Mr Robinson* Jean-Marc Barr, *narrator* John Hurt, *with* Geoffrey Bateman, Virgile Bramly, Ruben Brinkman, Jeremy Davies, Zeljko Ivanek, Teddy Kemper, Udo Kier, Clive Rowe, Chloë Sevigny, Nina Sosanya.

• *Dir* and *Screenplay* Lars von Trier, *Pro* Vibeke Windeløv, *Ex Pro* Peter Aalbæk Jensen and Lene Børglum, *Line Pro* Signe Jensen, *Ph* Anthony Dod Mantle, *Art Dir* Peter Grant, *Ed* Molly Malene Stensgaard, *Costumes* Manon Rasmussen, *Sound* Kristian Eidnes Anderson and Per Streit.

Zentropa Entertainments13 ApS/Isabella Films, etc-Metrodome. 138 mins. Denmark/Sweden/France/UK/Germany/ Netherlands/Finland/Italy. 2005. Rel: 3 March 2006. Cert. 15.

March of the Penguins ★★★★

There is a novelty about watching a National Geographic

documentary unfolding on the big screen. Somehow, the scope of the cinema brings a more deserving sweep to the incomprehensible world of nature. Here, the French documentarian Luc Jacquet gives us the unique story of the emperor penguin, the only living creature foolhardy and stubborn enough to brave the Antarctic winter. For over an entire year, Jacquet and his crew camped out in the frozen continent to capture the extraordinary annual cycle of the birds, which routinely walk seventy miles just to eat. And all this sacrifice just to hatch one egg per year. Never before has the camera been able to chronicle the rituals of the emperor penguin in such detail, from its tender lovemaking, to its resignation to the impact of 100mph blizzards, to its underwater fishing practices. This is truly a technological marvel and a cinematic miracle. Original title: *La Marche de l'Empereur*. JC-W

• *Narration*: Morgan Freeman.

• *Dir* Luc Jacquet, *Pro* Yves Darondeau, Christophe Lioud and Emmanuel Priou, *Ex Pro* Ilann Girard, *Ph* Laurent Chalet and Jerôme Maison, *Narration written by* Jordan Roberts, based upon the screenplay by Jacquet and Michel Fessler, *M* Alex Wurman.

Warner Independent Pictures/National Geographic Feature Films/Wild Bunch/Buena Vista International/ Canal Plus/French Polar Institute-Warner.
80 mins. France/USA. Rel: 9 December 2005. 2005. Cert. U.

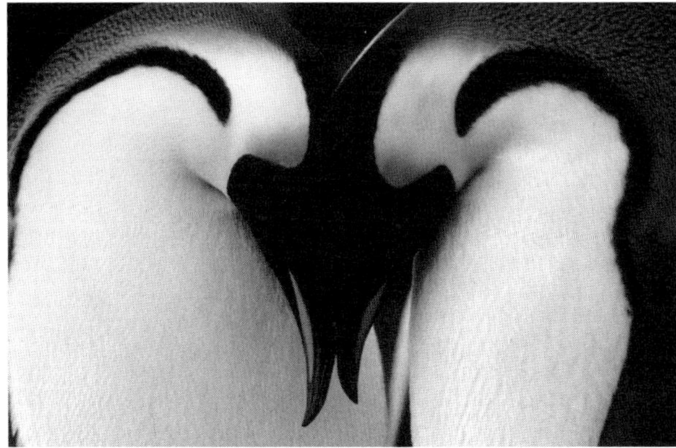

Love in a cold climate: Luc Jacquet's amazing and miraculous *March of the Penguins* (from Warner)

Mariscos Beach

See *Cockles & Muscles*.

The Matador ★★

Julian Noble has everything that a 50-year-old man could want: good looks, a globetrotting lifestyle and more money than he knows what to do with. But when he finds himself at a loose end on his birthday in Mexico City, he discovers that he has nobody to celebrate with. So, encountering a mild-mannered salesman in a bar, he decides to concoct a bit of male bonding. At first unnerved by Julian's obnoxious grandstanding, Danny

Wright is gradually drawn to the enigmatic stranger. After all, he's never met a hitman before… With its flashy opening and scenery-chewing turn from Pierce Brosnan (obviously relishing the chance to subvert his Bond persona), *The Matador* promises a lot of fun. However, around the halfway mark it becomes apparent that this is a one-joke movie with nowhere to go. In spite of exotic locations stretching from Mexico to Budapest via Denver, the film too often falls back on clumsy flashbacks and close-ups of Brosnan's impenetrable eyes. It's a bold concept, but one mired in inelegant execution. JC-W

• *Julian Noble* Pierce Brosnan, *Danny Wright* Greg Kinnear, *Bean Wright* Hope Davis, *Mr Randy* Philip Baker Hall, *Lovell* Dylan Baker, *Phil Garrison* Adam Scott, *with* Azucena Medina, Portia Dawson, Claudia Lobo.

• *Dir* and *Screenplay* Richard Shepard, *Pro* Pierce Brosnan, Beau St Clair, Sean Furst and Bryan Furst, *Ex Pro* Bob Yari, Mark Gordon, Adam Merims, Andreas Thiesmeyer, Josef Lautenschlager and Andy Reimer, *Ph* David Tattersall, *Pro Des* Rob Pearson, *Ed* Carole Kravetz-Akyanian, *M* Rolfe Kent, *Costumes* Catherine Thomas.

Weinstein Co./Miramax/Stratus Film Co./Irish Dreamtime-Buena Vista International.
96 mins. USA/Germany/Ireland/Australia. 2004.
Rel: 24 February 2006. Cert. 15.

Match Point ★★

Teaching tennis to the rich and pampered during the day and swatting up on opera and Dostoevsky at night, Chris Wilton is a man with an agenda. Masterfully unassuming and confident of his good looks, he quickly infiltrates the impossibly wealthy Hewett clan and lures Chloe Hewett into his bed. Then he meets Chloe's future sister-in-law, Nola, a beautiful, self-assured actress from Colorado… After Woody Allen's interminable cycle of neurotic, Jewish, Manhattan-bound comedies, it's good to see him trying something totally fresh: a London-set drama. However, his Richard Curtis-inflected view of England is at times quite laughable. Here, he's stumbled on a stratum of English life preoccupied with tennis, opera, grouse shooting, polo matches and the like, while his dialogue is laboured and overwritten. It's unfortunate, too, that Jonathan Rhys Meyers – who usually makes a good villain – is so charmless as the social-climbing opportunist. Indeed, in the wake of *Closer*, Mike Nichols' take on deceit and passion in modern London, *Match Point* seems all rather stilted and redundant. JC-W

• *Alec Hewett* Brian Cox, *Tom Hewett* Matthew Goode, *Nola Rice* Scarlett Johansson, *Chris Wilton* Jonathan Rhys Meyers, *Chloe Hewett Wilton* Emily Mortimer, *Eleanor* Penelope Wilton, *Inspector Dowd* Ewen Bremner, *Det. Banner* James Nesbitt, *with* Rupert Penry-Jones, Margaret Tyzack, Alexander Armstrong, Paul Kaye, Geoffrey Streatfield, John Fortune, Patricia Whymark, Rose Keegan, Zoë Telford, Selina Cadell, Georgina Chapman, Colin Salmon, Steve Pemberton.

• *Dir* and *Screenplay* Woody Allen, *Pro* Letty Aronson, Gareth Wiley and Lucy Darwin, *Ex Pro* Stephen Tenenbaum, *Co-Pro*

Helen Robin and Nicky Kentish Barnes, *Co-Ex Pro* Jack Rollins and Charles H. Joffe, *Ph* Remi Adefarasin, *Pro Des* Jim Clay, *Ed* Alisa Lepselter, *M* various, *Costumes* Jill Taylor.

BBC Films/Thema Prods/Jada/Kudu Films-Icon. 123 mins. UK/USA/Luxemburg. 2005. Rel: 6 Hanuary 2006. Cert. 12A.

Me and You and Everyone We Know ★★★½

A woman dons socks on her ears in a shoe shop. A shoes salesman pours lighter fluid over his hand and sets fire to it. A goldfish in a bag is left on the roof of a car and ends up on the boot of another. A seven-year-old boy rights scatological messages to a correspondent on the Internet. Yes, it's another typical day in an American suburb… An ensemble fable about people trying to connect with each other, *Me and You…* is a remarkable directorial debut for the performance artist Miranda July. Not only has July elicited exemplary performances from her unknown cast (including three children), she herself takes the central role of a young woman looking for love while staying true to her own vision. Quirky, funny, disconcerting and daringly original, the film occupies its own surreal universal while connecting on an entirely imaginable level. Of course, everybody is somebody else's weirdo and this extraordinary film goes to the heart of the human condition.
JC-W

• *Ellen* Ellen Geer, *Richard Swersey* John Hawkes, *Andrew* Brad William Henke, *Christine Jesperson* Miranda July, *Shamus* Jordan Potter, *Peter Swersey* Miles Thompson, *Robby Swersey* Brandon Ratcliff, *Chad* Jason A. Rice, *Heather* Natasha Slayton, *Rebecca* Najarra Townsend, *Sylvie* Carlie Westerman.

• *Dir* and *Screenplay* Miranda July, *Pro* Gina Kwon, *Ex Pro* Jonathan Sehring, Caroline Kaplan, Holly Becker, Iliana Ninkolic and Peter Carlton, *Assoc Pro* Mary Prendergast and Suzi Yoonessi, *Ph* Chuy Chavez, *Pro Des* Aran Mann, *Ed* Andrew Dickler and Charles Ireland, *M* Michael Andrews, *Costumes* Christie Wittenborn.

IFC Prods/FilmFour/Sundance Institute-Optimum Releasing. 91 mins. USA/UK/Japan. 2005. Rel: 19 August 2005. Cert. 15.

Memoirs of a Geisha ★★★

Japan; 1929-the 1940s. Sayuri Nitta tells us that, 'a story like mine should never be told…' Yet she tells it anyway, revealing the secrets of the world of the Japanese geisha, a tradition cloaked in mystery, competition, self-sacrifice and high personal stakes. Sold to a geisha house at the age of nine, Sayuri is separated from her family forever and, at great personal cost, learns the etiquette and pain of being a fashionable hostess… Arthur Golden's best-selling novel of 1997 is a big story and director Rob Marshall seems in a hurry to unfold it. Even before we know who Sayuri is (aged nine, she is called 'Chiyo'), we are hurled into the bustling back alleys of Kyoto and, like our young heroine, dazzled by all the new sights and sensations. As he revealed in his first film, *Chicago*, Marshall is a propulsive filmmaker, although one misses the beautiful narrative pauses of traditional Japanese cinema (Ozo this is not). At its best, this *Geisha* is

Japanese story: Ziyi Zhang and Ken Watanabe in Rob Marshall's bustling, propulsive *Memoirs of a Geisha* (from Sony Pictures)

a dazzling firework display, but the result is more impressive than actually engaging. JC-W

• *Chiyo* aka *Sayuri Nitta* Ziyi Zhang, *Chairman* Ken Watanabe, *Mameha* Michelle Yeoh, *Nobu* Koji Yakusho, *Pumpkin* Youki Kudoh, *mother* Kaori Momoi, *Hatsumomo* Gong Li, *Auntie* Tsai Chin, *the Baron* Cary-Hiroyuki Tagawa, *with* Randall Duk Kim, Mako, Kenneth Tsang, Ted Levine.

• *Dir* Rob Marshall, *Pro* Lucy Fisher, Douglas Wick and Steven Spielberg, *Ex Pro* Roger Birnbaum, Gary Barber, Patricia Whitcher and Bobby Cohen, *Co-Pro* and *Choregraphy* John DeLuca, *Screenplay* Robin Swicord and Doug Wright, *Ph* Dion Beebe, *Pro Des* John Myhre, *Ed* Pietro Scalia, *M* John Williams; *cello solos* Yo-Yo Ma, *violin solos* Itzhak Perlman, *Costumes* Colleen Atwood, *Sound* Harry Cohen, *Geisha Consultant* Liza Dalby.

Columbia/DreamWorks/Spyglass Entertainment/Amblin Entertainment-Columbia TriStar.
145 mins. USA. 2005. Rel: 13 January 2006. Cert. 12A.

Merry Christmas ★★★★½

As Christmas approaches in the trenches of the First World War, the war-weary troops on all sides wonder if they'll live long enough to `celebrate' the season. Then, out of the blue, a common fraternity breaks out of the fear and hatred… Both the subject matter and implementation of this Franco-Anglo-German co-production is unique. When in the history of recorded warfare did three armies put down their weapons to exchange gifts, photographs and refreshment in the reflected glow of Christmas? First chronicled in Richard Attenborough's *Oh! What a Lovely War*, this extraordinary event is now given its own movie, and extremely well executed it is. Gloriously photographed in Romania and featuring a cast of authentic European actors, the film pulls no punches but focuses on the human face of the bitterest of all wars. As three indoctrinated schoolboys from France, Scotland and Germany recite their loathing of the enemy, the film establishes its non-partisan agenda. We then cut to the Western front, where the reality of war is deftly drawn, where there are no villains, just a few misguided souls... This really should be compulsive viewing for schools throughout the European Union. Original title: *Joyeux Noël*. JC-W

• *Anna Sörensen* Diane Krüger, *Nikolaus Sprink* Benno Fürmann, *Lieutenant Audebert* Guillaume Canet, *Palmer* Gary Lewis, *Ponchel* Dany Boon, *Lieutenant Horstmayer* Daniel Brühl, *Gordon* Alex Ferns, *Jonathan* Steven Robertson, *Gueusselin* Lucas Belvaux, *French general* Bernard Le Coq, *the bishop* Ian Richardson, *William* Robin Laing, *with* Michel Serrault, Suzanne Flon, Frank Witter, Christopher Fulford.

• *Dir* and *Screenplay* Christian Carion, *Pro* Christophe Rossignon, *Ex Pro* Eve Machuel, *Ph* Walther Vanden Ende, *Art Dir* Jean Michel Simonet, *Ed* Andréa Sedlacková, *M* Philippe Rombi; *Anna Sörensen's songs performed by* Natalie Dessay, *Costumes* Alison Forbes Meyler.

Nord-Ouest/Senator Film/Artemis Prods/Canal Plus, etc-

Columbia TriStar.
115 mins. France/Germany/UK/Belgium/Romania.
Rel: 14 December 2005. Cert. 12A.

The Mighty Celt ★★★½

When he's not in school or playing on the streets of Dublin, 14-year-old Donal works for gruff Good Joe, a greyhound owner. When the latter is about to destroy an animal he deems useless, Donal makes him a bet: if he can train the dog to win three races, he gets to keep him. Reluctantly, Good Joe agrees and Donal names his new charge the Mighty Celt… Handsomely mounted in and around the verdant vistas of Dublin and well played by a first-rate cast, *The Mighty Celt* is a credible, fiercely non-sentimental modern fable. First-time director Pearse Elliott (who previously scripted Paddy Breathnach's greyhound-racing drama *Man About Dog*), shows a growing maturity with his material, neatly balancing his human drama with a cinematic varnish. Above all, he is rewarded by the central presence of newcomer Tyrone McKenna, a natural actor with an innate pluck and winning self-assurance. JC-W

• `O' Robert Carlyle, *Kate* Gillian Anderson, *Donal* Tyrone McKenna, *Good Joe* Ken Stott, *Turlough* Kevin Elliott, *Ronan* Richard Dormer, *the Mighty Celt* Pal, *with* Sean McGinley, Bernard Manning, John Travers, Alison Finnegan, Maureen Dow.

• *Dir* and *Screenplay* Pearse Elliott, *Pro* Robert Walpole, Paddy McDonald and Paddy Breathnach, *Co-Pro* Michael Casey, *Assoc Pro* Helen Murray, *Ph* Seamus Deasy, *Pro Des* Tom McCullagh, *Ed* Dermot Diskin, *M* Adrian Johnston, *Costumes* Hazel Webb-Crozier.

BBC Films/Bord Scannán na hÉireann/Irish Film Board/ Treasure Entertainment-Metrodome.
81 mins. Ireland/UK. 2005. Rel: 26 August 2005.
Cert. 12A.

Mirrormask ★★★★

Helena is 15 and feeling claustrophobic working in the circus run by her parents. Then, when her mother collapses and is taken to hospital, Helena runs away and finds herself in a world far stranger than any contained in the big top…
While, perhaps inevitably, *Mirrormask* recalls the illusory worlds of others (think Lewis Carroll, Roald Dahl, Terry Gilliam) and reflects the visual aesthetic of everybody from Escher to Henry Moore, it is nonetheless a true original. All the more surprising is that it's British (not, say, Czech or Japanese) and is geographically set in Brighton. Films like this don't come from Britain: it's not cheesy, provincial nor mired in a TV sensibility; its flights of imagination know no bounds. Thus, we have flocks of books, schools of aerial fish and calligraphical landscapes, all unfolding in a dream-like, multi-levelled universe of Helena's psyche. Had the film been just a tad shorter (without a conventional narrative, it does outstay its welcome), it would have been perfect. JC-W

• *Helena Campbell/Anti-Helena* Stephanie Leonidas, *Valentine* Jason Barry, *Morris Campbell* Rob Brydon, *Joanne Campbell*

Gina McKee, *Auntie Nan* Dora Bryan, *librarian* Stephen Fry, *Small Hairy* Andy Hamilton, *cops 1-4* Lenny Henry, *nurse* Victoria Williams, *with* Simon Harvey, Robert Llewellyn, Eryl Maynard, Eve Pearce, Simon Schofield, Mark Tate, Kate Robbins.

• *Dir* and *Design* Dave McKean, *Pro* Simon Moorhead, *Ex Pro* Lisa Henson, Michael Polis and Martin G. Baker, *Screenplay* Neil Gaiman, from a story by McKean and Gaiman, *Ph* Antony Shearn, *Ed* Nicolas Gaster, *M* Iain Ballamy, *Costumes* Robert Lever, *Sound* Hugh Johnson and Barnaby Smith, *CGI* Max McMullin.

Destination Films/Jim Henson-Tartan Films. 101 mins. UK/USA. 2004. Rel: 3 March 2006. Cert. PG.

Mission: Impossible III ★★★½

Breaking the cardinal rule of IMF operatives, Ethan Hunt decides to settle down and marry the woman of his dreams. Then he accepts a mission to kidnap a world-class marketeer, who promptly turns the tables on Hunt by abducting the agent's new wife... Tom Cruise enters the Vatican by striding up the sheer face of an outer wall. While driving across the Chesapeake Bay Bridge, he is literally blown into the side of a van. In Shanghai, he breaks into one skyscraper by swinging from another. The `wow factor' is certainly much in evidence in *M: I III*, which should thrill fans of the first two entries. However, its attempts at injecting a note of humanity into the character of Ethan Hunt is entirely superficial, included purely to service the plot and to crank up the emotional traction. In fact, first-time collaborator J.J. Abrams (TV's *Alias* and *Lost*) makes a critical misjudgement by dispensing with the traditional prologue in favour of a scene that actually takes place 95 minutes into the movie. This turns the bulk of *M: I III* into a flashback and robs it of much of its suspense and immediacy. The violence, while tailored to the requirements of a 12A, is also particularly gratuitous, leaving a remarkably nasty taste in the mouth. JC-W

• *Ethan Hunt* Tom Cruise, *Owen Davian* Philip Seymour Hoffman, *Luther* Ving Rhames, *Musgrave* Billy Crudup, *Julia* Michelle Monaghan, *Declan* Jonathan Rhys Meyers, *Lindsey* Keri Russell, *Zhen* Maggie Q, *John Brassel* Laurence Fishburne, *Benji* Simon Pegg, *with* Eddie Marsan, Bahar Soomekh, Carla Gallo, Sabra Williams, Sasha Alexander, Aaron Paul, Paolo Bonacelli, José Zuniga.

• *Dir* J.J. Abrams, *Pro* Tom Cruise and Paula Wagner, *Ex Pro* Stratton Leopold, *Screenplay* Abrams, Alex Kurtzman and Roberto Orci, *Ph* Dan Mindel, *Pro Des* Scott Chambliss, *Ed* Maryann Brandon and Mary Jo Markey, *M* Michael Giacchino, *Costumes* Colleen Atwood, *Visual Effects* Roger Guyett, *Special Effects* Dan Sudick, *Second Unit Dir* Vic Armstrong.

Paramount/Cruise/Wagner-UIP. 125 mins. USA. 2006. Rel: 4 May 2006. Cert. 12A.

The Mistress of Spices ★½

Tilo is a beautiful Indian woman who works in a small store in San Francisco called *The Spice Bazaar*. There she offers her expert advice and supplies all sorts of remedies, from spices to her clients... Paul Mayeda Berges' debut as a director comes as a disappointment despite a fascinating story. The script and direction are unimaginative and the attractive leads look uncomfortable in their underwritten roles. The supporting characters are also thinly sketched and verge on the stereotypical. As Tilo, Aishwarya Rai looks stunning but lacks the emotional depth to convey her dilemma in choosing between her duty and her love for a handsome American. GS

• *Tilo* Aishwarya Rai, *Doug* Dylan McDermott, *Haroun* Nitin Ganatra, *Kwesi* Adewale Akinnuoye-Agbaje, *Myisha* Caroline Chikezie, *Hameeda* Ayesha Dharker, *Jagjit* Sonny Gill Dulay, *Geeta's grandfather* Anupam Kher, *Geeta* Padma Lakshmi, *with* Nina Young, Toby Marlow, Zohra Sehgal.

• *Dir* Paul Mayeda Berges, *Pro* Deepak Nayar and Gurinder Chadha, *Ex Pro* Hannah Leader, Duncan Reid, Steve Christian, James Clayton, Jane Barclay and Susan Cartsonis, *Screenplay* Berges and Chadha, based on the novel by Chitra Banerjee Divakaruni, *Ph* Santosh Sivan, *Pro Des* Amanda McArthur, *Ed* Alexander Rodríguez, *M* Craig Pruess, *Costumes* Stewart Meachem.

Kintop Pictures/Balle Pictures/Capitol Films/Ingenious Film Partners/Isle of Man Film-Entertainment. 95 mins. UK/Germany. 2005. Rel: 21 April 2006. Cert. 12A.

The Moguls ★★

Andy Sargentee is a nice, kind, regular guy. He is the sort of salt-of-the-earth character that even his ex-wife is pleased to see. But then Andy decides he's had enough of not having enough. So he galvanises his close circle of loyal losers into filming a feature-length 'porno'... Set in the sunny environs of small-town Butterface Fields, California, this bizarre ensemble comedy thinks it's Frank Capra with an edge. The charm is laid on with a JCB and while there's the occasional funny and poignant moment, most of the comedy feels forced. Ted Danson reprises his role as Sam Malone in *Cheers* – but with a gay twist – and Jeff Bridges grounds much of the farce in a semblance of credibility. But even though there's no real naughty action, there is something dispiritingly smutty about a group of likeable folk talking about 'carpet munching', 'honey pots' and penis size. JC-W

• *Andy Sargentee* Jeff Bridges, *Moose* Ted Danson, *Otis* William Fichtner, *Emmett* Patrick Fugit, *Barney Macklehatton* Tim Blake Nelson, *Some Idiot* Joe Pantoliano, *Helen Tatelbaum* Glenne Headly, *Peggy* Lauren Graham, *Thelma* Jeanne Tripplehorn, *Homer* Isaiah Washington, *V* Valerie Perrine, *Moe* John Hawkes, *Ellie* Judy Greer, *with* Eileen Brennan, Tom Bower, Brad Henke, Steven Weber, Alex D. Linz, Elden Henson.

• *Dir* and *Screenplay* Michael Traeger, *Pro* Aaron Ryder, *Ex Pro* Michael Kuhn, Malcolm Ritchie and Jill Tandy, *Ph* Denis Maloney, *Pro Des* Bob Ziembicki, *Ed* Raúl Dávalos, *M* Nic. tenBroek, *Costumes* Ernesto Martinez.

Qwerty Films/N1 European Film Produktions/
Raygun-UIP.
96 mins. USA/UK/Germany. 2005. Rel: 28 April 2006.
Cert. 15.

Mrs Henderson Presents ★★★

London; the late 1930s. Following the death of her husband,
Laura Henderson, at 69, finds herself independently wealthy
and very bored. So, on a whim, she purchases the Windmill
Theatre in London's Soho and, with the help of theatrical
manager Vivian Van Damm, turns it into a showcase for non-
stop revue. However, when other theatres follow suit, the
Windmill suffers losses of £20,000. Then Mrs Henderson hits
on the idea of exhibiting naked girls… With Judi Dench,
ample nudity and a script dripping with priceless one-liners,
Mrs Henderson Presents would seem to be a recipe cooked up in
celluloid heaven. Indeed, Dame Judi is at the top of her form,
the nudity is tasteful and natural, while Martin Sherman's
script is a gift to his actors (Bob Hoskins: 'We must have
British nipples!'). There are also fascinating insights into the
bureaucracy of Britain at the time (nudity is permissible, but
only if the actresses don't move), while the use of newsreel
footage is very effective. Even so, there's an air of whimsy that,
at times, is quite suffocating. Based on a true story. JC-W

• *Laura Henderson* Judi Dench, *Vivian Van Damm* Bob
Hoskins, *Bertie* Will Young, *Maureen* Kelly Reilly, *Lord Cromer*
Christopher Guest, *Lady Conway* Thelma Barlow, *Doris* Anna
Brewster, *with* Rosalind Halstead, Sarah Solemani, Natalia
Tena, Doraly Rosen, Sir Thomas Allen, Ralph Nossek, Matthew
Hart, Toby Jones, Michael Culkin, Waris Hussein, Anne
Lambton, Joseph Long, Patti Love.

• *Dir* Stephen Frears, *Pro* Norma Heyman, *Ex Pro* Bob
Hoskins, David Aukin, David M. Thompson, Tracey Scoffield,
François Ivernel and Cameron McCracken, *Screenplay* Martin
Sherman, *Ph* Andrew Dunn, *Pro Des* Hugo Luczyc-Wyhowski,
Ed Lucia Zucchetti, *M* George Fenton, *Costumes* Sandy Powell,
Choreography Eleanor Fazan and Debbie Astell.

Pathé/BBC Films/Future Films/Micro-Fusion/
Weinstein Co/UK Film Council-Pathé.
102 mins. UK/USA. 2005. Rel: 25 November 2005.
Cert. 12A.

Munich ★★★★

Following the murder of nine Israeli athletes at the 1972
Munich Olympics, Golda Meir's former bodyguard, Avner
Kauffman, is called in for an audience. He is instructed to
leave behind his pregnant wife and hunt down the eleven
Palestinian perpetrators of the massacre. Money is no problem,
the mission could take years and he is to become invisible to
the Israeli government… There is an air of *The Day of the Jackal*
about *Munich*. It has the same clinical, methodical pacing and
a lot of European actors (not to mention the reacquisition of
Michael Lonsdale). Besides, the title seems a misnomer as the
film is set in Geneva, Frankfurt, Rome, Paris, Cyprus, London,
Tel Aviv, Beirut, Athens, New York… Indeed, there is a real

Dripping with one-
liners: Kelly Reilly
in Stephen Frears'
theatrical, whimsical
*Mrs Henderson
Presents* (from
Pathé)

international feel to the movie (although only shot in Malta,
Hungary and France), even if its moments of excitement are
punctuated by longueurs of political pontificating and soul-
searching. It's also been accused of inaccuracy, but then that
comes with the territory of the medium. If you want the real
story, check out Kevin Macdonald's slick, Oscar-winning
documentary on the subject, *One Day in September*. For now,
though, Spielberg's measured, gripping and inevitably overlong
treatise will do very nicely. JC-W

• *Avner Kauffman* Eric Bana, *Steve* Daniel Craig, *Carl* Ciarán
Hinds, *Robert* Mathieu Kassovitz, *Hans* Hanns Zischler,
Daphna Ayelet Zurer, *Ephraim* Geoffrey Rush, *Avner's mother*
Gila Almagor, *Papa* Michael Lonsdale, *Louis* Mathieu Amalric,
Jeanette Marie-Josée Croze, *Golda Meir* Lynn Cohen, *with* Moritz
Bleibtreu, Valeria Bruni-Tedeschi, Meret Becker, Yvan Attal,
Ami Weinberg, Amos Lavie, Lisa Werlinder, Robert John
Burke, Sasha Spielberg.

• *Dir* Steven Spielberg, *Pro* Spielberg, Kathleen Kennedy,
Barry Mendel and Colin Wilson, *Screenplay* Tony Kushner and
Eric Roth, from the book *Vengeance* by George Jonas, *Ph* Janusz
Kaminski, *Pro Des* Rick Carter, *Ed* Michael Kahn, *M* John
Williams, *Costumes* Joanna Johnston, *Sound* Ben Burtt.

DreamWorks/Universal/Amblin Entertainment/Kennedy/
Marshall/Alliance Atlantis-UIP.
163 mins. USA/Canada. 2005. Rel: 27 January 2006.
Cert. 15.

Murderball ★★★

This oddball American documentary about quadriplegic rugby players is, perhaps surprisingly, as entertaining as it is inspirational. The *Mad Max*-y idea is you have to smash your armour-plated wheelchair into your opponent's before he can get two wheels over the try-line while holding the ball. Despite the ferocity of all the action in the arena, the guys' hilarious self-deprecating humour means they come over very sympathetically – even though their tough nut of a coach, Joe Soares, turns out to be the film's star. A big crowd-pleaser, *Murderball* was not only nominated for an Oscar but was a favourite at the Sundance Festival, where it won the Audience Award and Special Jury Prize.
DW

• *With*: Keith Cavill, Andy Cohn, Scott Hogsett, Christopher Igoe, Bob Lujano, Joe Soares, Robert Soares, Patti Soares, Mark Zupan, Jessica Wampler.

• *Dir* Henry Alex Rubin, Jeffrey Mandel and Dana Adam Shapiro, from an article by Shapiro, *Pro* Jeffrey V. Mandel and Dana Adam Shapiro, *Ex Pro* Micah Green, Randy Manis, Jeff Sackman and Mark Urman, *Ph* Henry Alex Rubin, *Ed* Conor O'Neill and Geoffrey Richman, *M* Jamie Saft, *Sound* Patrick Donahue, *Animation* David Egan.

ThinkFilm/MTV Films-Optimum Releasing. 85 mins. USA/Canada. 2005. Rel: 4 November 2005. Cert. 15.

Must Love Dogs ★★★

Sarah Nolan and Jake Anderson are both drowning in the backwash of their respective divorces. She's a Montessori teacher, he's a boat builder and neither feels ready for romance. But thanks to the interference of friends and family, they find themselves reluctant entrants in a website called perfectmatch.com… Because of his obvious intelligence and cynicism, John Cusack excels in romantic comedy, being the perfect grit that activates the oyster. Meanwhile, Diane Lane – after a protracted term in the trenches – has sidled her way into the pantheon of Hollywood's finest fortysomething actresses. Here, she's handed a peach of a character and nails it with meticulous comic timing, batting off Cusack with a champion's backspin. However, while there's an abundance of chuckles and richly defined character turns, the direction of TV scenarist Goldberg is disappointingly pedestrian. *Must Love Dogs* had the potential to be smart and sensational; as it stands, it's smart and cute. JC-W

• *Sarah Nolan* Diane Lane, *Jake Anderson* John Cusack, *Bob Connor* Dermot Mulroney, *Carol* Elizabeth Perkins, *Dolly* Stockard Channing, *Bill* Christopher Plummer, *Christine* Ali Hillis, *Leo* Brad William Henke, *with* Julie Gonzalo, Will McCormack, Ted Griffin, Marylouise Burke, Brad Hall, Tony Bill, Laura Kightlinger, Colin Egglesfield.

• *Dir* and *Screenplay* Gary David Goldberg, from the novel by Claire Cook, *Pro* Goldberg, Suzanne Todd and Jennifer Todd, *Ex Pro* Brad Hall and Ronald G. Smith, *Ph* John Bailey, *Pro Des* Naomi Shohan, *Ed* Eric Sears and Roger Bondelli, *M*

Darcy's diaper: Colin Firth struggles with parenthood in Kirk Jones' silly, heavy-handed *Nanny McPhee* (UIP)

Craig Armstrong; tracks performed by Linda Ronstadt, Sheryl Crow, Aubergine 3, Supreme Beings of Leisure, Joan Jett and the Blackhearts, Stephanie Bentley, Joey Altruda, Vinnie Zummo, Rilo Kiley, Dengue Fever, Ryan Adams and The Cardinals, Susie Suh, etc, *Costumes* Florence-Isabelle Megginson and Gamila Smith.

Warner/UBU/Team Todd-Warner.
97 mins. USA. 2005. Rel: 16 September 2005. Cert. 12A.

Nanny McPhee ★½

Mr Brown, who runs the local funeral parlour, is at his wit's end. Since his wife died a year ago, his seven children – the unruliest in the world – have disposed of 17 nannies and if he doesn't find a new wife in one month, his allowance will be withdrawn. Then, seemingly out of nowhere, the serene, incredibly ugly Nanny McPhee turns up on his doorstep… Having won an Oscar for her first screenplay ten years ago, Emma Thompson has taken her time in finding a suitable project to follow. However, where *Sense and Sensibility* was timeless, sensitive and witty, *Nanny McPhee* is dated, heavy-handed and silly. Adapted from the *Nurse Matilda* children's books by Christianna Brand, the film boasts a mouth-watering cast and looks wonderful but lacks the mix of credibility and magic that it cries out for. Relying on slapstick, animated animals and over-acting, it may appeal to the very young, but not for long. JC-W

• *Mr Brown* Colin Firth, *Nanny McPhee* Emma Thompson, *Aunt Adelaide* Angela Lansbury, *Evangeline* Kelly Macdonald, *Mrs Blatherwick* Imelda Staunton, *Simon Brown* Thomas Sangster, *Mr Wheen* Derek Jacobi, *Tora Brown* Eliza Bennett, *Lily Brown* Jenny Daykin, *Eric Brown* Raphaël Coleman, *with* Samuel Honywood, Holly Gibbs, Hebe and Zinnia Barnes, Celia Imrie, Elizabeth Berrington, Patrick Barlow, Adam Godley, and *the voice of Mrs Partridge* Phyllida Law.

• *Dir* Kirk Jones, *Pro* Lindsay Doran, Tim Bevan and Eric Fellner, *Ex Pro* Debra Hayward and Liza Chasin, *Co-Pro* Glynis Murray, *Screenplay* Emma Thompson, *Ph* Henry Braham, *Pro Des* Michael Howells, *Ed* Justin Krish and Nick Moore, *M* Patrick Doyle, *Costumes* Nic Ede.

Universal/StudioCanal/MGM/Working Title-UIP.
97 mins. UK/France/USA. 2005. Rel: 21 October 2005. Cert. U.

The New World ★★★½

In 1607 three ships from London arrived on the shores of what was to become Virginia. There, the explorers found a land rich in virginal beauty and a native people lacking in guile, deceit or envy. The 'naturals' treated the newcomers with curiosity, but hoped they wouldn't stay too long… There is an enormous purity to Terrence Malick's vision. Dispensing with conventional cinematic narrative, the director doesn't so much let his story unfold as trickle, gush and splash, like an unpredictable stream of consciousness. While painting the screen with remarkable imagery, Malick is just as concerned with the sound of his film, enriching it with birdsong, the play of water, the swish of a sword and the rustle of wind in the grass. In fact, so dedicated is Malick to the perfect aural landscape that he insisted on a replica of the sound of the Carolina parakeet, even though it is extinct (in the end, sound editor Skip Lievsay had to contact Cornell University's Lab of Ornithology). The resulting experience is quite dream-like, and often rather inscrutable, although the authentic Virginian locations and the presence of the 15-year-old Peruvian actress Q'orianka Kilcher bring the film an extraordinary resonance. Only Colin Farrell, with his modern tattoos and unintelligible diction, sounds a note of spuriousness. JC-W

• *John Smith* Colin Farrell, *Captain Christopher Newport* Christopher Plummer, *John Rolfe* Christian Bale, *Powhatan* August Schellenberg, *Opechancanough* Wes Studi, *Pocahontas* Q'orianka Kilcher, *Wingfield* David Thewlis, *Captain Argall* Yorick van Wageningen, *with* Ben Mendelsohn, Raoul Trujillo, Brían F. O'Byrne, John Savage, Irene Bedard, Jamie Harris, Noah Taylor, Ben Chaplin, Janine Duvitski, Eddie Marsan, Myrton Running Wolf, Jesse Borrego, Raynor Scheine, *King James* Jonathan Pyce, *Queen Anne* Alexandra Malick.

• *Dir* and *Screenplay* Terrence Malick, *Pro* Sarah Green, *Ex Pro* Toby Emmerich, Rolf Mittweg, Mark Ordesky and Trish Hoffmann, *Ph* Emmanuel Lubezki, *Pro Des* Jack Fisk, *Ed* Richard Chew, Hank Corwin, Saar Klein and Mark Yoshikawa, *M* James Horner, *Costumes* Jacqueline West, *Sound* Craig Berkey, *Choreography* Raoul Trujillo.

New Line Cinema/First Foot Films-Entertainment.
150 mins. USA. 2005. Rel: 27 January 2006. Cert. 12A.

Niagara Motel ★★

The Niagara Motel is not the most salubrious accommodation within the romantic environs of Niagara Falls. The Serbian owner is in a perpetual rage, the janitor is a woeful drunk and the pregnant waitress is about to embark on a career in homemade porn. But these are cheerful creatures compared to the guests staying there… Montreal-born director Gary Yates has assembled some intriguing stories for his low-rent *Grand Hotel* (the Greta Garbo-Joan Crawford ensemble), but has failed to find a convincing tone. While pitched on the right side of farce, it is still beyond the realms of credibility. The result is a bouquet of whimsy teetering on the edge of the morose, underlined by an insistent cello on the soundtrack. Sadly, the latent comedy never finds its stride, although there are worthwhile performances from Anna Friel and Caroline Dhavernas. JC-W

• *Phillie Phillips* Craig Ferguson, *Denise* Anna Friel, *Michael* Kevin Pollak, *Lily* Wendy Crewson, *Loretta* Caroline Dhavernas, *Henry* Peter Keleghan, *R.J.* Kris Holden-Ried, *Dave* Tom Barnett, *Sophie* Catherine Fitch, *Helen Mackie* Janet-Laine Green, *Sandy* Krista Bridges, *Gilles* Normand Daneau, *with* Damir Andrei, Pierre Collin, Daniele Lorain.

• *Dir* Gary Yates, *Pro* Bernard Zukerman, Michael Prupas,

Terence S. Potter and Phyllis Laing, *Ex Pro* Jacqueline Quella and Tom Parkhouse, *Screenplay* George F. Walker and Dani Romain, from Walker's *Suburban Motel* plays, *Ph* Ian Wilson, *Pro Des* Deanne Rohde, *Ed* Simon Cozens, *M* Guy Fletcher, *Costumes* Linda Haysman.

India Grove/Muse Entertainment/Buffalo Gal Pictures/ Télèfilm Canada/Aquarius Films, etc-Soda Pictures. 88 mins. UK/Canada. 2004. Rel: 11 November 2005. Cert. 15.

The Night of Truth ★★★★

Although set in a fictional African country this assured debut dealing with rival races locked in a power struggle echoes *Hotel Rwanda* but it's made by a woman, Fanta Régina Nacro, who is herself African. Covering a short period of time, the film shows the tensions that threaten to undermine the peace pact that both sides have finally subscribed to in order to achieve stability in their country. With both sympathetic and unappealing characters in each camp, the film shows us in an almost Shakespearean way the tragedy that stems from the difficulty in moving beyond past atrocities to the forgiveness necessary if peace is to be cemented. There may be a touch of contrivance in the drama but the harrowing climax comes directly from a reality known to the film-maker's own family. A powerful, impressive first feature. Original title: *La Nuit de la Verite*. MS

• *Edna* Naky Sy Savané, *Colonel Theo* Commandant Moussa Cissé, *Soumari* Georgette Paré, *President Miossoune* Adama Ouédraougo, *Tomota* Rasmané Ouedraogo, *Fatou* Sami Rama Goumbané.

• *Dir* Fanta Régina Nacro, *Pro* Nacro and Claire-Agnès Lajoumard, *Screenplay* Nacro and Marc Gautron, *Ph* Nara Keo Kosal, *Pro Des* Bill Traore, *Ed* Andrée Davanture, *M* Troupe Naba Yaadega, Sami Rama and Los Tres Amigos;

Les Films du Defi/Acrobates Films/France 3 Cinéma-BFI. 99 mins. France/Burkina Faso. 2004. Rel: 9 September 2005. Cert. 18.

Night Watch ★★½

One thousand years ago the forces of good and evil settled on a truce. Then, as foretold by an ancient prophecy, a being that is neither Dark nor Light turns up in contemporary Moscow. It is he alone who can decide the tide of the opposing forces. Will he chose good or will he chose evil? In spite of rave endorsements from Danny Boyle and Quentin Tarantino – and the obliteration of box-office records in Russia – *Night Watch* is not the miracle one might have hoped for. While visually it is the most amazing film to hail from the former Soviet Union, and at times it recalls the fevered imagination of Jean-Pierre Jeunet and the Wachowski brothers, its non-stop set pieces of grandstanding bravado get quite wearisome. Still, considering it was made for just $4 million, it is something of a cinematic marvel, although the prospect of two more chapters of the trilogy is a daunting one. FYI: This is the sixth film to be called *Night Watch* since 1973. Original title: *Nochnoi Dozor*. JC-W

• *Anton Gorodetsky* Konstantin Khabensky, *Geser* Vladimir Menshov, *Kostya's father* Valery Zolotukhin, *Svetlana* Maria Proshina, *Olga* Galina Tunina, *Kostya* Alexei Chadov, *Andrei*

Smoke Gets In Your Eyes: A typical scene from Timur Bekmambetov's visually awesome, gruelling *Night Watch* (from Fox)

Ilia Lagutenko.

• *Dir* Timur Bekmambetov, *Pro* Antaoly Maximov and Konstantin Ernst, *Line Pro* Alexei Kublitsky and Varya Avdyushko, *English Screenplay Adaptation* Bekmambetov and Laeta Kalogridis, from the novel by Sergei Lukyanenko, *Ph* Sergei Trofimov, *Art Dir* Valery Victorov and Mukhtar Mirzakeyev, *Ed* Dmitri Kiselev, *M* Yuri Poteyenko, *Costumes/ Style* Varya Avdyushko.

Channel One Russia/Tabbak/ Fox Searchlight-Fox. 114 mins. Russia. 2004. Rel: 7 October 2005. Cert. 15.

The Night We Called It a Day ★★

Sydney, Australia; 1974. Rock promoter Rod Blue is in debt and can't rest on his laurels (Black Sabbath, The Doobie Brothers) forever. Then, after losing the confidence of one final financier, he flies to Los Angeles and convinces Frank Sinatra to sing in Sydney. Rod's future would seem assured, but Sinatra comes with his own set of monumental problems… In the film, he is described as, 'the biggest star on earth.' Today, Frank Sinatra may not be as recognisable as Madonna or Michael Jackson, but he is still an iconic image, before and with the hairpiece. Inevitably, then, casting a well-known actor like Dennis Hopper is going to be problematic, aggravated in this instance by poor lip-synching. In fact, little rings true in this amiable fiasco, Joel Edgerton fails to capture our sympathies (in spite of his character's Herculean resolve) and Rose Byrne – the film's true star – is given too little to do. JC-W

• *Frank Sinatra* Dennis Hopper, *Barbara Marx* Melanie Griffith, *Hilary Hunter* Portia De Rossi, *Rod Blue* Joel Edgerton, *Audrey Rose Appleby* Rose Byrne, *Mickey Rudin* David Hemmings, *Bob Hawke* David Field, *Penny* Victoria Thaine, *Jilly Rizzo* Stephen O'Rourke, *Kerry Packer* Max Fairchild, *Frank Sinatra's singing voice dubbed by* Tom Burlinson, *with* Nicholas Hope, Tony Barry, Vincent Ball, Jennifer Hagan.

• *Dir* Paul Goldman, *Pro* Emile Sherman, Nik Powell and Peter Clifton, *Ex Pro* Jonathan Shteinman, Michael Thomas III, Gary Smith, Bill Alan and Emma Hayter, *Line Pro* Barbara Gibbs, *Screenplay* Michael Thomas and Peter Clifton, *Ph* Danny Ruhlmann, *Pro Des* Michael Philips, *Ed* Stephen Evans, *M* Rupert Gregson-Williams, *Costumes* Emily Seresin.

Film Finance Corp. Australia/Baker Street-Content Film. 95 mins. Australia/UK. 2003. Rel: 26 December 2005. Cert. 15.

No Rest for the Brave ★★★

This piece from writer-director Alain Guiraudie is a real oddity about a youth in a French village who comes to believe that he will never awaken if he falls asleep. The filmmaker has a way with words and obtains good performances, but the universe he creates – all his own – is bemusingly weird. The youth in what could be his own fantasy of the outside world reappears under another name, has a gay relationship with an older man, seems to be a mass killer and gets caught up with gangsters. It doesn't really add up but Guiraudie gives himself to it wholeheartedly

and there are memorable moments of gentle comedy: when did you last see a shot of gangsters in the rain sheltering under umbrellas? Original title: *Pas De Repos Pour Les Braves*. MS

• *Basile/Hector* Thomas Suire, *Igor* Thomas Blanchard, *Johnny Got* Laurent Soffiati, *Bodowski* Vincent Martin, *Sorano* Pierre-Maurice Nouvel, *Roger* Roger Guidone, *Lydie* Nicole Huc, *Dede* Jean-Claude Baudracco, *Daniel* Bruno Izarn.

• *Dir* and *Screenplay* Alain Guiraudie, *Pro* Natalie Eybrard and Jean-Philippe Labadie, *Co-Pro* Gabriele Kranzelbinder and Alexander Dumreicher-Ivanceanu, *Line Pro* Marie-Rose Eybrard, *Ph* Antoine Heberle, *Pro Des* Eric Moulard, *Ed* Pierre Molin, *M* Bruno Izarin and Jacques Mestres, *Costumes* Karine Vintache.

Coproduction Office/Paulo Films/ARTE France Cinéma/ Canal Plus-Tartan Films. 104 mins. France/Austria. 2003. Rel: 26 August 2005. No Cert.

North Country ★★★★

Northern Minnesota; 1989. The mother of two illegitimate children, Josie Aimes is hardly the poster child for buttoned-up feminism. Even her own family – her parents, her kids – seems unsympathetic to the mess she's got herself into. But after running away from her abusive husband, Josie is determined to pay her own way in society. So, taking advantage of the new enforced quotas for women, she signs up for a job in the iron mine at which her increasingly distant father works. As winter blankets the bleak landscape, so Josie finds an even more desolate reception for her at the mine, as she becomes a target for her co-workers' openly aggressive and cruel male chauvinism. But she's not going to take any of it lying down… Inspired by the book *Class Action: The Landmark Case That Changed Sexual Harassment Law*, Niki Caro's *North Country* is a sobering indictment of the American working man. While the film's first quarter is overly slow and the finale a little rushed, its overall emotional impact is considerable. And it's a work of huge cinematic accomplishment, from the flawless performances of the female cast to Chris Menges' eloquent cinematography to Gustavo Santaolalla's effectively minimal score. JC-W

• *Josie Aimes* Charlize Theron, *Glory* Frances McDormand, *Kyle* Sean Bean, *Hank Aimes* Richard Jenkins, *Bobby Sharp* Jeremy Renner, *Sherry* Michelle Monaghan, *Bill White* Woody Harrelson, *Alice Aimes* Sissy Spacek, *Karen Aimes* Elle Peterson, *Leslie Conlin* Linda Emond, *Arlen Pavich* Xander Berkeley, *with* Thomas Curtis, James Cada, Rusty Schwimmer, Chris Mulkey, John Aylward, Tom Bower.

• *Dir* Niki Caro, *Pro* Nick Wechsler, *Ex Pro* Helen Bartlett, Nana Greenwald, Doug Claybourne and Jeff Skoll, *Screenplay* Michael Seitzman, *Ph* Chris Menges, *Pro Des* Richard Hoover, *Ed* David Coulson, *M* Gustavo Santaolalla, *Costumes* Cindy Evans.

Warner/Participant Prods-Warner. 126 mins. USA. 2005. Rel: 3 February 2006. Cert. 15.

Novo ★★

A competent cast cannot disguise the banality of this film with its utterly unlikely tale of a man suffering from short-term memory loss. In *Memento* that condition was central to an absorbing tale of vengeance, but here it's just an excuse for a sex drama. The man's state may prevent him from remembering that he has a wife eager for his cure but it doesn't discourage other women from making a play for him. In a very French way the film poses some philosophical questions among the general silliness, but it's really no more than an excuse for the players to shed their clothes. MS

• *Pablo* aka *Graham* Eduardo Noriega, *Irène* Anna Mouglalis, *Sabine* Nathalie Richard, *Fred* Éric Caravaca, *Isabelle* Paz Vega, *Antoine* Leny Bueno, *Julie* Julie Gayet, *Dr Sagem* Bernard Bloch.

• *Dir* Jean P. Limosin, *Pro* Hengameh Panahi, *Co-Pro* Valerio De Paolis, *Screenplay* Limosin and Christophe Honoré, *Ph* Julien Hirsch, *Art Dir* Jimmy Vansteenkiste, *Ed* Cristina Otero Roth, *M* Loik Dury and Mathieu Dury aka Kouz-1.

Lumen Films/Alta Prods/Amka Films/ Canal Plus-Tartan Films. 98 mins. France/Spain/Switzerland/Italy/Canada/Benelux/ Japan. 2002. Rel: 8 July 2005. Cert. 18.

Offside ★★★½

Offside not only conveys the extraordinary excitement of and passion for international football, but shows the hideous discrimination of Iranian society. As the whole country is roused into a state of frenzy as Iran prepares to play Bahrain in a World Cup qualifier, girls disguise themselves as boys so as to sneak into the stadium to watch the game live. Having paid a scalp more than three times the market price for a ticket, Sima is escorted to a holding pen with other girls disguised as boys. There, the disappointed fans argue with their uniformed captors about the inequality of the social status quo, while the electric atmosphere around them gradually intoxicates them all. A totally believable snapshot of contemporary Iran, *Offside* is an insightful and touching film (with considerable humour) from one of the country's most acclaimed neorealistic commentators. FYI: In spite of Jafar Panahi's international standing, none of his films have been screened in his own country. JC-W

• *With*: *first girl* Sima Mobarak Shahi, *Azari soldier* Safar Samandar, *smoking girl* Shayesteh Irani, *Mashadi soldier* M. Kheyrabadi, *girl soccer player* Ida Sadeghi, *girl with chador* Golnaz Farmani, *soldier girl* Mahnaz Zabihi.

• *Dir, Pro* and *Ed* Jafar Panahi, *Screenplay* Panahi and Shadmehr Rastin, *Ph* Mahmood Kalari, *Set Des* Iraj Raminfar.

Jafar Panahi-Artificial Eye. 88 mins. Iran. 2006. Rel: 9 June 2006. Cert. PG.

Oliver Twist ★½

An orphan boy escapes from the workhouse and flees to London where he's adopted by a ragbag gang of pickpockets… Some films are director-driven, others actor-driven. Considering that this ninth big-screen adaptation of Charles Dickens' 1939 novel is directed by the Oscar-winning Roman Polanski and stars the Oscar-winning Ben Kingsley, one might have hoped for a bit of both. As it is, it is composer-driven, with Rachel Portman's meddlesome score blindly choking the life out of this grim call-to-arms for the abolition of Britain's workhouses. So as poor Oliver drinks water from a puddle, we have Portman whipping up her favourite sunny phrases from *Emma* and *Chocolat*. But then the film is hardly helped by its actors: Ben Kingsley gets lost in a pantomimic mix of Shylock and Wilfred Brambell, Jamie Foreman is scruffy and petulant (when he should've been terrifying), and young Harry Eden – so good in Gillies MacKinnon's *Pure* – is badly miscast as the Artful Dodger. Oliver himself, played with angel-faced vapidity by Barney Clark, all but disappears in the final act as the film slows to an interminable limp. JC-W

• *Fagin* Ben Kingsley, *Oliver Twist* Barney Clark, *Bill Sykes* Jamie Foreman, *Nancy* Leanne Rowe, *Artful Dodger* Harry Eden, *Charley Bates* Lewis Chase, *Mr Brownlow* Edward Hardwicke, *Mr Bumble* Jeremy Swift, *Toby Crackit* Mark Strong, *Barney* Jake Curran, *Bet* Ophelia Lovibond, *Mrs Bedwin* Frances Cuka, *Mr Sowerberry* Michael Heath, *Mrs Sowerberry* Gillian Hanna, *Mr Fang* Alun Armstrong, *with* Chris Overton, Teresa Churcher, Patrick Godfrey, Ian McNeice, Paul Brooke, Timothy Bateson, Liz Smith, Andy de La Tour, Peter Copley, Frank Mills, John Nettleton, Gerard Horan.

• *Dir* Roman Polanski, *Pro* Polanski, Robert Benmussa and Alaine Sarde, *Ex Pro* Timothy Burrill and Petr Moravec, *Screenplay* Ronald Harwood, *Ph* Pawel Edelman, *Pro Des* Allan Starski, *Ed* Hervé de Luze, *M* Rachel Portman, *Costumes* Anna Sheppard.

Alain Sarde/Robert Benmussa/RP Films/Pathé/Future Films, etc-Pathé. 130 mins. UK/France/Czech Republic. 2005. Rel: 7 October 2005. Cert. PG.

On a Clear Day ★★½

Too serious and genuine an actor to suit a feel-good movie (which this seeks to be), Peter Mullan in Ken Loach mode plays a 50-five-year old made redundant and at odds with his surviving son whose sibling drowned. Dad tries to prove himself and regain self-respect by swimming the Channel. Elsewhere there's broad comedy and big fictional-sounding scenes set up to move the audience before sending them out with a glow. The echoes of *The Full Monty* are inescapable and, if the mix is difficult to bring off, that film shows how well something like it can work. Here, however, the clashing styles collide in a way that sinks the project despite the good efforts from the cast MS

• *Frank* Peter Mullan, *Joan* Brenda Blethyn, *Eddie* Sean McGinley, *Rob* Jamie Sives, *Danny* Billy Boyd, *Norman* Ron Cook, *Angela* Jodhi May, *Chan* Benedict Wong, *Michelle*

Gotta pick a pocket or two: Barney Clark is chased through the streets of the Big Smoke in Roman Polanski's sub-standard *Oliver Twist* (from Pathé)

Swimming upstream: Brenda Blethyn in
Gaby Dellal's incongruous and contrived
On a Clear Day (from Icon)

Anne-Marie Timoney, *Observer* Shaun Dingwall, *Merv the Perv* Tony Roper, *Mad Bob* Paul Ritter.

• *Dir* Gaby Dellal, *Pro* Sarah Curtis and Dorothy Berwin, *Ex Pro* Bill Allan, Steve Christian, Lenny Crooks, Emma Hayter, Nick Hill and Andy Mayson, *Co-Pro* Martha Coleman, *Assoc Pro* Amy Lo, *Screenplay* Alex Rose, *Ph* David Johnson, *Pro Des* Mark Leese, *Ed* Robin Sales, *M* Stephen Warbeck, *Costumes* Kate Hawley.

Take Film Partnerships/Isle of Man Film/Glasgow Film Finance/Royal Bank of Scotland/Scottish Screen/Icon Entertainment-Icon.
98 mins. UK. 2004. Rel: 2 September 2005.
Cert. 12A.

Once In a Lifetime: The Extraordinary Story of the New York Cosmos ★★★★

Made with an admirable slickness, this documentary feature narrated by Matt Dillon tells the story of the New York Cosmos, the soccer team that for a while (in the seventies) won over the Americans to a sport never truly entrenched in the USA. The team's history is retold with *Rashomon*-like variations and gives a revealing portrait of the commercialism inherent in such promotions. There's an appropriate irony in the fact that the failure to maintain the support built up was due to the game's lack of appeal on American television. Even without any contribution from Pelé who declined to be interviewed, this is a documentary that in taking us behind the scenes provides much interest for viewers irrespective of their feelings about soccer. MS

• *With*: Johann Cruyff, Franz Beckenbauer, Shep Messing, Werner Roth, Giorgio Chinaglia, Ahmed Ertegun, Clive Toye, Phil Woosnam, Jay Emmett, Raphael de la Serra, David Hirshey, Mark Ross, Carlos Alberto, Pepe Pinton. *Narrator*: Matt Dillon.

• *Dir* Paul Crowder and John Dower, *Pro* John Battsek, Fisher Stevens and Tim Williams, *Ex Pro* John Penotti, Julie Goldman, Andrew Ruhemann, Michael Davies, Vicki Cherkas, Cedric Jeanson, Nick Fraser and Richard Klein, *Co-Ex Pro* Krysanne Katsoolis and Caroline Stevens, *Screenplay* Mark Monroe, based on a story by Dower and Monroe, *Ph* Nick Bennett, *Ed* Crowder, *M* Matter

GreenStreet Films/Passion Pictures/Cactus Three/BBC/Cosmos Soccer Club-Pathé.
97 mins. USA/UK. 2006. Rel:19 May 2006. Cert. 15.

One Day in Europe ★★★

Writer-director Hannes Stöhr is adept at using locations well and here he has four of them, for this is a portmanteau feature made up of consecutive tales set in Moscow, Istanbul, Santiago de Compostela and Berlin. They are linked by the fact that all take place on the same day, that of an international soccer match. But since this sporting element is virtually ignored, one searches in vain for anything significant that will bring further coherence to the quartet. Admittedly each one features either a robbery or a scam based on a supposed robbery, but so what? The individual tales are mildly agreeable but totally unmemorable. MS

• *Kate* Megan Gay, *Elena* Luidmila Tsvetkova, *Rokko* Florian Lukas, *Celal* Erdal Yildiz, *Gabor* Peter Scherer, *Sergeant Barreira* Miguel de Lira, *Rachida* Rachida Brakni, *Claude* Boris Arquier.

• *Dir* and *Screenplay* Hannes Stöhr, *Pro* Anne Lepin and Sigrid Hoerner, *Co-Pro* Anton Reixa and Eoin Moore, *Ph* Florian Hoffmeister, *Pro Des* Andreas Olshausen, *Ed* Anne Fabini, *M* Florian Appl, *Costumes* Daniela Selig.

moneypenny filmproduktion, etc-Peccadillo Pictures. 95 mins. Germany/Spain. 2004. Rel: 19 May 2006. No Cert.

One Dollar Curry ★★½

If *Jaya Ganga* (1998) revealed Vijay Singh as a man with a flair for atmospheric art-house cinema, this popular-style comedy set in Paris shows that he is much less adept attempting mainstream fare. It's the story of an Indian immigrant featured in a TV programme after pretending to be a chef of distinction and the first half is reasonably engaging in its naive yet warm fashion. Thereafter, however, the going gets increasingly silly, stupid rather than comic and with contrived interludes for classical dance and a Bollywood-style song. The film means well for it makes serious underlying points in favour of a cosmopolitan mix but it comes across as amateurish and uneasy save for the assured performance of Trevor Stephens. MS

• *Nishan Singh* Vikram Chatwal, *Nathalie* Gabriella Wright, *Yamini* Smriti Mishra, *Fixer* Trevor Stephens, *with* Benoît Etchart-Solès, Lakshantha Abenayake, Stéphanie Guieu.

• *Dir, Pro* and *Screenplay* Vijay Singh, *Ph* Benoît Chamaillard, *Pro Des* Jean-Marc Trau Tan Ba, *Ed* Nadine Verdier, *M* Zakir Hussain and Taufiq Qureshi, *Costumes* Cedric Grenapin.

Silhouette Films/Zee Network/France 2 Cinéma-Silhouette Films. 89 mins, Fravce/India/UK.2004. Rel: 23 September 2005. Cert. 12A.

One Love ★½

Reggae musician Kassa and gospel singer Serena are just two of the entrants in a major musical competition calling itself Talent Jamaica. When the self-conscious Serena takes her time in the recording studio, Kassa hears her heavenly voice and believes she will be the perfect front woman for his band Freedom City. But Serena is the daughter of a devout Pentecostal preacher and is not allowed to sing anything but gospel… What a wonderful idea: a romance played out against the clash of in-bred cultures as seen through their respective musical forms set on the picturesque island of Jamaica. Better still, get Bob Marley's son to play the Rastafarian Romeo to a beautiful gospel-singing Juliet and you have the makings of a modest, sure-fire hit. But romance without a spark of human chemistry, undermined by

some ill-advised comic buffoonery, is not the best way to go about it. Furthermore, Ky-mani Marley looks drugged and anything but in love, while the film's one saving grace – its music – is all but relegated to the background. No music no try. JC-W

• *Kassa* Ky-mani Marley, *Serena* Cherine Anderson, *Aaron* Idris Elba, *Scarface* Vas Blackwood, *Selector G* Winston `Bello' Bell, *Pastor Johnson* Winston Stona, *Obeah man* Carl Bradshaw.

• *Dir* Rick Elgood and Don Letts, *Pro* Yvonne Deutschman, Shelaagh Ferrell and Bjorn Eivind Arskog, *Co-Pro* Ola K. Hunnes, *Screenplay* Trevor Rhone, *Ph* John Christian Rosenlund, *Pro Des* Elgood, *Ed* Jon Endre Mørk, *M* Simon Bass; tracks performed by Bob Marley, Stena, Innocent Kru, Luciano, The Revolutionaries, Sons & Daughters, Wayne Marshall, Elephant Man, Sean Paul, Cherine Anderson, Sandra Melody, Ky-mani Marley, Spice, Chaka Demus & Pliers, Bounty Killer, Cecile, Square One, Shaggy, Wayne Wonder, etc, *Costumes* Tasha Hussey.

Film Council/Baker Street/BV International/Take 4/One Love Films/Euromax/Exposed-Blue Dolphin. 94 mins. UK/Norway. 2003. Rel: 15 July 2005. Cert. 12A.

One Night in Mongkok ★★★½

Original title: *Mongkok Hakye.*
Mongkok, Kowloon; Hong Kong; today. Following a showdown between rival Triad gangs, a contract killer is hired from mainland China to knock off Triad head honcho Carl. However, the police get wind of the intrigue and appoint officer Lai Fu to intercept the assassin… Derek Yee's policier is, on one level, depressingly routine. Yet beneath its tapestry of crime, prostitution, assassins, gangsters and overcrowded streets, it expresses an aching, moving melancholy. It's also directed with an accomplished lucidity, a clarity of vision that unites the story's myriad threads with a satisfactory momentum. And the film's refusal to exploit its inherent violence is commendable. Original title: *Mongkok Hakye.* CB

• *Lai Fu* aka 'Roy' Daniel Wu, *Dandan* Cecilia Cheung, *Officer Milo* Alex Fong, *Dep. Lee* aka `Brandon' Chin Ka-lok, *with* Ken Wong, Lam Suet, Anson Leung, Monica Chan, Alex Chan, Henry Fong, Sam Lee, Austin Wei, Pau Hei-ching, Cha Chuen-yee.

• *Dir* and *Screenplay* Derek Yee, *Pro* Dau Sau-fong and Daniel Lam, *Ex Pro* Henry Fong, *Ph* Venus Keung, *Pro Des* Bruce Yu, *Ed* Cheung Ka-fai, *M* Peter Kam, *Costumes* William Feng and Mabel Kwan.

Film Unlimited-Tartan Films. 110 mins. Hong Kong. 2004. Rel: 23 September 2005. No Cert.

Out on a Limb ★★

West London; today. Felix Limb is an arrogant TV chef who has begun to rest on his laurels. Then, shortly before he is to host a prestigious dinner party, he discovers that his show has been cancelled. Then his most important guests bale out, his wife finds out that he has been having an affair with his PA and armed kidnappers interrupt the party. The 'terrorists' have actually broken into the wrong house, but armed police have already surrounded the premises… There is a great idea running through the script to this outrageous black comedy. A biting commentary on the cult of celebrity, a celebration of good food and a siege thriller all rolled into one, *Out on a Limb* should've been a riot. Unfortunately, it's played too heavily for laughs, there is a certain slackness in the pacing and an annoying soundtrack of Greatest Classical Hits. Still, to give it credit, it was shot in 17 days in South Africa by a first-time director. JC-W

• *Felix Limb* Henry Goodman, *Simon* Neil Stuke, *Michelle Limb* Julianne White, *Vaughn* Costa Milton, *Ramsey Harrison* Jeremy Crutchley, *Bruce Ash* Peter Gevisser, *Isabelle Leach* Bo Peterson, *Amy Hardcastle* Rolanda Marais, *with* Hakeem Kae-Kazim, Robyn Scott, André Jacobs, Miranda Sawyer, Bob McCabe, Rob Churchill, Anthea Thompson.

• *Dir* Robert Heath, *Pro* Costa Milton, Joy Mellins and Dave Shanks, *Ex Pro* Christopher Theo, Costa John Theo and Ronnie Apteker, *Line Pro* Diana Keam, *Screenplay* Bob McCabe and Rob Churchill, *Ph* Mike Downie, *Pro Des* Hayden Griffin, *Ed* Jackie Le Cordeur, *M* Andrew Ford, *Costumes* Dihantus Engelbrecht, *Sound* Stef Albertyn.

Theta Films/Faith Creations-Guerilla Films.
102 mins. UK/South Africa. 2004. Rel: 14 October 2005.
Cert. 15.

Overcoming ★★★½

A belated follow-on from Claude Lelouch's short piece *For A Yellow Jersey* (1965), this is a documentary feature about the Tour de France made by Denmark's Tómas Gislason. In recording the fortunes of a Danish owner team, CSC run by former biker Bjarne Riis, the film shows warmth of feeling and in looking at the individuals involved it emphasises the sense of team effort generated. However, a cycle race does not particularly lend itself to exciting cinematic presentation and elements of stylised direction and a music score that tries too hard to whip up dramatic tension only serve to limit further the film's effectiveness. *Overcoming* is over-stretched and uneven but there's also quite a lot about it that is pleasing. MS

• *With*: Lance Armstrong, Michelle Bartoli, Ivan Basso, B.S. Christiansen, Ole Kåre Føli, Brian Nygaard, Andrea Peron, Bjarne Riis, Carlos Sastre, Jens Voigt.

• *Dir* and *Screenplay* Tómas Gislason, *Pro* Stine Boe Jensen and Mikael Rieks, *Ex Pro* Kim Magnusson, *Ph* Mads Thomsen, *Ed* Gislason, Cathrine Ambus, Rikke Selin Lorentzen and Valdís Óskarsdóttir, *M* Tobias Marberger.

Nordisk Film/The Danish Film Institute/TV Fond-Soda Pictures.
105 mins. Denmark/Norway.Finland/Sweden. 2005. Rel: 28 April 2006. No Cert.

Overnight ★★★½

Filmed as it happened by two colleagues of Troy Duffy, this documentary records how this unknown sold a film script to Miramax and secured an astonishing deal. Although without any formal training, he was to direct the movie himself, cast it, use his own band on the soundtrack and even have final cut. Film fans will readily identify with what seemed a dream come true, only to find themselves backtracking – not simply because the movie, *The Boondock Saints*, seems to have been a stinker that barely got a release but on account of Duffy's character. This may be a movie about the heartless buck-making ways of Hollywood but it's also about megalomania with Duffy himself proving abusive, self-centred and totally unfeeling in his treatment of his colleagues. Cut his expletives and the film would scarcely run to feature length. However, this documentary has its own weakness: the absence of a wider picture. There are no clips from Duffy's movie, no explanation of what drew actors such as Willem Dafoe and Billy Connolly and no explanation from Miramax as to why they did what they did. We have only half the story, but what's there is fascinating. MS

• *With*: Troy Duffy, Taylor Duffy, Gordon Clark, Jimi Jackson, Chris Brinker, Mark Brian Smith, Tony Montana, Mark Wahlberg, Jake Busey, Paul Ruebens, Willem Dafoe, Billy Connolly, Ron Jeremy.

• *Dir, Pro* and *Ed* Mark Brian Smith and Tony Montana, *Ex Pro* Montana, *Co-Pro* Todd Fossey, *Ph* Smith, *M* Duotone Audio Group.

Black & White Pictures/Ronnoco Prods/Ether Films-Metrodome.
82 mins. USA. 2004. Rel: 8 July 2005. Cert. 15.

Over the Hedge ★★★½

On the face of it, the suburbs are a Mecca of grub. The inhabitants – who are just as frightened of the surrounding wildlife as it is of humans – order food to the door, throw food out and wear food on their faces (cucumber sandwich anyone?). However, the manicured lawns, household pets and towering presence of The Verminator prove to be a major menace to the creatures that have just lost their foraging grounds to civic encroachment… There's a big message here, not least the unsavoury effects of salt, sugar and unsaturated fats on their unsuspecting consumers. And there's much ingenuity at play as the loveable animals dream up fantastic ways to bypass the obstacle course of the housing development that has enveloped their world. A witty critique on American consumerism, *Over the Hedge* is full of virtuoso moments, with fireflies standing in for the proverbial light bulbs of inspiration and a superb sequence in which time stands still as a squirrel dosed on caffeine quietly goes about his business. Even so, there's something quite charmless about the wisecracking critters while the maudlin homily on family values is predictably banal. JC-W

• *Voices*: *RJ the raccoon* Bruce Willis, *Verne the turtle* Garry Shandling, *Hammy the squirrel* Steve Carell, *Ozzie the possum*

William Shatner, *Vincent the bear* Nick Nolte, *Dwayne, The Verminator* Thomas Haden Church, *Lou the porcupine* Eugene Levy, *Penny the porcupine* Catherine O'Hara, *Heather the possum* Avril Lavigne, *Stella the skunk* Wanda Sykes, *Tiger the housecat* Omid Djalili, *Gladys the human being* Allison Janney, with Sami Kirkpatrick, Shane Baumel, Madison Davenport, Nicholas Guest, Sandra Holt.

• *Dir* Tim Johnson and Karey Kirkpatrick, *Pro* Bonnie Arnold, *Ex Pro* Bill Damaschke, *Screenplay* Len Blum, Lorne Cameron, David Hoselton and Karey Kirkpatrick, based on the comic strip by Michael Fry and T. Lewis, *Pro Des* Kathy Altieri, *Ed* John K. Carr, *M* Rupert Gregson-Williams; songs performed by Ben Folds, *Visual Effects* Craig Ring, *Layout* Damon O'Beirne.

DreamWorks-UIP.
83 mins. USA. 2006. Rel: 30 June 2006. Cert. U.

Paradise Now ★★★★½

For Saïd and Khaled, existence on the West Bank is all but intolerable. Between the rubble, roadblocks, occasional mortar attack and dire prospects of gainful employment, life has become 'worthless.' Friends since childhood, Saïd and Khaled have vowed to die together, for a cause to liberate the suffering of their people. Then, out of the blue, they are chosen to sign on for 'Paradise'… Filmed on the West Bank and in Tel Aviv, *Paradise Now* is a timely commentary on the peace process in Palestine. And between the film's success at the Berlin Film Festival and its release in the UK, Hamas won over the Palestinian electorate and Steven Spielberg's pro-Israeli *Munich* skewered five Oscar nominations. Had *Paradise Now* not been so articulate, gripping and well made, it would still have been an important film. Addressing incendiary issues with a clear head, it focuses a potent spotlight on an unsustainable situation, which can only be exacerbated by more violence. Even so, the film gives a human face to the suicide bomber – and let us not forget that they are human – and even has the courage to introduce humour. JC-W

• *Saïd* Kais Nashef, *Khaled* Ali Suliman, *Suha* Lubna Azabal, *Jamal* Amer Hlehel, *Saïd's mother* Hiam Abbass, *Abu-Karem* Ashraf Barhoum.

• *Dir* Hany Abu-Assad, *Pro* Bero Beyer, Hengameh Panahi, Amir Harel, Gerhard Meixner and Roman Paul, *Assoc Pro* Hamoudi Buqai, *Screenplay* Hany Abu-Assad and Bero Beyer, *Ph* Antoine Heberlé, *Pro Des* Olivier Meidinger, *Ed* Sander Vos, *Costumes* Walid Maw'ed.

Augustus Film/Lama Films/Razor Film/Lumen Films/
Arte France Cinéma/Hazazah Film-Warner.
90 mins. France/Germany/Netherlands/Israel. 2005.
Rel: 14 April 2006. Cert. 15.

Pavee Lackeen The Traveller Girl ★★★½

Back in 1951 it took British director Paul Rotha to make a film about Irish tinkers (*No Resting Place*) and now Shropshire-born Perry Ogden has made this piece about gypsies in Dublin and sensibly the film is sub-titled for clarity. Taking Alan Clarke as his model, Ogden's approach is to minimalise fiction, to eschew sentimentality and to present the material as naturalistically as any documentary. He uses non-professional players who are, in effect, recreating their own lives, and at the centre is ten-year-old Winnie Maughan whose mother receives an eviction notice in respect of the trailer where she lives with her brood of children. The film's tone, never condescending, is exactly right but without bringing in anything too fictitious it should have been possible to round off the piece effectively instead of letting it fade away obliquely. MS

• *Winnie* Winnie Maughan, *Leroy* Paddy Maughan, *Rosie* Rosie Maughan, *Mum* Rose Maughan, *Uncle Martin* Michael Collins, *Marie* Helen Joyce, *Shannon* Abbie Spallen.

• *Dir, Pro* and *Ph* Perry Ogden, *Co-Pro* Martina Niland, *Screenplay* Ogden & Mark Venner, *Assoc Pro* John Rocha, *Ed* Breege Rowley.

An Lár Films/Bord Scannán na hÉireann/Irish Film Board-Verve Pictures.
88 mins. Ireland. 2005. Rel: 17 February 2006. Cert. 15.

The Perfect Catch ★★

Boston; the present. Having decided that the gap between their earning power is not a problem, business consultant Lindsey Meeks falls hard for the funny, gallant schoolteacher Ben Wrightman. He's sweet, honest and great with kids. So, what's the catch? Well, things prove too good to be true until the Boston Red Sox baseball team starts their new season. Suddenly, for Ben there's little room for anything else in his life… What is it about Nick Hornby and American brothers who direct? Having hit pay dirt with the film version of *About a Boy* – helmed by the New York-born siblings Chris and Paul Weitz – writer and executive producer Hornby has offered the second big-screen version of his 1992 novel to Bobby and Peter Farrelly. Jettisoning the naturalism, charm and understatement that distinguished the British edition (scripted by Hornby himself), the Farrellys squeeze their movie dry of both distinction and credibility. In addition, they have abandoned their trademark bad taste for a cloying sweetness that has become the norm for the Drew Barrymore canon. She tamed Adam Sandler and now, as producer, she has emasculated the Farrellys. US title: *Fever Pitch*. JC-W

• *Lindsey Meeks* Drew Barrymore, *Ben Wrightman* Jimmy Fallon, *Robin* KaDee Strickland, *Molly* Ione Skye, *Sarah* Marissa Jaret Winokur, *Doug Meeks* James B. Sikking, *Maureen Meeks* JoBeth Williams, *with* Jack Kehler, Willie Garson, Siobhan Fallon Hogan, Andrew Wilson, Jason Varitek, Johnny Damon, Jackie Burroughs, Dennis Eckersley, Keith MacWhorter, Peter Gammons, Harold Reynolds, Jordan Leandre.

• *Dir* Peter and Bobby Farrelly, *Pro* Alan Greenspan, Amanda Posey, Gil Netter, Drew Barrymore, Nancy Juvonen and Bradley Thomas, *Ex Pro* Nick Hornby, David Evans and Marc S. Fischer, *Screenplay* Lowell Ganz and Babaloo Mandel, *Ph* Matthew F. Leonetti, *Pro Des* Maher Ahmad, *Ed* Alan

Here lies Hilary Duff (right) as Vanessa Lengies (left) just laughs it off – in Mark Rosman's gossamer *The Perfect Man* (from UIP)

Baumgarten, *M* Craig Armstrong; tracks performed by The Standells, Porterville, The Silicone Teens, Ivy, J. Geils Band, Chic, Neil Diamond, The Human League, Nick Drake, Tears for Fears, Jonathan Richman, etc, *Costumes* Sophie de Rakoff.

Fox 2000 Pictures/Flower Films/Wildgaze Films-Fox. 103 mins. USA. 2005. Rel: 12 August 2005. Cert. PG.

The Perfect Man ★★

Like Kimberly J. Brown in *Tumbleweeds* and Natalie Portman in *Anywhere But Here*, Hilary Duff has a mom who just can't settle down to one place and one guy. So when Jean Hamilton nails a job as a baker in Brooklyn, Hilary's Holly concocts a perfect suitor for her mother via e-mail. Quite how Jean falls for the ruse may explain why men keep such a wide berth... It took three writers to come up with this story? Like a premise lifted from a teen novel and served up sitcom cute, *The Perfect Man* is undemanding fare for Hilary Duff fans. It's sad to see Heather Locklear – Sammy Jo in *Dynasty* – showing such signs of wear and tear, but she can cook up a mean tart. JC-W

• *Holly Hamilton* Hilary Duff, *Jean Hamilton* Heather Locklear, *Ben Cooper* Chris Noth, *Lenny Horton* Mike O'Malley, *Adam Forrest* Ben Feldman, *Amy Pearl* Vanessa Lengies, *Gloria* Caroline Rhea, *Dolores* Kym Whitley, *Zoe Hamilton* Aria Wallace.

• *Dir* Mark Rosman, *Pro* Marc Platt, Dawn Wolfrom and Susan Duff, *Ex Pro* Billy Higgins and Adam Siegel, *Screenplay* Gina Wendkos, from a story by Michael McQuown, Heather Robinson and Katherine Torpey, *Ph* John R. Leonetti, *Pro Des* Jasna Stefanovich, *Ed* Cara Silverman, *M* Christophe Beck, *Costumes* Marie Sylvie Deveau.

Universal/Marc Platt-UIP. 100 mins. USA. 2005. Rel: 19 August 2005. Cert. PG.

The Piano Tuner of Earthquakes ★★★½

Since this new feature by the Quay Brothers finds them being true to themselves, it follows that this strange imaginative work is of specialised appeal. The one real surprise is that the plot line echoes *The Phantom of the Opera* although the 'Scope format is also unexpected. One Dr Droz, a scorned opera composer, seizes a singer who has collapsed on stage as though dead so that she can perform his music, but the piano tuner summoned to service the doctor's seven automata proves to be the singer's lover out to rescue her. Music plays an integral role here and the cast, including Fassbinder's Gottfried John who has a powerful presence as Dr Droz, is adroitly chosen, but neither plot nor ideas register memorably. It's easier to admire the film's integrity than to be really caught up by it. MS

• *Malvina van Stille* Amira Casar, *Dr Emmanuel Droz* Gottfried John, *Assumpta* Assumpta Serna, *Filesberto/Adolfo* Cesar Sarachu.

Pillock in a pillbox: Steve Martin in Shawn Levy's *The Pink Panther* (from Fox)

• *Dir* Brothers Quay (i.e. Stephen and Timothy Quay), *Pro* Keith Griffiths, Alexander Ris and Hengameh Panahi, *Ex Pro* Terry Gilliam and Paul Trijbits, *Screenplay* Brothers Quay and Alan Passes, *Ph* Nic Knowland, *Art Dir* Eric Veenstra, *Ed* Simon Laurie, *M* Trevor Duncan and Christopher Slaski,

Mitteldeutsche Medienförderung GmbH/National Lottery-Artificial Eye.
99 mins. UK/France/Germany/Japan/Switzerland. 2005. Rel: 17 February 2006. Cert. 12A.

Pierrepoint ★★★★½

England; 1932-1956. The title character is a private, modest and moral man who takes enormous pride in his work. Meticulous to the point of obsession, he documents every encounter with his customers and defends their sanctity in no uncertain terms. And, after his job is done, he is no longer Britain's most popular hangman, but loveable Albert again… Considering how many hangings have been recorded by the cinema, little thought has ever been given to the hangman. And Albert J. Pierrepoint was a very real figure, a man whose deadly trade moved alongside many historical moments in British history. Adrian Shergold's film is a fascinating character study of as man who works outside the norm of convention and has to find ways to deal with that. From the thorough attention to the minutiae of hanging itself, to Timothy Spall's commanding interior performance, *Pierrepoint* is a film of uncommon distinction. JC-W

• *Albert J. Pierrepoint* Timothy Spall, *Annie Fletcher* Juliet Stevenson, *James 'Tish' Corbitt* Eddie Marsan, *Jessie Kelly* Claire Keelan, *Charlie Sykes* Christopher Fulford, *Uncle Tom* Bernard Kay, *Monty* Clive Francis, *Ruth Ellis* Mary Stockley, *Timothy Evans* Ben McKay, *with* Cavan Clerkin, Ian Shaw, Maggie Ollerenshaw, Frances Gold, Rodney Litchfield, Tim Woodward, Nicholas Blane, Anthony Denham, Robin Soans, Tobias Menzies, Ann Bell.

• *Dir* Adrian Shergold, Pro Christine Langan, *Ex Pro* Paul Trijbits, Andy Harries, Rebecca Eaton and Jeff Pope, *Line Pro* Claudine Sturdy, *Screenplay* Pope and Bob Mills, *Ph* Danny Cohen, *Pro Des* Candida Otton, *Ed* Tania Reddin, *M* Martin Phipps, *Costumes* Mary Jane Reyner.

UK Film Council/Capitol Films/Granada/Masterpiece Theatre-Redbus.
95 mins. UK/USA. 2005. Rel: 7 April 2006. Cert. 15.

The Pink Panther ★★½

When the Pink Panther – a priceless diamond ring – is stolen during the climax of an international football match, Chief Inspector Dreyfus sees it as a chance to ensnare the *Légion d'honneur*. So, for a decoy, he hires the historically inept Jacques Clouseau to hunt down the Panther, while he, Dreyfus, moves behind the scenes… When writer-director Blake Edwards was casting the original *Pink Panther* back in 1963, he envisaged Peter Ustinov in the role of Inspector Clouseau. Since then Peter Sellers has played the bumbling detective six times (once posthumously), Alan Arkin and

Roger Moore once each and Roberto Benigni his son. In Hollywood's quest to extend the franchise, Kevin Spacey, Mike Myers and Chris Tucker were all seriously mooted to take over Sellers' mantle, when, in November of 2003, Steve Martin stepped in. Now, Martin is making a career out of remakes, usually to disastrous ends, but here he retains a straight face and is as often hilarious as embarrassing. This says a lot for the comic durability of the original character, but you have to hand it to Martin that when he's not manipulating the obvious he can be seriously funny. Ponton: 'He was found dead.' Clouseau: 'Was it fatal?' Ponton: 'Yes.' Clouseau: 'How fatal?' Ponton: 'Completely.' JC-W

• *Inspector Jacques Clouseau* Steve Martin, *Chief Inspector Dreyfus* Kevin Kline, *Gilbert Ponton* Jean Reno, *Nicole* Emily Mortimer, *Yuri* Henry Czerny, *Xania* Beyoncé Knowles, *Cherie* Kristin Chenoweth, *Larocque* Roger Rees, *with* Philip Goodwin, Henri Garcin, William Abadie, Daniel Sauli, Anna Katarina, Charlotte Maier, and (uncredited) *Nigel Oswald 006* Clive Owen, *Yves Gluant* Jason Statham.

• *Dir* Shawn Levy, *Pro* Robert Simonds, *Ex Pro* Tracey Trench and Ira Shuman, *Screenplay* Len Blum and Steve Martin, from a story by Blum and Michael Saltzman, *Ph* Jonathan Brown, *Pro Des* Lilly Kilvert, *Ed* George Folsey Jr and Brad E. Wilhite, *M* Christophe Beck; *Pink Panther* theme Henry Mancini, *Costumes* Joseph G. Aulisi, *Main Titles* Kurtz & Friends.

MGM/Columbia Pictures-Fox.
92 mins. USA. 2006. Rel: 17 March 2006. Cert. PG.

Pleasant Days ★★★½

This Hungarian feature is our introduction to the work of Kornél Mundruczó who has a real sense of cinema. What one questions apart from an over-the-top start is why he should choose to tell such a despairing story. It features a youngster fresh from jail, Peter (Tamás Polgár), his sister so desperate for a child that she buys one from a young mother initially willing to sell, and the young mother herself, Maya (Orsolya Tóth). The women are hardly sympathetic and Peter proves to be an outsider closer to Camus's infamous character than to an appealing rebel. But Polgár is iconic and it's no surprise that Mundruczó is working with Tóth again, since she has a presence reminiscent of such fine actresses as Harriet Andersson and Eva Mattes in their youth. MS

• *Peter* Tamás Polgár, *Maja* Orsolya Tóth, *Maria* Kata Wéber, *János* Lajos Ottó Horváth, *Ákos* András Réthelyi, *Józsi* Károly Kuna.

• *Dir* Kornél Mundruczó, *Pro* Zsofia Kende, Viktoria Petranyi and Kornel Sipos, *Screenplay* Mundruczo, Viktoria Petranyi and Sandor Zsoter, *Ph* Andras Nagy, *Visual Des* Agnes Szabo, *Ed* Vanda Aranyi, *Costumes* Janos Brecki.

Coproduction Office/Laurinfilm-Tartan Films.
103 mins. Hungary/Germany. 2002. Rel: 22 July 2005. No Cert.

Poseidon ★★

In the middle of the North Atlantic, just minutes into New Year's Day, a rogue wave upturns the luxury cruise ship Poseidon. For many it's instant death, but there are survivors and they need to get to the bottom of the ship – now on top… The opening shot is terrific. The camera swoops down on the eponymous liner, picks up a jogging Josh Lucas, settles on his face and then soars off again. But after that everything else is CGI-tweaked mediocrity. A dozen or so characters are sketched in, the tsunami hits the ship and for the rest of the time we watch some people we don't really care about thrashing their way through a honeycomb of ballast tanks. With no plot, personality or good jokes (except when the captain declares, 'we *will* be safe'), *Poseidon* is a deeply joyless experience. JC-W

• *Dylan Johns* Josh Lucas, *Robert Ramsey* Kurt Russell, *Richard Nelson* Richard Dreyfuss, *Jennifer Ramsey* Emmy Rossum, *Maggie James* Jacinda Barrett, *Christian* Mike Vogel, *Elena* Mía Maestro, *Conor James* Jimmy Bennett, *Captain Michael Bradford* Andre Braugher, *Lucky Larry* Kevin Dillon, *Valentin* Freddy Rodriguez, *Gloria* Stacy Ferguson, *with* Kirk B.R. Waller, Kelly McNair, Gabriel Jarret.

• *Dir* Wolfgang Petersen, *Pro* Petersen, Duncan Henderson, Mike Fleiss and Akiva Goldsman, *Ex Pro* Kevin Burns, Jon Jashni, Sheila Allen and Benjamin Waisbren, *Screenplay* Mark Protosevich, base don the novel by Paul Gallico, *Ph* John Seale, *Pro Des* William Sandell, *Ed* Peter Honess, *M* Klaus Badelt, *Costumes* Erica Edell Phillips.

Warner/Virtual Studios/Radiant Prods/Next Entertainment/Irwil Allen/Synthesis Entertainment-Warner.
98 mins. USA. 2006. Rel: 1 June 2006. Cert. 12A.

Pretty Persuasion ★★★★½

Kimberly Joyce, 15, is the evil queen of Roxberry High, Beverly Hills. Insanely intelligent and preternaturally alluring, she uses her gifts to step on others so that she can attain her goal of complete supremacy. No strategy is too mean and no outcome too tragic for Kimberly's path to revenge and national celebrity… *Pretty Persuasion* is not the first black comedy to feature a manipulative vixen, but it's one of the best. Its power is that it uses comedy like a knife and wields a very sharpened blade. The film's other ace is Evan Rachel Wood, a young actress of limitless range and conviction (see *Thirteen, The Missing, Down in the Valley*) who is intelligent enough to let her words to do the talking. There's also some terrific dialogue ('Listen. [silence] That's the sound of me not caring'; 'You are my dyke in shining armour,' etc), but it's the unexpected, virtually unseen moments that reap the greatest force. You know exactly why Kimberly is the way she is from a single phone call – a one-sided conversation with her absent mother. Heart-breaking, daring, perceptive, shocking and wickedly funny. JC-W

• *Kimberly Joyce* Evan Rachel Wood, *Percy Anderson* Ron Livingston, *Hank Joyce* James Woods, *Emily Klein* Jane Krakowski, *Brittany Wells* Elisabeth Harnois, *Grace Anderson* Selma Blair, *Roger* Danny Comden, *Troy* Stark Sands, *headmaster Charles Meyer* Michael Hitchcock, *Kathy Joyce* Jaime King, *Randa Azzouni* Adi Schnall, *with* Robert Joy, Josh Zuckerman, Clyde Kusatsu, Alex Désert, Cody McMains, Johnny Lewis, James Snyder.

• *Dir* Marcos Siega, *Pro* Siega, Todd Dagres, Carl Levin and Matthew Weaver, *Ex Pro* Jason Barhydt, Eric Kopeloff, Robert Ortiz and Joni Sighvatsson, *Co-Pro* and *Screenplay* Skander Halim, *Ph* Ramsey Nickell, *Pro Des* Paul Oberman, *Ed* Nicholas Erasmus, *M* Gilad Benamram, *Costumes* Danny Glicker.

Prospect Pictures-Metrodome.
110 mins. USA. 2005. Rel: 23 June 2006.
Cert. 18.

Pride & Prejudice ★★★★★

England; the late 18th century. When the handsome, genial and very rich Charles Bingley moves into a neighbouring estate, Mrs Bennet – mother of five girls – sees an opportunity of marriage for one of her brood. Bingley is a huge success, although Elizabeth, Mrs Bennet's second eldest, takes an immediate dislike to Bingley's friend, the aloof and supercilious FitzWilliam Darcy… It's such a damned good story. Not filmed since the 1940 version with Greer Garson and Laurence Olivier (excluding all the TV editions), Jane Austen's most beloved novel is given a consummate treatment here. From the gorgeous locations to the sumptuous photography, from the exquisite production design to Dario Marianelli's inspirational score and Tothill's elegant editing, the film is a triumph of cinema. And with a Lizzie and Darcy of the right age, it is loyal to Austen's vision. And there are some wonderful characterisations here: Donald Sutherland's long-suffering Mr Bennet, Judi Dench's indomitable Lady de Bourg and Tom Hollander's wretched Mr Collins all steal their scenes with aplomb. Brenda Blethyn rather overdoes Mrs Bennet's gaucherie and the Bennet sisters hardly resemble each other, but these are minor quibbles in such an accomplished feast. JC-W

• *Elizabeth Bennet* Keira Knightley, *FitzWilliam Darcy* Matthew Macfadyen, Brenda Blethyn, *Mr Bennet* Donald Sutherland, *William Collins* Tom Hollander, *Jane Bennet* Rosamund Pike, *Lydia Bennet* Jena Malone, *Lady Catherine de Bourgh* Judi Dench, *Mary Bennet* Talulah Riley, *Charles Bingley* Simon Woods, *Kitty Bennet* Carey Mulligan, *Charlotte Lucas* Claudie Blakley, *Caroline Bingley* Kelly Reilly, *Mr Wickham* Rupert Friend, *Miss de Bourg* Rosamund Stephen, *Mrs Gardiner* Penelope Wilton, *Mr Gardiner* Peter Wight, *Georgiana Darcy* Tamzin Merchant, *with* Sylvester Morand, Pip Torrens, Roy Holder, Meg Wynn Owen, Moya Brady.

• *Dir* Joe Wright, *Pro* Tim Bevan, Eric Fellner and Paul Webster, *Ex Pro* Debra Hayward and Liza Chasin, *Co-Pro* Jane Frazer, *Screenplay* Deborah Moggach, *Ph* Roman Osin, *Pro Des* Sarah Greenwood, *Ed* Paul Tothill, *M* Dario Marianelli, performed on piano by Jean-Yves Thibaudet, *Costumes* Jacqueline Durran.

Universal/StudioCanal/Working Title/Scion Films-UIP.
127 mins. USA/UK/France. 2005. Rel: 16 September
2005. Cert. U.

Prime ★★★

Dr Lisa Metzger is a Jewish therapist who has formed
an attachment to her patient Rafi Gardet, a top fashion
executive. When Rafi divorces her husband of nine years, Lisa
`unequivocally' endorses Rafi's fling with David, a man 14
years her junior. However, Lisa changes her mind when she
discovers that David is her son… As Rafi wrestles with issues
of age, Lisa is consumed by the fact that her son is involved
with a woman who isn't Jewish. Thankfully, Meryl Streep
doesn't overdo the Jewishness (she leaves that to David's
grandparents), while Uma Thurman is touching and credible
as a woman in the throes of second love. The trouble is that
the film plays like a comedy (and a farce at that), and the
laughs aren't always forthcoming. FYI: Sandra Bullock was
poised to play Rafi, but pulled out of the film just two weeks
before start of production. JC-W

• *Lisa Metzger* Meryl Streep, *Rafi Gardet* Uma Thurman,
David Bloomberg Bryan Greenberg, *Morris* Jon Abrahams,
Katherine Annie Parisse, *Randall* Zak Orth, *Michelle* Aubrey
Dollar, *Sam* Jerry Adler, *with* Doris Belack, David Younger,
Madhur Jaffrey, Will McCormack.

• *Dir* and *Screenplay* David Younger, *Pro* Jennifer Todd and
Suzanne Todd, *Ex Pro* Mark Gordon and Bob Yari, *Co-Pro*
Anthony Katagas and Brad Jenkel, *Ph* William Rexer, *Pro Des*
Mark Ricker, *Ed* Kristina Boden, *M* Ryan Shore,

Costumes Melissa Toth.

Universal/Stratus Film/Team Todd/Younger Than
You-Momentum Pictures.
105 mins. USA. 2005. Rel: 12 May 2006. Cert. 12A.

Primer ★½

Abe and Aaron, engineers working for a faceless corporation,
take from their surroundings what they need and make of
it something more. Strapped for cash, the colleagues scrape
together components from car engines, household appliances
and the shelves of their local Wal-Mart to construct a unique
machine. They're not entirely sure what they're making, but
they know it's something that could make them extremely
rich. However, the side effects of their invention prove to
be decidedly sinister… Proudly, Shane Carruth, the writer,
producer and director of *Primer*, states that his film cost
about, `the price of a used car.' Unfortunately, it looks like
a used car. Shot in the sterile industrial outskirts of Dallas
on Super 16mm – blown up to 35mm – it is visually
muddy and amateur with a soundtrack to match. But the
film's worst failing is its perverse abstruseness, providing
an incomprehensible narrative that, through techno-speak,
muffled dialogue and erratic camera moves, renders the film
all but impenetrable. Carruth, who had no prior experience
as a filmmaker, genned up on all aspects of his craft and has
fashioned a calling card printed on fog. JC-W

• *Aaron* Shane Carruth, *Abe* David Sullivan, *Robert* Casey
Gooden, *Philip* Anand Upadhyaya, *Kara* Carrie Crawford,
with John Carruth, Samantha Thomson, Chip Carruth.

Desk set: Nathan Lane and Matthew Broderick take cover in Susan Stroman's dynamic if stage-bound *The Producers* (from Sony Pictures)

• *Dir, Pro, Screenplay, Pro Des Ed, M* and *Sound* Shane Carruth.

Shane Carruth-Tartan Films.
77 mins. USA. 2004. Rel: 19 August 2005. Cert. 12A.

Princess Raccoon ★★½

The veteran Japanese director Seijun Suzuki, more usually associated with violent thrillers, here offers something wholly different. This is a highly colourful musical in which the players, including Zhang Zizi from *Crouching Tiger, Hidden Dragon* and *House of Flying Daggers*, are dwarfed by the spectacle. But initial enthusiasm soon wanes for Suzuki filming on sets has no feel for cinematic choreography and many of the songs are too brief to register. The story, that of a seemingly impossible love between a human prince and a princess who is also a raccoon, places this halfway between *Cinderella* and *Romeo and Juliet*. These universal elements should combine with something quintessentially Japanese but, where *Spirited Away* felt authentic, this piece with its Western–style music score comes across as ersatz. It's homogenised, international populism of a kind that is the enemy of true art. Original title: *Operetta tanuki goten*. MS

• *Tanuki-hime, 'Princess Raccoon'* Zhang Ziyi, *Prince Amechiyo* Joe Odagiri, *Hagi* Hiroko Yakushimaru, *Biruzen* Baba Saori Yuki, *with* Mikijiro Hira, Hibari Misora, Federico Aletta.

• *Dir* Seijun Suzuki, *Pro* Satoru Ogura and Ikki Katashima, *Ex Pro* Nobuyuki Tohya, *Screenplay* Yoshio Urasawa, *Ph* Yonezou Maeda, *Pro Des* Takeo Kimura, *Ed* Nobuyuki Ito, *M* Michiru Oshima and Ryomei Shirai, *Costumes* Sachiko Ito, *Choreography* Mitsuko Tanizawa.

Geneon Entertainment/Dentus Inc/Nipon Herald Films-Yume Pictures.
110 mins. Japan. 2005. Rel: 30 June 2006. Cert. PG.

The Producers ★★★½

Broadway, New York; 1959. Theatrical impresario Max Bialystock and his accountant Leo realise that they could actually make more money mounting a flop than a hit. So they go in search of the worst script they can find and hire the worst director and actors to create a musical extravaganza called *Springtime for Hitler*… Considering the classic status of the original film and the prizes heaped on the musical remake, the film of the show of the film had to have something going for it. As it is, it is blessed with a killer premise, irrepressible energy, endless wit and a refreshing tastelessness (Leo: 'What is that, Max?' Max: 'It's called an erection.'). Above all, though, the film is carried by Nathan Lane, who brings a gusto, professionalism and comic expertise that demolishes any cynicism in its path. In addition, Uma Thurman is a revelation as Ulla, dancing, singing and mugging her way onto a new career arc, while supporting turns from Gary Beach and Roger Bart (repeating their Broadway routines) keep the laughs coming. In spite of all this, the film is never more than a brilliant trailer for a terrific stage musical and never really takes off as a cinematic experience in its own right. And good as Matthew Broderick is as the flustered accountant Leopold

Bloom, he can but dredge up happy memories of Gene Wilder's incomparable performance in the original. JC-W

• *Max Bialystock* Nathan Lane, *Leo Bloom* Matthew Broderick, *Ulla* Uma Thurman, *Franz Liebkind* Will Ferrell, *Carmen Ghia* Roger Bart, *Roger De Bris* Gary Beach, *Hold Me-Touch Me* Eileen Essel, *Mr Marks* Jon Lovitz, *Kiss Me-Feel Me* Andrea Martin, *Lick Me-Bite Me* Debra Monk, *with* David Huddleston, Michael McKean, Marilyn Sokol, Mike McGowan, Fred Applegate, John Barrowman, Ronn Carroll, Thomas Meehan, Mel Brooks.

• *Dir* and *Choreography* Susan Stroman, *The Producers* Mel Brooks and Jonathan Sanger, *Co-Pro* Amy Herman, *Screenplay* Brooks and Thomas Meehan, *Ph* John Bailey and Charles Minsky, *Pro Des* Mark Friedberg, *Ed* Steven Weisberg, *M* and *lyrics* Brooks, *Costumes* William Ivey Long, *Creature Effects* Jim Henson's Creature Shop.

Universal/Columbia/Brooksfilms-Columbia TriStar.
134 mins. USA. 2005. Rel: 26 December 2005. Cert. 12A.

Proof ★★★★

Chicago; today. Catherine is to turn 27 on the day of her father's funeral. It's not a birthday she's looking forward to as her father, a mathematical genius, achieved his greatest success by the age of 26. Prior to his death, Catherine nursed her father through the worst stages of his dementia and is beginning to think she has inherited his condition. But has she also inherited his genius? A notebook containing a revolutionary theorem could contain the proof… *Proof* seldom tears itself away from the limitations of the proscenium arch. An adaptation of David Auburn's Tony-winning play – in which Gwyneth Paltrow starred during its London run – the film seems content to remain within a very narrow dramatic context. But it's a wonderful play and director John Madden (*Shakespeare in Love*, *Captain Corelli's Mandolin*) has channelled the sunlight of cinema into its heart. Once again Paltrow confirms her status as one of the finest actresses of her generation, conveying a natural beauty, emotional instability and latent intelligence. Furthermore, Anthony Hopkins is wise enough not to play the insanity of his mad old professor and is all the more moving because of it. JC-W

• *Catherine* Gwyneth Paltrow, *Robert* Anthony Hopkins, *Hal* Jake Gyllenhaal, *Claire* Hope Davis, *Professor Bhandari* Roshan Seth, *with* Gary Houston, Colin Stinton, Leland Burnett.

• *Dir* John Madden, *Pro* Jeffrey Sharp, John N. Hart Jr., Robert Kessel and Alison Owen, *Ex Pro* Bob Weinstein, Harvey Weinstein, Julie Goldstein and James D. Stern, *Co-Ex Pro* Michael Hogan, *Co-Pro* Mark Cooper, *Screenplay* David Auburn and Rebecca Miller, *Ph* Alwin Küchler, *Pro Des* Alice Normington, *Ed* Mick Audsley, *M* Stephen Warbeck, *Costumes* Jill Taylor.

Miramax/Endgame Entertainment/Hart Sharp Entertainment-Buena Vista International.
100 mins. USA/UK. 2004. Rel: 10 February 2006. Cert. 12A.

A brilliant madness: Anthony Hopkins as the mathematical genius in John Madden's articulate, thought-provoking *Proof* (from Buena Vista International)

The Proposition ★★★★

Following the horrific rape and murder of a family of English settlers, police captain Maurice Stanley captures two members of the gang responsible. However, Stanley is more interested in bringing the ringleader to trial and makes the bushranger Charlie Burns a proposition: if he can track down his evil brother and kill him, Stanley will spare Charlie's younger brother from the gallows… With Aborigines killing whites, Irish outlaws preying on the English and with the police routinely executing the natives, Australia of the 1880s is depicted as a brutal, unforgiving domain. Capturing the heat, omnipresent flies and barren landscape of the Outback, *The Proposition* is a bracing slice of Australian history. With Guy Pearce as the token Eastwoodian antihero (in a surprisingly shadowy contribution), Ray Winstone and Emily Watson provide a nice touch of balance in nature's cruel backyard. In fact, this is Winstone's film, whose initially vicious law enforcer ('I *will* civilise this land') is rendered humane in the Victorian environs of his domestic oasis. This is powerful stuff – and sensationally photographed – that opens a new window on Australia as a last frontier. JC-W

• *Charlie Burns* Guy Pearce, *Captain Maurice Stanley* Ray Winstone, *Arthur Burns* Danny Huston, *Jellon Lamb* John Hurt, *Eden Fletcher* David Wenham, *Martha Stanley* Emily Watson, *Brian O'Leary* Noah Taylor, *with* Shane Watt, Robert Morgan, David Gulpilil, Oliver Ackland, David Vallon, Daniel Parker, Gary Waddell, Ralph Cotterill.

• *Dir* John Hillcoat, *Pro* Chiara Menage, Cat Villiers, Chris Brown and Jackie O'Sullivan, *Ex Pro* Sarah Giles, Michael Hamlyn, Chris Auty, Norman Humphrey, James Atherton, Michael Henry and Robert Jones, *Screenplay* Nick Cave, *Ph* Benoit Delhomme, *Pro Des* Chris Kennedy, *Ed* Jon Gregory, *M* Cave and Warren Ellis, *Costumes* Margot Wilson.

UK Film Council/Surefire Films/Autonomous/Pictures in Paradise-Tartan Films.
104 mins. UK/Australia. 2005. Rel: 10 March 2006. Cert. 18.

Pusher II : With Blood on My Hands ★★★½

The Danish filmmaker Nicolas Winding Refn has a sense of cinema that enables him to bring not just efficiency but individuality to genre pieces. It's not merely a matter of style because his personal approach extends to presenting low-life characters in a sympathetic yet unsentimentalised way. This is best seen in the original *Pusher* (1996) and especially in *Bleeder* (1999). The present tale of criminals in Copenhagen is centred on a father-son relationship and on a criminal's response to becoming a father but the material as a whole is less striking here. It's more a retreat onto safer ground after the adventurous but only partly successful attempt to make an American movie, 2002's *Fear X*. The acting is strong. MS

• *Tonny* Mads Mikkelsen, *Smeden* Leif Sylvester Petersen, *Charlotte* Anne Sørensen, *KusseKurt* Kurt Nielsen, *Ø* Oyvind Hagen-Traberg, *with* Zlatko Buric, Maria Erwolter, Karsten Schroder.

• *Dir* and *Screenplay* Nicolas Winding Refn, *Pro* Winding Refn and Henrick Danstrup, *Ex Pro* Kenneth D. Plummer and Kim Magnusson, *Ph* Morten Søborg, *Pro Des* Rasmus Thjellesen, *Ed* Anne Østerud and Janus Billeskov Jansen, *M* Peterpeter, *Sound* Jens Bønding.

NWR Films ApS/Pusher II Ltd/TV2 (Denmark)-
Vertigo Films.
96 mins. Denmark. 2005. Rel: 16 September 2005.
Cert. 18.

Quo Vadis, Baby? ★★★

Gabriele Salvatores is a filmmaker whose diverse work carries
no personal stamp and who has yet to match his *Mediterraneo*
(1991). Here he echoes Mario Martone's 1995 *L'Amore Molesto*
with the tale of a woman (Angela Baraldi) investigating
the death of a relative and uncovering unsavoury family
truths. It's a watchable but not very suspenseful mix that has
extra elements added: the work of the heroine as a private
investigator, pop songs on the soundtrack and a fascination
with cinema (a clip from *Last Tango in Paris* is incorporated
to prove that the film's title is a quote from it). Later on
we are treated to a highly condensed version of Fritz Lang's
M which brings an improbable tale to an unlikely end and
ironically leaves one wishing that it were Lang's film that one
was watching! This could be much worse but nothing about it
lingers in the mind. MS

• *Giorgia* Angela Baraldi, *Andrea Berti* Gigio Alberti, *Ada*
Claudia Zanella, *Lucio* Elio Germano, *Commissario Bruni* Andrea
Renzi, *with* Luigi Maria Burruano, Alessandra D'Elia, Stella
Vordemann.

• *Dir* Gabriele Salvatores, *Pro* Maurizio Totti, *Line Pro* Antonio
Tacchia, *Screenplay* Salvatores and Fabio Scamoni, *Ph* Italo
Petriccione, *Pro Des* Rita Rabassini, *Ed* Claudio Di Mauro,
M Ezio Bosso, *Costumes* Patrizia Chericoni and Florence Emir.

Colorado Film/Medusa Film-Yume Pictures.
102 mins. Italy. 2004. Rel: 12 May 2006. Cert. 15.

Rag Tale ★

With the prospect of a knighthood in the offing, the chairman
of *The Rag* reverses his paper's anti-monarchy stance. However,
the editor, Eddy Taylor, goes ahead with a front-page story
suggesting that Buck Palace should be turned into a public
facility… In a cut-and-paste job reminiscent of the tackiest
tabloid, director Mary McGuckian throws her film together
in a welter of close-ups, spastic zooms and tilted camera
angles. Designed to conjure up an aura of caffeine/coke-fuelled
dementia, the effect makes the film virtually unwatchable. But
even without such an approach, *The Rag* would have been a
naïve, ludicrous and misguided satire with barely any rooting
in reality. That an editor of a national newspaper should be
ignorant of the wonders of photographic manipulation is
beyond belief, while his misuse of the word `infer' suggests he
is not even literate. As the newspaper's proprietor, Malcolm
McDowell certainly looks the part but comes off implausibly
powerless. This is a mess in every sense of the word. JC-W

• *Eddy Somerset Taylor* Rupert Graves, *Mary Josephine 'MJ'
Morton* Jennifer Jason Leigh, *Richard 'The Chief' Morton* Malcolm
McDowell, *Cormac 'Fat Boy' Rourke* Simon Callow, *Debbs* Lucy
Davis, *Peach James Taylor* Kerry Fox, *Morph* Ian Hart, *Geoff 'P3'
Randal* David Hayman, *Paul `Mac' Macavoy* Cal Macaninch,

Tulloch 'Lucky' Lloyd Bill Paterson, *Felix Miles Sty* John Sessions,
Sally May Ponsonby Sara Stockbridge.

• *Dir* Mary McGuckian, *Pro* Mary McGuckian, Jeff Abberley
and Tom Reeve, *Ex Pro* Julia Blackman, Garrett McGuckian,
Romain Schroeder and James D. Stern, *Co-Pro* Elvira Bolz and
Douglas E. Hansen, *Line Pro* Robert How, *Screenplay* Mary
McGuckian in collaboration with the cast, *Ph* Mark Wolf, *Pro
Des* Max Gottlieb, *Ed* Kant Pan and Danny B. Tull, *M* Nick
'Mischief' Shaw, *Costumes* Sally O'Sullivan and Uli Simon.

Rag Tale/Carousel Picture Company/Scion Films/Endgame
Entertainment/Pembridge Pictures-Metrodome.
123 mins. UK/Luxembourg/USA/Ireland. 2005.
Rel: 7 October 2005.
Cert. 15.

Red Eye ★★½

As she juggles her professional and private commitments on
her mobile, Lisa Reisert is only too aware that she could miss
her plane to Miami. But, as luck would have it, her flight is
delayed and she ends up in the calming company of one Jackson
Rippner. Then, once on the plane, they discover that they are
sitting next to each other. Of course, this is not a coincidence…
Taking a break from the horror oeuvre for which he is famous,
Wes Craven gives a passable crack at the genre of psychological
thriller. Nicely laying on the suspense and periodically turning
the tables on his audience, Craven has fashioned a lean,
sweaty thriller that really does sustain the interest. But at 76
minutes (minus the leisurely end credits), it does feel rather
undernourished. JC-W

• *Lisa Reisert* Rachel McAdams, *Jackson Rippner* Cillian
Murphy, *Joe Reisert* Brian Cox, *Cynthia* Jayma Mays, *Charles
Keefe* Jack Scalia, *nice lady* Angela Paton, *with* Laura Johnson,
Suzie Plakson, Teresa Press-Marx, Robert Pine, Dey Young,
Tom Elkins, Beth Toussaint Coleman.

• *Dir* Wes Craven, *Pro* Chris Bender and Marianne Maddalena,
Ex Pro Bonnie Curtis, Jim Lemley, JC Spink and Mason
Novick, *Screenplay* Carl Ellsworth, from a story by Ellsworth
and Dan Foos, *Ph* Robert Yeoman, *Pro Des* Bruce Alan Miller,
Ed Patrick Lussier and Stuart Levy, *M* Marco Beltrami, *Costumes*
Mary Claire Hannan.

DreamWorks/Benderspink-UIP.
84 mins. USA. 2005. Rel: 2 September 2005. Cert. 12A.

Reeker ★★

First there was *The Fog*. Then the remake. Now comes the
reeker, an evil miasma that dispatches our comely pleasure
seekers of choice. As five partygoers find themselves stranded
in the Californian desert without fuel, they get wind of
something very, very smelly. There are apparitions, too, no
reception on their 'phones and not even a signal on the radio…
To give *Reeker* its due, its desert terrain is sharply evoked and
the young protagonists are a few degrees more savoury than in
your average slasher. But an overblown score and a nebulous
aggressor undermine the suspense from the get-go. Even by

the end, it's unclear exactly what caused or motivated the miasma, resulting in much frustration and head scratching. But then all may be explained by catching the vastly superior – and virtually identical – *Dead End* (2003). JC-W

• *Jack* Devon Gummersall, *Nelson* Derek Richardson, *Gretchen* Tina Illman, *Trip* Scott Whyte, *Cookie* Arielle Kebbel, *Henry* Michael Ironside, *Radford* Eric Mabius, *the deer* Lambert.

• *Dir* and *Screenplay* Dave Payne, *Pro* Payne, Tina Illman and Amanda Klein, *Ex Pro* Ronnie Apteker, *Co-Pro, Ed* and *Visual Effects* Dan Barone, *Ph* Mike Mickens, *Pro Des* Paul Greenstein, *M* Dave Payne, *Costumes* Marco Marco and Nicole Abel-Emery.

The Institution/Primal Pictures-Pathé. 91 mins. USA. 2005. Rel: 23 June 2006. Cert. 15.

Rent ★★½

The year is 1989 and the Bohemian masses of New York's East Village are finding it hard to meet their rent. In fact, poverty, Aids and heroin addiction can have a dampening effect on the colourful, transsexual, creative inhabitants of the Big Apple... Seldom has death, Aids and heroin addiction seemed so cosy, so nostalgic, so much *fun*. But then it is Chris Columbus (*Home Alone, Mrs Doubtfire, Stepmom*) behind the camera of this much-anticipated film version of the long-running Broadway musical. Echoing *Hair* in its harmonies and tribal liberalism, it all feels so terribly contrived and fey, complete with Hollywood backlot street scenes and computer-generated wisps of breath. Rosario Dawson and the original cast members all give spirited turns, and there's a couple of stand-out numbers – 'Seasons of Love' and 'Without You' – but the rest feels like an extended, outmoded sitcom in the tenor of *Happy Days*. FYI: The musical's author, Jonathan Larson, died of Marfan's syndrome the night of the final dress rehearsal. JC-W

• *Mimi Marquez* Rosario Dawson, *Mark* Anthony Rapp, *Roger* Adam Pascal, *Tom Collins* Jesse L. Martin, *Angel Shunard* Wilson Jermaine Heredia, *Maureen* Idina Menzel, *Joanne* Tracie Thoms, *Benjamin Coffin III* Taye Diggs, *with* Aaron Lohr, Sarah Silverman, Wayne Wilcox, Anna Deveare Smith, Daryl Edwards, Daniel London, Eleanor Columbus, Brendan Columbus.

• *Dir* Chris Columbus, *Pro* Columbus, Jane Rosenthal, Robert De Niro, Mark Radcliffe and Michael Barnathan, *Ex Pro* Jeffrey Seller, Kevin McCollum, Allan S. Gordon and Lara Ryan, *Co-Pro* Julie Larson, *Co-Ex Pro* Tom Sherak, *Screenplay* Stephen Chbosky, from the book by Jonathan Larson, *Ph* Stephen Goldblatt, *Pro Des* Howard Cummings, *Ed* Richard Pearson, *M* and *lyrics* Jonathan Larson, *Costumes* Aggie Guerard Rodgers, *Choreography* Keith Young.

Revolution Studios/1492 Pictures/Tribeca-Columbia TriStar. 134 mins. USA. 2005. Rel: 7 April 2006. Cert. 12A.

Death con: Ray Liotta exacts a terrible price in Guy Ritchie's stylish if impenetrable *Revolver* (from Redbus Film Distribution)

Revolver ★★★½

Jake Green has spent seven years behind bars on behalf of Vegas kingpin (Mr) Dorothy Macha. Now he's out and he wants revenge. Meanwhile, a couple of loan sharks, who seem to know every inside move of Macha's, offer Jack protection in exchange for *all* his money and his services as a carrier. Biding his time, Jack goes along with the ruse while plotting the ultimate comeback... Guy Ritchie's fourth movie is about the con of all cons and many suggest it's the audience that's being swindled. But Ritchie is still a very stylish filmmaker, and even when he falls back on his formula of the voice-over, slow motion and so forth, he enriches his own cinematic vocabulary with the odd amazing shot. And while one's puzzling over the Tarantino/Fincher allusions and the plot's impenetrable, chess-like parallels (the official term is 'scacchic'), there are many moments to cherish: the shoot-out in a restaurant (in which only the assassin and the victim know what's going on), a torture sequence of horrifying ingenuity (involving a box of matches and an axe) and a priceless hit man supplied by Mark Strong, a bespectacled, nerdy and ruthless gunman with a conscience. JC-W

• *Jake Green* Jason Statham, *Dorothy Macha* Ray Liotta, *Zack* Vincent Pastore, *Avi* Andre Benjamin, *French Paul* Terrence Maynard, *Billy* Andrew Howard, *Sorter* Mark Strong, *Lily Walker* Francesca Annis, *with* Anjela Lauren Smith, Elana Binysh, Bill Moody, George Sweeney.

• *Dir* and *Screenplay* Guy Ritchie, *Pro* Luc Besson and Virginie Silla, *Ex Pro* Steve Christian, *Co-Pro* Pierre Spengler, *Line Pro* Steve Clark-Hall, *Ph* Tim Maurice-Jones, *Pro Des* Eve Stewart, *Ed* James Herbert, Ian Differ and Romesh Aluwihare, *M* Nathaniel Mechaly; Vivaldi, Beethoven, *Costumes* Verity Hawkes.

Luc Besson/EuroCorp/Revolver Pictures/Toff Guy Films/ Canal Plus-Redbus Film Distribution. 114 mins. UK/France. 2005. Rel: 22 September 2005. Cert. 15.

The Ringer ★★½

Having agreed to pay the medical bills of an employee he was meant to have fired, Steve Barker needs some money fast. So, at the suggestion of his uncle, he pretends to be mentally disabled so that he can compete in the Special Olympics and, with his high school record for athletes, should be able to win the event and clean out the bookies… Produced by the Farrelly brothers Peter and Bobby, *The Ringer* is another attempt to poke fun at those who poke fun at the intellectually challenged. However, sitcom plotting and an irrelevant, mawkish romance scupper the comedy's un-PC stance. And while *The Ringer*'s intentions are admirable – and some of the performances of the real-life contestants genuinely funny – Barry W. Blaustein's direction is woefully unimaginative and Johnny Knoxville's central turn rather dull. EB

•• *Steve Barker* Johnny Knoxville, *Gary Barker* Brian Cox, *Lynn Sheridan* Katherine Heigl, *Winston* Geoffrey Arend, *Billy* Edward Barbanell, *Thomas* Bill Chott, *with* Leonard Flowers, Leonard Earl Howze, Steve Levy, Jesse Ventura.

• *Dir* Barry W. Blaustein, *Pro* Peter Farrelly, Bobby Farrelly and Bradley Thomas, *Ex Pro* Tim Shriver, *Co-Pro* Marc S. Fischer and Clemens Emanuel Franke, *Screenplay* Ricky Blitt, *Ph* Mark Irwin, *Pro Des* Arlan Jay Vettier, *Ed* George Folsey Jr., *M* Mark Mothersbaugh, *Costumes* Lisa Jensen.

Fox Searchlight/Conundrum Entertainment-Fox. 94 mins. USA/Germany. 2004. Rel: 24 March 2006. Cert. 12A.

Rize ★★★½

The pop photographer David LaChapelle made his name shooting the eccentric and famous, the fashionable and off-kilter. With this, his first feature-length documentary, he suppresses his more satirical flights of fancy and explores a story of hope, vitality and community. Out of the ashes of the Rodney King riots in 1992, South Central Los Angeles found a saviour in Tommy Johnson – aka Tommy the Clown – the self-styled 'hippest clown in Los Angeles.' A former drug dealer, Johnson became a clown to enliven children's birthday parties and with it introduced a dance largely inspired by tribal African ritual. The act caught on and as LaChapelle shows, there are now fifty clown troupes in South Central, 'clowning' and 'klumping' their hearts out. More of a creed than a craze, the movement has channelled the surplus energy of the young and disenfranchised into a liberating mode of self-expression. FYI: None of the dance sequences in the film have been speeded up which, considering the dynamism of the participants, is nothing short of astonishing. JC-W

• *With*: Tommy the Clown (aka Tommy Jonson), Dragon, Larry, Larry's mom, Lil Tommy, True Clowns, Homeboy the Clown, Swoop, Miss Prissy, etc.

• *Dir* David LaChapelle, *Pro* LaChapelle, Marc Hawker, Ellen Jacobson-Clarke, Richmond Talauega and Tone Talauega, *Ex Pro* Jacobson-Clarke, Ishbel Whitaker, Barry Peele, Stavros Merjos and Rebecca Skinner, *Line Pro* Coleen Haynes, Walid J. Mouaness, Drew Carolan and Scott Kaplan, *Ph* Morgan Susser, *Ed* Fernando Villena, *M* Amy Marie Beauchamp and Jose Cancella.

HIS/DarkFibre-Redbus Film Distribution. 86 mins. USA/UK. 2005. Rel: 30 December 2005. Cert. PG.

Rock School ★★★

Philadelphia inspirational music guru Paul Green teaches 120 nine-year-old to 17-year-old after-school students some of the greatest rock ever written, made famous by such leading lights as Ozzy Osborne, Santana, Frank Zappa and Black Sabbath. Green's teaching methods may be a shade questionable and his language inappropriate, but you can't complain about the results and it all seems to work out well as the kids play in the hard rockin' finale, at a Zappa festival in Germany. In a class of its own, this hard-swearing but thoroughly engaging and entertaining rock doc is head-bangingly good. DW

• *With*: Paul Green, C.J. Tywoniak, Will O'Connor, Madi Diaz Svalgard, Tucker Collins, Asa Collins, Napoleon Murphy Brock, Eric Svalgard, Andrea Collins, Chris Lampson, Monique Del Rosario, Brandon King, Lisa Rubens, Lisa Green, Jimmy Carl Black, Don Argott.

• *Dir* and *Ph* Don Argott, *Pro* Argott and Sheena M. Joyce, *Ed* Demian Fenton, *M supervisor* Charles Raggio, *Sound* Efrain Torres.

Newmarket Films/9.14 Pictures/A&E IndieFilms-Icon. 93 mins. USA. 2004. Rel: 9 September 2005. Cert. 15.

The Rocky Road to Dublin & The Making of Rocky Road ★★★★

Accompanied by a rewarding new half hour featurette, Paul Duane's *The Making of Rocky Road* (★★★★) which puts it in context, this feature documentary of 1968 arrives here at last. Banned for many years in Ireland because of its stance critical of the role of the Catholic Church, it may seem small beer for audiences who have seen *The Magdalene Sisters* (2002). However, it also captures the popular culture and life-style of its day and is historically significant. This applies cinematically as well as historically since first time director Peter Lennon called on the services of France's great cameraman Raoul Coutard and the result is a film which in style and outlook is a fascinating pendant to the British Free Cinema films of the late 1950s, not least Karel Reisz's *We Are The Lambeth Boys* as photographed by another European great, Walter Lassally. MS

• *With*: Sean O'Faoláin.

• *Dir* and *Screenplay* Peter Lennon, *Pro* Victor Herbert, *Ph* Raoul Coutard, *Ed* Lila Biro.

ICA/Soda Pictures.
69 mins (total: 99 mins). Ireland. 1968.
Rel: 16 September 2005. Cert. 12A.

Rolling Family

See *Familia Rodante*.

Rollin With the Nines ★

'Too Fine' is murdered by a gang after failing to pay his share from a drugs deal and his sister Hope pays for the debt by being brutally attacked. She then decides to take her revenge… This extremely violent film about the gun and drug culture in Britain tries to be another *Lock, Stock…* – as well as copying American gangster movies – but fails miserably on both counts. It lacks focus and a sense of humour, the script is written by numbers and it is difficult to care about these totally unsympathetic and stereotypical characters. However, Naomi Taylor does her best in an underwritten role. GS

• *Finny* Vas Blackwood, *Pushy* Robbie Gee, *Hope* Naomi Taylor, *Det. Andy White* Terry Stone, *Too Fine* Simon Webbe, *David Brumby* Billy Murray, *Captain Flemyng* Jason Flemyng, *with* George Calil, Dominic Alan-Smith, Rodney P, Dizzee Rascal, Heartless Crew.

• *Dir* Julian Gilbey, *Pro* Geoff Austin, James Hutchins, Pikki and Alexander Rofaila, *Ex Pro* Neil Dunn, Paul Lowin, Lawrence Mortorff, Nick Fearon and Terry Stone, *Screenplay* and *Ed* Julian Gilbey and William Gilbey, *Ph* Ali Asad, *Pro Des* Nataasha Van Kampen, *M* Sandy McLelland; tracks performed by Dizzee Rascal, Kano, Rodney P, Simon Webbe, Sizzla, Life, Ms Dynamite, etc, *Costumes* Shireena Facey.

Framework Entertainment/Flakjacket Films-Maiden Voyage Pictures.
96 mins. UK. 2005. Rel: 21 April 2006. Cert. 18.

Romance & Cigarettes ★★★★

Queens, New York; today. Nick and Kitty Murder are a working-class couple with three grown-up daughters still living at home. Now, Nick and Kitty are a pretty solid double-act, but when Kitty finds out that Nick is having an affair with the flame-haired Tula, all hell breaks loose… Director John Turturro began writing the outline for *Romance & Cigarettes* while in character as *Barton Fink*. Filmed typing at his vintage Underwood, Fink/Turturro conjured up the title, idea and first scene of this 'down and dirty' blue-collar musical – so it's apt that the Coen brothers (who made *Barton Fink*) should end up producing *Romance & Cigarettes*. With Turturro's all-star cast singing along to established hits by Elvis, Tom Jones and Engelbert Humperdinck, the film unfolds like a stellar karaoke session. And with its inventive choreography and revelatory performances (Kate Winslet as the sluttish Tula is a particular stand-out), the film is a real original, like *Moulin Rouge!* with the sophistication scrubbed off. Much of the dialogue is composed of song titles, and much of it is unduly sordid, but there's a gritty truth behind the cheap theatrics that culminates in a surprisingly poignant finale. JC-W

• *Nick Murder* James Gandolfini, *Kitty* Susan Sarandon, *Tula* Kate Winslet, *Angelo* Steve Buscemi, *Fryburg* Bobby Cannavale, *Baby* Mandy Moore, *Constance* Mary-Louise Parker, *Rosebud* Aida Turturro, *Cousin Bo* Christopher Walken, *Nick's mother* Elaine Stritch, *Gene Vincent* Eddie Izzard, *Gracie* Barbara Sukowa, *Roe* Cady Huffman, *Louis* Tony Goldwyn, *with* Amy Sedaris, P.J. Brown, Adam Lefevre, Tonya Pinkins, David Thornton, Amedeo Turturro, Jacob Lumet-Cannavale, Diego Turturro, Katherine Turturro, Katherine Borowitz, James Borowitz.

• *Dir* and *Screenplay* John Turturro, *Pro* Turturro and John Penotti, *Ex Pro* Jana Edelbaum, Matthew Rowland, Nick Hill, Joel Coen and Ethan Coen, *Ph* Tom Stern, *Pro Des* and *Costumes* Donna Zakowska, *Ed* Ray Hubley, *M* tracks performed by Engelbert Humperdinck, Dusty Springfield, Elvis Presley, Cyndi Lauper, Mandy Moore, Aida Turturro and Mary-Louise Parker, Bruce Springsteen, Buena Vista Social Club, Janis Joplin, Bobby Cannavale, Tom Jones, Connie Francis, James Brown, James Gandolfini and Susan Sarandon, Havrey & the Moonglows, Vikki Carr, Erma Franklin, Katherine Borowitz, etc, *Choreography* Tricia Brouk and Margie Gillis.

United Artists/Icon/GreenStreet Films-Icon.
106 mins. USA/UK. 2005. Rel: 24 March 2006. Cert. 15.

R-Point ★★

Original title: *Arpointeu*.

Vietnam; 1972. When the Korean military start receiving pleading radio communications from the island of R-Point, they are mystified. According to an eyewitness, the platoon sent there was completely massacred. So, a fresh outfit lands on the island and finds itself subjected to distressing visions and the fresh remains of recently butchered soldiers… With its novel perspective of the Vietnam war, interesting locations and atmospheric photography, *R-Point* promises much. It's a shame to report, then, that after the film's auspicious start, its one-dimensional characters and duff dialogue quickly

undermine any initial sense of dread –
or interest. Original title: *Arpointeu*. CB

• *Lt. Choi Tae-in* Kham Woo-sung, *Sergeant Jin* Sohn Byung-
ho, *Sergeant Jang* Oh Tae-kyung, *Sergeant Mah*
Park Won-sang, *with* Lee Seon-gyun, Ahn Na-sang,
Kim Byeong-cheol.

• *Dir* Kong Su-chang, *Pro* Choe Kang-Hyuk, *Ex Pro* Chang
Youn-Hyun, *Screenplay* Kong and Pil Young-woo, *Ph* Suk
Hyung-jing, *Art Dir* Ha Soo-min, *Ed* Nam Na-yeong,
M Dal Pa-ran, *Visual Effects* Park Ju-hye.

Cinema Service/C & Film-Tartan Films.
107 mins. South Korea. 2004. Rel: 16 September 2005.
Cert. 15.

Rumor Has It... ★★

At the wedding of her younger sister in Pasadena, California,
Sarah Huttinger learns that her mother was the inspiration for
the Katharine Ross character in *The Graduate*. Furthermore,
Sarah realises that she was born out of wedlock and that
her mother had a pre-marital fling with Dustin Hoffman,
er, Benjamin Braddock, or at least Beau Burroughs, now an
Internet millionaire… As sequels go, this is one of the most
ingenious. Proposing that *The Graduate* was inspired by a true
story, the film takes up the lives of the real characters who have
been affected by their fictionalised counterparts. So, thirty years
on Dustin Hoffman has been transposed into Kevin Costner (a
nice stretch) and Shirley MacLaine plays the real Anne Bancroft
(being the latter's co-star from *The Turning Point*). But all the
ingenuity in the world cannot save a dish as flat as this. While
there is no perceivable chemistry between Costner and Aniston,
Mark Ruffalo's Jeff is the only character who seems to mean
what he says. Aniston just seems lost in a post-Rachel Green
daze, while La MacLaine acts as if she's in a 1950s' sitcom. The
rest is just dead space.
JC-W

• *Sarah Huttinger* Jennifer Aniston, *Beau Burroughs* Kevin
Costner, *Katharine Richelieu* Shirley MacLaine, *Jeff Daly* Mark
Ruffalo, *Earl Huttinger* Richard Jenkins, *Annie Huttinger* Mena
Suvari, *Roger McManus* Christopher McDonald, *Scott* Steve
Sandvoss, *Aunt Mitzi* Kathy Bates, *with* Mike Vogel, Lisa
Vachon, Jenny Wade, Googy Gress, Clyde Kusatsu, Lyman
Ward, Jordan Lund, and (uncredited) Colleen Camp, George
Hamilton.

• *Dir* Rob Reiner, *Pro* Paula Weinstein and Ben Cosgrove, *Ex
Pro* George Clooney, Steven Soderbergh, Jennifer Cox, Michael
Rachmil, Len Amato, Robert Kirby and Bruce Berman, *Co-Pro*
Frank Capra III, *Screenplay* T.M. Griffin,
Ph Peter Deming, *Pro Des* Tom Sanders, *Ed* Robert Leighton, *M*
Marc Shaiman, *Costumes* Kym Barrett.

Warner/Village Roadshow/Section Eight/
Spring Creek-Warner.
96 mins. USA. 2005. Rel: 27 January 2006.
Cert. 12A.

Running Scared ★½

Joey Gazelle, in the words of his wife, is 'shady, sleazy and
mixed-up' – but he's a good husband, a decent provider.
However, when the Mob give him an incriminating snub-
nosed .38 to dispose of, the gun ends up in the hands of his
son's ten-year-old best friend, Oleg. And after Oleg shoots his
father with it, Joey has to find Oleg – and the gun – pronto…
Having established his filmmaking mettle with *The Cooler*
(for which Alec Baldwin snared an Oscar nomination), Wayne
Kramer blows his reputation to pieces with this insane cartoon.
Not only does he undermine the action by presenting the
whole thing as a flashback (why?), but he introduces a series
of characters and situations that are so far-fetched they are
laughable. Everybody is either twisted, criminal or downright
depraved – and packs a gun – while the only people who seem
remotely normal turn out to be purveyors of kiddie snuff
movies. Ultimately, violence just for violence's sake gets very
boring. JC-W

• *Joey Gazelle* Paul Walker, *Oleg Yugorsky* Cameron Bright,
Teresa Gazelle Vera Farmiga, *Det. Rydell* Chazz Palminteri, *Nicky
Gazelle* Alex Neuberger, *Tommy 'Tombs' Perello* Johnny Messner,
Ivan Yugorsky John Noble, *Anzor 'Duke' Yugorsky* Karel Roden,
Mila Yugorsky Ivana Milicevic, *with* Michael Cudlitz, Arthur
Nascarella, Idalis DeLeon, Bruce Altman, Elizabeth Mitchell,
Tod Kramer.

• *Dir* and *Screenplay* Wayne Kramer, *Pro* Michael A.
Pierce, Brett Ratner and Sammy Lee, *Ex Pro* Andrew Pfeffer,
Andreas Grosch, Andreas Schmid, Matt Luber and Stewart
Hall, *Co-Pro* Kevan Van Thompson, *Ph* James Whitaker, *Pro
Des* Toby Corbett, *Ed* Arthur Coburn, *Costumes* Kristin Burke.

New Line Cinema/Media 8 Entertainment/
True Grit-Entertainment.
121 mins. USA. 2005. Rel: 6 January 2006. Cert. 18.

Russian Dolls ★★★½

Closing in on thirty, Xavier is beginning to feel the pinch.
His life doesn't amount to much and all he's got to show for
it is a string of broken relationships. Hoping to make his
name as a novelist, he's merely found himself on the books of a
publisher as a ghostwriter and as the scripter to the sequel of a
TV romance. He's told, 'not to be afraid of clichés', but Xavier
thinks art would be more interesting without the postcard
sunset. Wendy, his English collaborator, would tend to agree…
While set in Paris, London, Moscow and St. Petersburg, *Russian
Dolls* is the polar opposite of the Europudding, preferring to
embrace the multi-culturalism of the new Europe. Indeed, the
film's referencing of all things international is part and parcel
of its appeal. And if the buzzing street scenes aren't engaging
enough, there is the roster of attractive women who fill Xavier's
frantic life. Playful, cynical and romantic, *Russian Dolls* may
outstay its welcome – and Xavier himself is often an irritant –
but the collision of pictorial and intellectual flavours make for a
memorable banquet. Original title: *Les Poupées Russes*. JC-W

• *Xavier* Romain Duris, *Martine* Audrey Tautou, *Isabelle
Wauquaire* Cécile De France, *Wendy* Kelly Reilly, *William* Kevin

Bishop, *Natacha* Evguenya Obraztsova, *Neus* Irene Montalà, *Edward* Gary Love, *Celia Shelton* Lucy Gordon, *Kassia* Aïssa Maïga, *with* Olivier Saladin, Martine Demaret, Nicholas Day, Amanda Boxer.

• *Dir* and *Screenplay* Cédric Klapisch, *Pro* Bruno Lévy, *Ex Pro* Elena Tarasova and Yelena Yatsura, *Ph* Dominique Colin, *Pro Des* Marie Cheminal, *Ed* Francine Sandberg, *M* Loïc Dury and Laurent Levesque, *Costumes* Anne Schott, *Choreography* Bernard Lebeau.

StudioCanal/Lunar Films/France 2 Cinéma-Cinefile World.
129 mins. France/UK. 2005. Rel: 5 May 2006. Cert. 15.

RV ★★

Facing the prospect of losing his job, Bob Munro switches the family vacation in Hawaii for a road trip to Colorado in an outsize recreational vehicle. His plan is to effect some quality time with his wife and two kids, while making the deadline for a crucial merger in the Centennial State – without his family's knowledge. However, the cumbersome caravan threatens to demolish both of Bob's goals... On the face of it a critique of the environmentally unfriendly RV, this is really just another excuse to espouse certain family values and to poke fun at the great unwashed of America's highways and byways. But whereas Chevy Chase played on the smugness and arrogance of his family man in *National Lampoon's Vacation*, Robin Williams comes off as reckless and tired in a weak variation of his madcap persona. It's certainly a sad day when a 15-year-old pop star – JoJo – gets more laughs than her overpaid leading man. JC-W

• *Bob Munro* Robin Williams, *Travis Gornicke* Jeff Daniels, *Jamie Munro* Cheryl Hines, *Mary Jo Gornicke* Kristin Chenoweth, *Cassie Munro* Joanna 'JoJo' Levesque, *Carl Munro* Josh Hutcherson, *Moon Gornicke* Chloe Sonnenfeld, *Todd Mallory* Will Arnett, *Howie* Brendan Fletcher, *with* Hunter Parrish, Rob LaBelle, Brian Markinson, Ty Olsson, *Irv* Barry Sonnenfeld.

• *Dir* Barry Sonnenfeld, *Pro* Lucy Fisher and Douglas Wick, *Ex Pro* Bobby Cohen and Ryan Kavanaugh, *Co-Pro* Graham Place, *Screenplay* Geoff Rodkey, *Ph* Fred Murphy, *Pro Des* Michael Bolton, *Ed* Kevin Tent, *M* James Newton Howard, *Costumes* Mary E. Vogt.

Columbia Pictures/Relativity Media/Red Wagon-Columbia TriStar.
98 mins. USA. 2006. Rel: 9 June 2006. Cert. PG.

Saraband ★★½

If ever a film could be described as Bergmanesque, this is it. Opening with a black screen accompanied by the solitary moan of a cello, the film – or, in this case TV drama – sets the scene for the gloom to come. Picking up from Bergman's harrowing, penetrating *Scenes from a Marriage* 32 years ago, *Saraband* is introduced by Liv Ullmann's Marianne talking directly to camera (à la Shirley Valentine). She is updating us

on her life, leafing through old photographs and preparing for a trip to visit her now decrepit ex-husband, Johan (Josephson). Johan is at last financially independent but is locked in a bitter hostility with his son, Henrik. Henrik is still mourning the loss of his wife two years previously and has staked all his future happiness on his teenage daughter, Karin. It is all a most unsatisfactory state of affairs... More of a play than a film, *Saraband* – which takes its name from a stately Spanish dance – is divided into ten acts (or 'dialogues') and explores Bergman's favourite themes of mortality, betrayal, infidelity, grief, suicide and death. There are moments of trenchant, devastating drama but they are few and far between. P.S. Bergman has stated categorically that this will be his last directorial assignment.
JC-W

• *Marianne* Liv Ullmann, *Johan* Erland Josephson, *Henrik* Börje Ahlstedt, *Karin* Julia Dufvenius, *Martha* Gunnel Fred.

• *Dir* and *Screenplay* Ingmar Bergman, *Ex Pro* Pia Ehrnvall, *Ph* Per Sundin, *Art Dir* Göran Wassberg, *Ed* Sylvia Ingemarsson, *M* J.S. Bach, Bruckner, and Brahms, *Costumes* Inger Pehrson.

SVT Fiction/DR/NRK, etc-Tartan Films.
107 mins. Sweden/Denmark/Norway/Italy/Finland/Germany/Austria. 2003. Rel: 7 October 2005. Cert. 15.

Saw II ★★★

The sickest man of the new millennium is back – and sicker than ever. With his cancer significantly advanced, John Kramer – aka 'Jigsaw' – is playing a new game. He has locked eight people into a room seeping with sarin gas and has left little clues to aid their escape. Meanwhile, Jigsaw's arresting officer, Eric Matthews, watches on helplessly – via a bank of TV monitors – as his own teenage son waits for a very painful death... Fans of torture, ingenious mayhem and the original *Saw* (2004), should get a kick out of this accomplished sequel that devises a few new inventive ways of tormenting the helpless. But while the film retains an unrelenting grip on the gut, the characters remain one-dimensional stereotypes that we don't really care about. The fun is in the dispatch and the new ringleader, co-scenarist and first-time director Darren Lynn Bousman, delivers the goods in a tight, edgy and visually proficient package. JC-W

• *Eric Matthews* Donnie Wahlberg, *Amanda* Shawnee Smith, *'Jigsaw'/John Kramer* Tobin Bell, *Xavier* Franky G, *Jonas* Glenn Plummer, *Laura* Beverley Mitchell, *Kerry* Dina Meyer, *Addison* Emmanuelle Vaugier, *Daniel Matthews* Erik Knudsen, *Obi* Timothy Burd, *with* Lyriq Bent, Naom Jenkins, Tony Nappo.

• *Dir* Darren Lynn Bousman, *Pro* Mark Burg, Gregg Hoffman and Oren Koules, *Ex Pro* James Wan, Leigh Whannell, Stacey Testro, Peter Block and Jason Constantine, *Co-Pro* Daniel Jason Heffner and Greg Copeland, *Screenplay* Bousman and Leigh Whannell, *Ph* David A. Armstrong, *Pro Des* David Hackl, *Ed* Kevin Greutert, *M* Charlie Clouser, *Costumes* Alex Kavanaugh.

Twisted Pictures-Entertainment.
92 mins. USA/Canada. Rel: 28 October 2005. Cert. 18.

Scary Movie 4 ★½

There are brief moments in this laboured spoof of *War of the Worlds*, *The Village* and *The Grudge* when director Zucker and his frequent scenarist Jim Abrahams remind us of the comic skill they once exercised on the likes of *Airplane!* But for the most part *Scary Movie 4* is a series of running gags in which old people and young children get beat up to the accompaniment of loud sound effects. The rest is just ham-fisted and puerile parody. And the humour of recognition (oh, I get it, two cowboys getting out the K-Y jelly – must be *Brokeback Mountain*) wears terribly thin after a while. JC-W

• *Cindy Campbell* Anna Faris, *Brenda* Regina Hall, *Tom Ryan* Craig Bierko, *Henry Hale* Bill Pullman, *Mahalik* Anthony Anderson, *Holly* Carmen Electra, *President Baxter Harris* Leslie Nielsen, *with* Chris Elliott, Beau Mirchoff, Patrice O'Neal, Simon Rex, Shaquille O'Neal, Molly Shannon, Dr Phil McGraw, Kevin Hart, Michael Madsen, Chingy, Lil' Jon, Fabolous, Youngbloodz, Cloris Leachman, Holly Madison, Bridget Marquardt, Kendra Wilkinson, Charlie Sheen, Conchita Campbell, Doug Abrahams, and (uncredited) *narrator* James Earl Jones.

• *Dir* David Zucker, *Pro* Robert K. Weiss and Craig Mazin, *Co-Pro* Grace Gilroy, *Screenplay* Mazin, Pat Proft and Jim Abrahams, *Ph* Thomas Ackerman, *Pro Des* Holger Gross, *Ed* Craig Herring and Tom Lewis, *M* James L. Venable, *Costumes* Carol Ramsey.

Miramax/Dimension Films-Buena Vista International.
83 mins. USA. 2006. Rel: 13 April 2006.
Cert. 15.

Scorched ★

Scorched tries so hard to be funny that it's painful to watch. There are pratfalls, zany fantasy sequences, bouncy pop songs and silly sound effects, but all to no avail. Set in a nondescript town in the Californian desert, the film focuses on a gaggle of misfits who work in a bank. Routinely humiliated by the bank's smarmy manager, the various employees plot to rob the establishment with audacious and independent schemes. How were they to know that they were all planning to rob it over the same weekend? This is not a bad idea *per se*, but the film is a mess from the get-go. Cluttered with flashbacks, captions and irrelevant characters, *Scorched* lurches along in a variety of directions with little pace or cohesion, grinding to a halt on a number of occasions. A reasonable ensemble of actors do their best to inject humour into their roles, but it's one of those films that looks like it was directed by an over-zealous film buff. When the only laugh comes from John Cleese hissing 'bitch!' at a Girl Scout, you know you're in trouble. JC-W

• *Sheila Rilo* Alicia Silverstone, *Shmally* Rachael Leigh Cook, *Jason 'Woods' Valley* Woody Harrelson, *Charles Merchant* John Cleese, *Rick* Joshua Leonard, *Stuart Stein* Paulo Costanzo, *Max Stein* David Krumholtz, *Mark* Ivan Sergei, *Carter Doleman*

Marcus Thomas, *with* Jeffrey Tambor, Max Wein, Gavin Grazer, Al Corley.

• *Dir* Gavin Grazer, *Pro* Al Corley, Bart Rosenblatt and Eugene Musso, *Ex Pro* Max Wein, Cindy Cowan, Daniel Sherman and Kyle Lundberg, *Screenplay* Joe Wein, *Ph* Bruce Douglas Johnson, *Pro Des* Patti Podesta, *Ed* Kathryn Himoff, *M* John Frizzell, *Costumes* Heather Goodwin and Cassendra De La Fortrie.

Neverland Films/Winchester Films-Feature Film/
Content Film.
94 mins. USA/UK. 2002. Rel: 9 December 2005.
Cert. 12A.

Screaming Masterpiece ★★½

An odd title, perhaps, for a documentary chronicling Iceland's music scene. Still, the insightful reflections of Björk, the devastating land- and seascapes of the island itself and the piercingly original sound of contemporary Icelandic rock make for an engaging portrait. Much of it tongue-in-cheek, some of it quite educational (out of a population of 300,000, 400 orchestras and marching bands have sprung up), *Screaming Masterpiece* opens up an interesting subject with humour and poetry. If the imagery hadn't been quite so murky (the film was transferred from DV to 35mm), it would've been a documentary to recommend. JC-W

• *With*: Björk, Minus, Mugison, Mum, Sigur Rós, Slowblow, The Sugarcubes, Amína, Apparat Organ Quartet, Bang Gang, Hilmar Örn Hilmarsson, Barði Jóhannsson, Odin's Raven Magic, Egill Sæbjörnsson, Singapore Sling, Vinyl, etc.

• *Dir* and *Screenplay* Ari Alexander and Ergis Magnusson, *Pro* Alexander, Magnusson and Sigurjon Sighvatsson, *Ex Pro* Thor S. Sigurjonsson and Skuli Fr Malmquist, *Ph* Bergsteinn Bjorgulfsson, *Ed* Jon Yngvi Gulfason, *M* Thor Eldon.

Ergis Filmproduction/Zik Zak Filmworks/Eurimages-
Soda Pictures.
88 mins. USA/Iceland/Denmark/Netherlands/Norway.
2005. Rel: 16 December 2005. Cert. 12A.

The Secret Lives of Dentists ★★½

Those two talented players Hope Davis and Campbell Scott play dentists who are also a married couple and, initially, Alan Rudolph's film promises to be an engaging black comedy. But all too soon its portrayal of the husband's suspicions of infidelity yield to a view that sees marriage as a mistake and family life as unendurable. Viewers who have reached such conclusions for themselves already may warm to the film's endorsement of their beliefs, but for others this would-be tragi-comedy will be inadequately amusing and insufficiently effective dramatically. The players help, but this is a depressing experience not helped by the notion of turning a patient (Denis Leary) into a kind of ghostly alter ego of the husband and thus adding a layer of inappropriate stylisation. MS

• *David Hurst* Campbell Scott, *Dana Hurst* Hope Davis, *Slater*

Denis Leary, *Laura* Robin Tunney, *Lizzie Hurst* Gianna Beleno, *Leah Hurst* Cassidy Hinkle, *Stephanie Hurst* Lydia Jordan, *Mark* Jon Patrick Walker, *Dr Danny* Kevin Carroll, *Elaine* Kate Clinton, *with* Peter Samuel, Adele D'Man, Susie Essman.

• *Dir* Alan Rudolph, *Pro* Campbell Scott and George VanBuskirk, *Ex Pro* Martin Garvey, David Newman, Bruce Cowen and Michael Lauer, *Co-Pro* Jonathan Filley, *Screenplay* Craig Lucas, based on the novella *The Age of Grief* by Jane Smiley, *Ph* Florian Ballhaus, *Pro Des* Ted Glass, *Ed* Andy Keir, *M* Gary DeMichele, *Costumes* Amy Westcott.

Hole Digger Films/ReadyMade-Tartan Films.
104 mins. USA. 2003. Rel: 12 August 2005. Cert. 15.

Secret Things ★★½

Yet another adaptation of *Les Liaisons Dangereuses*, this is given a contemporary Parisian setting and is much freer than that other recent take on Laclos, *Untold Scandal*. The two schemers here are both women (Sabrina Seyvecou and Coralie Revel). They set out initially to defy the conventions and rules of society and then aim to get to the top of the family business where they work as secretaries by seducing the men able to promote them. The film is technically competent which counts for something but what it offers is porn proffered as profundity. In reality it's male voyeurism designed to titillate, right down to scenes of lesbian sex. The tone is quintessentially French but on this occasion that's no recommendation, and I suspect that even Catherine Breillat might well find it obscene. Original title: *Choses Secretes*. MS

• *Natalie* Coralie Revel, *Sandrine* Sabrina Seyvecou, *Delacroix* Roger Mirmont, *Christophe* Fabrice Deville, *Charlotte* Blandine Bury, *with* Olivier Soler, Viviane Theophilides, Dorothee Picard.

• *Dir* and *Screenplay* Jean-Claude Brisseau, *Pro* Jean-Francois Geneix and Jean-Claude Brisseau, *Ph* Wilfred Sempe, *Pro Des, Ed* and *Costumes* Maria-Luisa Garcia, *Ed* Garcia, *M* J.S. Bach, Purcell, Vivaldi, and Handel.

Les Aventuriers de l'Image/La Sorciere Rouge-Tartan Films.
113 mins. France. 2002. Rel: 22 July 2005. Cert. 18.

Secuestro Express ★★

In theory, this thriller centred on a kidnapping in Venezuela is a serious statement about life in Caracas because it echoes real life cases that, occurring in their hundreds, stress the gap between the haves and have-nots. In practice, however, this is an exploitation movie that incorporates speeded-up footage and split-screen techniques and revels in the brutality of what is being depicted. Mía Maestro as the unfortunate heroine kidnapped with her boyfriend deserves better, for if director Jonathan Jakubowicz keeps things moving that is the film's only virtue. There's a homophobic feel to the piece too, and a number of plot contrivances. Only one moment near the close – showing the well-off heroine against a backdrop of her city that has fully revealed its dark side – carries the resonance that would justify those who have acclaimed this movie. MS

• *Carla* aka 'Princess' Mía Maestro, *Trece* Carlos Julio Molina, *Budú* Pedro Perez, *Niga* Carlos Madera, *Martín* aka `Teddy Bear' Jean Paul Leroux, *Sergio, Carla's father* Ruben Blades.

• *Dir* and *Screenplay* Jonathan Jakubowicz, *Pro* Jonathan Jakubowicz, Sandra Condito and Salomón Jakubowicz, *Ex Pro* Elizabeth Avellán and Eduardo Jakubowicz, *Ph* David Chalker, *Pro Des* Andres Zawisa, *Ed* Ethan Maniquis Jakubowicz, *M* Angelo Milli, *Costumes* Anabella Almena.

Tres Malandros-Buena Vista International.
87 mins. Venezuela. 2004. Rel: 9 June 2006. Cert. 18.

Seducing Doctor Lewis ★★★★

The remote community of St. Marie-la-Mauderue has little to offer. The houses are ugly, the cuisine medieval and maybe there are just two computers on the entire island. But the villagers have to find a doctor if they are to qualify for the construction of a new factory. Done for cocaine possession, Dr Lewis is forced to serve a month on St. Marie – and that's all the time the villagers have to win him round to a stay on for a permanent basis… With a strong flavour of Gallic charm (underlined by a winsome score), this award-winning film from Quebec is a delightful fable of small-town dynamics *vis-à-vis* the slick, sexy outside world. Recalling *Local Hero* and the Irish *The Closer You Get* in feel, the film shows enormous affection for its scheming villagers and a balanced perspective of a grass-roots mentality in awe of a nebulous urban sophistication. As it turns out, human beings are just as duplicitous whether they live in the city or in the middle of nowhere. Original title: *La Grande séduction*. JC-W

• *Germain Lesage* Raymond Bouchard, *Christopher Lewis* David Boutin, *Henri Giroux* Benoît Brière, *Ève Beauchemin* Lucie Laurier, *Yvon Brunet* Pierre Collin, *Steve Laurin* Bruno Blanchet, *Monsieur Dupré* Donald Pilon, *Hélène Lesage* Rita Lafontaine, *little Germain* Dominic Michon-Dagenais, *Roland Lesage* Guy-Daniel Tremblay, *Simone Lesage* Nadia Drouin, *Richard Auger* Ken Scott.

• *Dir* Jean-François Pouliot, *Pro* Roger Frappier and Luc Vandal, *Screenplay* Ken Scott, *Ph* Allen Smith, *Pro Des* Normand Sarrazin, *Ed* Dominique Fortin, *M* Jean-Marie Benoît, *Costumes* Louise Gagné, *Sound* Marcel Pothier.

Alliance Atlantis Vivafilm/Max Films/Télèfilm Canada-Dogwoof Pictures.
109 mins. Canada. 2003. Rel: 14 April 2006. Cert. 15.

Separate Lies ★★★½

James Manning is a successful corporate lawyer who shares a fine house in London – and another one in the country – with his loyal, attentive wife, Anne. Theirs would seem to be an ideal existence, although James does seem to spend more time in the office than Anne would like. Then, out of the blue, a hit-and-run accident tears apart the fabric of their lives… The erstwhile actor Julian Fellowes, who won an Oscar for his screenplay to *Gosford Park*, is, as a scenarist, a consummate craftsman. Here, he makes his directorial debut, shaping a taut, tight little drama from Nigel Balchin's novel *A Way Through the Woods*. While furnished with the ingredients of an Agatha Christie potboiler – a killing, a tenacious detective, country houses – Fellowes has elevated the story to credible drama pierced with observational humour. He's helped, of course, by such wonderful actors as Watson and Wilkinson, and glorious locations in London, Paris and the Buckinghamshire countryside. If the film fails to connect on an emotional level, it's because the milieu itself seems to be rooted in an Englishness that no longer really exists. JC-W

• *Anne Manning* Emily Watson, *James Manning* Tom Wilkinson, *Bill Bule* Rupert Everett, *Maggie* Linda Bassett, *Priscilla* Hermione Norris, *Inspector Marshall* David Harewood, *Lord Rawston* John Neville, *with* John Warnaby, Richenda Carey, Jeremy Child.

• *Dir* and *Screenplay* Julian Fellowes, *Pro* Christian Colson and Steve Clark-Hall, *Ex Pro* Paul Smith, *Ph* Tony Pierce-Roberts, *Pro Des* Alison Riva, *Ed* Alex Mackie and Martin Walsh, *M* Stanislas Syrewicz, *Costumes* Michele Clapton.

Fox Searchlight/Celador Films/DNA Films/UK Film Council/Film Four-Fox.
84 mins. UK/USA. 2004. Rel: 18 November 2005. Cert. 15.

Serenity ★★★½

Five hundred years in the future mankind has colonised outer space and now The Alliance is calling the shots. But somehow the battered old transport craft-cum-pirate ship *Serenity* just gets by. However, when it picks up a telepathic 17-year-old girl, The Alliance moves in for the kill... There was much favourable buzz surrounding *Serenity* before it opened. While the Fox TV series from which it was taken (*Firefly*) was cancelled mid-season, the subsequent DVD attracted positive reviews and a huge cult following. And the resultant film is a blast. With a sensational pre-credit sequence (setting a new benchmark for delivering exposition), the film cuts to the chase with aplomb. And there's plenty to cherish here: the futuristic, pared-down dialogue, an abundance of Oriental imagery, the anthropomorphic spacecraft, a peerless villain (albeit with an English accent) and an underlying black humour. Even so, *Serenity* does lack suspense and the 'wow factor', while the presence of a hunky white male as the ship's captain is retrograde to say the least. JC-W

• *Captain Malcolm Reynolds* Nathan Fillion, *Zoe* Gina Torres, *Wash* Alan Tudyk, *Jayne* Adam Baldwin, *Kaylee* Jewel Staite, *Simon* Sean Maher, *River Tam* Summer Glau, *The Operative* Chiwetel Ejiofor, *Inara* Morena Baccarin, *Shepherd Book* Ron Glass, *Mr Universe* David Krumholtz, *with* Michael Hitchcock, Sarah Paulson, Yan Feldman

• *Dir and Screenplay* Joss Whedon, *Pro* Barry Mendel, *Ex Pro* Christopher Buchanan, David Lester and Alisa Tager, *Ph* Jack Green, *Pro Des* Barry Chusid, *Ed* Lisa Lassek, *M* David Newman, *Costumes* Ruth Carter.

Universal-UIP.
119 mins. USA. 2005. Rel: 7 October 2005. Cert. 15.

Private lies: Emily Watson and Tom Wilkinson in Julian Fellowes' taut and credible *Separate Lies* (from Fox)

Seven Swords ★★★½

Following the Manchu invasion of China in the 1660s, the Ming dynasty was replaced by the Qing dynasty. However, rebellious factions throughout the land challenged the new leadership, so an Imperial Edict was issued to ban all martial arts. After making his fortune bringing the outlaws to justice (the price of one head netting him 300 pieces of silver), the warlord Fire-wind sets his sights on the remote outpost of the so-called Martial Village. But seven consummate warriors, each bequeathed with a sword of mythic proportions, protect the settlement… A grandiose restyling of *Seven Samurai* – according to the rules of *wuxia* cinema – Tsui Hark's *Seven Swords* is an epic very much in the tradition of *Crouching Tiger* and *House of Flying Daggers*. That is, it is stunning to behold, with a sweeping historical canvas and combat sequences to raise the bar of the martial arts genre. Yet even as we marvel at the souped-up action sequences and sophisticated weaponry (lethal crossbows, blade-loaded nets, circular-saw shields), the arc of the story gets a little lost in the clutter of subplots and characters. Magnificent, breathtaking, but at times maddeningly confusing. Original title: *Qi Jian*. JC-W

• *Chu Zhao Nan* aka 'The Dragon Sword' Donnie Yen, *Yang Yunchong* aka 'The Transience Sword' Leon Lai, *Wu Yuanyin* aka 'The Heaven's Fall Sword' Charlie Young, *General Fire-Wind* Sun Honglei, *Han Zhibang* aka 'The Deity Sword' Lu Yi, *Green Pearl* Kim So-Yeun, *Fu Qingzhu* Lau Kar-leung, *Liu Yufang* aka 'Fang' Zhang Jingchu.

• *Dir* Tsui Hark, *Pro* Tsui, Lee Joo-Ick, Pan Zhizhong and Ma Zhong Jun, *Ex Pro* Raymond Wong, Hong Bong-Chul and Zhang Yong, *Screenplay* Tsui, Cheung Chi-sing and Chun Tin-nam, *Ph* Keung Kwok-Man, *Pro Des* Eddy Wong, *Ed* Angie Lam, *M* Kenji Kawai, *Costumes* Poon Wing-Yan, *Action Choreography* Stephen Tung (aka Tung Wai) and Xiong Xinxin, *Image design* Shirley Chan.

Beijing Ciwen Film & TV Prods/Boram Entertainment/City Glory Pictures-Contender Entertainment.
140 mins. Hong Kong/China/South Korea. 2005. Rel: 24 February 2006. Cert. 15.

The Shaggy Dog ★★½

Los Angeles; today. Hotshot lawyer Dave Douglas is caught up defending a firm against accusations of animal testing and is neglecting the home front. Then, when he is turned into a sheepdog, he recognises his shortcomings as a homo sapien… For a Disney comedy, *The Shaggy Dog* rides pretty roughshod over sensitive ground: not least American interference in Tibet, marital breakdown and experimenting on animals. But, hey, kids, this is a comedy and to see a creature mutated into a toad-cum-bulldog is not to be taken too seriously. *The Shaggy Dog* is actually funnier than it deserves to be, thanks largely to the effortless comic skill of Tim Allen, who can purloin a smile just by asking Judge Claire Whittaker for a treat. It's pretty nuts-and-bolts stuff (with a terrible soundtrack), but it slips down with the comfortable ease of fast food. FYI: This is the fifth instalment in *The Shaggy Dog* franchise, the original starring Fred MacMurray and being Disney's first film to be set in the present day (1959, back then). JC-W

• *Dave Douglas* Tim Allen, *Dr Kozak* Robert Downey Jr, *Rebecca Douglas* Kristin Davis, *Ken Hollister* Danny Glover, *Josh Douglas* Spencer Breslin, *Judge Claire Whittaker* Jane Curtin, *Carly Douglas* Zena Grey, *Lance Strictland* Philip Baker Hall, *with* Joshua Leonard, Shawn Pyfrom, Craig Kilborn, Laura Kightlinger.

• *Dir* Brian Robbins, *Pro* David Hoberman and Tim Allen, *Ex Pro* Robert Simonds, Todd Lieberman, William Fay and Matthew Carroll, *Screenplay* The Wibberleys [Cormac Wibberley and Marianne Wibberley], Geoff Rodkey, Jack Amiel and Michael Begler, *Ph* Gabriel Beristain, *Pro Des* Leslie McDonald, *Ed* Ned Bastille, *M* Alan Menken; Vivaldi; tracks performed by Akon, John Travolta, The Rascals, Baha Men, Rosario Sasso and Georgio Rosciglione, Percy Sledge, The Beach Boys, Click Five, etc, *Costumes* Molly Maginnis.

Walt Disney Pictures/Mandeville Films/Boxing Cat Films-Buena Vista International.
98 mins. USA. 2006. Rel: 31 March 2006. Cert. U.

Shake Hands With the Devil: The Journey of Roméo Dallaire ★★★★

Rather than being unnecessary in the wake of *Hotel Rwanda*, this fine documentary by Peter Raymont complements it. We accompany General Roméo Dallaire, the UN official in charge at the time of the genocide, on his return to Rwanda ten years later. It had been a decade during which he had suffered traumatically, his sense of guilt over the lives he had been unable to save having resulted in a suicide attempt, but he had also written a book about his experiences entitled *Shake Hands with the Devil*. This film, while clearly sympathetic to Dallaire, doesn't hide criticisms made over deaths he might have prevented and, with footage from 1994 incorporated, it both revisits the tragedy – clarifying its roots in the process – and shows its effect on one man more hero than devil. It's a little too long and the personal perspective would be clearer if Dallaire's religious beliefs were more fully investigated. Nevertheless, this documentary portrait (of the man who served as the model for Nick Nolte's character in *Hotel Rwanda*) illustrates the power of a film possessed of the raw edge of truth. MS

• *With*: Lt. Gen. Romeo Dallaire.

• *Dir* and *Pro* Peter Raymont, *Ph* John Westheuser, *Ed* Michele Hozer, *M* Mark Korven.

Canadian Broadcasting Corp/Societe Radio Canada/Rogers Documentary Fund/Canadian Television Fund-ICA Cinema.
91 mins. Canada. 2004. Rel: 5 August 2005. No Cert.

Shallow Ground ★★½

Just as a police station in a rural backwater of the US is

Cat attack: Tim Allen gets ready to pounce in Brian Robbins' insensitive but quite funny remake, *The Shaggy Dog* (from Buena Vista International)

closing down, a naked, blood-spattered boy emerges from the woods. It turns out the teenager has a way with blood and a lot of corpses start turning up. Wrong place, wrong time… Micro-budget renaissance man Sheldon Wilson makes up for limited funds with intensity and atmosphere in this rather disturbing if nonsensical horror film. Referencing the classics as he goes along – and obviously influenced by others – Wilson brings a surprising degree of originality to his supernatural tale. It's just a shame he can't wrest a decent performance out of his cast. CB

• *Sheriff Jack Sheppard* Timothy V. Murphy, *Stuart Dempsey* Stan Kirsch, *Laura Russell* Lindsey Stoddart, *Helen Reedy* Patty McComack, *with* Rocky Marquette, Natalie Avital, Chris Hendrie, John Kapelos.

• *Dir, Screenplay* and *Ed* Sheldon Wilson, *Pro* Wilson, Martin Mathieu, John Tarver and Jason Ninness, *Ex Pro* William Mendel, Pierre David and Lawrence Goebel, *Ph* Tarver, *Pro Des* Don Clark, *M* Steve London, *Sound* Richie Nieto, *Special Effects Make-Up* Patrick Magee.

Imagination Worldwide/Deco Filmworks-Anchor Bay Entertainment UK.
96 mins. USA. 2004. Rel: 29 July 2005. Cert. 18.

She's the Man ★½

When Viola Hastings hears that the girls' football sessions have been eliminated from the school curriculum, she is devastated. But when she discovers that her brother Sebastian is on a secret trip to London (to further his musical aims), she disguises herself as him so as to compete in his team… In his time Shakespeare cooked up some pretty fanciful plots, albeit reinforced by his timeless verse ('If music be the food of love…'). One of his more outrageous conceits, *Twelfth Night* worked as a joke-within-a-joke as the female parts were already played by men. By transferring the action to an American high school the joke is turned into farce, amplified by Amanda Bynes' baboon-like mugging (Felicity Huffman she is not). In addition, the supporting grotesques and caricatures are really quite offensive. JC-W

• *Viola Hastings* Amanda Bynes, *Duke* Channing Tatum, *Olivia* Laura Ramsey, *Coach Dinklage* Vinnie Jones, *Justin* Robert Hoffman, *Monique* Alex Breckenridge, *Daphne* Julie Hagerty, *Principal Gold* David Cross, *Sebastian Hastings* James Kirk, *Eunice* Emily Perkins, *with* Jonathan Sadowski, Amanda Crew, Jessica Lucas, Robert Torti.

• *Dir* Andy Fickman, *Pro* Lauren Shuler Donner and Ewan Leslie, *Ex Pro* Tom Rosenberg, Gary Lucchesi and Marty Ewing, *Screenplay* Leslie, Karen McCullah Lutz and Kirsten Smith, *Ph* Greg Gardiner, *Pro Des* David J. Bomba, *Ed* Michael Jablow, *M* Nathan Wang, *Costumes* Katia Stano.

Lakeshore Entertainment/DreamWorks/Donners' Co.-Entertainment.
105 mins. USA. 2005. Rel: 7 April 2006. Cert. 12A.

Shooting Dogs ★★★★

Ecole Technique Officielle, Rwanda; April 1994. As the
United Nations quibbled over the semantics of genocide,
the Hutu population of Rwanda hacked to death 800,000 of
its Tutsi compatriots, with the police, army and members of
the public taking machetes to men, women and children. It's
inconceivable that all this happened just twelve years ago and
that no foreign government saw fit to intervene. With UN
forces in the thick of the action, they did nothing. They were
there not to 'enforce' peace but to 'monitor' it. And a great
lot of good that did to the butchered citizens of the country.
This is a true episode in the mayhem, the story of an English
priest and an English teacher who try to make a difference.
However, they are all but helpless when Belgian soldiers feel
they can bend the rules to shoot dogs – which prove a health
risk – but cannot protect a single child. *Hotel Rwanda* was a
hard act to follow, but this really is the better film. While
igniting the same incendiary material, but less afraid to pull
its punches where it matters, *Shooting Dogs* finds the optimum
balance between the emotive and the exploitative. JC-W

• *Father Christopher* John Hurt, *Joe Conner* Hugh Dancy,
Capitaine Delon Dominique Horwitz, *Sibomana* Louis Mahoney,
François David Gyasi, *Rachel* Nicola Walker, *Marie* Clare-Hope
Ashitey, *with* Steve Toussaint, Susan Nalwoga, Victor Power,
Jack Pierce, Musa Kasonka Jr.

• *Dir* Michael Caton-Jones, *Pro* David Belton, Pippa Cross
and Jens Meurer, *Ex Pro* David M. Thompson, Paul Trijbits,
Ruth Caleb, Karsten Stöter and Richard Alwyn, *Line Pro*
Andrew Wood, *Screenplay* David Wolstencroft, *Ph* Ivan
Strasburg, *Pro Des* Bertram Strauss, *Ed* Christian Lonk,
M Dario Marianelli, *Costumes* Dinah Collin.

Crossday/Egoli Tossell/BBC Films
National Lottery-Metrodome.
115 mins. UK/Germany/France. 2005.
Rel: 31 March 2006. Cert. 15.

Shopgirl ★★

Mirabelle Butterfield works as a shopgirl at the exclusive
Saks Fifth Avenue in Los Angeles. Desperate for love and
companionship, she finds herself with two romantic options.
There's the goofy, unwashed Jeremy, whose idea of a dream
date is to sit outsidse a cinema admiring the neon fonts. The
other is Ray Porter, a mysterious millionaire who lavishes
expensive gifts on Mirabelle, but is old enough to be her
father. So, what is a girl to do? Steve Martin would've been
wise to look at *Lost in Translation* before embarking on
this adaptation of his novella. But then he wouldn't have
had a movie. Still, it might have been better with another
actor – Richard Gere, say – and another actress (the bright
and beautiful Claire Danes does not convince as a lonely
wallflower). With Martin's character so underwritten he
could be a metaphor, there's no stuff of real life in the central
romance (how did Ray make his money again?); while, surely,
Jonathan Schwartzman's repellent and hopeless Jeremy cannot
be redeemed by self-help and yoga tapes? As it is, this seedy,
humourless film feels like a self-indulgent fantasy written as a
piece of menopausal wish-fulfilment.
JC-W

Game for a scream: Jodelle
Ferland in Christopher Gans'
beautifully shot but trite *Silent
Hill* (from Pathé)

• *Ray Porter* Steve Martin, *Mirabelle Butterfield* Claire Danes, *Jeremy* Jason Schwartzman, *Lisa Cramer* Bridget Wilson-Sampras, *Catherine Butterfield* Frances Conroy, *Dan Butterfield* Sam Bottoms, *Christie Richards* Rebecca Pidgeon, *with* Gina Doctor, Clyde Kusatsu, Samantha Shelton, Richard Fancy.

• *Dir* Anand Tucker, *Pro* Ashok Amritraj, Jon Jashni and Steve Martin, *Ex Pro* Andrew Sugarman, *Co-Pro* Marcus A. Viscidi, *Ph* Peter J. Suschitzky, *Pro Des* William Arnold, *Ed* David Gamble, *M* Barrington Pheloung, *Costumes* Nancy Steiner.

Touchstone Pictures/Hyde Park Entertainment/Brass Hat Films-Fox.
103 mins. USA/UK. 2004. Rel: 20 January 2006. Cert. 15.

Silent Hill ★★★½

Rose Da Silva, a young wife and mother, follows her daughter into a twisted version of our own reality inhabited by a miscellany of weirdoes… The latest in a long line of videogame adaptations, *Silent Hill* is distinguished by a suitably bedraggled and desperate central performance from Radha Mitchell, along with some particularly inventive and nasty visual effects. However, it's done a disservice by a truly awful script by Roger Avary (*Pulp Fiction*), which dares to use such lines as, 'something bad happened here' and 'I've got a bad feeling about this…' Even so, the film looks truly beautiful and, thankfully, allows its scares to creep up on one rather than beating the viewer over the head with its shocks effects. IP

• *Rose Da Silva* Radha Mitchell, *Christopher Da Silva* Sean Bean, *Cybil Bennett* Laurie Holden, *Dahlia Gillespie* Deborah Kara Unger, *Officer Thomas Gucci* Kim Coates, *with* Tanya Allen, Alice Krige, Jodelle Ferland.

• *Dir* Christopher Gans, *Pro* Samuel Hadida and Don Carmody, *Ex Pro* Andrew Mason, Victoria Hadida and Akira Yamaoka, *Screenplay* Roger Avary, based on the game by Konami, *Ph* Dan Lausten, *Pro Des* Carol Spier, *Ed* Sebastien Prangere, *M* Jeff Danna, *Costumes* Wendy Partridge, *Creature Design* Patrick Tatopoulos.

TriStar Pictures/Samuel Hadida/Davis Films-Pathé.
125 mins. Canada/France. 2006. Rel: 21 April 2006. Cert. 15.

Silver City ★★

Basking in the political reflection of his senatorial father, Dickie Pilager is a none-too-bright, verbally challenged candidate for the governorship of Colorado. The perfect puppet for the devious practitioners of local big business – with whom his father is irrevocably linked – Pilager would appear to be a shoo-in. Then, while promoting his environmental concerns for the camera, Pilager stands in front of a beautiful lake and, with fishing rod in hand, reels in a corpse… With films like *Matewan*, *City of Hope* and *Sunshine State*, John Sayles has earned a reputation for independent, pertinent and socially conscientious cinema. Now actors of a certain calibre line up to work with him (for peanuts) and he turns out large ensemble pieces almost every year. In his own insular way, John Sayles has become as automatic as Woody Allen, albeit of a very different stripe. *Silver City* is old hat, flatly edited and visually muddy; it's *Bob Roberts* without the laughs. Any Michael Moore documentary is more entertaining – and more relevant. If nothing else, Sayles shouldn't edit his own films – his narrative rhythm has become deadly. JC-W

• *Nora Allardyce* Maria Bello, *Karen Cross* Thora Birch, *Dickie Pilager* Chris Cooper, *Chuck Raven* Richard Dreyfuss, *Maddy Pilager* Daryl Hannah, *Danny O'Brien* Danny Huston, *Wes Benteen* Kris Kristofferson, *Mitch Paine* Tim Roth, *Chandler Tyson* Billy Zane, *Cliff Castleton* Miguel Ferrer, *Casey Lyle* Ralph Waite, *Tony Guerra* Sal López, *Sheriff Joe Skaggs* James Gammon, *Lupe Montoya* Alma Delfina, *Vince Esparza* Luis Saguar, *with* David Clennon, Michael Murphy, Mary Kay Place, Aaron Vieyra, Hugo Carbajal.

• *Dir* and *Screenplay* John Sayles, *Co-Pro* Maggie Renzi and Lansing Parker, *Ph* Haskell Wexler, *Pro Des* Toby Corbett, *Ed* Sayles and Renzi, *M* Mason Daring, *Costumes* Shay Cunliffe.

Anarchists' Convention-Tartan Films.
128 mins. USA. 2004. Rel: 22 July 2005. Cert. 15.

The Sisterhood of the Traveling Pants ★★★★

This being an American story, the pants of the title are actually a pair of jeans. But these are no ordinary jeans; they are magic denims that manage to fit all the various sizes of four inseparable girlfriends. Since birth, Carmen, Bridget, Lena and Tibby have been through a number of personal crises but have always been there for one another. Now, aged 17, they are to spend their first summer apart, as Carmen visits her divorced father, Bridget joins soccer camp in Mexico, Lena visits her grandparents in Greece and Tibby stocks shelves in the local supermarket. But to keep in touch, they decide to share their magic pants for one week at a time… Taking into account its target audience, *The Sisterhood…* is rather wonderful. Yes it's slick, corny and hackneyed, but it also tackles pertinent issues and does so with heart and a level head. Above all, though, it speaks to a contemporary teenage audience and does so without condescension or sensationalism. It's also skilfully put together, brightly and convincingly acted and once it gathers steam is hugely moving. JC-W

• *Tibby* Amber Tamblyn, *Carmen* America Ferrera, *Bridget* Blake Lively, *Lena* Alexis Bledel, *Al* Bradley Whitford, *Lydia Rodman* Nancy Travis, *Carmen's mother* Rachel Ticotin, *Bailey* Jenna Boyd, *Eric* Mike Vogel, *Kostas* Michael Rady, *Bridget's father* Ernie Lively, *with* Leonardo Nam, Maria Konstandarou, George Touliatos, Kyle Schmid, Erica Hubbard, Emily Tennant, Jacqueline Stewart, Sarah-Jane Redmond, Kristie Marsden, Patricia Mayan Salazar, Patricia Drake, Katie Stuart, Jonathon Young, Mary Black.

• *Dir* Ken Kwapis, *Pro* Debra Martin Chase, Denise di Novi, Broderick Johnson and Andrew A. Kosove, *Ex Pro* Leslie

Morgenstein, Kira Davis and Alison Greenspan, *Co-Pro* Christine Sacani, Steven P. Wegner and Melissa Wiechmann, *Screenplay* Delia Ephron and Elizabeth Chandler, *Ph* John Bailey, *Pro Des* Gae Buckley, *Ed* Kathryn Himoff, *M* Cliff Eidelman, *Costumes* Lisa Jensen.

Alcon Entertainment/Alloy Entertainment-Warner. 118 mins. USA. 2005. Rel: 26 August 2005. Cert. PG.

16 Blocks ★★★

Det. Jack Mosley has run to seed. He's got a gammy leg, a drinking problem and a surplus of cynicism. And, having been on duty all night, he just wants to go home. But he's given one last errand – to escort grand jury witness Eddie Bunker the 16 blocks from the police station to the courthouse. However, in New York, 16 blocks can seem like an eternity... Paunchy and unshaven, Bruce Willis's Jack Mosley is like a rusty old spring. But there's still some tension in his coil... Willis pretty much holds this potboiler together, his eyes saying more than all the irritating patter of co-star Mos Def (in a surprisingly misjudged performance). In fact, the first half of *16 Blocks* – unfolded in real time – is terrific, aided by above-average camera work and a canny score from Klaus Badelt. Then, past the halfway mark, the film loses momentum and credibility and slouches into a formulaic and predictable policier. JC-W

• *Jack Mosley* Bruce Willis, *Eddie Bunker* Mos Def, *Frank Nugent* David Morse, *Diane Mosley* Jenna Stern, *Captain Gruber* Casey Sander, *Jimmy Mulvey* Cylk Cozart, *Robert Torres* David Zayas, *Jerry Shue* Robert Racki.

• *Dir* Richard Donner, *Pro* Jim Van Wyck, John Thompson, Arnold Rifkin, Avi Lerner and Randall Emmett, *Ex Pro* Andreas Thiesmeyer, Josef Lautenschlager, Danny Dimbort, Trevor Short, Boaz Davidson, George Furla and Hadeel Reda, *Co-Pro* Derek Hoffman and Brian Read, *Co-Ex Pro* Gerd Koechlin and Manfred Heid, *Screenplay* Richard Wenk, *Ph* Glen Macpherson, *Pro Des* Arv Greywal, *Ed* Steven Mirkovich, *M* Klaus Badelt, *Costumes* Vicki Graef.

Alcon Entertainment/Millennium Films/Emmet/Furla Films/Cheyenne Enterprises-Warner. 101 mins. USA/Germany. 2006. Rel: 28 April 2006. Cert. 12A.

The Skeleton Key ★★

Disillusioned with her job as a nurse at a New Orleans hospital, Carrie takes a private position caring for an old man who's suffered a debilitating stroke. Stuck out in the middle of nowhere, Carrie feels far from welcome by the man's wife, who is suspicious of outsiders. But soon she discovers that there are other reasons for the old woman's uneasiness... The silt is rich but you can't smell the swamp in this half-baked Gothic thriller. Much of the problem is in the details, few of which ring true: for instance, Gena Rowlands' dotty Violet complains that Carrie doesn't have a Southern accent but can barely keep her own drawl functioning; and The Dixie Cups' 'Iko Iko' is presented as this obscure Southern anthem (it's actually a New Orleans standard heard on the soundtracks of

The Big Easy, *Rain Man*, *M:I-2*, etc). Besides, the plotting is so formulaic and the 'surprises' so contrived, that it's all about as frightening as a bowl of gumbo. It certainly isn't a patch on Wes Craven's terrifying voodoo thriller *The Serpent and the Rainbow* (1988). JC-W

• *Caroline* Kate Hudson, *Violet* Gena Rowlands, *Luke* Peter Sarsgaard, *Ben* John Hurt, *Jill* Joy Bryant, *Mama Cynthia* Maxine Barnett, *with* Fahnlohnee Harris, Tom Uskali, Isaach De Bankolé.

• *Dir* Iain Softley, *Pro* Softley, Daniel Bobker, Michael Shamberg and Stacey Sher, *Ex Pro* Clayton Townsend, *Screenplay* Ehren Kruger, *Ph* Dan Mindel, *Pro Des* John Beard, *Ed* Joe Hutshing, *M* Edward Shearmur, *Costumes* Louise Frogley, *Sound* Harry Cohen and Ann Scibelli.

Universal/Shadowcatcher Entertainment/ Double Feature Films-UIP. 104 mins. USA. 2005. Rel: 29 July 2005. Cert. 15.

Sky Blue ★★

Earth; 2142 AD. The city of Ecoban, an organic metropolis genetically engineered to withstand global contamination, is occupied by the elite. Outside, mining the carbon supplies essential to maintaining Ecoban's existence, are the 'diggers', labourers who once sought asylum within the city's walls. When Jay, a 19-year-old trooper from Ecoban, witnesses a wanton act of industrial sabotage aimed at undermining the diggers, she takes stock of her loyalties. Shua, Jay's childhood sweetheart, is at the heart of a rebellion against the city and Jay must choose between what is safe and what is right... Great idea this, and one pegged to an exciting new animation process calling itself 'multimation'. With the human characters portrayed in the simple pen-and-ink of traditional anime, the backgrounds are composed of a variety of fabulous cityscapes, skylines and aquatic effects. But however heady the visuals of any cartoon may be, they're not worth a jot if the story doesn't hold up. Here, the plotting is convoluted, the characters one-dimensional and the whole experience quite baffling – and soporific. JC-W

• *Voices*: *Jay/young Shua/Cheyenne* Catherine Cavadini, *Shua* Marc Worden, *Cade* Kirk Thornton, *Commander Locke/Dr Noah* David Naughton, *Moe* Karl Wiedergott, *Woody/young Jay* Rebecca Wink, *Goliath/governor/Typon* Bob Papenbrook, *Maya* Sunmin Park.

• *Dir* Moon Sang Kim; *American version*: Sunmin Park, *Pro* Hwang Kay, Sunmin Park and Lee Kyeong Hag, *Ex Pro* Stephen Kim, Victoria Shin and Jimin Park, *Screenplay* Moon Sang Kim, Un Young Park and Sunmin Park, *Ph* Lee Sun-kwan, *Pro Des* Lee Soug-young, *M* Won II, *Animation Dir* Yoon Young-ki.

Samsung Venture Investment/Korea Culture/Contents Agency-Tartan Films. 85 mins. South Korea/USA. 2003. Rel: 8 July 2005. Cert. 15.

Sky High ★★★

The son of the world's two greatest superheroes, Will Stronghold must hide the fact that he has no super-powers of his own (particularly as he attends a secret high school that specializes in training young heroes). Even as Will deals with the standard angst of burgeoning pubescence, high school cliques, and his own embarrassing role as a 'sidekick', he manages to thwart a villainous plot to destroy both Sky High and his own parents. The obvious caste system of the school is disturbing and goes way beyond the 'in crowd' and 'geek' dynamics of standard high school set fare. Still, this is a charming effort and a much softer, family friendly super-hero flick than the gritty *X-Men* franchise. Seeing Kurt Russell in a Disney movie is always a joy and casting Lynda Carter as the school's principal was simply brilliant! Young Michael Angarano (Jack's son from TV's *Will & Grace*) hits all the right marks as Will. SWM

• *Steve Stronghold/The Commander* Kurt Russell, *Josie Stronghold/Jetstream* Kelly Preston, *Will Stronghold* Michael Angarano, *Layla* Danielle Panabaker, *Ron Wilson, bus driver* Kevin Heffernan, *Principal Powers* Lynda Carter, *Gwen Grayson* Mary Elizabeth Winstead, *Coach Boomer* Bruce Campbell, *Mr. Boy* Dave Foley, *with* Steven Strait, Dee-Jay Daniels, Nicholas Braun, Kelly Vitz, Jim Rash, Jake Sandvig, Will Harris, Kevin McDonald, Cloris Leachman, *voice of Royal Pain* Patrick Warburton.

• *Dir* Mike Mitchell, *Pro* Andrew Gunn, *Ex Pro* Mario Iscovich and Ann Marie Sanderlin, *Screenplay* Paul Hernandez, Bob Schooley and Mark McCorkle, *Ph* Shelly Johnson, *Pro Des* Bruce Robert Hill, *Ed* Paul Amundson, *M* Michael Giacchino, *Costumes* Michael Wilkinson.

Walt Disney Pictures/Gunn Films-Buena Vista International.
99 mins. USA. 2005. Rel: 21 October 2005.
Cert. PG.

Slither ★★★

In what appears to be a meteor, an alien parasite lands in the woods of Middle America and soon takes the form of a giant worm. Local businessman Grant Grant is in the woods (trying to have sex with a woman he has picked up in a bar) and gets infected by the parasite… This is a welcome addition to the horror-comedy genre, directed by James Gunn with a great sense of fun and invention. A zombie film which also pays tribute to films like *The Fly* and *The Thing*, *Slither* works because it doesn't take itself too seriously. See it but make sure you stay until the end of the credits. GS

• *Sheriff Bill Pardy* Nathan Fillion, *Starla Grant* Elizabeth Banks, *Jack MacReady* Gregg Henry, *Grant Grant* Michael Rooker, *Kylie Strutemyer* Tania Saulnier, *Brenda Gutierrez* Brenda James, *Wally* Don Thompson, *with* Jennifer Copping, Jenna Fisher, Haig Sutherland, Lloyd Kaufman.

• *Dir* and *Screenplay* James Gunn, *Pro* Paul Brooks and Eric Newman, *Ex Pro* Marc Abraham, Thomas A. Bliss, Norman Waitt and Scott Niemeyer, *Co-Pro* Jeff Levine, *Ph* Gregory Middleton, *Pro Des* Andrew Neskoromny, *Ed* John Axelrad, *M* Tyler Bates, *Costumes* Patricia Louise Hargreaves.

Universal/Gold Circle Films/Strike Entertainment-Entertainment.
95 mins. USA/Canada. 2006. Rel: 28 April 2006. Cert. 15.

Song of Songs ★★½

This ambitious British debut by Josh Appignanesi, an impassioned writer-director, has two great assets in the performances of Joel Chalfen and Natalie Press portraying a brother and sister. The setting is North London and the piece, deeply Jewish in concerns and expression, presents them as contrasted siblings. She is devoted to looking after their deeply religious and dying mother while he, estranged from the family home, posits alternative ideas (he speaks up for the concept of a messiah who is a transgressor and, echoing Cocteau's *Les Enfants Terribles*, sees incest with his sister as a way forward). Even without its background emphasis on hostilities and atrocities by way of news bulletins, this is an over-complex work puzzlingly obscure in its aims – unless that is a Jewish viewer can find the key that would unlock it. MS

• *Ruth Cohen* Natalie Press, *David Cohen* Joel Chalfen, *Sarah Cohen* Julia Swift, *Rabbi Berg* Leon Lissek, *Abigail* Felicite du Jeu, *Rachel Silverbaum* Amanda Boxer, *with* Amber Agar, Philip Dunbar, Sue Kelvin, Justine Mitchell.

• *Dir* Josh Appignanesi, *Pro* Gayle Griffiths, *Line Pro* Tracy O'Riordan, *Screenplay* Josh Appignanesi and Jay Basu, *Ph* Nanu Segal, *Pro Des* Erik Rehl, *Ed* Nicolas Chaudeurge, *M* John Roome, *Costumes* Katy Howkins.

Wild Horses Film Co-Soda Pictures.
82 mins. UK. 2005. Rel: 10 February 2006. Cert. 15.

Sophie Scholl – The Final Days ★★★★

The commercial success of *Downfall* suggests that there are young audiences around who now welcome the opportunity to learn more about Hitler's Germany. They will be able to identify even more closely with this debut film by Marc Rothemund because in this true story the central figure, Sophie Scholl, is a 21-year-old student. Merely for involving herself in written protests against the route down which Hitler was leading her country, she was executed by the Nazis in 1943. The film's title foretells her demise but nevertheless this film which presents events from her viewpoint grips hard every step of the way. Julia Jentsch's performance in the title role achieves an intensity that makes us share fully in the tragedy, but the over-emphatic music score is a misjudgment. Original title: *Sophie Scholl – Die letzten Tage*. MS

• *Sophie Scholl* Julia Jentsch, *Robert Mohr* Alexander Held, *Hans Scholl* Fabian Hinrichs, *Christoph Probst* Florian Stetter, *Else Gebel* Johanna Gastdorf, *Robert Scholl* Jörg Hube, *Will Graf* Maximilian Brückner, *Roland Freisler* André Hennicke, *with* Johannes Suhm, Lilli Jung, Klaus Händl.
• *Dir* Marc Rothemund, *Pro* Christoph Müller, Sven

Burgemeister, Marc Rothemund and Fred Breinersdorfer, *Screenplay* Fred Breinersdorfer, *Ph* Martin Langer, *Pro Des* Jana Karen-Brey, *Ed* Hans Funck, *M* Johnny Klimek and Reinhold Heil, *Costumes* Natascha Curtius-Noss, *Sound* Alex Saal and Daniel Dietenberger.

Goldkind Film/Broth Film-ICA Projects.
120 mins. Germany/France. 2005. Rel: 28 October 2005. Cert. PG.

The Squid and the Whale ★★★½

Park Slope, Brooklyn, New York; 1986. Bernard and Joan Berkman have been together for 17 years. He is a writer of some experience and renown but is unable to find a publisher for his latest novel. She, wriggling free from the constraints of motherhood, is finding her own voice in the publishing world and with some success. Meanwhile, the Berkmans' marriage is coming apart at the seams… With raw, economic brushstrokes, writer-director Baumbach vacuum-packs his autobiographical fable with a number of memorably painful and embarrassing moments. Every minute, every scene cuts to the emotional and comic truth of this dysfunctional, very human quartet trapped in a void of self-deception. Jeff Daniels' Bernard and Jesse Eisenberg's Walt, the son who takes the former's side, are particularly delusional yet poignantly real mirror images of the fragile male psyche. However, at just 80 minutes this is only half the film it could have been, with the emotional closure it cries out for hanging in the balance. JC-W

• *Bernard Berkman* Jeff Daniels, *Joan Berkman* Laura Linney, *Walt Berkman* Jesse Eisenberg, *Frank Berkman* Owen Kline, *Ivan* William Baldwin, *Sophie Greenberg* Halley Feiffer, *Lili* Anna Paquin, *Carl* David Benger, *with* Bo Berkman, James Hamilton, Peggy Gormley, Peter Newman, Greta Kline, Nico Baumbach.

• *Dir* and *Screenplay* Noah Naumbach, *Pro* Wes Anderson, Peter Newman, Charlie Corwin and Clara Markowicz, *Ex Pro* Reverge Anselmo, Miranda Bailey, Greg Johnson and Andrew Lauren, *Co-Ex Pro* Jennifer M. Roth, *Ph* Robert D. Yeoman, *Pro Des* Anne Ross, *Ed* Tim Streeto, *M* Britta Phillips and Dean Wareham; Brahms; with tracks performed by Pink Floyd, Jesse Eisenberg, Bert Jansch, Tangerine Dream, Bryan Adams, John Phillips, Loudon Wainwright III, Kate McGarrigle and Anna McGarrigle, Greta Kline, The Cars, The Feelies, Blossom Dearie, and Lou Reed, *Costumes* Amy Westcott.

Samuel Goldwyn Films/Sony Pictures Releasing/ Destination Films/Original Media/Ambush Entertainment-Columbia TriStar.
80 mins. USA. 2005. Rel: 7 April 2006. Cert. 15.

Stay ★★

New York; the present. When psychiatrist Sam Foster stands in for an indisposed colleague, he takes on the case of Henry Letham. A precocious art student, Henry has decided to take his own life the following Saturday, on the eve of his 21st birthday. As Sam immerses himself in Henry's case, so he finds his parameters of reality increasingly challenged… There are a lot of interesting things going on in *Stay*, but for the most part it is maddeningly abstruse. With background figures dressed in identical outfits and computer-generated switches between character and place, the film unfolds like a pretentious music video. And it's this very technical sleight of hand that undermines the drama. With characters sacrificed on the altar of picturesque manipulation, there's little human meat to get one's teeth into. Once again, Ryan Gosling (*The Believer, Murder by Numbers*) provides a mesmerising portrait

Broken-hearted in Brooklyn: Jeff Daniels and Laura Linney in Noah Baumbach's raw, observant and poignant *The Squid and the Whale* (from Sony Pictures)

of disturbed karma, but the wonderful Naomi Watts is wasted and Ewan McGregor seems to be a paradoxical joke. JC-W

• *Sam Foster* Ewan McGregor, *Lila Culpepper* Naomi Watts, *Henry Letham* Ryan Gosling, *Dr Beth Levy* Janeane Garofalo, *Dr Ren* B.D. Wong, *Dr Leon Patterson* Bob Hoskins, *Mrs Letham* Kate Burton, *Athena* Elizabeth Reaser, *with* Jessica Hecht, Mark Margolis, Michael Gaston, Isaach De Bankolé.

• *Dir* Marc Forster, *Pro* Arnon Milchan, Tom Lassally and Eric Kopeloff, *Ex Pro* Bill Carraro and Guymon Casady, *Screenplay* David Benioff, *Ph* Roberto Schaefer, *Pro Des* Kevin Thompson, *Ed* Matt Chessé, *M* Asche & Spencer, *Costumes* Frank Fleming, *Visual Effects* Kevin Tod Haug.

Regency Enterprises/New Regency-Fox.
98 mins. USA. 2005. Rel: 3 March 2006. Cert. 15.

Stealth ★★½

US Navy test pilots Ben Gannon, Kara Wade and Henry Purcell are the best of the best. Firm friends, they thrive on their team spirit so are somewhat taken aback when a fourth pilot is entered into their winning equation. Yet this newcomer is not human, being a state-of-the-art computer dubbed 'EDI'. EDI has none of the failings of a human pilot but, it transpires, does have a mind of its own… Squinting his infinite blue eyes, flyboy superjock Ben Gannon tells his commander, 'I don't think war should become a video game.' Yet *Stealth* is just that, a jingoist, computer-animated romp across the world's more dubious nations, be they Myanmar, Tajikistan, North Korea or Alaska (*Alaska?*). Considering the material they're given, human stars Josh Lucas, Jessica Biel (especially Jessica Biel) and Jamie Foxx make the most of their characters, injecting shots of humanity with nano-second precision. Otherwise, the stars are just puppets in the adrenaline-powered, breakneck-paced

shenanigans that draw liberally on the cultural fusillade of *2001*, *Top Gun* and *Rambo*. It's a fun, exhausting ride, although when Ms Biel crashes into North Korea and Sam Shepard informs an aide that America has 'no diplomatic relations with *that* country', you wonder what halfwits the US Navy is employing. JC-W

• *Ben Gannon* Josh Lucas, *Kara Wade* Jessica Biel, *Henry Purcell* Jamie Foxx, *Captain George Cummings* Sam Shepard, *Captain Dick Marshfield* Joe Morton, *Dr Keith Orbit* Richard Roxburgh, *Tim* Ebon Moss-Bachrach, *Ray* David Andrews, *voice of EDI* Wentworth Miller, *with* Ian Bliss, Alexandra Davies, Caroline de Souza, Jason Lee, Nicholas Hammond.

• *Dir* Rob Cohen, *Pro* Laura Ziskin, Mike Medavoy and Neal H. Moritz, *Ex Pro* E. Bennett Walsh and Arnold W. Messer, *Screenplay* W.D. Richter, *Ph* Dean Semler, *Pro Des* J. Michael Riva and Jonathan Lee, *Ed* Stephen Rivkin, *M* BT, *Costumes* Lizzy Gardiner.

Columbia Pictures/Original Film/Phoenix Pictures-Columbia TriStar.
120 mins. USA. 2005. Rel: 5 August 2005. Cert. 12A.

Stoned ★★

Rolling Stones guitarist Brian Jones' decline and fall gets a rather tedious and muddled dramatisation in this slackly written biopic that suggests why Jones was found dead at the bottom of his swimming pool just after being dumped from the band in 1969. Paddy Considine plays a builder who is hired to make alterations on Jones' country estate and ends up being a fixture there, consumed by the singer's lifestyle, while Jones looks for sex and drugs in Marrakesh. Leo Gregory plays the latter in a trance-like way that induces boredom, then sleep, and frustratingly the look-alike actors playing the rest of the

Pilot lights: Jamie Foxx, Jessica Biel and Josh Lucas in Rob Cohen's dumb but entertaining *Stealth* (from Sony Pictures)

band have only a handful of lines in total. It's clearly a labour of love by producer-director Stephen Woolley, but the film's at its best in conjuring up the background situations of mood, atmosphere, clothes and accessories of the times, a credit to the cinematographer, production designer and art director. DW

• *Brian Jones* Leo Gregory, *Frank Thoroggod* Paddy Considine, *Tom Keylock* David Morrisey, *Keith Richards* Ben Whishaw, *Anna Wohlin* Tuva Novotny, *Janet* Amelia Warner, *Anita Pallenberg* Monet Mazur, *Mick Jagger* Luke de Woolfson, *with* David Walliams, Gary Love, Johnny Shannon, Melanie Ramsay, Ralph Brown, Lisa Dolan, Simon Chandler, Nathalie Cox, Tim Flavin.

• *Dir* Stephen Woolley, *Pro* Woolley and Finola Dwyer, *Ex Pro* Gary Smith and Paul White, *Line Pro* Charles Salmon, *Co-Pro* and *Screenplay* Neal Purvis and Robert Wade, *Ph* John Mathieson, *Pro Des* John Beard, *Ed* Sam Sneade, *M* David Arnold, *Costumes* Roger Burton.

Intadem Films/Audley Films/Number 9 Films/National Lottery/UK Film Council-Vertigo Films. 102 mins. UK. 2005. Rel: 18 November 2005. Cert. 15.

Strayed ★★

France; 1940. With her husband killed in action, Odile flees the Nazi occupation of Paris with her two children, 13-year-old Philippe and seven-year-old Cathy. When a German bomber destroys their car, they flee into nearby woods for cover where they befriend an enigmatic young man, Yvan. The latter's knowledge of the wilderness helps them survive on berries and wild rabbits and so a hesitant bond is formed…
In spite of the luxurious imagery of the French countryside, there is little sense of place in this wartime parable. Incongruous newsreel footage punctuates the action, but the Elysian woods could be anywhere, in any period. In fact, the film's time span is also problematic, the events seemingly trapped in a temporal vacuum. But the main trouble is the film's turgid pacing, generating a dramatic stasis unrelieved by a potentially intriguing human dynamic. JC-W

• *Odile* Emmanuelle Béart, *Yvan* Gaspard Ulliel, *Philippe* Grégoire Leprince-Ringuet, *Cathy* Clémence Meyer, *Georges* Jean Fornerod.

• *Dir* André Téchiné, *Pro* Jean-Pierre Ramsay Levi, *Ex Pro* David Rogers, *Screenplay* Téchiné and Gilles Taurand, from the novel *Le Garçon aux Yeux Gris* by Gilles Perrault, *Ph* Agnés Godard, *Art Dir* Zé Branco, *Ed* Martine Giordano, *M* Phiilippe Sarde, *Costumes* Christian Gasc.

Jean-Pierre Ramsay Levi/FTI Prods/Spice Factory/France 2 Cinéma/Canal Plus-Soda Pictures. 95 mins. France/UK. 2003. Rel: 24 March 2006. Cert. 15.

Summer Storm ★★★½

This is a German take on adolescence largely set in a summer camp where a rowing competition is being organized. It's centred on a youth, Tobi (Stadlober), coming to terms with the fact that he is gay. Well photographed and decidedly likable, it adopts a relatively light-hearted tone without failing to recognise the serious issues at stake. Indeed, its evident sympathy for the characters seems to link with the acknowledgment of filmmaker Marco Kreuzpaintner that this is a partly autobiographical work. The second half is at times more overtly dramatic and less individual but the film is never less than agreeable and a pleasing alternative to Hollywood's teenage movies. Original title: *Sommersturm*. MS

• *Tobi* Robert Stadlober, *Achim* Kostja Ullmann, *Anke* Alicja Bachleda-Curus, *Malte* Hanno Kofler, *Georg* Tristano Casanova, *Hansi* Jürgen Tonkel, *Sandra* Miriam Morgenstern.

• *Dir* Marco Kreuzpaintner, *Pro* Uli Putz, Thomas Wöbke and Jakob Claussen, *Screenplay* Kreuzpaintner and Thomas Bahmann, *Ph* Daniel Gottschalk, *Art Dir* Heike Lange, *Ed* Hansjörg Weißbrich, *M* Niki Reiser, *Costumes* Anke Winckler.

X-Verleih, etc-Peccadillo Pictures. 98 mins. Hungary/Germany. 2002. Rel: 26 August 2005. Cert. 15.

The Sun ★★★★

Hardly an undemanding film, this is nevertheless far more accessible than much of Alexander Sokurov's work. Finely played by Issey Ogata, it offers a study of Emperor Hirohito in 1945 and a portrait of a man caught in his own destiny. Somebody who would be content not to be a ruler, Hirohito questions the traditional view of the emperor's divinity but because of the people's belief in it he can save his country by capitulating to the Americans, although that act in itself betrays the Japanese belief in fighting to the death. Presented as a chamber work, this is a telling minimalistic drama, sombre but not without touches of humour. The personal risk taken by the emperor in accepting responsibility for his nation's actions is not investigated fully and that leaves the film short of being a masterpiece, but it is intensely yet quietly compelling. Original title: *Solntse*. MS

• *Emperor* Issey Ogata, *General MacArthur* Robert Dawson, *Empress* Kaori Momoi, *Chamberlain* Shiro Sano, *old servant* Shinmei Tsuji, *director of the institute* Taijiro Tamura, *adjutant of general* Georgy Pitskhelauri.

• *Dir* and *Ph* Alexander Sokurov, *Pro* Igor Kalenov, Andrey Sigle and Marco Mueller, *Co-Pro* Alexander Rodnyansky, Andrey Zertsalov and Antoine de Clermont-Tonnerre, *Screenplay* Yury Arabov, *Pro Des* Yury Kuper, *Ed* Sergey Ivanov, *M* Andrey Sigle, *Costumes* Lidia Krukova.

Nikola-Film/Proline-Film/Downtown Pictures/MACT Prods-Artificial Eye. 114 mins. Russia/Italy/France/Switzerland. 2005. Rel: 2 September 2005. Cert. PG.

Corrupt horizons: George Clooney in Stephen Gaghan's provocative, intellectually gripping *Syriana* (from Warner)

Sympathy for Lady Vengeance
See *Lady Vengeance.*

Syriana ★★★★
'Syriana' is a term used in Washington to describe a hypothetical reshaping of the Middle East. Here, it could equally stand for the name of a fictitious Persian Gulf country on the verge of switching its allegiance in a global oil franchise. Meanwhile, an ageing CIA agent, an ambitious energy consultant, an idealistic Arab prince and a conscientious attorney get caught in the backwash… Stephen Gaghan won an Oscar for his screenplay to *Traffic* and returns to the socio-political ensemble format for this, his second film as director. With private access to oil traders, CIA operatives, arm dealers and Islamic principals, Gaghan certainly knows his territory and spent a year travelling round Europe, the Middle East and Africa for his research. Recalling *Traffic* and Spielberg's *Munich* in its international sweep and multi-layered structure – not to mention its lucid narrative, economic storytelling and desaturated colour palette – *Syriana* unfolds like a tightly coiled spring. While not as emotionally engaging as, say, *Traffic* or *Crash*, it remains a provocative, intellectually gripping ride for viewers who like a bit of kick and polish with their CNN. Defining line: 'Corruption is our protection. Corruption keeps us safe and warm. Corruption is why we win…' JC-W

• *Bob Barnes* George Clooney, *Bryan Woodman* Matt Damon, *Bennett Holiday* Jeffrey Wright, *Jimmy Pope* Chris Cooper, *Stan* William Hurt, *Wasim* Mazhar Munir, *Danny Dalton* Tim Blake Nelson, *Julie Woodman* Amanda Peet, *Dean Whiting* Christopher Plummer, *Prince Nasir* Alexander Siddig, *Robbie Barnes* Max Minghella, *Prince Meshal* Akbar Kurtha, *Saleem Ahmed Kahn* Shahid Ahmed, *Bennett Holiday Snr* William C. Mitchell, *Farooq* Sonnell Dadral, *Mussawi* Mark Strong, *with* Kayvan Novak, Amr Waked, Robert Foxworth, Nicky Henson, Jayne Atkinson, Tom McCarthy, Jamey Sheridan, Nadim Sawalha, David Clennon, Donna Mitchell.

• *Dir* and *Screenplay* Stephen Gaghan, from the nonfiction book *See No Evil* by Robert Baer, *Pro* Jennifer Fox, Michael Nozik and George Kacandes, *Ex Pro* George Clooney, Steven Soderbergh, Ben Cosgrove and Jeff Skoll, *Ph* Robert Elswit, *Pro Des* Dan Weil, *Ed* Tim Squyres, *M* Alexandre Desplat, *Costumes* Louise Frogley.

Warner/Participant Prods/4M/Section Eight-Warner. 127 mins. USA. 2005. Rel: 3 March 2006. Cert. 15.

Take the Lead ★★½
This is inspired by the true story of Pierre Dulaine who, at a New York inner-city high school, volunteered his services to students serving detention and taught ballroom dancing. Antonio Banderas is well cast as the dashing teacher and his image as a modern day Valentino is used to great effect. He is supported by a talented and highly accomplished group of young actor and/or dancers. It is of course very predictable but fun and some of the set pieces are quite exciting, particularly towards the end. Interestingly, it covers very similar territory to the recent but much superior documentary *Mad Hot Ballroom.* MS

• *Pierre Dulaine* Antonio Banderas, *Rock* Rob Brown, *LaRhette* Yaya DaCosta, *Ramos* Dante Basco, *Mr Temple* John Ortiz, *Augustine James* Alfre Woodard, *with* Lauren Collins, Brandon D. Andrews, Jonathan Malen, Anna Dimitrie Melamed.

• *Dir* Liz Friedlander, *Pro* Diane Nabatoff, Michelle Grace and Christopher Godsick, *Ex Pro* Toby Emmerich, Matt Moore, Mark Kaufman, Ray Liotta and Mathew Hart, *Screenplay* Dianne Houston, *Ph* Alex Nepomniaschy, *Pro Des* Paul Denham Austerberry, *Ed* Robert Ivison, *M* Aaron Zigman and Swizz Beatz, *Costumes* Melissa Toth, *Choreography* JoAnn Fregalette Jansen.

New Line Cinema/Tiara Blu Films-Entertainment. 117 mins. USA. 2006. Rel: 14 April 2006. Cert. 12A.

Tell Me Something ★★½
Seoul, South Korea; today. A male body lies on a table and an unidentified figure picks up a scalpel and slices off the body's left arm, shoulder and all. Shortly afterwards, a black bin liner turns up, containing the severed remains of a corpse. Then another one, and then another one. But the twist is that each bag contains different parts of three men and it takes a small army of Seoul police to piece together the limbs, heads and internal organs… Quite frankly, the title of this 1999 Korean suspenser is about as baffling as its plot. Featuring a Rubik's cube of severed human anatomy, and with much of the action acted out in the dark, the thing unfolds like a mathematical equation dripping in blood. Even so, it is stunningly shot in the nocturnal, rain-soaked streets of Seoul and as such is an object lesson in pictorial, moody *film noir.* Original title: *Tel mi sseomting.* JC-W

• *Detective Cho* Han Suk-gyu, *Chae Soo-yeon* Shim Eun-ha, *Detective Oh* Jang Hang-seun, *Sung-Min Oh* Yum Jang-ah, *Kim Ki-Yeon* Yu Jun-sang.

• *Dir* Chang Yoon-hyun, *Pro* Chang and Koo Bon-Han, *Ex Pro* Choi Gwi-Duk, *Screenplay* Chang, Kong Su-Chang, In Eun-Ah, Shim Hae-Weon and Kim Eun-Jung, based on a story by Koo Bon-Han, *Ph* Kim Sung-Bok, *Art Dir* Chung Ku-Ho, *Ed* Kim Sang-Bum, *M* Cho Young-Ook and Bang Joon-Suk.

Koo & C Film Co/Cinema Service and Koomin Venture Capital-Tartan Films. 116 mins. South Korea. 1999. Rel: 16 September 2005. No Cert.

Tell Them Who You Are ★★★★
Haskell Wexler photographed *The Conversation, One Flew Over the Cuckoo's Nest, Days of Heaven* and *Matewan* and won Oscars for *Who's Afraid of Virginia Woolf* and *Bound for Glory.* Although one of the most feted cinematographers of his era, Wexler would like to be remembered best as the person

behind the talent. However, Mark Wexler seems more in awe of the Hollywood icon than the man he calls father. Difficult, plain-speaking and opinionated, Haskell Wexler is a crusty and arrogant individual and will probably be the first to admit it. Norman Jewison bluntly tells Haskell's son that his father 'was a pain-in-the-ass to work with', while the likes of Michael Douglas, Milos Forman and Jane Fonda provide mixed reviews. Part character study, part showbiz résumé and part family album, *Tell Them Who You Are* is an extraordinary document. Like Nathaniel Kahn's equally riveting *My Architect*, the film is ultimately an attempt at personal closure by the subject's own son, who seeks to understand his father through candid cinematic autobiography. JC-W

• *With*: Haskell Wexler, Mark Wexler, Peter Bart, Verna Bloom, Bill Butler, Billy Crystal, Michael Douglas, Jane Fonda, Milos Forman, Troy Garity, Conrad L. Hall, Conrad W. Hall, Tom Hayden, Dennis Hopper, Ron Howard, Norman Jewison, Irvin Kershner, George Lucas, Albert Maysles, Paul Newman, Sidney Poitier, Julia Roberts, John Sayles, Martin Sheen, Lee Tamahori, Studs Terkel, Joanthan Winters, Pamela Yates, etc.

• *Dir, Pro* and *Ph* Mark S. Wexler, *Assoc Pro* Sarah Levy, *Narration scripted by* Mark S. Wexler and Robert DeMaio, *Ed* DeMaio, *M* Blake Leyh.

Wexler's World-Metrodome.
94 mins. USA. 2004. Rel: 2 June 2006. Cert. 15.

10th District Court ★★★

In 2003 French documentarian Raymond Depardon was allowed to film in a Paris courtroom conditional on those seen giving their approval. Depardon eventually chose twelve out of 169 defendants filmed for his final cut, the charges ranging from drunken driving and harassment to drug-dealing and carrying weapons. The French character of the hearings comes across, together with a marked female presence among the lawyers while Madame Justice Michèle Bernard-Requin presides. But the film does indeed offer only 'moments of trial' so while the people make their mark there's never the detail of complex, involving cases that made Frederick Wiseman's *Juvenile Court* (1973) a classic. Furthermore, the film lacks any sense of shape, seeming so arbitrary that you would do just as well visiting a local court for free. MS

If the blue shirt fits: Legendary cinematographer Haskell Wexler makes a point to his son Mark S. Wexler in the latter's extraordinary *Tell Them Who You Are* (from Metrodome)

• *A film by* Raymond Depardon, *Ed* Simon Jacquet and Lucile Sautarel.

Claudine Nougaret/Palmeraie/France 2 Cinéma/CanalPlus-ICA Projects.
105 mins. France. 2004. Rel: 16 June 2006. No Cert.

Thank You For Smoking ★★★★

Variously described as the Colonel Sanders of nicotine, a yuppie Mephistopheles or, in his own words, a man with 'moral flexibility', Nick Naylor is officially the chief spokesman for the Academy of Tobacco Studies. It is his job to lobby for the legitimacy of cigarettes in a country that still recognises people's right to personal choice. And proud of his silver tongue and the comfortable lifestyle it provides him, Naylor is happy to be able to defend a practice that kills 1,200 Americans a day... Slick, thought provoking and very, very funny, *Thank You For Smoking* is an extremely well-written adaptation of Christopher Buckley's 1994 novel of the same name. Like every great villain, Nick Naylor is entirely loveable, just because he so wholeheartedly believes in himself and has so much positive can-do energy. But the film is replete with great performances, from Rob Lowe as a feng shui-obsessed tycoon (who sleeps on Sundays) to William H. Macy as a highly rattled senator ('The great state of Vermont will not apologize for its cheese!'). JC-W

• *Nick Naylor* Aaron Eckhart, *Polly Bailey* Maria Bello, *Joey Naylor* Cameron Bright, *Jack* Adam Brody, *Lorne Lutch* Sam Elliott, *Heather Holloway* Katie Holmes, *Bobby Jay Bliss* David Koechner, *Jeff Megall* Rob Lowe, *Senator Ortolan Finistirre* William H. Macy, *BR* J.K. Simmons, *Captain* Robert Duvall, *Ron Goode* Todd Louiso, *Jill Naylor* Kim Dickens, *with* Joan Lunden, Marianne Muellerleile, Alex Diaz, Daniel Travis, Connie Ray, Dennis Miller, Aaron Lustig, Melora Hardin, Michael Mantell, Catherine Reitman, Sean Patrick Murphy.

• *Dir* and *Screenplay* Jason Reitman, *Pro* David O. Sacks, *Ex Pro* Peter Thiel, Elon Musk, Max Levchin, Mark Woolway, Edward R. Pressman, John Schmidt, Alessandro Camon and Michael Beugg, *Co-Pro* Daniel Brunt, Daniel Dubiecki, Mindy Marin and Michael R. Newman, *Co-Ex Pro* David J. Bloomfield, *Assoc Pro* Eveleen Anne Bandy and Stephen Belafonte, *Ph* James Whitaker, *Pro Des* Steve Saklad, *Ed* Dana E. Glauberman, *M* Rolfe Kent, *Costumes* Danny Glicker.

Fox Searchlight/Room 9 Entertainment/Content Film-Fox.
92 mins. USA. 2006. Rel: 16 June 2006. Cert. 15.

These Foolish Things ★

Diana, a young and struggling actress, wants to follow her mother's footsteps on the London stage and hopes that her chance encounters with a playwright and a director will help her fulfil her dream... This badly written, directed and acted film is a strong contender for Turkey of the Year. Only Terence Stamp manages to bring some fun into his role as the butler, but he seems to be in a different film entirely. It is sad to see Anjelica Huston and Lauren Bacall sink so low. GS

• *Lottie Osgood* Anjelica Huston, *Diana Shaw* Zoe Tapper,

Christopher Lovell Andrew Lincoln, *Robin Gardner* David Leon, *Baker* Terence Stamp, *Dame Lydia Simons* Lauren Bacall, *Albert* Joss Ackland, *Garstin* Leo Bill, *Everard Carter* Jamie Glover, *Douglas Middleton* Mark Umbers, *Miss Abernethy* Julia McKenzie, *Lily Evans* Charlotte Lucas, *with* Craig Rooke, Roisin Goodall, Sinead Goodall, Jordan Metcalfe, Joanna David, Graham Seed, Joan Blackham, Paul Sarony, Nickolas Grace, Haydn Gwynne, Roy Dotrice.

• *Dir* and *Screenplay* Julia Taylor-Stanley, *Pro* Taylor-Stanley and Paul Sarony, *Ex Pro* Keith Northrop, Neil Dunn, Carola Ash and David Jones, *Ph* Gavin Finney, *Pro Des* Chris Townsend,
Ed David Martin, *M* Ian Lynn, *Costumes* Frances Tempest.

Swipe Films/Porpoise Prods-Swipe Films.
106 mins. UK. 2005. Rel: 10 March 2006. Cert. 12A.

The Thief Lord ★★½

Recalling their mother's love of Venice, the orphaned brothers Prosper and Bo flee there to escape the tyranny of Bo's foster parents. Once in Venice, the boys are adopted by an enigmatic teenager in a mask going by the name of The Thief Lord. While Prosper abhors the principle of unethical requisition, he warms to his new companion and moves in with the latter's motley gang of orphaned petty thieves… An unusual hybrid of *Oliver Twist* and *The Magic Roundabout*, *The Thief Lord* has much to recommended it. Of course, the canals and alleyways of Venice are a major asset, there are agreeable turns from Jim Carter and Caroline Goodall as the 'good' grown-ups and nine-year-old Jasper Harris (as the six-year-old Bo) is a real find. The underlying theme of adults scrambling for a chance to re-live their childhood and children wanting nothing more than to be grown-up is also ripe for the exploiting. However, the film does suffer from uneven pacing, some wooden acting and several rather awkward attempts at slapstick. JC-W

• *Victor Getz* Jim Carter, *Ida* Caroline Goodall, *Scipio* Rollo Weeks, *Prosper* Aaron Johnson, *Riccio* George MacKay, *Bo* Jasper Harris, *Hornet* Alice Connor, *Mosca* Lathaniel Dyer, *Esther Hartlieb* Carole Boyd, *Max Hartlieb* Bob Goody, *Dottor Massimo* Robert Bathurst, *Barbarossa* Alexei Sayle, *Sister Antonia* Vanessa Redgrave, *with* Geoffrey Hutchings, Malcolm Turrner, Ann Comfort, Anita Wright.

• *Dir* and *Pro* Richard Claus, *Ex Pro* John Buchanan, Alexander Buchman, Jimmy De Brabant, Michael Dounaev and Gary Hamilton, *Co-Pro* Kwesi Dickson and Daniel Musgrave, *Co-Ex Pro* Avi Bouhadana and Michael Halimi, *Line Pro* Patricia McMahon, *Screenplay* Musgrave and Claus, *Ph* David Slama, *Pro Des* Matthias Kammermeier, *Ed* Peter R. Adam, *M* Nigel Clarke and Michael Csányi-Wills, *Costumes* Stepahnie Collie.

Warner/Comet Films/DeLux Prods/Fern Gully Films/ Arclight Films/Blue Rider Pictures, etc-Warner.
98 mins. UK/Germany/Luxembourg/Australia. 2005. Rel: 26 May 2006.
Cert. PG.

Things To Do Before You're 30 ★★

Cass, Dylan, Adam, Colin, Billy and Johnny have been playing football on Sunday since they were boys. But the twin pressures of adulthood and responsibility are beginning to impede on their weekly bouts of carousing. And, approaching thirty, Colin still hasn't experienced a 'threesome'… Simon Shore's first film, *Get Real* (1998), was a touching, funny, painful and insightful exploration of an English schoolboy coming to terms with his burgeoning homosexuality. It's a shame, then, that Shore has taken on more than he can handle with this, his second outing, a breezy but superficial ensemble piece. There are just too many characters to get a handle on with any resonance, resulting in a melodrama of stock situations that plays like an extended episode of a TV soap. There a few nice touches, to be sure, but for the most part this is a glib, stereotypical affair. JC-W

• *Cass* Dougray Scott, *Dylan* Jimi Mistry, *Kate* Emilia Fox, *Adam* Shaun Parkes, *Vicky* Billie Piper, *Don* Georges Innes, *Dylan's dad* George Irving, *Colin* Bruce MacKinnon, *Billy* Roger Morlidge, *Johnny* Danny Nussbaum, *Rosie* Rosie Cavaliero, *Claire* Nina Young, *Fiona* Donna Alexander, *Sheera* Keira Malik, *Danny* Charlie Cox, *Tina Mellor* Stacy Hart, *with* David Paul Wesat, Chris Polick, Sophie McConnell.

• *Dir* Simon Shore, *Pro* Marc Samuelson and Peter Samuelson, *Ex Pro* Sally Caplan, Syteve Christian, Rolf Koot, David Kosse, Donald A. Starr and Daniel J.B. Taylor, *Line Pro* Leontine Ruette, *Screenplay* Patrick Wilde, based on *All Stars* by Jean van de Velde and Michiel Alexander, *Ph* Mike J. Fox, *Pro Des* Mark Leese, *Ed* Barrie Vince, *M* Daniel Teper, *Costumes* Sarah Burns.

Momentum Pictures/First Choice Films/Isle of Man Film-Momentum Pictures.
101 mins. UK/Netherlands/USA. 2004. Rel: 2 June 2006. Cert. 15.

Thirst

See *Atash*.

13 Tzameti ★★½

Set in France, this first work from Georgian filmmaker Géla Babluani features his brother George as a 22-year-old immigrant who, sensing that big money is involved, takes over the role of a dead man who has been summoned to a mysterious rendezvous outside Paris. What is involved turns out to be a deadly game based on rounds of Russian roulette with gambling on the outcome. It's only fair to say that the film has been much praised but its black-and-white imagery on cheap sets suggests the 'B' pictures of yesteryear, the need for the central figure to survive (at least until the last round) minimises suspense and horror addicts will surely deplore the lack of gore. Add that the plot often feels contrived and I find it difficult to understand why this has been so admired. Even the director's declaration that he was seeking to echo Soviet silent cinema prompts the reflection that the same aim was better realised in *Of Freaks and Men* (1998). MS

• *Sébastien* George Babluani, *Master of Ceremonies* Pascal Bongard, *José* Augustin Legrand, *Jean François Godon* Philippe Passon, *Jacky, player No. 6* Aurélien Recoing, *Alain* Fred Ulysse, *godfather* Nicolas Pignon.

• *Dir* and *Screenplay* Géla Babluani, *Pro* Babluani, Jean-Baptiste Legrand and Fanny Saadi, *Ph* Tariel Meliava, *Art Dir* Bernard Péault, *Ed* Noémie Moreau, *M* East (Troublemakers).

Les Films de la Strada/Quasar Pictures/MK2/
Canal Plus-Revolver Entertainment.
93 mins. France/Georgia. 2005. Rel: 6 January 2006.
Cert. 15.

36 ★★★★½

Prior to his retirement, police commissioner Robert Mancini is determined to catch the gang responsible for a series of ruthless armed robberies. So he offers his job to whichever cop is the first to apprehend the gang. It's the touchpaper for a showdown that has little place for legal ethics… If *36* were a book, it would be a beautifully tooled read with every nuance and character placed for the greatest narrative effect. That the film is inspired by real events – the director was a policeman who served in the same force as his subject – is nothing short of shocking. Marchal's friend, Dominique Loisseau, collaborated on the screenplay and is the template for the character played by Daniel Auteuil. To this day, Loisseau remains unpardoned and although a registered skipper is unable to fly the French flag on his boats because of his fabricated police record. As a piece of cinema, *36* is uncompromisingly gripping, atmospheric and authentic, with Depardieu bringing a haunted credibility to his rogue cop seldom witnessed in the thriller genre. Original title: *36: Quai Des Orfevres*. JC-W

• *Léo Vrinks* Daniel Auteuil, *Denis Klein* Gérard Depardieu, *Robert Mancini* André Dussollier, *Hugo Silien* Roschdy Zem, *Camille Vrinks* Valeria Golino, *Eddy Valence* Daniel Duval, *Titi Brasseur* Francis Renaud, *Eve Verhagen* Catherine Marchal, *Francis Horn* Alain Figlarz, *Lola Vrinks, aged 17* Aurore Auteuil, *Christo* Olivier Marchal, *Manou Berliner* Mylène Demongeot, *with* Guy Lecluyse, Vincent Moscato, Anne Consigny, Solène Biasch,

• *Dir* Olivier Marchal, *Pro* Cyril Colbeau-Justin, Jean-Baptiste Dupont and Franck Chorot, *Ex Pro* Hugues Darmois, *Screenplay* Marchal, Franck Mancuso and Julien Rappeneau, *Ph* Denis Rouden, *Art Dir* Ambre Fernandez, *Ed* Hachdé, *M* Erwann Kermorvant and Axelle Renoir, *Costumes* Nathalie du Roscoät, *Technical Adviser* Frédéric Tellier.

LGM Cinema KL/Gaumont/TF1 Films/Un Etoile 2/Canal Plus-Tartan Films.
111 mins. France. 2004. Rel: 2 June 2006. Cert. 15.

Three ★

And then there were three… Or two idiots and a bimbo stranded on a tropical island. This really is a laughable, silly excuse for real-life lovebirds Billy Zane and Kelly Brook to sun it in the Bahamas and get paid for it. Kelly looks like she's advertising Malibu rum rather than roughing it on the edge of survival, while Billy looks even odder in his Seventies' sideburns and handlebar moustache. And to think Guy

Kelly Brook clings to life in the lamentable *Three* (from Cinemavault)

Ritchie's *Swept Away* went straight to video… JC-W

• *Jack Matson* Billy Zane, *Jenny* Kelly Brook, *Manuel* Juan Pablo Di Pace, *Maria* Victoria Di Pace, *Captain Richards* Gary 'Tex' Brockette.

• *Dir* and *Screenplay* Stewart Raffill, *Pro* Albert Martinez-Martin, Heinz Thym and Michael Dounaev, *Ex Pro* Diane Kirman and Jimmy De Brabant, *Ph* Tony Imi, *Pro Des* Jon Bunker, *Ed* Nick Rotundo, *M* Richard A. Harvey and A.A. McLelland.

Cinemavault Releasing/Therma Prods/T Films/Future Films-The Works UK.
95 mins. UK/Luxembourg/Germany/Canada. 2006.
Rel: 5 May 2006. Cert. 15.

3-iron ★★

Korea's Kim Ki-duk struck gold with *Spring Summer Autumn Winter… and Spring* and all of his films look splendid, but much of his work is pretentious and obscure. So it is here with the story of a young man who breaks into houses which he inhabits in their owners' absence and in one of which he meets an abused wife. There's no explanation of his motives and virtually no dialogue between these two leading characters who fall in love. It's all very slow and eventually comes to carry echoes of *Blow-Up* and *The Green Mile*, but there's no depth in the characterisations and no charisma. As for the golfing metaphor indicated in the title it remains impenetrable. Stylish, yes, but this seems a pointless exercise. Original title: *Bin-Jip*. MS

• *Sun-hwa* Lee Seung-yeon, *Tae-suk* Jae Hee, *Min-kyu* Kwon Hyeok-ho, *Det. Cho* Joo Jin-mo, *jailor* Choi Jeong-ho, *with* Lee Ju-suk, Lee Mi-suk, Mun Sung-hyeok, Park Ji-ah, Jang Jae-yong, Lee Da-hae, Kim Han, Park Se-jin, Park Dong-jin.

• *Dir, Pro, Screenplay* and *Ed* Kim Ki-duk, *Pro Ex Pro* Michio Suzuki and Choi Yong-bae, *Ph* Jang Seung-beck, *Art Dir* Kim Hyun-joo, *M* Slvian, *Costumes* Koo Jea-heon.

Happinet Pictures/ Kim Ki-duk Film-Optimum Releasing.
87 mins. South Korea/Japan. 2004. Rel: 15 July 2005. Cert. 15.

The Three Burials of Melquiades Estrada ★★★★

When his good friend Melquiades Estrada, an illegal immigrant, is found dead in the desert, ranch foreman Pete Perkins is determined to find out why. Whatever it takes, Pete will procure justice and honour his friend… Unfolded like a novel, Tommy Lee Jones' theatrical directorial debut is full of understated moments, rich observation and arid black comedy. On one level a companion piece to Hitchcock's *The Trouble With Harry* and the jokey *Weekend at Bernie's* – in which a corpse becomes a comedy prop – and on another level an absorbing fable about respect and redemption, *Three Burials* is a beautiful piece of cinema. Matching

the unforgiving terrain of West Texas and Mexico with a performance every bit as rugged and taciturn, Jones has never been better (and won the best actor award at Cannes). However, credit, too, must go to Barry Pepper, whose willingness to be subjected to such epic physical punishment must have been no mean feat. FYI: Jones previously directed the 1995 TV movie *The Good Old Boys*. JC-W

• *Pete Perkins* Tommy Lee Jones, *Mike Norton* Barry Pepper, *Melquiades Estrada* Julio Cesar Cedillo, *Belmont* Dwight Yoakam, *Lou Ann Norton* January Jones, *Rachel* Melissa Leo, *old blind man* Levon Helm, *with* Mel Rodriguez, Cecilia Suarez, Gnacio Guadalupe, Vanessa Bauche, Richard Jones, Barry Tubb.

• *Dir* Tommy Lee Jones, *Pro* Jones, Michael Fitzgerald, Luc Besson and Pierre-Ange le Pogam, *Screenplay* Guillermo Arriaga, *Ph* Chris Menges, *Pro Des* Merideth Boswell, *Ed* Roberto Silver, *M* Marco Beltrami, *Costumes* Kathleen Kiatta.

EuropaCorp/Javelina Film Co-Optimum Releasing.
121 mins. USA/France. 2005. Rel: 31 March 2006. Cert. 15.

Thumbsucker ★★½

Justin Cobb is 17, diffident, awkward with girls and still sucks his thumb. Diagnosed with Attention Deficit Hyperactivity Disorder, he is prescribed Ritalin and overnight becomes a star pupil at school, particularly excelling in his debating classes. However, his erstwhile thumb-sucking would appear to have been emblematic of deeper problems, with the new drug merely a stopgap… Reflecting the newness of the Cobbs' neighbourhood cut into the Oregon wilderness, Justin's family home is bereft of paintings, household pets and clutter. It's a sterile, unlived-in environment that reflects the tone of the film, a wise, impeccably structured conceit without a breath of reality. With its artfully posed tableaux and underlined quirkiness, it's a handsome calling card for its writer-director, with the occasional insight, the odd good joke and some polished performances. It's also an emotional wasteland. FYI: Scarlett Johansson was originally cast in the role of Rebecca, but withdrew at the last minute. JC-W

• *Justin Cobb* Lou Pucci, *Audrey Cobb* Tilda Swinton, *Mr Geary* Vince Vaughn, *Mike Cobb* Vincent D'Onofrio, *Dr Perry Lyman* Keanu Reeves, *Matt Schraam* Benjamin Bratt, *Rebecca* Kelli Garner, *Joel Cobb* Chase Offerle, *with* Kit Koenig, Nancy O'Dell, Bob Stephenson, Colton Tanner.

• *Dir* and *Screenplay* Mike Mills, from the novel by Walter Kirn, *Pro* Bob Stephenson and Anthony Bregman, *Ex Pro* Anne Carey, Ted Hope, Bob Yari and Cathy Schulman, *Co-Ex Pro* Tilda Swinton and Jay Shapiro, *Line Pro* Callum Greene, *Ph* Joaquín Baca-Asay, *Pro Des* Judy Becker, *Ed* Haines Hall and Angus Wall, *M* Tim DeLaughter, performed by The Polyphonic Spree, *Songs* Elliot Smith, *Costumes* April Napier.

Bob Yari Prods/This is That/Cinema-Go-Go-Columbia TriStar.
95 mins. USA. 2004. Rel: 28 October 2005. Cert. 15.

Tickets ★★★★

In an echo of those portmanteau films popular in the 1950s, this feature is the work of three directors, but instead of offering three totally distinct segments, *Tickets*, while telling each tale in turn, sets all three on the same long-distance train journey to Rome. Indeed there are some preparatory and connecting scenes where you can't be certain who directed them. Even so, Ermanno Olmi's piece about an elderly professor (Carlo Delle Piane) half-fantasizing his romantic feelings for a helpful P.R. assistant (Valéria Bruni-Tedeschi) comes first, although it's the other two sections by Abbas Kiarostami and Ken Loach that work really well and give a unity to the work as a whole. Kiarostami shows us a young man on National service assigned to looking after the formidable widow of a general and Loach features Scottish youths en route to a football league final coming face to face with Albanians who could be conning them but may be in desperate need. In these two sections the audience is confronted both by moral issues and by the way in which appearances can be deceptive (the latter the more pertinent because there's a post 9/11 feel to this movie). Uneven though it is (the Olmi episode is able but doesn't really fit), *Tickets* grows in impact as it proceeds and at long last – and proving that it works perfectly – Loach has one of his works featuring Scottish accents presented as he wanted it with sub-titles. MS

• *professor* Carlo Delle Piane, *PR lady* Valéria Bruni Tedeschi, *Italian lady* Silvana De Santis, *Filippo* Filippo Trojano, *Jamesy* Martin Compston, *Frank* William Ruane, *spaceman* Gary Maitland, *Albanian girl* Blerta Cahani, *Albanian boy* Klajdi Qorraj.

• *Dir* Ermanno Olmi, Abbas Kiarostani and Ken Loach, *Pro* Carlo Cresto-Dina, Babak Karimi, Rebecca O'Brien and Domenico Procacci, *Screenplay* Ermanno Olmi, Abbas Kiarostami and Paul Laverty, *Ph* Fabio Olmi, Mahmud Kalari and Chris Menges, *Pro Des* Alessandro Vannucci, *Ed* Giovanni Ziberna, Babak Karimi and Jonathan Morris, *M* George Fenton, *Costumes* Maurizio Basile.

Sixteen Films/Fandango/UK Film Council/Medusa Film/ Sky/National Lottery-Artificial Eye.
109 mins. Italy/UK. 2005. Rel: 2 December 2005.
Cert. 15.

Time To Leave ★★★★

Paris; the present. Romain Brochant is a successful fashion photographer who lives with Sasha, his beautiful German boyfriend. He leads a comfortable, superficial life and is then told he has terminal cancer and has just a few months to live… In stark contrast to *Last Holiday* (released just eight weeks before this), *Time To Leave* is an unsentimental contemplation of a young life *in extremis*. Contrary to heroes of popular fiction in similar circumstances, Romain unleashes his true feelings and retreats into himself. Indeed, it is far more intellectually engaging to share time with a character who acts against the natural order and so with morbid fascination we follow Romain's journey from denial and anger through to depression and acceptance. Perhaps the film's most moving scene is when Romain confides his fate to his grandmother (sublimely played by the 78-year-old Jeanne Moreau). When she asks him why she, of all people, should be let into his secret, he tells her: `because you are like me – you will die soon.' Intelligent, bracing, thought-provoking cinema. Original title: *Le temps qui reste.* JC-W

• *Romain Brochant* Melvil Poupaud, *Laura* Jeanne Moreau, *Jany* Valéria Bruni-Tedeschi, *the father* Daniel Duval, *the mother* Marie Rivière, *Sasha* Christian Sengewald, *Sophie* Louise-Anne Hippeau, *the doctor* Henri de Lorme, *Bruno* Walter Pagano.

• *Dir* and *Screenplay* François Ozon, *Pro* Olivier Delbosc and Marc Missonnier, *Ph* Jeanne Lapoirie, *Art Dir* Katia Wyszkop, *Ed* Monica Coleman, *Costumes* Pascaline Chavanne.

Fidélité/France 2 Cinéma/CanalPlus-Artificial Eye.
81 mins. France. 2005. Rel: 12 May 2006.
Cert. 18.

Tiresia ★★★

A man hovers around a wood in Paris, singling out a prostitute. He opts for a tall Brazilian beauty whom he takes home with him. But far from laying a hand on her, he locks her in a room and spies on her through the door. Later, as she takes a wash, she turns from her ablutions to reveal that she has a penis… As powerful and shocking as it is stilted, *Tiresia* should be forgiven its more bizarre flights of pretension just because it is so compelling and original. Writer-director Bonello, who previously brought us the morose and aimless *The Pornographer*, here transposes the Greek myth of Tiresias to contemporary Paris. In the legend – several versions of which exist – a Theban seer is turned into a harlot for killing a female serpent while it was copulating with a male. Ultimately, the film is little more than an intellectual exercise and the employment of Laurent Lucas as the two ambiguous faces of good and evil is a disastrous and indulgent stroke of miscasting. The film works better as a potent exploration of sexual identity and is distinguished by the extraordinary presence of its three

A puff of the old post-coital: Melvil Poupaud takes a break as Valéria Bruni-Tedeschi looks on, in François Ozon's intelligent and bracing *Time to Leave* (from Artificial Eye)

newcomers, Choveaux, Teles and Catalifo. JC-W

• *Terranova/Father François* Laurent Lucas, *Tiresia 1* Clara Choveaux, *Tiresia 2* Thiago Teles, *Anna* Célia Catalifo, *Charles* Lou Castel.

• *Dir* and *Screenplay* Bertrand Bonello, from a story by Luca Fazzi, *Pro* Carole Scotta and Simon Arnal-Szlovak, *Co-Pro* Luc Dery, *Ph* Josee Deshaies, *Pro Des* Romain Denis, *Ed* Fabrice Rouaud, *M* Albin de la Simone and Laurie Markovitch, *Costumes* Dorothee Guiraud.

Haut et Court/micro_scope/Arte France Cinéma/Canal Plus-Tartan Films.
115 mins. France/Canada. 2003. Rel: 15 July 2005.
No Cert.

Tony Takitani ★★★★

This extraordinary example of stylised minimal cinema from Japan will inevitably not appeal to all but Jun Ichikawa's adaptation of Haruki Murakami's novel is a major achievement. It's a study of a loner who succeeds in business but is approaching middle age before he meets and marries a woman 15 years his junior. Despite comparisons with Hitchcock's *Vertigo* (understandable given the film's development but misleading since this is not a thriller), *Tony Takitani* is a contemplative work about loneliness and loss beautifully acted (both leading players have dual roles) and quintessentially Japanese. The obvious stylisations, with narrative largely replacing dialogue and a Brechtian use of panning shots beginning and ending with an empty screen,

capture the formality of Japanese life but follow Ozu in never squashing the depth of feeling that lies within. MS

• *Tony Takitani/ Takitani Shozaburo* Issey Ogata, *Konuma Eiko/ Saito Hisako* Rie Miyazawa, *young Tony Takitani* Nishijima Hidetoshi, *narrator* Hidetoshi Nishijima, *with* Shinohara Takahumi, Shihodo Wataru, Kino Hana, Kusano Toru, Oyamada Sayuri, Tanigawa Saho, Yamamoto Koji, Shioya Keiko, Nekota Nao, Mizuki Kaoru.

• *Dir* and *Screenplay* Jun Ichikawa, from the novel by Haruki Murakami, *Pro* Ishida Motoki, *Ex Pro* Hashimoto Naoki and Yonezawa Keiko, *Ph* Hirokawa Taishi, *Pro Des* Ichida Yoshikazu, *Ed* Sanjyo Tomoo, *M* Sakamoto Ryuichi.

Wilco Co./Ichikawa Jun Office-Axiom Films.
76 mins. Japan. 2004. Rel: 21 April 2006.
Cert. U.

Transamerica ★★★½

After years of saving up for her sexual reassignment surgery, Bree Osbourne – formerly Stanley – is told that she has a son. Refused permission for the operation by her therapist unless she embraces her parental responsibility, Bree flies from Los Angeles to New York. There, she finds a mutinous teenager with a drug problem locked behind bars… A lot of attention has been heaped on *Transamerica* for its startling performance by Felicity Huffman as a man becoming a woman. Yes, but… In a dream role, Ms Huffman certainly rises to the occasion, but even as she begins to resemble a man by the film's second half, the actress's vocal monotony takes its toll

After Stanley: Felicity Huffman and Kevin Zegers in Duncan Tucker's brave and fascinating *Transamerica* (from Pathé)

on the patience. *Transamerica* also has a tendency to swing into Mike Leigh caricature (particularly the section featuring Bree's parents), and for a road movie its visual palette is surprisingly drab. Even so, this is a brave, fascinating film and one of enormous integrity, insight and humour. JC-W

• *Bree Osbourne* Felicity Huffman, *Toby* Kevin Zegers, *Elizabeth* Fionnula Flanagan, *Margaret* Elizabeth Peña, *Calvin Many Goats* Graham Green, *Murray* Burt Young, *Sydney* Carrie Preston, *hitchhiker* Grant Monohon, *with* Venita Evans, Jon Budinoff, Raynor Scheine.

• *Dir* and *Screenplay* Duncan Tucker, *Pro* Linda Moran, Rene Bastian and Sebastian Dungan, *Ex Pro* William H. Macy, *Assoc Pro* Lucy Cooper, *Ph* Stephen Kazmierski, *Pro Des* Mark White, *Ed* Pam Wise, *M* David Mansfield; Massenet, Chopin, Purcell; tracks performed by Dolly Parton, Lucinda Williams, The Nitty Gritty Dirt Band, David Poe, Larry Sparks, The Wildlife Band, Wylie and the Wild West, Jean Grae, Miriam Makeba, Old Crow Medice Show, Duncan Sheik, Heather Myles, Lola Beltran, etc, *Costumes* Danny Glicker.

Belladonna Prods-Pathé.
103 mins. USA. 2005. Rel: 24 March 2006.
Cert. 15.

Transporter 2 ★★★

Special Forces veteran and getaway driver Frank Martin has relocated to Miami but still adheres rigidly to his rules. As a favour, he's currently babysitting the six-year-old son of a senator and is teaching the kid a whole new set of codes ('greet the driver, respect the car, fasten your seatbelt…'). Then Frank's charge is kidnapped and the police suspect that he is in on the deal… Another guilty pleasure from action auteur Luc Besson, *Transporter 2* is a slick, lean, take-no-prisoners jolt of escapist nirvana. Besson dreams up delicious stories, even though this one mirrors Tony Scott's *Man On Fire* (itself a remake) a little too closely. The stunts are gobsmacking (watch Statham jump out of the way of a head-on collision and then land neatly on the crushed bonnets), and there's a priceless *femme fatale* in the chiselled form of model-singer Kate Nauta who wears precious little while gunning down her victims. Unfortunately, the action eventually flattens everything in its path and does get very silly.
JC-W

• *Frank Martin* Jason Statham, *Gianni* Alessandro Gassman, *Audrey Billings* Amber Valletta, *Lola* Kate Nauta, *Jefferson Billings* Matthew Modine, *Dimitri* Jason Flemyng, *Stappleton* Keith David, *Tarconi* François Berléand, *with* Hunter Clary, Shannon Briggs, Raymond Tong, Marc MacAulay.

• *Dir* Louis Leterrier, *Pro* Luc Besson and Steven Chasman, *Ex Pro* Terry Miller, *Screenplay* Besson and Robert Mark Kamen, *Ph* Mitchell Amundsen, *Pro Des* John Mark Harrington, *Ed* Christine Lucas-Navarro and Vincent Tabaillon, *M* Alexandre Azaria, *Costumes* Bobbie Read, *Martial Arts* Cory Yuen.

Europacorp/TF1 Films/Current Entertainment/Canal Plus/ TPS Star-Fox.
87 mins. France/USA. 2005. Rel: 25 November 2005.
Cert. 15.

The rules of action: Jason Statham dives for cover in Louis Leterrier's slick, take-no-prisoners *Transporter 2* (from Fox)

Isolde by any other name: Sophia Myles in Kevin Reynolds' good-looking *Tristan + Isolde* (from Fox)

Tristan + Isolde ★★½

Under constant attack from the Irish, Lord Marke of Cornwall seeks to unite the tribes of England to form an independent nation. With the heroic Tristan at his side, he believes he would make a wise and stalwart king. But then in an Irish attack Tristan is felled by a poisoned sword and is given a Viking's funeral, his burning pyre pushed out to sea. Then, washed ashore in Ireland, Tristan is nursed back to life by Isolde who, unbeknownst to him, is the daughter of Donnchadh, the merciless king of Ireland… With Ridley and Tony Scott on board as executive producers, this evocation of England in the Dark Ages inevitably looks magnificent. The scenes of combat are also exceptionally well staged, but then this is a story of ill-crossed love and is exactly where the film falls down. While Sophia Myles makes a compelling and plucky Isolde (recalling Kate Winslet *circa* 2000), standard American import James Franco is an emotional black hole. Following the Josh Hartnett route of glum and serious, Franco gives a one-note performance of noble constipation, but passion isn't on his menu. Still, it's good to see Rufus Sewell in a sympathetic role, while the villainous Irish remind us that Kevin Reynolds previously directed *Robin Hood: Prince of Thieves*. JC-W

• *Tristan* James Franco, *Isolde* Sophia Myles, *Lord Marke* Rufus Sewell, *King Donnchadh* David Patrick O'Hara, *Wictred* Mark Strong, *Melot* Henry Cavill, *Bragnae* Bronagh Gallagher, *Morholt* Graham Mullins, *Simon* Leo Gregory, *Anwick* Jamie King, *young Tristan* Thomas Sangster, *with* Ronan Vibert, Lucy Russell, J.B. Blanc, Dexter Fletcher, Richard Dillane, Hans Martin-Stier, Thomas Morris, Isobel Moynihan.

• *Dir* Kevin Reynolds, *Pro* Moshe Diamant, Elie Samaha, Lisa Ellzey and Giannina Facio, *Ex Pro* Ridley Scott, Tony Scott, Jim Lemley, Frank Hübner, John Hardy and Matthew Stillman, *Co-Pro* Anne Lai and Jan Fantl, *Screenplay* Dean Georgaris, *Ph* Arthur Reinhart, *Pro Des* Mark Geraghty, *Ed* Peter Boyle, *M* Anne Dudley, *Costumes* Maurizio Millenotti

Fox/ApolloProMedia-MFF/Scott Free-Fox.
125 mins. USA/UK/Germany/Czech Republic. 2005. Rel: 24 March 2006. Cert. 12A.

The Truth ★★½

Candy, a young disabled woman, joins a group of people in a serenity lodge in the Highlands for a week, in the hope that it will change her life. The group is led by the pretentious American guru Donna, whose programme – Adventures in Truth – aims to make everyone speak the truth at all times. Then, halfway through, the film changes gear and becomes a murder mystery… *The Truth*, a quite original satire, is shot on video and is too long but there is plenty here to enjoy – the script is very funny, the characters clearly defined and the acting excellent. GS

• *Scott* William Beck, *Candy* Elaine Cassidy, *Felix* Stephen Lord, *Donna* Elizabeth McGovern, *Mia* Lea Mornar, *Martha* Rachael Stirling, *Blossom* Zoe Telford, *Spud* Karl Theobald, *Candy's mother* Amelia Bullmore, *Candy's father* Sean Murray.

• *Dir* George Milton, *Pro* Julie-anne Edwards, *Ex Pro* Milton, George Lenz and Martino Sclavi, *Assoc Pro* Tilton, Andrew J. Curtis and Kenton Allen, *Line Pro* Siobhan Lyons, *Screenplay* Milton and Mark Tilton, *Ph* Nick Tebbet, *Pro Des* Jonnie Elf, *Ed* Marco van Welzen, *M* Dominik Scherrer, *Costumes* Fiona Chilcott, *Sound* Annabelle Pangborn.

2 Many Executives-Guerilla Films.
118 mins. UK. 2005. Rel: 13 January 2006. Cert. 15.

Tsotsi ★★★★½

Tsotsi, 19, has obliterated his past, adopting for his name the local vernacular for a black urban criminal. Living in a corrugated shack on the outskirts of Johannesburg, he will stop at nothing to line his pockets, to pay for the modern amenities that clutter his home. Then, after car-jacking a BMW and shooting down its female occupant, he finds a baby in the back seat… A sublimely realised story of violence and salvation, *Tsotsi* is arguably the finest film to emerge from South Africa. Stylishly shot in 'scope and confidently paced, it is an updating of Athol Fugard's 1980 novel (which the playwright actually wrote in the early 1960s), a story as pertinent today as it ever was. With billboards claiming that, 'We Are All Affected by HIV and AIDS', the film plunges us into the South Africa of the 21st century, where life comes very cheap. Tsotsi's redemption is perhaps a little speeded-up for plausibility, but the film's scenes of violence, suspense, tenderness – and hope – more than make up. JC-W

• *Tsotsi/David* Presley Chweneyagae, *Miriam* Terry Pheto, *Aap* Kenneth Nkosi, *Boston* Mothusi Magano, *Butcher* Zenzo Ngqobe, *Fela* Zola, *John* Rapulana Seiphemo, *Captain Smit* Ian Roberts, *Soekie* Thembi Nyandeni, *young Tsotsi* Benny Moshe, *with* Nambitha Mpumlwana, Jerry Mofokeng, Percy Matsemela, Owen Sejake, Israel Makoe, Sindi Khambule.

• *Dir* and *Screenplay* Gavin Hood, *Pro* Peter Fudakowski, *Ex Pro* Sam Bhembe, Robbie Little, Doug Mankoff, Basil Ford, Joseph D'Morais, Alan Howden and Rupert Lywood, *Co-Pro* Paul Raleigh, *Assoc Pro* Janine Eser and Henrietta Fudakowski, *Line Pro* Gavin Joubert, *Ph* Lance Gewer, *Pro Des* Emelia Weavind, *Ed* Megan Gill, *M* Mark Kilian and Paul Hepker, featuring the voice of Vusi Mahlasela, *Costumes* Nadia Kruger and Pierre Vienings.

UK Film & TV Prod. Co/Moviworld-Momentum Pictures.
94 mins. South Africa/UK. 2005. Rel: 17 March 2006. Cert. 15.

Twentynine Palms ★★★½

The third feature by the controversial French director Bruno Dumont although largely subtitled was mainly shot in Joshua Tree National Park. Both sound and image are richly atmospheric as we share a journey undertaken by a couple whose violent love making cannot bridge the space that exists between them. The film, short on actual plot, is about that gap but also about space in another sense, since these are figures in a landscape dwarfed by nature and shown to be ephemeral. Dumont has a great instinct for placing his camera interestingly and his film evokes both Antonioni and Godard, but it's eclipsed by Breillat's *A Ma Soeur!* His unexpected ending is less meaningful than hers and Dumont fails to sustain interest in the scenes just prior to the climax. But if it's flawed it is also fascinating and, unless this is the kind of film that does nothing for you, it's far more rewarding than early dismissive reviews had suggested. MS

• *Katia* Katia Golubeva, *David* David Wissak.

• *Dir* and *Screenplay* Bruno Dumont, *Pro* Jean Brehat and Rachid Bouchareb, *Ex Pro* Muriel Merlin and Darren Goldberg, *Co-Pro* Christoph Thoke, Axel Moebius and Christel Brunn, *Assoc Pro* Allen Bain, Jesse Scolaro and Darren Goldberg, *Ph* Georges Lechaptois, *Ed* Dominique Petrot, *M* Takashi Hirayasu and Bob Brozman; J.S. Bach; *Costumes* Yasmine Abraham.

3B Prods/Canal Plus-Tartan Films.
114 mins. France/Germany/USA. 2003. Rel: 29 July 2005. Cert. 18.

Two For the Money ★½

Walter Abrams, a recovering addict, runs the biggest sports advisory service in the country. Then he hires golden boy Brandon Lang, who has the ability to consistently pick football winners... D.J. Caruso's film about greed, power and addiction lacks focus, excitement and danger. It also encourages Al Pacino to give another of his now very familiar over-the-top performances where he shouts a lot. Matthew McConaughey looks too pleased with himself and his contract must have stipulated endless scenes with his shirt off pumping iron. His character is thinly drawn and his relationship with Abrams fails to convince. GS

• *Walter Abrams* Al Pacino, *Brandon Lang/John Anthony* Matthew McConaughey, *Toni Abrams* Rene Russo, *Novian* Armand Assante, *Jerry* Jeremy Piven, *Alex* Jaime King, *with* Kevin Chapman, Ralph Garman, Gedde Watanabe.

• *Dir* D.J. Caruso, *Pro* James G. Robinson and Jay Cohen, *Ex Pro* Dan Gilroy, Rene Russo, Guy McElwaine and David C. Robinson, *Co-Pro* Wayne Morris, *Screenplay* Gilroy, *Ph* Conrad W. Hall, *Pro Des* Tom Southwell, *Ed* Glen Scantlebury, *M* Christophe Beck, *Costumes* Marie-Sylvie Deveau.

James G. Robinson/Morgan Creek-UIP.
122 mins. USA. 2005. Rel: 10 March 2006. Cert. 15.

U-Carmen eKhayelitsha ★★

Khayelitsha, South Africa; the present. After a fracas with a co-worker, the hotheaded Carmen is arrested by Jongikhaya, a God-fearing police sergeant. However, Jongikhaya is struck by Carmen's womanly wiles and falls for her big time, leading to inevitable tragedy and a lot of singing... While director Dornford-May's transposition of *Carmen* to a South African township is a brave attempt to revitalise Bizet's opera, it is unlikely to sit well with all but the most dedicated opera buff. At the best of times, opera can seem ludicrous, but plonked in such a naturalistic setting merely points up such absurdity. With Carmen herself played by a woman whose dimensions cause concern for the health of her heart, the femme fatale's turn of phrase — translated into the local click-punctuated Xhosa — is nothing short of arch. Switching from rampant ardour, Carmen tells her paramour Jongikhaya (standing in for Don José): 'I don't love you anymore. Piss off!' JC-W

• *Carmen* Pauline Malefane, *Jongikhaya* Andile Tshoni, *Amanda* Andiswa Kedama, *Nomakhaya* Lungelwa Blou, *Lulamile Nkomo* Zorro Sidloyi, *Bra Nkomo* Andries Mbali, *Captain Gantana* Zamile Gantana, *Pinki* Ruby Mthethwa.

• *Dir* Mark Dornford-May, *Pro* Dornford-May, Camilla Driver and Ross Garland, *Ex Pro* Garland, *Line Pro* Niki Hall-Jones, *Screenplay* Dornford-May, Andiswa Kedama and Pauline Malefane, *Ph* Giulo Biccari, *Set Design* Craig Smith, *Ed* Ronelle Loots, *M* Georges Bizet, *Costumes* Jessica Dornford-May, *Sound* Barry Donnelly, *Choreography* Joel Mthethwa.

Nando's Arts Initiative/Spier Films/Dimphio Di Kopane-Tartan Films.
127 mins. South Africa. 2004. Rel: 21 April 2006. Cert. 12A.

Ultranova ★★★★

This debut feature from Bouli Lanners is a contemporary tragic-comedy shot near Liège and built around characters, mainly young, who are unfulfilled. Dimitri, whose work involves the sale of new purpose-built houses quite lacking in individuality, might however break through his reserve to achieve a meaningful relationship with a local girl, Cathy. But this is essentially a film of mood rather than plot. There's a Tati-like precision in its laid back comedy timing and an underlying sense of pathos reminiscent of Kaurismäki or Mike Leigh's *Bleak Moments*. This movie is a small work but it's well played and decidedly individual with the 'Scope images wonderfully evocative of the loneliness that lies at the heart of Lanners's vision. MS

• *Dimitri* Vincent Lécuyer, *Cathy* Hélène De Reymaeker, *Phil* Michaël Abiteboul, *Jeanne* Marie Du Bled, *Verbrugghe* Vincent Belorgey, *man with dog* Philippe Grand'henry.

• *Dir* and *Screenplay* Bouli Lanners, *Pro* Jacques-Henri Bronckart, *Ph* Jean-Paul De Zaeytijd, *Art Dir* Paul Rouschop, Didier Smidts and Igor Gabriel, *Ed* Ewin Ryckaert, *M* Jarby McCoy, *Costumes* Elise Ancion.

Versus Prods/Prime Time/RTBF
83 mins. France/Belgium. 2005. Rel: 16 December 2005. No Cert.

Ultraviolet ★

In the late 21st century, the world is run by a tyrannical administration that has developed a secret weapon to rid the planet of its last remaining 'hemophages' (a pedantic

The bottom dollar: Al Pacino chases the high life in D.J. Caruso's limp, unfocused *Two for the Money* (from UIP)

word for vampires). So ace assassin Violet (odd name for a 21st-century assassin, but don't get me started) infiltrates a government facility to steal the weapon. As it turns out, the latter is a little boy, a clone of the guv'nor... For a 13-year-old lad, Cameron Bright is exceptionally young to be typecast as a clone (he played one in the Robert De Niro thriller *Godsend*). And Milla Jovovich has already done the kick-ass video game heroine to death (cf. *Resident Evil* and *Resident Evil: Apocalypse*). But originality is in short supply in this bum-shifting, mind-numbing cartoon, which, like *Sky Captain* before it, adopts the annoying technique of placing live actors into animated backdrops. It's like participating in a video game in which the joystick has been confiscated. JC-W

• *Violet* Milla Jovovich, *Six* Cameron Bright, *Daxus* Nick Chinlund, *Garth* William Fichtner, *Nerva* Sebastien Andrieu, *young Violet* Ida Martin, *with* David Collier, Kieran O'Rorke, Digger Mesch, Mike Smith, Kurt Wimmer.

• *Dir* and *Screenplay* Kurt Wimmer, *Pro* John Baldecchi, *Ex Pro* T.C. Wang, Charles Wang, Tony Mark and Sue Jett, *Ph* Arthur Wong Ngok Tai, *Pro Des* Choo Sung Pong, *Ed* William Yeh, *M* Klaus Badelt, *Costumes* Joseph Porro.

Screen Gems-Columbia TriStar.
87 mins. USA. 2005. Rel: 23 June 2006. Cert. 15.

Underworld: Evolution ★

A centuries-old feud between the rival races of Vampire and Lycan continues apace as Selene discovers some disturbing secrets about her past. As she and the Hybrid Michael (who's part-vampire, part-werewolf) get it together, so the thoroughly unprincipled Vamp Marcus attempts some total domination... With its heavy-handed dependence on loud sound effects, computer-generated bloodstreams and shocking acting (Bill Nighy, how could you?), this sorry sequel descends into the mire of derivative, mind-numbing, pointless and incomprehensible video fodder. A real endurance test. JC-W

• *Selene* Kate Beckinsale, *Michael* Scott Speedman, *Marcus Corvinus* Tony Curran, *Kraven* Shane Brolly, *Adrian Tanis* Steven Mackintosh, *Alexander Corvinus* Derek Jacobi, *Viktor* Bill Nighy, *William* Brian Steele, *Amelia* Zita Gorog, *young Selene* Lily Mo Sheen, *with* Scott McElroy, John Mann, Michael Sheen, Sophia Miles.

• *Dir* Len Wiseman, *Pro* Tom Rosenberg, Gary Lucchesi, David Coatsworth and Richard Wright, *Ex Pro* Wiseman, Skip Williamson, Henry Winterstern, Terry A. McKay, Danny McBride and James McQuade, *Screenplay* McBride, *Ph* Simon Duggan, *Pro Des* and *Creatures* Patrick Tatopoulos, *Ed* Nicolas De Toth, *M* Marco Beltrami, *Costumes* Wendy Partridge.

Lakeshore Entertainment/Screen Gems-Entertainment.
106 mins. USA. 2005. Rel: 20 January 2006. Cert. 18.

An Unfinished Life ★★★

Wyoming rancher Einar Gilkyson has never forgiven his
daughter-in-law, Jean, for the death of his only son. Resigned
to selling off his cattle and attending to the needs of his only
friend, a ranch hand crippled by a bear, Einar has all but
given up on life. Then Jean turns up out of the blue, trailing
a granddaughter that Einar never knew he had… The awe-
inspiring scenery, gentle strains of Christopher Young's music
and pitch-perfect performances from Morgan Freeman and the
14-year-old Becca Gardner almost disguise the predictability
of this old-fashioned weepy. The sort of 'true life' story you'd
once stumble across in *Reader's Digest*, *An Unfinished Life* is
flush with noble intentions and has enough of a pedigree
to make it all seem worthwhile. It's a bonus to see Redford
playing his age for once – and an unsympathetic character
at that – and the hoary sentiments of the original novel are
subtly tempered. You just can't help liking it. JC-W

• *Einar Gilkyson* Robert Redford, *Jean Gilkyson* Jennifer
Lopez, *Mitch Bradley* Morgan Freeman, *Crane Curtis* Josh
Lucas, *Griff Gilkyson* Becca Gardner, *Gary Winston* Damian
Lewis, *Nina* Camryn Manheim, *Kitty* Lynda Boyd, *with* Rob
Hayter, P. Lynn Johnson, Byron Lucas, Bart the Bear.

• *Dir* Lasse Hallström, *Pro* Leslie Holleran, Kellian Ladd and
Alan Ladd Jr., *Ex Pro* Michelle Raimo, Meryl Poster, Harvey
Weinstein, Bob Weinstein, Matthew Rhodes, Mark Rydell,
Graham King and Joe Roth, *Co-Pro* Su Armstrong, *Screenplay*
Mark Spragg and Virginia Korus Spragg, from the novel by
Mark Spragg, *Ph* Oliver Stapleton, *Pro Des* David Gropman,
Ed Andrew Mondshein, *M* Christopher Young, *Costumes*
Tish Monaghan.

Miramax/Revolution Studio/Initial Entertainment/Ladd
Co.-Buena Vista International.
107 mins. USA. 2004. Rel: 16 June 2006. Cert. 12A.

United 93 ★★★★

On September 11, 2001, 37 passengers and seven crew
members settled down for a routine flight from Newark
International airport to San Francisco. As the staff of the
Federal Aviation Administration struggled to comprehend the
repercussions of a hijack – the first in twenty years – United
93 set off, forty minutes late, on a calm autumn morning…
The third film to chronicle the fate of the fourth hijacked
plane on September 11 – *Flight 93* and *The Flight That Fought
Back* were made for television – *United 93* is a predictably
harrowing drama, all the more effective for its documentary-
style realism. Ben Sliney – who took over the job of manager
of the FAA command centre in Herndon, Virginia, on
September 11 – is an impressive presence playing himself,
along with a dozen or so personnel recreating their real-life
roles. The moment when they realise something historical
is taking place would be unbelievable were it not for the
corroboration of hindsight. While the outcome is inevitable

– and the Boeing's passengers implausibly pleasant – many
of the sequences are virtually unbearable in their intensity.
JC-W

• *Todd Beamer* David Alan Basche, *William Joseph Cashman*
Richard Bekins, *Jane Folger* Susan Blommaert, *Joseph DeLuca*
Ray Charleson, *Thomas E. Burnett Jr* Christian Clemenson,
Ziad Jarrah Khalid Abdalla, *Saeed Al Ghamdi* Lewis Alsamari,
Ben Sliney Ben Sliney, *Major James Fox* Major James Fox,
Sandra Bradshaw Trish Gates, *Colonel Robert Marr* Gregg
Henry, *Donald Freeman Greene* David Rasche, *Ahmed Al
Haznawi* Omar Berdouni, *Captain Jason M. Dahl* J.J. Johnson,
Deborah Welsh Polly Adams, *Thomas Roberts* Thomas Roberts,
with Gary Commock, Opal Alladin, Nancy McDoniel, Libby
Morris, Rebecca Schull, Leigh Zimmerman, Jamie Harding.

• *Dir* and *Screenplay* Paul Greengrass, *Pro* Greengrass, Lloyd
Levin, Tim Bevan and Eric Fellner, *Ex Pro* Debra Hayward
and Liza Chasin, *Ph* Barry Ackroyd, *Pro Des* Dominic
Watkins, *Ed* Clare Douglas, Christopher Rouse and Richard
Pearson, *M* John Powell, *Costumes* Dinah Collin.

Universal/StudioCanal/Sidney Kimmel Entertainment/
Working Title-UIP.
110 mins. UK/USA/France. Rel: 2 June 2006.
Cert. 15.

The United States of Leland ★★

For no apparent reason, even to himself, Leland P. Fitzgerald
stabs a retarded boy to death. Why? Good point. First-time
director Matthew Ryan Hoge unravels the intricate layers
of human ambiguity and fallibility in a thought-provoking
treatise that probes the complexities of good and evil. But
that's part of the film's problem – it feels like a dissertation.
Hoge's characters, in spite of wholesome appearances, all
harbour dark secrets: Becky Pollard is a heroin addict,
Pearl Madison cheats on his girlfriend, Albert Fitzgerald
has abandoned his son, Leland Fitzgerald kills a boy on a
Nietzschean whim and even the steadfast, upstanding Allen
Harris is not without his criminal potential. It gets to the
point where we're actually waiting for the next transgression.
Hoge, who previously spent two years as a teacher in the Los
Angeles juvenile court system, is obviously a writer of some
intelligence, but as a director he lacks a touch of cinematic
drama. Talky, self-indulgent and even soporific, *The United
States of Leland* is like a discussion on the equivocality of
ethics delivered by exceptionally fine actors without a referee.
JC-W

• *Pearl Madison* Don Cheadle, *Leland P. Fitzgerald* Ryan
Gosling, *Allen Harris* Chris Klein, *Becky Pollard* Jena Malone,
Marybeth Fitzgerald Lena Olin, *Albert T. Fitzgerald* Kevin
Spacey, *Julie Pollard* Michelle Williams, *Harry Pollard* Martin
Donovan, *Karen Pollard* Ann Magnuson, *Ayesha* Kerry
Washington, *Mrs Calderon* Sherilyn Fenn, *Elden* Ron Canada,
with Matt Malloy, Wesley Jonathan, Michael Peña, Michael
Welch, Jim Haynie, Kimberly Scott, Jim Metzler, Angela
Paton, Clyde Kusatsu.

• *Dir* and *Screenplay* Matthew Ryan Hoge, *Pro*
Bernie Morris, Jonah Smith, Kevin Spacey and Palmer West,
Ex Pro Mark Damon, Stewart Hall and Sammy Lee, *Co-Pro* Dara
Weintraub, *Ph* James Glennon, *Pro Des* Edward T. McAvoy, *Ed*
Jeff Betancourt, *M* Jeremy Enigk, *Costumes* Genevieve Tyrrell.

MDP Worldwide/Thousand Words/Trigger Street-
Momentum Pictures.
104 mins. USA. 2003. Rel: 1 July 2005. Cert. 15.

Unknown White Male ★★★

Filmmaker Rupert Murray, a friend of Doug Bruce, learnt
how the latter while in New York had suddenly experienced
amnesia so total that he was left with no awareness of his
past life or even of his identity. The situation of someone
becoming an unknown white male has the potential to make an
intriguing drama, so Murray decided to tell his friend's story
in documentary form. However, the potential is not realised
due to his self-consciously stylised direction which draws
attention to itself distractingly. Furthermore, the film fails to
be as informative as one would wish and ends up more self-
indulgent than revealing, especially when compared to *Black
Sun* which also looks at a moment of crisis in a man's life. Not
uninteresting, then, but disappointing all the same. MS

• *With*: Doug Bruce, Lt. Peña, Professor Daniel Schacter,
Dr Leonid Vorobyev, Lily Frost, Rupert Murray, etc. *Narrator*
Rupert Murray.

• *Dir* and *Ed* Rupert Murray, *Pro* Beadie Finzi, *Ph* Orlando
Stuart, *Design* Tony Brook, *M* Mukul; Dvořák, Mascagni,
Sibelius, Shostakovich, Stravinsky, etc.

FilmFour/Spectre/Wellspring/Court TV-Word of Mouth.
91 mins. UK/USA. 2005. Rel: 7 April 2006. Cert. 12A.

Unleashed ★★★½

Glasgow; today. Danny was brought up as a dog by his 'Uncle
Bart'. He lives in an underground cage, eats directly from cans
of meat and wears a metal collar. When, in the appropriate
circumstances, his collar is removed, Danny turns into a
ferocious pit bull, disabling anybody in his path. Quite how he
perfected his supernatural martial skills is not explained, yet
in spite of his diminutive stature he can kill his most fearsome
opponents in seconds. Then, one day, he meets a kind, blind
piano tuner who introduces him to the rapture of Mozart…
With its gratuitous violence and self-indulgent sentimentality,
Unleashed is an entertainment that will incense the critics and
delight its fans. Yet it is an unusual, engrossing story painted
in broad, colourful brushstrokes. In addition, it almost has its
cake and devours it. White initially serving up bone-crunching
violence for our delectation – expertly staged by the great Yuen
Wo-ping (*The Matrix*, *Kill Bill*) – it turns us off it once Danny
has found a gentler, more rewarding life. In this respect, the
film shares elements with *Fight Club* and even *A Clockwork
Orange*, although its psychological profundities may leave a lot
to be desired. Now 42, Jet Li looks a bit incongruous as a man-

Barking mad: Jet Li gets very, very angry in Louis Leterrier's
engrossing, whizz-bang *Unleashed* (from UIP)

child, while an ear-punching scale of sound effects takes up the slack of his advancing years. Original title: *Danny the Dog*. JC-W

• *Danny* Jet Li, *Sam* Morgan Freeman, *Bart* Bob Hoskins, *Victoria* Kerry Condon, *Raffles* Vincent Regan, *Lefty* Dylan Brown, *Georgie* Tamer Hassan, *with* Michael Jenn, Phyllida Law, Carole Ann Wilson, Georgina Chapman, Danielle Louise Harley, Andy Beckwith.

• *Dir* Louis Leterrier, *Pro* Luc Besson, Jet Li and Steven Chasman, *Co-Pro* Pierre Spengler, *Screenplay* Besson, *Ph* Pierre Morel, *Pro Des* Jacques Bufnoir, *Ed* Nicolas Trembasiewicz, *M* Massive Attack, *Costumes* Olivier Beriot, *Martial Arts Choreography* Yuen Wo-ping, *Artistic Consultant* Robert Mark Kamen.

Rogue Pictures/EuropaCorp/Canal Plus/Glasgow Film Office-UIP.
101 mins. UK/France/USA. 2004. Rel: 19 August 2005.
Cert. 18

Ushpizin ★★★½

Jerusalem; the present. In the Jewish calendar, Succoth is a fitting occasion in which to show one's blessings to God. To commemorate the shelter of the Children of Israel in Egypt, eight days are set aside to erect temporary dwellings and, God willing, to share one's food with 'holy guests', or *ushpizin*. Moshe Bellanga is too poor to buy meat, let alone a temporary dwelling (a `succah'), but his prayers are answered when he becomes the recipient of an anonymous donation from a local charity. And then an old drinking acquaintance, on the run from prison, turns up looking for asylum… Made according to the rules of the Torah, *Ushpizin* is the first film to star and be written by a genuine Orthodox Jew. A former actor who previously appeared in director Gidi Dar's *Eddie King*, Shuli Rand has fashioned a simple but effective fable that could only come to pass within the traditions of the Orthodox community. Told with humour, compassion and restraint, *Ushpizin* not only sheds light on a world largely ignored by the cinema, but brings it vividly and engagingly to life. Indeed, it's a testament to the film's facility that one should end up caring so much for a citron fruit, one of the four sacred 'species' of the Succoth. JC-W

• *Moshe Bellanga* Shuli Rand, *Rand Malli Bellanga* Michael Bat Sheva Rand, *Eliyahu Scorpio* Shaul Mizrahi, *Yossef* Ilan Ganani, *Ben Baruch* Avraham Abutbul, *with* Yonathan Danino, Daniel Dayan.

• *Dir* Gidi Dar, *Pro* Rafi Bukaee and Gidi Dar, *Line Pro* Gadi Levy, Shlomit Smadja and Ziv Ben Zvi, *Screenplay* Shuli Rand, *Ph* Amit Yasur, *Art Dir* Ido Dollev, *Ed* Nadav Harel and Isaac Sehayek, *M* Nethaniel Mechaly, Iosif Bardanashvili and Adi Ran, *Sound* Chen Harpaz.

Gilgamesh Prods/Eddie King Ltd-Redbus.
92 mins. Israel. 2004. Rel: 17 March 2006.
Cert. PG.

V for Vendetta ★★★★½

In the not-too-distant future, the former United States is engaged in civil war and England is run by a totalitarian government. Following riots in Leeds and certain disorder in Hendon and Islington, Islam and homosexuality has been outlawed, the death sentence reinstated and nocturnal curfews enforced. In retaliation, an enigmatic figure in a Guy Fawkes mask blows up the Old Bailey and kidnaps Evey Hammond, a dogsbody working for the omnipotent British Television Network… An ambitious, stylish, literate and forthright adaptation of the graphic novel by Alan Moore and David Lloyd, *V for Vendetta* succeeds where previous forays into the medium have failed. Grounded by a committed performance from Natalie Portman (employing a region-less English accent), the film displays a genuine human passion and a rooting in the recognisable, underscored by numerous cultural touchstones and authentic London locations (indeed, for the film's *tour-de-force*, Whitehall was closed off for the first time in its history). The result is a dizzying cocktail of *1984*, *A Clockwork Orange* and *The Legend of Zorro*, with a reverence for revolution, Shakespeare and Benny Hill. Stunning. JC-W

• *Evey Hammond* Natalie Portman, 'V'/ *William Rockwood* Hugo Weaving, *Finch* Stephen Rea, *Deitrich* Stephen Fry, *Adam Sutler* John Hurt, *Creedy* Tim Pigott-Smith, *Dominic* Rupert Graves, *Lewis Prothero* Roger Allam, *Dascomb* Ben Miles, *Delia Surridge* Sinead Cusack, *with* Natasha Wightman, Eddie Marsan, Billie Cook, John Standing, Guy Henry, Juliet Howland, Malcolm Sinclair, Derek Hutchinson.

• *Dir* James McTeigue, *Pro* Joel Silver, Grant Hill, Andy and Larry Wachowski, *Ex Pro* Benjamin Waisbren, *Co-Pro* Roberto Malerba, Henning Molfenter and Carl L. Woebcken, *Screenplay* Andy and Larry Wachowski, *Ph* Adrian Biddle, *Pro Des* Owen paterson, *Ed* Martin Walsh, *M* Dario Marianelli, *Costumes* Sammy Sheldon, *Sound* Glenn Freemantle.

Warner/Virtual Studios/Silver Pictures/Anarchos Prods-Warner.
131 mins. USA/Germany. 2005. Rel: 17 March 2006.
Cert. 15.

Wah-Wah ★★

South East Africa; 1969-1972. With his mother an adulteress and his father an alcoholic, young Ralph Compton is finding life hard in Swaziland. Then, returning from boarding school, he finds that his father has married an American air stewardess who just refuses to fit in with the dying embers of colonial protocol… In keeping with its period and the far-flung corner of the British empire that it documents, *Wah-Wah* seems to adhere to a bygone brand of cinema. In fact, cinema seems to have little to do with this provincial melodrama which, peppered with grotesque caricatures, would not seem out-of-place in an end-of-pier production. The problem is that debutant writer-director Richard E. Grant has tried to cram too much of his eventful childhood into 99 minutes. And even though Grant shot the film in South Africa and his native Swaziland, a sense of real Africa eludes it. JC-W

V for v-neck: Hugo Weaving shows off
Natalie Portman's décolletage in James
McTeigue's stylish and literate *V for
Vendetta* (from Warner)

• *Harry Compton* Gabriel Byrne, *Ruby Compton* Emily Watson, *Gwen Traherne* Julie Walters, *Ralph Compton* Nicholas Hoult, *Lauren Compton* Miranda Richardson, *Lady Riva Hardwick* Celia Imrie, *Charles Bingham* Julian Wadham, *June Broughton* Fenella Woolgar, *Vernon* Sid Mitchell, *young Ralph Compton* Zachary Fox, *with* John Carlisle, Olivia Grant, John Matshikiza, Mathokoza Sibiya, Ian Roberts.

• *Dir* and *Screenplay* Richard E. Grant, *Pro* Marie-Castille Mention-Schaar, Pierre Kubel and Jeff Abberley, *Ex Pro* Joel Phiri, Jeremy Nathan and Ronnie Apteker, *Ph* Pierre Aïm, *Pro Des* Gary Williamson, *Ed* Isabelle Dedieu, *M* Patrick Doyle, *Costumes* Sheena Napier.

Loma Nasha Prods/Scion Films-Lionsgate. 99 mins. UK/France/South Africa. 2005. Rel: 2 June 2006. Cert. 15.

Waiting... ★

Wet-behind-the-ears, new employee Mitch is shown the ropes of the chain restaurant ShenaniganZ by cynical waiter Monty. However, Monty seems more interested in putting his ward off the place – unless, that is, Mitch is into baring his genitals in the line of duty... If you think obnoxious losers scratching their scalp and emptying their nostrils over a plate of food is funny, then maybe this is just what you've been waiting for. Gestated from years of waiting tables in Florida, *Waiting...* is a leaden, unsavoury attempt at blue-collar farce in the spirit of *Clerks*. However, the dialogue is uninspired, the characters tedious stereotypes and the plotting nonexistent. Still, it could do to themed restaurants what *Super Size Me* did for McDonald's, which may not be a bad thing. JC-W

• *Monty* Ryan Reynolds, *Serena* Anna Faris, *Dean* Justin Long, *Dan* David Koechner, *Raddimus* Luis Guzman, *Bishop* Chi McBride, *Mitch* John Francis Daley, *Tyla* Emmanuelle Chriqui, *Naomi* Alanna Ubach, *Calvin* Robert Patrick Benedict, *Natasha* Vanessa Lengies, *with* Kaitlin Doubleday, Andy Milonakis, Jordan Ladd, Wendie Malick.

• *Dir* and *Screenplay* Rob McKittrick, *Pro* Adam Rosenfelt, Stavros Merjos, Jay Rifkin, Jeff Balis and Rob Green, *Ex Pro* Thomas Augsberger, Paul Fiore, Sam Nazarian, Malcolm Petal, Marc Schaberg, Chris Moore and Jon Shestack, *Co-Pro* Dean Shull, Randy Winogard and Chris Fenton, *Line Pro* Jacky Lee Morgan, *Ph* Matthew Irving, *Pro Des* Devorah Herbert, *Ed* David Finfer and Andy Blumenthal, *M* Adam Gorgoni, *Costumes* Jillian Kreiner.

Lions Gate/Eden Rock Media/Element Films-Momentum Pictures. 94 mins. USA/Australia. 2004. Rel: 19 May 2006. Cert. 15.

Walk On Water ★★½

Bizarrely overpraised in some quarters, this is a political thriller about the tracking down of a now aged Nazi war criminal by a Jewish would-be assassin who finds himself reconsidering his attitudes. Substitute Iran and those for and against the Ayatollah and you have similarities with the excellent Iranian film *The Mission* (1983), but here the plot is full of contrivances and improbabilities and the direction is misjudged. Equally misguided is the symbolical ending as reconciliation by the Sea of Galilee borrows from the Biblical miracle of walking on water. The actors deserve better. Even so, one of them is particularly good, and that's the unhappily yet memorably named Knut Berger. Original title: *Lalecet al Hamaim*. MS

• *Eyal* Lior Ashkenazi, *Axel Himmelman* Knut Berger, *Pia Himmelman* Carolina Peters, *Menachem* Gidon Shemer, *Alfred Himmelman* Ernest Lenart, *Jello* Eyal Rozales, *with* Yousef (Joe) Sweid, Imad Jabarin, Sivan Sasson, Nataly Szylman.

• *Dir* Eytan Fox, *Pro* Amir Harel and Gal Uchovsky, *Ex Pro* Moshe Edery, Leon Edery, Dodi Zilber and Micky Rabinovitz, *Screenplay* Gal Uchovsky, *Ph* Tobias Hochstein, *Art Dir* Avi Fahima and Christoph Merg, *Ed* Yosef Grunfeld, *M* Ivri Lider, *Costumes* Rona Doron and Peter Pohl.

Hot/Israel Film Fund/Medea-Redbus. 103 mins. Israel. 2004. Rel: 1 July 2005. Cert. 15.

Walk the Line ★★★½

Forever branded `the bad son' by his strict, unloving father, Johnny Cash grows up into an angry, rebellious singer of the blues. However, his spleen and uncompromising singing style make him a unique and popular musical act, although his demons repeatedly sabotage his private and professional life... With the recent spate of musical biographies (headed by *Ray*, *Beyond the Sea* and *Stoned*), it's hard to adapt to Joaquin Phoenix as Johnny Cash. But Phoenix has a way of creeping up on you and he seems to become more and more like Cash as the film progresses, catching the singer's pulses and rough edges with surprising verisimilitude. There are several electric moments here – Cash's audition for Sam Phillips is a highlight, as is his subversive concert appearance at Folsom Prison – Reese Witherspoon turns in the performance of her career and the music is great. It's the formula itself – the dirt-poor childhood, the race through the charts, the descent into drug addiction – that is all so achingly familiar. JC-W

• *Johnny R. Cash* Joaquin Phoenix, *June Carter* Reese Witherspoon, *Vivian Cash* Ginnifer Edwards, *Ray Cash* Robert Patrick, *Sam Phillips* Dallas Roberts, *Luther Perkins* Dan John Miller, *Carrie Cash* Shelby Lynne, *Elvis Presley* Tyler Hilton, *Jerry Lee Lewis* Waylon Malloy Payne, *Waylon Jennings* Shooter Jennings, *young J.R.* Ridge Canipe, *young Jack Cash* Lucas Till, *with* Sandra Ellis Lafferty, Dan Beene, James Keach.

• *Dir* James Mangold, *Pro* Cathy Konrad and James Keach, *Ex Pro* John Carter Cash and Alan C. Blomquist, *Assoc Pro* Lou Robin, *Screenplay* Mangold and Gill Dennis, from *Man in Black* and *Cash the Autobiography* by Johnny Cash, *Ph* Phedon Papamichael, *Pro Des* David J. Bomba, *Ed* Michael McCusker, *M* T. Bone Burnett, *Costumes* Arianne Phillips.

Fox 2000/Tree/Line/Catfish-Fox. 137 mins. USA. 2005. Rel: 3 February 2006. Cert. 12A.

Cash flow: Joaquin Phoenix as Johnny C and Reese Witherspoon as June Carter in James Mangold's Oscar-winning *Walk the Line* (from Fox)

Wallace & Gromit:
The Curse of the Were-Rabbit ★★★½

With the Giant Vegetable Competition approaching, Wallace has become something of a local hero with his high-tech *Anti-Pesto* enterprise, which rids his neighbours' gardens of marauding rabbits. But when a much larger – and considerably more destructive – cottontail turns up, Wallace finds his ingenuity stretched to its limits… Sometimes a subject lends itself to the short film format. Such is the case of Wallace and Gromit, who charmed the world in Nick Park's Oscar-nominated *A Grand Day Out* (1989) and the Oscar-winning *The Wrong Trousers* (1993 and *A Close Shave* (1995). Here, there are heavy-handed allusions to the classic Universal horror films of the 1930s – along with a huge debt to *King Kong* – and much silliness, especially in the closing chapters. Even so, Wallace and Gromit are such engaging creations and the incidental humour so consistently inventive, that it's hard not to love it to bits. From the handcrafted appeal of the puppets (complete with their creators' visible thumbprints) to the welter of visual puns, this is a triumph of Plasticine over CGI.
JC-W

• *Voices*: *Wallace* Peter Sallis, *Victor Quartermaine* Ralph Fiennes, *Lady Tottington* Helena Bonham Carter, *PC Mackintosh* Peter Kay, *Rev. Clement Hedges* Nicholas Smith, *Mrs Mulch* Liz Smith, *and* John Thomson, Mark Gatiss, Gferaldine McEwan, Ben Whitehead, Christopher Fairbank.

• *Dir* Nick Park and Steve Box, *Pro* Park, Peter Lord, David Sproxton, Claire Jennings and Carla Shelley, *Ex Pro* Michael Rose and Cecil Kramer, *Screenplay* Box, Park, Bob Baker and Mark Burton, *Ph* Dave Alex Riddett and Tristan Oliver, *Pro Des* Phil Lewis, *Ed* David McCormick and Gregory Perler, *M* Julian Nott, *Animation* Loyd Price, *Models* Jan Sanger.

Aardman/DreamWorks-UIP.
84 mins. UK/USA. 2005. Rel: 14 October 2005.
Cert. U.

Wal-Mart:
The High Cost of Low Price ★★

Wal-Mart, like Hitler, is bad. And it's an easy target for indignant denunciation. The superstore exploits Third World employees, promotes dishonesty as standard policy, sponges on the government to compensate its underpaid workforce, is a threat to the environment and is a breeding ground for rape and assault. Interestingly, Robert Greenwald's cheesy, one-dimensional and shabby documentary fails to accuse the franchise of genocide, nor does it enumerate the miseries of shopping at Wal-Mart, a bastion of tack that parades tabloid literature near its checkout tills. But then Greenwald's film is just the sort of tawdry trash that Wal-Mart dishes out to its trailer park demographic. With lazy condescension and fact stacking, this is Michael Moore-land without the scope or entertainment value. A sense of irony or perspective might have helped.
JC-W

• *Dir* Robert Greenwald, *Pro* Greenwald, Jim Gilliam and Devin Smith, *Co-Pro* Sarah Feeley, Caty Borum, Kerry Candaele and Luisa Dantas, *Ph* Kristy Tully, *Ed* Chris Gordon, Douglas Cheek, Jonathan Brock and Robert Florio, *M* John Frizzell, *Lead Research* Meleiza Figueroa.

Retail Project-Tartan Films.
99 mins. USA. 2005. Rel: 12 May 2006.
Cert. PG.

War of the Worlds ★★★★½

For Ray Ferrier, divorcee, dockworker and unsatisfactory father, the weekend starts off pretty much like any other. This time, though, he's looking after his teenage son and 11-year-old daughter, but there's not much excitement he can offer them. Then there's a sudden lightning storm, although the wind seems to be blowing *towards* the epicentre. That's odd. And so is the hole that appears at an intersection near his New Jersey home… 'Based' on H.G. Wells' 1898 novel ('inspired by' would've been more accurate), *War of the Worlds* takes the apocalyptic grandeur of *Independence Day*, *Deep Impact* and *The Day After Tomorrow* and channels it through the personal nightmare of Ray Ferrier and his two kids. This is the flip side of Spielberg's *E.T. The ExtraTerrestrial* and *Close Encounters* and possibly the darkest popcorn blockbuster of all time (and the goriest to receive a 12A certificate). After the temperance of *Catch Me if You Can* and *The Terminal*, Spielberg has sharpened his nails to claw back his commercial viability – and he doesn't hang around for the shark to appear in the middle act. From the first appearance of the terrible alien tripod, through to the capsizal of a crowded ferry and on to the nerve-racking refuge in a farm basement, *WOFT* delivers the goods. Ingenious, spectacular and simply breathtaking escapism – with a powerful political agenda.
JC-W

• *Ray Ferrier* Tom Cruise, *Rachel Ferrier* Dakota Fanning, *Mary Ann* Miranda Otto, *Ogilvy* Tim Robbins, *Robbie Ferrier* Justin Chatwin, *Vincent* Rick Gonzalez, *grandfather* Gene Barry, *grandmother* Ann Robinson, *with* Yul Vázquez, Lenny Venito, Lisa Ann Walter, Terry Thomas, *narrator* Morgan Freeman.

• *Dir* Steven Spielberg, *Pro* Kathleen Kennedy and Colin Wilson, *Ex Pro* Paula Wagner, *Screenplay* Josh Friedman and David Koepp, *Ph* Janusz Kaminski, *Pro Des* Rick Carter, *Ed* Michael Kahn, *M* John Williams, *Costumes* Joanna Johnston, *Visual Effects* Dennis Muren.

Paramount/DreamWorks/Amblin Entertainment/Cruise/Wagner Prods-UIP.
116 mins. USA. 2005. Rel: 1 July 2005. Cert. 12A.

The Weather Man ★★½

In spite of a healthy pay cheque and a relatively cushy job ('it's not neurosurgery'), TV weather presenter Dave Spritz is finding life a bit of a downer. He's divorced from the wife he still loves, his daughter is 'grossly overweight' and his father is dying from lymphoma. 'I'm not a hill of beans,' Dave Spritz

Time zone: Michael Caine and Nicolas Cage wait for the inevitable in Gore Verbinski's contemplative but rather insipid *The Weather Man* (from Momentum Pictures)

intones over the soundtrack, 'but I have a plan'… American cinema is littered with films about ordinary men facing domestic meltdown and this is no *About Schmidt*. Nicolas Cage hangs on to the same hangdog expression throughout the movie, but is well supported by an impeccable cast. And there are moments to cherish here, both comic and acerbic. In a father-son talk, Michael Caine (very good) tells Cage's Dave that, '"easy" doesn't enter into grown-up life' – but Dave Spritz is too powerless to make any uncomfortable stands. And there's a very funny scene at a 'trust' therapy class. Yet the film lacks teeth and momentum and is belittled by a running joke in which Spritz is bombarded by fast food from passing vehicles. By the end, it seems as if the viewer himself is being accosted by the product placement. JC-W

• *Dave Spritz* Nicolas Cage, *Robert Spritz* Michael Caine, *Noreen* Hope Davis, *Mike Spritz* Nicholas Hoult, *Don* Gil Bellows, *Russ* Michael Rispoli, *Shelly Spritz* Gemmenne de la Pena, *Lauren* Judith McConnell, *with* Chris Marrs, Dina Facklis, Joe Bianchi, Jason Wells, Bryant Gumbel, Ed McMahon.

• *Dir* Gore Verbinski, *Pro* Todd Black, Steve Tisch and Jason Blumenthal, *Ex Pro* David Alper, William S. Beasley and Norm Golightly, *Co-Pro* and *Screenplay* Steven Conrad, *Ph* Phedon Papamichael, *Pro Des* Tom Duffield, *Ed* Craig Wood, *M* Hans Zimmer, *Costumes* Penny Rose.

Paramount/Escape Artists-Momentum.
101 mins. USA/Germany. 2004. Rel: 3 March 2006.
Cert. 15.

Wedding Crashers ★★★½

No longer in the first flush of youth, divorce mediators and best buddies Jeremy Grey and John Beckwith crash weddings to pick up chicks. Regardless of the size or ethnicity of the event, John and Jeremy have become past masters at fitting in, taking the microphone, dancing with the kids and zeroing in on the impressed, young and inebriated womenfolk. With their acumen for background research and human knowledge, they have turned a rare form of partying into an art; an art that comes with its own set of very strict rules… It's a funny, outrageous concept and Vince Vaughn and Owen Wilson bring an in-built energy and chemistry to the proceedings. With its vibrant soundtrack, comic timing and endless inventiveness, it's a romp that only occasionally outstays its welcome. And remember, 'a friend in need is… a pest.' JC-W

• *John Beckwith* Owen Wilson, *Jeremy Grey* Vince Vaughn, *Secretary Cleary* Christopher Walken, *Claire Cleary* Rachel McAdams, *Gloria Cleary* Isla Fisher, *Kathleen Cleary* Jane Seymour, *Randolph* Ron Canada, *Sack Lodge* Bradley Cooper, *Grandma Mary Cleary* Ellen Albertini Dow, *Father O'Neil* Henry Gibson, *Todd Cleary* Keir O'Donnell, *with* Dwight Yoakam, Rebecca De Mornay, David Conrad, Rachel Sterling, and (uncredited) *Chaz* Will Ferrell.

• *Dir* David Dobkin, *Pro* Peter Abrams, Robert L. Levy and

Andrew Panay, *Ex Pro* Guy Riedel, Toby Emmerich, Richard Brener and Cale Boyter, *Screenplay* Steve Faber and Bob Fisher, *Ph* Julio Macat, *Pro Des* Barry Robison, *Ed* Mark Livolsi, *M* Rolfe Kent; Mozart, Haydn, Mendelssohn, Richard Wagner; tracks performed by Matter, The Isley Brothers, Mungo Jerry, Guster & Ben Kweller, Coldplay, Shanna Carlson, Crumb, Faces, The Weakerthans, Jont, and Robbers On High Street, *Costumes* Denise Wingate, *Sound* Tim Chau and Nils Jensen.

New Line Cinema/Tapestry Films-Entertainment.
118 mins. USA. 2005. Rel: 14 July 2005. Cert. 15.

When a Stranger Calls ★★

High school student Jill Johnson gets to explore a palatial, mountain residence in Colorado when she is called on to baby-sit. However, as a storm brews, she becomes unnerved when a stranger calls on her best friend's mobile… The original *When a Stranger Calls*, released in 1979 and starring Carol Kane and Charles Durning, wasn't very good, which shows the lengths that filmmakers will got to find anything to scare contemporary teens. The set-up of the telephone stalker has since been much utilised in the cinema, notably in the opening sequence of *Scream*, in which Drew Barrymore met her comeuppance. Here, that very scenario is extended to breaking point as the inevitable twist is kept at arm's length to wearying effect. EB

• *Jill Johnson* Camilla Belle, *Stranger* Tommy Flanagan, *Scarlet* Tessa Thompson, *Bobby* Brian Geraghty, *Mr Johnson* Clark Gregg, *Dr Mandrakis* Derek de Lint, *Mrs Mandrakis* Kate Jennings Grant, *voice of the Stranger* Lance Henriksen, *with* David Denman, Arthur Youngf, Madeline Carroll, Steve Eastin.

• *Dir* Simon West, *Pro* John Davis, Wyck Godfrey and Ken Lemberger, *Ex Pro* Paddy Cullen, *Screenplay* Jake Wade Well, *Ph* Peter Mezies Jr, *Pro Des* Jon Gary Steele, *Ed* Jeff Betancourt, *M* James Dooley, *Costumes* Marie Sylvie Deveau.

Screen Gems/Davis Entertainment-Columbia TriStar.
87 mins. USA. 2006. Rel: 12 May 2006. Cert. 15.

When Will I Be Loved? ★★★

Spoilt Vera Barrie has a luxurious loft apartment in New York and a scheming hustler, Ford Welles, for a boyfriend, who informs her that an Italian media tycoon wants to meet her… Cult writer-director James Toback's weird take on the old tale of a young woman being lured into a money deal with a rich man is a deliberately odd and alienating film, with its hard and unedifying characters, none more so than Neve Campbell's Vera. It's a tough stretch for the star, but she acquits herself well and so does Toback himself as a college professor. Strong, esoteric stuff with much to recommend it – and nobody can say that Toback is neither intelligent nor ambitious. Mike Tyson appears as himself. DW

• *Vera Barrie* Neve Campbell, *Ford Welles* Frederick Weller, *Count Tommaso Lupo* Dominic Chianese, *Ashley* Ashley Shelton, *Alexandra Barrie* Karen Allen, *Victor* Barry Primus, *Richard*

Turley Richard Turley, *Michael Burke* Michael Mailer, *homicide detective* Jason Pendergraft, *Joelle* Joelle Carter, *with* James Toback, Damon Dash, Alex Feldman, Oliver `Power' Grant, Mike Tyson, Lori Singer.

• *Dir* and *Screenplay* James Toback, *Pro* Ron Rotholz, *Ex Pro* Robert Bevan, Keith Hayley and Charlie Saville, *Co-Pro* Petra Hoebel and Piers Tempest, *Ph* Larry McConkey, *Pro Des* Ernestor Solo, *Ed* Suzie Elmiger, *M* Oli `Power' Grant, *Costumes* Luca Mosca.

International Film Collective/Rotholz Pictures-
Verve Pictures.
80 mins. UK/USA. 2003. Rel: 23 September 2005.
Cert. 15.

Where the Truth Lies ★★

The 1950s-1970s; Los Angeles. It's hard to imagine that our idols may indulge in less than perfect behaviour behind our backs. In the 1950s, Lanny Morris and Vince Collins were the golden boys of American television, as famous for their witty repartee as for their acts of charity. However, when the ambitious young journalist Karen O'Connor persuades a publisher to let her 'ghost' Vince's autobiography, she finds his past holds some hideous secrets… So, why are period films always swathed in music? Atom Egoyan, one of the most daring and original directors in the world, takes a giant step backwards to worship at the shrine of Hitchcock. While serving up his characteristic stew of shady characters, dark secrets and

emotional subterfuge, Egoyan embalms it all in Hitchcockian cliché: the insistent Bernard Hermannesque score, the icy manipulative blonde and a cumbersome variety of alternating flashbacks (not to mention some wobbly sets). Still, there is the novelty of watching Colin Firth try to mount Kevin Bacon. JC-W

• *Lanny Morris* Kevin Bacon, *Vince Collins* Colin Firth, *Karen O'Connor* Alison Lohman, *Maureen* Rachel Blanchard, *Reuben* David Hayman, *Sally Sanmarco* Maury Chaykin, *Alice* Kristin Adams, *with* Sonja Bennett, Deborah Grover, Beau Starr, Arsinée Khanjian, Don McKellar, David Hemblen.

• *Dir* and *Screenplay* Atom Egoyan, from the novel by Rupert Holmes, *Pro* Robert Lantos, *Ex Pro* Egoyan, Colin Leventhal, Daniel J.B. Taylor and Donald A. Starr, *Ph* Paul Sarossy, *Pro Des* Phillip Barker, *Ed* Susan Shipton, *M* Mychael Danna, *Costumes* Beth Pasternak, *Sound* Steven Munro.

Serendipity Point Films/First Choice Films/The Movie
Network/Télèfilm Canada/Ego Film Arts/Grosvenor
Park-Momentum.
107 mins. Canada/UK. 2005. Rel: 2 December 2005.
Cert. 18.

Whisky ★★★★

Small-scale but delightfully engaging, this is a quiet, laid-back tale about people well into middle age. Jacobo owns an ailing sock factory in Montevideo and awaits the arrival of his

Hitchcock blonde: Alison Lohman with Kevin Bacon
in Atom Egoyan's desperately disappointing *Where
the Truth Lies* (from Momentum Pictures)

brother for a ceremony at the grave of their dead mother. To impress his more successful sibling, Jacobo persuades his long-serving employee Marta to pose as his wife. The mixture of humour and pathos recalls Kaurismäki, the minimalistic style has echoes of Ozu and the comic touches sometimes seem Tatiesque. The deliberately open ending is rather abrupt, but the players and the directors Stoll and Rebella are wholly at one. Although the film may not suit all tastes, this Uruguayan oddity has a quality at once humane and haunting. MS

• *Jacobo Köller* Andrés Pazos, *Marta Acuña* Mirella Pascual, *Herman Koller* Jorge Bolani, *Don Ivan* José Pedro Bujaruz, *young married couple* Ana Katz, Daniel Hendler.

• *Dir* Juan Pablo Rebella and Pablo Stoll, *Pro* Fernando Epstein, *Screenplay* Rebella, Stoll and Gonzalo Delgado Galiana, *Ph* Barbara Alvarez, *Art Dir* Delgado Galiana, *Ed* Fernando Epstein, *M* Pequena Orquesta Reincidentes, *Costumes* Adelaida Rodríguez.

Control-Z Films/Fernando Epstein/Rizoma Films/Hernan Musaluppi/Pandora Filmproduktion-Artificial Eye. 98 mins. Uruguay/Argentina/Germany/Spain/France/ USA/Japan. 2004. Rel: 29 July 2005. Cert. 15.

The White Countess ★★

Shanghai; the late 1930s. When Todd Jackson lost his sight in a terrorist bombing, he was forced to give up his post as an American ambassador to China. Stubbornly indifferent to his blindness, he now dreams of opening his own nightclub in Shanghai. And when he meets Sofia Belinskya, a Russian émigré reduced to prostituting herself to feed her family, he finds his perfect muse: an alluring woman of tragedy and weariness. So he names his establishment after her... Ralph Fiennes has repeatedly confirmed his status as one of the world's most consummate actors, but there are many fine American actors, too. So, just as one has recovered form the shock of three Redgraves displaying throaty Russian accents, it's discomfiting to encounter Fiennes with his American twang. Still, the pre-war, cosmopolitan nightclub scene of Shanghai is an intriguing milieu, even though it is rendered somewhat stilted and claustrophobic here. It's not until the final act that Christopher Doyle's painterly compositions find their voice, but by then the film has lost any emotional traction it might have had. JC-W

• *Todd Jackson* Ralph Fiennes, *Countess Sofia Belinskya* Natasha Richardson, *Princess Vera Belinskya* Vanessa Redgrave, *Olga Belinskya* Lynn Redgrave, *Matsuda* Hiroyuki Sanada, *Samuel Feinstein* Allan Corduner, *Kao* Ying Da, *Katya* Madeleine Daly, *Grushenka* Madeleine Potter, *with* Dan Herzberg, Jean-Pierre Lorit, Lee Pace, John Wood, Dragan Micanovic, Terence Harvey, Alexandar Richardson.

• *Dir* James Ivory, *Pro* Ismail Merchant, Ren Zhonglun and Andreas Grosch, *Ex Pro* André Morgan, Andreas Schmid, Marcus Schöfer, Wang Tianyun, Fu Wenxia, Patrick Ko and Wang Daqing, *Screenplay* Kazuo Ishiguro, *Ph* Christopher Doyle, *Pro Des* Andrew Sanders, *Ed* John David Allen,

Shanghai dreams: Ralph Fiennes in James Ivory's stilted and claustrophobic *The White Countess* (from Sony Pictures)

M Richard Robbins and John Huie, *Costumes* John Bright.

Merchant Ivory/Sony Pictures Classics/Shanghai Film Group Corp-Columbia TriStar.
135 mins. UK/USA/Germany/China. 2005. Rel: 31 March 2006. Cert. PG.

Who Killed Bambi? ★★★½

'Bambi' is the condescending nickname given to the student nurse Isabelle by the charismatic Dr Philipp. Adverse to the sight of blood and suffering from dizzy spells, Isabelle is a vulnerable fawn in the big new forest of corridors that hold so many dreadful secrets. But Isabelle is no idiot and soon she is piecing together the fragments of a mystery involving a vanished Chinese invalid and the fact that patients are waking up under the surgeon's knife… Only in France would you find quite so many attractive female patients in one hospital, but for the most part this is a credible thriller in the Hitchcock mould (albeit without The Master's leavening of humour). First-time director Gilles Marchand exhibits a remarkable skill for setting up a scene and shows a maturity by refusing to clutter his film with false alarms and melodramatic music. It is this confidence in the material that makes *Who Killed Bambi?* so gripping, along with the strong premise of an inexperienced nurse pitted against a respected and unimpeachable authority figure. Original title: *Qui a tué Bambi?* JC-W

• *Isabelle* aka *'Bambi'* Sophie Quinton, *Dr Philipp* Laurent Lucas, *Véronique* Catherine Jacob, *Sami* Yasmine Belmadi, *Ms Vachon* Michèle Moretti, *Nathalie* Valérie Donzelli, *with* Jean-Claude Jay, Lucienne Moreau, Dominique Charmet.

• *Dir* Gilles Marchand, *Pro* Caroline Benjo and Carole Scotta, *Ex Pro* Barbara Letellier, *Screenplay* Marchand and Vincent Dietschy, *Ph* Pierre Milon, *Pro Des* Laurent Deroo, *Ed* Robin Campillo, *M* Doc Matéo, Alex Beaupin, Lily Margot, Carlos Dalton and François Eudes; Vivaldi, *Costumes* Virginie Montel and Isabelle Pannetier.

Haut et Court/M6 Films/Canal Plus-Tartan Films.
126 mins. France. 2002. Rel: 1 July 2005. No Cert.

The Wild ★★

Life would seem to be just peachy for Samson, Benny, Bridget, Nigel and Larry. A lion, squirrel, giraffe, koala and anaconda leading the life of Riley at New York Zoo, the critters have all the latest commodities and all the food they can eat. But when Samson's cub, Ryan, runs off and is accidentally shipped off to the wild, the quarrelsome quintet head off to rescue him and find that life can be a zoo out there…
Ten years in development and the biggest animated production to come out of Canada, *The Wild* defies one's most generous instincts. While much of the CGI wizardry is amazing in its detail, the characters are charmless, the dialogue lame and the story a poor combination of *Madagascar* and *Finding Nemo*. The film is also undone by its cacophonous soundtrack and slapstick that would look OTT in a third-rate circus. Thank St. Francis, then, for Eddie Izzard, who brings some humour to his contemptuous koala (although why does this koala have an English accent?). JC-W

• *Voices*: *Samson* Kiefer Sutherland, *Benny* Jim Belushi, *Nigel* Eddie Izzard, *Bridget* Janeane Garofalo, *Kazar* William Shatner, *Ryan* Greg Cipes, *Larry* Richard Kind, *Blag* Patrick Warburton, *with* Colin Hay, Miles Marsico, Jack De Sena, Jonathan Kimmel, Jason Connery, Nicholas Guest, Jess Harnell, Laraine Newman, Steve 'Spaz' Williams

• *Dir* Steve 'Spaz' Williams, *Pro* Clint Goldman and Beau Flynn, *Ex Pro* Kevin Lima, Will Vinton and Stefan Simchowitz, *Screenplay* Ed Decter, John J. Strauss, Mark Gibson and Philip Halprin, *Pro Des* Chris Farmer, *Ed* V. Scott Balcerek and Steven L. Wagner, *M* Alan Silvestri; songs performed by Coldplay, Everlife, Lifehouse, Big Bad Voodoo Daddy, Minnie Riperton, Tony Phillips, Eric Idle and John Du Prez, and Joey Miskulin, *Sound* Andy Newell.

Walt Disney Pictures/Hoytyboy Pictures/Sir Zip Studios/ Contafilm-Buena Vista International.
81 mins. USA. 2006. Rel: 26 May 2006. Cert. U.

The Wild Parrots of Telegraph Hill ★★★★

Initially one fears that a film about a man looking after a flock of parrots on San Francisco's Telegraph Hill may be more suited to TV, and possibly even to a ten-minute slot. But such doubts soon fade, banished by the way in which this film develops. It's not only fascinating on a personal level (the man is Mark Bittner, an engaging, rather eccentric middle-aged loner) but as a film concerning love for animals, parrots or otherwise. The fact that Bittner acknowledges that he could be accused of anthropomorphism adds to our willingness to credit what he has to say about the parrots' responses to him. In short, this movie is an animal lover's delight, but even if you are not in that category the film's warmth is irresistible and there's a final real-life twist that would be the envy of any fiction writer. MS

• *With*: Mark Bittner (human); parrot stars: Connor (blue-crowned conure), Olive (mitred conure), Mingus, Picasso & Sophie, Pushkin, and Tupelo (cherry-headed conures); *urban legends* Ivan Stormgart, Maggie McCall, Gary Thompson, Elizabeth Wright, Jamie Yorck.

• *Dir, Pro* and *Ed* Judy Irving, *Ph* Irving, James Attwood, Howard Munson, Mark Bittner and Jacquelyne Cordes, *M* Chris Michie.

Pelican Media-ICA Projects.
83 mins. USA. 2004. Rel: 9 December 2005. No Cert.

William Eggleston: In The Real World ★★

Born in 1939, the photographer William Eggleston, who attempts to pin down what is strange and mysterious in everyday life, has known both the vehement abuse of sceptics and the unstinted praise of admirers. He is said to have influenced such filmmakers as David Lynch and Sofia Coppola. However, on paper, Michael Almereyda is the perfect director to study him on film, being an offbeat artist himself and one with a strong visual eye. What we have, however, is probably the most uninformative documentary about an artist ever made. Following Eggleston around reveals little and when he opens his mouth his laconic manner and his inability – or refusal – to explain his art although occasionally hilarious is more often boring. Interviewing others about him and his life might have yielded something, but Almereyda stays close to his man and it's fatal. MS

• *With*: William Eggleston, Winston Eggleston, Haizlip Leigh, Bruce Wagner, Rosa Eggleston; narrator Michael Almereyda.

• *Dir* and *Ph* Michael Almereyda, *Pro* Almereyda, Jesse Dylan and Anthony Katagas, *Ex Pro* Donald Rosenfeld and Alex Zoullas, *Ed* Susan Choy, Joshua Falcon and Johannes Weuthen, *M* Simon Fisher Turner.

High Line Prods/Keep Your Head Prods-ICA Projects. 86 mins. USA. 2005. Rel: 18 November 2005. No Cert.

The Wind That Shakes the Barley ★★

Ireland; 1920. As Ireland prepares for its independence, Britain dispatches 10,000 'Black and Tan' soldiers to contain any potential rebellion. But far from enforcing capitulation, the invaders rouse an unquenchable anger… While it's always a pleasure to encounter a Ken Loach film – if only for the thoughtful characterisation and consummate craftsmanship – the director is at his best with intimate scenarios. Here, as in his Spanish Civil War treatise *Land and Freedom* (1995), Loach takes on a larger canvas. The result, with its abundance of characters, political debates and almost comical action scenes, is not great cinema. In addition, several sequences of uncompromising barbarity might well put off even the director's most devoted followers. JC-W

• *Damien* Cillian Murphy, *Teddy O'Donovan* Pádraic Delaney, *Dan* Liam Cunningham, *Sinead* Orla Fitzgerald, *Peggy* Mary Riordan, *Finbar* Damien Kearney, *Chris* John Crean, *Sir John Hamilton* Roger Allam, *Lily* Fiona Lawton, *with* Mary Murphy, Laurence Barry, Frank Bourke, Peggy Lynch, Sabrina Barry, William Ruane, Sean McGinley, Tom Charnock.

• *Dir* Ken Loach, *Pro* Rebecca O'Brien, *Ex Pro* Ulrich Felsberg, Andrew Lowe, Nigel Thomas and Paul Trijbits, *Co-Pro* Redmond Morris, *Screenplay* Paul Laverty, *Ph* Barry Ackroyd, *Pro Des* Fergus Clegg, *Ed* Jonathan Morris, *M* George Fenton, *Costumes* Eimer Ní Mhaoldomhnaigh.

Sixteen Films/Matador Pictures/Regent Capital/ UK Film Council/ Bord Scannán na hÉireann/I rish Film Board-Pathé. 124 mins. Ireland/UK/Germany/Italy/Spain. Rel: 23 June 2006. Cert. 15.

With Blood on My Hands

See *Pusher II : With Blood on My Hands*.

Wolf

See *Lobo*.

Wolf Creek ★★★★

Western Australia; 1999. Liz and Kristy are two English backpackers in their twenties. Accompanied by Ben, a Sydney native, they head out to Wolf Creek National Park. Then the weather turns, their watches stop and the battery of their car appears to die… *Wolf Creek* is an exceptionally well-crafted thriller. Besides the astonishing skyscapes of the Outback, the authentic banter between the young protagonists and the almost documentary-like feel to its set-up, the film's later passages are chillingly executed for the greatest effect. If you can win an audience around to like and believe in the main characters, then the methodical butchery of them is bound to be shocking. But what's really upsetting is that the film's publicity claims the story is based on 'actual events'. Bollocks. While British backpackers have been murdered in Australia (notably Peter Falconio in 2001), this has as much rooting in real life as *Psycho* had to the exploits of Ed Gein. JC-W

• *Mick Taylor* John Jarratt, *Liz Hunter* Cassandra Magrath, *Kristy Earl* Kestie Morassi, *Ben Mitchell* Nathan Phillips, *with* Gordon Poole, Guy O'Donnell, Phil Stevenson.

• *Dir* and *Screenplay* Greg McLean, *Pro* David Lightfoot, *Ex Pro* Gary Hamilton, Simon Hewitt, Martin Fabinyi, George Adams and Michael Gudinski, *Co-Pro* Matt Hearn, *Ph* Will Gibson, *Pro Des* Robert Webb, *Ed* Jason Ballantine, *M* François Tétaz, *Costumes* Nicola Dunn.

Darclight/Mushroom Pictures/FCC/ True Crime Channel-Optimum Releasing. 98 mins. Australia. 2004. Rel: 16 September 2005. Cert. 18.

The World's Fastest Indian ★★★½

For 25 years the eccentric inventor Burt Munro has worked on cranking up the performance of his 1920 Indian Twin Scout motorcycle. With dogged determination, imagination and sheer graft, he finely perfects his dream speed machine and in 1967 sets off with it from New Zealand to Los Angeles. Then all he has to do is get it to the Bonneville Salt Flats in Utah… The title sort of gives the game away but then there wouldn't be a film without the real-life achievement of this remarkable Kiwi. The pleasure is the journey that Munro takes, along with his irrepressible bonhomie and ability to make sporting history with mere gumption and various household appliances. It takes a while to get used to Anthony Hopkins' New Zealand accent – not to mention his transformation into a speed freak – but he wins you over and makes you care: FYI: Director Roger Donaldson, who emigrated to New Zealand in 1965, actually befriended Burt Munro back in 1971. JC-W

• *Burt Munro* Anthony Hopkins, *Ada* Diane Ladd, *Tom* Aaron Murphy, *Fernando* Paul Rodriguez, *Fran* Annie White, *Bob Higby* Chris Bruno, *Jerry* Bruce Greenwood, *Jim Moffet* Chris Lawford, *with* Carlos La Camara, Jessica Cauffiel, Patrick Flueger, William Lucking.

• *Dir* and *Screenplay* Roger Donaldson, *Pro* Donaldson and Gary Hannam, *Ex Pro* Megumi Fukasawa, Charles Hannah,

Kiwi fruitcase: Anthony Hopkins' Burt Munro dreams of breaking records in Roger Donaldson's endearing *The World's Fastest Indian* (from Icon)

Masaharu Inaba, Satoru Isaka and Barrie M. Osborne, *Co-Pro* John J. Kelly, *Ph* David Gribble, *Pro Des* J. Dennis Washington (USA) and Rob Gillies (NZ), *Ed* John Gilbert, *M* J. Peter Robinson, *Costumes* Nancy Cavallaro (USA) and Jane Holland (NZ), *Visual Effects* Kent Houston.

OLC/Rights Entertainment/Tanlay AG/3 Dogs & A Pony, etc-Icon.
126 mins. New Zealand/Japan/Switzerland/USA. 2005. Rel: 10 March 2006. Cert. 12A.

X-Men The Last Stand ★★½

Things are looking up for the mutant minority. Not only is the US President now an ally, but there's a mutant in the cabinet. Then a cure is discovered, a catalyst that divides those who think mutancy is a curse and those who think it's a gift… The potent underlying themes of race, individuality and the importance of `being oneself' are becoming increasingly diluted in deference to the almighty special effect. But, in the age of the CGI, such effects are no longer special. Once Ian McKellen's Magneto has torn the Golden Gate Bridge off its moorings and dumped it on to the island of Alcatraz, there's hardly anywhere else to go. However, after such a cataclysm, a terrified motorist's instinctive locking of her car door is a nice touch. It is such minor details that distinguish the *X-Men* franchise from its bombastic brethren, although apocalyptic excess is taking over. JC-W

• *Logan/Wolverine* Hugh Jackman, *Ororo Munroe/Storm* Halle Berry, *Eric Lehnsherr/Magneto* Ian McKellen, *Jean Grey/Phoenix* Famke Janssen, *Marie/Rogue* Anna Paquin, *Dr Henry `Hank' McCoy/Beast* Kelsey Grammer, *Scott Summers/Cyclops* James Marsden, *Raven Darkholme/Mystique* Rebecca Romijn, *Bobby Drake/Iceman* Shawn Ashmore, *John Allerdyce/Pyro* Aaron Stanford, *Cain Marko/Juggernaut* Vinnie Jones, *Professor Charles Xavier* Patrick Stewart, *Kitty Pryde* Ellen Page, *Warren Worthington III/Angel* Ben Foster, *Callisto* Dania Ramirez, *Warren Worthington II* Michael Murphy, *the President* Josef Sommer, *Jimmy/Leech* Cameron Bright, *with* Shohreh Aghdashloo, Bill Duke, Daniel Cudmore, Eric Dane, Kea Wong, Connor Widdows, Julian Richings, Ken Leung, Anthony Heald, R. Lee Ermey, Stan Lee, and (uncredited) Olivia Williams.

• *Dir* Brett Ratner, *Pro* Lauren Shuler Donner, Ralph Winter and Avi Arad, *Ex Pro* Stan Lee, Kevin Feige and John Palermo, *Co-Pro* Ross Fanger, Kurt Williams and James M. Freitag, *Screenplay* Simon Kinberg and Zak Penn, *Ph* Dante Spinotti, *Pro Des* Edward Verreaux, *Ed* Mark Helfrich, Mark Goldblatt and Julia Wong, *M* John Powell, *Costumes* Judianna Makovsky, *Visual Effects* John Bruno.

Fox/Marvel Entertainment-Fox.
103 mins. USA/UK. 2006. Rel: 25 May 2006. Cert. 12A.

A Year Without Love ★★½

Buenos Aires; 1996. Gradually succumbing to Aids, the gay poet Pablo Pérez ekes out a living as a French teacher. Incongruously sharing a cramped apartment with his dotty aunt, Pablo divides his spare time between visits to the hospital, writing up a diary on his disintegrating life and cruising the gay clubs of the capital. As his health deteriorates, the writer finds an unexpected salvation in becoming the slave to an underground group of S&M practitioners… Well, you can't accuse *A Year Without Love* of sentimentality. With its jaundiced colour palette and constant urban noise, it is a grim adaptation of the published diary of Pablo Pérez (who collaborated on the screenplay with the first-time director). Yet such verisimilitude does not excuse a movie of such unremitting ugliness. No doubt a marginalized gay demographic will be drawn to the material, and director Berneri does create an aura of bracing authenticity, but the film's non-judgemental attitudes towards promiscuity, perversion and dying is unlikely to appeal to any but the most dedicated S&M crowd. Original title: *Un año sin amor.* JC-W

• *Pablo Pérez* Juan Minujín, *Martín* Javier Van der Couter, *Pablo's aunt* Mimí Ardú, *Nicolás* Carlos Echevarría, *Julia* Bárbara Lombardo, *Báez* Osmar Nuñez, *father* Ricardo Merkin.

• *Dir* Anahí Berneri, *Pro* Diego Dubcovsky, Daniel Burman and Maximiliano Pelosi, *Ex Pro* Dubcovsky and Sebastián Ponce, *Screenplay* Berneri and Pablo Pérez, *Ph* Lucio Bonelli, *Art Dir* Maria Garcia Eugenia Sueiro, *Ed* Alex Zito, *M* Leo Garcia, *Costumes* Roberta Farina.

BD Cine/WAP/Aleph Media-Parasol Peccadillo Releasing.
96 mins. Argentina. 2004. Rel: 28 April 2006. Cert. 18.

Yes ★★

'No' is not an option. As the film's Greek chorus, a self-styled 'dirt consultant' (impishly played by Shirley Henderson), says, 'I think that "no" does not exist – there's only "yes".' An Irish-American molecular biologist trapped in a lifeless marriage cannot say `no' to the advances of a sweet-talking chef. She needs his attention and the comfort of his skin. But she is a Westerner and he is a Muslim and, inevitably, their cultural differences will prove a problem… There is little real about *Yes*. The domestic staff stare defensively at the camera, the walls are bereft of pictures and the characters speak in rhyme. The director, Sally Potter, explains that her film, 'is about becoming naked – the human commonality beyond our cultural and political differences.' Written in the wake of September 11, the script's iambic structure emerged in order to express ideas that, `might otherwise be indigestible, abstract or depersonalised.' It's a courageous conceit – and starkly original – and wilfully pretentious. There's a moving, lyrical sequence in which Sheila Hancock talks of her hopes while on the cusp of death – but it's an oasis in a sea of inscrutability. JC-W

• *She* Joan Allen, *He* Simon Abkarian, *Anthony* Sam Neill, *cleaner* Shirley Henderson, *aunt* Sheila Hancock, *Kate* Samantha Bond, *Grace* Stephanie Leonidas, *Billy* Gary Lewis, *Virgil* Wil Johnson, *Whizzer* Raymond Waring.

Domestic disharmony: Rene Russo and Dennis Quaid slum it in Raja
Gosnell's lazy, redundant *Yours, Mine & Ours* (from Sony Pictures)

• *Dir* and *Screenplay* Sally Potter, *Pro* Christopher Sheppard and Andrew Fierberg, *Ex Pro* John Penotti, Paul Trijbits, Fisher Stevens and Cedric Jeanson, *Line Pro* Nick Laws, *Ph* Alexei Rodionov, *Pro Des* Carlos Conti, *Ed* Daniel Goddard, *Costumes* Jacqueline Durran.

Greenstreet Films/UK Film Council/
Adventure Pictures-Optimum Releasing.
100 mins. UK/USA. 2004. Rel: 5 August 2005. Cert. 15.

Yours, Mine & Ours ★

This lame romantic comedy tells the story of two single parents who get married and end up with 18 children between them. So they move into a big house and chaos ensues. Yet another unnecessary remake. The original was made in 1968 after the success of *The Sound of Music*, when films with large families were popular. Raja Gosnell's indifferent piece with a lazy script has nothing going for it at all. It is dated, unfunny and boring. Once upon a time ... Dennis Quaid and Rene Russo used to make good films. GS

• *Frank Beardsley* Dennis Quaid, *Helen North* Rene Russo, *Commandant Sherman* Rip Torn, *Mrs Munion* Linda Hunt, *Max* Jerry O'Connell, *Darrell* David Koechner, *with* Sean Faris, Katija Pevec, Dean Collins, Danielle Panabaker, Drake Bell, Miki Ishikawa, Josh Henderson, Bradley Gosnell.

• *Dir* Raja Gosnell, *Pro* Robert Simonds and Michael Nathanson, *Ex Pro* Ira Shuman, Richard Suckle and Tracey Trench, *Screenplay* Ron Birch and David Kidd, *Ph* Theo Van De Sande, *Pro Des* Linda DeScenna, *Ed* Stephen A. Rotter and Bruce Greeen, *M* Christophe Beck, *Costumes* Marie-Sylvie Deveau.

Paramount/MGM/Nickelodeon Movies/Columbia-Columbia TriStar.
88 mins. USA. 2005. Rel: 31 March 2006. Cert. PG.

Zathura: A Space Adventure ★★½

When their single father dashes out of the house for ten minutes, Danny and Walter – rival siblings – are left to their own devices. Danny wants to play; Walter just wants to watch sport on TV. Then Danny stumbles across an old board game in the basement, a game so realistic that Walter is forced to join in. It takes two to play and the stakes appear to be deadly... When Chris Van Allsburg sat down to write *Jumanji* – the story of a board game that comes to life – he can have little realised the monster he was creating. *Jumanji* was made into a successful movie in 1995 (with Robin Williams and Kirsten Dunst) and Van Allsburg set about writing *Zathura*, the story of a board game that comes to life. Ten years after *Jumanji* the special effects seem less amazing but the domestic dynamic is more interesting and is well played by the nine-year-old Jonah Bobo and 12-year-old Josh Hutcherson. However, there's something inescapably frustrating about watching people play a game that, as a viewer, you are unable to participate in. JC-W

• *Danny* Jonah Bobo, *Walter* Josh Hutcherson, *the astronaut* Dax Shepard, *Lisa* Kristen Stewart, *Dad* Tim Robbins, *voice of robot* Frank Oz.

• *Dir* Jon Favreau, *Pro* William Teitler, Scott Kroopf and Michael De Luca, *Ex Pro* Ted Field and Louis D'Esposito, *Co-Pro* Peter Billingsley, *Screenplay* David Koepp and John Kamps, *Ph* Guillermo Navarro, *Pro Des* J. Michael Riva, *Ed* Dan Lebental, *M* John Debney, *Costumes* Laura Jean Shannon.

Columbia/Radar Pictures/Teitler Film-Columbia TriStar.
101 mins. USA. 2005. Rel: 3 February 2006. Cert. PG.

Games that children play: Dax Shepard in Jon Favreau's frustrating *Zathura: A Space Adventure* (from Sony Pictures)

DVD Premieres

A selection of films released direct to DVD in the UK between July 2005 and June 2006.

by Daniel O'Brien

AMERICAN CRIME

A plucky TV journalist (Rachael Leigh Cook) pursues a serial killer who likes to videotape his crimes. Low on gore, this routine thriller has little new to offer. The media's exploitation – and glamorisation – of real-life crime has been better explored elsewhere. Connoisseurs of the daft may enjoy Cary Elwes' British 'True Crime' TV host.

Directed by Dan Mintz. Also starring Annabella Sciorra, Kip Pardue.
High Fliers. September 2005. Cert 15.

AMERICAN PIE PRESENTS: BAND CAMP

Clumsy title aside, this fourth instalment in the pastry humping franchise is woefully thin on laughs. Stifler's younger brother (Tad Hilgenbrinck) is sent to summer band camp, where he has fun with hidden cameras until true love turns his head. Series regular Eugene Levy does what he can with the substandard material. Former porn star Ginger Lynn Allen plays the camp nurse. A tired collection of sniggering hijinks, *Band Camp* seems to have a following among 15-year-old boys.
Note: This is the cut version of the film, trimmed to obtain an R rating in the US. At present, the full version is only available on Region 1 DVD.

Directed by Steve Rash. Also starring Arielle Kebbel, Jason Earles, Jun Hee Lee. Universal Pictures Video. October 2005. Cert 15.

ANIMAL

A ruthless criminal (Ving Rhames) reforms in prison, helped by a veteran black revolutionary (Jim Brown). Released on probation, he tries to prevent his son making the same mistakes. While the script is formulaic, committed performances give this urban crime drama an edge. Some accuse the film of PC propaganda, blaming all the characters' problems on institutional racism.

Directed by David J. Burke. Also starring Terrence Howard, Chazz Palminteri. High Fliers. January 2006. Cert 15.

ARAHAN

In this South Korean action comedy, a bumbling cop finds his career advancing when he learns the tai chi 'palm blast'. Fun enough, though we've been here many times before.

Directed by Ryu Seung Wan. Starring Jung Doo Hong, Ryu Seung Beom, Yoon So Yi. Optimum. July 2005. Cert 15.

BACK IN THE DAY

A young black man (Ja Rule), who escaped a life of poverty and crime, finds the past catching up when his affluent father is murdered. Looking for revenge, he recruits an ex-con friend (Ving Rhames), whose schemes extend beyond personal vengeance. A strong cast do their best with familiar material, as long-standing friendships are put to the test. Rapper Ja Rule is ably supported by Ving Rhames, still getting medieval after all these years.

Directed by James Hunter. Also starring Pam Grier, Frank Langella, Joe Morton, Tia Carrere.
High Fliers. August 2005. Cert 15.

BECAUSE OF WINN-DIXIE

Director Wayne Wang has abandoned the edge of his earlier work (*Eat a Bowl of Tea*, *Life is Cheap…But Toilet Paper is Expensive*, *Smoke*) for mainstream fare. *Because of Winn-Dixie* is at least an improvement on *Maid in Manhattan*. Anna Sophia Robb stars as a preacher's daughter, who wishes for a new best friend. Encountering a mind-reading dog in a Winn-Dixie supermarket, she takes him home. Based on a popular book, this amiable family comedy delivers an effective dose of feel-good entertainment. Taking their cue from *Pollyanna*, girl and dog bring happiness into lonely people's lives. Also starring Jeff Daniels, Eva Marie Saint, Cicely Tyson.

Twentieth Century Fox Home Entertainment. February 2006. Cert U.

BETWEEN YOUR LEGS

Made in 1999, this steamy Spanish thriller pays lavish homage to *Vertigo*. Director Manuel Gomez Pereira gets off to a strong start, with Victoria Abril and Javier Bardem as sex addicts whose affair leads to blackmail and murder. Unfortunately, the initial intrigue and tension are dissipated by redundant characters and subplots. Plausibility flies out of the window and the big payoff is an anticlimax. For all the surface dazzle and smoulder, the end result isn't in the Hitchcock league.

Also starring Carmelo Gomez.
Nucleus Films. September 2005. Cert 18.

BLACK DAWN

Steven Seagal is Jonathan Cold, ex CIA agent. Hoping for a quiet life, Cold is forced back into action when terrorists plot a nuclear explosion in Los Angeles. Standard Seagal fare, with the star over-reliant on his stunt double. Not to be confused with *Red Dawn*.

Directed by Alexander Gruszynski. Also starring Warren Derosa, Tamara Davis, Timothy Carhart.
Sony Pictures Home Entertainment. March 2006. Cert 15.

BLIND BEAST

Made in 1969, Yasuzo Masumara's bizarre psycho-drama remains a tense, unsettling experience. A blind sculptor (Eiji Funakoshi) obsessed with the female form kidnaps a young model (Mako Midori). Their subsequent relationship takes a very dark turn. Not for all tastes, but far more than mere sado-sexploitation.

Also starring Noriko Sengoku.
Yume Pictures. May 2006.
Cert 18.

THE BODYGUARD

An enjoyable Thai action comedy, directed by and starring Petchtai Wonghamlau. A bodyguard is fired after his employer's murder. He gets a chance to redeem himself when his dead boss' son is also threatened. Wonghamlau co-starred opposite Tony Jaa in the action smash hit *Ong Bak*. Jaa's cameo appearance in *The Bodyguard* will both intrigue and disappoint fans hoping for more of the new martial arts sensation.

Also starring Pumwaree Yodkamol.
Momentum Asia. September 2005. Cert 15.

BOY EATS GIRL

This Irish horror comedy is aimed straight at the teen market. A mother resurrects her dead son with a voodoo handbook from her local church. What could possibly go wrong? Hoping for another *Shaun of the Dead*, director Stephen Bradley delivers a patchy zombie farce with some questionable casting. Good title, though.

Starring Samantha Mumba, David Leon, Deirdre O'Kane, Sara James, Bryan Murray.
High Fliers. February 2006. Cert 18.

BRAM STOKER'S THE BURIAL OF THE RATS

Inspired by a Stoker short story, this 1995 schlock horror features the author as a character. Unfortunately, the good ideas end there. Set in 19th century France, the film has young Stoker (Kevin Alber) tangling with a man-hating cult of women and their army of rats. Can his literary skills save him from a lethal gnawing? Co-star Adrienne Barbeau – who appeared in John Carpenter's *The Fog* and *Escape from New York* and George Romero's *Creepshow* – plays the cult leader, who controls the rats with a flute. The black leather bikinis may not be historically accurate. Executive producer Roger Corman has been churning out this kind of stuff since the 1950s. Director Dan Golden has a cameo as 'Man with knife in back'. He deserved it. Some interpret the film as a feminist allegory. Yeah, right.

Also starring Maria Ford, Olga Kabo.
Anchor Bay UK. June 2006. Cert 18.

THE BROWN BUNNY

Existential masterpiece or self-indulgent drivel? Following its disastrous Cannes premiere in 2003, *The Brown Bunny* was re-edited – and tightened – to its current version. Producer-writer-director-cameraman-editor-star Vincent Gallo plays a motorbike racer on a cross country trip to nowhere. The main selling points are the striking landscapes and a notorious hardcore sex scene with Chloe Sevigny. While not in the same league as Gallo's *Buffalo 66*, *The Brown Bunny* is no disaster. As downbeat road movies go, there are certainly worse.

Also starring Cheryl Tiegs, Elizabeth Blake, Anna Vareschi.
Sony Pictures Home Entertainment.
October 2005. Cert 18.

COLD & DARK

When a vigilante starts killing London's biggest villains, Detective Luke Goss is put on the case. He soon learns that the culprit isn't quite human. Director Andrew Matthew Goth provides visual flair but little sense of pace. The script is often weak, leaving Goss – a competent actor – on his own. *Little Britain*'s Matt Lucas makes a cameo appearance as a wacky doctor.

Also starring Kevin Howarth, Carly Jane Turnball.
High Fliers. April 2006. Cert 18.

THE COLLINGSWOOD STORY

This imaginative low budget horror movie was a big hit on the festival circuit. Directed by Michael Costanza, the film focuses on a young student (Stephanie Dees) staying in a town with a bad past. Told entirely through webcams, *The Collingswood Story* builds the tension and sense of menace with some skill.

Also starring Johnny Burton, Grant Edmonds.
Anchor Bay UK. June 2006. Cert 18.

THE COMMITMENT

Set in Bangkok, this supernatural tale explores the problem of exam pressure in modern Thailand. Sort of. Desperate to get good grades, a group of friends make a reckless bargain with the spirit of a shrine in a derelict house. Bad idea. An effective teen horror from a different perspective.

Directed by Montri Kong Im. Starring Prangthong Changthom, Pinsuda Tanphairoh.
Anchor Bay UK. August 2005. Cert 18.

CONVICTED

A jaded ex-lawyer (Aidan Quinn) befriends and exploits death-row convicts, selling their last letters to the media. His latest target is a young woman (Connie Nielsen) awaiting execution for the murder of a child. Looking for another quick buck, he becomes convinced that she is innocent, protecting the real killer for reasons unknown. Offered a shot at redemption, he fights to prevent a miscarriage of justice before time runs out. Director Bille August conjures a gripping tale from a script by James Bond regulars Neal Purvis and Robert Wade. Quinn and Nielsen give strong performances, transcending the standard legal thriller formula. Original title: *Return to Sender*.

Also starring Kelly Preston.
High Fliers. November 2005. Cert 15.

THE CUTTING EDGE 2

A belated 'sequel' to the 1992 film, starring Christy Carlson Romano as the daughter of the original skating duo. This uptight princess is paired with a rollerblading jock (Ross Thomas) to compete for the figure skating gold medal. Clashing on and off the rink, the reluctant couple must put aside their differences and work as a team. Predictable – to say the least – this inferior sporting romance makes the original look a whole lot better. Also known as *The Cutting Edge – Going for Gold*.

Also starring Christine Lakin.
MGM Home Entertainment. February 2006. Cert 12.

THE DARK HOURS

The Canadian horror cinema has thrived – on and off – since the late 1960s, from David Cronenberg to *Ginger Snaps*. This psychological horror is a solid addition to the sub-genre. A psychiatrist with health problems is stalked by an ex-patient - a rapist and murderer – convinced she messed with his head during therapy sessions. Now it's his turn to play mind games. Largely confined to a remote rural cabin, the film is tense, claustrophobic and uncomfortable viewing. Whether or not that makes it good is another matter.

Directed by Paul Fox. Starring Kate Greenhouse, Aidan Devine, Iris Graham. Anchor Bay UK. June 2006. Cert 18.

DARK TALES OF JAPAN

Produced for Japanese television, this horror anthology offers five stories: 'The Spiderwoman', 'Crevices', 'The Sacrifice', 'Blond Kwaidan' and 'The Presentiment', linked by a spooky bus journey. As with most compendium films, the end result is uneven, with some weak scripts and rushed episodes. At least they saved the best till last. Shot on digital video.

Directed by Takashi Shimizu, Norio Tsuruta, Masayuki Ochiai, Yoshihiro Nakamura, Koji Shiraishi. Anchor Bay UK. February 2006. Cert 18.

DEAD & BREAKFAST

A wedding party road trip goes badly wrong in a small Texas town besieged by zombies. Horror comedies are difficult to pull off and this gory effort is decidedly uneven. The end result feels like a half hour short stretched to feature-length. Exploitation veteran David Carradine makes a cameo appearance, but *Dead & Breakfast* is no *Kill Bill*.

Written and directed by Matthew Leutwyler. Starring Erik Palladino, Jeremy Sisto, Portia de Rossi, Ever Carradine (David's niece). Anchor Bay UK. April 2006. Cert 18.

DEMON HUNTER

The Catholic Church uses Jake Greyman (Sean Patrick Flannery) to take out the demons its exorcists can't handle. Jake is half-human, half-demon, which gives him a certain edge. Arch-demon Asmodeus (Billy Drago) has evil designs on LA's most attractive hookers. Who you gonna call? Borrowing heavily from *Blade*, *Angel* and *Constantine*, *Demon Hunter* is a second rate shocker. Even Jake's nun sidekick can't save it.

Directed by Scott Ziehl. Anchor Bay UK. May 2006. Cert 18.

DIVERGENCE

A burnt-out cop is haunted by memories of his girlfriend, who disappeared ten years earlier. After meeting her 'double', the fiancée of a ruthless businessman, he becomes determined to solve the mystery. The success of *Infernal Affairs* spawned a rash of Hong Kong cop movies. Efficiently made, *Divergence* suffers from a convoluted script and a slow pace. Director Benny Chan has made some fine films, notably *A Moment of Romance*. This isn't even close.

Starring Aaron Kwok, Ekin Cheng, Daniel Wu. Momentum Asia. February 2006. Cert 15.

DOUBLE BANG

In this average thriller, honest cop William Baldwin must break the rules to avenge his corrupt partner's death. While the clichés come thick and fast, director Heywood Gould delivers an entertaining movie. Viewers seeking an in-depth study of police ethics will probably be disappointed. *Trivia:* Heywood Gould co-scripted *Rolling Thunder* (1977), one of Quentin Tarantino's favourite movies.

Also starring Elizabeth Mitchell, Adam Baldwin, Jon Seda Anchor Bay UK. October 2005. Cert 15.

DR. DOLITTLE 3

Dr. Dolittle's teenage daughter (Kyla Pratt) has the same ability to communicate with animals. Troubled at home, she's sent to the country, where she uses her gift to help an old farmer save his ranch. This second sequel continues the series without Eddie Murphy (what no cameo?), though Kristen Wilson returns as Mrs Dolittle. Kyla Pratt contends with a by-the-numbers script. Efficiently made, with an unsubtle message about finding yourself, the film trundles along to no great purpose.

Directed by Rich Thorne. Also starring John Amos. Twentieth Century Fox Home Entertainment. May 2006. Cert PG.

DRACULA 3000

This German-South African co-production is a science fiction spin on the Dracula story. Van Helsing (Casper Van Dien) is now a starship captain, who encounters something nasty in a derelict spacecraft. Could it be Count Dracula himself?

Ripping off Stoker, *Alien* and *Pitch Black*, this risible concoction doesn't even score as a camp classic. The actors look embarrassed and the rushed ending suggests the producers ran out of money. German actor Udo Kier, who played the Count in *Blood for Dracula* (1974), is wasted in a cameo role. Former Starship Trooper Van Dien deserves better than this.

Directed by Darrell Roodt. Also starring Erika Eleniak, Coolio. Anchor Bay UK. October 2005. Cert 15.

8MM 2 – VELVET SIDE OF HELL

An unrelated sequel to the less than wonderful 1999 film. In sunny Budapest, a US diplomat (Johnathon Schaech) and his fiancée (Lori Heuring) – the ambassador's daughter – engage in a threesome with a gorgeous 'model' (Zita Gorog). It turns out that a blackmailer filmed this steamy encounter. Faced with career ruin and social disgrace, the desperate couple are plunged into Budapest's seedy porn underworld. An uninspiring mixture of intrigue and soft porn, with the obligatory twist ending. Apparently, the film was shot as *The Velvet Side of Hell*, acquiring its sequel status at the last minute.

Directed by J.S. Cardone. Also starring Bruce Davison, Julie Benz. Sony Pictures Home Entertainment. December 2005. Cert 18.

END GAME

Cuba Gooding Jr.'s Oscar-win for *Jerry Maguire* didn't put him on Hollywood's A-list. This dismal political 'thriller' won't help his cause. When the US President is assassinated, a secret service agent and investigative journalist uncover a massive conspiracy. A reasonable premise is lost in a welter of poor dialogue, wooden acting and stilted direction. Cast as the guilt-ridden agent, who drinks to ease his pain, Gooding Jr. acts on autopilot. Co-stars James Woods and Burt Reynolds look like they'd rather be elsewhere. Watch *The Manchurian Candidate*, *The Parallax View*, *Blow Out*, *JFK* or just about anything else.

Directed by Andy Cheng. Also starring Patrick Fabian, Anne Archer, Jack Scalia. Sony Pictures Home Entertainment. May 2006. Cert 12.

THE FALLEN ONES

Produced, written, directed and edited by Kevin Van Hook, this old style monster movie boasts a 42ft mummy. Casper Van Dien makes a suitably dashing lead, ably supported by veterans Robert Wagner, Tom Bosley, and Geoffrey Lewis. Can our heroes avert a biblical apocalypse? Watch and see.

Also starring Kristen Miller, Carel Struycken (Lurch in the *Addams Family* movies).
Anchor Bay UK. May 2006. Cert 12.

FAT ALBERT

Fat Albert (Kenan Thompson) and friends leave their TV cartoon for the real world to help a lonely girl (Kyla Pratt). Based on the popular 1970s show, *Fat Albert* is fair family entertainment with a positive message. Bill Cosby, who created the original series, co-wrote the script and appears in a cameo. Apparently, Fat Albert and the gang have been toned down from the TV show to appease PC sensibilities. At least he's not called 'Differently Sized Albert'.

Directed by Joel Zwick. Also starring Keri Lynn Pratt.
Twentieth Century Fox Home Entertainment. March 2006. Cert U.

FLIGHT 93

The story of the 'fourth plane' on 9/11 is already the stuff of legend. This efficient TV movie has been overshadowed by Paul Greengrass' *United 93*. Given the subject matter and the times, it's hard to judge this dramatisation of a real-life tragedy by normal standards. Some feel the script veers into cliché and melodrama. Others claim the film is factually suspect. That said, it has undeniable power.

Directed by Peter Markle. Starring Jeffrey Nordling, Brennan Elliott, Colin Glazer, Monnae Michaell, April Talek.
Metrodome. May 2006. Cert 12.

FRANKENSTEIN

This update of Mary Shelley's novel was devised by horror author Dean Koontz, who left the project after creative differences. Intended as the pilot for a TV series, *Frankenstein* is set in New Orleans, where a serial killer is operating with surgical precision. Could he be harvesting body parts to create new super beings? Director

Marcus Nispel helmed the *Texas Chain Saw Massacre* remake. Working with more modest resources, he delivers an interesting variation on the *Frankenstein* myth that never fulfils its potential. Executive producer Martin Scorsese is a fan of Hammer horror films. Perhaps he should have given Nispel a few pointers.

Starring Parker Posey, Adam Goldberg, Michael Madsen, Vincent Perez, Thomas Kretschmann.
High Fliers. November 2005. Cert 18.

FREAK OUT

Four years in the making, on a budget of £30,000, this engaging British horror comedy sends up the slasher sub-genre. While none too polished, *Freak Out* transcends its no-budget origins, delivering gory laughs aplenty. Director Christian James, who also co-wrote the script, deserves full marks for effort.
Starring James Heathcote, Dan Palmer, Yazz Fetto.
Anchor Bay UK. May 2006. Cert 15.

THE GHOSTS OF EDENDALE

A young couple (Steven Wastell and Paula Ficara) move to Los Angeles, hoping to break into the movie business. Strange things happen in their new home, linked with the death of cowboy star Tom Mix many years before. Working on a miniscule budget, writer-director Stefan Avalos offers an intriguing premise, playing on the disparity between Mix's good guy persona and his less savoury real-life character. Playing on fantasy and illusion, Hollywood has more than its share of dark secrets. Unfortunately, the film turns into a low-rent retread of *The Shining*, losing much of its early interest.
Anchor Bay UK. April 2006. Cert 15.

THE GOOD SHEPHERD

A Catholic priest (Christian Slater) investigates a murder that prompted the suicide of a close friend. This Canadian-made drama falls flat in all departments. The mystery element and Catholic backdrop are equally perfunctory. Slater's worldly priest is about as convincing as his novice monk in *The Name of the Rose*. Also known as *The Confessor*.

Directed by Lewin Webb. Also starring Stephen Rea, Molly Parker, Gordon

Pinsent, Nancy Beatty.
Momentum. December 2005. Cert 15.

THE HAUNTING OF HELL HOUSE

Trite title aside, this is a fair adaptation of Henry James' story 'The Ghostly Rental'. Producer Roger Corman recaptures some of the style of his 1960s Edgar Allan Poe films starring Vincent Price. The Irish locations provide a sense of mood and atmosphere sometimes lacking in the script. Not to be confused with *The Haunting*, *The Legend of Hell House*, *House on Haunted Hill* or Corman's own *The Haunted Palace*.

Directed by Mitch Marcus. Starring Michael York, Claudia Christian, Jason Cottle.
Anchor Bay UK. June 2006. Cert 15.

HAZE

A man (Shinya Tsukamoto) wakes up in a cramped concrete cell, slowly bleeding to death from a stomach wound. Seeking a way out, he's confronted by hellish visions. Running just 49 minutes, this creepy tale is a mini *tour de force* from writer-director-star Tsukamoto. Despite nods to *Cube*, *Saw* and *Oldboy*, *Haze* is an original, unsettling piece of work.

Also starring Kahori Fujii, Takahiro Kandaka.
Terra. May 2006. Cert 18.

HELL

In this Bangkok ghost story, survivors of a mini-van crash find themselves in limbo, caught between life and death. Unfortunately, they are not alone. Effective, if familiar, low budget Eastern horror. Just don't expect in-depth characterisation.

Directed by Thanit Jitnukul. Starring Nathawan Woravit, Kom Chauncheun, Wuttinan Maikan.
Anchor Bay UK. June 2006. Cert 15.

HOBOKEN HOLLOW

Deep in the heart of Texas, a crazed family with a dark secret prey on hitchhikers. Sound familiar? Based on real events, this derivative shocker is unpleasant without being interesting. Writer-director Glen Stephens serves up the usual atrocities with little conviction and less effect. Leading man C. Thomas Howell did much better in *The Hitcher* (1986).

Also starring Michael Madsen, Dennis Hopper, Jason Connery, Robert Carradine, Dedee Pfeiffer (Michelle's sister). High Fliers. April 2006. Cert 18.

THE HOUSE ON TERROR TRACT

This horror anthology stars the late John Ritter as an estate agent trying to shift some troublesome properties. These Houses That Dripped Blood prompt three stories, 'Nightmare', 'Bobo' and 'Come to Granny'. While the episodes are uneven, the last instalment delivers some chills. Ritter gives a game performance as the realtor from hell (figuratively or otherwise).

Directed by Lance W. Dreesen & Clint Hutchison. Also starring Bryan Cranston, Allison Smith, Brenda Strong. Original title: *Terror Tract*. Anchor Bay UK. October 2005. Cert 15.

ICE PRINCESS

A teenager (Michelle Trachtenburg) whose mother pushes her to excel at school dreams of becoming a skating star. A feelgood family movie about the pressures of parental ambition and the importance of finding your own way in life. Passable entertainment for fans of ice skating or Trachtenburg, late of *Buffy the Vampire Slayer*.

Directed by Tim Fywell. Also starring Joan Cusack, Kim Cattrall. Buena Vista Home Entertainment. August 2005. Cert U.

KARLA

This grim drama tells the real-life story of Karla Homolka (Laura Prepon) and Paul Bernardo (Mischa Collins), Canada's most notorious serial killers. A respectable, well-liked couple, Paul was an abusive womaniser, while Karla became increasingly desperate – and ruthless – to hold on to him. Paul kidnapped, drugged, raped and murdered three woman, helped by Karla. One of the victims was her younger sister. While they were caught and convicted, many feel that justice wasn't done. Director Joel Bender, who also co-wrote, avoids sensationalism and the lead performances are chilling. Whether *Karla* needed to be made at all is another matter. This controversial film was shot in the US, as no-one in the Canadian film industry would get involved.

Also starring Tess Harper, Patrick Bauchau. High Fliers. June 2006. Cert 18.

THE LAST SIGN

A young widow (Andie MacDowell) is haunted by the spirit of her abusive alcoholic husband (Tim Roth), recently killed in a car crash. This substandard ghost story wastes a good cast. Roth has little screen time, French actor Samuel Le Bihan is dubbed and Margot Kidder is confined to a pointless cameo. MacDowell, who peaked with *Groundhog Day*, can't carry the film single-handed. While the themes of loss, regret and forgiveness have potential, the script isn't up to the job.

Directed by Douglas Law. High Fliers. October 2005. Cert 15.

LILO & STITCH 2: STITCH HAS A GLITCH

The May Day hula competition is threatened when Stitch suffers a malfunction. Can Lilo help her alien friend and triumph on the big day? This amiable cartoon sequel should please fans of the original. That said, some feel Dakota Fanning's voice is wrong for Lilo. Never fear, Daveigh Chase returns for the next sequel.

Directed by Michael LaBash, Anthony Leondis. Also starring Christopher Sanders, Tia Carrere, Jason Scott Lee, David Ogden Stiers. Buena Vista Home Entertainment. August 2005. Cert U.

THE LITTLE NORSE PRINCE

This 1968 animated feature places Japanese mythology in a Norse backdrop. A young boy seeks the demon who killed his father, learning some valuable life lessons along the way. Directed by Isao Takahata, *The Little Norse Prince* is a charming fantasy, with interesting design and first rate animation. Three years in the making, the film had a troubled production, which explains the use of static images in one scene. A box-office flop in Japan, *The Little Norse Prince* quickly became a cult favourite. The key animator was Hayao Miyazaki, who went on to direct such classics as *Kiki's Delivery Service*, *Laputa*, *Porco Rosso* (see below), *Princess Mononoke* and *Spirited Away*. Optimum Home Entertainment. October 2005. Cert U.

LIZARD WOMAN

A remote cave contains a sacred box. Inside the box is a carved stone lizard. Can gory demonic possession be far away? A solid, if bloody chunk of Thai horror.

Written and directed by Manop Udomdej. Starring Rungravee Brijindakul, Pete Thongchua. Anchor Bay UK. May 2006. Cert 18.

LONG DISTANCE

After dialling a wrong number, a young woman finds herself talking to a serial killer. He subsequently calls her back, from the scenes of his murders. As the killings continue, he gets closer and closer. Average thriller, with a big twist.

Directed by Marcus Stern. Starring Monica Keena, Ivan Martin, Tamala Jones, Kevin Chapman. High Fliers. May 2006. Cert 15.

MALEVOLENCE

After a botched heist, bank robbers take hostages and look for a hideout. Unfortunately, they pick a house where bad things happened ten years earlier. This throwback to 1980s slasher movies is watchable but very familiar.

Directed by Stevan Mena. Starring Brandon Johnson, Heather Magee, Richard Glover, Samantha Dark. Anchor Bay UK. September 2005. Cert 15.

MAN THING

This eco horror movie is based on a Marvel Comics character. In swamp-infested Louisiana, locals are disappearing, only to return as mangled corpses. Has the local oil tycoon upset something more lethal than the environmentalists? Looks like it. Viewers of *Frogs*, *Squirm*, *Prophecy* and *Humanoids from the Deep* will have a fair idea what to expect. Filmed in Australia (it's cheaper).

Directed by Brett Leonard. Starring Matthew Le Nevez, Rachael Taylor, Jack Thompson. Optimum. May 2006. Cert 15.

THE MARKSMAN

Oh Wesley Snipes, where did it all go wrong? With the *Blade* franchise out of gas/guts, Snipes looks set for a long stretch on the 'B' list. After this movie, he'll be lucky to make the 'Z' list. When Chechen terrorists threaten to blow up a nuclear plant, our man Wesley is put on the case. Having thwarted their plot, he finds himself in the middle of a double-cross. Feeble in all departments.

Directed by Marcus Adams.
Also starring Anthony Warren,
Emma Samms (from *Dynasty*).
Sony Pictures Home Entertainment.
December 2005. Cert 15.

MY NAME IS MODESTY

This super-agent movie originated with Quentin Tarantino, a big fan of Peter O'Donnell's comic strip heroine (check out John Travolta's bathroom reading in *Pulp Fiction*). Persuading Miramax to buy the rights, Tarantino had problems with the script, placing the project on hold. To retain their option on the franchise, Miramax produced this low budget 'B' version. Tarantino agreed to the 'Quentin Tarantino Presents' banner, which may mislead some viewers into thinking he was involved with the film. Shot in Bucharest, Romania, *My Name is Modesty* explores the character's origins, which prove uninteresting. Director Scott Spiegel shows little flair for the material and Alexandra Staden is inadequate as the eponymous heroine. It doesn't even have the camp/nostalgia appeal of Joseph Losey's 1966 film.

Also starring Nikolaj Coster-Waldau, Raymond Cruz, Fred Pearson.
Buena Vista Home Entertainment.
June 2006. Cert 18.

THE NET 2.0

A young computer analyst (Nikki Deloach) takes a new job in Istanbul, only to find her identity stolen and the cops on her tail. A lacklustre 'sequel' to the 1995 Sandra Bullock movie, itself no classic. Director Charles Winkler is the son of producer Irwin Winkler, who directed the original movie.

Also starring Derret Akbag, Neil Hopkins, Sebnem Donmez.
Sony Pictures Home Entertainment.
February 2006. Cert 15.

ONCE UPON A TIME IN HIGH SCHOOL

A South Korean coming-of-age tale, with romance and punch-ups. In 1978, a shy teenage boy (Kwon Sang Woo) enrols in a harsh new high school, where the staff are scarier than the bullies. Inspired by Bruce Lee, our hero uses his martial arts skills to fight back. Alas, his dream girl fancies his more charismatic best friend. Nothing new, but generally well done. Just don't expect non-stop kung fu action.

Written and directed by Ha Yu. Also starring Lee Jung Jin, Han Ga In.
Premier Asia. April 2006. Cert 15.

OUT FOR BLOOD

The already stretched LAPD is faced with an outbreak of vampire attacks. Luckily, these bloodsuckers can be found at the local Goth fetish club. Where else? When cop Kevin Dillon is bitten, he must fight both the undead and his own bloodlust. Having already faced *The Blob*, Dillon returns to monster fighting with dogged professionalism. The rest of the film is a familiar trawl through the vampire basics. Also known as *Vampires: Out for Blood*.

Written and directed by Richard Brandes. Also starring Lance Henriksen, Vanessa Angel.
Anchor Bay UK. July 2005. Cert 18.

THE PEACOCK KING

This Hong Kong-Japanese fantasy stars Yuen Biao, Gloria Yip and Gordon Liu, recently seen in *Kill Bill*. Mankind's depravity is causing the Four Holes of Hell to open up. When the last hole is opened, Hell King will be unleashed on the world. Only brave monks Peacock (Yuen) and Lucky Fruit (Hiroshi Makami) can stop him. The most memorable character is demonic *femme fatale* Raga (Pauline Wong) who literally eats men alive. Director Nam Nai Choi made such exploitation classics as *The Ghost Snatchers*, *The Seventh Curse*, *Erotic Ghost Story* and *The Story of Ricky*. *The Peacock King* has some great scenes, despite peaking too early. As apocalyptic action movies go, this is pretty good. Beware the dreadful sequel, *Saga of the Phoenix*.
Hong Kong Legends. June 2006. Cert 15.

PORCO ROSSO

Japanese animator Hayao Miyazaki achieved his western breakthrough with *Princess Mononoke* and *Spirited Away*. This 1992 production is regarded as one of his best films. Set in 1920s Italy, it follows the adventures of Porco Rosso, a part-man part-pig aviator. A World War I veteran, he now earns a meagre living fighting sky pirates. Porco Rosso's friends include a young female mechanic, who fixes his damaged plane. Set against the rise of fascism, *Porco Rosso* is filled with quirky characters and exciting aerial sequences. Presumably, Porco's piglike features – explained by a curse - are a metaphor for the traumatic effects of war. This charming, one-of-a-kind film is well worth a look.
Optimum Home Entertainment.
January 2006. Cert PG.

REBOUND

This family comedy is a cynical piece of filmmaking-by-committee. Martin Lawrence stars as an arrogant basketball coach whose bad attitude has stalled his career. Obliged to coach a high school team, he turns a group of no-hopers into winners, regaining his integrity in the process. Stale and predictable.

Directed by Steve Carr. Also starring Wendy Raquel Robinson, Breckin Mayer, Oren Williams.
Twentieth Century Fox. February 2006.
Cert PG.

SAINTS AND SOLDIERS

This low budget World War II drama has been acclaimed as a 'sleeper' classic. In 1944 Belgium, a group of American POWs escape a German massacre. Struggling to get behind Allied lines, they encounter a British intelligence officer who holds vital information. Filmed in Utah, *Saints and Soldiers* favours characters over action. Generally well made, it revisits familiar themes – duty versus survival, the thin line between friend and foe – with modest success. Some claim the film is a vehicle for the makers' Mormon beliefs.

Directed by Ryan Little. Starring Corbin Alfred, Alexander Niver, Kirby Heybourne, Lawrence Bagby, Peter Holden.
Metrodome. January 2006. Cert 15.

SAMURAI COMMANDO: MISSION 1548

Japanese soldiers are sent back in time to the feudal era. This causes mini black holes to appear in modern Japan, threatening the entire planet. A second squad travel through time on a rescue mission that could reverse the effect. It's a long shot but it just might work. This big budget fantasy is a remake of the Sonny Chiba film *Timeslip* (1979), aka *GI Samurai*, itself based on a popular book by Ryo Hanmura. *Samurai Commando* lacks the visceral quality of Chiba's version, but it's not bad as time travel paradox action movies go.

Directed by Masaaki Tezuka.
Starring Yosuke Eguchi, Kyoka Suzuki, Haruka Ayase.
Momentum Asia. May 2006. Cert 15.

SECOND IN COMMAND

The US embassy in an East European country is besieged by trigger-happy rebels. Second in command Sam Keenan (Jean-Claude Van Damme) fights back with his formidable martial arts skills. Frankly, it's no contest. An above average Van Damme vehicle, with solid production values. After a run of poor movies (*Derailed* anyone?), the veteran action star seems to have his act together. Just don't expect subtlety.

Directed by Simon Fellows. Also starring Julie Cox., William Tapley.
Sony Pictures Home Entertainment.
May 2006. Cert 15.

SEOUL RAIDERS

This Hong Kong action comedy is a sequel to *Tokyo Raiders*. Tony Leung Chiu Wai returns as the agent-for-hire, backed by Shu Qi and Richie Ren. Director Jingle Ma delivers some reasonable action set-pieces against the South Korean backdrop. Watchable, but there are much better Hong Kong thrillers on the market.
Hong Kong Legends. February 2006.
Cert 12.

SHE SHOOTS STRAIGHT

This 1990 Hong Kong cop movie was a vehicle for Australasian actress Joyce Godenzi. An ambitious police officer must contend with vicious crooks and hostile in-laws, who despise her mixed-race ancestry. Directed by Cory Yuen, *She Shoots Straight* is a fair action movie with domestic asides. It's also one of the few Hong Kong films to touch on Chinese racism. Godenzi's forceful performance balances her limited fighting ability.

Also starring Tony Leung Ka Fai, Carina Lau, Sandra Ng, Yuen Wah, Sammo Hung (also the producer and Godenzi's husband).

Hong Kong Legends. May 2006. Cert 15.

SHOOTING GALLERY

Down in New Orleans, a young pool hustler (Freddie Prinze Jr.) must contend with a treacherous mentor and corrupt vice cop. Touted as a change of pace for lightweight star Prinze Jr., this routine thriller hardly bears comparison with *The Color of Money*, let alone *The Hustler*. Any dramatic potential is dissipated by fidgety direction and lacklustre performances. Prinze Jr. looked more comfortable in the *Scooby Doo* movies.

Written and directed by Keoni Waxman.
Also starring Ving Rhames, Devon Sawa, Roselyn Sanchez.
High Fliers. December 2005. Cert 15.

SILVER HAWK

Michelle Yeoh has been a star in the Far East for over twenty years. She stole *Tomorrow Never Dies* and *Crouching Tiger, Hidden Dragon* from Pierce Brosnan and Chow Yun Fat. A charismatic performer, Yeoh is also an action star of the first rank. That said, she's
appeared in some real duds and *Silver Hawk* is a prime example. Based on a Chinese comic book, this is a limp superheroine fantasy, unworthy of Yeoh's talent. The plot, involving brainwashing via mobile phone, is as perfunctory as the action set-pieces. Yeoh covered similar ground to much better effect in *The Heroic Trio* and its sequel *The Executioners*.
Note: Silver Hawk was released in both English and Cantonese versions. This is the English version, with Yeoh and co-star Luke Goss dubbing themselves.

Directed by Jingle Ma. Also starring Michael Jai White, Richie Jen Hsien Chi. Momentum Asia. September 2005. Cert 15.

SNUFF BOTTLE CONNECTION

This 1977 martial arts drama is a good example of the genre. During the Ching Dynasty, a government agent investigates a corrupt magistrate and his Russian ally. The fight scenes were staged by Yuen Woo Ping, now internationally famous for his work on *The Matrix, Crouching Tiger, Hidden Dragon, Kill Bill* and many more.

Directed by Lui Le Le and Tung Kan Wu. Starring John Liu, Jang Lee Hwang, Roy

Horan, Yuen Biao.
Soul Blade. May 2006. Cert 15.

SOUTH OF HEAVEN, WEST OF HELL

Made in 2000, this turgid western was a vanity project for country music star Dwight Yoakam, who co-wrote, directed and co-stars. In old Arizona, an honest marshal (Yoakam) goes up against the murderous Henry Gang, his former childhood friends. A familiar premise is sunk by the poor script, sluggish pacing and excessive length. Yoakam wastes a strong cast, including Billy Bob Thornton, Vince Vaughn, Bridget Fonda, Peter Fonda and Luke Askew. Nice photography, though.
High Fliers. December 2005. Cert 18.

STRANGELAND

This gory shocker was written and produced by Dee Snider, frontman of glam metal band Twisted Sister. Snider also stars as Captain Howdy, a serial killer with a liking for the internet and extreme S/M. While derivative in the extreme, with nods to *The Exorcist* and *Silence of the Lambs*, *Strangeland* is good nasty fun.

Directed by John Pieplow. Also starring Robert Englund, Linda Cardellini, Elizabeth Pena.
Anchor Bay UK. May 2006. Cert 18.

STUART LITTLE 3: CALL OF THE WILD

This animated sequel features the voices of original stars Michael J. Fox, Geena Davis and Hugh Laurie. While the story and design are nothing special, the end result is solid family entertainment.

Directed by Audu Paden.
Also starring Wayne Brady, Virginia Madsen.
Sony Pictures Home Entertainment.
February 2006. Cert U.

SUBMERGED

A submarine is trapped on the ocean floor, filled with terrorists, traitors and a deadly bio weapon cargo. Outside lurk monsters and a hostile navy destroyer. Looks like a job for Steven Seagal and luckily he's the star of this film. Directed and co-scripted by Anthony Hickox, *Submerged* is a mishmash of elements from every other film set underwater. Seagal relies heavily on stunt and doubles, though apparently this wasn't his decision. A British-Bulgarian co-production.

Also starring Vinnie Jones, Christine Adams, Nick Brimble, P.H. Moriarty, Gary Daniels.
Sony Pictures Home Entertainment. September 2005. Cert 15.

SURVIVE STYLE 5+

Directed by Gen Sekiguchi, this Japanese spin on *Pulp Fiction* blends thrills, horror and comedy with some success. The various storylines eventually come together for a satisfying payoff. Stylish and hugely enjoyable. Vinnie Jones plays one of those philosophical hitmen who make people think before blowing their heads off.

Also starring Tadanobu Asano, Sonny Chiba.
Manga. May 2006. Cert 18.

TRACKS

This gruelling drama was a personal exorcism for producer-writer-director Peter Wade, who based the script on his own experiences. A gang of New Jersey teenagers play a dangerous prank which causes a fatal accident. Tried as adults, they are given harsh prison sentences. The main character struggles to adjust to life inside while dealing with his guilt. Though not avoiding cliché, *Tracks* is an effective film, reflecting Wade's obvious sincerity.

Starring Chris Gunn, Ice T, John Heard.
High Fliers. March 2006. Cert 15.

THE UGLIEST WOMAN IN THE WORLD

Set in 2010 Madrid, this science fiction comedy thriller satirizes society's obsession with physical beauty. The hero is a toothless, one-eyed detective. Director Miguel Bardem hedges his bets, creating a film that can be read as both misogynist and feminist.

Starring Roberto Alvarez, Elia Galera, Hector Alterio.

Nucleus. September 2005. Cert 15.

VOODOO MOON

A brother and sister (Eric Mabius and Charisma Carpenter) with special powers return to their home town, where a demon slaughtered the rest of the population twenty years earlier. It's payback time. This derivative shocker is weak in all departments. Even a cameo from Jeffrey *Reanimator* Combs can't save it. Hopefully just a glitch in Charisma Carpenter's post *Buffy/Angel* career. That said, she's getting a little old for this kind of role.

Written and directed by Kevin Van Hook. Also starring Geoffrey Lewis, Rik Young.
Anchor Bay UK. June 2006. Cert 18.

WAKE OF DEATH

An ex-mob enforcer (Jean-Claude Van Damme) pursues the triad kingpin responsible for his wife's death. Despite a troubled production, this dark, tense thriller was hailed as a comeback by Van Damme fans. He gives a more nuanced performance than usual, with first rate support from Hong Kong star Simon Yam. Certainly worth a look for those who'd lost faith in the Brussels butt-kicker.

Directed by Philippe Martinez (and Ringo Lam, uncredited). Also starring Philip Tan, Valerie Jian, Burt Kwouk, Jacqui Chan (sic).
Sony Pictures Home Entertainment. August 2005. Cert 18.

WHITE DRAGON

A period kung fu comedy, involving a noblewoman and a warrior. Directed and co-written by Wilson Yip, the film offers good action scenes and a lot of turgid romance. Hong Kong comedy remains an acquired taste for most western viewers.

Starring Cecilia Cheung, Francis Ng, Andy On.
Sony Pictures Home Entertainment. March 2006. Cert 12.

ZERO DAY

After a high school massacre, the killers' video diary is found. Inspired by the Columbine murders, this unsettling drama eschews the lyricism of Gus Van Sant's *Elephant*. Telling the story from the killers' perspective, writer-director Ben Coccio refuses to demonise or explain them. Andre Keuck and Calvin Robertson are chilling as the teenage gunmen, fatally disconnected from the world around them. *Note:* The BBFC have cut a hefty 3m, 18s from this release, to remove details of making explosive devices and evading capture.

Also starring Rachel Benichak.
High Fliers. June 2006. Cert 18.

ZOMBIE HONEYMOON

Honeymooning newlyweds are attacked by a zombie, who bites the husband. As he transforms into one of the undead, his wife stands by him. Fans of writer-director David Gebroe's horror comedy praise its romanticism and emphasis on character. Others may feel it's a one idea movie, neither original nor well done. Connoisseurs of obscure horror may recall *Neither the Sea Nor the Sand* (1972), which plays the same story with a straight face. Starring Graham Sibley, Tracy Coogan, Tonya Cornelisse, David M. Wallace.
High Fliers. March 2006. Cert 15.

Faces of the Year

AMY ADAMS

Born: 20 August 1975 in
Vicenza, Italy

In a nutshell: After small roles in Steven
Spielberg's *Catch Me if You Can* and
the British romcom *The Wedding Date*,
Amy Adams joined the ensemble in
Junebug. A low-budget, highly personal
film from first-time director Phil
Morrison, *Junebug* was a comic, tender
and terribly real portrait of the divide
between the Deep South and urban
enlightenment. As the eager-to-please,
voluble and very pregnant Ashley, Amy
Adams was funny and heart-breaking.
The performance won the actress – who
grew up in Colorado – a Special Jury
Prize at Sundance and the award for
Best Supporting Actress from the
National Society of Film Critics. More
significantly, it brought her an Oscar
nomination and a slew of upcoming
projects, including Mike Nichols'
Charlie Wilson's War with Tom Hanks,
Julia Roberts and Philip Seymour
Hoffman.

STEVE CARELL

Born: 16 August 1963 in Acton,
Massachusetts

In a nutshell: *Premiere* magazine dubbed
him Hollywood's New King of Comedy
and rated him a hotter star than his good
friend Will Ferrell. A couple of years
ago, the mild-mannered actor could
never have imagined his meteoric rise
to comedic supremacy. Having played
the droll support for 15 years – he had a
delicious turn as a non sequitur-spouting
weatherman in *Anchorman: The Legend
of Ron Burgundy* – Carell starred in the
American remake of the BBC's *The Office*
and *The 40-Year-Old Virgin*. The latter
grossed $177million worldwide and
turned Carell into a box-office entity. He
followed this with an inspired supporting
turn in one of the finest comedies of
2006, *Little Miss Sunshine* – as a suicidal
authority on Marcel Proust – and played
a squirrel introduced to the joys of
caffeine in the enormously successful *Over
the Hedge*. He now has six major projects
lined up, notably the sequel *Evan*

Almighty (taking over from Jim Carrey's
Bruce) and *Get Smart*.

HUGH DANCY

Born: 19 June 1975 in Stoke-on-Trent,
Staffordshire, England

In a nutshell: With his dashing good
looks and appealing demeanour, Hugh
Dancy is in danger of becoming the next
Orlando Bloom. However, in spite of
doing time in such lightweight vehicles
as *Ella Enchanted*, *King Arthur* and *Basic
Instinct 2*, Dancy proved his acting chops
in Michael Caton-Jones' searing, very
human take on the Rwandan genocide,
Shooting Dogs. Having carved his name
in the TV classics (he was on the cover
of the reissued paperbacks of both *David
Copperfield* and *Daniel Deronda*), Dancy
is moving in even bigger circles and
will next be seen in the films *Blood and
Chocolate*, *Shamrock Bay* and, opposite
Claire Danes, Toni Collette and Vanessa
Redgrave, in Lajos Koltai's *Evening*.

NAOMIE HARRIS

Born: 6 September 1976 in London

In a nutshell: In the year's most successful movie, *Pirates of the Caribbean: Dead Man's Chest*, Naomie Harris played the seductive voodoo sorceress Tia Dalma. Then, four weeks after *Pirates* had shattered box-office records, the film was knocked off the number one spot by *Miami Vice* – also featuring Ms Harris. In the latter she played Jamie Foxx's alluring colleague and girlfriend who gets to shoot big guns and, in a steamy shower scene, to reveal all. However, before that Ms Harris had already clocked up notable appearances in *28 Days Later*, *Trauma* and *A Cock and Bull Story*, revealing a grounded sexuality and astonishing versatility. She also played Clara in the Channel Four adaptation of Zadie Smith's *White Teeth* and will next appear in sequels to both *28 Days* and *Pirates*.

SCOTT MECHLOWICZ

Born: 17 January 1981 in New York City

In a nutshell: A cross between a young Anthony Perkins and Brad Pitt, Scott Mechlowicz made his presence felt in three distinctly different movies. After a supporting turn in the fantasy *Neverland*, he landed the lead in *EuroTrip*, playing a horny Yank in pursuit of his German e-pal. While adhering to the gross-out template of current teen comedies, *EuroTrip* did boast a certain comic creativity as well as a beguiling energy. Then, in the critically praised *Mean Creek*, Mechlowicz won plaudits for his role as a youth with unpredictable currents of violence, made all the more chilling by the actor's innate stillness. He expanded on this style – with an added dash of charm – for the Anglo-Australian *Gone*, an average thriller more than elevated by his presence. Next, he stars opposite Nick Nolte in the German-American drama *Peaceful Warrior*.

MICHELLE MONAGHAN

Born: 23 March 1976 in Winthrop, Iowa

In a nutshell: Not unlike a young Kathleen Turner, Michelle Monaghan turned in a socking portrayal of humour, grit and sensuality in Shane Black's witty and irreverent *Kiss Kiss Bang Bang*. Had the film been a bigger hit, Monaghan would already be a star. In the words of the designer Sari Gueron, Monaghan 'effortlessly combines old Hollywood glamour and New York cool', while Charlize Theron went on record as saying that she's 'one of the funniest people I've ever met in my life.' Although thirty, Monaghan changed gear dramatically as a 19-year-old mine worker in *North Country* (who is memorably humiliated in a portaloo) and then played Tom Cruise's captivating wife in *Mission: Impossible III*. Next, she will be seen in Ben Affleck's directorial debut, *Gone, Baby, Gone*, and opposite Ben Stiller in the Farrelly brothers' *Seven Day Itch*.

KELLY REILLY

Born: 18 July 1977 in Surrey, England

In a nutshell: Although Kelly Reilly had made her film debut back in 2000 – in Ben Elton's *Maybe Baby* – few noticed her until five years later when, suddenly, she seemed to be everywhere. She played Caroline Bingley in the enormously popular *Pride & Prejudice*, took her clothes off in *Mrs Henderson Presents*, paid oral service to Johnny Depp in *The Libertine* and bolstered Anglo-French relations in the playful and romantic *Russian Dolls*. On stage, she was nominated for an Olivier award in Patrick Marber's *After Miss Julie* and, at the time of writing, was romantically linked with the actor J.J. Feild. Next, she stars in the Somerset-set thriller *Puffball* directed by none other than Nicolas Roeg.

ELLEN PAGE

Born: 21 February 1987 in Halifax, Nova Scotia

In a nutshell: In her native Canada, Ellen Page had already made an impact at the age of eleven, landing the part of Maggie MacLean in the TV series *Pit Pony* and later winning the Genie – the Canadian Emmy – for her guest role in the sci-fi series *ReGenesis* (2005). However, it wasn't until 2006 that the actress, now 18, took the world of international cinema by storm. In the tense, claustrophobic and hair-raising *Hard Candy*, Miss Page played a precocious 14-year-old seductress called Hayley Stark. Then, in an astonishing about-face, Hayley turns into a ruthless predator who may or may not have her reasons, let alone any sense of morality. And for those who failed to catch her in one of the year's most arresting indies, she showed up in *X-Men: The Last Stand* playing Shadowcat, a mutant who can levitate and pass through walls. Next, she starred opposite Catherine Keener in Tommy O'Haver's *An American Crime*, a true story of the unlawful incarceration of the teenager Sylvia Likens.

BRANDON ROUTH

Born: 9 October 1979 in Des Moines, Iowa

In a nutshell: Brandon Routh was working in a bowling alley when he was first approached to play the Man of Steel. The casting process took seven months, from the time Routh spilled coffee over director Bryan Singer (a perfect Clark Kent moment) to the signing of the contract. Well, the wait seemed to pay off as Routh – bearing a striking resemblance to Christopher Reeve – won laudatory reviews, prompting *The Daily Telegraph* to gush that he 'is terrific, the heartbeat of an exhilarating film.' At the time of writing, *Superman Returns* had racked up $340 million worldwide.

BEN WHISHAW

Born: 14 October 1980 in the UK

In a nutshell: Having played Keith Richards in Stephen Woolley's *Stoned*, Whishaw moved on to the lead in *Perfume: The Story of a Murderer*. In the latter, he plays Jean-Baptiste Grenouille, the amoral protagonist of Patrick Süskind's acclaimed novel, a perfumer who kills people in order to own their scent. The German director Tom Tykwer (*Ron Lola Run*, *Heaven*) calls the shots, while Whishaw's co-stars include Alan Rickman, Rachel Hurd-Wood and Dustin Hoffman. Whishaw, who played Hamlet at the Old Vic aged 23, is accruing enormous interest in the industry and has also appeared in the films *The Trench*, *Enduring Love* and *Layer Cake*. Next, he joins Richard Gere, Cate Blanchett, Julianne Moore, Heath Ledger and Christian Bale in Todd Haynes' Bob Dylan biopic *I'm Not There*.

Hugh Dancy

Naomie Harris

Scott Mechlowicz

Michelle Monaghan

Kelly Reilly

Ellen Page

Brandon Routh

Ben Whishaw

Film World Diary
July 2005 – June 2006

JULY 2005

Fantastic Four grosses $100 million in the US – in ten days • **Jude Law** publicly acknowledges that he has cheated on fiancée **Sienna Miller** with his children's nanny, Daisy Wright, a 26-year-old au pair. Sienna is so upset that she cancels her appearance in the London production of *As You Like It* • **Haley Joel Osment**, the angel-faced star of *The Sixth Sense* and *A.I. Artificial Intelligence*, is hospitalised after losing control of his car in Pasadena, California. Apparently, Osment's 1995 Saturn was hit by a brick pillar and 'flipped' • **Daniel Baldwin**, member of the once-idolised sibling clan, is hospitalised after losing control of his car in Los Angeles, California. Apparently, Baldwin's Ford Thunderbird was hit by two parked cars when the actor was speeding down a street at 129 kilometres per hour in the company of an unnamed female passenger. He was driving with a suspended licence and is suffering back and neck pain • **Angelina Jolie** adopts a baby girl, Zahara Marley Jolie, from Ethiopia. Zahara, whose parents died from Aids, will join Angelina's three-year-old adopted son Maddox at their Buckinghamshire home • **Colin Farrell** is granted a temporary restraining order to prevent former girlfriend **Nicole Narain**, Playboy's Miss January 2002, from selling or distributing a 15-minute home video of them having sex • *War of the Worlds* grosses $200m in the US • *Charlie and the Chocolate Factory* grosses $100m Stateside – in under ten days.

AUGUST 2005

Scarlett Johansson puts paid to rumours that she had sex with **Benicio Del Toro** in the lift at Los Angeles' Chateau Marmont hotel. 'If you've ever been in a Chateau Marmont elevator, you'll know,' the actress set the record straight. 'You can barely stand, let alone do anything like that' • In a candid interview in the *New York Daily News*, **Joaquin Phoenix** denies that he suffered a nervous collapse while working on *Walk the Line*. The actor was alleged to have broken down while filming a scene in which Cash recalls the death of his older brother from a wood saw accident. Joaquin, whose own brother River died from a drugs overdose, remonstrated that, 'the press has imposed upon me the title of "mourning brother". I don't need to pull from my experience for a character – I've never understood why actors would, except for a lack of ability, imagination or research' • **Eddie Murphy**'s wife Nicole files for divorce, citing 'irreconcilable differences' • **Scarlett Johansson** rams her Mercedes into another car outside Disneyland while escaping paparazzi, who had been trailing her for 45 minutes.

SEPTEMBER 2005

Chad Michael Murray and **Sophia Bush**, co-stars of TV's *One Tree Hill*, decide to call it a day. The couple have been married five months • **Sean Penn** hires a boat and rows into New Orleans to help survivors of Hurricane Katrina. *Rolling Stone* journalist **Douglas Brinkley** was impressed: 'I witnessed him rescuing up to forty people. He was an American hero.' • **Jennifer Jason Leigh** and filmmaker **Noah Baumbach** (*The Squid and the Whale*) tie the knot over the Labour Day weekend • **Ashton Kutcher** and **Demi Moore** tie the knot in a Kabbalah ceremony at the couple's Beverly Hills home. This is Moore's third marriage, having previously been wed to the musician Freddie Moore (1980-84) and **Bruce Willis** (1987-2000) • The model-turned-actress **Rebecca Romijn**, 32, and actor **Jerry O'Connell**, 31, are engaged after a year of serious dating. Romijn, who was previously married to the actor **John Stamos**, used the name Rebecca Romijn-Stamos to appear in such movies as *X-Men*, *Rollerball*, *Godsend* and *The Punisher*. O'Connell has been a

Brad Pitt with Angelina
Jolie and her children
Maddox and Zahara

star since he was eleven, when he played Vern Tessio in *Stand by Me* ● **Renée Zellweger** files for an annulment of her marriage to Country singer **Kenny Chesney**, whom she married in May. She cites 'fraud' as the reason for the nuptial breakdown ● *Wedding Crashers* grosses $200 million at the US box-office ● Having made the quintessentially English Bridget Jones her own, **Renée** Zellweger signs on to play Beatrix Potter in a new film biography. *Miss Potter*, who wrote of Peter Rabbit, Tabitha Twitchit and Squirrel Nutkin, made her home in the Lake District.

OCTOBER 2005

The 40-Year-Old Virgin grosses $100 million in the US ● Country singer **Kenny Chesney** releases a statement concerning his failed marriage to **Renée Zellweger**. In his defence, he cites a case of being too busy to make his marriage work… ● A fire sweeps through a warehouse in Bristol containing drawings, figures and props used by Aardman Animation. According to spokesman Arthur Sheriff, the warehouse held virtually everything Aardman had created in its 30-year-history: 'Everything from Morph to *Creature Comforts* to Wallace and Gromit were there' ● **Katie Holmes**, 27, reveals that she is pregnant by her fiancé, **Tom Cruise**. While the actress vowed that she wouldn't lose her virginity until her wedding day, she apparently succumbed to Cruise's eagerness to cement their bond ● The sperm of actor **Vincent Gallo** (*Buffalo '66*, *The Brown Bunny*) is auctioned on eBay at a starting bid of $1 million. A spokesman for Gallo promises that the actor is 'drug, alcohol and disease free' and is hoping for a Jewish recipient ● **Gérard Depardieu** announces his retirement from acting.

NOVEMBER 2005

George Clooney makes the front pages of the tabloid press in Britain following a drunken fracas in London's Soho district. Apparently abandoned in a back alley after avoiding the paparazzi, he attacked a security guard for not coming to his rescue ● Seven months after **Denise Richards** filed for divorce from **Charlie Sheen**, the actor reveals that their relationship is now 'really good' ● **Brad Pitt** and **Angelina Jolie** reportedly exchange vows during a Buddhist matrimonial ceremony in Malibu ● *Harry Potter and the Goblet of Fire* grosses $101.4 million in its first three-day weekend in the US, the most money any film has made in that time outside the June-July period ● *Chicken Little* grosses $100m in the US * **Nicole Kidman** is allegedly engaged to the Country singer **Keith Urban** ● In a Manhattan criminal court, **Russell Crowe** pleads guilty to assaulting a New York hotel clerk. He is subsequently charged with a third degree misdemeanour assault, enabling him to avoid a custodial sentence or probation. His punishment is a conditional discharge ● *Harry Potter and the Goblet of Fire* grosses $200m in the US – in ten days ● **Robert Blake** is ordered to pay $30 million in damages to the children of his late wife after being found guilty of her murder by a civil jury ● **Daniel Radcliffe** is named Britain's richest teenager, with a personal fortune of £23 million. For the first *Harry Potter* film, Radcliffe received 'just' £150,000, but for *Harry Potter and the Order of the Phoenix* he is reported to be pocketing £8 million ● *Hollywood Reporter* publishes its annual table of the world's highest paid female stars, with **Julia Roberts** once again lodged firmly at the top of the heap. With an earning power of $16-17 million a movie, **Nicole Kidman** comes second, followed by **Reese Witherspoon**, **Drew Barrymore**, **Renée Zellweger**, **Angelina Jolie**, **Cameron Diaz**, **Jodie Foster**, **Charlize Theron** and **Jennifer Aniston**.

DECEMBER 2005

Having played St Peter in the TV movie *San Pietro*, **Omar Sharif** is issued a death threat by a radical Islamic website. As Sharif reveals that he may re-embrace Christianity (he was born a Christian but later converted to Islam), the website claims he has offended Islam ● The government offers the British film industry a new tax credit scheme, offering 16% to films with budgets of more than £20 million and 20% to films below that figure. Producer **Timothy Burrill** is not impressed: 'We're not clear what the proposed rules really are,' he admitts, 'but it appears that co-productions would need to spend 40 per cent of their budget in the UK in order to receive just 10 per cent of their UK spend.' The industry soldiers on ● The actor **Lillo Brancato Jr** is charged with the second degree murder of a New York policeman after he and an accomplice shot the officer

A lift with Benicio and car trouble: Scarlett Johansson makes the headlines

dead when the latter disturbed them during a burglary. Brancato played the central role of Calogero Anello in **Robert De Niro**'s directorial debut, *A Bronx Tale* (1993) ● **Matt Damon** weds his girlfriend of two years, Luciana Bozan, in a private Manhattan ceremony. The couple met in Miami Beach in 2003 when Damon was filming *Stuck On You* ● In an admittedly limited release, *Brokeback Mountain* still manages to break box-office records. Not only is the film scoring the highest screen average take of any film in 2005, but the highest screen average take of an adult drama in history.

JANUARY 2006

The three highest-grossing films of 2005 in the US are *Star Wars: Episode III – Revenge of the Sith*, *The Chronicles of Narnia: The Lion, the Witch and the Wardrobe* and *Harry Potter and the Goblet of Fire*. Interestingly, they all top-bill British stars: **Ewan McGregor**, **Tilda Swinton** and **Daniel Radcliffe** ● Shortly after leaving rehab, **Lindsay Lohan** paints the town red with her new friend **Kate Moss**. According to onlookers, she and Kate put on an impromptu pole-dancing show for clients at a New York strip club. Then, in the same the evening, Ms Lohan is alleged to have scrawled 'Scarlet is a c**t' in lipstick on a mirror in the ladies' room. Girls will be girls ● After months of speculation, **Gwyneth Paltrow**, wife of Coldplay singer **Chris Martin**, confirms that she is pregnant with their second child ● **Joaquin Phoenix** totals his car on Sunset Strip and is pulled clear of the wreckage by a neighbour, none other than the German filmmaker **Werner Herzog**.

Renée Zellweger: nuptial breakdown, major payday and an assignation with Squirrel Nutkin

FEBRUARY 2006

Walk the Line grosses $100 million in the US • *Fun With Dick and Jane* grosses $100 million in the US • **Lee Tamahori**, in a black wig and off-the-shoulder dress, approaches an undercover police officer on Santa Monica Boulevard, in Los Angeles. Arrested for 'soliciting and loitering with intent to commit prostitution,' the New Zealand director (*Die Another Day*, *xXx 2: The Next Level*) is freed on $2,000 bail • Four actors who play al-Qaida suspects in **Michael Winterbottom**'s award-winning *The Road to Guantánamo* are stopped by police at Luton airport. A spokesperson for Bedfordshire police explains that the actors were questioned 'under the counter-terrorism act' • **Sandra Bullock** reveals that she is to blow up her new house in Austin, Texas. After designing the lakeside mansion herself – complete with towers, spires and private cinema – she found that the £4 million 'dream home' was a death trap, with a leaking roof, toxic mould and faulty wiring. So after successfully suing her builders to the tune of £3.9m, she is planning to start again from scratch • **Sean Connery** has a tumour removed from his kidney. The operation, performed by a team of specialists in New York, is a total success • After eleven years together, **Ralph Fiennes** and **Francesca Annis** are to split, following revelations that Fiennes had a ding-dong with a Romanian singer thirty years Ms Annis' junior.

MARCH 2006

Reese Witherspoon is crowned 'highest paid actress in the world' after signing a deal for $29 million to star in the horror film *Our Family Trouble* • **Uma Thurman** breaks off her relationship with the hotelier **Andre Balazs** • Following his no contest plea to a drunk-driving charge in a Los Angeles court, **Brad Renfro** (*Telling Lies in America*, *Apt Pupil*, *Bully*) starts a ten-day jail term. The actor was also fined, ordered to take 18 months of alcohol education classes and sentenced to five years' probation • The rumour mill kicks in as **Jennifer Aniston** and **Vince Vaughn** appear to be preparing for married bliss • **Randy Quaid** sues *Brokeback Mountain* producer **James Schamus** and Focus Features' co-president **David Linde** for £5.7 million, saying that he was lured to do *Brokeback* for a low fee because it was an 'art house' production. In legal papers, Quaid accuses the producers of 'movie laundering'.

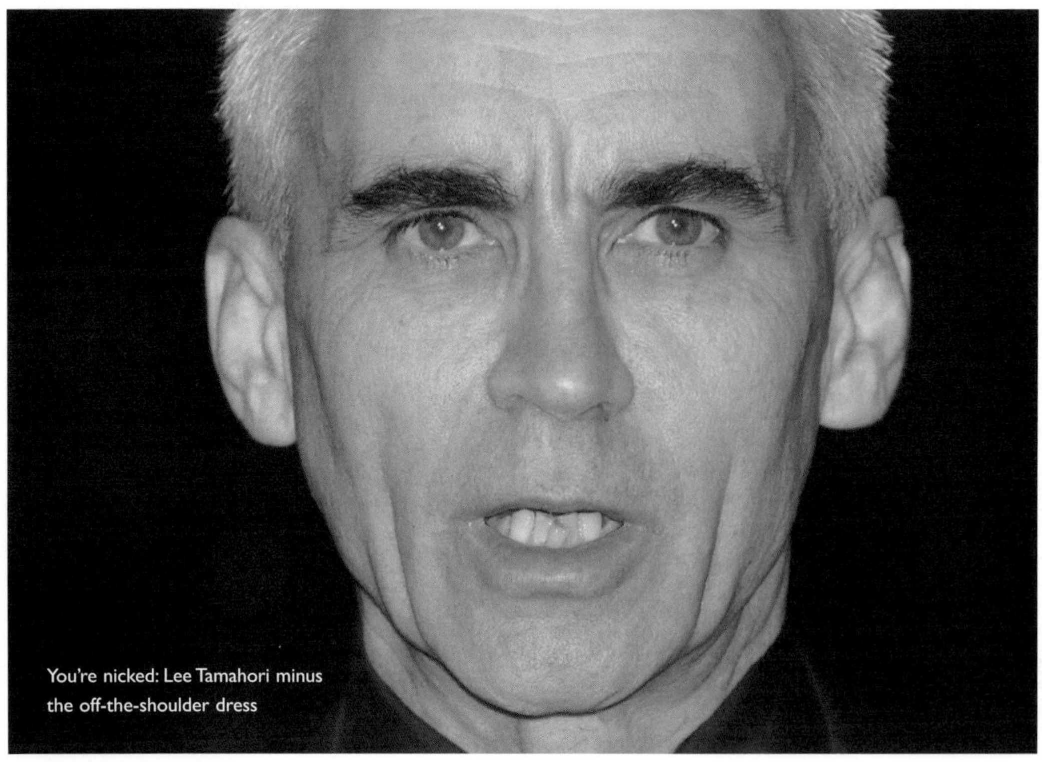

You're nicked: Lee Tamahori minus the off-the-shoulder dress

Tom Cruise and Katie Holmes:
virginity lost and Suri gained

Ken Loach: he's finally
got that winning feeling
— at Cannes, no less

APRIL 2006

The 16th century thatched cottage of **Ken Russell**, in which he has lived for 20 years, is burned down. Returning from a doctor's appointment, Russell saw flames engulfing his home and rushed in to rescue his wife, Elize. However, she had already escaped, having leaped from her bath stark naked • *Ice Age: The Meltdown* grosses over $100m in its first ten days, making the Fox cartoon the first break-out hit of 2006 • **Gwyneth Paltrow** gives birth to a baby boy, Moses, in New York • Loving couple **Maggie Gyllenhaal** (*Donnie Darko,* *Secretary*) and **Peter Sarsgaard** (*Kinsey, Jarhead*) announce that they are engaged and expecting a baby • The trailer for **Paul Greengrass**'s *United 93* is banned in the US after upsetting cinema patrons • Disney's big CGI 'toon *The Wild* grosses $9.5m in its opening weekend, somewhat less than its rival Fox's $70.5m for *The Meltdown* • **Tom Cruise** and **Katie Holmes** are the proud parents of a baby girl, Suri, the first biological child for both parents • **Kevin Costner** is named as the 'A-list' celebrity who exposed himself and performed a lewd act in front of a masseuse at a Scottish hotel. The incident allegedly occured two years ago – while the star was honeymooning with his second wife, Christine Baumgartner – but Costner's name had been withheld for legal reasons. Costner denies that he abused himself in front of the hotel employee • **Keira Knightley** is chosen as the new face of the Chanel scent *Coco Mademoiselle*. Earning a reported £559,597 for her one-year endorsement, the 21-year-old actress ousts former Chanel face **Kate Moss**.

MAY 2006

Adam Sandler and his wife, Jackie, are the proud parents of a baby girl • **Michelle Williams** is to play Charlotte Brontë in a new biography, **Angela Workman**'s *Brontë*. The Montana-born actress joins **Renée Zellweger** and **Anne Hathaway** in the growing list of Americans playing British literary figures, with Ms Zellweger playing Beatrix Potter (in *Miss Potter*) and Hathaway limning Jane Austen in *Becoming Jane* • *Mission: Impossible III* grosses $100m in the US – in its third week • **Nicole Kidman** confirms that she is engaged to the Country singer **Keith Urban** • In Cannes, **Todd Haynes** – director of *Far from Heaven* and *Velvet Goldmine* – unveils his new project, *I'm Not There*. An authorised biography of **Bob Dylan** – who is giving Haynes access to his entire catalogue *gratis* – the film will star **Cate Blanchett**, while **Richard Gere, Heath Ledger** and **Christian Bale** play the singer-songwriter at various points in his life. **P.J. Harvey** and **Michael Stipe** will do the actual singing • *The Da Vinci Code* grosses $100m in its first week on release in the US • **Brad Pitt** and **Angelina Jolie** are in the news again, this time as the proud parents of Shiloh Nouvel Jolie-Pitt. Shiloh is born on Sunday, 27 May, at 01:40 local time in Namibia, per the country's deputy environment minister, **Leon Jooste** • A few hours later, **Ken Loach** wins the Palme d'Or at Cannes for *The Wind That Shakes the Barley*, having been nominated seven times previously for the prestigious festival award • After a rather unexciting start to the popcorn summer (all of *Mission: Impossible III, Over the Hedge* and *Poseidon* have under-performed), *X-Men The Last Stand* shatters box-office records, grossing more than $120 million in its opening Memorial weekend in the US • *Over the Hedge* grosses $100m in the US – in just over two weeks.

JUNE 2006

The Omen, opening on the sixth of the sixth month, 2006, breaks box-office records, raking in $12,633,666 (at 2,660 screens) on its first day, a Tuesday. Numerologists will note that the figure ends in three sixes, the devil's own number. Then of course 12 is half six and three and three make six and… • **Hugh Jackman** joins **Nicole Kidman** in **Baz Luhrmann**'s as-yet-untitled period epic after **Russell Crowe** drops out • **Ryan Reynolds**, the hunky Canadian star of *The Amityville Horror* remake and *Just Friends*, splits up with his fiancée, superstar Canadian singer **Alanis Morissette**. The couple were engaged for two years and dated for two years before that • *X-Men The Last Stand* grosses $200m in the US – the first 2006 release to do so • **Elisabeth Shue** and her husband, director **David Guggenheim**, are the proud parents of a baby girl, Agnes Charles Guggenheim • *Cars* grosses $100m in ten days, becoming the sixth film to clock up that figure this year • **Nicole Kidman** marries Country singer **Keith Urban** in Sydney, in a candlelit ceremony at the beach-side suburb of Manley. **Russell Crowe, Hugh Jackman, Baz Luhrmann, Philip Noyce** and **Naomi Watts** are in attendance • *The Break-Up* grosses $100 million in the US • *The Da Vinci Code* grosses $200m in the US • *Superman Returns* grosses $100m in the US.

Soundtracks

by Daniel O'Brien

In June 2006, the estate of Gustav Holst announced it was suing composer Hans Zimmer. The estate claimed that Zimmer's *Gladiator* score plagiarised the 'Mars, Bringer of War' suite from Holst's *The Planets*. Whatever the outcome of this legal action, it raises an interesting question. At what point does inspiration or *homage* become outright theft? Italian composer Ennio Morricone quoted Beethoven, Mozart and Wagner in his scores for *The Big Gundown* (1966), *A Fistful of Dynamite* (1971) and *My Name is Nobody* (1973).

The cult horror *Re-Animator* (1985) borrows elements of Bernard Herrmann's *Psycho* score. Jerry Goldsmith's music for *Total Recall* (1990) was possibly inspired by Basil Poledouris' classic *Conan the Barbarian* (1982) score. Come to think of it, the opening of Led Zeppelin's 'Immigrant Song' sounds a bit like the start of the *South Pacific* overture. It will be intriguing to see if the outcome of the Holst versus Zimmer affair sets any precedents. Anyway, on to business.

BREAKFAST ON PLUTO

Neil Jordan's tale of a sweet transvestite in 1970s Ireland cried out for a bittersweet pop nostalgia soundtrack. We get The Rubettes' 'Sugar Baby Love' (which lingered at number one for an eternity), Harry Nilsson's 'You're Breakin' My Heart' and 'Me and My Arrow', Patti Page's '(How Much Is) That Doggy in the Window', Dusty Springfield's 'Windmills of Your Mind' (superior to the Noel Harrison original), T-Rex's 'Children of the Revolution' and Don Partridge's 'Breakfast on Pluto'. To Jordan's credit, the choice of songs amounts to more than a marketing tool. 'Me and My Arrow' comes from Nilsson's concept album *The Point*, the story of a boy victimised for being different. For copyright reasons, this release is missing several songs, notably Van Morrison's 'Madam George' and Buffalo Springfield's 'For What It's Worth'. Rhino. January 2006.

BROKEBACK MOUNTAIN

The score for this sleeper hit blends folk and bluegrass standards with original music by Argentine composer Gustavo Santaolalla. Highlights include Willie Nelson's version of the Bob Dylan classic 'He Was a Friend of Mine'. Emmylou Harris performs Santaolalla's haunting theme song, 'A Love That Will Never Grow Old', with lyrics by Bernie Taupin. For copyright reasons, several songs are absent from this release, notably Tammy Wynette's 'D.I.V.O.R.C.E.' and Roger Miller's 'King of the Road', replaced with a cover version by Teddy Thompson and Rufus Wainwright. Verve. November 2005.

BROKEN FLOWERS

This soundtrack is a great showcase for Ethiopian musician Mulatu Astatke. Having studied in the US, Astatke blends jazz with traditional Ethiopian music. The hypnotic end result carries an intriguing but unfocussed movie that depends more on mood than substance. The eclectic yet harmonious score also features Marvin Gaye's 'I Want You', Holly Golightly's 'Tell Me Now So I Know' and Sleep's 'Dopesmoker', a potent extract from the original one hour piece. Oh, and Faure's 'Requiem'. Whatever one's opinion of the film, director Jim Jarmusch knows how to pick his tracks.
Decca. October 2005.

CHARLIE AND THE CHOCOLATE FACTORY

Tim Burton and Danny Elfman have been pretty much inseparable since *Pee-wee's Big Adventure* (1985). Elfman's score for *Charlie and the Chocolate Factory* is as charming, quirky and lyrical as expected. As with *The Nightmare Before Christmas*, Elfman also provides some first class vocals, singing the five Oompa Loompa songs. Four of these feature lyrics taken from Roald Dahl's original text. There's also a nod to Queen's glam rock classic 'Bohemian Rhapsody'. While opinion is divided on Johnny Depp's Willy Wonka, Elfman's music compares favourably with the Leslie Bricusse-Anthony Newley score for the 1971 film version.
Warner Home Vision. July 2005.

CINDERELLA MAN

Thomas Newman's score has a tenderness and poignancy that Ron Howard's boxing biopic never quite achieves. The soundtrack also includes Depression-era standards – notably Bud Freeman's 'Tillie's Downtown Now' and Eddie Cantor's 'Cheer Up, Smile, Nertz' – and traditional Irish tunes, including 'Londonderry Air', whistled by co-star Paul Giamatti.
Decca. September 2005.

THE CORPSE BRIDE

Danny Elfman's score for Tim Burton's macabre puppet fantasy boasts some stellar British voices: Albert Finney, Joanna Lumley, Tracey Ullman, Paul Whitehouse, Jane Horrocks and Helena Bonham Carter. Furthermore, they can all sing, to varying degrees. The Gothic styling is impeccable, favouring harpsichord and organ. Elfman also plays Bonejangles, displaying his vocal skills on 'Remains of the Day'. Other highlights include 'The Piano Duet' and 'Tears to Shed', featuring a touching contribution from Bonham Carter. Cynics feel that Elfman has rehashed his music for *The Nightmare Before Christmas*, to diminishing returns. Maybe so, but the end result is still a winner.
WEA. October 2005.

THE DA VINCI CODE

Hans Zimmer lays on the soaring choirs and plaintive violin solos for the stodgy movie of the crummy book. The sombre, subdued end result is suitably mock spiritual, if hardly inspired. Highlights include 'L'Esprit des Gabriel'. Lowlights include Tom Hanks' hair. *PS* Did you know that Da Vinci's Mona Lisa is actually John the Baptist? It was someone else's head on the plate, you see, and John escaped to Rome where he fell in with Caligula and Elvis Presley…
Decca. May 2006.

THE DUKES OF HAZZARD

Like movie, like soundtrack, a cynical package deal hung on an old TV show. Jessica Simpson's 'These Boots are Made for Walkin'' isn't fit to kiss the feet of the Nancy Sinatra original. There's a fair, if random collection of 70s and 80s classics, notably Lynyrd Skynyrd's 'Call Me The Breeze', Ram Jam's 'Black Betty' and Molly Hatchet's 'Flirtin' With Disaster'. The most successful fusion of TV/movie and actor/singer is Willie Nelson's 'Good Ol' Boys' theme, which bears comparison with the Waylon Jennings version. Channelling the spirit of Denver Pyle, Nelson also makes a pretty good Uncle Jesse. By and large, one for undiscriminating moonshiners and demolition derby fanatics.
Sony. August 2005.

THE FANTASTIC FOUR

The long-gestating superhero movie gets a solid, if unexceptional top'o'the pops score. The good stuff includes T.F.F.'s hard rockin' 'I'll Take You Down', 'Everything Burns' by Ben Moody with Anastacia, and the hip-hop curiosity 'Kirikirimai', by Japanese band Orange Range. Joss Stone's 'Whatever Happened to the Heroes' shouldn't be confused with the Stranglers classic of the same name. Frankly, the latter still has the edge.
Sony. July 2005.

GET RICH OR DIE TRYIN'

Looking for another *8 Mile*, 50 Cent ended up with rap's answer to *Can't Stop the Music*. The Artist Formerly Known As Curtis Jackson retold his life story as a shapeless bag of clichés. The soundtrack is more successful, though 50 Cent's smooth delivery and non-life threatening lyrics aren't hardcore enough for some rap fans. He's joined by Spider Loc, Lloyd Banks, Mobb Deep, Nate Dogg, Olivia (not Newton John), Young Buck, Tony Yayo and Ma$e. Explicit Content, as the sticker says.
Interscope. November 2005.

GOOD NIGHT, AND GOOD LUCK

A superb collection of jazz standards from singer Dianne Reeves and arranger-saxophonist Matt Catingub. The 50s-60s cabaret style is an ideal vehicle for Reeves' rich, expressive contralto. Highlights include 'You're Driving Me Crazy', 'Pick Yourself Up', 'Into Each Life Some Rain Must Fall', 'One For My Baby' and the sole instrumental piece, 'When I Fall in Love'. *Note:* Ed Murrow, the film's central figure, was a big jazz fan, profiling Duke Ellington and Louis Armstrong in his TV series *See It Now* (1951) and producing the documentary *Satchmo the Great* (1958).
Concord. February 2006.

HARRY POTTER AND THE GOBLET OF FIRE

The fourth *Harry Potter* movie sees John Williams making way for Patrick Doyle, whose score is supplemented by three Jarvis Cocker songs. Best known for his work with Kenneth Branagh, Doyle has a distinguished Hollywood track record, including *Carlito's Way* and *Donnie Brasco*. He certainly delivers the *Potter* goods, though Williams devotees will probably argue otherwise. Whatever its faults, Doyle's score captures the darkness, romance and humour of Potter #4. Cocker's Wyrd Sisters songs, including the catchy 'Hippogriff', work better as stand alone tracks than in the movie. Reprise. November 2005.

A HISTORY OF VIOLENCE

Howard Shore has been David Cronenberg's regular composer since *The Brood* (1979), a tale of family breakdown and homicidal midgets. His score for *Dead Ringers* (1988) is one of the finest ever written, carrying a fascinating yet self-destructing narrative. While *A History of Violence* needs no such support, Shore's music captures the dark side of

Americana, ominous, romantic and subtle. Not an essential purchase, perhaps, but a welcome contrast to the pick'n'mix pop soundtracks all too prevalent in Hollywood movies.
Silva Screen. October 2005.

JARHEAD

Most critics received Sam Mendes' Gulf War epic as a would-be instant classic that didn't deliver. Thomas Newman's score doesn't really work as a stand-alone piece, despite some intriguing Middle Eastern influences. The obligatory pop anthems include T-Rex's 'Get It On' and Public Enemy's 'Fight the Power'. Gung ho? Hip? Ironic? Whatever. Fans of the movie will probably hold off for the DVD release. Others won't be bothered either way.
Decca. January 2006.

KING KONG

When Peter Jackson got the greenlight for his cherished *King Kong* remake, he hired *Lord of the Rings* composer Howard Shore to provide the score. So far, so epic. Jackson then rejected Shore's work at the last minute, giving replacement James Newton Howard a matter of weeks to compose a new score. Frankly, it shows. The end result is competent, but impersonal, with little sense of the film's 1930s setting. Pushed for time, Newton Howard relies on generic Hollywood scoring, especially during the action scenes. Apparently, Shore recorded much of his *Kong* music before leaving the project. Whether or not it will ever be released is another matter. In the meantime, Max Steiner's iconic 1933 score still reigns supreme.
Decca. December 2005.

KINKY BOOTS

Much of this soundtrack is a vehicle for star Chiwetel Ejiofor, who performs such classics as 'Whatever Lola Wants' and 'I Want to Be Evil' with aplomb. He also tackles the 70s disco standards 'Together We Are Beautiful' and 'Yes Sir I Can Boogie'. There are well-chosen contributions from Kirsty MacColl ('In These Shoes'), James Brown ('It's a Man's, Man's, Man's World'), Nina Simone ('I Put a Spell on You') and David Bowie ('The Prettiest Star'). Inevitably, Ejiofor takes a shot at 'These Boots are Made for Walkin'', with honourable results. Surprisingly, there's no cover of 'Kinky Boots', the Patrick Macnee/Honor Blackman camp classic spun off from *The Avengers*. Surely the rights weren't that expensive?
Hollywood. October 2005.

MUNICH

Another Steven Spielberg movie, another John Williams score. Ever since *The Sugarland Express* (1974), director and composer have been more or less inseparable. The perfect complement to Spielberg's style, Williams' orchestrations shift from lush to spare at the drop of a hat, hitting all the right emotional buttons. For *Munich*, he draws on Jewish and Middle Eastern influences, including the Israeli national anthem in the 'Hatikrah' track. The haunting vocals are performed by Lisbeth Scott. While Williams offers no surprises, his *Munich* score expertly matches the mood of the film.
Decca. January 2006.

THE NEW WORLD

Terrence Malick's atypically swift follow-up to *The Thin Red Line* came and went without leaving much impression. James Horner's simple, atonal score echoes Malick's slow, hypnotic style, which may or may not be a good thing. That said, much of the music on this release isn't in the film. Presumably, Malick was unhappy with the score, discarding Horner's work in favour of excerpts from Wagner and Mozart (not included here). Perversely, several Horner cues which *are* in the film are absent from the official soundtrack. On balance, it's hard to know who this release is aimed at. One for Horner completists, perhaps, but probably not for Malick fans.
Silva Screen. January 2006.

OLIVER TWIST

As performed by the Prague Philharmonic, Rachel Portman's score is charming but a touch too demure, given the subject matter. That said, some critics felt the same way about Roman Polanski's film, toned down for UK audiences. Aside from the lack of edge and darkness, some of the tracks are both superficial and repetitive.
Sony. October 2005.

THE OMEN

Marco Beltrami faced a tough task following Jerry Goldsmith's score for the original *Omen*. Goldsmith's pounding 'Ave Satani' theme proved an instant classic, winning the composer his only Academy Award. Favouring percussion, piano and woodwind, Beltrami fashions an assured creepy score, enhancing an otherwise colourless movie. Having studied with Goldsmith, Beltrami pays subtle homage to his mentor throughout the film. What the music lacks is the religious sense of Goldsmith's gloriously overblown score. The 'Ave Satani' theme kicks in over the end credits, too late for both Goldsmith fans and newcomers.
Varese Sarabande. June 2006.

THE PROPOSITION

This brutal Australian western was co-scripted by musician Nick Cave, who composed the score with former Bad Seeds collaborator Warren Ellis. *The Proposition* is Cave's third film with director John Hillcoat, following *Ghosts…of the Civil Dead* (1988) and *To Have & to Hold* (1996). The haunting, understated end result is as unsettling as the bleak Outback setting and the characters' wretched lives. Cave and Ellis, a gifted violin player, create an atmospheric, eerie and melancholy soundtrack.
Mute. March 2006.

STONED

How do you make a biopic of Rolling Stone Brian Jones without any Rolling Stones songs? Stephen Woolley's film never overcame this obstacle, though this proved only one of its problems. As a soundtrack per se, *Stoned* is a curious mix of contemporary covers and non-Stones 60s classics. The Counterfeit Stones deliver 'Little Red Rooster', while The Bees offer respectable takes on 'The Last Time', 'Not Fade Away' and 'Time Is On My Side'. The original tracks include The Small Faces' 'Lazy Sunday', Jefferson Airplane's 'White Rabbit' and Traffic's 'Paper Sun'. Robert Johnson's 'Stop Breakin' Down Blues' underlines Jones' main influence when he founded The Rolling Stones. A bluesman at heart, he became disenchanted when Jagger and Richards took the group in a different direction. *Stoned* works better as a soundtrack than a movie, but that's damning with faint praise.
Milan. November 2005.

UNITED 93

John Powell's score is as tense, ominous and dark as Paul Greengrass' film. Favouring background vocals, bass notes and horn, Powell enhances the action without lapsing into Hollywood melodrama. The solo vocal is performed by the composer's son, Oliver Powell. Mixed low in the film, the score comes alive on this soundtrack release. Not easy listening, to be sure, but a fine piece of work in its own right.
Varese Sarabande. June 2006.

WALK THE LINE

As actors, Joaquin Phoenix and Reese Witherspoon gave striking portrayals of country legends Johnny Cash and June Carter Cash. As inexperienced singers and musicians, they emerge with honour intact. While Phoenix lacks Cash's power and gravitas, especially on 'Ring of Fire', his 'Folsom Prison Blues' is more than respectable. Some prefer Witherspoon's singing to Carter Cash's style, though most country fans will dismiss this as heresy. Their joint highlights include 'It Ain't Me Babe'. For copyright reasons, the 'Times a Wastin" duet is missing from this release. There are contributions from co-stars Waylon Payne (Jerry Lee Lewis), Johnathan Rice (Roy Orbison), Tyler Hilton (Elvis Presley) and Shooter Jennings, cast as his dad Waylon. Wisely, the actors don't attempt imitations of the original stars. In terms of accomplishment, Shooter has a head start. Produced by T. Bone Burnett, best known for the bestselling *O Brother, Where Art Thou?* soundtrack. Sony. January 2006.

X-MEN – THE LAST STAND

Taking over from the late Michael Kamen and John Ottman, composer John Powell delivers a creditable superhero score. There are some interesting departures from the previous films and the 'Dark Phoenix' theme is a standout. Arguably, Powell's music carries the weaker scenes, which would flounder without his persuasive underscoring. Judged as a stand-alone score, some tracks are too similar, making repeat listening unlikely. Varese Sarabande. May 2006.

Leo Gregory, as Brian Jones (second left), leads a dodgy line-up of the Rolling Stones in *Stoned*. The *real* Counterfeit Stones play on the film's soundtrack

Awards and Festivals

Crash, winner of the Best Film Oscar for 2005

The 78th American Academy of Motion Picture Arts and Sciences Awards and Nominations ('The Oscars')
Kodak Theatre, Hollywood & Highland, Los Angeles, 5 March 2006

• Best Film: *Crash.* Nominations: *Brokeback Mountain, Capote, Good Night, and Good Luck, Munich*
• Best Director: Ang Lee for *Brokeback Mountain.* Nominations: Bennett Miller, for *Capote*, Paul Haggis, for *Crash,* George Clooney, for *Good Night, and Good Luck*, Steven Spielberg, for *Munich*
• Best Actor: Philip Seymour Hoffman, for *Capote.* Nominations: Terrence Howard, for *Hustle & Flow,* Heath Ledger, for *Brokeback Mountain*, Joaquin Phoenix, for *Walk the Line*, David Strathairn, for *Good Night, and Good Luck*
• Best Actress: Reese Witherspoon, for *Walk the Line.* Nominations: Judi Dench, for *Mrs Henderson Presents,* Felicity Huffman, for *Transamerica*, Keira Knightley, for *Pride & Prejudice*, Charlize Theron, for *North Country*
• Best Supporting Actor: George Clooney, for *Syriana.* Nominations: Matt Dillon for *Crash*, Paul Giamatti, for *Cinderella Man*, Jake Gyllenhaal, for *Brokeback Mountain*, William Hurt, for *A History of Violence*
• Best Supporting Actress: Rachel Weisz, for *The Constant Gardener.* Nominations: Amy Adams, for *Junebug*, Catherine Keener, for *Capote*, Frances McDormand, for *North Country*, Michelle Williams, for *Brokeback Mountain*
• Best Animated Feature: *Wallace & Gromit in The Curse of the Were-Rabbit.* Nominations: *Howl's Moving Castle*, *Tim Burton's Corpse Bride*
• Best Original Screenplay: Paul Haggis and Bobby Moresco, for *Crash.* Nominations: George Clooney and Grant Heslov for *Good Night, and Good Luck*, Woody Allen, for *Match* Point, Noah Baumbach, for *The Squid and the Whale*, Stephen Gaghan, for *Syriana*
• Best Adapted Screenplay: Larry McMurtry & Diana Ossana , for *Brokeback Mountain.* Nominations: Dan Futterman, for *Capote*, Jeffrey Caine, for *The Constant Gardener*, Josh Olson, for *A History of Violence*, Tony Kushner abd Eric Roth, for *Munich*
• Best Cinematography: Dion Beebe, for *Memoirs of a Geisha.* Nominations: Wally Pfister, for *Batman Begins*, Rodrigo Prieto, for *Brokeback Mountain*, Robert Elswit, for *Good Night, and Good Luck*, Emmanuel Lubezki for *The New World*
• Best Editing: Hughes Winborne for *Crash.* Nominations: Mike Hill and Dan Hanley for *Cinderella Man*, Claire Simpson for *The Constant Gardener*, Michael Kahn for *Munich*, Michael McCusker for *Walk the Line*
• Best Original Score: Gustavo Santaolalla for *Brokeback Mountain.* Nominations: Alberto Iglesias for *The Constant Gardener*, John Williams for *Memoirs of a Geisha,* Dario Marianelli for *Pride & Prejudice*
• Best Original Song: Jordan Houston, Cedric Coleman and Paul Beauregard for 'It's Hard Out Here for a Pimp' from

Left: *Memoirs of a Geisha*, winner of the Best Cinematography Oscar

Right: Costume designer Sandy Powell was Oscar-nominated for *Mrs Henderson Presents*

Hustle & Flow. Nominations: Kathleen 'Bird' York and Michael Becker for 'In the Deep' from *Crash*, Dolly Parton for 'Travelin' Thru', from *Transamerica*
• Best Art Direction: John Myhre and Gretchen Rau for *Memoirs of a Geisha*. Nominations: Jim Bissell and Jan Pascale for *Good Night, and Good Luck*, Stuart Craig and Stephenie McMillan for *Harry Potter and the Goblet of Fire*, Grant Major, Dan Hennah and Simon Bright for *King Kong*, Sarah Greenwood and Katie Spencer for *Pride & Prejudice*
• Best Costume Design: Colleen Atwood for *Memoirs of a Geisha*. Nominations: Gabriella Pescucci for *Charlie and the Chocolate Factory*, Sandy Powell for *Mrs Henderson Presents*, Jacqueline Durran for *Pride & Prejudice*, Arianne Phillips for *Walk the Line*
• Best Sound: Christopher Boyes, Michael Semanick, Michael Hedges and Hammond Peek for *King Kong*. Terry Porter, Dean A Zupancic and Tony Johnson for *The Chronicles of Narnia: The Lion, the Witch and the Wardrobe*, Kevin O'Connell, Greg P Russell, Rick Kline and John Pritchett for *Memoirs of a Geisha*, Paul Massey, DM Hemphill and Peter F Kurland for *Walk the Line*, Andy

Nelson, Anna Behlmer and Ronald Judkins for *War of the Worlds*
• Best Sound Effects Editing: Mike Hopkins and Ethan Van der Ryn for *King Kong*. Nominations: Wylie Stateman for *Memoirs of a Geisha*, Richard King for *War of the Worlds*
• Best Makeup: Howard Berger and Tami Lane for *The Chronicles of Narnia: The Lion, the Witch and the Wardrobe*. Nominations: David Leroy Anderson and Lance Anderson for *Cinderella Man*, Dave Elsey and Nikki Gooley for *Star Wars: Episode III – Revenge of the Sith*
• Best Visual Effects: Joe Letteri, Brian Van't Hul, Christian Rivers and Richard Taylor for *King Kong*. Nominations: Dean Wright, Bill Westenhofer, Jim Berney and Scott Farrar for *The Chronicles of Narnia: The Lion, the Witch and the Wardrobe*, Dennis Muren, Pablo Helman, Randal M Dutra and Daniel Sudick for *War of the Worlds*
• Best Animated Short Film: *The Moon and the Son: An Imagined Conversation* by John Canemaker and Peggy Stern. Nominations: *Badgered* by Sharon Colman, *The Mysterious Geographic Explorations of Jasper Morello* by Anthony Lucas, *9* by Shane Acker, *One Man Band*

by Andrew Jimenez and Mark Andrews
• Best Live Action Short Film: *Six Shooter* by Martin McDonagh. Nominations: *Ausreisser (The Runaway)* by Ulrike Grote, *Cashback* by Sean Ellis and Lene Bausager, *The Last Farm* by Rúnar Rúnarsson and Thor S. Sigurjónsson, *Our Time Is Up* by Rob Pearlstein and Pia Clemente
• Best Documentary Feature: *March of the Penguins* by Luc Jacquet and Yves Darondeau. Nominations: *Darwin's Nightmare* by Hubert Sauper, *Enron: The Smartest Guys in the Room* by Alex Gibney and Jason Kliot, *Murderball* by Henry-Alex Rubin and Dana Adam Shapiro, *Street Fight* by Marshall Curry
• Best Documentary Short: *A Note of Triumph: The Golden Age of Norman Corwin* by Corinne Marrinan and Eric Simonson. Nominations: *The Death of Kevin Carter: Casualty of the Bang Bang Club* by Dan Krauss, *God Sleeps in Rwanda* by Kimberlee Acquaro and Stacy Sherman, *The Mushroom Club* by Steven Okazaki
• Best Foreign Language Film: *Tsotsi* (South Africa). Nominations: *Don't Tell* (Italy), *Joyeux Noël* (France), *Paradise Now* (The Palestinian Territories), *Sophie Scholl – The Final Days* (Germany)
• Honorary Award: Robert Altman

The 6th American Film Institute Awards
13 January 2006

AFI Movies of the Year: Official Selections

• *Brokeback Mountain*
• *Capote*
• *Crash*
• *The 40-Year-Old Virgin*
• *Good Night, And Good Luck*
• *A History of Violence*
• *King Kong*
• *Munich*
• *The Squid and the Whale*
• *Syriana*

The 47th Australian Film Institute Awards
25-26 November 2005

- **Best Film**: *Look Both Ways*
- **Best Actor**: Hugo Weaving, for *Little Fish*
- **Best Actress**: Cate Blanchett, for *Little Fish*
- **Best Supporting Actor**: Anthony Hayes, for *Look Both Ways*
- **Best Supporting Actress**: Noni Hazlehurst, for *Little Fish*
- **Best Director**: Sarah Watt, for *Look Both Ways*
- **Best Original Screenplay**: Sarah Watt, for *Look Both Ways*
- **Best Screenplay Adaptation**: Robert Connolly and Elliot Perlman for *Three Dollars*
- **Best Cinematography**: Benoît Delhomme, for *The Proposition*
- **Best Editing**: Alexandre de Franceschi ASE and John Scott ASE, for *Little Fish*
- **Best Music**: Nick Cave and Warren Ellis, for *The Proposition*
- **Best Costumes**: Margot Wilson, for *The Proposition*
- **Best Foreign Film**: *House of Flying Daggers*

- **Best Documentary**: Dennis O'Rourke, for *Land Mines – A Love Story*
- **Best Direction in a Documentary**: Jabe Babe, for *A Heightened Life Janet Merewether*
- **Best Short Fiction Film**: Tony Krawitz, for *Jewboy*
- **Best Screenplay in a Short Fiction Film**: Tony Krawitz, for *Jewboy*
- **Best Cinematography in a Non-Feature Film**: Greig Fraser, for *Jewboy*
- **Best Editing in a Non-Feature Film**: James Bradley, for *Mr Patterns*
- **Best Short Animation**: Anthony Lucas, for *The Mysterious Geographic Explorations of Jasper Morello*
- **AFI Internetional Aware for Best Actor**: Russell Crowe, for *Cinderella Man*
- **AFI Internetional Aware for Best Actress**: Emily Browning, for *Lemony Snicket's A Series of Unfortunate Events*

The 56th Berlin International Film Festival
18 February 2006

- **Golden Bear for Best Film**: *Grbavica*, by Jasmila Zbanic
- **Silver Bear, Grand Jury Prize (shared)**: *En Soap*, by Pernille Fischer Christensen

and *Offside*, by Jafar Panahi
- **Silver Bear, Best Director**: Michael Winterbottom and Mat Whitecross, for *The Road to Guantanamo*
- **Silver Bear, Best Actor**: Moritz Bleibtreu, for *Elementarteilchen*
- **Silver Bear, Best Actress**: Sandra Huller, for *Requiem*
- **Silver Bear for Individual Artistic Contribution**: Jurgen Vogel as Actor, Co-Author and Co-Producer of the film *Der Freie Wille (The Free Will)* by Matthias Glasner
- **Silver Bear for Best Film Music**: Peter Kam for *Isabella* by Pang Ho-Cheung
- **Silver Bear, Best Film Music**: Peter Kam, for *Isabella*
- **Alfred Bauer Prize**: *El Custodio*, by Rodrigo Moreno
- **The Best First Feature Award**: *En Soap* by Pernille Fischer Christensen
- **Golden Bear for Best Short Film**: *Aldrig Som Forsta Gangen! (Never Like the First Time!)* by Jonas Odell
- **Silver Bear for Best Short Film (shared)**: *Gratte-Papier (Penpusher)* by Guillaume Martinez and *Our Man in Nirvana* by Jan Koester
- **Silver Berlin Bear (Special Mention)**:

El Dia Que Mori (The Day I Died) by Maryam Kewshavarz
• **Panorama Short Film Award:** *Tes Cheveux Noirs Ihsan (Your Dark Hair Ihsan)* by Tala Hadid
• **Panorama Special Mention:** *Love This Time* by Rhys Graham
• **UIP Berlin Award:** *El Cerco (The Fence)* by Ricardo Iscar and Nacho Martin
• **DAAD Short Film Award:** *Barburot (Swanettes)* by Rony Sasson
• **Glass Bear for Best Feature Film:** Niels Arden Oplev, for *Drommen*
• **Glass Bear, Special Mention Feature Film:** Auraeus Solito, for *Ang Pagdadalaga Ni Maximo Oliveros (The Blossoning of Maximo Oliveros)*
• **Glass Bear for Best Short Film:** Cameron B Alyasin, for *Aldrig En Absolution (Never An Absolution)*
• **Glass Bear, Special Mention Short Film:** Irina Boiko, for *O Kleftis (The Thief)*
• **Ecumenical Jury Prize:** Jasmila Zbanic, for *Grbavica*
• **Forum:** Khalo Matabane, for *Conversations on a Sunday Afternoon*
• **Panorama:** Feliks Falk, for *Komornik (The Collector)*
• **FIPRESCI Prizes:**
• **Competition:** *Requiem*, by Hans-Christian Schmid
• **Panorama:** *Knallhart (Touch Enough)*, by Detlev Buck
• **Forum:** *In Between Days*, by So Yong Kim
• **German Arthouse Cinemas Guild:** Matthias Glasner for *Der Freie Wille (The Free Will)* .
• **Panorama:** *Kan Shang Qu Hen Mei (Little Red Flowers)*, by Zhang Yuan
• **Forum:** *Karov La Bayit (Close to Home)*, by Dalia Hager and Vidi Bilu
• **Gay Teddy Bear Award, Best Feature:** Auraeus Solito, for *Ang Pagdadalaga Ni Maximo Oliveros (The Blossoning of Maxomo Oliveros)*
• **Gay Teddy Bear Award, Best Documentary:** Olivier Meyrou, for *Au-Dela De La Haine (Beyond Hatred)*
• **Wolfgang Staudt Award:** Tizza Covi and Rainer Frimmel, for *Babooska*
• **Peace Film Prize:** Jasmila Zbanic, for *Grbavica*
• **Panorama Audience Award:** Tomer Heymann, for *Bubot Niyar (Paper Dolls)*
• **Panorama Audience Award for Short Film:** Talya Lavie, for *Hayelet Bodeda (The Substitute)*

Jury: Charlotte Rampling, Matthew Barney, Yash Chopra, Marleen Gorris, Janusz Kaminski, Lee Young-ae, Armin Mueller-Stahl, Fred Roos

The 2005 British Academy of Film and Television Arts Awards ('The BAFTAs')
Odeon Leicester Square, London, 19 February 2006

• **Best Film:** Diana Ossana amd James Schamus, for *Brokeback Mountain*
• **David Lean Award for Direction:** Ang Lee, for *Brokeback Mountain*
• **Best Original Screenplay** Paul Haggis and Bobby Moresco, for *Crash*
• **Best Adapted Screenplay:** Larry McMurtry and Diana Ossana, for *Brokeback Mountain*
• **Best Actor:** Philip Seymour Hoffman, for *Capote*
• **Best Actress:** Reese Witherspoon, for *Walk the Line*
• **Best Supporting Actor:** Jake Gyllenhaal, for *Brokeback Mountain*
• **Best Supporting Actress:** Thandie Newton, for *Crash*
• **Best Cinematography:** Dion Beebe, for *Memoirs of a Geisha*
• **Best Production Design:** Stuart Craig, for *Harry Potter and the Goblet of Fire*
• **Best Editing:** Claire Simpson, for *The Constant Gardener*
• **Anthony Asquith Award for Film Music:** John Williams, for *Memoirs of a Geisha*
• **Best Costumes:** Colleen Atwood, for *Memoirs of a Geisha*
• **Best Sound:** Paul Massey, DM Hemphill, Peter F.Kurland and Donald Sylvester, for *Walk The Line*
• **Best Special Visual Effects:** Joe Letteri, Christian Rivers, Brian Van't Hul and Richard Taylor, for *King Kong*
• **Best Make Up/Hair:** Howard Berger, Gregory Nicotero and Nikki Gooley, for *The Chronicles of Narnia: The Lion, The Witch and the Wardrobe*
• **Alexander Korda Award for Best British Film:** *Wallace & Gromit: The Curse of the Were-Rabbit*
• **Best Foreign Language Film:** *De Battre Mon Coeur S'est Arrete (The Beat That My Heart Skipped)*
• **Best Short Film:** *Antonio's Breakfast*
• **Best Animated Short:** *Fallen Art*
• **Carl Foreman Award for the Most Promising Newcomer:** Joe Wright (director), for *Pride & Prejudice*

• **The Orange Rising Star Award:** James McAvoy
• **Michael Balcon Award:** Robert (Chuck) Finch and Bill Merrell
• **BAFTA Fellowship:** Lord Puttnam

The 26th Canadian Film Awards ('The Genies')
Toronto, 13 March 2006

• **Best Film:** *C.R..A.Z.Y.*
• **Best Director:** Jean-Marc Vallee, for *C.R..A.Z.Y.*
• **Best Actor:** Michel Cote, for *C.R..A.Z.Y.*
• **Best Actress:** Seema Biswas, for *Water*
• **Best Supporting Actor:** Denis Bernard, for *L'Audition*
• **Best Supporting Actress:** Danielle Proulx, for *C.R..A.Z.Y.*
• **Best Original Screenplay:** Jean-Marc Vallee and Francois Boulay, for *C.R..A.Z.Y.*
• **Best Adapted Screenplay:** Atom Egoyan, for *Where The Truth Lies*
• **Best Cinematography:** Giles Nuttgens, for *Water*
• **Best Editing:** Paul Jutras, for *C.R..A.Z.Y.*
• **Best Art Direction:** Patrice Vermette, for *C.R..A.Z.Y.*
• **Best Music (Original Score):** Mychael Danna, for *Water*
• **Best Music (Original Song):** Glenn Buhr and Margaret Sweatman, 'Seven Times Lucky', from *When Wintertime*
• **Best Costumes:** Ginette Magny, for *C.R..A.Z.Y.*
• **Best Sound Editing:** Francois Sauve, for *C.R..A.Z.Y.*
• **Best Overall Sound:** Yvon Benoit, Daniel Bisson, Luc Boirdrais, Berbard Gariepy Sttrobl , for *C.R..A.Z.Y.*
• **Best Documentary:** *Sacredsacred*, by Velcrow Ripper, Tracet Friesen, Cari Green and Harry Susterland
• **Best Live-Action Short:** *Milo55160*, by David Ostry and Matthew Cervi
• **Best Animated Short:** *CNote*, by Chris Hinton and Michael Fukushima

The 59th Cannes Film Festival Awards
17-28 May 2006

• **Palme d'Or for Best Film:** *The Wind That Shakes the Barley*, by Ken Loach
• **Grand Prix du Jury:** *RedRoad*, by Andrea Arnold
• **Best Actor (ensemble award):** Jamel Debbouze, Samy Naceri, Roschdy Zem,

Samy Bouajila and Bernad Blancan for
Indigenes
• **Best Actress (ensemble award):**
Penbelope Cruz, Carmen Maura, Lola
Duenas, Blanca Portillo, Yohana Cobo and
Chus Lampreave for *Volver*
• **Best Director:** Alejenadro Gonzalez
Inarritu, for *Babel*
• **Best Screenplay:** Pedro Almodovar, for
Volver
• **Palme d'Or for Best Short:** *Sniffer*, by
Bobbie Peers
• **Technical Prize:** Stephen Mirrione, for
Babel
• **Prix du Jury:** *Red Road*, by Andrea
Arnold
• **Camera d'Or** (for first feature): *A Fost
Sau N-a Fost?* by Corneliu Porumboiu
• **Awards Cinéfondation:**
• **First Prize:** *Ge & Zeta*, by Gustavo Riet
• **Second Prize:** *Mr Schwartz, Mr Hazen
and Mr Horlocker*, by Stefan Mueller
• **Third Prize:** *Mother*, by Siân Heder; *A
Virus (The Virus)*, by Agnes Kocsis
• **Prix Un Certain Regard – Fondation
Gan pour le Cinéma:** *Luxury Car*, by Chao
Wang
• **Une Certain Regard Special Jury
Prize:** *Ten Canoes (10 canoes, 150 Lances et 3
Epouses)*, by Rolf De Heer
• **Une Certain Regard:** *Luxury Car*, by
Chao Wang
• **Une Certain Regard Award for Best
Actress:** Dorotheea Petre, for *Cum Mi-Am
Petrecut Sfarsitul Lumii*
• **Une Certain Regard Award for Best
Actor:** Don Angel Tavira, for *El Violin*
• **Prix du Président du Jury Un Certain
Regard:** *Meurtrieres* by Grandperret Patrick
• **Grand Prix:** *Flandres, by Bruno Dumont*

Juries:
*Feature Flms Jury: President of the Jury: Wong
Kar-Wai; Members of the Jury: Elia Suleiman,
Helena Bonham-Carter, Lucrecia Martel,
Monica Bellucci, Patrice Leconte,
Samuel L Jackson, Tim Roth, Zhang Ziyi
Cinefindation and Short Films Jury: President
of the Jury: Andreï Konchalovsky; Members of
the Jury: Daniel Bruhl, Sandrine Bonnaire,
Souleymane Cisse, Tim Burton,
Zbigniew Preeisner
Un Certain Regard Jury: President of the Jury:
Monte Hellman; Members of the Jury: Jean-
Pierre Lavoignat, Lars-Olav Beier,
Laura Winters, Marjane Satrapi,*
Maurizio Cabonat
*Camera D'Or Jury: President of the Jury: Jean-
Pierre et Luc Dardenne; Members of the Jury:*

Alain Riou, Frédéric Maire, Jean Louis
Vialard, Jean-Paul Salome,
Jean-Pierre Neyrac, Luiz Carlos Merten,
Natacha Laurent

50th David Di Donatello Academy Awards ('The Davids')
Rome, 21 April 2006

• **Best Film:** *Il Caimano (The Alligator)*,
by Angelo Barbagallo and Nanni Motetti
• **Best Director:** Nanni Motetti,
for *Il Caimano (The Alligator)*
• **Best New Director:** Fausto Brizzi, for
*Notte prima degli esami (First Night of the
Exams)*
• **Best Screenplay:** Stefano Rulli, Sandro
Petraglia, Giancarlo De Cataldo, with
the collaboration of Michele Placido, for
Romanzo Criminale (Crime Novel)
• **Best Producer:** Angelo Barbagallo and
Nanni Motetti, for *Il Caimano
(The Alligator)*
• **Best Actor:** Silvio Orlando,
for *Il Caimano (The Alligator)*
• **Best Actress:** Valeria Golino,
for *La Guerra di Mario (Mario's War)*
• **Best Supporting Actor:** Pierfrancesco
Favino, for *Romanzo Criminale (Crime Novel)*
• **Best Supporting Actress:** Angela
Finocchiaro, for *La Bestia nel cuore (The
Beast in the Heart)*

• **Best Cinematography:** Luca Bigazzi,
for *Romanzo Criminale (Crime Novel)*
• **Best Music:** Franco Piersanti,
for *Il Caimano (The Alligator)*
• **Best Original Song:** 'Arrividetrci
Amore, Ciao', by Caterina Caselli
• **Best Production Design:** Paola
Comencini, for *Romanzo Criminale
(Crime Novel)*
• **Best Costume Design:** Nicoletta
Taranta, for *Romanzo Criminale (Crime Novel)*
• **Best Editing:** Esmeralda Calabria, for
Romanzo Criminale (Crime Novel)
• **Best Sound:** Alessandro Zanon,
for *Il Caimano (The Alligator)*
• **Best Visual Effects:** PROXIMA, for
Romanzo Criminale (Crime Novel)
• **Best Documentary Feature:** *Il Bravo
Gatto Prende I Topi (The Brave Cat Gets the
Mice)*, by Francesco Conversano and Nene
Grignaffini
• **Best Short:** *Un Inguaribile Amore
(An Incurable Love)*, by Giovanni Covini
• **Best European Union Film:** *Match
Point*, by Woody Allen
• **Best Foreign Film:** *Crash*, by Paul
Haggis
• **Young David:** *Romanzo Criminale
(Crime Novel)*, by Michael Placido
• **Critics' Award:** *La Guerra di Mario
(Mario's War)*, by Antonio Capuano
• **Special Awards of the Fiftieth
Anniversary:** Gina Lollobrigida, Piero

Tosi, Peppino Rotunno, Ennio Morricone, Dino De Laurentiis, Francesco Rosi, Suso Cecchi d'Amico, Mario Garbuglia

The 32nd Deauville Festival of American Cinema
2-11 September 2005

• **Grand Prix for Best Film**: *Crash*, by Paul Haggis
• **Jury Prize**: *Keane*, by Lodge H Kerrigan; *On The Outs*, by Lori Silverbush and Michael Skolnik
• **Best Screenplay**: *Transamerica*, by Duncan Tucker
• **International Critics Award**: *Keane*, by Lodge H. Kerrigan
• **Premiere Award**: *Reefer Madness: The Movie Musical,* by Andy Fickman
• *Canal+ Award*ward: *Enron: The Smartest Guys in the Room, by Alex Gibney*

Jury: Alain Corneau (Head of Jury); *Members of the Jury*: Melvil Poupaud, Dominique Blanc, Romane Bohringer, Rachida Brakni, Dominik Moll, Brigitte Roüan, Enki Bilal, Christophe

The 20th European Film Awards ('The Felixes')
Arena, Berlin, 3 December 2005

• **Best European Film**: *Cache (Hidden)*
• **Best European Director**: Michael Haneke, for *Cache (Hidden)*
• **Best European Actor**: Daniel Auteuil, for *Cache (Hidden)*
• **Best European Actress**: Julia Jentsch, for *Sophie Scholl, Die Letzen Tage (Sophie Scholl, the Final Days)*
• **Best European Screenplay**: Hany Abu-Assad and Bero Beyer, for *Paradise Now*
• **Best European Cinematographer**: Franz Lustig, for *Don't Come Knocking*
• **Best European Music**: Rupert Gregson-Williams and Andrea Guerra, for *Hotel Rwanda*
• **Best Best European Editor**: Michael Hudecek & Nadine Muse, for *Cache (Hidden)*
• **Best Best European Production Design**: Aline Bonetto, for *Un Long Dimanche De Fiancailles (A Very Long Engagement)*
• **European Film Academy Lifetime Achievement Award**: Sir Sean Connery
• **Best Achievement in World Cinema**: Maurice Jarre
• **Discovery of the Year (Fassbinder Award)**: *Anklaget (Accused),* by Jakob Thuesen
• **Critics Award, Prix Fipresci**: Michael Haneke, for *Cache (Hidden)*
• **Documentary, Prix Arte**: *Un Dragon Dans Les Eaux Pures Du Caucase (The Pipeline Next Door),* by Nino Kirtadzé
• **Short Film, Prix UIP**: *Undressing My Mother,* by Ken Wardrop
• **Non-European Film, Prix Screen International**: *Good Night, and Good Luck,* by George Clooney
• **The Jameson People's Choice Awards**:
• **Best European Director**: Marc Rothemund for *Sophie Scholl, Die Letzen Tage (Sophie Scholl, the Final Days)*
• **Best European Actor**: Orlando Bloom, for *Kingdom of Heaven*
• **Best European Actress**: Julia Jentsch for *Sophie Scholl, Die Letzen Tage (Sophie Scholl, the Final Days)*

The Golden Raspberries ('The Razzies')
Ivar Theatre, Hollywood, 4 March 2006

• **Worst Picture**: *Dirty Love*
• **Worst Actor**: Rob Schneider
• **Worst Actress**: Jenny McCarthy
• **Worst Supporting Actor**: Hayden Christensen
• **Worst Supporting Actress**: Paris Hilton
• **Worst Director**: John Asher

Screen couple Nicole Kidman and Will Ferrell won a Razzie for their performance in *Bewitched*

• Worst Screenplay: *Dirty Love*
• Worst Remake or Sequel:
Son of the Mask
• Worst Screen Couple: Will Ferrell and
Nicole Kidman
• Most Tiresome Tabloid Targets: Tom
Cruise and Katie Holmes

The 63rd Hollywood Foreign Press Association Awards ('The Golden Globes')
15 January 2006

• Best Motion Picture – Drama:
Brokeback Mountain
• Best Motion Picture – Musical or
Comedy: *Walk The Line*
• Best Director: Ang Lee, for *Brokeback Mountain*
• Best Performance by an Actor in a
Motion Picture – Drama: Philip Seymour
Hoffman, for *Capote*
• Best Performance by an Actress in
a Motion Picture – Drama: Felicity
Huffman, for *Transamerica*
• Best Performance by an Actor in
a Motion Picture – Comedy/Musical:
Joaquin Phoenix, for *Walk the Line*
• Best Performance by an Actress in a
Motion Picture: Reese Witherspoon for
Walk the Line
• Best Performance by an Actor in a
Supporting Role: George Clooney for
Syriana
• Best Performance by an Actress in
a Supporting Role – Motion Picture:
Rachel Weisz for *The Constant Gardener*
• Best Foreign Language Film:
Paradise Now

• Best Screenplay: Larry McMurtry and
Diana Ossana, for *Brokeback Mountain*
• Best Original Score: John Williams, for
Memoirs of a Geisha
• Best Original Song: Gustavo Santaolalla,
Bernie Taupin ('A Love That Will Never
Grow Old'), from *Brokeback Mountain*
• Best Television Series – Drama: *Lost*
• Best Television Series – Musical or
Comedy: *Desperate Housewives*
• Best Mini-Series or Motion Picture
made for Television: *Empire Falls*

The 26th London Film Critics' Circle Awards
**The Dorchester, London,
8 February 2006**

• Best Film: *Brokeback Mountain*
• Best Actor: Bruno Ganz, for *Der Untergang*
• Best Actress: Naomi Watts, for *King Kong*
• Best Director: Ang Lee, for *Brokeback Mountain*
• Best Screenwriter: Paul Haggis and
Robert Moresco, for *Crash*
• Best British Film: *The Constant Gardener*
• Best British Director: Joe Wright, for
Pride & Prejudice
• Best British Producer: Simon
Channing-Williams, for *The Constant Gardener*
• Best British Actor: Ralph Fiennes, for
The Constant Gardener
• Best British Actress: Rachel Weisz, for
The Constant Gardener
• Best British Supporting Actor: Tom
Hollander, for *Pride & Prejudice*

• Best British Supporting Actress:
Thandie Newton, for *Crash*
• Best British Newcomer: Kelly Reilly,
for *Mrs Henderson Presents*
• Best Foreign Language Film: *Der Untergang*
• Dilys Powell Award: Bryan Forbes

The Los Angeles Film Critics' Association Awards
**Park Hyatt Hotel, Los Angeles,
17 January 2006**

• Best Picture: *Brokeback Mountain*
• Best Actor: Phillip Seymour Hoffman,
for *Capote*
• Best Actress: Vera Farmiga, for *Down to the Bone*
• Best Supporting Actor: William Hurt,
for *A History of Violence*
• Best Supporting Actress: Catherine
Keener, for *The 40-Year-Old Virgin*, *Capote*,
The Ballad of Jack and Rose and *The Interpreter*
• Best Director: Ang Lee, for *Brokeback Mountain*
• Best Screenplay (tied): Dan Futterman,
for *Capote* and Noah Baumbach, for *The Squid and The Whale*
• Best Foreign Film: *Cache*
• Best Documentary: *Grizzly Man*
• Best Cinematography: Robert Elswit,
for *Good Night, and Good Luck*
• Best Music: Joe Hisaishi, for *Howl's Moving Castle*
• Best Production Design: William
Chang, for *2046*
• New Generation Award:
Terrence Howard

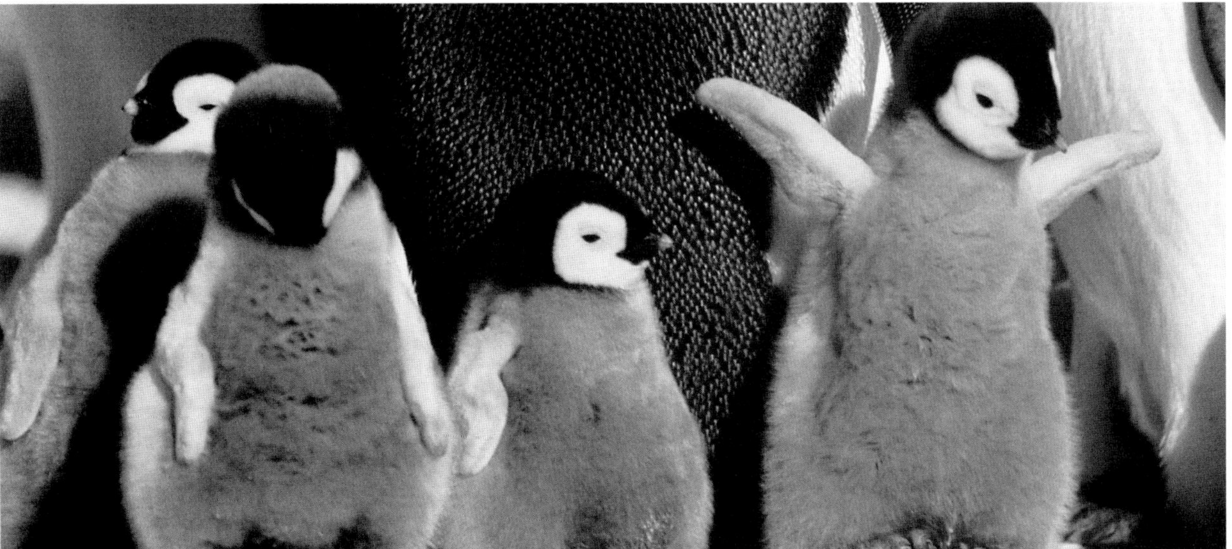

These youngsters celebrate the victory of *March of the Penguins*
at the National Board of Review of Motion Picture Awards

Reese Witherspoon (right) won numerous awards for her performance in *Walk the Line*

• **Best Animation**: *Wallace & Gromit in The Curse of the Were-Rabbit*
• **Career Achievement Award**: Richard Widmark
• **Special Citation**: to Kevin Thomas for his contribution to film culture in Los Angeles. To David Shepard, Bruce Posner and the Anthology Film Archive to honour *Unseen Cinema*, a seven-disc collection of avant garde films dating from 1894 to 1941

14th MTV Movie Awards
Sony Pictures Studio, Culver City, California, 3 June 2006

• **Best Movie**: *Wedding Crashers*
• **Best Performance**: Jake Gyllenhaal, for *Brokeback Mountain*
• **Best Comedic Performance**: Steve Carell, for *The 40-Year Old Virgin*
• **Best Onscreen Team**: Vince Vaughn and Owen Wilson, for *Wedding Crashers*
• **Best Breakthrough Performance**: Isla Fisher, for *Wedding Crashers*
• **Best Villain**: Hayden Christensen, for *Star Wars Episode III: Revenge of the Sith*
• **Best Hero**: Christian Bale, for *Batman Begins*

• **Sexiest Performance**: Jessica Alba, for *Sin City*
• **Best Fight**: Angelina Jolie vs Brad Pitt, in *Mr & Mrs Smith*
• **Best Kiss**: Jake Gyllenhaal and Heath Ledger, in *Brokeback Mountain*
• **Best Frightened Performance**: Jennifer Carpenter, in *The Exorcism of Emily Rose*
• **MTV Generation Award**: Jim Carrey
• **mtvU Student Filmmaker Award**: Joshua Caldwell (Fordham University), for *A Beautiful Lie*

The 95th National Board of Review of Motion Picture Awards
Tavern on the Green, New York, 12 December 2005

• **Best Film**: *Good Night, and Good Luck*
• **Best Actor**: Philip Seymour Hoffman, for *Capote*
• **Best Actress**: Felicity Huffman, for *Transamerica*
• **Best Supporting Actor**: Jake Gyllenhaal, for *Brokeback Mountain*
• **Best Supporting Actress**: Gong Li, for *Memoirs of a Geisha*

• **Best Director**: Ang Lee, for *Brokeback Mountain*
• **Best Adapted Screenplay**: Stephen Gaghan, for *Syriana*
• **Best Original Screenplay**: Noah Baumbach, for *The Squid and the Whale*
• **Best Ensemble Cast**: *Mrs Henderson Presents*
• **Best Foreign Language Film**: *Paradise Now*
• **Best Animated Feature**: *Tim Burton's Corpse Bride*
• **Best Documentary**: *The March of the Penguins*
• **Breakthrough Performances (Actor)**: Terrence Howard, for *Crash*, *Get Rich or Die Tryin'* and *Hustle & Flow*
• **Breakthrough Performances (Actress)**: Q'Orianka Kilcher, for *The New World*
• **Best Directorial Debut**: Julian Fellowes, for *Separate Lies*
• **Best Made-for-Cable Movie/Miniseries**: *Lackawanna Blues*
• **Career Achievement Award**: Jane Fonda
• **Career Achievement – Music Composition**: Howard Shore
• **Billy Wilder Award for Excellence in Directing**: David Cronenberg

• Outstanding Achievement in Special Effects: *King Kong*
• William K Everson Award for Film History: George Feltenstein
• Special Achievement in Producing: Saul Zaentz
• Special Recognition of Films that Reflect the Freedom of Expression: *Innocent Voices, The Untold Story of Emmett Louis Till*
• Special Mention for Excellence in Filmmaking: *Breakfast on Pluto, Cape of Good Hope, The Dying Gaul, Everything is Illuminated, Hustle & Flow, Junebug, Layer Cake, Lord of War, Nine Lives, The Thing About My Folks, The Upside of Anger*

The 40th National Society of Film Critics' Awards
New York, 7 January 2006

• Best Film: *Capote*
• Best Actor: Philip Seymour Hoffman, for *Capote*
• Best Actress: Reese Witherspoon, for *Walk the Line*
• Best Director: David Cronenberg, for *A History of Violence*
• Best Supporting Actor: Edharris, for *A History of Violence*
• Best Supporting Actress: Amy Adams, for *Junebug*
• Best Screenplay: Noah Baumbach, for *The Squid and the Whale*
• Best Cinematography: Christopher Doyle II, Pung-Leung Kwan and Yiu-Fai Lai, for *2046*
• Best Foreign Film: *Gegen die Wand*
• Best Non-Fiction Film: *GrizzlyMan*
• Special Citation: Kenneth Turan
• Special Award: To David Shepard, Bruce Posner and the Anthology Film Archive, a Special Heritage Award for the *Unseen Cinema* DVD collection.

The 71st New York Film Critics' Circle Awards
Algonquin Hotel, New York, 12 December 2005

• Best Film: *Brokeback Mountain*
• Best Actor: Heath Ledger, for *Brokeback Mountain*
• Best Actress: Reese Witherspoon, for *Walk the Line*
• Best Supporting Actor: William Hurt, for *A History of Violence*
• Best Supporting Actress: Maria Bello,

for *A History of Violence*
• Best Director: Ang Lee, for *Brokeback Mountain*
• Best Screenplay: Noah Baumbach, for *The Squid and the Whale*
• Best Cinematographer: Christopher Doyle, Lai Yiu Fai and Kwan Pun Leung, for *2046*
• Best Foreign Film: *2046*
• Best Nonfiction Film (tie): *Grizzly Man* and *White Diamond*
• Best Animated Film: *Howl's Moving Castle*
• Best First Feature: *Capote*

The 22nd Sundance Film Festival
Park City, Utah, 28 January 2006

• The Documentary Grand Jury Prize: *God Grew Tired of Us*, by Christopher Quinn
• The Dramatic Grand Jury Prize: *Quinceañera*, by Wash Westmoreland and Richard Glatzer
• Audience Award – Documentary: *God Grew Tired of Us*, by Christopher Quinn
• Audience Award – Dramatic: *Quinceañera*, by Wash Westmoreland and Richard Glatzer
• Special Jury Prize – Dramatic: Best Ensemble Performance: *Cast of A Guide to Recognizing Your Saints*, by Dito Montiel
• Special Jury Prize – Dramatic: Independent Vision: *In Between Days*, by So Yong Kim
• Special Jury Prize – World Cinema Documentary: *Into a Great Silence*, by Philip Groening
• Special Jury Prize – World Cinema Documentary: *Dear Pyongyang*, by Yonghi Yang
• Jury Prize – World Cinema Dramatic: *13 Tzameti*, by Géla Babluani
• Special Jury Prize – World Cinema Dramatic: *Eve & the Fire Horse*, by Julia Kwan
• Jury Prize – World Cinema Documentary: *In the Pit*, by Juan Carlos Rulfo
• Audience Award – World Cinema Documentary: *De Nadie*, by Tin Dirdamal
• Audience Award – World Cinema Dramatic: *No. 2*, by Toa Fraser
• Directing Award – Documentary: James Longley, for *Iraq in Fragments*
• Directing Award – Dramatic: Dito Montiel, for *A Guide to Recognizing Your Saints*
• Cinematography Award –

Documentary: James Longley, for *Iraq in Fragments*
• Cinematography Award – Dramatic: Tom Richmond, for *Right at Your Door*
• Waldo Salt Screenwriting Award: Hilary Brougher, for *Stephanie Daley*
• Documentary Jury – Special Jury Prize: *American Blackout*, by Ian Inaba; *TV Junkie* by Michael Cain and Matt Radecki
• Jury Prize – Short Filmmaking: *Bugcrush*, by Carter Smith and *The Wraith of Cobble Hill*, by Adam Parrish King
• Jury Prize – International Short Filmmaking: *The Natural Route*, by Alex Pastor
• Honorable Mention – Short Filmmaking: *Before Dawn,* by Bálint Kenyeres
• Honorable Mention – Short Filmmaking: *Preacher With an Unknown God*, by Rob VanAlkemade
• Honorable Mention, Short Filmmaking: *Undressing My Mother,* by Ken Wardrop
• Documentary Film Editing: Billy McMillin, Fiona Otway, and James Longley, for *Iraq in Fragments*
• Sundance/NHK International Filmmakers Award: Patrice Toy, for *The Spring Ritual;* Fernando Eimbcke, for *Lake Tahoe;* Cruz Angeles, for *Don't Let Me Drown;* Kanji Nakajima, for *The Clone Returns to the Homeland*

Juries:
Jury, Independent Film Competition: Documentary: Joe Bini, Zana Briski, Andrew Jarecki, Alexander Payne, Heather Rae
Jury, Independent Film Competition: Dramatic: Miguel Arteta, Terrence Howard, Alan Rudolph, Nancy Schreiber, Audrey Wells
Jury, World Cinema Competition: Documentary: Kate Amend, Jean-Xavier de Lestrade, Rachel Perkins
Jury, World Cinema Competition: Dramatic: Irene Bignardi, Lu Chuan, Thomas Vinterberg
Jury, Shorts Competition: Georgia Lee, Sydney Neter, John Vanco
Alfred P Sloan Feature Film Prize Jury: John Underkoffler, Greg Harrison, Lynn Hershman Leeson, Antonio Demasio

In Memoriam
by Daniel O'Brien

MOUSTAPHA AKKAD

Born: 1 July 1930*, in Aleppo, Syria.
Died: 11 November 2005, from injuries sustained in a terrorist explosion in Amman, Jordan.
Job description: Producer and director
A graduate of the UCLA and USC film schools, Moustapha Akkad was best known for *The Message* (1976), which chronicles the birth of Islam. As Islamic law forbids any depiction of the Prophet Mohammad, Akkad employed some unusual POV shots. He followed *The Message* with *Lion of the Desert* (1981), a biopic of Bedouin warrior Omar Mukhtar, who battled Mussolini's armies in Libya. Akkad enjoyed his biggest commercial success as the executive producer of the *Halloween* series (1978-2002).
(*Some sources list 1935)

KEITH ANDES

Born: 12 July 1920, in Ocean City, New Jersey, USA.
Died: 11 November 2005, a suicide, in Canyon Country, California, USA.
Birth name: John Charles Andes
Job description: Actor
A busy character actor, Keith Andes spent much of his career in television. His film credits include *Clash by Night* (1952), *Away All Boats* (1956), *Interlude* (1957), *Tora!, Tora!, Tora!* (1970) and *...And Justice for All* (1979).

AVRIL ANGERS

Born: 18 April 1918, in Liverpool, England.
Died: 9 November 2005, of pneumonia, in London, England.
Birth name: Avril Florence Angers
Job description: Actress
A gifted comedienne, Avril Angers appeared in such films as *Miss Pilgrim's Progress* (1950), *The Green Man* (1956), *The Family Way* (1966) and *There's a Girl in My Soup* (1970).

JARBAS BARBOSA

Born: 1927, in Campina Grande, Paraiba, Brazil.
Died: 9 December 2005, in Recife, Pernambuco, Brazil.
Job description: Producer
Jarbas Barbosa was a key player in Brazil's Cinema Novo ('New Cinema') movement of the 1960s. Made on low budgets, many of his films dealt with social, political and historical issues. Barbosa's credits include *The Rifles* (1963), *Ganga Zumba* (1963), *God and the Devil in the Land of the Sun* (1964), *Carnaval Barra Limpa* (1967), *The Inheritors* (1970), *Ali Baba and the Forty Thieves* (1972), *Aladdin and His Marvellous Lamp* (1973) and *Xica da Silva* (1976). He was the younger brother of Chacrinha, a well known television presenter.

RONNIE BARKER

Born: 25 September 1929, in Bedford, Bedfordshire, England.
Died: 3 October 2005, from heart failure, in Addersbury, Oxfordshire, England.
Birth name:
Ronald William George Barker
Job description: Actor, writer and one half of the comedy duo The Two Ronnies. Active mainly in television, Ronnie Barker appeared in a handful of films, notably *The Bargee* (1964), *The Magnificent Seven Deadly Sins* (1971), *Robin and Marian* (1976), as Friar Tuck, and *Porridge* (1979), reprising his popular TV character Norman Fletcher.

BARBARA BEL GEDDES

Born: 31 October 1922, in New York, New York, USA.
Died: 8 August 2005, from lung cancer, in Northeast Harbor, Maine, USA.
Job description: Actress
An acclaimed stage and television actress, Barbara Bel Geddes is best known as Miss Ellie in *Dallas*. Her film credits include *Panic in the Streets* (1950), *Vertigo* (1958), as James Stewart's confused girlfriend, and *The Todd Killings* (1971).

PETER BENCHLEY

Born: 8 May 1940, in New York, New York, USA.
Died: 11 February 2006, of idiopathic pulmonary fibrosis, in Princeton, New Jersey, USA.
Job description: Writer
A former political speechwriter, Peter Benchley enjoyed his biggest success with *Jaws* (1974), a pulp classic about a rampaging Great White Shark that sold 20 million copies. He co-scripted Steven Spielberg's 1975 film version, making a cameo appearance as a television reporter. The movie was a box-office sensation, establishing Benchley as a hot Hollywood property. He followed *Jaws* with *The Deep* (1976) and *The Island* (1979), both bestsellers. Benchley was paid $1 million to co-write the film of *The Deep* (1977), sold largely on the strength of Jacqueline Bisset's wet t-shirt. He took sole screenplay credit and a $4 million fee for *The Island* (1980), a grisly tale of an inbred pirate colony.

When it flopped, Benchley's film career ground to a halt. His subsequent books were adapted as more modest TV dramas. In later life, Benchley regretted perpetuating the negative image of sharks, campaigning for a greater understanding of the creatures.

ADRIAN BIDDLE

Born: 20 July 1952,
in London, England.
Died: 7 December 2005,
of a heart attack, in London, England.
Job description: Director of photography
Adrian Biddle got his break as a camera assistant with the 2nd unit for *On Her Majesty's Secret Service* (1969). Years later, Ridley Scott hired him as the focus puller for *The Duellists* (1977) and *Alien* (1979). Active in commercials, Biddle didn't embark on a full-time film career until the mid-1980s. Fittingly, he served as the cameraman on *Aliens* (1986), the belated sequel to Scott's hit. Showing a flair for fantasy, Biddle worked on *The Princess Bride* (1987) and *Willow* (1988). He reunited with Scott for *Thelma and Louise* (1991) and *1492: The Conquest of Paradise* (1992). Biddle's later credits included *Judge Dredd* (1995), *Event Horizon* (1997), *The Mummy* (1999) and *The Mummy Returns* (2001). He also shot the Bond movie *The World Is Not Enough* (1999), 30 years after his debut on *OHMSS*. Biddle's last film was *V for Vendetta* (2005).

LLOYD BOCHNER

Born: 29 July 1924,
in Toronto, Ontario, Canada.
Died: 29 October 2005, of cancer, in Santa Monica, California, USA.
Birth name: Lloyd Wolfe Bochner
Job description: Actor
An accomplished stage and television actor, Lloyd Bochner appeared in several notable films: *Point Blank* (1967), *The Detective* (1968) and *Ulzana's Raid* (1972). His later films included *Naked Gun 2 ½: The Smell of Fear* (1991).

TOMMY BOND

Born: 16 September 1926,
in Dallas, Texas, USA.
Died: 24 September 2005, of heart disease, in Northridge, California, USA.
Birth name: Thomas Ross Bond
Job description: Actor
A onetime child actor, Tommy Bond was best known for playing Butch the bully in the *Our Gang* films from 1937 to 1940.

JAMES BOOTH

Born: 19 December 1927,
in Croyden, Surrey, England.
Died: 11 August 2005,
in Hadleigh, Essex, England.
Birth name: David Geeves-Booth
Job description: Actor
James Booth's best known role was in *Zulu* (1964), as the insubordinate yet heroic Private Henry Hook. He also starred in *Sparrows Can't Sing* (1963), *French Dressing* (1964), *Robbery* (1967), *That'll Be the Day* (1973) and *Zorro, The Gay Blade* (1981). Booth's last film, dedicated to him, was the black comedy *Keeping Mum* (2005), in which he played the profoundly deaf neighbour of Rowan Atkinson.

WALERIAN BOROWCZYK

Born: 2 September 1923,
in Kwilicz, Poland.
Died: 3 February 2006, of congestive heart failure, in Paris, France.
Job description: Animator and director
Walerian Borowczyk was famous – and notorious - for his stylish, erotically charged films. Based in France, he started out as an animator, winning acclaim for *Les Jeux des anges* (1964), among others. Moving into live action, Borowczyk made *Goto, Island of Love* (1968) and *Blanche* (1971), downbeat fables of frustrated desire. The more explicit *Immoral Tales* (1974), *The Beast* (1975) and *Doctor Jekyll and the Women* (1981) tempered their sexual content with irony, black comedy, social commentary and an impressive visual sense. Always on the fringes of the film industry, Borowczyk was later restricted to picturesque soft-porn.

LORD JOHN BRABOURNE

Born: 9 November 1924,
in London, England.
Died: 22 September 2005,
in Kent, England.
Birth name: John Ulick Knatchbull
Job description: Producer
Lord Brabourne specialised in 'quality' films, often with a literary pedigree, big name director and all-star cast. His best known productions include *Sink the Bismarck!* (Lewis Gilbert, 1960), *Romeo and Juliet* (Franco Zeffirelli, 1968), *Tales of Beatrix Potter* (Reginald Mills, 1971), *Murder on the Orient Express* (Sidney Lumet, 1974), *A Passage to India* (David Lean, 1984) and *Little Dorrit* (Christine Edzard, 1988).

JOCELYN BRANDO

Born: 18 November 1919, i n San Francisco, California, USA.
Died: 27 November 2005, of natural causes, in Santa Monica, California, USA.
Job description: Actress
Best known as Marlon Brando's older sister, Jocelyn Brando had a long stage and television career, compromised by her alcohol dependency. Her sporadic film career included *The Big Heat* (1953), as Glenn Ford's ill-fated wife, and *Mommie Dearest* (1981), a much derided biopic of Joan Crawford. Jocelyn Brando appeared in two films with her brother, *The Ugly American* (1963) and *The Chase* (1966).

PHIL BROWN

Born: 30 April 1916,
in Cambridge, Massachusetts, USA.
Died: 9 February 2006, from pneumonia, in Woodland Hills, Los

Angeles, California, USA.
Job description: Actor
A solid character actor, Phil Brown made an early film appearance in *The Killers* (1946). Blacklisted in 1952, he spent the next 40 years based in London, England. Brown's later films included Charles Chaplin's *A King in New York* (1957), *The Camp on Blood Island* (1958), *Valdez is Coming* (1971), *Superman* (1978) and *Chaplin* (1992), Richard Attenborough's biopic of the comedy star. His best known film role was Luke Skywalker's Uncle Owen in *Star Wars* (1977), which made Brown a popular figure on the fan convention circuit.

HENRY BUMSTEAD

Born: 17 March 1915,
in Ontario, California, USA.
Died: 24 May 2006, of prostate cancer, in Pasadena, California, USA.
Birth name: Lloyd Henry Bumstead
Job description: Production designer
Henry Bumstead enjoyed fruitful collaborations with directors Alfred Hitchcock, George Roy Hill and Clint Eastwood, among others. His many credits include *Vertigo* (Hitchcock, 1958), *I Married a Monster from Outer Space* (Gene Fowler, Jr., 1958), *The Bellboy* (Jerry Lewis, 1960), *The War Lord* (Franklin J. Schaffner, 1965), *Slaughterhouse Five* (Hill, 1972), *High Plains Drifter* (Eastwood, 1973), *The World According to Garp* (Hill, 1982) and *Unforgiven* (Eastwood, 1992). He won Academy Awards for *To Kill a Mockingbird* (Robert Mulligan, 1962) and *The Sting* (Hill, 1973). Bumstead's final

project was Eastwood's two part war epic *Flags of Our Fathers* (2006) and *Red Sun, Black Sand* (2006).

EDDIE BUNKER

Born: 31 December 1933, in Hollywood, California, USA.
Died: 19 July 2005, of complications from cancer surgery, in Burbank, California, USA.
Job description: Writer and actor
A reformed criminal, Eddie Bunker co-scripted *Straight Time* (1978), based on his novel *No Beast So Fierce*. He also played a bit part, leading to a new career in acting. Bunker is best known as Mr Blue in *Reservoir Dogs* (1992). His other credits include *The Long Riders* (1980), *The Runaway Train* (1985), writing and acting, and *The Longest Yard* (2005). Bunker served as a consultant for *Heat* (1995), drawing on his experiences as an armed robber.

OLEG CASSINI

Born: 11 April 1913, in Paris, France.
Died: 17 March 2006, of complications from a stroke, in Long Island, New York, USA.
Birth name: Oleg Cassini Loiewski
Job description: Fashion designer
Oleg Cassini broke into films designing costumes for his wife, movie star Gene Tierney. Beginning with *The Shanghai Gesture* (1941), he supervised Tierney's wardrobe for ten years. When the marriage ended, Cassini left films to concentrate on his fashion empire. He later contributed to *Rampage* (1963) and *The Ambushers* (1967).

JACK COLVIN

Born: 13 October 1934, in Lyndon, Kansas, USA.
Died: 1 December 2005, of complications from a stroke, in North Hollywood, California, USA.
Job description: Actor
Jack Colvin was best known for the television series *The Incredible Hulk* (1977-82), playing reporter Jack McGee. A respected stage actor, director and teacher, he made several film appearances, including *Monte Walsh* (1970), *Jeremiah Johnson* (1972), *The Life*

and Times of Judge Roy Bean (1972), *Scorpio* (1973), *The Terminal Man* (1974), *Rooster Cogburn* (1975) and *Child's Play* (1988).

HUBERT CORNFIELD

Born: 9 February 1929, in Istanbul, Turkey.
Died: 18 June 2006, of heart failure, in Los Angeles, California, USA.
Job description: Director and writer
Hubert Cornfield specialised in low budget dramas with an unusual interest in character psychology. Many of his protagonists are low life criminals, undone by their greed and inner weakness. A Hollywood insider, Cornfield was friends with William Wyler, Billy Wilder and Joseph Mankiewicz, who all signed his application to join the Directors Guild. Cornfield drew attention with *Pressure Point* (1962), a gripping psychological thriller starring Sidney Poitier and teen idol Bobby Darin. Cornfield's best known film is *The Night of the Following Day* (1968), an offbeat kidnap drama with Marlon Brando. While production proved a nightmare, the end result is strangely memorable. Latterly based in France, Cornfield retired from film-making after *Les Grands moyens* (1975).

PATRICK CRANSHAW

Born: 17 June 1919,
in Bartlesville, Oklahoma, USA.
Died: 28 December 2005, of natural causes, in Fort Worth, Texas, USA.
Job description: Actor
A busy character actor, Patrick Cranshaw appeared in *Bonnie and Clyde* (1967), *Sergeant Pepper's Lonely Hearts Club Band* (1978), *Pee-Wee's Big Adventure* (1985), *Ed Wood* (1994), *Best in Show* (2000) and *Herbie Fully Loaded* (2005).

CONSTANCE CUMMINGS

Born: 15 May 1910,
in Seattle, Washington, USA.
Died: 23 November 2005,
in Oxfordshire, England.
Birth name: Constance Halverstadt
Job description: Actress
Constance Cummings had a brief taste of Hollywood stardom, appearing in

The Criminal Code (1931), with Walter Huston, and *Movie Crazy* (1932), with Harold Lloyd. Relocating to England, she became a respected actress on the London stage. Cummings' later films included *Blithe Spirit* (1945) and *Sammy Going South* (1963).

DAN CURTIS

Born: 12 August 1927,
in Bridgeport, Connecticut, USA.
Died: 27 March 2006, from a brain tumour, in Brentwood, California, USA.
Birth name: Daniel Mayer Cherkoss
Job description: Producer, writer and director
Active largely in television, Dan Curtis created *Dark Shadows* (1966-71), a gothic daytime soap opera. Its popularity prompted two film spin-offs, *House of Dark Shadows* (1970) and *Night of Dark Shadows* (1971). The latter was hacked about by distributor MGM, destroying Curtis' original vision. He returned to the horror genre with *Burnt Offerings* (1976), a crudely effective tale of family breakdown. Curtis produced the more 'respectable' TV mini-series *The Winds of War* (1983) and its sequel *War and Remembrance* (1988).

FRANCESCO DE MASI

Born: 11 January 1930, in Rome, Italy.
Died: 6 November 2005, of cancer, in Rome, Italy.
Job description: Composer
One of Italy's most prolific film composers, Francesco De Masi profited

from the 1960s boom in horror films and 'spaghetti' westerns. His more notable credits were *The Ghost* (1963), *Johnny Hamlet* (1968), *The Arena* (1974), a US co-production, and *The New York Ripper* (1982). De Masi also scored the Chuck Norris hit *Lone Wolf McQuade* (1983), a homage to the Italian western.

TONINO DELLI COLLI

Born: 20 November 1922,
in Rome, Italy.
Died: 16 August 2005,
from a heart attack, in Rome, Italy.
Birth name: Antonio Delli Colli
Job description: Director of photography
One of Italy's leading cameramen, Tonino Delli Colli worked with Roberto Rossellini, Pier Paolo Pasolini, Sergio Leone, Federico Fellini and Roman Polanski. His best known films include *Accatone* (Pasolini, 1961), *The Gospel According to St. Matthew* (Pasolini, 1964), *The Good The Bad and The Ugly* (Leone, 1966), *Once Upon a Time in the West* (Leone, 1968), *The Canterbury Tales* (Pasolini, 1972), *Lacombe, Lucien* (Louis Malle, 1974), *Salo, or The 120 Days of Sodom* (Pasolini, 1975), *Once Upon a Time in America* (Leone, 1983), *Ginger and Fred* (Fellini, 1986) and *Death and the Maiden* (Polanski, 1994). Delli Colli's last film was the Oscar-winning *Life is Beautiful* (Roberto Benigni, 1997).

JAMES DOOHAN

Born: 3 March 1920,
in Vancouver, British Columbia, Canada.
Died: 20 July 2005, from pneumonia and Alzheimer's disease, in Redmond, Washington, USA.
Birth name: James Montgomery Doohan
Job description: Actor
A jobbing television actor, James Doohan achieved lasting fame in *Star Trek* (1966-69), as Chief Engineer Montgomery 'Scotty' Scott. After the franchise was relaunched with *Star Trek: The Motion Picture* (1979), Doohan stayed with the film series up to *Star Trek: Generations* (1994). His non-*Trek* film credits include *The Satan Bug* (1965), *Pretty Maids All in a Row* (1971) and *Man in the Wilderness* (1971).

HENRY FARRELL

Born: 27 September 1920,
in Madera County, California, USA.
Died: 29 March 2006, in Pacific Palisades, California, USA.
Birth name: Charles Henry Myers
Job description: Writer
Henry Farrell got an early break writing stories for pulp magazines. His best known novel was *Whatever Happened to Baby Jane?* (1960), a tale of faded Hollywood glamour, sibling rivalry and creeping insanity. Producer-director Robert Aldrich bought the rights and his 1962 film version proved a hit, reviving the careers of Bette Davis and Joan Crawford. Farrell co-scripted the follow-up, *Hush… Hush, Sweet Charlotte* (Aldrich, 1964), based on his story 'Whatever Happened to Cousin Charlotte?'. He wrote an original script for *What's the Matter with Helen?* (Curtis Harrington, 1971), a belated entry in this sub-genre. Francois Truffaut adapted Farrell's novel *Such a Gorgeous Kid Like Me* (1967) as the black comedy *Une belle fille comme moi* (1972).

CY FEUER

Born: 15 January 1911,
in Brooklyn, New York, USA.
Died: 17 May 2006, of bladder cancer, in New York, New York, USA.
Birth name: Seymour Arnold Feuer
Job description: Producer
Cy Feuer began his film career as a composer for Saturday morning serials, notably *The Adventures of Captain Marvel* (1941). Back in New York, he became

a successful producer of Broadway musicals. Feuer's later film credits included *Cabaret* (1972) and *A Chorus Line* (1985).

GERALDINE FITZGERALD

Born: 24 November 1913, in Dublin, Ireland.
Died: 17 July 2005, of Alzheimer's disease, in New York, New York, USA.
Job description: Actress
A respected stage and television actress, Geraldine Fitzgerald made intermittent film appearances, including *Wuthering Heights* (1939), *Wilson* (1944), *The Pawnbroker* (1964), *Rachel, Rachel* (1968) and *Arthur* (1981).

RICHARD FLEISCHER

Born: 8 December 1916, in Brooklyn, New York, USA.
Died: 25 March 2006, of 'natural causes', in Woodland Hills, Los Angeles, California, USA.
Job description: Director
The son of animation pioneer Max Fleischer, Richard Fleischer became a successful director in his own right. A fine craftsman, he drew attention with *The Narrow Margin* (1952), a superior B movie. Fleischer was promoted to the A list with Disney's *20,000 Leagues Under the Sea* (1954), followed by *The Vikings* (1958) and *Compulsion* (1959). His best films include *Barabbas* (1962), an intelligent epic, and *The Boston Strangler* (1968), a chilling account of the notorious serial killer. He also directed the cult fantasies *Fantastic Voyage* (1966) and *Soylent Green* (1973). The controversial *Mandingo* (1975) was widely condemned as racist trash, though some critics acclaimed the film as a misunderstood masterpiece. While Fleischer's later films were disappointing, both *Amityville 3-D* (1983) and *Conan the Destroyer* (1984) have their moments.

ANTHONY FRANCIOSA

Born: 25 October 1928, in New York, New York, USA.
Died: 19 January 2006, from a massive stroke, in Los Angeles, California, USA.
Birth name: Anthony Papaleo

Job description: Actor
A successful Broadway actor, Anthony Franciosa got his film break with *A Hatful of Rain* (1957), reprising his stage role. He co-starred in *The Long, Hot Summer* (1958), playing second fiddle to Paul Newman, Joanne Woodward and a barnstorming Orson Welles. Regarded as a 'difficult' actor, Franciosa struggled to sustain his film career. A brief marriage to Shelley Winters drew extensive media coverage, much of it unfavourable. His commitment to the civil rights movement also caused friction with more staid Hollywood figures. Relegated to the B list, Franciosa gave creditable performances in *Rio Conchos* (1964) and *Across 110th Street* (1972). His best role was in Dario Argento's *Tenebre* (1982), as a crime writer with something to hide. Franciosa's last notable film was *City Hall* (1996).

ARTHUR FRANZ

Born: 29 February 1920, in Perth Amboy, New Jersey, USA.
Died: 16 June 2006, from emphysema, in Oxnard, California, USA.
Job description: Actor
A dependable character actor, Arthur Franz co-starred in several fantasy cult classics: *Abbott and Costello Meet the Invisible Man* (1951), as the title character, *Invaders from Mars* (1953), *Monster on Campus* (1958) and *The Atomic Submarine* (1959). Franz's favourite role was *The Sniper* (1952), as a disturbed war veteran who goes on a murderous rampage. His more mainstream films included *The Sands of Iwo Jima* (1949), *The Caine Mutiny* (1954), *The Young Lions* (1958) and *The Carpetbaggers* (1964). Franz's last film was *That Championship Season* (1982).

PAUL GLEASON

Born: 4 May 1944, in Jersey City, New Jersey, USA.
Died: 27 May 2006, of lung cancer, in Burbank, California, USA.
Birth name: Paul Xavier Gleason
Job description: Actor
Paul Gleason's film career got off to a shaky start with *Doc Savage: The Man of Bronze* (1975), a deserved flop. Employed largely in television, Gleason gave solid performances in *Arthur* (1981), *Trading Places* (1983), *The Breakfast Club* (1985) and *Die Hard* (1988).

GUY GREEN

Born: 5 November 1913, in Somerset, England.
Died: 14 September 2005, of heart and kidney failure, in Beverly Hills, Los Angeles, California, USA.
Job description: Cinematographer, producer, writer and director
Guy Green was the first British cameraman to win an Oscar, for David Lean's *Great Expectations* (1946). His other credits as director of photography include Carol Reed's *The Way Ahead* (1944), Lean's *Oliver Twist* (1948) and Raoul Walsh's *Captain Horatio Hornblower R.N.* (1951). As a director, he made *River Beat* (1954), *Sea of Sand* (1958), *The Angry Silence* (1960), *The Mark* (1961), *Diamond Head* (1963), *A Patch of Blue* (1965), from his own screenplay, *The Magus* (1968), *A Walk in the Spring Rain* (1970) and *The Devil's Advocate* (1977). From the mid-1970s, Green worked largely in American television. He was awarded the OBE in 2004.

KENNETH GRIFFITH

Born: 12 October 1921, in Tenby, Pembrokeshire, Wales.
Died: 25 June 2006, in London, England.
Job description: Actor
A fine character actor, Kenneth Griffith enjoyed a long career in British films.

He excelled at quirky, idiosyncratic characters, sometimes with sinister undertones. Adept at comedy, Griffith was a favourite of the Boulting Brothers, appearing in *Private's Progress* (1956), *Lucky Jim* (1957), *I'm All Right Jack* (1959) and *Heaven's Above!* (1963). His other credits included *Love on the Dole* (1941), *Fame is the Spur* (1946), *A Night to Remember* (1958), *The Two-Headed Spy* (1958), as a plausible Hitler, *Only Two Can Play* (1962), *The Whisperers* (1967), *The Lion in Winter* (1968), *The Wild Geese* (1978), lending humanity to a stereotypical 'queen' role, *Who Dares Wins* (1982) and *Four Weddings and a Funeral* (1994). Television credits included two episodes of *The Prisoner* (1968), 'The Girl Who Was Death' and 'Fall Out', which he also co-wrote, uncredited. Griffith was well known for his anti-establishment politics, especially his support for Irish Unification. His film about Michael Collins, *Hang Up Your Brightest Colours* (1973), was banned by ATV boss Lew Grade, remaining unshown for 20 years.

VAL GUEST

Born: 11 December 1911, in London, England.
Died: 10 May 2006, of prostate cancer, in Palm Springs, California, USA.
Birth name: Valmond Maurice Grossman
Job description: Writer, director and producer
A former journalist, Val Guest got his film break writing scripts for Will Hay (*Oh, Mr Porter!*, 1937; *Ask a Policeman*,

1938) and The Crazy Gang (*Okay for Sound*, 1937; *The Frozen Limits*, 1939). As a director, he scored a hit with the comedy *Mr Drake's Duck* (1951). In the mid-1950s, Guest found a niche in intelligent, downbeat science fiction. Working with Hammer Films, he made *The Quatermass Xperiment* (1955), *Quatermass 2* (1957), and *The Abominable Snowman* (1957), all based on TV scripts by Nigel Kneale. Guest followed this trio with the BAFTA-winning *The Day the Earth Caught Fire* (1961), an apocalyptic fable that favoured characterisation over spectacle as it laid out the dangers of the nuclear arms race. Adept in all genres, he also made thrillers (*Hell is a City*, 1960), musicals (*Expresso Bongo*, 1960), spy spoofs (*Casino Royale*, 1967) and prehistoric sagas (*When Dinosaurs Ruled the Earth*, 1970). While Guest's career declined with the collapse of the British film industry, *Confessions of a Window Cleaner* (1974) remains a cult favourite. His last film, *The Boys in Blue* (1983), was an undernourished remake of *Ask a Policeman*.

JUNE HAVER

Born: 10 June 1926, in Rock Island, Illinois, USA.
Died: 4 July 2005, from respiratory failure, in Brentwood, California, USA.
Birth name: June Stovenour
Job description: Actress
Active in Hollywood for ten years, June Haver co-starred in *Irish Eyes Are Smiling* (1944), *The Dolly Sisters* (1945), *Scudda Hoo! Scudda Hay!* (1948) and *Love*

Nest (1951). She made her last screen appearance in 1953, marrying actor Fred MacMurray in 1954.

GREGG HOFFMAN

Born: 1963, in Phoenix, Arizona, USA.
Died: 4 December 2005, of natural causes, in Los Angeles, California, USA.
Job description: Producer
A respected independent producer, Gregg Hoffman scored a sleeper hit with the horror movie *Saw* (2004), followed by the equally successful *Saw II* (2005).

WILLIAM HOOTKINS

Born: 5 July 1948, in Dallas, Texas, USA.
Died: 23 October 2005, of pancreatic cancer, in the Pacific Palisades, Santa Monica, California, USA.
Job description: Actor
A busy character actor, William Hootkins found cult fame as X-wing pilot Porkins, aka Red Six, in *Star Wars* (1977). His other films include *Flash Gordon* (1980), *Raiders of the Lost Ark* (1981), *Batman* (1989), *Dust Devil* (1992), *Funny Bones* (1995) and *Colour Me Kubrick* (2005).

AKIRA IFUKUBE

Born: 31 May 1914, in Kushiro, Hokkaido, Japan.
Died: 8 February 2006, from multiple organ failure, in Tokyo, Japan.
Job description: Composer
One of Japan's leading film composers,

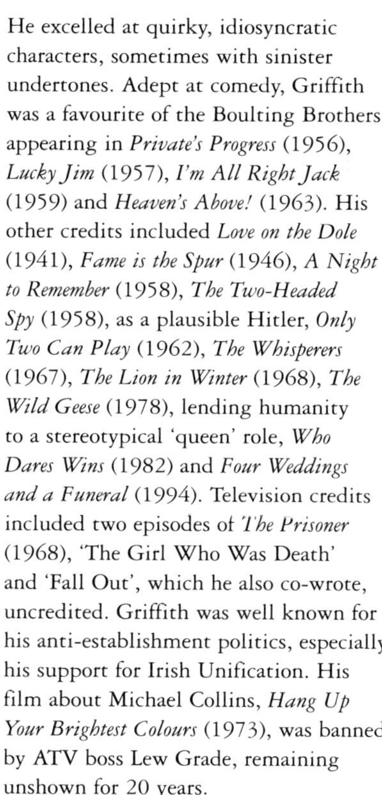

Akira Ifukube is best known for *Gojira* (1954), aka *Godzilla*. His stirring martial theme, enhanced by Godzilla's roars, remains a classic piece of film music. Ifukube's other credits include *The Burmese Harp* (1956), *Rodan* (1956), *Zatoichi* (1962), *Frankenstein Conquers the World* (1965), *War of the Gargantuas* (1966), *Daimajin* (1966) and *Godzilla versus Mechagodzilla* (1993). His fine score for *King Kong versus Godzilla* (1962) was largely dropped from the English-language version, replaced by cues from *The Creature from the Black Lagoon* (1954).

SHOHEI IMAMURA

Born: 15 September 1926, in Tokyo, Japan.
Died: 30 May 2006, of liver cancer, in Tokyo, Japan.
Job description: Director
Shohei Imamura was acclaimed for his unflinching, sympathetic depiction of Japan's underclass, often from a female perspective. His films include *Insect Woman* (1963), *The Pornographer* (1966), *Black Rain* (1989) and *Warm Water Under a Red Bridge* (2001). He twice won the Cannes Film Festival *Palme d'Or*, for *The Ballad of Narayama* (1983) and *The Eel* (1996).

ANDREAS KATSULAS

Born: 18 May 1946, in St. Louis, Missouri, USA.
Died: 13 February 2006, of lung cancer, in Los Angeles, California, USA.
Birth name: Andrew Katsulas
Job description: Actor
A gifted actor, Andreas Katsulas was often typecast in sinister roles: a mobster in *Someone to Watch Over Me* (1987), the one-armed man in *The Fugitive* (1993) and a terrorist leader in *Executive Decision* (1996). He enjoyed a (slight) change of pace as the alien G'Kar in the TV series *Babylon 5* (1994-98).

GEOFFREY KEEN

Born: 21 August 1916, in Wallingford, Surrey, England.
Died: 3 November 2005, in Northwood, Middlesex, England.
Job description: Actor
A dependable character actor, Geoffrey

Keen appeared in *The Third Man* (1949), *Treasure Island* (1950), *Doctor in the House* (1954), *Horrors of the Black Museum* (1959), *Doctor Zhivago* (1965) and *Born Free* (1966), among many others. He became a James Bond regular, as Sir Frederick Gray, from *The Spy Who Loved Me* (1977) to *The Living Daylights* (1985). Keen had one of his best roles in *Taste the Blood of Dracula* (1970), cast as a hypocritical Victorian libertine who gets on the wrong side of the Count.

DON KNOTTS

Born: 21 July 1924, in Morgantown, West Virginia, USA.
Died: 24 February 2006, of pulmonary and respiratory complications, in Los Angeles, California, USA.
Birth name: Jesse Donald Knotts
Job description: Comic actor
For non-American viewers, Thora Birch's Don Knotts fixation in *Ghost World* (2001) is doubly baffling. In fact, this rubber-faced comic was a US pop icon. A television regular, Knotts achieved stardom in *The Andy Griffith Show* (1960-65), winning three Emmys for his performance as Deputy Barney Fife. Knotts' nervous, 'reluctant hero' persona was popular enough to launch a film career. He starred in a series of family comedies, including *The Incredible Mr Limpet* (1964), *The Ghost and Mr Chicken* (1966) and *The Reluctant Astronaut* (1967). An attempt at 'adult' comedy with *The Love God?* (1969) proved less successful. In the 1970s, Knotts appeared in several Disney films, notably *The Apple

Dumpling Gang* (1974), *Herbie Goes to Monte Carlo* (1977) and *Hot Lead and Cold Feet* (1978). His other films include *No Time for Sergeants* (1958), *It's a Mad, Mad, Mad, Mad World* (1963, cameo), *Move Over Darling* (1963), *The Private Eyes* (1980), *Pleasantville* (1998) and *Chicken Little* (2005).

GAVIN LAMBERT

Born: 23 July 1924, in East Grinstead, Sussex, England.
Died: 17 July 2005, of pulmonary fibrosis, in Los Angeles, California, USA.
Job description: Writer
A respected novelist and journalist, Gavin Lambert wrote and directed *Another Sky* (1954), a tale of English repression and North African sensuality. A friend of Nicholas Ray, he co-scripted *Bitter Victory* (1957) for the director. Lambert also wrote *Sons and Lovers* (1960), *Inside Daisy Clover* (1965), based on his novel, and *I Never Promised You a Rose Garden* (1977).

MARC LAWRENCE

Born: 17 February 1910, in New York City, New York, USA.
Died: 27 November 2005, of heart failure, in Palm Springs, California, USA.
Birth name: Max Goldsmith
Job description: Actor.
Marc Lawrence's brooding features and pockmarked skin typecast him as a villain. Active in films from the 1930s, he played bit parts in *If I Had a Million* (1932), *Brigham Young* (1940), *This

Gun for Hire (1942), *Dillinger* (1945), *Key Largo* (1948) and *The Asphalt Jungle* (1950), among many others. Blacklisted in the early 1950s, Lawrence moved to Europe. His later appearances included *Helen of Troy* (1956), *Custer of the West* (1968), *Krakatoa – East* (sic) *of Java* (1969), *Diamonds Are Forever* (1971), *The Man with the Golden Gun* (1974), *Marathon Man* (1976), *The Big Easy* (1987), *From Dusk Till Dawn* (1996) and *The Shipping News* (2001). Lawrence also produced, wrote and directed *Nightmare in the Sun* (1965) and *Daddy's Deadly Darlings* (1972). The latter starred his daughter, Toni, with Lawrence in a supporting role.

ERNEST LEHMAN

Born: 8 December 1915, in New York, New York, USA.
Died: 2 July 2005, of a heart attack, in Los Angeles, California, USA.
Job description: Writer and producer
One of Hollywood's leading screenwriters, Ernest Lehman worked on *Sabrina* (1954), *Sweet Smell of Success* (1957), based on his novel, *North by Northwest* (1959), *West Side Story* (1961), *The Sound of Music* (1965), *Who's Afraid of Virginia Woolf?* (1966) and *Black Sunday* (1977). Lehman also directed *Portnoy's Complaint* (1972), a poorly received adaptation of Philip Roth's novel.

AL LEWIS

Born: 30 April 1910 **or** 30 April 1923*, in New York, New York, USA.
Died: 3 February 2006, of natural causes, in New York, New York, USA.
Birth name: Alexander Meister
Job description: Actor
Al Lewis achieved TV immortality playing Sam Dracula, aka Grandpa Munster in *The Munsters* (1964-66), a ghoulish sit-com for the whole family. He reprised the role in the film spin-off, *Munster, Go Home* (1966). Lewis' other film credits include *The World of Henry Orient* (1964), *They Shoot Horses, Don't They?* (1969), *They Might Be Giants* (1971), *Used Cars* (1980) and *Married to the Mob* (1988).
(*It's been suggested that Lewis added thirteen years to his age when auditioning for the role of Grandpa Munster. If 1923 is the correct date, Lewis was a year younger than screen daughter Yvonne De Carlo.)

SID LUFT

Born: 2 November 1915, in New York, New York, USA.
Died: 15 September 2005, of a heart attack, in Santa Monica, California, USA.
Birth name: Michael Sidney Luft
Job description: Producer
The one-time husband of Judy Garland, Luft produced *A Star is Born* (1954), her last major film. Luft's other film credits include *Kilroy Was Here* (1947) and *French Leave* (1948).

PAT McCORMICK

Born: 30 June 1927, in Lakewood, Ohio, USA.
Died: 29 July 2005, of 'natural causes', in Woodland Hills, California, USA.
Birth name: Arley McCormick
Job description: Comedy writer and performer
A television regular, Pat McCormick appeared in Robert Altman's *Buffalo Bill and the Indians* (1976) and *A Wedding* (1978), *Smokey and the Bandit* (1977), plus two sequels, and *Scrooged* (1988). He co-wrote and acted in *Under the Rainbow* (1981), a failed comedy about the making of *The Wizard of Oz*. In 1998, McCormick suffered a massive stroke, which left him paralysed and unable to speak.

DARREN McGAVIN

Born: 7 May 1922, in San Joaquin, California, USA.
Died: 25 February 2006, of 'natural causes', in Los Angeles, California, USA.
Job description: Actor
A prolific television and stage actor, Darren McGavin was best known as Carl Kolchak, the intrepid reporter who battles a vampire in the TV movie *The Night Stalker* (1972). He reprised the role in *The Night Strangler* (1973) and the series *Kolchak: The Night Stalker* (1974), a short-lived flop that now enjoys cult status. McGavin's film credits included *The Man With The Golden Arm* (1955), *Airport '77* (1977), *A Christmas Story* (1983), *The Natural* (1984, unbilled)

and *Raw Deal* (1986). He directed *Happy Mother's Day, Love George* (1973) and *American Reunion* (1976).

MATTHEW McGRORY

Born: 17 May 1973, in West Chester, Pennsylvania, USA.
Died: 9 August 2005, from natural causes, in Los Angeles, California, USA.
Job description: Actor
Standing 7'6", Matthew McGrory played memorable giants – good and bad – in *Men in Black II* (2002), *Big Fish* (2003), *House of 1000 Corpses* (2003), *Constantine* (2005) and *The Devil's Rejects* (2005).

CONSTANCE MOORE

Born: 18 January 1920, in Sioux City, Iowa, USA.
Died: 16 September 2005, of heart failure, in Los Angeles, California, USA.
Job description: Actress and singer
Constance Moore co-starred in *Buck Rogers* (1939, serial), with Buster Crabbe, *You Can't Cheat an Honest Man* (1939), opposite W.C. Fields, and *Charlie McCarthy, Detective* (1939). Her brief film career ended with *Hit Parade of 1947* (1947).

PAT MORITA

Born: 28 June 1932, in Isleton, California, USA.
Died: 24 November 2005, of 'natural causes', in Las Vegas, Nevada, USA.
Birth name: Noriyuki Morita
Job description: Actor

Pat Morita achieved cult status – and an Oscar nomination - as Mr Miyagi, the wise martial arts master in *The Karate Kid* (1984) and its sequels. He started out in the 1960s as a stand-up comic, billed as the 'Hip Nip'. Morita's other film credits included *Thoroughly Modern Millie* (1967), *Midway* (1976), *Full Moon High* (1981), *Honeymoon in Vegas* (1992), *Mulan* (1998) and *Brother* (2000).

NAUSHAD ALI

Born: 25 December 1919, in Lucknow (now Uttar Pradesh), India
Died: 5 May 2006, from natural causes, in Mumbai, India.
Job description: Composer
Naushad Ali was best known for his work with director Mehboob Khan, notably *Precious Time* (1946), *Aan* (1952) and *Mother India* (1957). His other credits included *Prem Nagar* (1940), *Son of India* (1962) and *Ganwaar* (1970).

ROBERT F. NEWMYER

Born: 30 May 1956, in Washington, D.C., USA.
Died: 12 December 2005, from a heart attack, in Toronto, Ontario, Canada.
Job description: Producer
A successful independent producer, Robert F. Newmyer came to notice with *sex, lies, & videotape* (1989). He scored his biggest hit with *The Santa Clause* (1994), followed by two sequels. Newmyer also produced *Don Juan DeMarco* (1995) and *Training Day* (2001).

SHEREE NORTH

Born: 17 January 1932, in Los Angeles, California, USA.
Died: 4 November 2005, from complications with cancer surgery, in Los Angeles, California, USA.
Birth name: Dawn Shirley Crang
Job description: Actress
A prolific television actress, Sheree North appeared in such films as *Living It Up* (1954), *Lawman* (1971) and *The Outfit* (1974). She was a favourite of director Don Siegel, who cast her in *Madigan* (1968), *Charley Varrick* (1973), *The Shootist* (1976) and *Telefon* (1977). In later years, North made a TV comeback in *Seinfeld*, playing Cosmo Kramer's mother.

JEAN PARKER

Born: 11 August 1915, in Butte, Montana, USA.
Died: 30 November 2005, of a stroke, in Woodland Hills, California, USA.
Birth name: Luis Stephanie Zelinska
Job description: Actress
Jean Parker started out as a sweeter-than-thou ingénue, appearing in *Little Women* (1933), *The Ghost Goes West* (1935), *The Flying Deuces* (1939) and *Bluebeard* (1944). She latterly played hard-bitten broads, notably in *The Gunfighter* (1950). Parker retired from films after 1966.
Note: Parker's birth name is sometimes given as Lois Mae Green, while her birthplace has been listed as Deer Lodge, Powell County, Montana.

GORDON PARKS

Born: 30 November 1912, in Fort Scott, Kansas, USA.
Died: 7 March 2006, of cancer, in New York, New York, USA.
Job description: Photographer, writer, composer and director
Gordon Parks was a world class photojournalist, employed for many years by *Life* magazine. As a director, he came to notice with *The Learning Tree* (1969, a tale of African American life, based on his novel. Parks got finance for the film from Warner Brothers, the first African American director to obtain major studio backing. He was best known for *Shaft* (1971), one of the first blaxploitation films. Though *Shaft* suffered from indifferent handling, its influence is undeniable. Parks directed the first sequel, *Shaft's Big Score* (1972), followed by *The Super Cops* (1974) and the biopic *Leadbelly* (1976). Retired from feature films, he made a cameo appearance in the *Shaft* remake (2000).

CHRIS PENN

Born: 10 October 1965, in Los Angeles, California, USA.
Died: 24 January 2006, from an enlarged heart, in Santa Monica, California, USA.
Job description: Actor
The brother of Sean Penn, Chris Penn emerged as a fine character actor in his own right. Penn's films include *Rumble Fish* (1983), *Footloose* (1984), *Pale Rider* (1985), *At Close Range* (1986), with Sean

Penn, *Reservoir Dogs* (1992), as Nice Guy Eddie, *True Romance* (1993), *Short Cuts* (1993), *The Funeral* (1996), *Starsky and Hutch* (2004) and *The Darwin Awards* (2006).

BROCK PETERS

Born: 2 July 1927, in New York, New York, USA.
Died: 23 August 2005, of pancreatic cancer, in Los Angeles, California, USA.
Birth name: George Fisher
Job description: Actor
Brock Peters was one of the first African American actors to establish a film career not dependent on stereotypical roles. His many credits include *Carmen Jones* (1954), *To Kill a Mockingbird* (1962), *The Pawnbroker* (1964), *Major Dundee* (1965), *Ace High* (1968), *Soylent Green* (1973),

Star Trek IV: The Voyage Home (1986) and *Star Trek VI: The Undiscovered Country* (1991).

INGO PREMINGER

Born: 25 February 1911, in Czernowitz, Austria-Hungary (now Cernovcy, Ukraine).
Died: 7 June 2006, in Pacific Palisades, California, USA.
Birth name: Ingwald Preminger
Job description: Agent and producer
The younger brother of director-producer Otto Preminger, Ingo Preminger was a respected Hollywood agent. His clients included writers Dalton Trumbo and Ring Lardner Jr., both blacklisted during the 1950s. Preminger kept them in work by arranging a series of pseudonyms and 'fronts'. He turned producer with *MASH* (1970), a modestly-budgeted black comedy. Based on a book by Richard Hooker, and a script by Lardner Jr., the film became a box-office hit and anti-establishment classic. *MASH* made stars of Donald Sutherland and Elliott Gould, and launched the career of Robert Altman, a former TV director whose earlier features had flopped. Preminger also produced *The Salzburg Connection* (1972), a routine thriller.

JAY PRESSON ALLEN

Born: 3 March 1922, in Fort Worth, Texas, USA.
Died: 1 May 2006, in Manhattan, New York, USA, from a stroke.
Job descripton: Writer
Jay Presson Allen was a leading screenwriter, latterly associated with director Sidney Lumet. Her credits include *Marnie* (1964), *The Prime of Miss Jean Brodie* (1969), *Cabaret* (1972), *Prince of the City* (Lumet, 1981) and *Deathtrap* (Lumet, 1982).

RICHARD PRYOR

Born: 1 December 1940, in Peoria, Illinois, USA.
Died: 10 December 2005, of a heart attack, in Encino, Los Angeles, California, USA.
Birth name: Richard Franklin Lennox Thomas Pryor III
Job description: Stand-up comic, writer

and actor
Richard Pryor was the archetypal troubled comic genius. A keen observer of human foibles – especially his own – he had an unmatched ability to make the most painful, humiliating situations uproariously funny. Sadly, the cinema rarely allowed him to show this talent. After a run of minor films, including *Wild in the Streets* (1968), Pryor co-wrote *Blazing Saddles* (1974) with Mel Brooks. While Brooks intended Pryor to star, backers were wary of this foul-mouthed chronicler of sex, drugs and racism. Pryor proved a credible straight actor in *Lady Sings the Blues* (1972), *Hit!* (1973) and *Blue Collar* (1978), a direction he didn't pursue. He stole *Uptown Saturday Night* (1974) from nominal stars Sidney Poitier and Bill Cosby, and played a lead role in the sleeper hit *Car Wash* (1976). Pryor's partnership with Gene Wilder brought mainstream success yet blunted much of his edge. While *Silver Streak* (1976) and *Stir Crazy* (1980) have their moments, the later Pryor-Wilder films are barely watchable. Audiences were given a sample of full-strength Pryor in *Richard Pryor – Live in Concert* (1979), the first and best of four concert films. Conversely, *Superman III* (1983) saw him unhappily cramped in a clumsy piece of family entertainment. Pryor wrote, directed and starred in *Jo Jo Dancer, Your Life is Calling* (1986), a flawed yet interesting semi-autobiography. Afflicted by multiple sclerosis from 1986, Pryor largely retired from the screen. His last notable role came in David Lynch's *Lost Highway* (1997).

RAJKUMAR

Born: 24 April 1928, in Gajanur, Karnataka, India.
Died: 12 April 2006, from a heart attack, in Bangalore, Karnataka, India.
Birth name: Mutturaju Singanalluru Puttaswamayya
Job description: Actor
One of India's best loved actors, Rajkumar appeared in films over five decades. His many credits included *Sodari* (1955), *Bhoodana* (1962), *Sakshatkara* (1972), *Aasha* (1980) and *Shabdavedi* (2000).

CHARLES ROCKET

Born: 24 August 1949, in Bangor, Maine, USA.
Died: 7 October 2005, a suicide, in Canterbury, Connecticut, USA.
Birth name: Charles Adams Claverie
Job description: Actor
A *Saturday Night Live* veteran, Charles Rocket had a successful, if low key film career. His credits included *Earth Girls Are Easy* (1988), *Dances with Wolves* (1990), *Short Cuts* (1993), *Dumb and Dumber* (1994) and *Shade* (2003).

VINCENT SCHIAVELLI

Born: 10 November 1948, in Brooklyn, New York, USA.
Died: 26 December 2005, of lung cancer, in Polizzi, Generosa, Sicily.
Job description: Actor
A distinctive character actor, Vincent Schiavelli was best known for his films with director Milos Forman: *Taking Off* (1971), *One Flew Over the Cuckoo's Nest* (1975), *Amadeus* (1984), *Valmont* (1989), *The People vs. Larry Flynt* (1996) and *Man on the Moon* (1999). Schiavelli's other credits included *Fast Times at Ridgemont High* (1982), *Ghost* (1990), *Batman Returns* (1992), *Tomorrow Never Dies* (1997) and *Death to Smoochy* (2002).

MOIRA SHEARER

Born: 17 January 1926, in Dunfermline, Fife, Scotland.
Died: 31 January 2006, of 'natural causes', in Oxford, Oxfordshire, England.
Birth name: Moira Shearer King
Job description: Ballerina and actress
Moira Shearer made an unforgettable

film debut in Michael Powell and Emeric Pressburger's *The Red Shoes* (1948), as the young ballet star who literally dances her way to tragedy. Committed to her stage career, Shearer made only a few more films, notably Powell and Pressburger's *Tales of Hoffmann* (1951), *The Man Who Loved Redheads* (1955) and Powell's *Peeping Tom* (1960). In the latter, she meets a gruesome end to match her fate in *The Red Shoes*.

VINCENT SHERMAN

Born: 16 July 1906, in Vienna, Georgia, USA.
Died: 18 June 2006, of natural causes, in Woodland Hills, Los Angeles, California, USA.
Birth name: Abram Orovitz
Job description: Director
Vincent Sherman was a gifted craftsman with no aspirations to *auteur* status. A former theatre actor, he took his stage name from his mother, Vinnie Schurman. After a few acting roles in Hollywood, Sherman was given a writing job by Warner Brothers, who placed him under contract. He turned director with *The Return of Dr. X* (1939), a B horror movie starring Humphrey Bogart. Having paid his dues, Sherman directed a series of superior melodramas and adventure films, including *Old Acquaintance* (1943), *Mr. Skeffington* (1944), *The Adventures of Don Juan* (1948) and *Harriet Craig* (1950). His leading ladies – and lovers – included Joan Crawford, Bette Davis and Rita Hayworth. During the early 1950s, Sherman was 'greylisted' for his

liberal sympathies. Dropped by Warner, he found employment in television. While Sherman returned to feature films, including Warner's *The Young Philadelphians* (1959), his career never regained momentum. His last film was *Cervantes* (1967), aka *Young Rebel*, a fanciful biopic of the Spanish writer. Sherman continued to work in television until 1983.

SHIN SANG OK

Born: 11 October 1926, in Chungjin, North Korea.
Died: 11 April 2006, of complications from a liver transplant, in Seoul, South Korea.
Job description: Producer, director and writer
A prolific film-maker in South Korea, Shin Sang Ok directed *Akya* (1952), *Madam White Snake* (1960) and *Ghosts of Chosun* (1970), among others. In the late 1970s, Shin and his wife were allegedly kidnapped and forced to make films for Kim Jong Il, movie-mad son of the North Korean dictator. During this period, Shin co-directed *Pulgasari* (1985), a bizarre combination of folktale, political allegory and *Godzilla* rip-off. The Shins escaped to the US in 1986. Shin Sang Ok's later films included *Mayumi* (1990) and *3 Ninjas Knuckle Up* (1995).

VILGOT SJOMAN

Born: 2 December 1924, in Stockholm, Sweden.
Died: 9 April 2006, from a cerebral haemorrhage, in Stockholm, Sweden.
Birth name: David Harald Vilgot Sjoman
Job description: Director
Vilgot Sjoman earned international notoriety with *I Am Curious (Yellow)* (1967). Devised as a political comedy, the film drew attention for its then daring nudity and sex scenes. A follow-up, *I Am Curious (Blue)* (1968) failed to repeat this success. Sjoman's later films included *The Garage* (1975), *The Pitfall* (1989) and *Alfred* (1995).

JOHN SPENCER

Born: 20 December 1946, in New York, New York, USA.

Died: 16 December 2005, of a heart attack, in Los Angeles, California, USA.
Birth name: John Speshock
Job description: Actor
A respected stage and television actor, John Spencer was best known for his roles in *L.A. Law* and *The West Wing*. He got an early break on *The Patty Duke Show* (1964-65), which launched his small screen career. Spencer's film credits included *War Games* (1983), *Sea of Love* (1989), *The Rock* (1996) and *Ravenous* (1999).

NORRIS SPENCER

Born: 1943
Died: 12 January 2006, of pneumonia, in London, England.
Job description: Production designer
Norris Spencer did his best known work with Ridley Scott: *Black Rain* (1989), *Thelma and Louise* (1991), *1492: The Conquest of Paradise* (1992) and *Hannibal* (2001). Formerly employed in commercials, he met Scott through the latter's younger brother, Tony Scott. Spencer also designed *Plunkett and Macleane* (1999), directed by Ridley's son Jake Scott, and Tony Scott's *Spy Game* (2001). Spencer's other credits included *Britannia Hospital* (1982) and *National Treasure* (2004).

WENDIE JO SPERBER

Born: 15 September 1958, in Hollywood, California, USA.
Died: 29 November 2005, of breast cancer, in Sherman Oaks, California, USA.
Job description: Actress
A gifted comedienne, Wendie Jo Sperber was best known as Linda McFly in Robert Zemeckis' *Back to the Future* (1985) and *Back to the Future III* (1990). Zemeckis had earlier cast her in *I Wanna Hold Your Hand* (1978) and *Used Cars* (1980). Sperber also appeared in *1941* (1979), co-scripted by Zemeckis, and *Love Affair* (1994).

RICHARD STAHL

Born: 4 January 1932, in Detroit, Michigan, USA.
Died: 18 June 2006, from Parkinson's disease, in Los Angeles, California, USA.

Job description: Actor
A prolific television actor, Richard Stahl had a lengthy, if intermittent film career, appearing in *Five Easy Pieces* (1970), *Billy Jack* (1971), *Slaughterhouse Five* (1972), *High Anxiety* (1977), *Nine to Five* (1980), *The Flamingo Kid* (1984), *L.A. Story* (1991) and *The American President* (1995).

ROBERT STERLING

Born: 13 November 1917, in New Castle, Pennsylvania, USA.
Died: 31 May 2006, from shingles, in Brentwood, California, USA.
Birth name: William Sterling Hart
Job description: Actor
A solid leading man, Robert Sterling worked in theatre, films and television without achieving star status. His film credits included *Blondie Meets the Boss* (1939), *Only Angels Have Wings* (1939), *Two-Faced Woman* (1941), *Show Boat* (1951), *Return to Peyton Place* (1961) and *Voyage to the Bottom of the Sea* (1961).

FRANKIE THOMAS

Born: 9 April 1921, in New York, New York, USA.
Died: 11 May 2006, from respiratory failure, in Los Angeles, California, USA.
Job description: Actor
A former child actor, Frankie Thomas appeared in *Boys Town* (1938), *The Angels Wash Their Faces* (1939) and *The Major and the Minor* (1942). He enjoyed his biggest success as *Tom Corbett, Space Cadet* (1950-55), a popular television series.

MICHAEL VALE

Born: 28 June 1922, in Brooklyn, New York, USA.
Died: 24 December 2005, of complications from diabetes, in New York, New York, USA.
Job description: Actor
A veteran of over 1300 television commercials, Michael Vale appeared in several films, including *A Hatful of Rain* (1957) and *Marathon Man* (1976).

ALIDA VALLI

Born: 31 May 1921, in Pola, Istria, Italy (now Pula, Istria, Croatia)
Died: 22 April 2006, in Rome, Italy.

Birth name: Alida Maria Laura von Altenburger
Job description: Actress
One of cinema's most beautiful women, Alida Valli achieved national stardom in *Manon Lescaut* (1939). She was placed under contract by producer David O. Selznick, who cast her in *The Paradine Case* (Alfred Hitchcock, 1947), a box-office flop. With the exception of *The Third Man* (Carol Reed, 1949), Valli's Hollywood career was short and undistinguished. Back in Italy, she was caught up in a 1954 scandal involving sex, drugs and murder in high society. Nevertheless, Valli made a series of distinguished films with some of Italy's leading directors: *Senso* (Luchino Visconti, 1954), *The Wide Blue Road* (Gillo Pontecorvo, 1957), *Il Grido* (Michelangelo Antonioni, 1957), *Oedipus Rex* (Pier Paolo Pasolini, 1968), *The Spider's Stratagem* (Bernardo Bertolucci, 1970) and *1900* (Bertolucci, 1976). She also appeared in several classic horror films: *Eyes Without a Face* (Georges Franju, 1959), *Lisa and the Devil* (Mario Bava, 1973), *Suspiria* (Dario Argento, 1977) and *Inferno* (Argento, 1980). Valli's last film was *Semana Santa* (2002).

DENNIS WEAVER

Born: 4 June 1924, in Joplin, Missouri, USA.
Died: 24 February 2006, of complications from cancer, in Ridgway, Colorado, USA.
Birth name: William Dennis Weaver
Job description: Actor

Dennis Weaver's biggest success was on television, in the long running series *Gunsmoke* (1955-64) and *McCloud* (1970-77). His film credits included *Dragnet* (1954), *Touch of Evil* (1958), *Duel at Diablo* (1965) and *Home on the Range* (2004). Weaver gave his best performance in Steven Spielberg's TV movie *Duel* (1971), as the hapless motorist pursued by a demonic truck.

JACK WILD

Born: 30 September 1952, in Royton, Lancashire, England.
Died: 2 March 2006, of mouth cancer, in Tebworth, Bedfordshire, England.
Job description: Actor
A classic case of too much, too soon, Jack Wild achieved stardom in *Oliver!* (1968) aged 15. He earned an Oscar nomination for his performance as the Artful Dodger, and never found another role to match it. Moving to the US, Wild starred in the children's TV series *H.R. Pufnstuf* (1969) and a 1970 film spin-off. Back in England, he reunited with *Oliver!* co-stars Ron Moody, in *Flight of Doves* (1971), and Mark Lester, in *Melody* (1971). Wild also appeared in *The Pied Piper* (1972), a largely forgotten flop. None of these did much for his film career, which soon stalled. As an adult, Wild worked largely in theatre and television. A heavy smoker and drinker, he soon looked much older than his years. Wild made a modest film comeback in *Robin Hood: Prince of Thieves* (1991).

SHELLEY WINTERS

Born: 18 August 1920,
in East St. Louis, Illinois, USA.
Died: 14 January 2006, of heart failure,
in Beverly Hills, California, USA.
Birth name: Shirley Schrift
Job description: Actress

A powerful actress with a tendency to
overplay, Shelley Winters first came to
notice in *A Double Life* (1947), opposite a
murderous Ronald Colman. For a while,
she seemed typecast as victims, meeting
bad ends in *A Place in the Sun* (1951) and
The Night of the Hunter (1955). Winters
played more assertive characters in
Lolita (1962), *Alfie* (1966), *Bloody Mama*
(1970), *The Poseidon Adventure* (1972),
The Tenant (1976) and *Delta Force* (1986).
Her last major role was in *The Portrait
of a Lady* (1996). Winters won Academy
Awards for her performances in *The Diary
of Anne Frank* (1959) and *A Patch of Blue*
(1965).

ROBERT WISE

Born: 10 September 1914, in
Winchester, Indiana, USA.
Died: 14 September 2005, of a heart
attack, in Los Angeles, California, USA.
Job description: Director

A meticulous craftsman, Robert Wise
directed some of Hollywood's best
loved films. He got his break at RKO,
editing *The Hunchback of Notre Dame*
(1939), *Citizen Kane* (1941) and *The
Devil and Daniel Webster* (1941). He recut
The Magnificent Ambersons (1942) after
negative previews. Accused of colluding
in the 'sabotage' of a masterpiece, Wise
placed the blame on director Orson
Welles, whose stubborn behaviour
alienated the studio. Promoted to
director, Wise made some stylish, hard-
hitting B movies, notably *The Body
Snatcher* (1945), *Born to Kill* (1947)
and *The Set-Up* (1949). He went on
to direct *The Day the Earth Stood Still*
(1951), a classic science fiction parable,
Somebody Up There Likes Me (1956), a
sentimental biopic, *The Haunting* (1963),
an atmospheric ghost story, *The Sand
Pebbles* (1966), a potent Vietnam allegory,
and *The Andromeda Strain* (1971), an
intellectual science fiction thriller. Wise
won Academy Awards for two musicals,
West Side Story (1961), co-directed by
Jerome Robbins, and *The Sound of Music*
(1965), arguably the most popular film
ever made. His last major film was *Star
Trek: The Motion Picture* (1979), regarded
by some as the best of the series.

Index

Charlize Theron struggles to shake off a butterfly on her arm in Karyn Kusama's enjoyably silly *Aeon Flux* (from UIP)

The uninvited guest: Bill Murray snoops on his past in Jim Jarmusch's deliciously observed *Broken Flowers* (from Moment Pictures). Frances Conroy holds the bouquet.

Trial by tinsel: Diane Keaton attempts to get into the spirit in Thomas Bezucha's painful and hilarious *The Family Stone* (from Fox)

Mixed doubles: Jonathan Rhys Meyers and Scarlett Johansson in Woody Allen's laboured and implausible *Match Point* (from Icon)

Guns 'n' poses: Pierce Brosnan inverts his Bond persona in Richard Shepard's one-joke *The Matador* (from Buena Vista International)

The French Inspector's Woman: Beyoncé Knowles does her thing in Shawn Levy's *The Pink Panther* (from Fox)

All in the family: Kevin Costner (right) works his way down from Shirley MacLaine to Jennifer Aniston (left) in *Rumor Has It*, Rob Reiner's limp development of *The Graduate* (from Warner)

Nathan Fillion as Malcolm Reynolds, captain of the transport-for-hire ship *Serenity* (from UIP)

Bog standard: Shaquille O'Neal and Dr Phil McGraw in David Zucker's ham-fisted and puerile *Scary Movie 4* (from Buena Vista International)

Hugo Weaving as the masked avenger in James McTeigue's *V for Vendetta* (from Warner)